The Child in the Bible

General Editor

Marcia J. Bunge

Coeditors

Terence E. Fretheim
Beverly Roberts Gaventa

WILLIAM B. EERDMANS PUBLISHING COMPANY
GRAND RAPIDS, MICHIGAN / CAMBRIDGE, U.K.

Published 2008 by
Wm. B. Eerdmans Publishing Co.
2140 Oak Industrial Drive N.E., Grand Rapids, Michigan 49505 /
P.O. Box 163, Cambridge CB3 9PU U.K.

Printed in the United States of America

19 18 17 16 15 14   8 7 6 5 4 3

Library of Congress Cataloging-in-Publication Data

The child in the Bible / general editor, Marcia J. Bunge;
    Terence E. Fretheim and Beverly Roberts Gaventa, coeditors.
        p.   cm.
    Includes bibliographical references and index.
    ISBN 978-0-8028-4835-2 (pbk.: alk. paper)
    1. Children in the Bible.   I. Bunge, Marcia J. (Marcia JoAnn), 1954-
    II. Fretheim, Terence E.   III. Gaventa, Beverly Roberts.

    BS576.C45   2008
    220.8′30523 — dc22

                                        2008013162

www.eerdmans.com

*In recognition of the dignity and humanity of
all the world's children*

and

Dedicated to our children and grandchildren

> *Anja and Isaac*
> > *Tanya, Andrea, Kelly, Shannon, and Emre*
> > *Matthew*

Contents

Acknowledgments

This volume reflects the efforts of many people from various disciplines and institutions. They contributed to this project because of their shared interest in strengthening biblical studies and childhood studies and their common concern and compassion for children themselves. I am deeply grateful to them for making the publication of this book possible and admire how all of them, in their own ways, are supporting children in their midst and around the world.

I wish to thank, first of all, the book's contributors and consultants. Most of them were able to meet in Chicago at the initial stages of this project, working together in a spirit of genuine collaboration. All of them strengthened the volume as a whole, and they are listed at the end of the volume.

I would like to thank especially the coeditors of this volume, Terence E. Fretheim and Beverly Roberts Gaventa, for their own outstanding essays and for their editorial suggestions for other chapters. My work as general editor of the volume was greatly eased because of their goodwill, attention to detail, and wisdom about the Bible.

My coeditors and I are delighted that the book has been published by Eerdmans Publishing Company. We would like to thank Jon Pott, editor-in-chief at Eerdmans, for his encouragement and support, and Jennifer Hoffman, the volume's editor, for diligently bringing the manuscript into its final form.

Contributors to and consultants for the volume were able to meet together in person because of a generous grant from the Lilly Endowment Inc. The grant also funded additional activities of contributors that helped them disseminate and develop further the ideas formulated in this volume. I therefore wish to express my deep appreciation to Craig Dykstra, Vice President for Religion, and Chris Coble, Program Director, for their support and for their own abiding commitment to children and young people.

This volume is one aspect of a larger project, The Child in Religion and Ethics Project, which is housed at my own institution and funded by the Lilly Endowment. Thus, through their support of this larger project, members of the Valparaiso University community have contributed to this volume in significant ways. Alan Harre, President of the University, and Mel Piehl, Dean of Christ College (the University's Honors College), have enthusiastically supported the publication of this volume and the related work of The Child in Religion and Ethics Project. Members of the University's finance office, including Nancy Stalbaum, Michelle Scott, and Charley Gillispie, effectively carried out their roles in administering the grant for the project.

Many of my students at Christ College also strengthened this project. Daniel Jarrett was my primary research assistant from 2004 to 2007, and he contributed significantly to the project in a number of ways. He is highly talented in all areas of communication and visual arts, and he established the project website, helped edit chapters, and produced all of the visual materials for the project. Libbi Bartelt and Bonnie Keane, also honors students, each served as research assistants for a semester, diligently proofreading chapters and the select bibliography. I also deeply appreciated the questions and insights of those who participated in my upper level seminars on children and childhood during the period of the grant.

Special thanks and recognition go to the project's administrative assistant, Vicki Brody. She was responsible for numerous details regarding the project's consultations and publications. She consistently carried out all aspects of her responsibilities effectively, enthusiastically, and with a sense of humor. She has not only devoted her time and significant talents to the publication of this particular book and to The Child in Religion and Ethics Project; she has also shared a passion for the overall aims of the project and helped to strengthen it in ways both large and small.

Several other colleagues and friends gave me sound advice about aspects of this book and the project. These include the project's two primary consultants, Don Browning (University of Chicago Divinity School) and Michael Welker (University of Heidelberg), as well as Dorothy Bass (Valparaiso University), Jerome Berryman (Center for the Theology of Childhood), and Walter Wangerin Jr. (Valparaiso University).

My own interest in and passion for this volume and the project as a whole are deeply connected to my own experiences with children. I am an "older mother" who has both given birth to and adopted children, and I am deeply grateful each and every day for Anja (7 years old) and Isaac (14), who have brought so many blessings and so much joy into my own life, our family, and our community. I am also an aunt to eight nieces and nephews, a godmother to three children, a sister to three siblings, and a child myself, deeply grateful for my parents (Myrene and Richard) and thankful that my mother (now 86) is still alive and well. I am privileged to know the friends of my children and the children of my friends. I enjoy and appreciate all of these relationships, and they have opened my heart and mind to the needs of other children in our community and around the world.

All contributors and consultants to this volume have held in mind, as they worked on the project, not only the children in their own immediate families but also children, near and far, who are our "neighbors" but are often treated "as the least of these." Thus, my coeditors and I have dedicated this book to our children and grandchildren, recognizing at the same time the deep needs, the amazing gifts, and the full humanity of all of the world's children.

Marcia J. Bunge
Christ College
Valparaiso University
April 14, 2008

Introduction

Marcia J. Bunge

The Bible is teeming with direct references to children, childhood, and adult-child relationships. Biblical passages refer to the conception, birth, and naming of children. They give accounts of childhoods, sibling relationships, and children's birth order. The Bible also portrays diverse, complex, and emotion-filled child-adult relationships. Some adults enjoy children, carry them on their shoulders, and hold them in their bosoms. Others reject children, abandon them, and plot their destruction. Various children in the Bible are blessed, touched, or healed. Others are cursed, victims of injustice, or murdered. Some are abandoned; others are adopted. They are treated by others as gifts and treasures as well as spoils and booties of war. Biblical texts also refer to adult obligations to children. Adults are commanded to teach, educate, and discipline children and to care for poor children and orphans. Other biblical texts outline children's own duties and responsibilities to parents, God, and the community. The actions and words of children themselves are varied and often central to biblical accounts of events or the stories of families, tribes, and nations. Children are depicted as singing, rejoicing, and praising God as well as rebelling, committing wrongs, and turning from God. They learn from adults yet also are recognized as prophets and models for adults.

Biblical texts also often refer indirectly or metaphorically to children and childhood. Individuals and nations are referred to as children of God and sons and daughters of God, with God as their father or, sometimes, mother. "Childlike" is used to refer to both immature as well as admirable behavior. A range of child-related terms and metaphors is used to articulate central themes or events. For example, Jesus bids farewell to his disciples by saying, "I will not leave you orphaned" (John 14:18). In his appeals to the Galatians, Paul speaks of them as his "little children," for whom he is "again in the pain of childbirth" (Gal. 4:19). The book of Proverbs depicts wisdom not only as a woman but also as a child growing up beside and playing before God (Prov. 8:27-31). Visions of peace, hope, and restoration are described with the help of images of children. "The wolf shall live with the lamb," and "a little child shall lead them" (Isa. 11:6); and "the streets of the city shall be full of boys and girls playing in its streets" (Zech. 8:5).

Growing Attention to Children and Childhood in Biblical Studies and the Academy Today

Although the biblical texts are flooded with both direct and indirect references to children and childhood, biblical scholars have generally neglected these themes. Certainly, they have explored issues related to children, such as biblical views of the family, sexuality, and gender relations, but they have rarely focused their attention directly on references to children and childhood and uses of child-related terms in the Bible. Furthermore, they have not explored how attention to children might shed light on other significant aspects of biblical texts. Until recently, most of the literature that has addressed any relationships between biblical texts and children has been written primarily by scholars in the areas of religious education or children's ministry.

However, biblical scholars, like scholars in many other fields and disciplines, have recently begun to turn their attention more directly to children and childhood, contributing to the new and burgeoning field of childhood studies. This interdisciplinary field has grown over the past few years, as scholars have undertaken studies on children and childhood not only in education and psychology but also in history, law, literature, philosophy, sociology, and anthropology.[1] This research is opening up new lines of inquiry, challenging preconceptions about children, and even, in some fields, reshaping research methodologies. These studies are also generating collaboration among scholars from several disciplines, leading in some cases to the develop-

---

1. For a brief account of the growth of childhood studies in several disciplines, see Scott Heller, "The Meaning of Children in Culture Becomes a Focal Point for Scholars," *The Chronicle of Higher Education*, August 7, 1998, pp. A14-A15. For an introduction to childhood studies with contributions from scholars from a range of academic disciplines, see, for example, Mary Jane Kehily, ed., *An Introduction to Childhood Studies* (Oxford: Open University Press, 2004); Peter B. Pufall and Richard P. Unsworth, eds., *Rethinking Childhood* (New Brunswick, NJ: Rutgers University Press, 2004); and Dominic Wyse, ed., *Childhood Studies: An Introduction* (Oxford: Blackwell, 2004). See also the interdisciplinary and international journals devoted to childhood studies, such as *Childhood* (published by Sage) or *Childhoods Today* (an on-line journal).

ment of interdisciplinary childhood studies programs or centers.[2] Since scholars working in the area of childhood studies, whatever their particular discipline or area of expertise, often share a concern for the situation of children today, they also are forging creative and cooperative relationships among scholars, child advocates, and public policy makers.

In line with these trends, scholars in diverse areas of biblical studies, religious studies, and theology are also beginning to focus attention directly on children and childhood.[3] For example, religious scholars have begun to explore more fully the role of children in the history and development of various religious traditions, thereby contributing to the history of religions as well as to the history of childhood in general.[4] Studies that compare conceptions of children and childhood across selected religious traditions are also beginning to be published.[5] Other interdisciplinary initiatives are examining the spiritual development and experiences of children and adolescents in various religions and cultures worldwide.[6] Scholars here and abroad in the areas

2. See, for example, the Center for Children and Childhood Studies (Rutgers University, United States); the Norwegian Centre for Child Research (Norwegian University of Science and Technology, Norway); the Centre for the Study of Childhood and Youth (University of Sheffield, United Kingdom); and the Department of Child Studies (Linköping University, Sweden).

3. For an overview of developments in these areas, see Marcia J. Bunge, "The Child, Religion, and the Academy: Developing Robust Theological and Religious Understandings of Childhood," *Journal of Religion* 86, no. 4 (October 2006): 549-79.

4. See, for example, in the areas of Judaism, Christianity, Islam, and Buddhism: Elesheva Baumgarten, *Mother and Children: Jewish Family Life in Medieval Europe* (Princeton: Princeton University Press, 2004); Ivan G. Marcus, *Rituals of Childhood: Jewish Acculturation in Medieval Europe* (New Haven: Yale University Press, 1998); O. M. Bakke, *Childhood in Early Christian Traditions*, trans. Brian P. McNeil (Minneapolis: Fortress, 2005); Marcia J. Bunge, ed., *The Child in Christian Thought* (Grand Rapids: Eerdmans, 2001); Philip Greven, *The Protestant Temperament: Patterns of Child-Rearing, Religious Experience, and the Self in Early America* (New York: Alfred A. Knopf, 1977); Avner Gil'adi, *Children of Islam: Concepts of Childhood in Medieval Muslim Society* (New York: St. Martin's, 1992) and *Infants, Parents, and Wet Nurses* (Leiden: Brill, 1999); Alan Cole, *Mothers and Sons in Chinese Buddhism* (Stanford: Stanford University Press, 1998); and Anne Behnke Kinney, *Representations of Childhood and Youth in Early China* (Stanford: Stanford University Press, 2003).

5. See, for example, *The Given Child*, ed. Trygve Wyller and Usha S. Nayar (Göttingen: Vandenhoeck and Ruprecht, 2007). See also *Children and Childhood in World Religions*, ed. Don Browning and Marcia Bunge (New Brunswick, NJ: Rutgers University Press, 2008); and *Children and Childhood in American Religions*, ed. Don Browning and Bonnie Miller-McLemore (New Brunswick, NJ: Rutgers University Press, 2008).

6. For example, the Search Institute has opened a new Center for Spiritual Development in Childhood and Adolescence and recently published two books on child spirituality: one focusing on social scientific research and the other on religious perspectives primarily within Buddhism, Christianity, Hinduism, Islam, and Judaism. See E. C. Roehlkepartain, P. E. King, L. M.

of ethics and systematic theology have also taken up the themes of children and childhood.[7] The American Academy of Religion, the Society of Biblical Literature, and other academic organizations are also devoting more sessions at their conferences and annual meetings to various themes of religion and childhood.[8] In all areas of biblical studies, theology, and religious studies,

---

Wagener, and P. L. Benson, eds., *The Handbook of Spiritual Development in Childhood and Adolescence* (Thousand Oaks, CA: Sage, 2006); and K.-M. Yust, A. N. Johnson, S. E. Sasso, and E. C. Roehlkepartain, eds., *Nurturing Child and Adolescent Spirituality: Perspectives from the World's Religious Traditions* (Lanham: Rowman & Littlefield, 2006). For more information on the project and the Search Institute, see http://www.Search-Institute.org.

7. Recent studies in the areas of Christian ethics and systematic and practical theology include, for example: Herbert Anderson and Susan B. W. Johnson, *Regarding Children* (Louisville: Westminster John Knox, 1994); Pamela Couture, *Seeing Children, Seeing God: A Practical Theology of Children and Poverty* (Nashville: Abingdon, 2000); Marva Dawn, *Is It a Lost Cause? Having the Heart of God for the Church's Children* (Grand Rapids: Eerdmans, 1997); Dawn DeVries, "Toward a Theology of Childhood," *Interpretation* 55, no. 2 (April 2001); Kristin Herzog, *Children and Our Global Future: Theological and Social Challenges* (Cleveland: Pilgrim, 2005); Timothy P. Jackson, ed., *The Morality of Adoption: Social-psychological, Theological, and Legal Perspectives* (Grand Rapids: Eerdmans, 2005); David H. Jensen, *Graced Vulnerability: A Theology of Childhood* (Cleveland: Pilgrim, 2005); Kathleen Marshall and Paul Parvis, *Honouring Children: The Human Rights of the Child in Christian Perspective* (Edinburgh: Saint Andrews Press, 2004); Martin E. Marty, *The Mystery of the Child* (Grand Rapids: Eerdmans, 2007); Joyce Ann Mercer, *Welcoming Children: A Practical Theology of Childhood* (St. Louis: Chalice Press, 2005); Bonnie Miller-McLemore, *Let the Children Come: Reimagining Childhood from a Christian Perspective* (San Francisco: Jossey-Bass, 2003); Jürgen Moltmann, "Child and Childhood as Metaphors of Hope," *Theology Today* 56, no. 4 (2000): 592-603; Deusdedit R. K. Nkurunziza, "African Theology of Childhood in Relation to Child Labour," *African Ecclesial Review* 46, no. 2 (2004): 121-38; Karen-Marie Yust, *Real Kids, Real Faith: Practices for Nurturing Children's Spiritual Lives* (San Francisco: Jossey-Bass, 2004). This list does not include a number of resources that focus primarily on marriage and family yet also refer to children. For a fuller discussion of current trends, see Bunge, "The Child, Religion, and the Academy," and John Wall, "Childhood Studies, Hermeneutics, and Theological Ethics," both in the *Journal of Religion* 86, no. 4 (October 2006).

8. The American Academy of Religion (AAR), the Society of Biblical Literature (SBL), the American Historical Association, the Society of Church History, and the Society of Christian Ethics have all recently devoted sessions at their national meetings to the themes of religion and childhood. Furthermore, in 2002 the Program Committee of the AAR approved a new program unit, the Childhood Studies and Religion Consultation, which is now providing a forum for a more focused and sustained interdisciplinary and interreligious dialogue about children and religion. For information on the Childhood Studies and Religion Consultation and the AAR annual meeting, see the website of the AAR (http://www.aarweb.org). In 2008 the Society of Biblical Literature (SBL) also approved a new program unit entitled "Children in the Biblical World." For more information about the SBL and its annual meeting, see its website (www.sbl-site.org). Several academic projects and initiatives in the United States, such as The Child in Law, Religion, and Society (Emory University; website is http://www.law.emory.edu/cslr) and The Child

journals are devoting entire issues to the theme of children,[9] and scholars are also finding many more opportunities to present work on childhood at professional meetings or through specially funded national and international symposia or research projects.

Primary Aim and Significance of This Volume

Although attention to children and childhood is also growing in the area of biblical studies,[10] this volume represents one of the first collaborative efforts by biblical scholars to provide a highly informed and focused study of biblical perspectives on children and childhood. The contributors to this volume reexamine selected biblical texts through the "lens" or category of "the child." In other words, they keep in mind or "foreground" questions and concerns about children and childhood as they interpret biblical texts. By using this "lens" or category of analysis, contributors not only explore passages directly about children and childhood but also consider how attention to children might shed new light on the structure and themes of a text as a whole. Thus, the chapters not only deepen our understanding of biblical conceptions of children and obligations to them but also provide a new angle of vision on other aspects of biblical texts. Furthermore, by exploring ancient texts and traditions through the lens of "the child," the chapters also challenge readers to reexamine their own contemporary conceptions about children and childhood. Thus, just as in the case of using the lens of "gender," "race," or "class" as categories of analysis, the lens of "the child" reveals unexplored or neglected aspects of a text or a tradition, exposes new and important methodological questions and concerns, and helps contemporary readers to reflect on their own attitudes and behaviors.

The chapters are written by highly respected biblical scholars who use the

---

in Religion and Ethics (Valparaiso University; website is http://www.childreligionethics.org), are also focusing on children and religion, generating new discussions and research opportunities for scholars in many areas of theology and religious studies.

9. See, for example, *Dialog* 37 (Summer 1998); *Interpretation* 55, no. 2 (2001); *Conservative Judaism* 53, no. 4 (Summer 2001); the *Jahrbuch für biblische Theologie* 17 (2002); *Christian Reflection* (July 2003); *The Living Pulpit* 12, no. 4 (2003); *Sewanee Theological Review* 48, no. 1 (2004) and 48, no. 4 (2005); *Theology Today* 56, no. 4 (2000); *African Ecclesial Review* 46, no. 2 (2004); and the *Journal of Religion* 86, no. 4 (October 2006).

10. For studies on children and childhood in the Bible, see the select bibliography in this volume and the excellent review article (also cited in the bibliography) by Reidar Aasgaard, "Children in Antiquity and Early Christianity: Research History and Central Issues," *Familia* [Salamanca, Spain] 33 (2006): 23-46.

lens of "the child" to reexamine a selected number of biblical texts and themes. Although few of the contributors writing for this volume had written previously on children or childhood, they had already published material on the particular strand of the biblical texts they address in this volume.

Although contributors focused on selected texts, and although the scope of the volume is necessarily limited, it examines a rich variety of biblical texts and approaches to them. The volume intentionally includes analyses of texts that speak directly about children or are highly quoted in relationship to children as well as texts that appear at first glance to have nothing to say regarding children. The volume also explores a variety of literary genres. Given the diversity of texts they are exploring and their own specific questions and concerns, the contributors have also taken a range of approaches to them, including historical-critical, literary, narrative, sociological, and theological. The Bible is, of course, a complex and ancient library of texts representing a variety of literary genres, and even the terms for and the contents of the "Bible" are variously defined by different religious traditions and communities. Thus, although this collection of essays cannot be exhaustive, it is nevertheless wide-ranging and illustrates diverse traditions within the Scriptures and approaches to them.

By offering close analyses of selected texts by respected biblical scholars, the volume fills a void in current scholarship in the area of biblical studies and enriches childhood studies as a whole. The book helps to establish "the child" as a legitimate area of intellectual inquiry in biblical studies, thereby encouraging further serious research on children and childhood in this field and in other areas of theology and religious studies. By providing highly informed scholarship on childhood in relation to several ancient periods and texts, the volume also contributes to the history of childhood and to childhood studies in general.

In addition to its significance for the academy, the volume speaks to a broad range of readers working with or on behalf of children here and abroad. For example, it serves as a foundational text for those working in the areas of religious education, youth and family ministries, or children's ministries. By exposing the depth and complexity of biblical thinking about children, the volume is also a resource for theologians and ethicists, especially within the Jewish and Christian traditions, who seek to articulate theological views of children and obligations to them that are both biblically sound and speak to contemporary issues and concerns. Since many contemporary Jewish, Christian, and Muslim communities around the world are highly informed by and critically appropriate ideas represented in biblical texts, this volume also assists religious leaders, child advocates, practitioners, and all those seeking to address the needs of children here and abroad. Furthermore, since biblical texts also inform varied religious responses to children's rights, the volume is a resource for those who are participating in national or international debates and consultations surrounding the *Millennium Development Goals* or the ratification and implementation of the *United Nations Convention on the Rights of the Child* (UNCRC).[11] Finally, the volume helps all readers, whatever their religious background, profession, or discipline, to take more seriously many issues regarding children and to reevaluate their own conceptions of children and the moral obligations of individuals, religious communities, and nations to children themselves.

In these and other ways, this volume is a valuable resource for a variety of audiences and contexts in the academy and the public sphere both nationally and internationally. Regardless of their religious commitments or backgrounds, scholars in all areas of childhood studies as well as all those concerned about children today need and appreciate in-depth and informed studies of religious understandings of children and childhood. The value of such scholarship for a range of audiences has been apparent in my own research on the history of childhood in various religious traditions and in my participation in national and international consultations on contemporary challenges facing children today. Given the tremendous significance and influence of biblical texts not only in religious communities and political debates today but also in the history of so many cultures and countries around the world, this volume should be a particularly useful resource in a variety of undergraduate and graduate courses on childhood as well as in national and international consultations on children organized by religious leaders, practitioners, or child advocates.

Guiding Questions

Although they examine different biblical texts and raise questions unique to those particular texts, contributors have all kept in mind some of the following general themes and questions:

1. Terminology: What terms are used to refer to children and young people? How are these terms used and defined? What are the various metaphorical and rhetorical uses of "children," "child," and "childhood"?
2. Nature and status of children: How are children depicted in the texts? How do the texts speak about the nature of children and about their sta-

---

11. The UNCRC was passed in 1989 by the UN General Assembly. Since then, it has been ratified by all but two nations: the United States and Somalia.

tus in and value to the community? How do biblical attitudes toward children differ from those expressed in documents from other ancient cultures and religious communities?

3. Adult responsibilities to children: How do the texts speak about the duties and responsibilities of parents and other adults to children? What are the particular responsibilities of the community to children, especially orphans and the poor?

4. Adult-child relationships, education, and formation: What do commonly cited biblical passages regarding adult-child relationships mean, especially those about "honoring parents," "obeying parents," "the rod," "teaching," "discipline," or "becoming like a child"? What does the Bible say more specifically about the education and spiritual formation of children and adults? What should children be taught? How should they be taught? What do children teach adults?

5. Children and their roles and responsibilities: How does the Bible speak about activities, thoughts, roles, duties, and responsibilities of children themselves? In what ways, if any, do children contribute to families or communities? What particular children are mentioned in the Bible? What does the Bible say about the character or agency of these children? What is the role of children in specific biblical narratives? How do children's words or actions help interpret events portrayed in the Bible?

6. Broader findings: Does attention to children and childhood shed new light on the overall structure, content, or historical context of selected biblical texts and passages?

These questions served as initial guidelines for contributors as they examined a variety of biblical sources, raising different questions as they explored these particular sources further.

Methodological Challenges

As they have examined these and other questions, contributors have recognized the limitations as well as the benefits of any study of children and childhood, whether one is exploring the past or today. As scholars in a number of fields have found, the study of children and childhood presents many methodological challenges. For example, it is much easier to study adult conceptions of children than the experiences of children themselves. Furthermore, it is difficult to know, even from contemporary accounts of adults or from conversations with children themselves, how children are actually treated and raised or how they actually think and behave. The questions we pose to children shape their responses, and adult preconceptions about children color the interpretations of these responses. We also disagree, even in contemporary legal, academic, and religious settings, about when childhood ends and adulthood begins, and we wonder whether or not in some fundamental ways childhood never ends.

All of these complex factors and questions are present and intensified whenever we attempt to study ancient texts and periods, and any study of children and childhood in biblical texts faces some specific challenges. Biblical interpreters must ask, for example: What was possibly lost in the oral transmission of the biblical materials to their written form? What version of the written text is being considered? How should the texts and terms regarding children be best translated? Who is writing about children, and were these authors interested in or in contact with children themselves? Where are the voices of children themselves in this material? How should ancient texts outside the various canonical sources inform the interpretation of these sources?

Despite these and many more difficult challenges and questions, the study of children and childhood certainly reaps tremendous rewards and benefits: intellectually, politically, morally, and spiritually. Such studies disclose new aspects of any subject, raise new questions, and check and challenge contemporary attitudes and behaviors toward children themselves. This is clearly the case in the study of children and childhood in the Bible, as the essays in this volume confirm.

Some Central Themes and Findings

Although contributors face various methodological challenges and lift up distinctive questions and insights, they do engage some common questions and themes, and their chapters, taken as a whole, provide a window into the complexity of biblical sources regarding children and childhood. What follows highlights a few of the central themes and findings of the volume that emerged in response to some of the guiding questions listed above.

1. Wide Range of Terms for Child, Children, and Childhood and Rhetorical and Metaphorical Uses of These Terms

The Bible uses a number of child-related terms. Such terms can be used to speak about a particular stage in life that one passes or about roles and relationships that one could take up at any stage of life. Furthermore, child-related terms often overlap, and they are used in a wide variety of categories or "semantic fields," such as inheritance, kinship, social position, formation, and belonging.[12] Given the complexity of child-related terms and their meanings, the contributors to the volume all address what particular terms are found in the specific texts they are examining and how these terms are defined or used. The range of references is astounding and includes particular Hebrew or Greek terms for stillborns, babies, very young children, little children, boys, girls, little girls, little boys, young heirs, heirs, young children, young people, orphans, firstborns, brothers, sisters, sons, daughters, siblings. All contributors also address metaphorical and rhetorical uses of these and other terms, and the essays by Reidar Aasgaard, Marianne Meye Thompson, and Brent A. Strawn address at length the complexity and power of child-related biblical metaphors.

2. Multifaceted Views of Children Themselves

The chapters also reveal that biblical views of and attitudes toward children themselves are more complex and multifaceted than readers might assume. Some of the commonly cited biblical texts regarding children point narrowly to one angle of vision. For example, some individuals or communities today tend to cite passages about children needing to be taught or disciplined, such as "train a child in the way he should go" (Prov. 22:6); or bring up children "in the discipline and instruction of the Lord" (Eph. 6:4). Others emphasize passages that depict children as active agents or even models for adults, such as the stories of God calling the "boy Samuel" (1 Sam. 3–4), the young David slaying Goliath (1 Sam. 17), and Jesus as a twelve-year-old in the temple (Luke 2:40-52), or passages in the New Testament, where Jesus himself welcomes children and claims, "Whoever becomes humble like this child is the greatest in the kingdom of heaven. Whoever welcomes one such child in my name welcomes me" (Matt. 18:2-5).

However, the Bible includes many such passages *both* about children needing instruction, training, or guidance *and* about children actively ministering to others, prophesying, or modeling faith. Furthermore, the Bible in-

---

12. In his chapter in this volume and also in his book, *"My Beloved Brothers and Sisters!" Christian Siblingship in Paul* (London: T&T Clark International; New York: Continuum, 2004), Reidar Aasgaard discusses these semantic fields directly, building on the work of Peter Müller, *In der Mitte der Gemeinde: Kinder im Neuen Testament* (Neukirchen-Vluyn: Neukirchener, 1992).

cludes many additional and rich terms and perspectives on children. They are often depicted, for example, as signs of divine blessing, rewards, gifts, or sources of joy. Other passages present a view of God as intimately forming the "inward parts" of every child and "knitting" them together in the womb (Ps. 139:13). Texts in Genesis also claim that all human beings are created in "the image of God," and W. Sibley Towner's essay helps to draw out some of the implications of this claim for understanding biblical views of children. Children are also recognized as being rebellious or sinful as well as highly vulnerable and sinned against, as the chapters by Terence E. Fretheim and Claire Mathews McGinnis especially help illustrate.

The chapters in this volume point out these and many other perspectives on children, and the volume as a whole cautions readers not to reduce biblical understandings of children and childhood to one perspective alone.

3. Adults Have Obligations to Their Own and to Other Children

The biblical texts express a number of responsibilities and obligations that adults have not only to their own children but also to children in their midst. The Bible includes explicit commands as well as general assumptions about the responsibilities of feeding, clothing, and protecting children and providing for their basic needs. Across many of the biblical texts there is also an emphasis on training and instructing children to fear and love God and to care for the stranger, the orphan, or others in need. Several important yet often neglected passages speak about adult responsibilities of protecting and preserving a child's inheritance. Such obligations extend not only to one's "own" children but also to children in the community and particular children in need, as the chapters by Walter Brueggemann and David Bartlett persuasively and forcefully illustrate.

4. Teaching, Training, and Disciplining Children Are Sophisticated and Multilayered Tasks

The specific themes of disciplining, teaching, or training children are taken up in many of the essays, especially those by Patrick D. Miller, William P. Brown, Joel B. Green, and Margaret Y. MacDonald. These and other contributors point out that "discipline" is far more than punishing children, and "teaching" is far more than repeating or memorizing the law. Central to many of the biblical texts on teaching are the questions of children themselves and stories passed onto them. Training children also involves initiating them into communal rituals and practices of study, worship, and prayer. The chapters also warn that terms often translated as "fear," "honor," "obedience," "discipline," "instruction," or "training" mean something quite different in the original Greek or Hebrew and in the context of the passages in which they were written than they do today. The chapters as a whole also challenge contemporary readers to revisit the multilayered and intricate approaches to the teaching and training of children that the biblical texts express.

5. Children are Complex Characters, Play Various Roles in Families and Communities, and Bear Responsibilities to Others

There are many references to and stories about particular children in the Bible. Some children are at the center of a narrative or event, and others are marginal characters or mentioned only in passing. Several chapters in this volume lift up often ignored names of children as well as explore more well-known child characters. The chapters expose "flat" or "watered-down" yet common interpretations of specific children in the Bible, revealing various sides of their character, agency, or place in the overall content or structure of text. The chapter by Esther M. Menn focuses specifically on narratives about children in the Bible, highlighting the range of biblical stories about children and exploring selected narratives about them, including those about the young David (1 Samuel 16–17) and Naaman's servant girl (2 Kings 5:1-19).

An emphasis on children's own obligations to God, families, communities, neighbors, and strangers can also be found in the biblical texts. Children, like adults, are to "fear" and love God and to study the law. Children are also commanded to "honor" father and mother, a duty that is understood to extend through adulthood (see, for example, Exod. 20:12 and Deut. 5:16). Although we see references to "honoring" parents in Greek and Hebrew texts, the specific command to "obey" parents is found only in the New Testament. Children also bear responsibilities to others and are commanded to love the neighbor.

Biblical texts also recognize potential conflicts between honoring or obeying parents and fearing God or following the law. The texts are also highly realistic and honest about failings, weaknesses, and injustices of parents themselves. John T. Carroll's chapter on Luke explores possible tensions between children and families at length, and throughout the volume many other dimensions of the responsibilities of young children as well as adult children are examined.

6. Children and Childhood Are Integrally Connected
to Other Central Biblical Themes

Several essays in the volume reveal that attention to child-related terms or themes can unexpectedly throw new light on other themes in a text or on its structure as a whole. Other chapters also show ways in which biblical themes generally not associated with children nevertheless contribute to and challenge contemporary perspectives on children. For example, William Brown's investigation of children and childhood in Proverbs sheds light on the text's language about wisdom. Jacqueline E. Lapsley illustrates the importance of children and child-related terms for understanding Isaiah's visions of God's judgment and promises and the text as a whole. Essays by John Carroll, Judith M. Gundry, and Keith J. White show how the Gospels integrally connect children and God's reign. The essay by Beverly Roberts Gaventa demonstrates how central theological themes in the letters of Paul, such as the cross and the body of Christ, have contributions to make to contemporary reflection about children, quite apart from Paul's explicit and implicit references to children.

Conclusion

The chapters in this volume add complexity to all of these general themes and findings and raise a number of additional questions and issues. Taken as a whole, the chapters provide an introduction to a vast array of themes and questions regarding children and childhood in the Bible; throw new light on biblical themes and religious practices beyond those generally associated with children; and prompt questions for further research. The chapters also invite readers to reconsider the roles that children can or should play in religious communities today. Furthermore, whatever the particular cultural or religious contexts of individual readers, these chapters also challenge each of us to reevaluate more seriously our own attitudes, behaviors, and obligations toward children themselves — whether children in our own homes, in our religious communities, in our neighborhoods, in our own countries, or across the world.

PART I

TEXTS FROM THE HEBREW SCRIPTURES

1 "God Was with the Boy" (Genesis 21:20): Children in the Book of Genesis

Terence E. Fretheim

The history of Hebrew children is fraught with turmoil and instability, as they suffered with their elders the effects of centuries of warfare, tumultuous upheavals, and aimless migration. Lamentations of their starvation, slaughter, and enslavement fill the pages of the Old Testament.[1]

The Bible contains many stories where children suffer and simply become dispensable objects in the telling of the story.[2]

Children take center stage in the book of Genesis.[3] This essay attends to those texts in Genesis that are especially important for thinking about the Bible's

---

1. A. R. Colon, *A History of Children: A Socio-Cultural Survey Across Millennia* (Westport, CT: Greenwood, 2001). Colon cites Nah. 3:10; Hos. 13:16; and Lam. 5:13; many other texts could also be cited. That children lived perilous lives can be observed in studies of several burial sites in Canaan. About one-third of the children buried at these sites had died before age 5, about half of them before age 18. See Carol Meyers, *Discovering Eve: Ancient Israelite Women in Context* (New York: Oxford University Press, 1988), p. 112.

2. Danna Nolan Fewell, *Children of Israel: Reading the Bible for the Sake of Our Children* (Nashville: Abingdon, 2003), p. 9. She has stories such as Sodom and Gomorrah in mind (pp. 28-29). The new heaven and new earth are marked by the end of infant mortality (Isa. 65:20), indirectly indicating the commonness of the death of young children.

3. It is difficult to know what period(s) of Israel's history are reflected in Genesis. Regarding Genesis 12–50, Walter Moberly (*The Old Testament of the Old Testament: Patriarchal Narratives and Mosaic Yahwism* [Minneapolis: Fortress, 1992]) has shown that some theological dimensions of these chapters seem to reflect a time before the development of much other Old Testament theology. For a careful and thorough sociological study of families in early Israel (which

portrayal of children. The first section focuses on Genesis 1–11; the balance of the article centers on Genesis 12–50 and the place of children among Israel's ancestors. Focused attention will be given to two endangered children: Ishmael and Isaac.

By reexamining Genesis through the lens of "the child," this essay invites readers to discover the critical role that children play in the opening book of the Bible. Children are created in the image of God, promised to barren ones, loved and enjoyed, vulnerable to violence, threatened with death, and engulfed in destructive events. Of special concern is a delineation of the role that Israel's God plays in the lives of these children and in the shaping of their stories.

Genesis 1–11: Children in the Image of God

In the language of Genesis 1:26-27, human beings are created in the image of God. We know from the larger context that human beings do not become an "image of God" only when they are adults; the image of God is not something that they "grow up into." This point is made clear in Genesis 5:1-3, the beginning of the genealogy of Adam. After noting that male and female were created in the image of God, the genealogical structure of this chapter makes God the "father" of Adam. Genesis 5:3 then states: "When Adam had lived 130 years, he became the father of a son in his likeness, according to his image, and named him Seth." Human beings are now the ones who create further images of God. In other words: this first generation of children *is* created in the image of God (even after the fall into sin). This inclusion of both God and Adam in the genealogy suggests that the procreation of children is a genuinely creative act (as Eve already recognized in Gen. 4:1: "I have created a man with the help of the Lord").

Everything that the image of God is, every child is. These Genesis texts claim that all human beings — regardless of gender, race, social status, or age — are created in the image of God from the beginning of their life. The image of God is democratized to include everyone — a move that kings and other elites probably did not appreciate. And so, every child is created in the image of God and, as such, has special dignity and value to God and for the world — a point made all too uncommonly.

---

may or may not correspond to familial life depicted in Genesis), see Carol Meyers, "The Family in Early Israel," in *Families in Ancient Israel,* ed. Leo Perdue et al. (Louisville: Westminster John Knox, 1997), pp. 1-47. Her references to Genesis are rare.

In the divine call to the first human beings in Genesis 1:28, as well as to the post-flood families in Genesis 9:1-7 ("be fruitful and multiply"), God builds into the very structures of creation the capacity for humans to bring children into being. Unlike the Canaanites, whose *gods* assumed responsibility to generate new life, human beings are here given that responsibility. By being the image of God they were created to be, human beings will naturally perpetuate their own kind. God will not be absent from the gestation and birthing process, as Psalm 139:13, among other texts, testifies: "You knit me together in my mother's womb." But human beings will do the procreating, not God!

Libraries are filled with literature about the "image of God," and Sibley Towner's essay in this volume reviews various interpretations of the image of God and addresses this theme at length. For the purposes of the present essay and in the context of this discussion of Genesis as a whole, it is important to note that remarkably little scholarly study on the image of God focuses on the word "God."[4] If one understands the word "God" in terms of its context in Genesis 1, God is one who creates. It would thus follow that human beings created in the image of God are fundamentally creative beings, and this includes children. When we see children play with whatever might be available, we are astonished at their creativity. Their imagination is a grand gift of God, and they demonstrate that they are created in the image of God in every such imaginative moment. Israel did not always honor this high status of children, often treating them as second-class citizens. Yet Israel stakes a claim that children are created in the image of God, and this enhances their stature as creative human beings.

Even more, the God who creates is a deeply relational God, evidenced in the "let us" of Genesis 1:26. This reference to the divine council demonstrates that the creation of humanity is the result of a dialogical act — an inner-divine consultation — rather than a monological one. Relationality is thus shown to be basic to the being of God, and hence it is intensely characteristic of all who are created in the divine image. The interrelational capacities of children may, in fact, be said to be a model for all human beings, of whatever age.

With this creativity and relationality in every child, no matter how old, it is no wonder that this world is not a static state of affairs, but a dynamic, relational process of becoming. And the fact that this process is somewhat disorderly, as children will often be, in fact makes excellence possible.[5] With all of

---

4. For the most up-to-date study of the image of God, with a thorough analysis of ancient Near Eastern and biblical literature, see J. Richard Middleton, *The Liberating Image: The Imago Dei in Genesis 1* (Grand Rapids: Brazos, 2005). For my own reflections, see Terence E. Fretheim, *God and World in the Old Testament: A Relational Theology of Creation* (Nashville: Abingdon, 2005), pp. 42-43, 48-56.

5. See W. Sibley Towner, *Genesis* (Louisville: Westminster John Knox, 2001), pp. 20-21.

these creative children, we have to do with, not automatons and a monotonous cycle of inevitability, but genuine newness at every step. This understanding of children as creative and relational stands as a grand claim about children at the beginning of the Bible. Whenever readers think about children in the Bible, they are called to think about relationality and creativity.

The concern for children in the balance of Genesis 1–11 is largely limited to their assumed presence in the several genealogies. Genesis 12–50 will introduce us to children more fully in the context of several stories.

Genesis 12–50

God, Children, and Promises

Children are the focus of God's promises to Abraham, Isaac, and Jacob, for the promise of many descendants obviously depends upon the birth of children.[6] But children are hard to come by in the family of Abraham. With all the emphasis upon generating children in the opening chapters of Genesis, it is striking that the chosen family experiences so much barrenness. Sarah, Rebekah, and Rachel all have such difficulties, and this reality regularly complicates the plot, putting pressure on the divine promises (Gen. 15:2-4; 18:1-15; 25:21; 30:1-8, 22-24).

Strikingly, such negative developments are not ascribed in any special way to the presence of sin in the world. It is as if these difficulties, not unlike pain in childbirth (see Gen. 3:16), were believed to be a normal part of God's world, though, in the wake of sin, they were intensified by moral factors. These recurrent difficulties regarding conception and birth were also exacerbated by the famine, disease, and violence of their world. Child mortality remained high throughout the biblical period. To move all the way through childhood in Israel was a major feat.

These various difficulties were of such intensity that special arrangements were at times made to ensure posterity. Concubines were not uncommon — usually female slaves owned by a household who bore children to assure the line of the patriarch and to add to the labor pool. For example, Sarah makes arrangements with her slave girl, Hagar, to be a surrogate wife for Abraham.

---

6. It is very difficult to determine the ages of children in the Old Testament. Over a dozen Hebrew words can be translated as infant, child, boy/girl, youth, the young, offspring, etc. The words are not age-specific and the stages of life not carefully factored out. Some educated guesswork will be necessary.

Jacob even made polygamous arrangements, including children born through the slave girls of Leah and Rachel. These sorts of arrangements were made without moral judgment being cast on the persons involved, probably because of the importance of assuring the production of needed children. A related practice was levirate marriage, built into the heart of Israel's laws (Gen. 38; Deut. 25:5-10); if a husband died, the husband's brother married his widow to raise legal descendants and to transmit the name of the deceased.

Aside from natural difficulties, human behaviors complicated the production of progeny. On three different occasions Sarah and Rebekah are endangered by their husbands (Gen. 12:10-20; 20:1-18; 26); related issues of paternity place further pressure on the promises.[7] The competing wives and concubines of both Abraham and Jacob vie for attention in and through their children (Gen. 16:1-6; 21:7-21; 29:31–30:24) and make issues of lineage and inheritance highly complex. Those children grow up to make their own contributions to the dysfunctionality of this family, including the continuing endangerment of children such as Joseph.

With these difficult realities of birthing and childhood, it is no wonder that God focuses on children in the ancestral promises. All the promises of God depend upon the birth and continuing life of children (see, e.g., Gen. 15:3-5; 22:17; 28:14). Abraham even gives such a high value to a biological heir that an adopted son will not do. The meaning of his life is closely bound up with *his* having children, and that is where God's promises center (Gen. 15:1-6).

The importance of children can also be seen in the seemingly endless references to blessing. For example, the blessing is spoken to Rebekah before she leaves home to become the wife of Isaac: "May you, our sister, become thousands of myriads" (Gen. 24:60). The patriarch is often the one who mediates the divine blessings from generation to generation. For example, Jacob "blesses" his grandsons in Genesis 48 with these words: "The God before whom my ancestors walked, the God who has been my shepherd all my life to this day, the angel who has redeemed me from all harm, bless the boys . . . and let them grow into a multitude on the earth" (48:15-16; Jacob blesses his sons in Gen. 49). So, children are the fulfillment of God's promises to these families, and they in turn carry on those promises of life and blessing into successive generations.

That children play such an important role in these stories can be seen even in the way the narratives are structured. For example, in the middle of the story of Jacob are listed the births of all of Jacob's children except Benjamin (Gen. 29:31–30:24). The narrative flows up to this point and then,

---

7. See also Gen. 25:1-6 and Abraham's six other children.

after the flurry of births, flows away from it. In verse after verse, rhythmic references are made to a child being born and being named, often with reference to God.[8] The reader is being told thereby that these children, the progenitors of the twelve tribes of Israel, are central, not only to the Genesis narrative, but to the entire story of God's people. The births of these children mean that this particular family is flourishing and God is fulfilling God's promises.

Gratitude to God is evident in the responses of these mothers to their newborn children, as elsewhere in the Old Testament. Again and again, children are the source of great joy. Especially to be noted is the response of Sarah to the birth of Isaac (Gen. 21:6): "God has brought laughter for me; everyone who hears will laugh with me."[9] Deep appreciation and love for children may also be seen in Jacob's reaction to the apparent death of Joseph (Gen. 37:33-35). He cries out for his child with deep intensity, with traditional signs of mourning, lamenting for many days, unable to be comforted by his other children. In another case, if Benjamin does not return with his older brothers, Jacob will be so distressed that he will die, "bringing the gray head of our father down to the grave in sorrow" (44:31). Love and affection for children are often noted in the Old Testament, with both tenderness and discipline evident.

At the same time, children bring great anxiety and, at times, experience remarkably poor parenting. (See examples of poor parenting by Jacob in Gen. 34; and by David in 2 Sam. 13-19). That more negative side of the story of children in Genesis will become evident shortly.

One other claim is made about the divine promises. God does not make promises of children only to members of the chosen line. The narrative in Genesis 16-21 is punctuated with references to God's promises to Hagar and Ishmael (I return to them below). Virtually the same language is used for them as in God's promises to Abraham and Sarah (see Gen. 16:10; 17:20; 21:13, 18).[10] That God makes promises of children to outsiders as well insiders is significant. Given the fact that God always keeps promises, how might one look for the descendants of Hagar and Ishmael through the centuries?

So God's promises to children and about children fill almost every scene in the book of Genesis. Without these ongoing divine blessings, life for this family and its children would be bleak indeed.

---

8. Note the differences in the reference to Jacob's one daughter, Dinah (Gen. 30:21).

9. Isaac was a typical Israelite child in remaining under the care of his mother until the time of weaning — about three years old (see Gen. 21:8).

10. The extensive genealogy of another outsider, Esau (Gen. 36), reveals that he is also a richly blessed man.

Abraham as Teacher of Children

God specifically commands Abraham to teach his children (Gen. 18:19). Abraham is chosen so that "he may charge his children and his household to keep the way of the Lord by doing righteousness and justice; so that the Lord may bring about for Abraham what he has promised him." Notably, the future of God's promise to Abraham is said to involve the teaching of Abraham's children. Abraham is later said to have kept this divine charge to be teacher of his children (Gen. 26:5). This divine charge to Abraham is focused on the children's religious education and its implications for their daily walk. The reference to "righteousness and justice" reminds the reader of the depth and breadth of this education. The "way of the Lord" that Abraham is called to teach the children consists, not simply of personal or spiritual issues, but also matters of justice. Abraham is charged to teach his children very public matters, which are understood to be key concerns for God. Or, in other terms, the teaching of children by the community of faith has a very public face that includes the entirety of life in relationship to others.

This Genesis theme is picked up especially in the books of Exodus and Deuteronomy (Exod. 12:26-27; 13:8-10, 14-16; Deut. 4:9-10; 6:4-9, 20-25; 11:13-21; 31:9-13; cf. Josh. 4:6-7, 21-24). Central to several of these texts are the questions of children, which in turn become the occasion for teaching. For example, Deuteronomy 6:20-25 reads, "When your children ask you in time to come, 'What is the meaning of the decrees . . . that God has commanded you, then you shall say. . . .'" The focus is not on simple repetition but on an *interpretation* of the tradition in view of the new times and places represented in the book of Deuteronomy.[11]

The Vulnerability and Endangerment of Children

The patterns of the endangerment of children begin in the Genesis texts and become a lens through which the reader can read subsequent texts that imperil children. One thinks of the suffering of children in the flood or in the destruction of Sodom and Gomorrah, for whom Abraham interceded before God, unsuccessfully. Elsewhere in Genesis, one thinks of Ishmael and Isaac, to whom we will return.

Beyond Genesis, the biblical texts often witness to the endangerment of children — chosen and non-chosen. Andreas Michel speaks of "almost 200

---

11. See the essay by Patrick Miller in this volume.

texts about violence against children in the Hebrew Old Testament, another fifty from the deutero-canonical writings."[12] The sources of the endangerment of children vary, from war to famine and, as we shall see, even God's action in such situations. Life for children gets so horrific at times that the texts even speak about eating children to survive (Lam. 4:10).

God is not removed from such adverse effects upon children. God, using human agents, is a key actor in the judgment of sins that adults have perpetrated (Lam. 1:15-16). While God does not directly perpetrate the violence, the children suffer severely in the wake of God's using human agents to exact judgment. The best modern example may be World War II, in which children suffered, not least because of Allied bombs; these allies could be interpreted as the agents of God against the evils of Hitler and his minions. This sin-consequence connection enables many difficult Old Testament texts to be understood, such as Exodus 20:5: "God visits the iniquity of the fathers upon the children." This claim is a basic statement about God's created moral order.[13] The moral order functions so that sin and evil do not go unchecked in the life of world. But that moral order does not cut clean, striking only those who are wicked.[14]

God also endangers children through divine choices made and not made. Who will be the son of promise? Ishmael or Isaac? Jacob or Esau? One of Jacob's sons, or all twelve? God chooses some children rather than others and so creates even further conflict within this family.[15] Indeed, God chooses younger children over older children (e.g., Isaac, Jacob), thereby overturning cultural expectations and disrupting family life. The question may legitimately be asked regarding these divine choices: Do they inevitably make life difficult for children?

12. Michel goes on to say that such violence against children occurs primarily "in the context of descriptions or threats of war, usually as brutal and deadly human violence: children become the victims of armed force, cannibalism, imprisonment, slavery and the extermination of dynasties" (p. 51). Andreas Michel, "Sexual Violence against Children in the Bible," in *The Structural Betrayal of Trust,* ed. R. Ammicht-Quinn, H. Haker, and M. Junker-Kenny, Concilium (London: SCM, 2004), pp. 51-71.

13. For a discussion of the created moral order, see Fretheim, *God and World in the Old Testament,* pp. 158-64. See also the essay by Patrick Miller in this volume.

14. Whole families suffer for the sins of parents — e.g., the rebellion of Korah (Num. 16); Achan (Josh. 7); sons of Saul (2 Sam. 21:1-9). David's child suffers and dies for David's sins, as do many others in the following generations (1 Sam. 12). We know today that the sins of parents often have deeply adverse effects on the children — witness alcoholism.

15. This theme is revealing of the fact that conflict in Genesis must *not* be studied simply in sociological or psychological terms. Familial conflict in Genesis has a theological component. Of course, what human beings do with God's choices can make things a lot worse than they normally would be.

Human beings, including parents, certainly do their share in jeopardizing the life and health of children in Genesis and elsewhere. One thinks of Joseph, whose life is threatened from within his own household (Gen. 37). Joseph's brothers become jealous of their father's favoritism. First they conspire to kill him, then instead they sell him into slavery — a remarkable interruption in his advantaged childhood. Themes in this story include sibling rivalry, parental partiality, and familial violence.[16] The story refuses to shy away from the issue of the child's own culpability in how he is being treated; he is named outright as a tattletale and interprets his dreams in a prideful way.

One also thinks of Benjamin, treated like a pawn in the midst of familial struggles (Gen. 43–44). One thinks of Lot's virgin daughters (Gen. 19); Lot endangers them by offering them to the men of Sodom for sexual pleasure. While their age is not specified, that they are betrothed and yet unmarried suggests that they are youth. Such horrendous actions on the part of a father! No amount of appeal to issues of hospitality will enable Lot to escape from the judgment of the narrator. The daughters he offers are *betrothed* (see the strictures in Deut. 22:23-29). Later he has sexual relations with each of them, even if under the influence of alcohol. The narrative judges Lot: just as Lot gave his daughters no voice in the matter of sexual relations, so he is placed in a comparable situation, where his daughters give him no voice. What goes around comes around.

Two Genesis stories regarding the endangerment of children (Isaac and Ishmael) have proved difficult for interpreters, and the story of each deserves special attention.

Two Stories about Children

The Eviction and Rescue of Ishmael

Bible readers should give more time and space to this child of Abraham and Hagar and to the stories associated with him. That so many have been so ne-

---

16. Danna Nolan Fewell states: "For children who have been the victims and survivors of domestic abuse and who are struggling with issues of forgiveness, the story of Joseph may offer a significant model of psychological and emotional interruption. For although Joseph claims when the brothers are at last reconciled that, though they meant their actions for evil, God used them for good, Joseph is still careful to forgive his brothers only after he is in a position of power, removed from any further abuse at their hands" (*Children of Israel*, p. 111). The question may be raised as to whether Joseph does not actually refuse to forgive his brothers, for he is "not in the place of God" (Gen. 50:19-20).

glectful of Ishmael's story is sad; we would have been much better prepared for post–September 11 events if we had paid attention to this child.

When it comes to issues relating to children, several verses from the second story of Hagar and Ishmael in Genesis 21:14-21 are particularly pertinent. This boy was Abraham's son, but not a member of the chosen line; God makes a covenant with Isaac, not Ishmael. Ishmael and Hagar are outsiders; indeed, they are twice specifically excluded from the chosen family (Gen. 16; 21).

Once again the structure of the Genesis narrative assists us. Prior to Genesis 17:15, Sarah has not been named as the potential mother of the children God has promised Abraham. The context shows that having this child via Hagar is Sarah's choice; yet, Abraham voices no objection whatsoever. No judgment is passed on either figure for this means of having children.[17]

After Isaac's birth, Sarah's decision to send Hagar and Ishmael away is contrary to Abraham's wishes, but because God sides with Sarah, they are banished into the wilderness. At this point, when the narrative takes a particularly poignant turn, how striking it is that God becomes so deeply involved in the life of this child, Ishmael. God had come to Hagar's aid earlier in the wilderness, when she had been excluded from the chosen family. At that point God had extended promises to her (Gen. 16:10): "I will so greatly multiply your offspring that they cannot be counted for multitude." And a chapter later, when God makes it clear for the first time that Sarah is to be the mother of Isaac, God does not forget Ishmael. Indeed, God reiterates those promises to him in even sharper detail (17:20): "As for Ishmael, I have heard you. I will bless him and make him fruitful and exceedingly numerous; he shall be the father of twelve princes, and I will make him a great nation." Now, in the context of those ringing promises to Hagar and Ishmael, the story of Hagar and Ishmael takes a special turn in Genesis 21:14-20.

Notice the specific actions of God and recall the setting — away from the chosen people and out in the wilderness.

1. God hears the voice of the boy; the point is twice spoken. God hears the cries of children; God is not deaf to the seemingly "minor" wailings of the little ones. We are not given Ishmael's words here; there may not even have been words, only cries in the night. In any case, God hears his voice and moves to help him and his mother. Notably, God hears the voice of the boy "where he is" (Gen. 21:17). That is, God does not deal with the issue of a desperate child from afar; God goes where the troubled child is. Hagar and Ishmael do not

---

17. This also happens later with Jacob (Gen. 30); it is a practice known in other parts of that world.

have to find God and bring him on the scene. God is already there, quite apart from the ministrations of the chosen family. This theme of divine presence is especially striking in Genesis 21:22. Abimelech tells Abraham, "God is with you in all that you do." The same language that was used of Ishmael in 21:20 is here used of God's servant Abraham. The chosen family does not have a corner on the presence of God.

2. God uses human agents to bring the child through the crisis. God makes use of what is available; in this case, it is Ishmael's mother Hagar and a well of water. God tells Hagar: "Come lift up the boy and hold him fast with your hand, for I will make a great nation of him" (Gen. 21:18). Lift up this boy; hold this child fast. God opens her eyes, and she spots a well of water and gives him to drink. God does not perform a miracle, manufacturing a well of water out of thin air. Rather, God opens Hagar's eyes to see a well, a resource already available in God's good creation, but unable to be seen in the midst of all the trouble. Hagar, this outsider, becomes God's agent. God provides for the children, even for those who are not from the chosen line. But the importance of the agent should not be diminished; God always acts in and through available creaturely agents. God does not do these caring actions alone.

3. God was with the boy (Gen. 21:20). What follows are implications of God's "being with": Ishmael grows up, even in the godforsaken place of the wilderness. He receives an education, becoming an expert in the bow, a key means of food-gathering in that context. His mother continues to be an agent of God in his life; she takes advantage of her Egyptian heritage to acquire a wife for him.

And so here God is involved in the life of an unchosen child. God's will for this child is evident in several ways, but, most basically, the following: that the child live, that the child no longer be deprived, and, more generally, that he thrive in a life of stability. This is a massive testimony to God as one who cares for all children, not just those who are members of the chosen line. Out in the middle of nowhere, God is with this excluded child, a child excluded by good, religious people; God provides for him through means that are available quite apart from a religious community. This text is testimony that God is present and active out and about in neglected parts of the world, providing for the health and welfare of children, both insider and outsider. Wherever the chosen may traverse across the face of the earth, they encounter a God who has long been at work for good in the lives of even the most deprived of people, including children.

This text about Ishmael in Genesis is a lens through which to read the many references to orphans and other underprivileged children in the Old

Testament, for he is the first such biblical individual.[18] Stories like those of Ishmael may reflect the development of Israel's special concern about orphans and other such children. The theme of "widows and orphans" becomes a prominent biblical lens for thinking about God's relationship with children (see, e.g., Exod. 22:21-24). The mistreatment of children becomes a sign of the unfaithfulness of adults to their God (even among the chosen people!). Images of healthy, thriving children are a divine concern, and sharp penalties are prescribed for those who flaunt it, even if it means that the children of the privileged will in turn be orphaned. God will not tolerate the mistreatment of homeless children.

The Near-Sacrifice of Isaac

Contemporary Questions Raised by the Story

I focus here on the most difficult text regarding children in Genesis 12–50, namely, the near-sacrifice of Isaac.[19]

Genesis 22 is a deeply troubling text, even a hurtful text; it must be used with great care.[20] Religious interpretations, especially since Søren Kierkegaard's *Fear and Trembling*,[21] seem often to intensify the contradictoriness of the story, perhaps in the interests of heightening the mystery of God's ways. While the reader should not discount the unusual, even frightening character

18. An orphan is defined as one who has lost one or both parents. See the essay by Walter Brueggemann in this volume.

19. Estimates of the age of Isaac vary. On the one hand, he was old enough to carry wood and ask questions that assume a capacity to analyze a situation and potential problems relating to it (Gen. 22:6-7). On the other hand, God refers to him as a "boy" (22:12), and he calls out "Father" to Abraham (22:7). I think of a boy that is 12 to 13 years old. For a more complete study, see Terence E. Fretheim, *Abraham: Trials of Family and Faith* (Columbia: University of South Carolina Press, 2007), pp. 118-39.

20. In the Revised Common Lectionary, the text is appointed for Easter vigil; in the Jewish community, it is annually read on Rosh Hashanah. Repeated efforts have been made to soften the impact of the story; for example, God's test of Abraham was to see whether he would refuse to go forward with the sacrifice of his son. Whatever the interpretation, it must be consistent with God's commendation of Abraham for proceeding with the sacrifice.

21. Søren Kierkegaard, *Fear and Trembling: A Dialectical Lyric* (Princeton: Princeton University Press, 1941). For a critical analysis of Kierkegaard, see Jon Levenson, "Abusing Abraham: Traditions, Religious Histories, and Modern Misinterpretations," *Judaism* 47 (1998): 259-77. For Levenson, the "teleological suspension of the ethical" says too much. Because God's commands in the Bible are not grounded in some universal morality, Abraham is not suspending ethical foundations or "relying on a faith that transcends and diminishes ethical action" (p. 270).

of God's command, it must not be exaggerated either, not least because the narrator gives Abraham no explicit emotional reaction.

While this text has long occasioned theological and pastoral problems for interpreters, readerly anxieties have intensified over the course of the last century or so, not least because of the focus given to the abuse of children. Interrelated issues have been raised with respect to each of the three main characters: God, Abraham, and Isaac.

God What kind of God would command the sacrifice of a child? What does this command say about God's character? Even if God does not intend Abraham to follow through and, finally, slaughter his child, what kind of God would test Abraham in such a violent way? This God promises a son, proceeds to fulfill that promise, and then seems to take it back. Can this God be trusted?

Various responses to such questions have been suggested over the years. Sometimes it is thought that, if we consider the text offensive, then the problem is with us and with our relationship with God, and not with the text. A faithful one will follow where God leads, or at least where God is thought to lead, and especially what God commands — come what may. Such a perspective, however, seems to grant to faith in God a blank check; the ethical can be suspended whenever one thinks that that faith is being served. Jonestown and Waco, to name but two examples, seem not too far away.

Abraham What kind of faith does Abraham have? A blind faith? No questions are asked and no objections are raised. In fact, he shows no emotion whatsoever, though many retellings of the story have portrayed an agonized Abraham. Earlier in the narrative (Gen. 18; cf. 15:2, 8), Abraham could raise sharp questions with God about the fate of the righteous in Sodom and Gomorrah, but he is strangely passive when it comes to his own child. The narrator assures readers that Abraham loves his son (22:2). Yet Abraham apparently thinks nothing of putting him through the trauma that must have been involved. Is this not child abuse? Or is Abraham (and the culture of which he is a part) oblivious to such a reality? If so, does that make the issue of child abuse irrelevant?[22]

A suggestion might be made as to why Abraham raises no objection. It may be that the narrator intends that the *reader,* having learned from Abraham in Genesis 18 how to question God, is the one to ask the questions on this

---

22. See Phyllis Trible, "The Sacrifice of Sarah," in *'Not in Heaven': Coherence and Complexity in Biblical Narrative*, ed. J. Rosenblatt and J. Sitterson (Bloomington: Indiana University Press, 1991).

occasion. If so, the narrator has been immensely successful! Initially, one might suggest that Genesis 22:8 (and 22:5) is a delayed clue to Abraham's silence on this occasion: Abraham obeyed because he trusted that, given his prior experience, God would provide a way through this moment that would not entail giving up on the promise.

From another perspective, interpreters can get into a kind of quantitative game; does Abraham love God *more than* he loves his son (his love for Isaac is recognized in 22:2)?[23] But this story should not be reduced to a matter of how much love Abraham has for one or the other. To be a genuine sacrifice, it must be an act of faith and love of God, a giving back to God what is truly dear and costly. And so for the sacrifice to be genuine, must not Abraham's love for Isaac and Abraham's love for God be comparably great at the end of the day? Would not, then, issues of the degree of Abraham's love of God compared to his love for his child be beside the point?

Isaac   What kind of son is this who asks only one question and exhibits no struggle? Does this behavior reveal a child who is completely cowed by an authoritarian, if loving father? Or is this a son who trusts his father as his father trusts God?

Is This Child Abuse?

This story has occasioned deep readerly concern about Isaac, especially in this time when the abuse of children has screamed its way into the modern consciousness.[24] A 1990 book by Alice Miller, a Swiss psychoanalyst, has put the question sharply before us.[25] Miller suggests that this text has contributed in subtle ways to an atmosphere in church and society that makes it possible to justify the abuse of children. She grounds her reflections on some thirty artistic representations of this story over the centuries. This includes two of Rembrandt's paintings, in which Abraham is faced toward the heavens rather than toward Isaac, as if in blind obedience to God and oblivious to what he is about to do to Isaac. Abraham has his hands over Isaac's face, seemingly pre-

---

23. See the argument of Phyllis Trible, "The Sacrifice of Sarah," who thinks that the issue is idolatry, becoming more attached to Isaac than to God. On Trible's questionable analysis of "love" in v. 2, see Walter Moberly, *The Bible, Theology, and Faith: A Study of Abraham and Jesus* (Cambridge: Cambridge University Press, 2000), pp. 163-68.

24. This story has, of course, long raised troubling issues, but they have largely been focused on the dilemma faced by the parent in the wake of the divine command.

25. Alice Miller, *The Untouched Key: Tracing Childhood Trauma in Creativity and Destructiveness* (New York: Doubleday, 1990). She has been joined by many others.

venting him from seeing or raising a cry. Not only is Isaac silenced; in addition, only his torso is visible, so that his personal features are obscured. Miller says: Isaac "has been turned into an *object*. He has been dehumanized by being made a sacrifice; he no longer has a right to ask questions and will scarcely even be able to articulate them to himself, for there is no room in him for anything besides fear."[26] Even if she is wrong about Isaac asking no questions, does she not raise an important issue?

We have the testimony of a few parents who have in fact killed their children and ascribed the act to obedience to a divine command.[27] It will not do for us simply to dismiss this negative impact of Genesis 22; it would not be the first time that the Bible has been used knowingly or unknowingly in such distorted ways. Hard as it may be to hear, traditional understandings of this text may in fact have contributed to this more recent reading of the text: *the place of the child has been sorely neglected in a centuries-long focus on the trusting response of Abraham to God's testing.*

It seems clear that more recent problems with Genesis 22 have been sparked by the increasing recognition of the lack of societal attention to the issues children face.[28] Such realities of our own context have sharpened our reading experience of Genesis 22. Meanings of texts are always, of course, the product of the interaction of the text and the reader and his or her experience. At the same time, the issue cannot simply be laid at the feet of readers; at the least, the text does not provide safeguards against negative interpretations. Even if child abuse was not in the mind of the narrator or those who heard this text in ancient Israel, what modern readers hear is not totally irrelevant. Indeed, the language of the text itself can contribute to such an understanding, for God asks and then twice commends Abraham for not withholding his son, his only son, "from me" (Gen. 22:2, 12, 16). It is as if the child is simply a pawn in the hands of an issue between "adults" (God and Abraham). Of course,

26. Miller, *The Untouched Key*, p. 139.

27. See Wayne Oates, *The Bible in Pastoral Care* (Philadelphia: Westminster, 1953), who tells the story about a mother's response to hearing a sermon on this text. On California trials, see Carol Delaney, *Abraham on Trial: The Social Legacy of Biblical Myth* (Princeton: Princeton University Press, 1998). Moberly's claim, "There is *no* recorded example of Jews or Christians using the text to justify their own abusing or killing of a child," is insufficiently researched (*The Bible, Theology, and Faith*, p. 129).

28. More broadly, one might cite twentieth-century experiences of poverty, homelessness, and violence that have so often caught up the young. Or one thinks of the sending of young men and women into battle to settle conflicts that adults have failed to resolve; or the saturation bombings of cities that wipe out large numbers of children; or the death camps and gas chambers that snuff out the lives of children; or the virtual ignoring of genocidal activities in far-off lands (e.g., Rwanda, Darfur). Sadly, one could go on.

modern adults have little room to criticize either God or Abraham, given the extent to which we remain silent about child abuse among us.[29] But some room exists for an evaluative stance on the basis of the Bible's larger perspective regarding children. If the child in the text (Isaac) is carefully and concernedly remembered, can we ignore this direction of reflection regarding abuse?

History and Metaphor

Reading this text in view of the issue of child abuse has not been common among interpreters until quite recently.[30] In response, several scholars have claimed that this approach is a misuse, even gross misuse of the text.[31] Two directions of response to the "charge" of child abuse might be especially noted: the historical context of the text; and the text as metaphor. Neither approach, in my opinion, finally succeeds in setting aside the issue that has been raised.

The Historical Context Jon Levenson has been particularly concerned to draw out the religio-historical dimensions of the text. His discussion is often helpful. Initially, the text speaks of Isaac as a "burnt offering" (Gen. 22:2; see Exod. 29:38-46; Lev. 1:3-17 for details) and a "substitute" sacrifice is finally given (Gen. 22:13).[32] These bookends of the story place the episode within the context of the sacrificial system. This reality should be placed alongside the fact (known from other texts) that child sacrifice was an important part of the context within which Genesis 22 was written.[33] More specifically, "the first-born son was long and widely believed to belong to God and must be offered to him, either through literal sacrifice (rarely, as in Genesis 22) or

---

29. A related theme is present in twentieth-century war literature, e.g., the poem of Wilfrid Owen, who died fighting for England in 1917, "The Parable of the Old Man and the Young." Appended to a posthumous edition was this line: "The willingness of the older generation to sacrifice the younger." See also Danny Siegel's 1969 look at this text in poetic form: "Father Abraham Genesis 22 — Slightly Changed."

30. See T. Fretheim, "God, Abraham, and the Abuse of Isaac," *Word and World* 15 (1995): 49-57. See also the survey in Moberly, *The Bible, Theology, and Faith.*

31. Especially to be noted are Jon Levenson, "Abusing Abraham," in *The Death and Resurrection of the Beloved Son: Child Sacrifice and Its Transformation in Judaism and Christianity* (New Haven: Yale University Press, 1993); Moberly, *The Bible, Theology, and Faith*, pp. 127-31, 162-83, who follows Levenson. Levenson describes this approach in these terms: Abraham's action has been "increasingly and loudly developed into an interpretation of the last trial as an act of unspeakable cruelty, a paradigm not of love, faith, and submission to God, as in Judaism, Christianity, and Islam, in their traditional formulations, but of hatred, mental illness, and even idolatry" (p. 262).

32. On whether it is appropriate to use the language of substitution, see below.

33. It should be noted that we do not know when this chapter was written.

through one or another of the rituals by which a substitution was made" (e.g., Exod. 22:28-29; cf. Ezek. 20:25-26). The firstborn son was to be thereby "redeemed" (Exod. 13:11-16; 34:20; Num. 3:40-51); in Genesis 22, God does just this in a *narrative equivalent of the ritual.* That is, God commands that Isaac be sacrificed and then provides an animal "instead of" Isaac.[34] To the father about to make the offering "the prospect was doubtless painful in the extreme, perhaps too painful for words, but it was *not* unconnected to the larger culture and its ethical and theological norms, nor was it incomprehensible or incommunicable to others in the same cultural universe." An important matter for Levenson is that, *"in the biblical text, sacrifice is not deemed unethical or irrational,"* and so it requires no more an act of faith to adhere to such demands than to ethical demands."[35] The texts generally recognize the difference between murder and sacrifice.[36]

For Levenson, that Abraham's response would not have been offensive in that era does not in any way imply that a contemporary person of faith should do likewise; in our culture it would rightly be considered murder. Between the Akedah and today lies the Torah, with its redemption of the firstborn, and the prophetic condemnation of child sacrifice (e.g., Jer. 9:3-6),[37] and hence one cannot read a validation of child abuse from the text. Levenson goes to great lengths in seeking to demonstrate that Abraham is not a child abuser; in fact, "it is a symptom of acute myopia and mind-numbing parochialism to think that this must also have been the case in a society that practiced sacrifice (even, on occasion and for a while, child-sacrifice) and did not confuse it with murder."[38]

---

34. Jon Levenson, "Abusing Abraham," pp. 270-71. He cites parallels in the ancient world in *Death and Resurrection*, pp. 3-24, 43-52. Child sacrifice in general is different and is prohibited in Lev. 20:2-5 and denounced by several of the prophets (e.g., Jer. 19:3-6).

35. Jon Levenson, "Abusing Abraham," p. 271 (emphasis his). These comments occur in a context of a critique brought against Søren Kierkegaard's *Fear and Trembling;* he claims that Kierkegaard fails to recognize this historical reality and hence "opens a door to those who judge Abraham to be an unbalanced person."

36. Jon Levenson suggests that this is a difference between Genesis 18:16-33, against which Abraham protests, and Genesis 22; the former is a "forensic" context (where the death of an innocent person is an outrage, and hence Abraham's intervention), while the latter is a sacrificial context.

37. It should be noted that child sacrifice was a sometime problem for Israel (cf. Lev. 20:2-5; 2 Kings 3:27; Jer. 7:31; 32:35), even if finally abhorrent.

38. Levenson, "Abusing Abraham," p. 271. Moberly *(The Bible, Theology, and Faith)* is comparably sharp: "To disregard the context which enabled the meaningful preservation of a story about child sacrifice, and then proclaim the story a problem for contemporary readers, is to create a more or less artificial problem. It exemplifies the truism that context is crucial for meaning" (p. 129).

Perhaps so, but I wonder if the factors cited are sufficient to shut down the conversation about abuse. First, three details might be more closely considered. (a) The text bears no explicit mark of being a polemic against child sacrifice (unlike the prophets, e.g., Jer. 19:3-6); Abraham, finally, is commanded not to sacrifice his son, but the text does not generalize the point. (b) The text makes no claim to being an etiology of the redemption of the firstborn.[39] Is it because Isaac is not a firstborn son? Is it because the ram is not clearly a "substitute" for Isaac?[40] (c) From another angle, while the factors relating to the emergence of laws prohibiting child sacrifice in Israel are unclear, might it have had to do, at least in part, with observed negative effects on the lives of children and their families?[41]

Second, to speak more generally, to say that the divine command would not have been offensive in Israel's world begs the question as to whether it *should* have been deemed so. Can evaluative judgments not be made of Israelite thought and practice? For example, patriarchy was characteristic of Israel's life, but does this mean that no evaluative words can be directed at those who exercised patriarchal practices?[42] Levenson and others are on target when they criticize those who speak of Abraham being mentally unbalanced or cruel. But if Abraham should not be criticized at those points, given the realities of sacrifice in that world, what of the practice itself? Perhaps even more importantly, the issue should not simply revolve around the issue of the behaviors of the "adults" involved (God and Abraham). Whatever the evaluation of their actions (on either side of the issue), the negative effects on the child (emotional and otherwise) should be placed front and center. Whatever Abraham's (and God's) intent, is it not likely that Isaac was traumatized by the threat of imminent and violent death at the hands of his father?[43]

---

39. The etiological reference in Genesis 22:14b is unclear, but it has no known reference to the redemption of the firstborn (see Claus Westermann, *Genesis 12–36: A Commentary* [Minneapolis: Augsburg, 1981], pp. 362-63).

40. See n. 47 below.

41. Jon Levenson ("Abusing Abraham," p. 277, n. 50), in considering the question of the emergence of the prohibition, considers basically cultic factors, with a mention of Genesis 9:6 and not shedding the blood of human beings made in the image of God. Given what we are told about the suffering of children in the fall of Jerusalem (e.g., Lam. 4:10) and our knowledge of children more generally, might the suffering of children have been a key factor? The point should at least be considered.

42. Generally on the issue of evaluation of biblical texts, see Terence E. Fretheim with Karlfried Froehlich, *The Bible as Word of God in a Postmodern Age* (Minneapolis: Fortress, 1988). See also Terence E. Fretheim, "Violence in the Old Testament," *Word and World* 24 (2004): 18-28.

43. That Isaac did not return with his father, though Abraham had promised that they would both return (Gen. 22:5), is sometimes cited as a sign of this, but that remains uncertain.

The Text as Metaphor   Moving beyond simple historical issues, Levenson promotes a metaphorical (he uses the term "symbolic") interpretation of the text. That the sacrificial death "is only symbolic, that the son, *mirabile dictu*, returns alive, is the narrative equivalent of the ritual substitutions that prevent the gory offering from being made."[44] Early in its history, Israel had prohibited child sacrifice as an abomination hateful to God; yet they could see in Abraham's deed "a paradigmatic disclosure of deeper truths." Among the truths he sees in the text: "all we have, even our lives and those of our dearest, belong ultimately to God; His claim must be honored; God's promises are often painfully at odds with empirical reality."[45]

Walter Moberly also speaks of a metaphorical understanding of Genesis 22, joining a long line of interpreters in the life of the church. He admits that the metaphor is a "dangerous" one, open to abuse on the part of the unscrupulous and misguided. But all metaphors are "in some way 'dangerous.'"[46] He summarizes the metaphorical value of this story in these terms:[47] (a) relinquishing to God that which is most precious (Isaac, the beloved son);[48] (b) self-dispossession of that on which one's identity and hopes are most deeply based (Isaac as hope for the future); (c) response to God as costly, or even more costly, at the end of one's life than it was earlier on; (d) the outcome of obedience is unknown and cannot be predicted in advance (a real

---

44. Jon Levenson, *Death and Resurrection*, p. 59. The force of the word "only" needs discussion.

45. Levenson, "Abusing Abraham," pp. 272-73.

46. Moberly, *The Bible, Theology, and Faith*, p. 130. I wonder whether this claim slides much too quickly over the vast difference among metaphors regarding their "danger."

47. Moberly, *The Bible, Theology, and Faith*, p. 182. The extent to which the language of self-sacrifice permeates his discussion deserves closer attention on his part. For example, Abraham is "required to sacrifice to God not only the centre of his affections but that which he has lived for and is the content of his hope and his trust in God" (p. 131). Or, "the whole burnt offering is symbolic of Abraham's self-sacrifice as a person who unreservedly fears God" (p. 118). He seems not to recognize the dangers of this kind of sacrificial language on the shape and character of the life of faith. It should be noted that, after discerning Abraham's faithfulness, God stopped him *before* the ram was spotted (Gen. 22:12-13). So the provision of the ram was not necessary to save Isaac. Indeed, Isaac's sacrifice was stopped independent of the role of the ram, so that "instead of" does not have a "substitutionary" sense. Why would the ram, then, be sacrificed? Is it because of the way in which Abraham states the trust in v. 8? Abraham has faith that God will provide an animal for the offering instead of his son, and so that is what God provides.

48. See the common theme of mourning over an only son. The question may be asked: Has Isaac been sacrificed? Certainly in some respects. Perhaps, as Janzen states (*Abraham and All the Families of the Earth: A Commentary on Genesis 12–50* [Grand Rapids: Eerdmans, 1993]), "Isaac has truly been sacrificed — truly given up and given over to God. The life he will go on to live is now wholly God's, and Abraham no longer has any claim to it" (pp. 80-81).

test); (e) the religious community cannot become complacent. In these terms, the story is "a paradigm of life with God." To that end, the "purpose of YHWH's testing is to promote such a way of living."[49] Though the "literal" practice had been set aside, the story as metaphor retained its power as a paradigm of religious life.[50]

In response, it must be said that these points of significance retain a focus on Abraham (the adult) and his faith, moving all too quickly past the child.[51] In any interpretation of the text as metaphor, it is important not to deplete the story of its sheer horror (remembering that metaphor does include a literal dimension). To identify the story as metaphor should not set readers' minds to looking for the "real" meaning of the text and away from the sacrifice of a child.[52] The potential sacrifice of an actual child is certainly intended to come to the mind of the reader, to confront the reader with the difficult nature of the divine command and the complexity of the journey with God. Readers may disagree with the narrator's strategy in doing that, but the point remains: a child has been abused.

Genesis 22 does not finally enable one to sit comfortably with the obvious abuse that Isaac undergoes. Readers have wondered whether this experience is evident in the fact that Isaac does not return with his father in 22:19 (though Abraham had so assured his servants in 22:5).[53] Abraham and Isaac

---

49. Moberly, *The Bible, Theology, and Faith,* p. 101. Moberly emphasizes *Abraham's* learning, though Genesis 22:12 stresses God's learning.

50. *If* one is to interpret the text as a metaphor for Israel's life with God, it seems to me necessary to understand that Israel is *both* Abraham and Isaac. And so Israel is not simply one who *makes* a sacrifice (Abraham); Israel is also the one who *is* the sacrifice (Isaac). Various issues related to the fall of Jerusalem would come into play at this point, including the Suffering Servant in Isaiah 53.

51. For *Israel* as the firstborn of God, see Exodus 4:22, an issue faced by the exiles (Jer. 31:9, 20; cf. 2:3). I have spoken of Genesis 22 as metaphor with reference to *Israel* as firstborn (Terence E. Fretheim, "The Book of Genesis," *The New Interpreter's Bible,* vol. 1 [Nashville: Abingdon, 1994], pp. 494, 499). See also Terence E. Fretheim, "Christology and the Old Testament," in *Who Do You Say That I Am? Essays on Christology in Honor of Jack Kingsbury,* ed. Mark A. Powell and David Bauer (Louisville: Westminster John Knox, 1999), pp. 201-15. The New Testament connections, which link Jesus with both Abraham and Isaac, should also be cited. For the parallels of Jesus and Abraham, see Ellen Davis, *Getting Involved with God: Rediscovering the Old Testament* (Cambridge: Cowley, 2001), p. 63.

52. I wonder whether Moberly understands metaphor in such a way that the actual sacrifice of the child is not to come to the mind of the reader.

53. For detail, see the discussion in Hemchand Gossai, *Power and Marginality in the Abrahamic Narrative* (Lanham, MD: University Press, 1995), pp. 158-60. Cf. also M. J. Kohn, "The Trauma of Isaac," *Jewish Bible Quarterly* 20 (1991-1992): 96-104. It has also been suggested that this experience may be related to an ineptitude on Isaac's part in Genesis 26–27.

never again converse in the narrative that follows, not even in connection with the search for a wife for Isaac (Gen. 24). While Isaac attends Abraham's funeral (25:9), he does not attend Sarah's or even return to her deathbed (Gen. 23). Moreover, why would God, but not Abraham, bless Isaac (25:11)?

Might this distancing between father and son have anything to do with the horrific experience on Mt. Moriah? Might these textual details, even if in subtle ways, recognize that a child has been abused?

What, Then, of the Future of Children for Genesis?

In the wake of such horrendous stories about children in Genesis, two notes of hope for children are lifted up for readers in the last chapter (Gen. 50).

Human Acts of Kindness as God's Agents for Good   When Joseph and his brothers are reconciled, he gives testimony that God has been at work for good in the midst of evil, "in order to preserve a numerous people" (Gen. 50:20). This goodness of God becomes immediately evident in Joseph's own words and actions (50:21): "So have no fear; I myself will provide for you and *your little ones*. In this way he reassured them, speaking kindly to them." Joseph does not retaliate but reaches out to those who have betrayed him and promises to take care of their children.

Ending on a Note of Promise   Joseph becomes the mediator of God's continuing promises to this people. He says, "God will surely come to you and fulfill the promises that God has extended to your ancestors." God will continue to be present and active in this family, in the midst of the worst the world may throw their way. God will do this on behalf of the divine mission, so often stated in Genesis: through you shall all the families of the earth be blessed, including their children.

Concluding Reflection

So, this essay ends precisely where the book of Genesis ends: on a note of hope for children in the wake of all the violence that they have experienced through the generations. Will that hope be realized?

2 Exodus as a "Text of Terror" for Children

Claire R. Mathews McGinnis

Introduction

The events recounted in the book of Exodus are central to the Bible's story of God's election of Israel. The book opens with the ruthless oppression of the Israelites by Pharaoh and the Egyptians, including the drowning of all Hebrew baby boys in the Nile. Moses famously escapes death when his mother places him in a papyrus basket by the shore, after which he is adopted by Pharaoh's daughter, met by God on Mt. Horeb in the burning bush, and commissioned to go to Pharaoh to ask him to "Let my people go" (Exod. 1–4). Pharaoh's repeated refusal to let the Israelites go, in spite of the sending of numerous plagues, culminates in one final act of God, the death of all the firstborn of Egypt, after which Pharaoh sends the Israelites away (chs. 5–13). He has a change of heart, though, and pursues them to the Sea, through which the Israelites pass unharmed on dry ground, while Pharaoh and his army are drowned (chs. 14–15). YHWH subsequently meets Moses and the Israelites on Mt. Sinai where a covenant is made, observance of which includes the Ten Commandments along with numerous other statutes and ordinances given to Moses on behalf of the entire people (chs. 19–24). The latter portion of Exodus contains detailed instructions for crafting the tabernacle and other apparatus, including the ark of the covenant, necessary for the cultic (liturgical) life of the Israelites en route to the promised land (chs. 25–30; 35–40). The book closes with the dramatic account of the glory of the LORD filling the tabernacle and of the cloud by day and fire by night that marked YHWH's presence among the Israelites on their journey (40:34-38).

The impact of the Exodus from Egypt on Israelite identity, including its role in shaping interpretation of later situations in Israel's history, is not easy to overstate. As Nahum Sarna has observed, the book's "central theme, God's redemption of His people from Egyptian bondage, is mentioned no less than one hundred and twenty times in the Hebrew Bible in a variety of contexts."[1] Of course, that the covenant at Sinai which is the focus of the second half of the book serves as the foundation for subsequent Israelite and Jewish observance is well known.

Children are particularly prominent in the first half of the book: in the genealogy that opens chapter 1 (and a second genealogy in ch. 6); in the story of Pharaoh's attempts at killing the Israelite male infants; in the birth and rescue of Moses in such a context; and especially in the final plague on Egypt in which the firstborn Egyptians are slain while the firstborn of the Israelites are "passed over." The prominence of children in this first part of the book, however, presents a paradox to the reader, for this story of deliverance is also very much a "text of terror" for children:[2] first Pharaoh seeks to kill them, and then so does YHWH, in the plague of the firstborn. The portrayal of God as one who would slaughter innocents (inasmuch as at least some of the Egyptian firstborn would still have been children) is very troubling indeed, and hence its "terror."

In examining the central role of children in the story of Exodus, this chapter will attempt to tease out some of the complexities of the place and significance of children within the covenant community. On the one hand, the biblical text displays recognition of the particular vulnerability and needs of children as they develop physically and socially. On the other hand, children are portrayed not primarily as a distinct demographic but as an integral element of a larger social and liturgical community, an element whose fortunes are tied to the fate and faith of that community. I will contend that understanding two things helps mitigate to some degree the terror of the text. The first of these is the distinct nature of the Israelite community as YHWH's elect or "firstborn"; the second is the way in which the consecration and redemption of firstborn in Israel signals God's sovereignty over the entire community. In the latter part of the chapter I will examine the celebration of the Passover enjoined by the book of Exodus in order to illustrate how those features that constitute Exodus's terror become the occasion for acknowledging the kinds of terror that children in certain communities continue to experience. I will also suggest ways in which Exodus's perspectives on children might inform our own understanding of our obligations to children today.

---

1. Nahum Sarna, *Exodus,* The JPS Torah Commentary (Philadelphia: The Jewish Publication Society, 1991), p. xii.

2. The description of certain biblical texts as texts of terror comes from Phyllis Trible, *Texts of Terror: Literary-Feminist Readings of Biblical Narratives,* Overtures to Biblical Theology (Minneapolis: Fortress, 1994).

Genealogy and Blessing

If one looks for children in Exodus, then one initially finds them embedded in a family line, in genealogy. The book of Exodus opens, "These are the names of the sons of Israel who came down to Egypt with Jacob, each with their household" (Exod. 1:1). The total number of persons, the sons and their households, is given as seventy (1:2-4). This genealogical information is an adaptation of materials from Genesis 46 and 35.[3] While it might strike today's reader as a very poor way to begin a book, the importance of place given to genealogy, both at the opening of Exodus and again in chapter 6, is suggestive of how children are viewed by the biblical writers: while a son or daughter remains a child for only a short time, the child's place in the nexus of extended familial relations — being a son or daughter of these particular parents, and from this particular household, clan, and tribe — situates one within the larger community.[4] Indeed, the Israelites in Egypt are delivered in part because of their lineage — because they are descendants of Abraham, Isaac, and Jacob (see Exod. 2:23b-25).

That one's familial connections are integral to one's identity within the larger community is likewise suggested by the subtle transformations in terminology exhibited in Exodus 1. Verses 1 and 7 both refer to the "sons of Israel" (*bᵉnê yiśrāʾēl*). In the first instance the reference is to Jacob's sons in particular; in the second, to their descendants, who were "fruitful and prolific." In verse 9, however, Pharaoh refers to these descendants as *ʿam bᵉnê yiśrāʾēl*, literally "*the people* (of) the sons of Israel."[5] Verse 12 then picks up again the shorter phrase "the sons of Israel." The construction "*people* (of) the sons of Israel" in verse 9 is an unusual one, and it helps to underscore the development that has taken place between verses 1 and 7 as well as the consequent shift in what the phrase "sons of Israel" now connotes. The sons of Jacob/Israel, who came down to Egypt as a family of seventy persons (vv. 1-6), have now become a body so large

---

3. See discussion in Brevard Childs, *The Book of Exodus*, The Old Testament Library (Philadelphia: Westminster, 1974), p. 2, and Gordon F. Davies, *Israel in Egypt: Reading Exodus 1–2*, Journal for the Study of the Old Testament — Supplement Series 135 (Sheffield: Sheffield Academic Press, 1992), pp. 32-34.

4. For a discussion of the household, clan, and tribe as the major components of kinship in Israel, see C. J. H. Wright, "Family," in *Anchor Bible Dictionary*, vol. 2, ed. David Noel Freedman (New York: Doubleday, 1992), pp. 761-69.

5. This is an example of Joüon's "genitive of proper noun" as exhibited also in phrases like "the river (of) Euphrates" and "the land (of) Canaan." Paul Joüon, S.J., and T. Muraoka, *A Grammar of Biblical Hebrew*, vol. 2, Subsidia Biblica 14 (Rome: Editrice Pontificio Istituto Biblico, 1991), p. 466.

it constitutes a "people" — the Israelites (v. 7).[6] This change in the meaning of the Hebrew phrase *b⁽ⁿê yiśrā'ēl* is reflected in English translations such as the NRSV, which renders the phrase in verse 1 as "the sons of Israel" and the phrase in verse 7 as "the Israelites."[7] Pharaoh's expression in verse 9 is appropriately rendered in English as "the Israelite people."

By summarizing the development of the sons of Israel into a people, the Israelites, the opening section of Exodus not only illustrates the way in which familial connections — being a son or daughter of this particular household, clan, and tribe — situates one within the Israelite community. It also moves the reader out of Genesis's stories of the individual patriarchs and their families and into Exodus's story of God's deliverance of a nation.

The Israelites' proliferation is described in Exodus 1 in a way that alludes both to the promises to the patriarchs and, even farther back in Genesis, to the blessings conferred on humanity at the creation of the world. Exodus 1:7 states that the Israelites "were *fruitful (pārû)* and *teemed (wayyišr⁽ṣû)* and *multiplied (wayyirbû)* and became *exceedingly numerous (wayya'aṣ⁽mû bim⁽'od m⁽'od)* so that the land *was filled (wattimālē')* with them." The first, third, and fifth terms ("fruitful," "multiply," "filled") are the very ones God uses in blessing humankind in Genesis 1:28, blessings that are reiterated after the flood (Gen 9:1-2). Three of these terms are also used in the blessings given to Abraham and his descendants.[8] By using such allusive language in describing the proliferation of the Israelites, the biblical writers signal that what God is doing for the Israelites in the book of Exodus is "conceived as a new act of God's creation," that "God's intentions in creation are being realized in this family."[9] Put another way, the language of creation and blessing taken up by

6. See Moshe Greenberg, *Understanding Exodus,* Part I, The Heritage of Biblical Israel, vol. II (New York: Behrman House for The Melton Research Center of the Jewish Theological Seminary of America, 1969), p. 20; J. Cheryl Exum, "'You Shall Let Every Daughter Live': A Study of Exodus 1:8–2:10," *Semeia* 28 (1963): 63-82 (here 66), reprinted in *A Feminist Companion to Exodus and Deuteronomy,* ed. Athalya Brenner (Sheffield: Sheffield Academic Press, 1994) 37-67; and Childs, *Exodus,* p. 2.

7. Greenberg, *Understanding Exodus,* p. 20, seems to suggest that the phrase is not to be rendered as "the Israelites" until after verse 7.

8. See Gen. 17:2, 6: "multiply," "be fruitful," and "become numerous." "Exceedingly" is also used here twice. See also Gen. 28:3; 35:1; and 48:4. The term "teemed" is used in the creation stories concerning animals.

9. James S. Ackerman, "The Literary Context of the Moses Birth Story (Exodus 1–2)," in *Literary Interpretations of Biblical Narratives,* ed. Kenneth R. R. Gros Louis, James S. Ackerman, and T. W. Warshaw (Nashville: Abingdon, 1974), pp. 74-75; Terence E. Fretheim, *Exodus,* Interpretation (Louisville: John Knox, 1991), p. 25. Both Ackerman's and Fretheim's works explore this aspect of the text at length.

the writer in Exodus 1:7 reminds readers that the gift of children in general, and of the Israelite children in particular, is a distinguishing, tangible manifestation of God's ongoing blessing of humankind.[10]

God's unfolding plan for Israel is opposed by the words and actions of the king of Egypt. Pharaoh attempts to suppress the burgeoning Israelite population — to counteract God's blessing through children — by means of forced labor and ultimately through infanticide.[11] Thus Pharaoh sets himself against the intentions and work of God, a fact that becomes increasingly clear as the narrative progresses.[12] That Pharaoh is no match for God is initially intimated by the fact that "the more [the Israelites] were oppressed, the more they multiplied and spread" (Exod. 1:12).

The developing contest between the God of the Israelites and the king of Egypt is designed to demonstrate to whom the Israelites' "service" rightfully belongs.[13] But it is the differing fates of the Egyptian and Israelite children through which the liberation from Egypt is to be won.[14] The Egyptian firstborn will be slain, while those of the Israelites will be passed over, demonstrating that it is God's prerogative not only to give life but also to take it away.

The Midwives and Moses' Birth, Rescue, and Redemption

Several studies have noted the prominent role played by women in Exodus 1:15–2:10, observing along the way that among the many unnamed characters in this portion of narrative — the Pharaoh, Moses' mother, father, and sister

---

10. In Genesis 1 God also blesses the sea creatures and birds, saying, "Be fruitful and multiply . . ."; thus it cannot be said that progeny is *the* distinguishing manifestation of God's blessing of humankind. (Indeed, what distinguishes the blessing of humans from that of animals is the addition of the blessing to subdue the earth and to have dominion over the other living things [Gen. 1:28].)

11. For discussion on the logic of using forced labor to decrease a population and having the male infants rather than female infants killed, see Exum, "'Let Every Daughter Live,'" p. 69; Ackerman, "Literary Context," p. 83; Greenberg, *Understanding Exodus,* p. 29, particularly n. 2; and William H. C. Propp, *Exodus 1–18,* Anchor Bible 2 (New York: Doubleday, 1999), p. 132.

12. James Ackerman demonstrates how this section of the narrative echoes the story of the tower of Babel and thereby participates in Exodus's many allusions to Genesis's creation narratives. See Ackerman, "Literary Context," pp. 78-82.

13. The Hebrew term ʿăbodāh can mean both servitude and worship, a feature that the narrative capitalizes on but that is much less apparent in English translations.

14. While not all of the firstborn of Egypt would still have been children, many would.

— it is the midwives whose names are given.[15] Even so, it is the children who are central to the story's plot, even if they are not those acting but being acted upon. The prominence of women in this section of the story is at least in part a function of the story's focus on bearing and nursing children.

The account of the midwives' role in preserving children's lives is richly allusive and full of dark humor.[16] The two women are able to dupe the wicked Pharaoh with their story of the Hebrew women being more "vigorous" than the Egyptians,[17] while their piety (they "feared God") resonates with other wisdom themes that run throughout this section of narrative.[18]

From a literary standpoint, the story helps to tie together the account of the Israelites' servitude, which precedes it, and the account of Moses' birth,

15. In addition to Exum, "'Let Every Daughter Live,'" see J. Cheryl Exum, "Mother in Israel: A Familiar Story Reconsidered," in *Feminist Interpretation of the Bible,* ed. Letty Russell (Philadelphia: Westminster, 1985), pp. 73-85; J. Cheryl Exum, "Secondary Thoughts about Secondary Characters: Women in Ex 1:8–2:10," in *A Feminist Companion,* pp. 75-87. As A. Brenner has suggested, Moses' story reflects a pattern of stories of the birth of a hero in the Bible. In this case Moses has three "mothers," a biological one, a sister who plays a protective role, and a foreign, adoptive mother. See Athalya Brenner, "Female Social Behavior: Two Descriptive Patterns within the 'Birth of the Hero' Paradigm," *Vetus Testamentum* 36, no. 3 (1986): 257-73.

16. Scholarly discussion of the story of the midwives has concerned why only two midwives are represented as serving such a large population. See, for instance, the discussion in Sarna, *Exodus,* p. 7, and Childs, *Exodus,* p. 16. Ackerman, "Literary Context," p. 85, suggests that there are only two because the story has narrowed its focus to a small locale. Discussion has also concerned whether "the midwives of the Hebrew women" were themselves Hebrew or Egyptian. See the discussion in Childs, *Exodus,* p. 16; Greenberg, *Understanding Exodus,* p. 26; Ackerman, "Literary Context," pp. 85-86; and Exum, "'Let Every Daughter Live,'" pp. 72-74. There has also been discussion concerning Pharaoh's command in 1:16, "when you see them *on the birthing stool* ('al-hā'ābnāyim) if it is a boy you shall kill him." The term 'abnāyim, literally, "two stones," but taken to mean birthing stool, refers elsewhere to a potter's wheel (Jer. 18:3). Thus Scott Morschauser argues that one finds here an "Egyptianism," given that "the 'potter's wheel' is regularly linked to pregnancy in ancient Egyptian religious literature and art." He suggests that the metaphor "refers to a gestating fetus *prior to parturition*," and that Pharaoh is telling the midwives to "terminate" the baby boys during prenatal exams. "Potters Wheels and Pregnancies: A Note on Exodus 1:6," *Journal of Biblical Literature* 122, no. 4 (2003): 731-33. Durham's commentary accepts the interpretation that the "two stones" refer to a boy's testicles, and that Pharaoh's intention is that they be killed at birth. See his discussion on pp. 11-12 of John I. Durham, *Exodus,* Word Biblical Commentary 3 (Waco, TX: Word, 1987).

17. The Hebrew term used here, ḥāyôt, is discssued in G. R. Driver, "Hebrew Mothers," *Zeitschrift für die alttestamentliche Wissenschaft* 67 (1955): 246-48. Renita Weems observes how the midwives' ruse capitalizes on Pharaoh's own prejudices about the Israelites' difference from Egyptians in "The Hebrew Women Are Not Like the Egyptian Women: The Ideology of Race, Gender and Sexual Reproduction in Exodus 1," *Semeia* 59 (1992): 25-34.

18. See the discussion on pp. 118-22 of Brevard S. Childs, "The Birth of Moses," *Journal of Biblical Literature* 84, no. 2 (1965): 109-22.

which follows.[19] With the latter, it shares the theme of the Pharaoh's attempt to kill the baby boys. With the former, it shares the theme of proliferation: verse 20 states that God "dealt well with the midwives; and the people multiplied and became very numerous" (using the Hebrew roots *rbb* and *ṣm* as in Exod. 1:7.) And in verse 21, God also gives the midwives enduring progeny.[20] But Exodus 1:15-21 is not *simply* a transitional piece. Through their courageous act of resistance, the midwives help "bring forth" the blessing of fruitfulness that God intends for Israel and humanity. Their actions are thus emblematic of the fact that, in the larger contest between YHWH and Pharaoh which the first half of Exodus is about, to side with YHWH results in the protection and nurture of children.[21] To side with Pharaoh is to acquiesce in their death.

When Pharaoh's attempt to decrease Israel's population through the midwives fails, he then commands the Egyptians to kill the baby boys by exposing them in the Nile (Exod. 1:22).[22] While this decree serves as necessary background to the story of Moses' being left in the Nile, it also functions as part of a progression through which the extent of Pharaoh's ruthlessness is unveiled and his opposition to God's intentions for Israel is increasingly unmasked. He begins by imposing forced labor on the Israelites, proceeds to seek the death of their boys in secret, and finally establishes an open pogrom against them.[23] Pharaoh's decree to have the baby boys killed also underscores the fact that the fate of children — Egyptian and Israelite alike — serves as the focal point of God's contest with Pharaoh to liberate the Israelites from bondage in Egypt.

Given that Moses is such a central figure in the Pentateuchal literature, it is not surprising that a story concerning this "hero's" birth should be found in the tradition. It has been widely observed that the story of Moses' rescue from

---

19. Exum, "'Let Every Daughter Live,'" p. 68, n. 6. Childs, following Gressman, suggests that the story of Moses' birth, although relatively late in the development of the traditions concerning Moses, is primary to the material in Exod. 1:15-22, which arose secondarily to explain why Moses' mother placed him by the shore of the Nile. See Childs, *Exodus*, p. 8, and "Birth of Moses."

20. The Hebrew reads *bāttîm*, "houses." The NRSV translates this as "families." For the rendering of "houses" as enduring progeny, see Greenberg, *Understanding Exodus*, p. 31.

21. Sarna, *Exodus*, cites an interesting midrash from the *Midrash Rabbah* on 1:19-20. It draws on the fact that the verbal for "let live," as in, "every daughter you shall let live" (1:17), can also mean to sustain life. According to Sarna, the midrash "sees the midwives actively providing the indigent mothers with food and shelter in addition to obstetric services."

22. See M. Cogan, "A Technical Term for Exposure," *Journal of Near Eastern Studies* 27 (1968): 133-35.

23. Exum, "'Let Every Daughter Live,'" p. 68. She also observes that Pharaoh "speaks" to the midwives but later "commands" the people, citing U. Cassuto, *A Commentary on the Book of Exodus*, trans. Israel Abrahams (Jerusalem: Magnes Press, 1967), p. 16.

a basket in the river exhibits many parallels with a story told of Sargon of Akkad, although Moses' story has its own distinct features.[24] For instance, while Moses' mother follows the letter of Pharaoh's command to expose the baby boys in the Nile, it is clear from the great care lavished in the preparation of the basket and from the attention of his sister that the spirit of her actions is in no way a true "exposure."[25] Striking, of course, is the fact that while Moses' mother fulfills the letter of Pharaoh's command, Pharaoh's own daughter knowingly goes against his decree in order to spare Moses. This contributes another irony to the story. In his two different instructions to kill the infant boys, Pharaoh rather redundantly specifies, "you shall let every daughter live." The story of Moses' birth is full of daughters — the daughter of a Levite (Moses' mother), her own daughter (Moses' sister), and Pharaoh's daughter, and it is these daughters who work together to spare the very infant boy who will later help bring about the Pharaoh's demise.[26]

It may be worth noting that the various accounts of the suffering of the Israelites in chapters 1 and 2 are not told by way of tortuous personal detail, but in broader sweeps. Even later at the death of the firstborn, a plague that afflicted the family of every Egyptian from "Pharaoh who sat on his throne to the prisoner who was in the dungeon" (Exod. 12:29), the writer is not concerned so much with the suffering per se as with the effect this suffering achieves in YHWH's contest with Pharaoh. This is not to suggest that the writer is callous by any means. Particular rhetorical aims call for particular rhetorical strategies. But at the same time, the brevity with which the events are recounted belies the ability of those events to vividly engage the imagination of the reader.

The writer does leave an opening or two for the reader to enter into the agonizing world of the story's suffering, and does so most noticeably in the story of Moses' birth. What parent does not feel pangs at the description of the young Levite woman who, "when she saw that he was a fine baby" *(kî tôv hû'),*[27] desperately and futilely hid him for three months? With what unbear-

---

24. See especially Propp, *Exodus 1–18*, pp. 155-59; Childs, "Birth of Moses"; and Donald B. Redford, "The Literary Motif of the Exposed Child," *Numen* 14, no. 1 (1967): 208-28.

25. So Ackerman, "Literary Context," p. 90; and Greenberg, *Understanding Exodus*, 40.

26. Ackerman, "Literary Context," p. 95. Although Moses' name is actually Egyptian, the narrative places a Hebrew etymology for it in the mouth of the Egyptian princess. It has been noted that the etymology given, "for I drew him out of the water," would properly be for the name *Mushay,* "the one drawn out (of the water"), not *Moshe,* which means "the one who draws out (from the water)."

27. Exodus 2:2, so NRSV. Childs, *Exodus,* p. 18, translates this as, "[When she saw] how healthy he was."

able agony must she have prepared the seaworthy basket for her precious son and placed it in the reeds? Is it because she could not bear the sound of his awakening cry that it was his sister, not she herself, who watched the basket from a distance?[28] With what joy must she have suckled him for Pharaoh's daughter — what bittersweet joy, knowing that she must part with him once he is weaned.[29] This is one of the few moments when Exodus invites the reader — and perhaps "invite" is too strong a word — to consider the child on an intimate, tender scale. The more obvious role of the birth of Moses story, however, is its ability to anticipate what is to come.

From his birth and rescue the reader is able to anticipate that Moses will play an important role in the coming chapters, and his survival seems a good omen. But it is only in retrospect that the reader understands how the fate of this child anticipates all that is to be experienced by the Israelites and their children in the chapters to follow. While it is common for commentators to treat Exodus 1–2 as a distinct section, a kind of prologue to the book,[30] Michael Fishbane has convincingly argued that chapters 1–4 as a whole — which include scenes from Moses' adult life — foreshadow the events and scenarios of the block of materials contained in chapters 5–19.[31]

When YHWH appears to Moses in Exodus 3–4, he commissions him to go to the Israelites to tell them of YHWH's coming deliverance and to seek from Pharaoh the release of the Israelites (3:7-10, 16-18). Moses objects, "Suppose [the Israelites] do not believe me or listen to me, but say, 'The LORD did not appear to you.'" To this God responds by giving him three signs: the ability to turn his staff into a snake and back again; the ability to turn his hand leprous and whole again; and the ability to turn the water of the Nile into blood by pouring it on the ground (4:2-9). At 4:21-23, God refers back to these signs ('ot) as "wonders" (moph^{e}tîm) and tells Moses,

---

28. Greenberg, *Understanding Exodus*, p. 39, notes Abarbanel's interpretation that if Moses were to die, his mother did not want him to die in her presence, citing Hagar's similar sentiment expressed in Gen. 21:16.

29. Greenberg, *Understanding Exodus*, p. 42, suggests that when Moses goes to live with Pharaoh's daughter he is older than weaning age (which would have been about three). He bases his argument on the fact that the Hebrew says *wayyigdal* (the boy grew) without *wayyiggāmal* (he was weaned.) The former can connote any age from boyhood to early manhood. The context and the presence of *wayyigdal* in the next verse indicate that he was a boy (but older than the age of weaning). Childs, "Birth of Moses," discusses the ways in which the negotiations between Pharaoh's daughter and Moses' mother are typical of a labor contract, as well as how the text may reflect features typical of an adoption, pp. 112-14.

30. So, for instance, Durham, *Exodus*; Greenberg, *Understanding Exodus*; Fretheim, *Exodus*.

31. Michael Fishbane, "Exodus 1–4: The Prologue to the Exodus Cycle," in *Text and Texture: Close Readings of Selected Biblical Texts* (New York: Schocken Books, 1979), pp. 63-76.

"When you go back to Egypt, see that you perform before Pharaoh all the wonders that I have put in your power; but I will harden his heart, so that he will not let the people go. Then you shall say to Pharaoh, 'Thus says the LORD: Israel is my firstborn son. I said to you, "Let my son go that he may worship me." But you refused to let him go; now I will kill your firstborn son.'" (4:21-23)[32]

Fishbane observes that this passage achieves two things. First, it indicates that the three signs already given to Moses are now "expressly intended for the Pharaoh as well." Second, the passage introduces yet a fourth sign explicitly for Pharaoh: the death of his firstborn. In this way, Fishbane argues, Exodus 4:21-23 establishes a pattern of three signs plus a climactic fourth (3 + 1).[33] The plague narrative of Exodus 7:8–12:36 follows a similar but expanded pattern of 3 + 3 + 3 + 1, again ending with a climactic "fourth" in the plague of the death of the firstborn.[34]

The three signs of the first triad and the 3 + 3 + 3 signs of the second, extended triad are expressly said to be for the benefit of both the Egyptians and the Israelites, Fishbane observes (see Exod. 7:3-5 and 10:1-2). This is not the case for the fourth signs, however. The fourth sign of the first triad — the death of the firstborn — is only for the Egyptians.[35] There is a fourth sign for the Israelites that accompanies the first triad of signs, however, in the following account of God's attempt to kill Moses:

On the way, at a place where they spent the night, the LORD met him and tried to kill him. But Zipporah took a flint and cut off her son's foreskin, and touched Moses' feet with it, and said, "Truly you are a bridegroom of blood to me!" So he let him alone. It was then she said, "A bridegroom of blood by circumcision." (Exod. 4:24-26, NRSV)

---

32. Space does not allow for a fuller discussion of the various roles of the series of plagues in this essay. It is worth noting, however, that this passage demonstrates that in the final form of the narrative they serve a larger purpose than to convince Pharaoh to let the people go, since it is already acknowledged here that they will not achieve this effect.

33. Fishbane, "Exodus 1–4," p. 69.

34. Fishbane, "Exodus 1–4," p. 70. Fishbane observes further that two shorter versions of this pattern are also found in Ps. 78:43-51 and Ps. 105:27-36.

35. As Greenstein observes, Exod. 4:21-23 specifies only the death of *Pharaoh's* firstborn, not of all the firstborn of Egypt. However, Fishbane understands Pharaoh's firstborn to be a "figure" of the death of the Egyptian firstborn. See the quote in the following paragraph. Edward L. Greenstein, "The Firstborn Plague and the Reading Process," in *Pomegranates and Golden Bells*, ed. David P. Wright, David Noel Freedman, and Avi Hurvitz (Winona Lake, IN: Eisenbrauns, 1995), pp. 555-68.

Fishbane argues that, "Just as 4:23 anticipates the death of the Egyptians through the figure of Pharaoh's firstborn, so do vv. 24-26 anticipate the redemption of the Israelites . . . by focusing on the salvation and protection effected for Moses by the blood of his own son's circumcision."[36] In other words, the sparing of Moses by means of his son's blood anticipates the sparing of the Israelite firstborn on the night of the first Passover, and it serves as the fourth sign for Israel, in distinction from the fourth sign for Egypt, the death of Pharaoh's firstborn. Thus, the events of Moses' life recounted in chapters 1–4, including his rescue from the reeds of the Nile (the Israelites are delivered at the Sea of Reeds in ch. 14) and his redemption from death through blood, are representative of the events that pertain to all of Israel in chapters 5–19.

The Death of the Firstborn

Appreciating how God's attack on Moses in chapter 4 fits into a particular anticipatory structure in the narrative helps make sense of how this particularly surprising and mysterious story found its way into the narrative. Grappling with the attack on Egypt's firstborn in the pursuant cycle of signs, however, and understanding precisely why children serve as the focal point of God's contest with Pharaoh in the cycle of plagues require further examination of the practices surrounding the firstborn in ancient Israel.

The firstborn son of an Israelite received a double portion of the father's inheritance, which, as M. Tsevat has argued, "is an expression of the exceedingly high esteem in which the first child is held, especially if it is a male." Tsevat goes even further to claim, "The first is the best," observing that the Hebrew term for the first, *rē'šît*, "has both of these meanings, and in the [biblical] expression 'the first of the (procreative) strength' the latter sense is quite clear." Thus *bekhor*, which is the Hebrew term for the firstborn, can also assume the meaning "excellent," as when used in Psalm 89:27[28] where it stands in a parallel position to "the highest" *(elyôn):* "I will make him the firstborn, the highest of the kings of the earth."[37] One might conclude from this that describing Israel as YHWH's firstborn in Exodus 4:22-23 is a way of speaking of its primacy in YHWH's eyes. Yet the laws on the consecration and redemption of the firstborn also have bearing on what is meant in Exodus when YHWH speaks of Israel in this way.

According to the various legal materials found in the books of Exodus, Le-

---

36. Fisbhane, "Exodus 1–4," p. 71.

37. M. Tsevat, *"bᵉkhôr,"* in *Theological Dictionary of the Old Testament,* rev. ed., vol. 2 (Grand Rapids: Eerdmans, 1977), pp. 121-27.

viticus, Numbers, and Deuteronomy, the firstfruits of an Israelite's produce, as well as the firstborn of one's animals and the firstborn male child, belong to God. Exodus 22:29-30 offers an example of such legislation:

> You shall not delay to make offerings from the fullness of your harvest and from the outflow of your presses.
> The firstborn *(b^ekôr)* of your sons you shall give to me. You shall do the same with your oxen and with your sheep: seven days it shall remain with its mother; on the eighth day you shall give it to me. (NRSV)

The specific language used here to describe the relationship of firstborn sons to YHWH is "give" *(tittēn-lî)*. Other phrases used with reference to firstborn include "consecrate to me" *(qadeš-lî;* Exod. 13:1) and "set apart" *(ha'ăbartā;* Exod. 13:12). Gershon Brin argues that these phrases all imply transferal to the domain of the divine. The nature of that transferal would be according to its kind. An animal, for instance, might have its fat burned and blood sprinkled on the altar. Brin hypothesizes that consecration of the firstborn sons would have meant giving them cultic functions, although, he admits, this was likely not consistently or widely practiced.[38] Several, although not all, of the instructions concerning the firstborn children provide for their redemption (Exod. 13:13, 15; 34:20).

One rationale for these firstfruit and firstborn practices is suggested by Deuteronomy 26, which describes the offering of firstfruits as an occasion for an Israelite to recall Jacob's descent into Egypt, the Exodus, and the entry into the promised land. The summary of God's acts ends with the profession that "The LORD . . . brought us into this place and gave us this land, a land flowing with milk and honey. So now I bring the first of the fruit of the ground that you, O LORD, have given me" (Deut. 26:9-10). This formulation would seem to confirm Roland de Vaux's suggestion that firstfruit and firstborn offerings served as acknowledgment that all things belong to, and come from, God, and therefore it is fitting to pay tribute. Thus, he asserts, the firstfruit and firstborn offerings serve as a "desecration" — in the sense of taking away something's consecrated character; "by giving a part to God, man 'desecrates' things and may use the rest as his own."[39] Walther Eichrodt offers a similar interpretation, suggesting that "The motive may be either to obtain God's

---

38. Gershon Brin, *Studies in Biblical Law: From the Hebrew Bible to the Dead Sea Scrolls,* Journal for the Study of the Old Testament — Supplement Series 176 (Sheffield: Sheffield Academic Press, 1994), pp. 217-20.

39. Roland de Vaux, *Ancient Israel,* vol. 2, *Religious Institutions* (New York: McGraw-Hill, 1961), p. 251.

blessing and sanctification of all one's property, or else to acknowledge that God is the real owner of all things, and only allows men to enjoy the fruits of the earth in return for a regular tribute."[40]

However, in Exodus 13:14-15 the reason given for the consecration of first-born sons is specifically tied to the death of the firstborn in Egypt:

> When in the future your child asks you, "What does this mean?" you shall answer, "By strength of hand the LORD brought us out of Egypt, from the house of slavery. When Pharaoh stubbornly refused to let us go, the LORD killed all the firstborn in the land of Egypt, from human firstborn to the firstborn of animals. Therefore I sacrifice to the LORD every male that first opens the womb, but every firstborn of my sons I redeem."[41]

On this basis C. J. H. Wright argues that the consecration of the firstborn "seems to have been a symbolic declaration of Israel's complete belonging to YHWH":

> The firstborn of Israel had been spared when the firstborn of Egypt had been slain. *Hence, those whom God had delivered from death belonged entirely to him.* And since the firstborn, like the firstfruits, represented the whole of which they were the part, this was the basis of the sanctification of the nation as a whole.[42]

With this idea we find ourselves having come full circle. Hoping to make sense of the terror of YHWH's slaying of the firstborn of Egypt, we set out to understand the significance of what it means for YHWH to describe Israel as his "firstborn son," inasmuch as the death of Pharaoh's firstborn, and by analogy, of all the firstborn of Egypt, is explained as retribution for Pharaoh having refused to let YHWH's firstborn son go. We have seen that the firstborn holds a certain primacy of place in the family, which includes receiving a double share of the father's inheritance. We have also seen that the firstborn belongs to YHWH. Yet the reason for the fact that the firstborn belongs to God is given in the firstborn plague in Egypt. It would seem tautological to say that in chapter 4 YHWH describes Israel as his firstborn *prior* to the death of the

---

40. Walther Eichrodt, *Theology of the Old Testament,* trans. J. A. Baker, vol. 1 (Philadelphia: Westminster, 1961), p. 152.

41. See also Num. 8:17: "For all the firstborn among the Israelites are mine, both human and animal. On the day that I struck down all the firstborn in the land of Egypt I consecrated them for myself." According to both Numbers 3 and 8 YHWH took all the Levites for himself in place of all the firstborn of Israel.

42. Wright, "Family," p. 765.

firstborn *because of* the death and redemption of firstborn in chapter 12, although this does seem to be the case. Short of such a tautology, however, it does seem apparent that in calling Israel his firstborn in Exodus 4, YHWH is asserting a claim of ownership: Israel belongs to YHWH, is consecrated to him, and is not for Pharaoh's profane use.

Such a conclusion would suggest that the plague of the firstborn serves both a retributive and a cultic function. As Edward Greenstein has observed, the impression that the plague is retributive is one the reader is able to form first on the basis of Exodus 4:23: "I said to you, 'Let my son go that he may worship me.' But you refused to let him go; now I will kill your firstborn son.'" However, once a reader arrives at Exodus 13, the final plague's cultic nature is signaled in part, Greenstein observes, by the fact that both the pronouncement of the coming plague and the plague itself mention the death not only of firstborn human beings *but of cattle as well* (Exod. 11:5; 12:29). If the death of the firstborn were simply retribution for the Pharaoh's refusal to let YHWH's firstborn son go, then only the death of Egypt's firstborn sons would have been called for. That firstborn animals are also taken suggests that the plague is an expression of the cultic practice of devoting all firstborn — humans and animals — to God. Greenstein supports this view by observing that both YHWH's demands to release the Israelites and Pharaoh's refusal to do so concern the worship of YHWH. Moses sets forth the demand, "Let my people go, *so that they may worship me*" (e.g., Exod. 9:1), and all negotiations concerning this potential pilgrimage are discussed in cultic terms: where the ritual will take place (8:24), who will participate (10:8-11), and what may be offered (10:24-26). Greenstein observes further that Moses even insists that Pharaoh provide the animals for sacrifice (10:25). Thus, he concludes that the climactic death of Egypt's firstborn is not only for retribution (although the impression that it is, in part, remains). The plague also demonstrates YHWH's sovereignty over Pharaoh, one of the major themes of the plague cycle as a whole. The firstborn of Israel belong to YHWH, which is why Exodus's legislation stipulates their consecration and the practice of their redemption. The firstborn of Egypt also belong to YHWH, and in the final plague YHWH demonstrates that this is so. Greenstein writes:

> Israel's firstborn are spared for now; they will be redeemed later. Egypt has no option of redemption. In the plague of the firstborn, YHWH exercises his proprietary prerogative to collect, as it were, all Egypt's unredeemed firstborn. By appropriating Egypt's firstborn, YHWH demonstrates his sovereignty over Pharaoh and his people.[43]

---

43. Greenstein, "The Firstborn Plague," p. 566.

The Passover: A Story for Children?

Every spring Jewish families around the world gather at the family table to recall the deliverance from Egypt by means of the Passover Seder. The Seder serves as much more than a mere recollection of deliverance from Egypt. A central part of the Haggadah, the retelling of those events, is the exhortation, "In every generation let one look on himself or herself as if *he or she* came forth out of Egypt."[44] The Haggadah continues:

> It was not only our fathers that the Holy One, blessed be he, redeemed, *but us as well did he redeem along with them.*
>
> Therefore, we are bound to thank, praise, laud, glorify, exalt, honor, bless, extol, and adore Him who performed all these miracles for our fathers *and for us.* He has brought *us* forth from slavery to freedom, from sorrow to joy, from mourning to holiday, from darkness to great light, and from bondage to redemption.[45]

In other words, the Passover Seder does not simply recount God's deliverance of the Israelites in the past; it brings the reality of that deliverance into the lives of the participants.[46]

This feature of the observance finds its origins in the book of Exodus itself, in two distinct ways. First, the narrative of Exodus is so structured as to have the reader contemplate an annual celebration of Passover (Exod. 12:1-20), not only even prior to the founding event, but prior even to Moses' instructions for that founding event (12:21-27)! Furthermore, when Moses does instruct the people concerning preparations for the first Passover night, his instructions take it for granted that commemoration of the night will continue in subsequent generations: "You shall observe this rite as a perpetual ordinance for you and your children" (12:24).

---

44. In this instance the term "haggadah" refers both to the account or retelling of the events of Exodus and, more technically, to the "manual" for its telling that has developed over the centuries. See *The Passover Haggadah*, ed. Nahum N. Glatzer (New York: Schocken Books, 1989), p. 5. In what follows I will use "Haggadah" to refer to the standardized text, and "haggadah" (without a capital H) to refer to the telling, more generally, as it may vary from family to family. The quotation, from Glatzer's Haggadah (p. 59), has been altered slightly to use inclusive language.

45. Glatzer, *The Passover Haggadah*, pp. 59-61; emphasis added.

46. For an excellent documentary and discussion of the Passover Haggadah and Seder as practiced by families throughout the world, and of how both instruct and involve children, see *Passover Traditions of Freedom*, produced and directed by Randy Goldman, 58 min., Owings Mills, MD: Maryland Public Television and Frappé, Inc., 1994, videocassette.

A second way in which the book of Exodus grounds the transformation of Passover from a celebration of the past into a celebration in the present is by its attention to the religious education of Israelite children. "When you come to the land that the LORD will give you, as he has promised," instructs Moses,

> you shall keep this observance. And when your children ask you, "What do you mean by this observance?" You shall say, "It is the Passover sacrifice to the LORD for he passed over the houses of the Israelites in Egypt, when he struck down the Egyptians but spared our houses." (Exod. 12:25-27a)

A similar instruction is given at 13:8: "You shall tell your child on that day, 'It is because of what the LORD did for me when I came out of Egypt.'"[47]

The Jewish Seder and its Haggadah incorporate the educational dimensions of the Exodus account in innovative ways. There is, for instance, the hiding of a piece of Matzoh — the Afikomen — at the beginning of the meal. This is a ritual to which the children pay great attention, for the Seder cannot end until the Afikomen has been found, and what child can resist a game of hide and seek? There are also the four questions, which, traditionally, are to be read by the youngest around the table:

> Why does this night differ from all other nights? For on all other nights we eat either leavened or unleavened bread; why on this night only un-leavened bread?
>
> On all other nights we eat all kinds of herbs; why on this night only bitter herbs?
>
> On all other nights we need not dip our herbs even once; why on this night must we dip them twice?
>
> On all other nights we eat either sitting up or reclining; why on this night do we all recline?[48]

And then there are the four children spoken of by the Haggadah: one intelligent, another wicked, a third simple, and the fourth who "does not yet know how to ask." The intelligent child is interested in learning more and asks (quoting intelligently from Deut. 6:20), "What mean the testimonies and the

---

47. The instructions for the consecration and redemption of firstborn animals and children in Exod. 13:11-16 actually speaks to future generations of children about the Exodus from Egypt as if in the present: "When in the future your child asks you, 'What does this mean?' you shall answer, 'By strength of hand the LORD brought *us* out of Egypt, from the house of slavery" (13:14; emphasis added).

48. Glatzer, *The Passover Haggadah*, p. 25.

statutes, and the ordinances which the LORD our God hath commanded you?" The wicked child, however, asks, "What is this service to you?" This is the question of a wicked child because he asks "What is this service *to you?*" "'To you,' and not to him," the Haggadah observes, as if the child were dissociating himself from the community:

> Since he removes himself from the group, and so denies God, you in return must set his teeth on edge, and answer him: "It is because of that which the LORD did for me when I came forth from Egypt" [Exod 13:8]. "For me," not for him. Had he been there, he would not have been redeemed.[49]

Of course, there are no real wicked children around the Seder table. The point is to further instruct the participants, and especially the children, about the importance of appropriating the Exodus story of oppression and deliverance into one's own life. But it is precisely this aspect of the Seder directed toward children, both young and old, that confronts the ongoing terror of the Exodus story directly, for the Haggadah also contains the following passage:

> For it was not one man only who stood up against us to destroy us; *in every generation they stand up against us to destroy us,* and the Holy One, blessed be he, saves us from their hand.[50]

Families whose members experienced the Holocaust, and those whose communities have recently experienced acts of anti-Semitism, may feel the sting of the truth of the Haggadah in a particularly sharp way. Learning when one is still a child that one can expect to be treated in ways less than human is its own kind of terror. Yet for many children, because of their skin color, their religious observance, or their country of origin, such lessons are necessary for survival. Thus, we see that for Jewish children participation in the Seder can serve as a deadly serious education in reality: the reality that "in every generation they stand up against us to destroy us" and that vigilance is required "lest from this we learned nothing."[51]

---

49. Glatzer, *The Passover Haggadah*, p. 33, text as well as notes.

50. Glatzer, *The Passover Haggadah*, p. 39.

51. This last phrase is from Abraham Shlonsky's "A Vow," which is recited at many Seders in the land of Israel:

> In the presence of eyes
> Which witnessed the slaughter,
> Which saw the oppression
> The heart could not bear,
> And as witness the heart

While remembering the suffering of the Israelites, the Haggadah likewise acknowledges the suffering of the Egyptians. One version includes the following passage from the Talmud:

> Our rabbis taught: When the Egyptian armies were drowning in the sea, the Heavenly Hosts broke out in songs of jubilation. God silenced them and said, "My creatures are perishing, and you sing praises?"[52]

It is also common practice to spill ten drops of wine, one for each plague, in recognition that in the suffering of others one's own joy is diminished. And so a version of the Haggadah includes the following group recitation:

> Though we descend from those redeemed from brutal Egypt,
> And have ourselves rejoiced to see oppressors overcome,
> Yet our triumph is diminished
> By the slaughter of the foe,
> As the wine within the cup of joy is lessened
> When we pour ten drops for the plagues upon Egypt.[53]

These pieces of haggadah recognize that Exodus is not only a story of deliverance but also of terror, and so one should rejoice in God's mighty deeds in a sober way. If Terence Fretheim is correct, then this instinct also finds its seeds in Exodus itself. For he sees in the instructions concerning the firstborn in chapter 13 a reminder of the cost at which the Israelite children were redeemed: namely, the lives of the firstborn of Egypt. He writes:

> That once taught compassion
> Until days came to pass
> That crushed human feeling,
> I have taken an oath: To remember it all,
> To remember, not once to forget! . . .
> An oath: Not in vain passed over
> The night of terror.
> An oath: No morning shall see me at flesh-pots again.
> An oath: Lest from this we learned nothing.

Translated by Herbert Bronstein; quoted in *A Passover Haggadah: The New Union Haggadah,* rev. ed., ed. Herbert Bronstein (New York: Central Conference of American Rabbis, 1975), p. 46. Goldman, *Passover Traditions of Freedom,* offers an excellent example of a family's discussion of how during the Holocaust grandparents (re)constructed a Haggadah, when none was available, as an act of resistance in occupied France.

52. Talmud Bavli, Sanhedrin 39b, as quoted in Bronstein, *A Passover Haggadah,* p. 48.

53. Bronstein, *A Passover Haggadah,* p. 47.

[Exodus 13:15-16] give a special twist to the issue of the firstborn. In essence, Israel is to continue to be attentive to its firstborn because of what the *Egyptian* firstborn have suffered. . . . This is thus an everlasting reminder in Israel at what cost Israel's firstborn were redeemed. The death of the firstborn of the Egyptians is thus not forgotten; it is seared on Israel's memory forever.[54]

Conclusion

This examination of children in the book of Exodus has shown that children are portrayed not so much as a distinct demographic as an integral element of a larger social and liturgical community whose fortunes are tied to the fate and faith of that community. This is not to say that the text fails to recognize the particular vulnerability and needs of children. On the contrary, the terror of Exodus derives in part from their extreme vulnerability and from the inability of the adult population to protect them from Pharaoh's designs of death.

The fate of children lies at the very heart of the contest between Pharaoh and YHWH that serves as a major theme of the book's first fifteen chapters. The reason children are at the center of the divine contest is precisely because the gift of children, established in God's blessing of creation (Gen. 1:28 and 9:1-2) and given central place in the Abrahamic promises (Gen. 17:2, 6; cf. 28:3; 35:1; 48:4), is a distinguishing, tangible manifestation of God's ongoing blessing of humankind. The story of Exodus is depicted as a new act of creation through which God's intentions in creation are being realized among the descendants of Abraham.[55]

The divine contest between YHWH and Pharaoh is necessitated by Pharaoh's opposition to YHWH's intentions for Israel, and it is intended to establish unequivocally YHWH's sovereignty, so that both the Egyptians and the Israelites might know the LORD. That YHWH chooses to establish his sovereignty through the death of Egypt's firstborn serves as another locus of the text's terror. Contemporary readers are apt to balk at YHWH's taking of innocent lives. Yet as our examination has suggested, YHWH's sovereignty over Pharaoh and the Egyptians can be fully displayed only through the death of the firstborn. For the offering of firstfruits and firstborn alike serves as the appropriate acknowledgment that all things come from and belong to God. In Israel, YHWH provides for the redemption of firstborn children. But be-

54. Fretheim, *Exodus*, p. 149.
55. See note 9, above.

cause the Pharaoh stubbornly refuses to acknowledge YHWH, YHWH "exercises his proprietary prerogative to collect" Egypt's firstborn.[56] The death of the firstborn contains within it a degree of retributive justice: because Pharaoh refused to let YHWH's firstborn son go that he might worship, YHWH now kills Pharaoh's firstborn son (Exod. 4:23). But the plague of the firstborn, both humans *and animals,* is primarily cultic in nature. Pharaoh repeatedly refuses to "Let my people go so that they may worship me," and he resists doing so in the negotiations concerning where this ritual will take place, who will participate, and what may be offered. In the end, YHWH establishes his sovereignty by taking that appropriately representative part of the whole — the firstborn.

The terror of the plague of the firstborn is thus symptomatic of the difficult but necessary truth that the same God who gives life also has the prerogative to take life away. Michael Fishbane, in his reading of the "bridegroom of blood" passage in Exodus 4:24-26, makes a similar argument with regard to Moses' understanding of God:

> Now, at this most decisive moment in his life, when he gathers his strength to submit himself fully to God as a faithful messenger, Moses is tested in his resolve, in his capacity to acknowledge that He who referred to Himself as *'eheye,* "I shall be," is the same One whether He promises life and redemption or causes death and destruction. A true messenger, one faithful to his task, would have to know this truth and not resist it.[57]

Our examination of Exodus also pointed out that in Israel a child's place in the nexus of extended familial relations helped situate him or her within the larger community. The opening passage of Exodus traces the transformation of the sons of Jacob from a household of seventy persons to a "people," whom YHWH delivers, and with whom YHWH covenants — as a people. Yet as the instructions concerning the annual observance of Passover demonstrate, the ongoing religious life of that covenant community depends on parents' obligations to instruct the next generation so that they may understand and observe the obligations of the covenant in their own lives. The Passover Haggadah reflects this obligation in its attention to instructing the children around the Seder table. But as we have seen, the instruction of children at the Passover Seder not only concerns what YHWH has done "for our fathers and for us" but also instructs children that "in every generation they stand up against us to destroy us, and the Holy One, blessed be he, saves us from their

56. Greenstein, "The Firstborn Plague," p. 566.
57. Fishbane, "Exodus 1–4," p. 71.

hand."[58] In this way the Haggadah does not flinch from acknowledging the terror of the text, inasmuch as one aspect of its terror, the sort perpetrated by Pharaoh, continues as a reality in the lives of children today. Instruction becomes a necessary form of vigilance. At the same time the Passover Haggadah engages in its celebration of God's deliverance through the sober recognition of the Egyptians' suffering. In this, it develops a reflex already found in Exodus's stipulations to "be attentive to [Israel's] firstborn because of what the Egyptian firstborn have suffered."[59]

Exodus's ability to inform our understanding of our own obligations to children arises, I would contend, from the very ways in which it depicts children as the locus of God's ongoing blessing to humanity, integrally situated within a larger communal context. In its portrayal of the fate of children as inextricable from that of the communities of which they are a part (Israelite and Egyptian), Exodus offers an invitation for parents to look beyond securing the future and well-being of their own children in a myopic way, to thinking about the ways in which our efforts at nurturing communal well-being at various levels — local, national, global — secures the future and wholeness, not only of one's own children, but of others' as well. The women of Exodus 1 and 2 may be emblematic in this regard. In their resistance to Pharaoh the midwives took sides with YHWH in the developing contest, and doing so meant being a protector and nurturer of children, even at great risk to themselves. Likewise, Pharaoh's daughter transgressed the boundaries imposed by her status as an Egyptian and member of Pharaoh's household in order to rescue the Hebrew foundling. Finally, Moses' wife, Zipporah, who enables YHWH to spare Moses by circumcising her son and placing the blood on Moses (Exod. 4:24-26), points us to the central obligation to acknowledge that even our own children do not "belong" to us but to God. Surely it is for this reason that the religious instruction of children is central to Exodus's preservation of the memory of the exodus.

---

58. Glatzer, *The Passover Haggadah*, p. 49.
59. See Exod. 13:15-16, and Fretheim, *Exodus*, p. 149.

3 That the Children May Know:
Children in Deuteronomy

Patrick D. Miller

Searching for the children of Scripture leads one rather quickly to the book of Deuteronomy. From beginning (Deut. 1:39) to end (Deut. 32:46) it gives prominent attention to children and especially to what and how they are taught. That concern has something to do with the character of the book itself. The role and significance of Deuteronomy raise the matter of the children and what they are taught because the book itself is so central to that teaching.

My starting point, therefore, is with Deuteronomy and some reflection on its character. I will then seek to identify who are the children so often mentioned in the book, what they should be taught and why, and who should teach them. A central dimension of Deuteronomy's guidance about instruction of the young is found in the variety of ways that such teaching goes on. Teaching is a complex endeavor that involves far more than "learning the rules," though that is a part of it. Coming to know the faith involves questioning, knowing the story behind the rules, and engaging in a range of familial and communal rituals and activities.

The Nature and Character of Deuteronomy

The genre of Deuteronomy has occasioned much discussion and debate. The very term "deuteronomy," or "second law," is indicative of the character of the book. It is a covenantal document and clearly sets forth a way of life for the people of Israel. One of the early characterizations of the book, going back at least as far as Josephus and reaffirmed in more recent times by S. Dean

McBride, is that it constitutes the "polity" of the covenant people.[1] It is law as polity or even constitution.[2] So one turns to it on the assumption that it is formative and foundational for the order and life of God's people as a socio-political community. One can say that about the Bible as a whole, but in this case the role given to the whole of Scripture is claimed explicitly by Deuteronomy for itself. The book of Deuteronomy climaxes in 30:15-20 with the call of Moses to the community:

> See, I have set before you today life and good, death and bad. . . . Therefore choose life so that you and your descendants may live, loving the Lord your God, obeying him, and holding fast to him; for that means life to you and length of days, so that you may live in the land that the Lord swore to give to your ancestors, to Abraham, to Isaac, and to Jacob.

To the question "How then shall we live?" Deuteronomy answers: Here is God's law. More specifically, here is your constitution, a manual or "book of order" for your life together from now on.

At the same time, the very term for "law" in Hebrew, *tôrâ*, points us to another significant dimension of Deuteronomy. Torah is at root "instruction" or "teaching." Moses' role in Deuteronomy is that of teacher, the one transmitting the divine instruction. So some interpreters rightly point to the didactic character of the book and identify its genre as catechesis or teaching rather than constitution or polity.[3] The reason this argument has arisen is because the book is in fact *both polity and instruction,* constitutional and catechetical. That dual character is crucial for understanding Deuteronomy and its importance, especially with regard to children. That is, the book is teaching and focuses upon instructing the people. In that context, the children come prominently into the picture. While the family context is central to Deuteronomy, the references to children are not simply to make that point or have them as part of the picture. They are there specifically because of the importance of

---

1. S. Dean McBride, "Polity of the Covenant People: The Book of Deuteronomy," *Interpretation* 41 (1987): 229-44; reprinted in *Constituting the Community: Studies on the Polity of Ancient Israel in Honor of S. Dean McBride,* ed. John T. Strong and Steven S. Tuell (Winona Lake: Eisenbrauns, 2005), pp. 17-33.

2. Moshe Weinfeld has argued that the book "fashions a national constitution under state-controlled officials" (*Deuteronomy and the Deuteronomic School* [Oxford: Clarendon, 1972], p. 168).

3. E.g., Dennis T. Olson, *Deuteronomy and the Death of Moses: A Theological Reading,* Overtures to Biblical Theology (Minneapolis: Augsburg Fortress, 1994), pp. 6-14. For further discussion of the issues, see Patrick D. Miller, "Constitution or Instruction? The Purpose of Deuteronomy," in Strong and Tuell, eds., *Constituting the Community,* pp. 125-41.

instruction. My aim here is less to point out the fairly obvious didactic and homiletical character of Deuteronomy than to look at its specific concern for teaching. Since, however, the book is both polity and catechesis, the substance of the book is as important as the process. That is, it does not simply lift up the teaching enterprise within the family. Its *content* is what is to be taught.

Who Are the Children?

One of the questions in thinking about the place of children in Scripture, and particularly in Deuteronomy where they are so much in view, is the question of what is meant by "children." Who is included in this designation? What are their ages? Is the term "children" primarily an age designation or a relational one? The answer to the last question is that both factors are important for Deuteronomy. A key text is 1:39, which refers to the "little ones" and then goes on to identify them as "your children who today do not yet know right from wrong." The term used for "little ones," *ṭappîm*, is a word that usually has in mind the young children in a family or a community, and in Deuteronomy it usually occurs in a sequence such as "men, women, and children" to speak of everyone or only the women and children. The term used for "children" in this verse is the large term *bānîm*, which can mean "children," "sons," or simply one who belongs to the category of whatever it is that appears in genitival relationship with the word, as, for example, "children of Israel," that is, the Israelites, and with no respect to age at all. It is this term that lies behind most of the substantive occurrences of the word "children" in Deuteronomy where something is being said specifically about children in distinction from the adults in the family.

Often, however, or at the same time, the distinction is meant to be a generational one. It may not have a specific age in mind. Or if it does, the critical thing is that it is the next generation or the next generations (children's children) more than it is the age. As one engages the various references to children, whatever term is used, it would seem that both the youthfulness or young age of the children and the relationship between them and their parents are critical to the perspective of Deuteronomy. The passage mentioned above (1:39) is crucial not only because it refers to both *ṭappîm* (young ones) and *bānîm* (children) but also because it is the one place where there is some definition of the term: "your little ones *(ṭappîm)* who you thought would become booty" and "your children *(bānîm)* who today do not know right and wrong." The descriptive phrases clearly have in mind those who in some sense are not responsible, too young to have been involved in the decision to rebel against the divine command, not yet at the age of moral discretion, or, like the women, vulnerable to being enemy spoil, which clearly does not mean mature adult males. From other parallel contexts, specifically Numbers 14:29 and 32:11, we learn that what is by the children here are those who are under twenty years of age.[4] We are thus given some indication of who is in view, and it clearly is the children and youth as those terms are used for age reference.

But even as we use the term "children" to refer to our progeny, whatever the age, that is also the case with Deuteronomy. There is some sense in which the term has in mind those who come after, who do not yet know, who have not yet learned, whatever age or generation. The "children" of Deuteronomy are both the next generation and the young.

What Is to Be Learned

What the children are to learn is the same as what the adults are taught: the polity or constitution of the people. Reference to teaching begins with chapter 4, the point in the book where Moses moves from his narrative memoir, recapitulating the story of the wilderness wandering, to the teaching of the divine instruction for their life in the land they are about to enter. Most of the rest of the book is devoted to that instruction. Chapter 4 makes this transition both by emphasizing the rest of what is given as teaching and by providing the first piece of that instruction with a sermon by Moses on the command-ment against making and worshiping idols (see vv. 15ff.). In 4:1, Moses tells the people to "listen to the statutes and ordinances that I am teaching you to do/observe." Then in verse 5 he reiterates the point: "See, I am now teaching you the statutes and ordinances, as the Lord my God charged me, for you to do/observe in the land you are going in to possess." Again in verse 14: "And the Lord charged me at that time to teach you statutes and ordinances for you to do/observe in the land that you are about to cross over into and occupy." At the beginning of chapter 5: "Hear, O Israel, the statutes and ordinances that I am addressing to you today; you shall learn them and observe/do them dili-gently." Again in 5:28 (Eng. 31) Moses is told by the Lord to stand with him to hear "all the commandments, the statutes and the ordinances, that you shall teach them, so that they may do them in the land that I am giving them to possess." And in 6:1: "Now this is the commandment — the statutes and the

---

4. For more extended discussion of this definition of the young as well as other references, see, e.g., Jeffrey Tigay, *Deuteronomy*, The JPS Torah Commentary (Philadelphia: The Jewish Publication Society, 1996), p. 20.

ordinances — that the Lord your God charged me to teach you to do/observe in the land."

It is clear, therefore, that the substance of what the people are being taught by Moses and are to learn is the whole of the statutes and ordinances presented in the book of Deuteronomy — in effect, what is found in Deuteronomy 12–26. Once one begins to think of Deuteronomy as polity or constitution, it is obvious why it is so important that the book be taught and learned. It is what is needed to make things work in the community that lives under the rule of God.

> *Learning the polity* of a community's life is a necessity for those who are responsible for leading the community. So it is that those who govern in a religious denomination are required to learn (and often be examined on) the polity of the denomination, so that they will know it and act according to it in all matters having to do with the governance of the different branches and institutions set forth in the polity. Many will keep a copy of the denomination's polity close at hand for reference when needed. In Deuteronomy, the whole assembly learns the polity, because one of the features of the social order is its highly democratic character and its concern for the well-being of each individual in the community.[5]

Learning the rules of the manual is necessary to accomplish the goal. Nothing at this point is said specifically about children. Moses is teaching everyone (see 5:1: "Moses convened all Israel . . .").

The children, however, come in quite specifically at several places and with regard to being taught or learning. In two of these instances (4:9-10 and 31:12-13), the issue is that the younger ones, the next generation, who will take over, have not been exposed to the teaching. So two things are urged upon the community: (1) to tell (literally, make known) the children who were not there about the appearance of the Lord on the mountain to give the commandments (4:9-10);[6] and (2) to recite or read the polity at regular intervals through the years so that future generations of children will come to know (31:12-13). In effect, the first passage speaks of the children coming to know the basic rules, the guidelines of the constitution, that is, the Ten Command-

---

5. Miller, "Constitution or Instruction?" p. 138.

6. With the expression "make them known to your children and your children's children" it is clear that all future generations are meant. The recounting of the Lord's appearance at Sinai to all the people is so formative and foundational that it is to be recounted and passed on to each generation forever (cf. Isa. 59:21 and Ezek. 37:25). If only a certain number of generations are meant, a modifying clause is added (e.g., Exod. 34:7; Job 42:16). See below.

ments, and the second passage has them come to know the whole polity that governs their life and that they are to follow.[7]

There is one other substantial element. The children do not simply learn the rules. They learn the *story behind the rules,* out of which they come and on which they are grounded. There are two passages that show this, one quite directly, the other more indirectly. In Deuteronomy 6:20-25 Moses tells the people to expect to be asked questions by their children: "When in the future your child asks you. . . ." The practices of family and community raise questions in the minds of the children — the perennial "Why?" — and become the occasion for teaching. In this instance the question arises out of the character of the book itself: "What are the decrees and the statutes and the ordinances that the Lord our God has commanded you?" Other ways of translating the sentence would be roughly: "What are all these statutes and laws that the Lord our God has commanded you?" or, "What about the decrees and statutes . . . ?" or, as in most translations: "What is the meaning of the decrees . . . ?"[8] The question seems not so much to be asking for a recitation of the various laws. Rather, it assumes the teaching mentioned above. That is, it presumes the child has in some sense been exposed to the various aspects of the polity, the teaching for life in the land, and wants now to know why it is that we do these things. What is all this about? At that point, as is well known, the answer is not a legal interpretation, not even a giving of information about the laws. It is telling the people's story, the account of God's deliverance of Israel from slavery and bringing them into the land. The decrees and statutes about which the child asks are the Lord's commands to be observed "to fear the Lord our God, for our good all the days of our life, as is now the case." The teaching of the child is thus responsive to the question, interprets what is going on (the way they have to live), roots it in the prior experience of God's deliverance, and provides implicit motivation for obedience by identifying the good that obedience accomplishes.

Such mode and content of instruction for the children are not confined to the book of Deuteronomy. On other occasions, it is presumed that the community's activities and rituals will evoke questions from the children who participate. This happens with regard to Passover (Exod. 12:25-27), Mazzot or

---

7. Deuteronomy 32:46 suggests that both the law and admonition or warning about keeping it were part of what was taught to the children. On this passage, see Moshe Weinfeld, *Deuteronomy 1–11,* Anchor Bible 5 (New York: Doubleday, 1991), pp. 261-62.

8. The ambiguity of the Hebrew should be acknowledged, that is, the character of the question as being both a content question and a why question. The common judgment that it is more the latter because of the context does not rule out the possibility that the child may ask "What are the rules?" as well as "What do the rules mean?"

Unleavened Bread (Exod. 13:7-8 — the question is implied, not spoken), the rituals of the firstborn (Exod. 13:14-16), and the stone monument erected after crossing the Jordan (Josh. 4:6-7, 21-24).[9]

In all of these instances, we are told that the children are going to ask "What does this mean?" and the answer is some part of the story of redemption. I have suggested elsewhere that there may be some inferences for our catechetical modes from this process:

> The answer to what and why and who in this Deuteronomic context is not a formulation of rational and abstract theological statement, though such means of teaching have value and place. Here the answer to the question is a story, a story of a people and of how by the grace of God they came to be and to be free. If catechisms are to tell us something of who we are and what we are to believe, they may need to begin in the story that does that. Further inferences may be drawn, as indeed they are in the Deuteronomic account (see verses 24-25). The biblical tradition seems to start everything in the experience of the grace of God and the calling of the one and the many into a new identity. . . . The catechism that will teach the next generation will be one that takes them back again to the questions of who they are and what it is that God has done for them.[10]

One also notes the way in which all of these teaching moments are question and answer in form; they arise, as do so many things in a child's education, from the child's "Why" question. That is, the education of the child responds to the child's curiosity and even waits for the strategic moment, the receptivity implied in the question. Further, instruction of the child is not simply in a classroom. It is highly contextual, growing out of context and practice. The religious and social practices of the community, when carried out in continuing and regular fashion, become the occasion for the young ones to learn who they are and whose they are. One may infer something here about the value of regular and repeated practices that are so much a part of the life of the family and the community that curiosity and interest in finding out what they are all about is almost inevitable. The line between practice and meaning is a direct one. The community's practices evoke the deeper questions of meaning and thus turn practice into something that is value-laden

---

9. Like Deuteronomy 4:9, all of these texts refer to "your children's children," that is, all future generations.

10. P. D. Miller, "Teaching the Faith," *Theology Today* 53 (1996): 146-47; reprinted in Miller, *Theology Today: Reflections on the Bible and Contemporary Life* (Louisville: Westminster John Knox Press, 2006), p. 25.

and not mechanical or technical. Instruction in the faith will go on in various ways, but what is suggested by these texts is that it may be most fruitful when it is connected to what we do and when the child is "ready," that is, wondering and curious enough to ask "Why?"[11]

A more indirect way the story is taught to the children is seen in Deuteronomy 11:2-7, which begins: "Know today that it is not your children who have not known and have not seen the discipline of the Lord your God, his greatness, his mighty hand and his outstretched arm, his signs and his deeds that he did in Egypt to Pharaoh, the king of Egypt and to all his land . . . but your eyes are the ones seeing all the great work of the Lord, which he did." The story is fleshed out in the intermediate verses in some detail. The question to be raised is why the children are even mentioned since they are in the story only as the ones who *did not* see. Why refer to them at all? I would presume that, at least, they are mentioned because, by the time the recitation of these verses is over, *the children now will have "seen."* That is, the recitation of the story, the reminder to the generation on the scene, serves now to retell the story to all the succeeding generations, to give them eyes now to see what happened then. In the process, the children will come to learn why their parents have kept the commandments (v. 8).[12]

---

11. Such curious questions about the faith are always a starting point for the nurture of the young, as much now as it was so clearly for ancient Israel. As I write, I remember hearing our son at the age of three or four ask his mother at bedtime prayers one evening: "Mom, what does God look like?" Not an easy question, but one that arose out of both childish curiosity and the practices of the faith.

12. The power of the stories of Scripture to shape the child's faith is suggested by Reynolds Price in his book *Letter to a Godchild: Concerning Faith* (New York: Scribner, 2006), pp. 13-14:

> My preparation for faith likely began with something as uncomplicated as the gift of two Bible-story books — one was a collection of Old Testament tales from my paternal grandmother when I was two or three years old. The second came a year or so later from my parents and was *Hurlburt's Story of the Bible*. The two books, both of which are still with me, proved to be long-range endowments for the only child I was then. . . . Though I owned other good books in my childhood, nothing else made me long to read for myself more powerfully than the chance of learning those ancient and immensely pregnant stories on my own. Even now I don't know why, beyond the fact that there are no better stories — literally none in our culture which can promise a child both a more fascinating tale and a glimpse at least of the footsteps of God, the motions of his hands.

A similar, and even more poignant, articulation of this same point in a personal fashion is found in Stephen Dunn's poem, "At the Smithville Methodist Church," in *New and Selected Poems 1974-1994* (New York: Norton, 1994), pp. 183-84.

The Aims of Instruction

Several related aims lie behind the instruction of the children, and they are no different for the adults. It is worth noting that, aside from the fact that the children do not know yet, there really is no difference between the teaching of the child and the teaching of the adult. At least, the aims and intentions of such teaching are constant.

The first and primary aim of this teaching — child and adult — is that they may *learn to fear the Lord*.[13] Again and again when the people, the king, and the children are called to hear and learn, it is said that they are to learn to "fear the Lord" (Deut. 4:10; 6:1-2; 14:23; 17:19; 31:12-13). Reverence for the Lord of Israel, who freed them and guides their life, is to be learned and appropriated in the process of learning the law. That is why the Shema is repeated and talked about day in and day out. The family business is the love of the Lord.

Closely related to this is the intention to bring about fear of or reverence for the Lord through observing or doing the law, all the instruction that has come from the Lord through Moses (e.g., Deut. 5:1, 31; 6:2, etc.). Over and over, literally, one hears that the people learn to fear by keeping the law that has been taught to them.[14] Obedience is the goal of the law but also the means by which the proper relation to the Lord is developed. Precisely in the nurture of the child, faith and obedience are so intricately tied together that it is not possible to set them in a chronological order.

Finally, one must not miss the utilitarian aim of learning to fear by observing. It is also so that the people may find, individually and corporately, the good and abundant life, that they may live long and well in the place God has provided for them (e.g., Deut. 4:1; 6:2, 24; 8:1; 11:9). The point is made rather dramatically at the end when Moses says to the people in what many would regard as the climax of the book: "See, I have set before you life and death. . . . Therefore, choose life . . ." (30:15). Observing this polity, keeping these instructions, is the way to life. So learning them is learning how to live — in both senses of the term, how to get by and how to flourish.

It is easy to ignore this dimension of the instruction, but it is too promi-

---

13. On the fear of the Lord and fear of the parents, see also the essay by William Brown on Proverbs in this volume.

14. Dietrich Bonhoeffer understood and expressed this relationship between faith, that is, the true fear of the Lord, and obedience when he wrote: "For faith is only real when there is obedience, never without it, and faith only becomes faith in the act of obedience. . . . Not only do those who believe obey, but only those who obey believe. In the one case faith is the condition of obedience, and in the other obedience the condition of faith." Dietrich Bonhoeffer, *The Cost of Discipleship* (New York: Macmillan, 1957), p. 56.

nent in Deuteronomy to dismiss. Learning to live this way, according to this instruction, opens a positive outcome for individual and community. That is indeed always the premise of good law. Its aim is to mark out a way for all to live together. There is no guarantee that misfortune may not occur, but good fortune is possible only along the path laid out in the divine instruction. The pragmatic implications of teaching the children to learn the fear of the Lord are not to be ignored.

The Components of Teaching and Learning

What goes into helping the children come to know? To some extent that question has guided the whole discussion to this point. Still, some effort to lift up the processes and modes of educating the children is necessary to make the picture complete, even as it involves reiteration of matters noted earlier.

1. *The family context and the learning of adults.* Teaching and learning happen in the community as a whole (Deut. 31:12-13; see below), but there are explicit indications that the learning of children takes place in the family context especially. One may assume that there were schools that provided instruction, but the whole orientation of Deuteronomy is toward teaching in the family context (4:10). That goes on in a variety of ways, as indicated below, from daily recitation in the family setting, with parents reciting the words of the law, the divine instruction, and having the children repeat them back (6:7a) to continued speaking out loud or meditating on the words of the law (6:7b)[15] to the family's participation in the religious life of the commu-

---

15. For detailed investigation of the language of Deuteronomy 6:6-9 and related passages to demonstrate that what is meant by talking about the words (6:7b) is more likely a continual meditation and recitation of them so that the children can learn them and take them to heart rather than general discussion or talking about the law, see Georg Fischer, S.J., and Norbert Lohfink, S.J., "'Diese Worte sollst du summen' Dtn 6,7 *wedibbartā bām* — ein verlorener Schlüssel zur meditativen Kultur in Israel," *Theologie und Philosophie* 62 (1987): 59-72; cf. Georg Braulik, *Deuteronomium 1-16,17,* Die Neu Echter Bibel Kommentar zum Alten Testament mit der Einheits-übersetzung (Würzburg: Echter Verlag, 1986), pp. 56-57. That such recitation and repeating of the words was the way in which they were taught is made even more explicit by Deuteronomy 11:19, which is another version of 6:6-9. There is much debate about what is meant by "these words" at the beginning of 6:6, whether only vv. 4-5 are meant, or the Decalogue, or the whole of the Deuteronomic law. More recent interpretation has tended to assume that the whole of the Deuteronomic law is in view, as Fischer and Lohfink have argued in the article referred to above; cf. Norbert Lohfink, "Glauben lernen in Israel," *Katechetische Blätter* 108 (1983): 92; reprinted in a revised version in Lohfink, *Das Jüdische am Christentum: Die verlorene Dimension* (Freiburg: Herder, 1987), pp. 154-55. For brief discussion of the matter,

nity (14:23; 31:10-13). Taking the divine instruction to heart also happens as it is literally and symbolically written on the structures of family life as well as in the minds and hearts of the parents and children (6:8-9). The adults have to learn also. In Deuteronomy 4:10, this all goes on at once. The adults' learning and their teaching the children are in tandem and go together.[16]

2. *Hearing (and reading)*. Again and again, the people are told to listen and hear (e.g., Deut. 4:10; 5:1; 6:4; etc.). Recitation of the Lord's instruction happens constantly and regularly. There is a specific requirement that it be read every seven years before the whole people (31:10-13). Particular reference is made in that context to the children who have not known it. In other words, what is recalled at the beginning of Deuteronomy as God's call to the people at Sinai to gather and hear "my words" to learn and teach them to the children (4:9-10) is, at the end of the book, regularized in the life of the community (31:10-13). There is something about the community regularly encountering the divine instruction that is important for its place in the minds and hearts of the people. Clearly this regular encounter is so that it will not be forgotten but also so that the children who do not know will get to know. Thus, they come to hear the "words" of the Lord's instruction in the daily life of the family and in the special but regular occasions of the community's listening to them as a congregation. The sabbath also serves as a time when the story and its implications are regularly heard and remembered by the family.[17]

3. *Remembering and not forgetting*. The point of regular reading and hearing of the law and the story out of which it comes is so that it will always be remembered and not forgotten. The recall of the story is fundamental to the learning process. Early on, Moses warns the people: "But take care and watch yourselves closely, so as neither to forget the things that your eyes have seen nor to let them slip from your mind all the days of your life; make them known to your children and your children's children" (4:9). Remembering

---

see Weinfeld, *Deuteronomy 1–11*, p. 340; and Richard D. Nelson, *Deuteronomy*, The Old Testament Library (Louisville: Westminster John Knox Press, 2002), p. 91.

16. The syntax of the sentence in 4:10 indicates that the learning of the adults and the teaching of the children are simultaneous actions, not sequential. The point is not elaborated, but the two acts go hand in hand. The parents are always learning to fear the Lord by listening to the Lord's words even as they are teaching the children those words as the way to learn to fear the Lord.

17. While it does not have to do directly with the instruction of the children, the so-called law of the king (Deut. 17:14-20) is important in this regard because it makes clear that the king's only responsibility is to have a copy of the law, keep it with him constantly, and read it regularly so that he may learn to fear the Lord. In other words, the king's duty is to model the obedience expected of every member of the community. Making sure this happens depends directly on a constant reading of the Lord's instruction so that it cannot be forgotten or set aside.

and not forgetting what the Lord has done is critical to the ongoing well-being of the people (e.g., Deut. 8).[18]

4. *Answering questions.* Instruction in response to the child's own questions has already been noted above. It is catechetical in some sense. In that the questions come from the child, they are not prior. They are prior, however, in that they can be anticipated and answers or responses provided, as they are in each instance in Exodus and Deuteronomy where the question is expected.

5. *Cultic context to precipitate the children's coming to know.* Various cultic activities and symbols — Passover, Unleavened Bread, the stone monument at the Jordan — in the community's life, both as family and as larger assembly, are a primary impetus to the education of the child. That is not only because these activities will provoke the "Why" questions but also because their regular enactment — presenting the tithe, for example — provides opportunity for the children to find out practices and their rationale whether or before any questions are asked. In Deuteronomy 14:23 the presentation of the tithe before the Lord is seen as an opportunity for the family as a whole, adults and children, to learn to fear the Lord. In regard to virtually all the regular festive occasions, the text in one way or another, explicitly or implicitly, prescribes a family gathering across the generations. The children are not excluded from the ritual acts of the congregation. They are present and learning.[19]

6. *Recitation and meditation.* The words of God's instruction are to be recited by the parents and repeated by the child until they are written on the heart (Deut. 6:7; 11:18-19).[20] Then they continue to be recited again and again, said out loud and reflected upon. It is what we call memorization, and in Deuteronomy such activity is central to the instruction of children. They hear the parents say the words to them and they repeat them. In the process the

---

18. I have suggested some of the ongoing significance of this focus on remembering and not forgetting in the following manner: "In a time of cultural exposure to so many stimuli and of the transiency of every moment accentuated in the rapidity of daily life and the rapidity of technological and social change, there needs to be within ourselves the possibility of holding and recalling the past, of living in the present and not simply by the present. Whether in the family, the community of faith, the political community, or simply the fellowship of friends, the remembrance of what has been done and said and experienced, whether in the immediate past or long past, will shape us now and in the future." Patrick D. Miller, "'A' Is for Augustine, Aquinas . . . ," *Theology Today* 55 (1998): 3; reprinted in Miller, *Theology Today: Reflections on the Bible and Contemporary Life,* p. 50.

19. One cannot resist noting how often in contemporary church services the children are excused from much of the liturgy and so lose the opportunity to ask and to learn.

20. Cf. Deuteronomy 30:14, which speaks of "the word," that is, the commandment(s), the law, being "very near to you; it is in your mouth and in your heart for you to observe." As "the word" is spoken with the mouth, it becomes embedded in the heart.

children appropriate these words so that they are like breathing. One never stops saying them, through the course of the day and in public and private (6:7). They have them for guidance all their lives. As Norbert Lohfink has put it, one lives in the text of these words as in a landscape.[21]

7. *Doing.* Keeping the statutes and ordinances serves to teach the children and adults what it is they need to know: the fear of the Lord. Observing or doing the law is thus both the aim of the teaching and a process for learning.

8. *Motivation.* Learning to keep the Lord's instruction is "for our lasting good" (Deut. 6:24). Over and over Deuteronomy points to positive outcomes for observing the law and negative ones for not doing so. One should not overlook the importance of urging and motivating the children and the adults by indicating the value and gains that come from learning what is being taught in all this instruction. That is a long-standing practice in families and religious communities, though perhaps neglected in more recent times. Deuteronomy affirms the significance of identifying the rich gains that come from learning the way. It claims also that to go another way will bring disaster. That is clearly a theological judgment in Deuteronomy. It is also a pragmatic reality.

9. *Learning for future catastrophe.*[22] It is necessary, therefore, also to learn the Lord's way to prepare for the possibility of future catastrophe, the failure of the people to keep the law and learn the fear of the Lord. The last two times that the children are specifically on the scene are in verses that bracket the Song of Moses in Deuteronomy 32. In Deuteronomy 31:21, that song is not to be forgotten "from the mouth of their descendants." It is to be recited again and again to prepare the people to comprehend and deal with their fate when they inevitably lose the way. Then in Deuteronomy 32:46, after Moses has sung the song, which recounts both the Lord's goodness and the people's disobedience leading to God's judgment upon them, it is taken up into the law to be learned by the children. As they learn the story from the past to comprehend why they are to keep the law, they recite or sing this song in the future to comprehend why the good that the Lord intends for them does not come to pass. The Song of Moses, therefore, stands as an enduring "witness against you" through the ongoing generations. The catastrophes of the future cannot be comprehended or overcome if the people do not learn and teach this part of the instruction as well as all the statutes and ordinances and the story behind them. Teaching the children is to bring about the good the Lord's way offers. It is also to prepare them for the bad when that way is lost.

---

21. Lohfink, "Glauben lernen in Israel," p. 93.
22. This rubric is drawn from Lohfink, "Glauben lernen in Israel," p. 94.

Honoring the Parents and Punishing the Children?

The children appear in Deuteronomy largely as the focus of teaching and learning, and that learning centers on the family and the family's participation in the larger religious life of the people. The children are also present, however, in one other context, though still very much as part of the family. It is the Ten Commandments. One would assume that the commandment requiring honor of parents would be the most direct word about and to children in the Decalogue if not in the book as a whole. That is deceptive, however, because the commandment to honor father and mother is not primarily directed at young children but at adult children whose parents are still living.

Such honoring, however, is learned early on. Because the term for honor, *kabbēd*, literally means "to make heavy," one may see in the commandment a call to the child to regard mother and father as worthy of weighty respect, that is, to treat them with high regard. Indeed, this word is also used for proper respect and honoring of God. Such honor when rendered to parents has to do with respect for the role and authority of the parents, listening to and obeying their wise counsel, and caring for them as they grow older. The negative counterparts, that is, examples of dishonoring parents, are expressed in references to striking or cursing parents (Exod. 21:15, 17); being rebellious, stubborn, and disobedient (Deut. 21:18-21); or treating parents lightly, shabbily.

While listening to and obeying parents is surely part of what is meant by honoring them, it is easy to assume that this means a kind of unconditional obedience of anything a parent says. That is not the point, however. It may be helpful to note that the Hebrew verb for "obey" is the same verb as "listen" (*šāma*). Perhaps the term "heed" may convey best both dimensions, that is, the need to pay attention to what the parents say and take it seriously but also the responsibility for doing what they say, not simply hearing and going one's own way. The son and daughter listen to and learn from their father and mother. That would certainly mean, as one learns from both Deuteronomy and Proverbs, listening to the wise counsel of father and mother and to the story they have to tell about the family and the faith, as described above. What is not meant is either a disinterested listening to a lecture or a mindless obedience to whatever is said, as if simply the act of obedience is all that matters. The importance of obedience is because the father and mother can teach the way to live. By virtue of their position and their experience, they have things to teach the child that will help him or her to live and prosper. Obeying father and mother is a claim that rests upon the coherence of position (father or mother) and teaching (wise, helpful). Children are to listen to, respect, and obey their parents in a manner that indeed may be compared to the way they revere and obey the Lord. The honor of parents is on analogy with the honor of God because it is derivative of that honor and representative of it. Implicit in the analogy is the assumption that the parents are faithful representatives of the Lord's way. When that is not the case, the children are not to heed their parents and follow their way (e.g., Ezek. 20:18-20a).

Children also come into the Commandments at another and rather disturbing point, however. At the conclusion of the commandment forbidding making and worshiping images of the Lord or other gods (Deut. 5:8-9a), a motivation clause is added as follows: "For I the Lord your God am a jealous God, visiting the iniquity of the parents upon the children, to the third and fourth generation of those who reject me, but showing steadfast love to the thousandth generation of those who love me and keep my commandments" (5:9b-10). Like the children in view in the commandment to honor parents, the reference to the children of the third and fourth generation most likely refers generally to adult children. Because, however, that is not necessarily always the case, this troubling promise of divine vengeance upon innocent children merits some attention even if it is not central to Deuteronomy's focus on children. To comprehend what is going on with this cross-generational consequence of both obedience and disobedience, love of the Lord and rejection of the Lord, one must view it within a large and rather extended trajectory of meaning and effects, on which Deuteronomy functions in a key role. Some of the points on that trajectory are as follows:

1. The principle of cross-generational consequences is not peculiar to Scripture, nor does it begin there. The negative effect of family solidarity on future generations is evident in both Hittite texts from the second millennium and Greek texts from much later.[23]
2. This principle is manifest in biblical literature in story (e.g., 2 Sam. 12:10 [David]; 1 Kings 14:7-18; 15:29-30 [Jeroboam]; 2 Kings 9:7-9 [Ahab]) and creedal-type formulations (e.g., Exod. 34:6-7; Num. 14:18) more than in law (Lev. 26:39-40).
3. The principle of later generations suffering for the sins of their ancestors undergoes significant development with explicit modifications to bring about a change in understanding. The starting point for seeing what happens to the principle is Exodus 34:6-7 (of which Num. 14:18 is a shortened version):

---

23. See, e.g., Weinfeld, *Deuteronomy 1–11*, pp. 297-98.

> The Lord, the Lord, a God merciful and gracious, slow to anger, and abounding in steadfast love and faithfulness, keeping steadfast love for the thousandth generation, forgiving iniquity and transgression and sin, yet by no means clearing the guilty, but visiting the iniquity of the parents upon the children and the children's children, to the third and fourth generation.

The text clearly calls for consequences to descendants for the ancestors' sins. At the same time, one notes that the clause "to the third and fourth generation" is a modification of the previous clause "upon the children and the children's children." The phrase "children's children" means all future generations (e.g., Ezek. 37:25). Only here and in Job 42:16 ("four generations") is that expression modified.[24] So even in this text, the strongest formulation of the principle, continuing consequences are restricted to those generations that would have been alive during the lifetime of the parent/ ancestor committing the sin.

4. One crucial modification of this formulation takes place in the Decalogue, in both the Exodus and Deuteronomy versions. Whereas Exodus 34:7 concludes its formulation with "to the third and fourth generation," Exodus 20:5 and Deuteronomy 5:9 add the phrase "of those who reject me."[25] That is, "cross generational retribution applies only to descendants who act as their ancestors did."[26] Or as one interpreter has put it: "These phrases look like explanatory glosses, which come to stress that God punishes only those of the sons [and daughters] who propagate the evil ways of their fathers [and mothers] . . . and keeps his kindness for those of the descendants who love God and keep his commandments."[27]

5. A further modification takes place in Deuteronomy, underscored by its implicit articulation in Moses' sermon in Deuteronomy 7:9-10 and its explicit legal formulation in Deuteronomy 24:16. In the former passage, we read:

> Know therefore that the Lord your God is God, the faithful God who maintains covenant loyalty with those who love him and keep his commandments, to a thousand generations, *and who repays in their own per-*

---

24. Cf. n. 6 above.

25. The same difference between Exodus 34 and the Decalogue version is found with regard to the positive outcome. Whereas Exodus 34:7 has "keeping steadfast love to the thousandth generation," the commandment version adds "of those who love me and keep my commandments."

26. Jeffrey H. Tigay, *Deuteronomy*, The JPS Torah Commentary (Philadelphia: The Jewish Publication Society, 1996), p. 437.

27. Weinfeld, *Deuteronomy 1–11*, p. 299.

son those who reject him. He does not delay but repays in their own person those who reject him.

As Dean McBride has noted, this is "an emphatic revision of 5:9b."[28] What was already freighted toward God's covenantal love and grace, even in the commandment, where the steadfast love of God is shown "to the thousandth generation of those who love me and keep my command-ments," is now modified so completely that the punishment is explicitly only for the individual offender. The point is emphasized with the repeated "in their own person." Nothing is said about punishment of further gener-ations. On the contrary, it is specifically the one who has rejected the Lord who is punished. This word is then reinforced within the realm of human law by the statute that appears in Deuteronomy 24:16: "Parents shall not be put to death for their children, nor shall children be put to death for their parents; only for their own crimes may persons be put to death."

6. The quotation of this Deuteronomic law in 2 Kings 14:6 reinforces the re-vision or elimination of the principle as a standing rule in Israelite theol-ogy and law.

7. The persistence of the principle (e.g., Lam. 5:7) and its emphatic rejection are identified more than once in the prophets. Both Jeremiah (31:29-30) and Ezekiel (18:1-24) explicitly deny the punishment or consequences of one's sins being carried forward to succeeding generations, the latter do-ing so at some length.[29]

In short, one may say that in Deuteronomy and the main traditions flowing out of it, children are freed from the consequences of their parents' deeds; they are held accountable for their own actions but not for those of other members of the family.

---

28. S. Dean McBride Jr., "Deuteronomy," in *The Harper Collins Study Bible* (New York: Harper Collins, 1989), pp. 280-81.

29. Note that each of the two prophets cites a proverb that makes the retributional point and obviously was widely known and accepted ("The parents have eaten sour grapes, and the children's teeth are set on edge"). So this retribution notion was something that did not belong only to theological claims about the nature of Israel's God and the covenantal requirements. It was also a part of common wisdom and, like the utilitarian motivations for keeping the law, re-flected not only a deep theological point but also a commonsense approach to the way things work in the world.

Conclusion

No single book of Scripture attends more directly and so often to the education of the children in the community of faith than Deuteronomy. It is itself a book of teaching and one that is deeply aware that the starting point for learning the faith is in the family circle and early in life. If the fear of the Lord — that is, reverence, obedience, and worship of the God who has saved and cared for us — is the aim of human existence, as it surely is for those who live by and with the Holy Scriptures, then that fear is something to be learned and developed from the earliest days onward. Such learning happens in many ways, as we have seen. It does not happen without the early attention of the parents and the continuing presence of the family in the worship life of the larger community.

Deuteronomy as a whole offers a cohesive and persuasive argument for the importance of excellent and comprehensive faith formation within families and communities. Reading this text as a parent or teacher or member of a religious community allows one to see more clearly the complex and communal process of children's instruction, nurture, and discipline today and in the past. It also invites one — indeed, pulls one — into the enterprise of teaching the young that they may be ready to serve the Lord as they grow older.

4 To Discipline without Destruction: The Multifaceted Profile of the Child in Proverbs

William P. Brown

Proverbs has much to say about children and, in fact, *to* children. Although predominantly the product of professional literati associated with the royal court, the book does not lose touch with the more mundane, intimate world of the family. Indeed, proverbial wisdom explicitly identifies its primary setting with the household. Whereas "king" is mentioned eighteen times in Proverbs, there are at least thirty-three explicit references to children.[1] The child remains a prominent figure throughout this diverse collection of literature, more so than even wisdom herself.

And what a varied corpus Proverbs is! This ancient book of wisdom is a collection of collections of didactic sayings, from extended lectures to pithy apothegms, brought together in self-nuancing, in some cases self-correcting, ways. The search for wisdom, according to Proverbs, is an open-ended, dynamic enterprise, one based on observation and inquiry in which there is no final word. The quest for understanding is ongoing.[2] As testimony to this, Proverbs bears its own self-critique, indicated no less by various incompatible sayings contained within the book (see, e.g., Prov. 26:4-5), ancient sayings collected over centuries on the part of the sages as testimony to the perennial quest for wisdom. Wisdom is thus both contextual and dynamic. To borrow its own metaphor in Proverbs, wisdom is a "pathway," and its direction is signaled at the outset in the book's stated objective:

---

1. See Carole R. Fontaine, "Wisdom in Proverbs," in *In Search of Wisdom: Essays in Memory of John G. Gammie*, ed. Leo G. Perdue et al. (Louisville: Westminster John Knox, 1993), pp. 105-6.

2. For the pedagogy of wisdom in Proverbs, see Charles F. Melchert, *Wise Teaching: Biblical Wisdom and Educational Ministry* (Harrisonburg, PA: Trinity Press International, 1998), pp. 47-73.

To appropriate wisdom and instruction,
    to understand insightful sayings;
To acquire effective instruction,
    righteousness, justice, and equity.
To teach prudence to the simple,
    and to the young knowledge in discretion.
Let the wise also attend and gain erudition,
    and the discerning acquire skill.

$$(1:2-5)^3$$

Proverbs is a book for young and old alike, for it is all about imparting prudential wisdom for the successful navigation of life. If Proverbs were marketed today, it would be found in the "self help" section of any bookstore.

Or, perhaps more likely, in the "family life" section. In contemporary discourse, Proverbs is often cited in the context of child-rearing. Typically, those proverbial sayings that commend physically harsh disciplinary measures are cited as proof texts to legitimate corporal punishment (e.g., 13:24; 22:15; 29:15). But lacking in such appropriation of these texts is an awareness of the sheer variety of perspectives contained in Proverbs regarding child development and discipline.

As nearly complex as the literature itself, the figure of the child assumes a multifaceted profile in Proverbs. Indeed, the label "child" (literally "son" in most instances in Proverbs) extends far beyond what is normally associated with childhood today. Those dimensions of this profile that highlight the complex and abiding relationship between child, parent, and wisdom constitute the focus of this essay.

The study will proceed in more historical than canonical order, and for good reason. I begin with a look at the *earliest* collections in Proverbs (chapters 10–30) and conclude with a look at the figure of the child in the *latest* phase of the book's formation (chapters 1–9 and 31). Such a historical approach coincides, not coincidentally, with a thematic progression that begins with a discussion of the child's status and value within the family, moves to matters of instruction and discipline, and concludes with a treatment of wisdom's relation to the child. This sequence of presentation is, moreover, hermeneutically governed. The first and final chapters define Proverbs as a book and therefore provide the overall hermeneutic for understanding the book *as a whole*. The bookends shape the book literarily and, in the end, theologically. Only by accounting for the book as a whole in all its richness and va-

---

3. Unless otherwise noted, all biblical translations are the author's.

riety can the reader accurately discern the insights Proverbs offers regarding the all-important task of raising children.

The Value and Status of Children

It is frequently claimed that children in antiquity took the bottom rung of the ladder of social value and sapiential worth. This is true to a degree within the scope of Proverbs, particularly among the earliest sayings.

Age before Wisdom

Among the early proverbs, age is valued more highly than youth, for the former is identified with wisdom.

> The crown of the wise is their wisdom,
>> but the folly of fools yields (only) folly.
>>> (Prov. 14:24)

> Gray hair is a crown of glory;
>> it is attained by a righteous life.
>>> (16:31)

Wisdom is not given at birth; it is cultivated in the process of maturation. Its full sign is "gray hair." As for children, their value is in part measured in terms of their ancestors:

> Grandchildren are the crown of the elders,
>> and the glory of children is their parents.
>>> (17:6)

The metaphor is telling, both negatively and positively: children are valued primarily in relation to their progenitors. As "crowns," they are worn, as it were, by their grandparents, and the "glory" of children resides in their parents, not in themselves. Parallel to "crown" in 17:6, the label "glory" marks something of supreme value and worth as well as indicating something of the subject's very essence. Glory radiates the subject's value and identity. When applied to children, "glory" imbues them with a worth that exceeds commercial value. Children are prized as the *crowning* achievement of a stable, fully intergenerational family. But the relationship between generations, between progenitors and progeny, is not one way: as the child's glory is identified with his or her parents, so the gleaming crown of grandparents reflects their grandchildren. Interrelated in the most intimate and rewarding way, the generations enjoy a reciprocity of value, a mutual "glory." Yet a qualitative distinction is made: whatever qualities children possess that would warrant the label "glory," those qualities do not include wisdom:

> The glory of youths *(bahûrîm)* is their strength,
>> but the beauty of the aged *(zĕqēnîm)* is their gray hair.
>>
>> (20:29)

Strength and wisdom are qualities that are found on nearly opposite ends of the spectrum of maturation.

Children and Slaves

In the earliest collections, the closest social equivalent given to the child is the slave. Slave status typically denoted the lowest social rung, the opposite of the king:

> Under three things the earth quakes;
>> under four it cannot bear up:
> a slave when he becomes king,
>> and a fool when sated with food;
> an unloved woman when she gets married,
>> and a maidservant when she displaces her royal mistress.
>>
>> (Prov. 30:21-23)

Two of the examples given above describe the overturning of the social and cosmic order by virtue of the lowest status (i.e., slave) assuming highest status (king and royal mistress or queen). Nevertheless, as one proverb imagines, the slave's social position is more fluid, for it can potentially overtake that of the child without causing tectonic tremors.

> A slave who deals wisely will rule over a child who acts shamefully,
>> and will share the inheritance as one of the family.
>>
>> (17:2)

The slave and the child can in principle trade positions within the family hierarchy. Determination of social position is not simply a matter of birth and inheritance; it depends also on character and conduct. Indeed, just as a "slave pampered from childhood will come to a bad end" (29:21), so also the child. Much, then, rests on the quality of upbringing.

Child as Bane or Blessing

Among the earliest proverbs in the book, we find that the child's (i.e., "son's") worth is frequently framed in view of the parents' emotional welfare.

> The wise child gladdens a father,
> but the foolish child is a mother's grief.
>
> (Prov. 10:1; cf. 17:25)

This proverb strikingly talks of the "wise child," whose wisdom has a direct impact upon the parents. The same goes for the foolish child. Depending on his conduct, the child counts as either bane or blessing for the family (see 15:20). Parental grief and gladness are dependent upon the child's prudential conduct.

The child's impact upon the parents, however, reaches beyond emotional measures:

> A foolish child is sheer calamity *(hawwôt)* to his father,
> and a wife's quarreling is a continual dripping of rain.
>
> (19:13)

A child steeped in folly is comparable to a contentious spouse. In both cases, the family's very stability is placed in jeopardy. Most threatening is the case of the violent son:

> The one who assaults his father and drives away his mother
> is a son who causes shame and dishonor.
>
> (19:26)

The violent child causes shame, but shame to whom? The son, to be sure, suffers disgrace, but the parents, indeed the whole family, are included within this sphere of shame, for all are implicated. And such shame bears tangible consequences.

Parental Investment and Children

In the agrarian world of antiquity, much of the family's economic well-being hung on the success of the annual harvest. All family members, young and old, male and female, did their part on behalf of the household, and failure brought about both shame and economic deprivation. Productive children contributed their vital share to the family's material welfare. The lazy child, however, was considered "out of sync" with the natural or seasonal rhythms of the agrarian household.

> A child who gathers in summer is prudent,
>> but a child who sleeps in harvest brings shame.
>>> (Prov. 10:5)

Together, these sayings cast the worth of children in terms of productive maturity, and falling short of the mark results in shame and calamity. The parable of the prodigal son in Luke's Gospel operates precisely within this system of values: the squandering of family wealth is tantamount to violence of the worst sort (Prov. 28:7, 24). And violence, indeed death, is threatened against the son who brazenly curses his parents.

> If one curses his father or his mother,
>> his lamp will be put out in utter darkness.
>>> (20:20)[4]

More gruesome is the following scene:

> The eye that mocks a father and scorns obedience due to a mother
>> should be pecked out by the ravens of the valley and devoured
>> by vultures.
>>> (30:17)

Constituting a dire threat to the family's integrity, disobedience is deliberately cast in the language of contempt. Disobedience itself, however, is not so much the problem as the scorn and mockery that can accompany it. Recall that the Decalogue stipulates "honor" for the parents, not submission (Exod. 20:12), and Leviticus 19:3, more to the issue here, enjoins "reverence" for mother and father.

In sum, the child's profile within the patriarchal household was a power-

---

4. Cf. Exodus 21:17; Deuteronomy 21:18-21.

ful one. Far from being irrelevant or peripheral, and much more than a commodity, the child was from the outset considered a vital contributor to the family's welfare, and much of the child's success as a contributor hinged on proper child-rearing. The child's profile in Proverbs is not that of willful disobedience or intractable defiance, although the sages fully acknowledged that children *can* be disrespectful, lazy, and selfish. Rather, the child is primarily educable. Discipline and instruction (one and the same thing, as we will see) were deemed the most important investment in the family's well-being. It was a matter of life and death.

Instruction, Discipline, and the Rod

The impact of the child's conduct upon the family as a whole and the parents' well-being in particular establishes a compelling need for proper discipline.

> Discipline your child, and he will give you rest;
> he will bring delight to your soul.
>
> (Prov. 29:17)

From the parents' standpoint, a properly disciplined child yields rest and joy. Discipline in Proverbs, and elsewhere in biblical tradition, conveys the basic meaning of correction aimed at the avoidance of moral fault and the acquisition of moral insight.[5] Simply put, discipline is a means to an end; its purpose is to foster moral integrity. Integrity in Proverbs is a wide-ranging concept that includes honesty and truthfulness (e.g., 12:17, 19; 14:25; 24:26), self-control (e.g., 12:16; 14:29; 29:11), and productivity (as opposed to laziness, e.g., 6:6-9; 12:24, 27; 31:27), as well as generosity (e.g., 11:25; 21:26; 22:9), piety (1:7; 2:5; 3:7; 8:13; 15:33; 31:30), and independence (6:1-3; 31:10-30).

With regard to children, Proverbs 22:6 sets the context for discipline and its future orientation.

> Train a child in the way he should go,
> and when he is old he will not depart from it.
>
> (22:6)

The conviction is that discipline, if administered rightly, is truly in the child's best interest, not just the parents' or the family's. Discipline is an essential in-

---

5. See Michael V. Fox, *Proverbs 1–9*, Anchor Bible Commentary 18A (New York: Doubleday, 2000), pp. 34-35.

vestment in the *child's* future; it is the means to his maturity and moral integrity. How such discipline is to be administered is the topic of several proverbs whose common motif is that of the "rod." (Contrary to popular opinion, the adage "Spare the rod and spoil the child" is *not* in the Bible.) Words alone are considered insufficient in the arduous task of discipline (29:19).

The Function of the Rod

The use of physical pain for disciplining children was widely accepted in the ancient Near East. In the Egyptian schoolbook *Papyrus Lansing,* from the New Kingdom (1570-1070 BCE), the teacher says to a recalcitrant student: "But though I beat you with every kind of stick, you will not listen. If I knew another way of doing it, I would do it for you that you might listen."[6] The student, later in the text, responds in praise of his teacher: "I grew into a youth at your side. You beat my back; your teaching entered my ear."[7] "Beating" a student was conducted to instill "listening," that is, a receptive disposition. The "stick" was employed also to teach "the fool" and "punish" the son,[8] as well as used as a means of protection, as indicated in *Papyrus Insinger,* the latest surviving Egyptian instruction, dated to the Demotic Period (1070-656 BCE).[9]

From another cultural context we have the Aramaic *Proverbs of Ahiqar* (sixth or fifth century BCE), which contains the admonition: "Spare not your son from the rod; otherwise, can you save him [from wickedness]?"[10] But perhaps the most vivid is the Syriac version of this proverb:

> My son, spare not thy son from stripes;
>> for the beating of a boy is like manure to the garden,
>> and like a rope to an ass,
>> and like a tether on the foot of an ass.[11]

Rich in mixed metaphors, the proverb likens physical discipline to horticultural cultivation, on the one hand, and animal training, on the other.

6. Miriam Lichtheim, *Ancient Egyptian Literature,* vol. 2: *The New Kingdom* (Berkeley: University of California Press, 1976), p. 169.

7. Lichtheim, *Ancient Egyptian Literature,* vol. 2, p. 172.

8. Miriam Lichtheim, *Ancient Egyptian Literature,* vol. 3: *The Late Period* (Berkeley: University of California Press, 1980), p. 192.

9. Lichtheim, *Ancient Egyptian Literature,* vol. 3, p. 196 (14:26).

10. James M. Lindenberger, *The Aramaic Proverbs of Ahiqar* (Baltimore: Johns Hopkins University Press, 1983), p. 49 (Saying 3).

11. Cited in Lindenberger, *The Aramaic Proverbs of Ahiqar,* p. 49.

Comparable reference to the use of the "rod" in matters of discipline can be found among the biblical proverbs.

Do not withhold *(mn')* discipline from a boy *(na'ar);*[12]
    if you strike him *(nkh)* with a *rod,* he will not die.
If you strike him with the *rod,*
    you will save *(nṣl)* his life from Sheol.

                            (Prov. 23:13-14)

He who withholds *(ḥśk)* the *rod* hates his child,
    but he who loves him seeks earnestly to discipline him.

                            (13:24)

Folly is bound up *(qšr)* in the heart of a boy *(na'ar),*
    but the *rod* of discipline removes *(rḥq)* it from him.

                            (22:15)

There is no question that the "rod" *(šebet)* refers to a physical instrument and that these proverbs commend its active use as a disciplinary measure.[13] The admonition cited first (Prov. 23:13-14) presents the rhetorically strongest case of using the "rod." The first line gives assurance that use of the rod will not kill the son. Far from it: the rod is meant to *save* the son from (premature) death ("Sheol"). The saying in 13:24 identifies negligence in using the rod as a sign of hatred rather than love for the child. The rod is emblematic of diligent discipline. The last saying cited above (22:15) highlights the *function* of the rod: the rod removes folly from the boy (compare 27:22). To mix metaphors, the rod performs, as it were, radical surgery. Elsewhere in Proverbs, physical blows against the body are considered cleansing: "Blows that wound cleanse away evil; beatings make clean the innermost parts" (20:3).

Of particular importance is the overall rationale these sayings provide in commending use of the "rod." Wielding the rod is meant to edify, that is, to save the child from, literally, grave danger. Love, not anger, is the fundamental reason or motivation. To refrain from discipline is to refuse to love. The sages condemn the lack of discipline as the manifestation of hatred, the abuse of negligence (see also Prov. 29:15b).

Also significant is what the sages do *not* say about discipline. Lacking in any of the sayings is the language of punishment.[14] Use of the rod upon the

---

12. The Hebrew *na'ar* can designate a boy from infancy to upper teenage years (e.g., Exod. 2:6; Gen. 37:2).

13. See also Proverbs 10:13; 14:3; 26:3.

14. See also Randall J. Heskett, "Proverbs 23:13-14," *Interpretation* 55 (2001): 182-84.

child is neither penalty nor punishment. Hence, "corporal punishment" does not technically apply in Proverbs. Physical discipline is meant to edify, not punish. Retaliation, even retribution, does not figure in the act of discipline. "Rod and reproof yield wisdom" (29:15a).

> Discipline your child while there is hope,
>> but do not set your heart on his destruction.
>
>   (19:18)

The proverb makes clear that discipline has nothing to do with destruction. Whenever malice enters into the act, discipline becomes abusive.

Parental Anger

The immediately following verse of the saying cited above, moreover, prohibits the use of anger as a possible motivation for wielding discipline:

> A violent tempered person will pay the penalty;
>> if you effect a rescue, you will only have to do it again.
>
>   (Prov. 19:19)

Any anger-inspired behavior, including discipline, is anathema in Proverbs; it denotes disruption of order and loss of control. In the case of child-rearing, proverbial wisdom takes pains to restrict the motivations that occasion usage of the rod. This is perhaps the most important lesson to be learned from Proverbs thus far: while the corporeal means of discipline is accepted in these sayings, biblical wisdom probes deeply into the rationales and motivations behind such usage with the effect of imposing limits: edification rather than punishment, love rather than hatred motivates acts of discipline. Anger, above all, is proscribed. Elsewhere in Proverbs, anger is regarded as a violent emotion, likened to a flood (27:4), that destroys relationships (21:19).[15]

Fear

Consonant with the widespread proscription of anger in Proverbs is the absence of any reference to the child's fear before the parents. Although the object of honor and respect, parents are never cast as the object of fear in pro-

---

15. See also Proverbs 15:18; 16:14; 19:11, 12; 21:19; 25:23; 27:3-4; 29:8, 22.

verbial wisdom. Fear, rather, is reserved for God, as perhaps the most famous of biblical proverbs attests:

> The fear of the LORD is the beginning of knowledge;
> fools scorn wisdom and instruction.
>
> (1:7; cf. 9:10)

Indeed, there is something distinctly didactic about godly "fear" even in the earliest proverbs; it is the means of knowledge and insight (see also 1:29; 2:5; 15:33). Fear of God is, moreover, eminently edifying and life-enhancing (e.g., 10:27; 14:27; 19:23). Such salutary consequences, as delineated in Proverbs, suggest a more positive translation of the Hebrew *yir'āh,* such as "reverence" or "awe." In any case, within the human realm, only the king is considered worthy of fear and hence of obedience (24:21). But as parents are also in a position to elicit obedience from the child, instilling fear is evidently not the means. "Fear" of God on the part of parents establishes security for their children.

> In the fear of the LORD there is strong confidence,
> and one's children will have refuge.
>
> (14:26)

Child as Every Person

Despite their intense focus on children, the sages of biblical antiquity acknowledged that discipline is not a matter that pertains exclusively to children. Discipline applies to everyone, both child and adult alike. As a "wise child loves discipline" (Prov. 13:1a), so "whoever loves discipline loves knowledge" (12:1a). The implication is that what is cultivated in the child, namely, a love for discipline, is carried into adulthood as a disposition for learning. The connection, in fact, is much clearer in the Hebrew, since the word for "discipline" is the same word for "instruction" *(mûsār).* Terminological distinction, for better or worse, is made in most English translations on the presumed basis of the age of the recipient: *mûsār* is translated as "discipline" for children and as "instruction" for adults. But such categorical divisions do not obtain in Proverbs. Even the wise must welcome the *discipline* of others (9:8; 10:17; 12:1; 17:10). Such "discipline," along with its attendant consequences (e.g., wisdom and prudence), is a perennial need that is never completely fulfilled within a lifespan. "Discipline" is a matter of lifelong learning, and accepting it is a mark of wisdom!

Through the bond of *mûsār*, the sages deliberately blur the pedagogical distinction between child and adult. The reader, regardless of age, is constantly addressed as "my child" (literally "my son"), and the source of such rhetoric is identified with a parental figure, as evidenced in the following sample of admonitions.

> Cease straying, my child, from the words of knowledge,
>   in order that you may hear instruction.
>
> (Prov. 19:27)

> My child, if your heart is wise,
>   my heart too will be glad.
>
> (23:15)

> Hear, my child, and be wise,
>   and direct your mind in the way.
>
> (23:22)

> My child, give me your heart,
>   and let your eyes observe my ways.
>
> (23:26)

> Be wise, my child, and make my heart glad,
>   so that I may answer whoever reproaches me.
>
> (27:11)

The speaker's identity, however, need not be a parent. The speaking voice could be, more generally, a teacher, while the student, as the recipient of instruction, is cast in the pedagogical role of the "son." The framework of education thus finds its model in the family. Throughout much of the ancient Near East, Israel included, education was an extension of the family hierarchy.[16] Rhetorically, every reader of these admonitions, whether ancient or modern, young or old, is put back into the role of the receptive child, the model child *and* student of learning, the one who gladly receives, indeed welcomes, "rebuke."

> Do not rebuke the scoffer lest he hate you;
>   rebuke the wise and he will love you.
>
> (9:8)

---

16. See James Crenshaw, *Education in Ancient Israel: Across the Deadening Silence,* Anchor Bible Reference Library (New York: Doubleday, 1998), pp. 15-16, 130-32, 187-89, 230.

The pedagogical parallel between child and adult is most clearly evinced in the tight juxtaposition found in the purpose statement that opens the book of Proverbs:

> To teach prudence to the simple,
>   and to the young knowledge in discretion.
> Let the wise also attend and gain erudition,
>   and the discerning acquire skill.

(1:4-5)

The young and the wise are bound together in Proverbs; they share in common the quest for wisdom, the need for instruction. While the young begin the journey, the wise never complete it. Thus, even the wise remain in need of further learning. The difference between the wise and the simple, the old and the young, is merely relative.

> Even a boy *(na'ar)* makes himself known by his acts,
>   by whether his deed is pure and right.

(20:11)

Like adults, children are moral agents in progress and thus bear to some degree the responsibilities of moral conduct. In Proverbs, there is no transitional period of development in which the child is *not* held accountable for his or her actions. Children are deemed to have the capacity to choose, and such capacity is most explicitly developed in the first nine chapters of Proverbs.

Wisdom and Child

With its extended lecture format, Proverbs 1–9 reflects the final stage of the book's composition, and it is here that a decidedly different profile of the child emerges. The lectures are framed by the rhetoric of direct address of a parental source to a receptive child. The admonition, "Hear, my son, your father's instruction, and do not reject your mother's teaching" (Prov. 1:8), opens the series of lectures that constitute these chapters.[17] The father figure addresses his "son" with words, not rods, and such words are designed precisely to *persuade* the son to walk in the pathway of wisdom. The father's discourse assumes that the son has the *capacity to choose* for himself; hence, much of his

---

17. See also Proverbs 2:1; 3:1, 11, 21; 4:1, 10, 20; 5:1, 7; 6:1, 3; 7:1, 24; 8:32.

"lecturing" is laced with conditional statements ("if you . . ." [e.g., 2:1-4; 3:24; 6:1]) in place of direct admonitions. Nothing is said, however, of how the son responds. That is left to the reader. Borrowing from the Marxist theoretician Louis Althusser, Carol Newsom suggests that this figure of the silent "son" serves as the "interpellated" subject of the reader.[18] The reader of Proverbs 1–9, whether male or female, young or old, is invited to take up the subject position of the "son" in relation to a parental figure.

Wisdom's Discourse

While the "son" is consistently cast as the addressee in Proverbs, the father is not the only source of authoritative discourse. His main counterpart is woman wisdom (Hebrew *ḥokmāh*, Greek *sophia*),[19] whose grammatically determined gender is "fleshed out" rhetorically and meta-narratively in Proverbs.[20] For the father and wisdom, words are the *only* means of discipline and instruction. Both parent and wisdom cajole, encourage, entice, plead, and issue an occasional rebuke (see, e.g., 1:22-31), but no threats of beatings or of bodily pain are made by either speaker. Rationale for such reticence in the use of physical force is perhaps indicated in Proverbs 17:10:

A rebuke strikes deeper into an intelligent person
than a hundred blows into a fool.

Reproving words ultimately carry greater weight than a multitude of beatings. Whereas 29:15a puts "rod" and "reproof" on the same pedagogical level ("Rod and reproof yield wisdom"), the saying in 17:10 holds clear preference for the verbal, rather than physical, form of instruction. Reproof or rebuke in Proverbs is to be equated not with mere scolding or harsh denunciation but rather with convictive, cajoling, urgent words of wisdom, the medium of discipline (see, e.g., 1:23, 25; 3:11-12): "For the commandment is a lamp and the teaching a light, and the reproofs of discipline are the way of life" (6:23). In-

18. Carol A. Newsom, "Woman and the Discourse of Patriarchal Wisdom: A Study of Proverbs 1–9," in *Gender and Difference in Ancient Israel*, ed. Peggy L. Day (Minneapolis: Fortress, 1989), p. 143.

19. It is possible that the speaker in Proverbs 7 is the mother. See Athalya Brenner, "Proverbs 1–9: An F Voice?" in *On Gendering Texts*, ed. A. Brenner and F. van Dijk-Hemmes (Leiden: Brill, 1993), pp. 113-30.

20. For the meta-narrative dimensions of wisdom in Proverbs 1–9, see William P. Brown, *Character in Crisis: A Fresh Approach to the Wisdom Literature of the Old Testament* (Grand Rapids: Eerdmans, 1996), pp. 36-41, 47-49.

deed, "better is open rebuke than hidden love" (27:5). The word, thus, is mightier than the rod! In Proverbs 1–9, the rebuke has replaced the rod. Recourse to words, and only words, in the task of discipline (a.k.a. instruction) marks the addressee, the child, as potentially intelligent or wise.

Within the discourse of both father and wisdom, persuasion is the means of instruction. Arguments, admonitions, observations, rebukes, and encouragement — these various rhetorical forms and strategies are deployed to bend the son's ear and form his character. Never does the father take for granted the child's receptivity, hence the relentless repetition and urgency that characterize his lectures. At one point, the father pleads, "Bind [your father's commandments] upon your heart always; tie them around your neck. When you walk, they will lead you; when you lie down, they will watch over you; and when you awake, they will talk with you" (Prov. 6:21-22). The father wants his son to travel in good company, namely, with his instruction ever before the son, the *torah* for the family (cf. Deut. 6:6-9).

Wisdom provides just such companionship, and of the most edifying kind. The father promises that wisdom will "enter into your heart and knowledge will be pleasant to your soul" (Prov. 2:10). She comes wielding not the rod of discipline but the power of persuasion, and of the most intimate kind. Indeed, the son is urged to call wisdom "sister" and "kin" (7:4). Elsewhere she is the gracious host, inviting her guests, her "children," to an open, lavish banquet (9:1-6). Whereas the father maintains his authoritative position above the son (see 3:11-12), wisdom positions herself as the son's intimate "equal."

In Proverbs 1–9, instruction or discipline is not so much an external force as a matter of internal suasion. At one point, the father recollects a time when he was a child:

> When I was son to my father,
>   the tender and favorite one of my mother,
> he taught me, saying to me, "Let your heart hold fast my words;
>   keep my commandments, and live.
> Acquire wisdom; acquire insight:
>   do not forget nor turn away from the words of my mouth.
> Do not forsake her, and she will keep you;
>   love her, and she will guard you."
>
>   (4:3-6)

Instead of recalling a childhood experience comparable to what his own sons may be facing, the father simply defers to the formative authority of his father. Any personal element is all but missing; nothing is particularly revealed about the father's childhood in relation to his sons' other than that he, too, had to carry the weight of tradition upon his shoulders, now transferred to his children (to be transferred to their progeny, and so on).

Wisdom as Child

Wisdom, however, proffers another approach. As the father makes clear, she is the goal of the son's quest, the object of his love, his companion and guardian. Most revealing is wisdom's lofty discourse on her character in Proverbs 8:22-31, part of her aretalogy or self-praise. Wisdom begins authoritatively enough: she is the first act of creation, created before everything else, thereby staking out her preeminent authority. Her age surpasses that of any parent, almost infinitely so. She is birthed by God, no less, and prior to all creation (vv. 23, 25). Wisdom, moreover, bears witness to God's creation of heaven and earth and so is intimately familiar with the workings of the cosmos. Next to God, she is most fully "in the know." But the manner in which she exercises her authority, in contrast to the father, derives not from familial hierarchy but from mutual kinship. Wisdom's discourse ends with a final, evocative image that cements an everlasting bond of shared identity with the child:

> When he established the heavens, I was there,
> > when he circumscribed the surface of the deep,
> when he secured the skies above,
> > when he stabilized the springs of the deep,
> when he assigned the sea its limit,
> > lest the waters transgress his command,
> when he carved out the foundations of the earth,
> > *I was beside him growing up,*[21]
> and I was his delight day by day,
> > playing before him always,
> playing in his inhabited world,
> > and delighting in the human race.
>
> (8:27-31)

---

21. NRSV: "a master worker." The term is actually a Qal infinitive absolute of *'mn,* whose root meaning is "support" or "nourish." For detailed linguistic discussion, see Michael V. Fox, "'Āmôn Again," *Journal of Biblical Literature* 115 (1996): 699-702; William P. Brown, *The Ethos of the Cosmos: The Genesis of Moral Imagination in the Bible* (Grand Rapids: Eerdmans, 1999), p. 274. The context, moreover, suggests the image of wisdom as a child "playing" before God.

Wisdom, too, is a child, playing, delighting, learning, and growing. Here, wisdom is created in the *imago nati,* an image underappreciated, if not dismissed, by interpreters such as R. B. Y. Scott:

> The fact is that the thought of Wisdom as a child playing is not really congruous with the total context in Prov. viii, and this suggestion, based on the metaphors of birth and play, is superficial. The first part of the chapter and the peroration in verses 32-36 appeal to men to listen to Wisdom because of her *primacy* in creation, which is expressed as *priority* in sequence. For this high claim to grave authority *the imagery of a gay, thoughtless childhood is inappropriate.*[22]

But are "primacy" and "playing" mutually exclusive? At the very least, wisdom *as child* in Proverbs 8 is able to forge a uniquely intimate bond with the child *as recipient* of wisdom's instruction and, yes, authority. At most, perhaps, such imagery highlights the primacy of play when it comes to the sapiential way of life. The authority that wisdom embodies is not "grave" but creative, and playfully so. But in any case, the image of wisdom playing cannot be gainsaid in this passage, for she frolics *before* God as much as she grows up *beside* God.[23] And such "child's play" takes on entirely cosmic dimensions; indeed, it is made possible by the established stability of God's creation. The cosmos is, as it were, child-proofed for wisdom's flourishing.

Where the father stops short of forging a bond of identification with his son, wisdom does so fully. Wisdom's approach is not meant to rival the father's authority but to complement it and extend it as the child grows into maturity. Nurtured in a life of delight in God and in creation, wisdom's growth beside God makes possible the child's growth with wisdom. Her discourse marks the culmination of the child's education *as a child.* Amid (and not despite) her unsurpassable authority, wisdom finds a way to bond with her audience, her "children" (v. 32), by revealing her own childlike nature. In the end, the child embarks on the pathway to maturity neither by the "rod of discipline" nor by harsh words, but by wisdom's inviting discourse, by the wisdom who shares with the child a delight in God's creation. That is to say, maturity in wisdom does not discount or outgrow wide-eyed wonder. Far from rejecting wonder, wisdom cultivates it.

---

22. R. B. Y. Scott, "Wisdom in Creation: The ʾĀmôn of Proverbs VIII 30," *Vetus Testamentum* 10 (1960): 218-19; italics added.

23. See the comparable image of a child featured at Jesus' side in Luke 9:47, as discussed in the essay by John T. Carroll in this volume.

Growing Up in Wisdom's Joy

As wisdom, daughter of God, "grows up," so also the child. It is wisdom, not the parent, not the rod, not the teacher, who ultimately leads the child onward toward maturity, establishing the most lasting of relationships for navigating the complexities of life, while preserving childlike delight all along the way. Like wisdom herself, the child in Proverbs exhibits various profiles, faced with both the end of a rod and wisdom's open, inviting hand (1:24). But wisdom, in all her authority and majesty as well as her childlikeness, *spares* the rod, and in so doing relativizes its use, much in tension with what we find in the earlier sayings of Proverbs. Hence, all references to "rod" (as noted above) must be read through wisdom's pedagogical approach, culminating in chapters 8 and 9, whereby both her delight and her passionate discourse outweigh the resort to corporal discipline as a means of instruction. Wisdom's way with the inhabited world gives sufficient reason to set aside the rod and replace it with powerful, directive, affirming, and, yes, critical words, such words that prove to be more palpably effective and enduring than any form of physical force. Such words are wisdom's words.

What, then, is the child's destination on the path of wisdom? What is the profile of maturity in Proverbs? The answer lies at the conclusion of the book, in the acrostic poem that pays homage to the "woman of strength" (Prov. 31:10-31). There, the son has become a husband, a father, and an "elder of the land" (vv. 11, 23, 28-29). He has married well, so well in fact that his spouse is tantamount to wisdom herself, incarnated in the household (vv. 17, 25-26).[24] The child has chosen the right path.

The book of Proverbs, in sum, is about instructing children *and* letting them go, both to play and to contribute to the larger community. As the son is ready to venture forth from home, the parent urges him to take on a companion who will guide him through the challenges and dangers of establishing himself in the larger community. The father's words in Proverbs 1–9 are parting words; wisdom's words, conversely, are welcoming, inviting words. And through it all, the child is a developing moral subject passed on from parent to spouse, from mother to wisdom, from home to community. Together, parents and wisdom establish an authoritative community in the best sense: one that provides both structure and warmth, one that *creates* an environment

---

24. For a full treatment of the connections between the "woman of strength" and wisdom, see Christine Yoder, *Wisdom as a Woman of Substance: A Socio-Economic Reading of Proverbs 1–9 and 31:10-31*, Beihefte zur Zeitschrift für die alttestamentliche Wissenschaft 304 (Berlin/New York: de Gruyter, 2001).

conducive to the child's development. The child is ever in process and on the move, "growing up," comparable to wisdom. As the son ventures farther away from his father's house, so he becomes more intimate with wisdom in her multi-pillared mansion (9:6). Wisdom begins in the home and radiates outward into the community.

Perhaps the greatest lesson Proverbs offers to every reader, both young and old, is its claim that what pertains to the child's growth in wisdom also applies to the adult (Prov. 1:5a), namely, instruction and joy. As wisdom's growth begins in joy, in playing with creation and God, may the delight shared by children never be lost on the wise. For there are no "grown-ups" in Proverbs. Progress along wisdom's path will always be marked with baby steps.

5 "Look! The Children and I Are as Signs and Portents in Israel": Children in Isaiah

Jacqueline E. Lapsley

The book of Isaiah is perhaps the most well known of the major prophets, and in the Christian tradition it has pride of place within the Old Testament as the "Fifth Gospel" due to its messianic prophecies that later interpreters (including the New Testament writers) understood in light of their experience of Jesus Christ and on account of its soaring words of comfort found especially in chapters 40–55.

Most scholars agree that the book of Isaiah may be divided into three parts according to different historical contexts. Most of Isaiah 1–39 (called First Isaiah) dates from the eighth century BCE and reports the activity of the prophet named Isaiah, whereas Isaiah 40–55 (Second Isaiah) is rooted in the experiences of exile in the sixth century, and Isaiah 56–66 (Third Isaiah) reflects a post-exilic context, when the people are back in the land of Israel and are struggling to sort out their communal life and its theological grounding. Since I am primarily interested in a literary-theological exploration of the children in Isaiah, I will nod to these traditional scholarly boundaries, but they will not restrict my inquiry. The whole book of Isaiah with all its sixty-six chapters offers images of children worth our attention.[1]

In this essay I examine a number of the images of children that appear in Isaiah, including the prophet's own children, his focus on orphans, and the way Israel itself is described metaphorically as a child in the book. The chil-

---

1. The division between the northern kingdom (sometimes called "Israel") and the southern kingdom (often called "Judah") took place in the tenth century BCE. Although the eighth-century prophet of First Isaiah is for the most part addressing the southern kingdom of Judah, to simplify usage and because it does not affect the discussion of children in Isaiah I use the generic term "Israel" to refer to the prophetic audience throughout the book of Isaiah, irrespective of the historical situation, whether pre-exilic, exilic, or post-exilic.

dren in Isaiah may at first appear to be background figures for the primary drama of God's judgment and promise of redemption, but upon closer reading they come to the fore. In the end I argue that they are not extraneous but rather serve as powerful indexes of God's judgment and promise. The fortunes and faithfulness of Israel are represented in the welfare of Israel's children. Yet they are not simply barometers; rather, children in the book of Isaiah are signs of and, in an important way, constitutive of the flourishing that God would have for Israel, and by extension, for all humanity.

Isaiah's More Familiar Children: The Named Children and the Orphans

Children as Signs: Isaiah's Named Children

To be sure, the book of Isaiah does not immediately appear to offer much raw material for reflection on children and theology, let alone anything as coherent as an explicit "theology of the child." Three memorably named children do appear in the book: Shear-jashub ("A remnant shall return"), Immanuel ("God with us"), and the unfortunate Maher-shalal-hash-baz ("Pillage hastens; looting speeds"). YHWH often commanded the Israelite prophets to express the divine will to the people through sign-acts: the divine will not simply expressed in words but *enacted* on the body. Usually this entailed the prophet himself physically undertaking unconventional behavior (e.g., Ezekiel lies on his side for 390 days to signify the number of years of Israel's punishment). The symbolic naming of a prophet's children is also a form of sign-act, wherein the deity's message to the Israelite people is conveyed through the birth of children who carry significant names. (In addition to Isaiah, the prophet Hosea also has children with symbolic names.)

Sign-acts reinforce the validity and power of the divine message to a reluctant audience; they are "visible evidence of the presence and purpose of God."[2] Yet Isaiah's children are more than simply a kind of papyrus for divine messages, as though the fact that they are children were utterly irrelevant. As I will argue below, form and content are inextricably intertwined here as elsewhere in the prophetic material — it matters that the divine message of both judgment and hope in Isaiah comes in the form of *children*.

Isaiah's children appear in chapters 7 and 8, the account of the prophet's

---

2. Bernard W. Anderson with Steven Bishop and Judith H. Newman, *Understanding the Old Testament*, 5th ed. (1998; Upper Saddle River, NJ: Pearson Prentice Hall, 2007), p. 68.

encounters with King Ahaz and the prophet's attempt to counsel the king during the Syro-Ephraimite War (735-32 BCE). The first to appear is Shear-jashub ("A remnant shall return"). The meaning of the child's name is ambiguous: some commentators understand the name as intended to provide some comfort to Ahaz, while other interpreters read the name as judgment against him (is it: "a remnant shall return — that's some comfort" or "*only* a remnant shall return — everyone else is defeated/killed"?).[3] In either case, Isaiah is attempting to dissuade Ahaz, who is trying to defend himself against external threats, from making foreign alliances; he needs to trust in YHWH instead. The child is present to embody that message. The next child whose name Ahaz is meant to ponder is the most famous of Isaiah's children (Isa. 7:14-17). His name, Immanuel ("God with us"), is less ambiguous: Ahaz is not to form a foreign alliance because YHWH is present in Jerusalem and Judah and will not allow his people to come to harm, provided Ahaz does not lose his faith and trust in YHWH. The name was later taken up in the Gospel of Matthew (1:23) to refer to Jesus' birth, and so it was forever immortalized in Western culture. Like Shear-jashub, the last of Isaiah's named children, Maher-shalal-hash-baz ("Pillage hastens; looting speeds"), offers an ambiguous message: is it a word of comfort or warning?[4] The name, mercifully, is not as well remembered as Immanuel.

Of these three "named children" most readers recall only Immanuel, and even then it is not the child but his name that is important — its messianic resonances gesturing forward to Jesus in the Christian tradition. The three children themselves seem to be quite dispensable, mere vessels for the names that convey God's judgment and promises to Israel. While these children are more helpful for thinking about biblical perspectives on children than they first appear, their meaning is not immediately apparent. The significance of these children and their names are thrown into greater relief by the other children appearing in Isaiah; thus I will return to them in the discussion below, once the other less well known children in Isaiah have been coaxed out of the shadows.

---

3. For an extended discussion, see Hans Wildberger, *Isaiah 1–12: A Commentary*, trans. Thomas H. Trapp (Minneapolis: Fortress, 1991), pp. 295-97. Walter Brueggemann understands the name as ominous in the eighth-century context but as reassuring in a later exilic setting (*Isaiah 1–39*, Westminster Bible Companion [Louisville: Westminster John Knox, 1998], p. 65).

4. Marvin A. Sweeney, *Isaiah 1–39: With an Introduction to Prophetic Literature*, Forms of the Old Testament Literature 16 (Grand Rapids: Eerdmans, 1996), p. 171.

Championing the Welfare of the Orphan

In addition to the symbolically named children, most people acquainted with biblical traditions recall that children also appear in Isaiah as the victims of injustice. The prophet famously excoriates the people for failing to execute justice for the widow and the orphan, the most vulnerable members of society (Isa. 1:17, 23; 10:2). Their vulnerability, which is social, but especially economic, stems from their lack of kinship ties to a male head of family. Orphans and widows are thus economically and socially marginal, and their very survival is at risk. YHWH indicts Judah for failing to champion[5] the welfare of the orphan (1:23) and exhorts them to do so (1:17). These failures are cited as a significant reason for the harsh divine judgment that Isaiah announces. The failure is not one of charity, as is commonly perceived in popular thought, but a failure of justice at the systemic level. The divine concern for orphans and widows in Isaiah and other prophetic texts has rightly been translated into the modern context as a theological imperative to ensure economic and social justice for all those persons who are most at risk of finding themselves at the edge of the social fabric.

In general, the Torah — that is, the legal and instructional material found in the first five books of the Bible — constitutes the legal and moral standard for dealing with widows and orphans. The overall thrust of that standard is summarized negatively in Exodus 22:22: "You shall not abuse any widow or orphan." All the laws concerning orphans and widows in the Torah are designed to safeguard them from being victimized by the greed of those with more power and social and economic capital (cf. Deut. 10:18; 14:29; 24:17-21; 26:12-13; 27:19). When the orphans and widows cry out to God at the injustices perpetrated against them, God will heed their cry (Exod. 22:23). As J. David Pleins observes: "Justice for the poor became self-consciously both a civil and religious matter in ancient Israel."[6]

Isaiah, then, implicitly judges Israel's treatment of orphans and widows against the Torah's teaching and legislation concerning them. The temptation is to use the term "rights" as in the "rights of the orphan," and this would not

5. The verb *shafat* that is repeatedly used in the context of what the people should do with respect to orphans is variously translated "to judge," "to uphold the rights of," and, in the Jewish Publication Society's translation of Psalm 10:18, "to champion." See below for my discussion of the terminology; see also the discussion in Moshe Weinfeld, *Social Justice in Ancient Israel and the Ancient Near East* (Minneapolis: Fortress, 1995), p. 40. Scripture translations are mine unless noted otherwise.

6. J. David Pleins, *The Social Visions of the Hebrew Bible: A Theological Introduction* (Louisville: Westminster John Knox, 2001), p. 53.

be far off the mark in one sense (indeed, this is the Jewish Publication Society's translation of Isa. 1:17). In the context of the Hebrew Scriptures, however, the term "rights" is somewhat misleading. Regarding the need to protect the powerless from the greed of the powerful, the emphasis in the Torah is less on rights and more on the responsibilities of those in power.[7] There is no single Hebrew word for "rights" corresponding to any modern sense of the word. The verb *shafat* in these contexts denotes the responsibility of making sure that the welfare of these vulnerable individuals be upheld according to the law.

While Patrick Miller is correct to observe that the Torah emphasizes the responsibility side of this relationship, the flip side is that these children and widows have a "right" to expect the championing of their cause, and certainly God expects that Israel will fulfill the Torah. The disappointment of that expectation is the main drama of the prophetic material. Having understood that responsibilities are emphasized in the Torah more than rights (what would this look like today?), "champion/uphold the rights of" is nonetheless an appropriate translation for *shafat* in these contexts since it helps to contrast the powerlessness of the children and widows over against the power of those in Israel who should have, and might have, acted differently.

So these are the most memorable children in Isaiah: the three named children of the prophet, and the victimized orphans. They are certainly the ones that came immediately to mind when I first began to reflect on Isaiah and children.

Concern for Orphans: A Second Look

It was only upon reading Isaiah again, actually looking for the presence of children, that I noticed that images of children appear much more prominently in the book than I had previously thought. It would be impossible within the scope of this essay to do justice to all the images of children appearing in Isaiah. Instead, I limit my discussion to two major areas.

The first is the way children's lives — how they are treated, the quality of their lives — indexes how far Israel is from embodying God's will. The fate of the children, the orphans in particular, is a barometer that indicates how far

---

7. Patrick D. Miller makes the point with reference to the Ten Commandments, but it applies to other legal material as well. See Patrick D. Miller, "'That It May Go Well with You': The Commandments and the Common Good," in his book *The Way of the Lord: Essays in Old Testament Theology* (Tübingen: Mohr Siebeck, 2004), pp. 141-43.

Israel is from keeping the Torah, from living as God would have them live. Isaiah searingly contrasts the Israelites' treatment of their own children with the vision of children in God's eschatological future, when no harm will come to even the most vulnerable.[8] Although I have already introduced Isaiah's concern for orphans above, below I focus particularly on the contrast between how Israel treats its orphans and how God would have them be treated.

The second major area to be addressed concerns the way Isaiah describes Israel itself as a child and the Israelites as children, with God as their parent. The relationship between the child Israel and God the parent is a fundamental one that pervades much of the Hebrew Bible. After a brief introduction to this metaphor, I focus on the way the metaphor functions in Isaiah, and specifically how it changes significantly over the course of the book. When tracked, the trajectory of that relationship reveals much about God, about Israel, about children, and about how we might reflect theologically on the relationships among the three. Following the course of that relationship will bring us back to Isaiah's three named children; we will reflect on why they figure so prominently as embodiments of God's judgment and hope and why Isaiah proclaims, "Look! The children . . . and I are as signs and portents in Israel!" (Isa. 8:18).

How the Israelites Treat Their Own Children

Much of the first chapters of the book of Isaiah announces God's judgment on Judah for failing to live by the instruction and word of YHWH. "They have rejected the teaching (Torah)[9] of YHWH of hosts, and the word of the Holy One of Israel they have spurned" (Isa. 5:24b). Already in the first chapter of the book the people are exhorted to change their treatment of those who have no social or economic support, the widows and orphans: "Champion the welfare [*shafat*] of the orphan; defend the cause [*rib*] of the widow" (1:17). The imperative implies that the welfare of orphans and widows is presently forgotten, neglected, perhaps willfully abandoned. Indeed, the indictment follows a few verses later, and the language is identical to that in the exhortation of verse 17: "They do not champion the welfare of the orphan, and the cause of the widow never comes to them" (1:23). When understood against the background of ancient Israelite law,

---

8. God's eschatological future is not here a promise of eternal life; the promises are meant for this world, albeit in a future that has not yet arrived.

9. "Torah" connotes more than law: it is also teaching, catechesis, instruction, with the force of law. For further reflection on its meaning, see Patrick D. Miller's essay, "That the Children May Know," in this volume.

it becomes apparent that the Israelite leaders' failure to champion the welfare of the orphan is not a result of passive neglect but a deliberate effort to subvert the law concerning the most vulnerable in their midst.

As mentioned above, the Hebrew words used here ("*champion* the *welfare of*," "the *cause* of the widow") are distinctively *legal* language; they refer to the Torah's requirements for treatment of widows and orphans. Justice is denied the most vulnerable members of society by perversion of the law itself. The Torah unequivocally — and repeatedly! — stipulates that food and clothing are to be provided, tithes are to be set aside, and gleanings are to be left so that the widows and orphans might "eat their fill" (Deut. 26:12; cf. Deut. 10:18; 14:29; 24:17-21; 26:12-13; 27:19). The Torah requires not that a few crumbs be given to the poor orphan, but that the orphan's life be marked by the satiety that marks the lives of everyone else. Orphans and widows are to live lives marked by fullness, just as fullness marks the lives of other members of Israelite society; there is one standard of living applicable to all.

The language of justice *(mishpat)* appears frequently in these Isaianic texts and is closely associated with widows and orphans. Isaiah charges that the law, designed to sustain widows and orphans generously within the fabric of society, is willfully forgotten, misapplied, and abused. Old Testament scholar Brevard Childs observes that the law is not understood in a narrow, legalistic sense, but rather "as imperatives commensurate with everything that Israel had learned from its long historical experience with its God."[10] Who is the "they" targeted in Isaiah's accusation of willful abuse? The charge is leveled not at ordinary folk for their refusal to lend a hand to the widows and orphans but at Judah's rulers, the people who lead, who set policy and make decisions. The beginning of the verse makes it clear: "Your rulers are rogues, and cronies of thieves; each and every one loves a bribe and runs after gifts" (Isa. 1:23). The issue is not the occasional refusal by ordinary people to lend a helping hand to a neighbor in need but the wholesale abandonment of the widows and orphans to a corrupt legal system where the leaders feather their own nests at the expense of the powerless. Concern for the public good has vanished. As Brueggemann observes: "Widows and orphans are the litmus test of justice and righteousness. . . . On this test, Jerusalem fails completely and decisively."[11]

The indictment against these leaders gets even more specific in Isaiah 10:1-2. "Ha! You who author sinful laws [*hakhoqeqim khiqqe-'awen*] and

---

10. Brevard S. Childs, *Isaiah*, Old Testament Library (Louisville: Westminster John Knox, 2001), p. 20.

11. Brueggemann, *Isaiah 1–39*, pp. 21-22.

who endlessly produce sinful decrees,[12] to subvert the poor from justice, and to rob of justice the needy of my people, to make widows their spoil, and orphans their prey!" Note the way the language here ("spoil" and "prey") echoes the language found in the name of one of the prophet's children: Maher-shalal (spoil)-hash-baz (prey). With "poetic justice" the Israelites will be subject to the same treatment at the hands of the Assyrians as they have inflicted on their own children. Even clearer in this verse than in the first chapter is the specific accusation that the ill treatment of orphans and widows takes place not randomly but by efforts to use the legal system to increase the wealth and power of the ruling elite at the expense of those with no power to challenge them.[13] The appearance here of "spoil" and "prey," which are wartime practices, signals that, far from engaging in benign neglect, the rulers are *waging war* against their own helpless women and children. Warfare may have been an all too common experience for peoples in the ancient Near East, but the idea that the enemies are one's own leaders is shocking indeed.

Children in the Eschatological Future

On either side of this indictment of the Israelite leaders' treatment of Israel's own women and children appear two sharply contrasting images of children. In Isaiah 9:5 the prophet announces that "a child has been born for us, a son given to us" — it is this child who will become the authoritative ruler who embodies God's grace and peace. The present situation where adult leaders maliciously pursue children as booty is entirely reversed — here it is a child who bears the divine promises. Such a vision portends a total reversal of the present situation described in 10:1-2. The other image of a child that contrasts sharply with the evils in 10:1-2 comes in the other famous messianic passage in chapter 11. The Davidic ruler described in 11:1-5 will inaugurate an era in which children feature prominently (11:6-9). First, the natural predatory conflicts are eradicated (wolf and lamb dwell together [v. 6]), and a child peacefully tends this bizarre herd. Ordinarily the child himself would become yet

---

12. Difficult to translate without emendation (see *Biblia hebraica stuttgartensia*), the word I translate "decrees" is *umekhattevim*, which, as a piel participle, suggests "constantly writing" — whence I take the sense of "endlessly" producing the self-serving decrees.

13. Childs notes that the reference is probably not to new laws; rather, the accusation is directed "against the judges and petty officials of the state who abuse the poor in the application of the law. Through directives and decrees, red tape and delay, they rob the widows and orphans of their rights" (*Isaiah*, pp. 86-87).

one more carcass in a scene of bloody carnage. But this is no ordinary scene, of course; this is life under God's messianic ruler.

Two infants appear next, both apparently playing near the dens of deadly snakes without fear or even consciousness of danger (v. 8). The first child, the little boy, is engaging in appropriate work that contributes to the life of the family and community (leading the animals). The two infants are not working of course, but playing — indeed, delighting in play (*sh'*)! But whether at work or at play, in all cases the children are safe and secure even in the most dangerous of circumstances. This vision does not describe life as it presently is, so searingly portrayed in 10:1-2, but life as God would have it be, when children work and play without fear and when "nothing evil or vile shall be done on all my holy mountain, for the land shall be filled with knowledge of YHWH as water covers the sea" (11:9).

Fittingly, the same vision is repeated and expanded at the end of the book, when, under the strains and woes of post-exilic restoration, YHWH promises a new heaven and a new earth (Isa. 65:17). In this new creation no one, including infants, will die prematurely, even centenarians will be considered young (65:20). Given the relatively high infant mortality, the mention of babies here is especially significant — it is not simply that people will live to very great ages once they are past the health dangers of childhood, but that everyone, including all the infants, will live long lives. God will delight in the people of Jerusalem (v. 18), and "they will not bear children for terror," that is, their children will no longer be subject to the terrors wrought by enemies, or to homegrown varieties of terror for that matter. Instead, YHWH will bless their children, who will no longer be subject to human depredations (v. 23). As Brevard Childs rightly cautions, the vision of chapter 65 should not be understood as "an apocalyptic flight into an imaginative world of fantasy."[14] It is rather the culmination of a vision begun at the beginning of the book and only now coming to fuller expression.

Reflecting back on the way the names of Isaiah's children conveyed God's judgment ("Pillage hastens; looting speeds") and God's promise ("God with us") in chapters 7 and 8, it is no longer tenable to think that the children are merely the vessels for these names, as though they might have been replaced by rocks that the prophet picked up and said, "This rock is called Maher-shalal-hash-baz because . . ." The children themselves are meaningful, especially in the context of the other images of children in the chapters that follow. In 8:18 Isaiah proclaims: "Look! The children, whom YHWH has given me, and I are as signs and portents in Israel. . . ." Children

---

14. Childs, *Isaiah*, p. 538.

embody the judgment and promise of God because they are intimately bound up with both the judgment of Israel and the promise of deliverance. The Israelites reveal the depth of their sin in their treatment of children, yet God's will for Israel is revealed in the safety and playfulness of children. Children are more than just things to which symbolic names can be attached; their welfare constitutes the heart of both God's judgment and the divine promises for deliverance.

Reconciliation of Parent and Child

The Parent-Child Metaphor

God is the parent, and Israel is the child. This powerful, flexible metaphor operates in a wide variety of biblical material, not only in the Hebrew Scriptures but also, and especially, in the New Testament. Indeed, while certainly not the only operative metaphor, the parent-child metaphor is one of the primary ways in which Israel understands itself in relation to its God.[15] The metaphor is flexible because it is capable of encompassing both divine care and love and also divine discipline and expectation. The early chapters of Deuteronomy offer one example among myriads of how the metaphor encompasses a variety of divine and human attitudes and postures: in the recital of God's story with Israel to date, Moses reminds Israel of YHWH's tender parental care: ". . . in the wilderness, where you saw how YHWH your God carried you, just as one carries a child, all the way that you traveled until you reached this place" (Deut. 1:31). God is a tender parent, and Israel is a little child. Yet exhortation is not far behind: "Know then in your heart that as a parent disciplines a child so YHWH your God disciplines you" (Deut. 8:5).

The metaphor of God as a loving but firm parent who disciplines when necessary lies in the background of Isaiah's theology.[16] In Isaiah's view, God loves and cares for Israel, but especially in First Isaiah Israel is expected to fulfill the "parental" expectations of obedience to the Torah, which can be summed up as the exclusive worship of YHWH and the keeping of the divinely given commandments. God gives Israel the commandments not as an arbitrary rulebook, but because they provide the means for the life-giving order-

---

15. See the essay by Brent A. Strawn, "'Israel, My Child': The Ethics of a Biblical Metaphor," in this volume.

16. The issue of the discipline meted out by human parents is addressed by William P. Brown in "To Discipline without Destruction: The Multifaceted Profile of the Child in Proverbs," in this volume.

ing of Israel's communal life. The commandments are a gift because they make possible the flourishing of all. Failure to obey the commandments consequently brings disciplinary action. In Second Isaiah especially, the emphasis is on God's unconditional love for Israel, however. Thus the relationship between the child Israel and YHWH the parent is multifaceted and complex in Isaiah, as both parenting and good theology always are.

The Rebellious Children

The entire book of Isaiah begins, after the informative superscription, with the image of Judah as a rebellious child and with God as the exasperated, frustrated parent. "I have reared and raised up children, but they have rebelled against me" (Isa. 1:2). In Second and Third Isaiah this image of the exasperated YHWH softens, as the children who refused the guiding, formative hand of YHWH in First Isaiah are welcomed and embraced anew. By the end of the book God has reclaimed and named the children of Israel, bearing them tenderly back to a revivified land, a major sign of whose renewed vitality is the presence of vast numbers of returning children, tenderly carried by those who care for them.

In the eschatological vision of chapter 11 that I discussed above, "nothing evil or vile shall be done" when the knowledge of YHWH pervades the land (Isa. 11:9). The verbs here are *ra'a'* and *shakhat*, the same verbs that describe what the Israelites, described metaphorically as children, are accused of doing in 1:4: "Woe, sinful nation! People heavy with iniquity! Brood of evildoers [*ra'a'*]! Depraved [*shakhat*] children! They have forsaken YHWH. . . ." The Israelites are children who refuse to heed the shaping instruction that God offers them through the Torah. "For it is a rebellious people, faithless children, children who refused to heed the Torah of YHWH" (30:9). Back in 1:3 the faithless Israelites are accused of being more stupid than the dumbest domestic animal — they do not understand the fundamental relationship of dependence upon God. This situation will be reversed when the knowledge of God is spread over the land, and the evil doings of these adults, who behave like unformed children — worse, like unthinking animals — cease.

As I have discussed above, Isaiah emphasizes the vulnerability of children, and especially orphans, and the need to see that their welfare is sustained. But children have other characteristics as well: they are by nature immature; for instance, they lack good judgment. Children are prone to disobey their parents, and it is this aspect of the metaphor that is working for Isaiah here.[17] A couple of things might be said about thinking about Israel this way. To be sure, conceiving of the Israelites as YHWH's children is meant to evoke the intimacy and history of their relationship, but it also emphasizes their *dependence* on YHWH for instruction, their need to be formed into a mature people who understand clearly the nature of the divine-human relationship.[18] The parent's role is to love the child in the bonds of intimacy, and part of that love involves teaching the child, yet Israel is pictured as refusing to acknowledge YHWH's role as parent and teacher.

Daughter Zion

In addition to the reference to Israel as "children" (literally, "sons"), on numerous occasions Isaiah speaks of "daughter Zion." In fact, this epithet is one of many textual features (including themes, vocabulary, etc.) appearing throughout the book of Isaiah that unify the otherwise distinct sections. "Daughter Zion" appears in all three of the recognized sections of Isaiah.[19] The daughter represents both the city of Jerusalem and her inhabitants who suffer the Babylonian exile. Within the metaphor, she is of course the daughter of YHWH, but she is also correspondingly portrayed, especially in Second Isaiah, as a parent, and specifically a mother who labors for her children. In a fascinating juxtaposition of images, Isaiah 42:13-14 portrays YHWH delivering Judah both as an enraged warrior, ready to do battle on behalf of his people, and as a woman who pants and gasps from labor pains:

> YHWH goes forth like a soldier,
>> like a warrior he stirs up his fury;
> he cries out, he shouts aloud,
>> he shows himself mighty against his foes.
> For a long time I have held my peace,
>> I have kept still and restrained myself;
> now I will cry out like a woman in labor,
>> I will gasp and pant.[20]

---

17. Other prophets do this as well (e.g., Jer. 3:14, 22; 4:22; Hos. 11:1). The parent-child metaphor for YHWH's relationship to Israel is a dominant one in the prophets.

18. See Patrick D. Miller, "That the Children May Know," in this volume.

19. Isaiah 1:8; 3:16, 17; 4:4; 10:32; 16:1; 37:2; 52:2; 62:11.

20. Cf. Isaiah 66:6-16 for similar imagery.

The two otherwise disparate images (warrior and woman in labor) are connected by the shouting — as the warrior cries out, so God cries out; as the woman in labor cries out, so God cries out.[21] The warrior god is a traditional image in the ancient Near East, but the god who delivers as a woman in labor pains is more unusual and suggestive for thinking about God as parent/mother who is delivering daughter Zion from all the distress of exile.

In an even more poignant passage, God is depicted as more maternal than any human mother ever could be:

> But Zion said, "YHWH has forsaken me,
>   my Lord has forgotten me."
> Can a woman forget her nursing child,
>   or show no compassion for the child of her womb?
> Even these may forget,
>   yet I will not forget you.
>
> (Isa. 49:14-15)

As inimitable as a human mother's ferocious love for her child is, and indeed it may seem like the fiercest force in all of creation, even this is surpassed by God's relentless and inexorable maternal love and compassion for daughter Zion.[22] Though the rebellious child in Isaiah 1 refuses to be formed by parental instruction, the angry, exasperated parent does not abandon that child but returns again to deliver her from all her enemies.[23]

---

21. Katheryn Darr stresses the auditory nature of the labor cries and argues that "the travailing woman underscores YHWH's power" (K. P. Darr, "Like Warrior, Like Woman: Destruction and Deliverance in Isaiah 42:10-17," *Catholic Biblical Quarterly* 49 [1987]: 560-71).

22. The maternal divine imagery is discussed in Leila Leah Bronner, "Gynomorphic Imagery in Exilic Isaiah (40-66)," *Dor le Dor* 12 (1983-84): 70; Mayer I. Gruber, "The Motherhood of God in Second Isaiah," *Revue Biblique* 90 (1983): 351-59; John J. Schmitt, "The Motherhood of God and Zion as Mother," *Revue Biblique* 92 (1985): 557-59; and the feminist classic of biblical interpretation, Phyllis Trible, *God and the Rhetoric of Sexuality* (Philadelphia: Fortress, 1978), pp. 64-67. For a discussion of similar images in other texts, see Walter Brueggemann's essay, "Vulnerable Children, Divine Passion, and Human Obligation," in this volume.

23. There is considerable slippage in the way the metaphor operates — that is, sometimes Zion is understood as daughter to YHWH, sometimes as wife. On this question and the various entities represented by Zion (Jerusalem, Israelite people, etc.), see John Goldingay, *The Message of Isaiah 40–55: A Literary-Theological Commentary* (London and New York: T&T Clark, 2005), pp. 384-85.

Being Named

Deliverance for Israel means being named and claimed by this same God whose love is greater than any mother's for her child.

> But now thus says YHWH —
> who created you, O Jacob,
> who formed you, O Israel?
> Do not be afraid, for
> I have redeemed you.
> I have called you by name — you are mine.
>
> (Isa. 43:1)

The parent who created and formed also lays claim to Israel through naming, a distinctively parental prerogative (cf. 49:1). Names in ancient Israel were usually markers of one's core identity; thus most Hebrew names in the Scriptures suggest key aspects of the character of the one who bears it. "Israel," for example, means to strive with God (cf. Gen. 32:29), thereby signifying one important aspect of Israel's relationship with YHWH over the millennia. The creation, redemption, and claiming of Israel by naming — "you are mine" — is here marked by overtones of the intimacy and ferocity associated with parental love and reaffirms Israel's core identity as YHWH's beloved child.

That God is here understood to be the parent is confirmed a few verses later when YHWH promises Israel's return to the land. In this passage the language of love is both pronounced and integral to the way the parent-child metaphor unfolds. Love — parental love — is the motivating force behind the divine will to restore Israel.

> Because you are precious in my sight,
> and honored, and I love you,
> I give people in return for you,
> nations in exchange for your life.
> I will say to the North, "Give back!"
> And to the South, "Do not withhold!"
> Bring my sons from afar
> and my daughters from the end of the earth,
> all who are called by my name.
>
> (Isa. 43:4-7a)

This image of the repopulation of the land with children recurs throughout Second and Third Isaiah: "Swiftly your children are coming . . ." (49:17; cf.

v. 20); "Your sons shall be brought from afar, your daughters like babes on shoulders" (60:4; cf. v. 9). What does deliverance look like? It is swarms of children returning to the land, *over*populating it.[24]

> The children born in the time of your bereavement
>   will yet say in your hearing:
> "The place is too crowded for me;
>   make room for me to settle."
>
> (49:20)

A dual image of children is at work here. First, the Israelites are YHWH's children, lovingly reclaimed by the mother who will not give them up, and second, YHWH will cause the Israelites' offspring to return in huge numbers and repopulate the land, giving abundant life to what was lifeless.

Children are the primary trope for representing most of the major aspects of deliverance in Second and Third Isaiah. In Isaiah 44:3-5 several of these aspects come together: YHWH's blessing, the renewed fruitfulness of the people, and being named and claimed by God.

> For I will pour water on the thirsty land,
>   and streams on the dry ground;
> I will pour my spirit upon your descendants,
>   and my blessing on your offspring.
> They shall spring up like grass,
>   like willows by flowing streams.
> This one will say, "I am YHWH's,"
>   another will be called by the name of Jacob,
> yet another will write on the hand, "YHWH's,"
>   and adopt the name of Israel.
>
> (44:3-5)

This generation, exiled from the land, which is Second Isaiah's primary audience, is not the focus of deliverance; or rather, deliverance for that generation is constituted by the deliverance of their children. YHWH's blessing will be upon their children; the children will be a vast multitude, "like grass," and they will all be called by YHWH's name. The preponderance of language connoting fecundity and the naming of children suggests mater-

---

24. Overpopulation seems a troubling image for deliverance only to moderns for whom it has become a problem. Overpopulation in a time of exile and war functions in the opposite way: it offers a vision of abundance and prosperity.

nal imagery: God is the mother, sometimes acting through human agents (e.g., Zion), who makes these children spring up and who names and claims them. The presence of large numbers of children represents both new life after death and devastation (e.g., the importance of children in Jewish communities after the Holocaust) and the possibility of a new relationship with YHWH, after the fracturing of that relationship and the exile that followed.

The book of Isaiah does not view children sentimentally,[25] but they do represent the possibility of a new beginning. With God's decisive action to save, the old brokenness is at an end: "I am about to do a new thing; now it *springs forth* (*tsamakh*), do you not perceive it?" (Isa. 43:19). The verb "to spring forth/up" (*tsamakh*) appears both with reference to the "new thing" God is doing, which is God's salvation ("let the skies rain down righteousness; let the earth open, that salvation may *spring up*" [45:8; cf. 42:9]), and with reference to children, as just observed in Isaiah 44:4: "they shall *spring up* like grass." God as mother acts, and children/salvation spring up. Children — and all the hope they represent — embody, or, to put it even more strongly, actually *constitute* God's gracious action that the Israelites are about to experience in dramatic fashion (the new exodus, the return to the land out of exile, the restored fecundity and fruitfulness of that land).

Adopted Children

I have already discussed the passage where the compassion of God for God's people is even more powerful and intense than a mother's love for her baby (Isa. 49:15). It is worth returning to the passage where this occurs in order to see how the images of parents and children unfold throughout the passage. The passage is lengthy (49:14-26) so I will not quote it in its entirety, but it begins with the voice of daughter Zion speaking, lamenting that YHWH has abandoned her. It is to this complaint that YHWH replies with the poignant assertion that the divine love is greater than that of any human mother ("I have engraved you on the palms of my hands" [49:16]). In what follows God promises Zion that her children will return swiftly and they will be like jewels

---

25. In Isaiah 3:1-5 the leaders of Jerusalem are excoriated for their poor leadership and told that, as punishment, children will rule over them. Rule by children is marked by oppression and bullying. This is not an indictment of children but of the leaders. Nonetheless, the view of the text affirms that children are not meant to have adult roles and responsibilities. Furthermore, in an account of Israel's history offered in Third Isaiah, YHWH initially thought the "children would not lie" (Isa. 63:8), but as events unfolded, this did not prove to be the case (63:10).

to her (49:17-18).[26] Those children, considered lost due to the conditions of the exile ("the children of your bereavement"), will return and require more space to settle — the repopulation of the land being a potent sign of God's deliverance (49:20).

Yet because she was in exile and bereavement, daughter Zion did not bear these children — they have been borne by others while she was grief-stricken and barren, unable to raise any children.

> Then you will say in your heart,
>   "Who has borne (*yld*) me these?
> I was bereaved and barren,
>   exiled and put away —
>   so who has reared these?
> I was left all alone —
>   where then have these come from?"
>
> (Isa. 49:21)

The reply to this question is unusual: daughter Zion's children, who will re-populate Jerusalem, have been provided by YHWH and apparently raised by *foreigners:*

> Thus says YHWH GOD:
> I will soon lift up my hand to the nations,
>   and raise my signal to the peoples;
> and they shall bring your sons in their bosom,
>   and your daughters shall be carried on their shoulders.
> Kings shall be your nursing fathers,
>   and their queens your nursing mothers.
>
> (49:22-23a)[27]

Historically, Zion's children are those Israelites living as exiles in foreign lands — they will be returning home to their "mother" Zion.[28] A little further

---

26. The RSV and NRSV translate "children" in 49:17 as "builders," following the Septuagint, but this renders the following verses confusing.

27. Goldingay and Oswalt both assume that YHWH has adopted these children on Zion's be-half and downplay the role of the foreigners in the raising of these children (Goldingay, *The Message of Isaiah 40–55*, p. 390; John N. Oswalt, *The Book of Isaiah: Chapters 40–66*, New International Commentary on the Old Testament [Grand Rapids: Eerdmans, 1998], pp. 308-9), but see Paul Hanson, who notes the role of the foreign rulers as "guardians and nurses of Zion's re-turning sons and daughters" (Paul D. Hanson, *Isaiah 40–66*, Interpretation [Louisville: West-minster John Knox, 1995], p. 134).

28. On the reversal of the exiles' status from slave and war booty to joyous homecoming, see

down, the image is summed up by the divine promise: "Your children *I* will deliver" (Isa. 49:25b). One of the major themes in Second Isaiah appears here — that is, YHWH's sovereignty over all nations, not simply Israel, although the image of foreigners, albeit foreign royalty, bearing and raising Israelite children is quite striking.[29] The role of the foreign sovereigns in bringing Zion's adopted children home clearly falls under the authority of, and at the behest of, the real sovereign, YHWH.[30]

God's Tender Bearing of the Child Israel

Children being lovingly carried is a recurring and powerful image in Isaiah. One of the most poignant portraits of God as the compassionate parent lovingly tending and delivering the child Israel/Zion occurs in two passages worth examining closely. The first appears in Isaiah 46:3-4:

> Listen to me, O house of Jacob,
> all the remnant of the house of Israel,
> who have been borne by me from your birth,
> carried from the womb;
> even to your old age I am he,
> even when you turn gray I will carry you.
> I have made, and I will bear;
> I will carry and will save.

The verbs used here, "to bear" and "to carry," seem to resonate with the images of children being carried back to the land from exile (e.g., Isa. 49:22; 60:4), and

---

Walter Brueggemann, *Isaiah 40–66*, Word Biblical Commentary (Louisville: Westminster John Knox, 1998), p. 118.

29. Some elements, and especially the ending of the passage ("I will make your oppressors eat their own flesh . . ." [49:26]), tend toward the triumphalistic, and due caution is in order when interpreting them in contemporary contexts.

30. The sovereignty and power of YHWH in Second Isaiah is complex. Obviously YHWH does not control the behavior of the Israelites, or their failure to keep the commandments would not have been so acutely problematic in Israel's history. On the other hand, Second Isaiah is keen to show that YHWH rules in a way that the Babylonians' so-called gods do not, and that historical political events that might otherwise appear random (e.g., the rise of Cyrus the Persian) are in fact brought about by the will of YHWH. Terence E. Fretheim (*God and the World in the Old Testament: A Relational Theology of Creation* [Nashville: Abingdon, 2005], pp. 184-87) argues that God's power in Second Isaiah is not principally revealed in political and military movements but in the forgiveness made possible through the suffering of God and of God's servant (Isa. 42:1-4; 49:1-6; 50:4-9; 52:13–53:12).

indeed the overall idea of children borne in the arms and on the shoulders of others does recall those joyous visions of the return of children into the land and all that the promise of such a return portends. The image here in chapter 46 is also a salvific image, of course, a profound sign and promise of God's acting to save Israel. Yet the image here is different, more somber, though the gravity is conveyed largely in the nuances of the verbs chosen. The verbs here, "to bear" ('ms) and "to carry" (sbl), do not evoke carefree pictures of toddlers on their daddies' shoulders. Rather, these verbs denote the carrying of *burdens*, things that are heavy and even painful to bear (of course, parents know that any child on their shoulders is not weightless!). The deliverance of God's people does not come without divine effort. And yet the promise that Israel, no matter what rebellions are fomented or idolatries are practiced, will always be carried by YHWH is one of the most profound assurances to appear in Scripture. As Frederick J. Gaiser argues, "God saves by carrying."[31] From the womb until old age and death, God bears Israel up, like a child.[32]

Throughout Isaiah, comforting and carrying children, whether at the hand of human beings or of God — images of unsentimental tenderness — function as the *normal, appropriate* way to treat children. The second passage evoking God's tender care for Israel occurs within a section where Jerusalem is described metaphorically as a mother who has been in labor, and now YHWH will serve as midwife for the delivery of her children (66:7-11).

> For thus says YHWH:
> I will extend prosperity [literally, *shalom*] to her like a river,
>   and the wealth [or: glory] of the nations like an overflowing stream;
> and you shall nurse [*ynq*] and be carried [*ns'*][33] on her arm,
>   and dandled [*sh'*] on her knees.
> As a mother comforts her child,
>   so I will comfort you;
>   you shall be comforted in Jerusalem.
>
> (66:12-13)

---

31. Frederick J. Gaiser, "'I Will Carry and I Will Save': The Carrying God of Isaiah 40–66," in *"And God Saw That It Was Good": Essays on Creation and God in Honor of Terence E. Fretheim*, ed. Frederick J. Gaiser and Mark A. Throntveit (St. Paul, MN: Word & World, Luther Northwestern Theological Seminary, 2006), p. 99. Gaiser understands the multiplicity of images for God in Isaiah 40–66 as moving toward incarnational theology.

32. Commentators regularly observe that YHWH's carrying of Israel contrasts sharply with the image a few verses later (Isa. 46:6-7) of human beings carrying their alleged "gods" on their backs. See, e.g., Childs, *Isaiah*, p. 360; Brueggemann, *Isaiah 40–66*, pp. 114-15.

33. This is not the verb denoting the bearing of burdens; rather, this verb is the more common and less weighted word meaning "to carry."

In verse 12 Jerusalem is the mother who will nurse and play with the newborn Israel upon her knees. This vision of normal, tender motherly care provides the template, the model for God's care for Israel. The juxtaposition of verses 12 and 13 suggests that just as Jerusalem is a good mother to her children, feeding and playing with them, so God is a good mother, not only feeding and playing, but also comforting the child Israel (notice the threefold repetition of "comfort" in v. 13). The verb translated by the NRSV as "dandled" is worth noting: it sometimes means "to take delight in," as in Psalm 119 where it describes the psalmist's relationship with Torah,[34] but it also appears in Isaiah 11:8, the eschatological vision of deliverance I discussed above: "The *nursing child* shall *play* over the hole of the asp." Once again the vision of wholeness, of peace, of salvation is one in which children — helpless, vulnerable nursing babes — are playing safely. In the chapter 66 passage, the form of the verb even emphasizes the relational nature of play: far from playing alone, mother and child are playing together, with the child securely and intimately held on her knees.

The book of Isaiah begins and ends with images of children: in Isaiah 1 YHWH laments that the children he has reared have rebelled, have refused to live in ways that are life-giving to all in Israel and that acknowledge the bonds of dependence and intimacy with God (1:2-4). The end of the book offers a strikingly different portrait of that relationship: God as a mother, tenderly holding and playing with Israel, as a human mother would her own child. Mother and child are now reconciled; their now healthy relationship exhibits the love, tenderness, and play that is normative for parent-child relationships in Isaiah. When Isaiah declares that "the children, whom YHWH has given me, and I are as signs and portents in Israel," the words refer not only to the three symbolically named children of the prophet but to all the children in the book of Isaiah — they are signs and portents of God's judgment (indeed, the book ends with a strong note of judgment)[35] and, even more clearly and emphatically, of God's promises.

Summary and Conclusion

Once we move beyond the initial three named children and begin to look more closely, the book of Isaiah seems to be veritably teeming with images of children, and especially young, nursing children carried on the shoulders and

---

34. Psalm 119:16, 47, 70.
35. See Isaiah 65:1-7; 66:1-4, 14-16, 24.

in the bosoms of adults. Children function in myriad ways in the book. They are the barometer of the health of the Israelites' relationship with God, revealed in how well they live according to the Torah. According to First Isaiah, failure to fulfill the commandments, and especially the laws that provide for the flourishing of orphans, crushes children. Isaiah then sketches an alternative vision in which children work and play and are loved as they ought to be. Images of safe, happy children are a principal means of expressing what God's salvation looks like — in stark contrast to the war Israel wages upon its own children.

At one time I thought that the naming of the prophet's children as a means of conveying messages to Israel was a form of creepy instrumentalism, but in the larger context of the book it seems that more is being said about the importance of children in God's economy than their role as mere papyrus for divine messages might imply. Not only do the named children convey the "content" of the messages ("A remnant shall return," etc.), but they themselves are part of the message: children, children, children — God is telling Israel throughout the book of Isaiah that children are central to salvation. How children are treated, both in the present and in the future, is essential to the divine vision of what God would have for Israel. In the alternative world that Isaiah envisions, God is a tender mother, whose fierce maternal love outstrips that of every human mother for her children. In that world children are not sentimentalized but are claimed, named, and blessed. They are abundant and protected. And they play and are played with by loving adults. God bears the Israelites up, and God does not give up on the task, even when it is deeply burdensome, because of the commitment to care for them from the womb until old age and death.

6 "Israel, My Child": The Ethics of a Biblical Metaphor

Brent A. Strawn

Even before they've been lived through, a child can sense the great human subjects: time which breeds loss, desire, the world's beauty.

Louise Glück, *Proofs and Theories*

The quality of childhood is largely determined by the care and protection children receive — or fail to receive — from adults.

Carol Bellamy, *The State of the World's Children 2005*

When the father dies he will not seem to be dead, for he has left behind him one like himself, whom in his life he looked upon with joy and at death, without grief. (Sir. 30:4-5, NRSV)

Introduction

The notion (really, metaphor) of God as a divine parent — typically a "father" — with human offspring is deeply embedded in numerous religions. In the Jewish and Christian traditions, this rootage stems from the metaphor's

---

My thanks to the members of the consultation for their helpful feedback, especially William P. Brown, Marcia J. Bunge, and Terence E. Fretheim. I also thank Bill T. Arnold, Steve Kraftchick, Mark Roncace, Brad D. Strawn, and Christine Roy Yoder for reading drafts of the paper and/or for discussing it with me. I dedicate this essay to my children, Caleb Verner, Hannah Jean, and Micah Reese, who, in this subject as in so many other subjects in life, have been my best teachers.

presence in Scripture, where it is found in both the Old Testament/Hebrew Bible and the New Testament (note also Wis. 14:3; Sir. 23:1, 4). Admittedly, it occurs with much greater frequency in the New Testament than in the Old,[1] and this fact is not without certain literary effects — one of which is that the New Testament presentation of God is, overall, far more "father-ish" than that of the Old.[2] Regardless, the metaphor's presence in both Testaments serves as a uniting factor between them and helps to explain the "fatherhood" of God as a common conception in Judaism and Christianity.

The metaphor is not only scriptural; it is powerful, and this is so in several ways. To mention but one example, many find it of great significance that in the New Testament Jesus often calls God "Father."[3] Whatever one might think about how this practice speaks to contemporary concerns over proper God-language — and whatever this practice's precedents in the Old Testament and elsewhere[4] — it is especially noteworthy that by means of this language Jesus is figured as (and figures himself as) God's *child*. Moreover, in the Lord's Prayer, according to both the Matthean and Lukan versions, Jesus encourages his followers to do the same by addressing God as "(our) Father" (Matt. 6:9; Luke 11:2). In this way, every Christian who prays this prayer becomes (is "metaphorized" as) the child of God. Not surprisingly, the children of God metaphor is found elsewhere in the New Testament (e.g., John 1:12; 1 John 3:1-2, 10; 5:2; Rom. 8:16; Phil. 2:15) and, of course, also in the Old.[5]

These examples — a few among many — demonstrate the significance of the divine parent–human child metaphor: it is deeply rooted, widely attested in Scripture, and legitimized by important figures and worship practices. In-

---

1. By Marjo Christina Annette Korpel's count there are 21 instances of God being figured as a father in the Old Testament vs. 255 instances in the New Testament (*A Rift in the Clouds: Ugaritic and Hebrew Descriptions of the Divine* [Münster: Ugarit-Verlag, 1990], p. 237). Both numbers would increase if one would include passages where parental imagery is alluded to or evoked in subtle ways.

2. Said differently, the Old Testament permits other metaphors more play; this functions to restrict and critique the father (alone) metaphor. See further Parts II-III below.

3. Some examples: Matthew 7:21; 10:32-33; 11:27; 12:50; 15:13; Mark 14:36; Luke 10:22; 22:29, 42; 23:46; 24:49; John 5:17; 6:32, 40; 8:19, 49, 54; 10:18, 29, 37; 15:8, 15, 23-24; 20:17. One should perhaps distinguish passages where Jesus calls God "my father" from those where Jesus speaks of God as a father more generally. See further the essays on the Gospels in the present volume.

4. On these points, see Marianne Meye Thompson, *The Promise of the Father: Jesus and God in the New Testament* (Louisville: Westminster John Knox, 2000).

5. For the Johannine texts, see the essay by Marianne Meye Thompson in the present volume. For the Old Testament, see Parts III and IV below. Note especially Isaiah 63:16, where Israel prays to YHWH, twice addressing God as "our father." A third instance, belonging to the same prayer, is found in Isaiah 64:8. See, most recently, Paul Niskanen, "Yhwh as Father, Redeemer, and Potter in Isaiah 63:7–64:11," *Catholic Biblical Quarterly* 68 (2006): 397-407.

deed, the metaphor is so compelling that the ultimate proof of its power may be that many devout persons do not realize that the statement "God is (my/our) (Heavenly) Father" is a metaphor in the first place. But it is. And it is a metaphor with profound effects, in part because of the power of major, macro-metaphors such as this one (see Part II below). The present study (re)considers some of the most important of these effects. Its thesis can be stated as follows:

Construing the relationship between YHWH and Israel as that between a parent (whether father or mother) and a child (whether daughter or son) has impact on at least two different areas:

1. explicitly, the metaphor shaped how Israel represented and understood God's actions toward itself and its actions toward God (see Part III) — making what might otherwise be misunderstood on both sides of the metaphor (parent and child) available, evocative, and insightful;
2. implicitly, the metaphor affected how Israelite parents may have (and ought to have) treated their own children, providing them a divine example to emulate at their (and its) best moments (see Part IV).

The first area concerns the theology (including the theological anthropology) of the parent-child metaphor; the latter has to do with the metaphor's ethics. The present essay will argue that the latter can be understood in positive ways with beneficial results. This leads to a final piece of the thesis — one closely related to the second element:

3. in its best aspects the God:Israel::parent:child analogy bears within itself ethical significance for present communities (and their families) that claim allegiance to these texts and the God they portray — offering them, like Israel, modes and models of action and relationship that can benefit all concerned (see Part IV).

This last item might be restated as a question: Does the portrayal of God as our parent make any difference when we consider our own relationship with our children? Once we have children of our own, do we parent differently and better if we believe that God is a parent both to us and to others?[6] Before proceeding any further in answering these questions or addressing the

---

6. God's parenthood of "other children" means that the ethics at work need not concern only one's own biological children. See further Part IV below and the essay by Walter Brueggemann in the present volume.

various parts of this thesis, it is imperative to acknowledge some important and far less positive assessments of the metaphor (Part I). Thereafter, I will discuss Wayne C. Booth's work on the ethics of metaphor (Part II) before I turn to the theology and ethics of the divine parent–human child metaphor proper (Parts III-IV, respectively).

Part I: Two Opposing Readings

In recent years vigorous criticism has been leveled at the God-as-parent metaphor, especially in its masculine-gendered version. Two writers can be lifted up as exemplary and paradigmatic. First, from a psychoanalytical perspective, is Sigmund Freud.[7] In several of his writings on religion, Freud argued that humanity (as species and civilization) evolved on analogy with the life of the individual. Consequently, the "traumata" associated with individual psyches were also present in larger, societal ways in extreme (prehistoric) antiquity. That ancient history was marked by the brutal rule of a tyrannical male father only belatedly conquered by a horde of victimized sons who wished both to be and to replace him. Reflexes of that drama (specifically, neurotic symptoms) were found by Freud in a number of religious systems and their beliefs. What is important for the present study is Freud's assertion that the problems manifested in both that tragic ancient history and in more recent religious phenomena stem from and pertain to the family, especially the father. Most striking in this regard is Freud's belief that the ancient despotic male ruler is ultimately what lies behind the (return of the) notion of "the one and only father deity whose power is unlimited" — namely, God the Father.[8]

Some fifty years later, writing from a feminist perspective, Mary Daly leveled a withering critique at "father religion." Like Freud before her, but in a different mode, Daly exposed the history of violence against women that has often accompanied the God-as-Father metaphor:

> If God in "his" heaven is a father ruling "his" people, then it is in the "nature" of things and according to divine plan and the order of the universe that society be male-dominated. Within this context a mystification of roles

---

7. For what follows, see Sigmund Freud, *Moses and Monotheism*, trans. Katherine Jones (New York: Vintage, 1939), esp. pp. 101-17, 164-76. Many of the ideas in that book are already found in his earlier *Totem and Taboo: Some Points of Agreement between the Mental Lives of Savages and Neurotics*, trans. and ed. James Strachey (German orig., 1912-13; New York: Norton, 1950), esp. p. 182.

8. Freud, *Moses and Monotheism*, p. 106.

takes place: the husband dominating his wife represents God "himself." . . . [I]f God is male, then the male is God.[9]

There can be no doubt that the critiques of Freud and Daly are on target on a number of points. Insofar as the God-as-father/parent metaphor has been associated with and served to legitimate inappropriate and unjust "rule" by male figures, especially fathers, the problems these writers are critiquing are longstanding and in gross need of rectification. It is especially noteworthy that the difficulties they have identified are not confined solely to issues of gender but also and obviously concern age and family relationships: it is the children — whether boys or girls — who have typically suffered the ill effects of the father (or mother). Not surprisingly, then, both Freud and Daly have worried about the metaphor's capacity to permanently confine humans to infantile status.[10]

However, simply because the metaphor has been problematic at points in the past does not constitute proof that it need necessarily be so always and everywhere. Freud's psychohistorical reconstruction, in particular, has been critiqued and challenged given its highly speculative nature.[11] Daly's gender-based argument is more substantial, but its conclusions, too, are neither exhaustive nor foregone. Some women and children can relate (and manifestly have done so) to the God-as-father metaphor with apparently no ill effects; conversely, some women and children (and men) cannot relate to the God-as-mother metaphor or have done so to ill effect.[12] Moreover, not all fathers are despotic — some have been known to be quite loving and nurturing (!); conversely, and unfortunately, even motherhood is not beyond the reach of

9. Mary Daly, *Beyond God the Father: Toward a Philosophy of Women's Liberation* (Boston: Beacon, 1985), pp. 13, 19. Among others, Karl Barth would debate Daly's equation of God and fathers; we only know fatherhood, he argues, because of God — not vice versa (see his *Credo* [New York: Scribner's, 1962], pp. 19-27). Cf. Ephesians 3:14-15.

10. See Freud, *Moses and Monotheism*, p. 172; Daly, *Beyond God the Father*, p. 25.

11. The post-Freudian developments and critiques are too numerous to list. For a beginning, see Stephen A. Mitchell and Margaret J. Black, *Freud and Beyond: A History of Modern Psychoanalytic Thought* (New York: Basic, 1995).

12. See Jane R. Dickie, Amy K. Eshleman, Dawn M. Merasco, Amy Shepard, Michael Vander Wilt, and Melissa Johnson, "Parent-Child Relationships and Children's Images of God," *Journal for the Scientific Study of Religion* 36 (1997): 25-43. This study of two diverse samples indicated that *both* fathers and mothers impact children's God-concepts. Interestingly, if the mother was perceived as powerful and the father as nurturing — a reversal, the authors note, of stereotypical gender roles — then God was perceived as both nurturing and powerful. Important for the conclusions of Daly is the fact that the children sampled tended to use God as an ideal substitute attachment figure, "the more perfect parent," even and especially if the actual parent was imperfect and/or absent (regardless of gender, though it was the fathers who were most often absent).

tyrants. What is crucial, regardless, is that we remember, despite the power of the God-as-father/mother/parent metaphor, that we are dealing with a *metaphor:* God, even in biblical construction, is beyond gender.[13] Metaphors, furthermore, function as tropes of both resemblance and dissemblance.[14] To say that God is a father is thus to say that God is both like and unlike fathers — especially, of course, fathers of the human variety.[15] The same holds true for the predication "God is a mother."

This is not to argue that the God-as-father metaphor (or God-as-parent metaphor, for that matter) is problem-free; on the contrary, it clearly has been problematic at many times and in various ways. That negative history lives on with us and in us such that the metaphor must always be viewed as potentially dangerous.[16] It is only to say that this negative reception of the

13. See Numbers 23:19; Hosea 11:9; Job 32:13; Tikva Frymer-Kensky, *In the Wake of the Goddesses: Women, Culture, and the Biblical Transformation of Pagan Myth* (New York: Free Press, 1992), esp. pp. 188-89; and Mayer I. Gruber, *The Motherhood of God and Other Studies,* South Florida Studies in the History of Judaism 57 (Atlanta: Scholars Press, 1992), p. 8; *contra* Daly, *Beyond God the Father,* pp. xxiii-xxiv. For the argument that the biblical authors knew they were speaking metaphorically when they spoke of God's fatherhood, see Korpel, *A Rift in the Clouds,* pp. 237, 263, and note the earlier, similar sentiments of Roland de Vaux, *Ancient Israel: Its Life and Institutions* (New York: McGraw-Hill, 1961), pp. 51-52; and W. Robertson Smith, *The Religion of the Semites: The Fundamental Institutions,* 2nd ed. (1894; New York: Schocken, 1972), pp. 41-42.

14. See Paul Ricoeur, *The Rule of Metaphor: Multi-Disciplinary Studies of the Creation of Meaning in Language,* trans. Robert Czerny et al. (Toronto: University of Toronto Press, 1977), pp. 6-7, 216-56, and *passim;* cf. Korpel, *A Rift in the Clouds,* p. 48. The dissimilarity or difference inherent in metaphor is what makes Daly's equation of "God = male, therefore male = God" logically unnecessary.

15. By itself, the term for "father" in Hebrew may not refer only to humans. The term used for animal mothers is the same as that used of human mothers: *'ēm* (see Exod. 22:29 [ET v. 30]; 23:19; 34:26; Lev. 22:27; Deut. 14:21; 22:6-7; cf. Job 17:14). While there is no clear reference in biblical Hebrew to a male animal by the term "father" (*'āb*), it is likely — given the use of *'ēm* — that an animal father would also have been called *'āb*. So, while it is common for readers, when hearing of God as father, to think of human fathers, it is possible that this was not always the case in ancient Israel. Note that some parental metaphors used of God are mammalian and are marked for gender (Nah. 2:13: male lion; Hos. 13:8: female bear).

16. The same is true for many metaphors; see Part II. For the history of violence against children remaining with us note the chilling remark of Alice Miller, *Thou Shalt Not Be Aware: Society's Betrayal of the Child,* trans. Hildegarde Hannum and Hunter Hannum (German orig., 1981; New York: Farrar, Straus and Giroux, 1998), p. 315: "The truth about our childhood is stored up in our body, and although we can repress it, we can never alter it. Our intellect can be deceived, our feelings manipulated, our perceptions confused, and our body tricked with medication. But someday the body will present its bill, for it is as incorruptible as a child who, still whole in spirit, will accept no compromises or excuses, and it will not stop tormenting us until we stop evading the truth." See further Alice Miller, *The Body Never Lies: The Lingering Effects of Cruel Parenting,* trans. Andrew Jenkins (New York: Norton, 2005).

metaphor need not be so, at least not always, and this judgment is due, in part, to the ethics of metaphor in general and the ethics of this particular metaphor — points that must now be addressed.

Part II: On the Ethics of Metaphors

It is imperative to assess the parent-child metaphor precisely because of its potential for abuse and real (mis)use *against* children. And yet, when the metaphor is seen through their eyes, a way forward might be found. It may be the case that, when viewed with children "foregrounded," this metaphor is revealed to be one with great potential for and real use *on behalf of* children. If so, a reexamination of this metaphor is imperative as it can benefit children everywhere.

Assessment of the parent-child metaphor is also required because every metaphor contains within itself ethical potential. Figurative language, of whatever stripe, is powerful: it can "figure" the mind in tenacious ways. Wayne C. Booth, in his noted work on the ethics of fiction, writes: "Every art of the imagination, benign or vicious, profound or trivial, can colonize the mind."[17] In this colonization process, the one who experiences the art becomes, as it were, a part of the work of art itself. The effort that is involved in engaging or resisting art (or, here, figurative language) means that it "will always figure the mind more incisively than plain language."[18] This leads to an equation of sorts: the more engaging the figure, the more ethical power is needed and exerted. Most engaging and most powerful of all figures — and therefore most representative of the power of figurative language — is metaphor: "the figure that we . . . conduct our lives *with* and *in*."[19]

Not all metaphors are created equal, however; some are more powerful than others. The most powerful "do not simply *allow*" one to engage them or to wonder about possible ethical outcomes; "they *require* every reader to do so."[20] Booth calls these especially large and generative metaphors "cosmic myths" or "macro-metaphors."[21] These metaphors are world-creators — or, perhaps better, world-devourers: they demand "a choice between . . . imagi-

---

17. Wayne C. Booth, *The Company We Keep: An Ethics of Fiction* (Berkeley: University of California Press, 1988), p. 298.

18. Booth, *The Company We Keep*, p. 298.

19. Booth, *The Company We Keep*, p. 300; his italics; cf. p. 304 and, further, George Lakoff and Mark Johnson, *Metaphors We Live By* (1980; Chicago: University of Chicago Press, 2003).

20. Booth, *The Company We Keep*, p. 331; his italics.

21. Booth, *The Company We Keep*, pp. 325-73.

native worlds. . . . . Each invites us to come and live within a given culture, sharing the assumptions of all who live there. Our entire way of life is thus at stake."[22] Metaphors derived from the sphere of the family and household are of this macro-type. Indeed, it is hard to imagine a more fundamental societal metaphor — whether we are speaking of antiquity or of today's world. The ethical assessment of metaphors drawn from the family sphere is thus particularly urgent. Such assessment has already taken place, especially around the problems of the gendered divine parent and *his* (!) human child. But Booth's work demonstrates that macro-metaphors are never taken in "as isolated propositions, nor even as developed fragments."[23] Instead, as we encounter them, we reconstitute them within "a vast articulated network of interrelated images, emotions, propositions, anecdotes, and possibilities. . . . We find ourselves dwelling in a newly created, animated *uni*-verse of possibilities, in which each particular obtains its full life by virtue of being *in* the whole."[24] Among other things, this means that, even if the God-as-parent metaphor is represented in gendered fashion, it cannot be simplistically interpreted as "God = Father/Male Superpower" and/or/therefore "Father/Male Superpower = God" in purely negative fashion. Instead, the larger context(s) of the metaphor means that more is happening in the construction and reception of the metaphor. That "more" in the case of this particular metaphor is that the world created by the metaphor is, in context and at root, *familial.* This means that not only fatherhood but also motherhood and even childhood are all on the table — the artist's table, as it were, taking their place in a larger, sculptured world.

That point being granted, macro-metaphors like those derived from the realm of the family remain powerful (and dangerous) precisely because of their capacity to co-opt the imagination and all other narratives completely. Once a macro-metaphor has been established and readers become aware of it (or entrapped by it), everything can and will be seen through its lens, even as that lens is modified and nuanced or reinforced and strengthened.[25] As Northrop Frye remarked: "In examining the relation of one subject to another, the initial choice of metaphors and conceptual diagrams is a fateful choice."[26] It is fateful because subsequent events, later metaphors, and succeeding images are all able to be read with — all *will* be read with — the initial choice. A macro-metaphor draws all narratives unto itself.

22. Booth, *The Company We Keep,* p. 335.
23. Booth, *The Company We Keep,* p. 336.
24. Booth, *The Company We Keep,* p. 336; his italics.
25. See Booth, *The Company We Keep,* p. 325.
26. Northrop Frye, "Expanding Eyes," *Critical Inquiry* 2 (1975): 204.

Part III: The Theology of the Divine Parent–Human Child Metaphor

Biblical family metaphors are macro-metaphors largely due to the importance of the family and household in the ancient world. In antiquity, it was, quite simply, family "all the way down."[27] While the larger familial context means that family metaphors are never solely a matter of fathers, it is nevertheless apparent that ancient Israel, like other ancient Near Eastern (and Mediterranean) societies, was "patri-central" — organized around a central male father figure. While traditional family structures have slowly changed in recent generations, especially in the industrialized world, it is no less true today that the family remains a (if not the) dominant nexus wherein humans live, move, and have their being. And every human being had parents, even if they played only biological functions. The sheer ubiquity of family, parents, and children — which is to say the human life-cycle and societal structures — means that family metaphors are set and function within a context that is quite literally everywhere. They are, as a result, eminently sensible. Construing God as a parent in this family-rich context is thus also thoroughly understandable. Indeed, the metaphor corresponds to such a degree with human society that — as noted above — many people do not realize that the construction is metaphorical in the first place.[28]

Writing directly of the Old Testament, Leo G. Perdue has argued that the family sphere had profound impact on the presentation of virtually all aspects of Israelite thought:

> Much of what the Old Testament says about the character and especially the activity of God is shaped by discourse concerning the family. . . . Major metaphors for Israel's self-presentation were drawn from household roles, especially those of the wife (the bride/wife of Yahweh), the son and the daughter,

27. See the massive study by J. David Schloen, *The House of the Father as Fact and Symbol: Patrimonialism in Ugarit and the Ancient Near East,* Studies in the Archaeology and History of the Levant 2 (Winona Lake: Eisenbrauns, 2001); as well as Mark S. Smith, *The Origins of Biblical Monotheism: Israel's Polytheistic Background and the Ugaritic Texts* (New York: Oxford University Press, 2001), pp. 54-66, 90-91, 102-3; Leo G. Perdue, Joseph Blenkinsopp, John J. Collins, and Carol Meyers, *Families in Ancient Israel* (Louisville: Westminster John Knox, 1997); and Karel van der Toorn, *Family Religion in Babylonia, Syria and Israel: Continuity and Change in the Forms of Religious Life,* Studies in the History and Culture of the Ancient Near East 7 (Leiden: Brill, 1996), *passim,* esp. p. 205.

28. Schloen, *The House of the Father,* p. 349, points out that the parent-child metaphor endures because it is not a "free invention of discourse but is 'bound' to actual preverbal experience of the world."

the impoverished kin (redeemed by Yahweh), and marginal members (debt servant, slave, resident alien, and sojourner). . . . Indeed, the household not only grounded Old Testament theology in Israel's social reality but also became the primary lens through which to view the character and activity of God, the identity and self-understanding of Israel in its relationship to God, the value and meaning of the land as the *naḥălāh* ["inheritance"] God gives to Israel, and Israel's relationship to the nations.[29]

Perdue's comment underscores for the Old Testament what we have already seen elsewhere: (1) the power of the family sphere to serve as a locus for major theological metaphors; and (2) the ability of the family metaphor to become all-powerful: a macro-metaphorical lens through which all else is viewed — God, Israel, the land, the nations.

And yet, interestingly enough, when we turn to Genesis, we do not encounter the family metaphor under discussion here, that of parent-child, in the beginning, where we might expect it. Instead, apart from creation, which in the ancient Near East was often associated with various gods' "fatherly" status,[30] we have no indication of God's "fathering" in the first book of the Bible.[31] The metaphor is withheld until Exodus 4. When it finally appears there, it is shocking in force:

> YHWH said to Moses: "When you return to Egypt, make sure that you do all the wonders that I have placed in your power before Pharaoh. But I will

---

29. Leo G. Perdue, "The Household, Old Testament Theology, and Contemporary Hermeneutics," in Perdue et al., *Families in Ancient Israel,* pp. 225-26; cf. pp. 251, 254.

30. That is, as begetter or engenderer. Some scholars (e.g., David R. Tasker, *Ancient Near Eastern Literature and the Hebrew Scriptures about the Fatherhood of God,* Studies in Biblical Literature 69 [New York: Peter Lang, 2004]) have argued that the avoidance of "father" language with reference to the creation of the world is a polemical move on Israel's part vis-à-vis its neighbors. This claim appears dubious in light of Deuteronomy 32:6, which employs *'āb* ("father") along with the verbs *qnh* ("to create"), *'śh* ("to do/make"), and *kwn* ("to establish"). Moreover, even if father-language is absent from Genesis, the power of the parent-child metaphor is such that the creation stories can easily be read through its lens. Cf. Malachi 2:10; 1 Corinthians 8:6.

31. A possible exception, depending on certain interpretations, would be the "God of the fathers" motif that recurs throughout Genesis. *Prima facie,* however, the metaphorical construction here appears different. Regardless, the power of the metaphorical lens means that these references can also be read as reflecting the parent-child metaphor. For example, covenant terminology in the ancient Near East and Old Testament often uses family terms, sometimes with adoption overtones. The covenant and calling of Abraham (e.g., Gen. 12:1-9; 15:1-21; 17:1-27), therefore, can be read (especially via the parent-child metaphor) as a kind of divine adoption. For more on the child in Genesis, see the essay by Terence E. Fretheim in this volume; for adoption, see the essay by David Bartlett.

harden his heart so that he will not release the people. Then say to Pharaoh, 'Thus says YHWH: Israel is my firstborn son [*bny bkry yśr'l*]. I said to you: Release my son [*bny*] that he might worship me, but you have refused to release him. So now I will kill your firstborn son [*bnk bkrk*].'" (Exod. 4:21-23)[32]

The placement of this metaphor is significant in at least two ways. The first is that it comes on the scene relatively early in the book of Exodus. The narrative of Moses' call and commission has only just finished in Exodus 4:17, and, though verse 20 indicates that Moses and his family went back to Egypt, the subsequent materials indicate that verses 21-23 occur (in narrative time) prior to the first encounter with Pharaoh (see vv. 21, 24, 27). These temporal and geographical confusions may reflect redactional seams and compositional layers; but even so, that judgment only serves to underscore the importance of the current canonical placement of verses 21-23. As it now stands in the book of Exodus, this unit is a summary of the showdown with Pharaoh *before the fact*, and the climax of that summary is the explanation offered in verses 22-23, predicated on the identification of Israel as YHWH's firstborn son.[33] This predication suggests that YHWH is Israel's parent, but no specific term for parent is used of YHWH until much later (Deut. 32:6: *'āb*, "father").[34] Whatever the case, the placement of the metaphor so early in the Exodus narrative (and the Pentateuch as a whole)[35] indicates that the metaphor should not be understood solely as a reflex of the covenant, nor simply as covenantal language.[36] For the book of Exodus (and the Pentateuch), God's parenting of

32. Translations are my own unless otherwise indicated.

33. The initial positioning of *bny bkry* and the double construction in verse 22 suggest emphasis: "*My son, my firstborn (son)* is Israel." The *inclusio* with verse 23 (which ends with *bnk bkrk*, "your son, your firstborn [son]") should not be missed. At the center of this structure is the command in verse 23a to "release my son *(bny)* that he might worship me." Pharaoh's refusal (*m'n*) to release leads directly to YHWH's statement that he will kill Pharaoh's firstborn. Everything hinges, then, on *bny*, "my son." What is done, or not done, to *bny*, "*my* son," directly affects *bnk*, "*your* [i.e., Pharaoh's] son." Cf. Jon D. Levenson, *The Death and Resurrection of the Beloved Son: The Transformation of Child Sacrifice in Judaism and Christianity* (New Haven: Yale University Press, 1993), p. 38: "In no small measure, the story of the Exodus turns on the contrast between the first-born son whom God enables to survive enslavement and attempted genocide and the first-born son whom he slays."

34. Cf., earlier, the metaphors in Deuteronomy 1:31; 8:5 (both of God, with *k'šr*, "just as"); and 14:1 (of Israel).

35. This early placement also means that the metaphor occurs early in the presentation of Israel as a nation-group (regardless of what that group is called) since that is often thought to lie in the book of Exodus itself (cf. *bny yśr'l* in Exodus 1:1 with 1:9 ['*m* "people"]) or in the Exodus event (see Exod. 15; esp. the use of *qnh*, "to create," in v. 16).

36. *Contra* F. Charles Fensham, "Father and Son as Terminology for Treaty and Covenant,"

Israel is earlier and prior to covenant-making. From whence the metaphor comes is not explicitly stated, though the use of the "God of the fathers" motif in Exodus 3:6, 15-16; 4:5, and throughout Genesis, is probably sufficient indication that it has to do with the ancestors (cf. Deut. 4:37; 7:8).[37] Regardless, in the narrative form of Exodus, the metaphor is not only covenantal, though it can easily include that. It is, at times at least, "literal" — that is, *real*, whether biological or adoptive.[38]

The second critical observation about the placement of Exodus 4:21-23 is that it occurs in the context of the Exodus event, with all that that means, both socio-politically and theologically. A large part of what that means is that God's parental claim of "child Israel" involves *protection and deliverance* of God's child. That these values are at work in the very first instance of the metaphor is of no small import. In Tasker's words, "when God liberates his people from bondage and allots them their inheritance, he is 'acting like a father.'"[39]

---

in *Near Eastern Studies in Honor of William Foxwell Albright,* ed. Hans Goedicke (Baltimore: Johns Hopkins University Press, 1971), pp. 121-35; Dennis J. McCarthy, "Notes on the Love of God in Deuteronomy and the Father-Son Relationship Between Yahweh and Israel," *Catholic Biblical Quarterly* 27 (1965): 144-47; Niskanen, "Yhwh as Father," pp. 397-407; and others. But, again, the covenant can be read with the parent-child metaphor and vice versa (see notes 30-31 above). In this light, one wonders if "becoming like a child" in the New Testament involves entering into relationship (or into covenant) with God (see Matt. 18:1-5; Mark 9:33-37; 10:15; Luke 9:46-48; 18:17; John 1:12; 12:36). For relationship *preceding* covenant, see Terence E. Fretheim, *God and World in the Old Testament: A Relational Theology of Creation* (Nashville: Abingdon, 2005), esp. pp. 14-16.

37. Cf. Schloen, *The House of the Father,* esp. pp. 345-60; and van der Toorn, *Family Religion,* pp. 155-60, on the West Semitic god *Ilib* (literally: "the god of the father" — that is, the divine ancestor), who was a primeval deity — father of the gods — at Ugarit and elsewhere. For the general antiquity of the parent-child metaphor in Israel and elsewhere, see McCarthy, "Notes on the Love of God," pp. 144-47; Tasker, *Ancient Near Eastern Literature;* Robertson Smith, *The Religion of the Semites,* pp. 41-48; Korpel, *A Rift in the Clouds,* p. 236; and Thorkild Jacobsen, *The Treasures of Darkness: A History of Mesopotamian Religion* (New Haven: Yale University Press, 1976), pp. 145-64, esp. 158-60. Note also Numbers 21:29, which applies the metaphor to the Moabite people and their god Chemosh.

38. For the latter option, see Janet L. R. Melnyk, "When Israel Was a Child: Ancient Near Eastern Adoption Formulas and the Relationship between God and Israel," in *History and Interpretation: Essays in Honour of John H. Hayes,* ed. M. Patrick Graham, William P. Brown, and Jeffrey K. Kuan, Journal for the Study of the Old Testament — Supplement Series 173 (Sheffield: Sheffield Academic Press, 1993), pp. 245-59. For the "literal" option, see Tasker, *Ancient Near Eastern Literature,* p. 191. Note also Fensham, "Father and Son," p. 132, who points out that Deuteronomy 32:19 cannot be a covenantal instance of the metaphor because it mentions daughters and "nowhere in the Old Testament or the ancient Near East is 'daughters' used as a covenant term." Of course, this verse could be the exception.

39. Tasker, *Ancient Near Eastern Literature,* p. 5. See also Niskanen, "Yhwh as Father," 406.

But note that Exodus 4:21-23 does *not* mention inheritance; instead, it is apparent that Tasker has succumbed to the power of the parent-child macrometaphor. Given its early placement in the Pentateuch and its conceptual, explanatory power, Tasker has read the entirety of the narrative of Exodus–Joshua through the metaphorical lens. Such is the power of a macrometaphor! Even so, the presence of protection and deliverance in the first clear instance of the parent-child metaphor in Scripture lends support to Tasker's further comment: "it appears that this metaphor was chosen by the Bible writers to best describe their experience of God's protection and care from the perspective of human fatherhood, as they knew it."[40] This statement is full of ethical potential for human parents (see Part IV below), but it also has ethical ramifications for this particular text. Quite apart from the vexed issue of the hardening of Pharaoh's heart (v. 21), the difficulty of verse 23 should not be skirted. To be sure, there is protection, care, and liberation for child Israel. But it comes at the expense of Pharaoh's (Egypt's) firstborn. Some children live, some die: both at the hands of the Parent who is YHWH. These two outcomes concerning the firstborn son are inextricably conjoined in this text. How, then, does this text speak for and about children (can it?), who in our day are so often the victims in armed conflicts not unlike (and certainly as deadly as) the battle between YHWH and Pharaoh?[41]

Exodus 4:21-23, like so many other difficult texts, cannot be "fixed," especially not easily, but it is worth paying attention to the fact that this first indication of YHWH's onslaught against Pharaoh and Egypt via the plague of the firstborn is crafted as a metaphor and, further, *as a metaphor* that highlights *the childlike status of Israel.* Perhaps we will never understand the hardening of Pharaoh's heart, the plague narratives, or, especially, the final plague, all of which testify to an odd, violent, and certainly biased deity. But we can understand or at least feel this metaphor with its evocation of childlike helplessness and parental passion. Children are the most vulnerable of human beings, easily preyed upon, most in need of protection. And what parent would not go to the end of the world to protect his or her child? Especially a child that has been imprisoned, beaten, enslaved, or worse? Who would not, if they could, wreak havoc (or at least wish to) on the perpetrator of their child's death?[42]

40. Tasker, *Ancient Near Eastern Literature,* pp. 5-6.

41. See Carol Bellamy, ed., *The State of the World's Children 2005: Childhood Under Threat* (New York: The United Nations Children's Fund [UNICEF], 2004), pp. 39-66; and Danna Nolan Fewell, *The Children of Israel: Reading the Bible for the Sake of Our Children* (Nashville: Abingdon, 2003), p. 19, for the grisly statistics. For the difficulties the book of Exodus poses for children, see Claire Mathews McGinnis's essay in the present volume.

42. Israel is, of course, a collective "child." For these children's deaths, see Pharaoh's at-

This does not fix a very difficult text, but seeing the violence of YHWH against Egypt through the metaphorical lens of the parent-child may make it more understandable and affective, even if it remains unpalatable.[43] (But is it unpalatable, when *our* children are at stake?)

Co-opting (All) Other Metaphors

Certainly more could be said about this text from Exodus 4. For now, however, it is important to reconsider the parent-child metaphor in Exodus in light of Booth's work on macro-metaphors. When this is done, the early placement of the metaphor in the book of Exodus, in the context of Egyptian slavery, takes on even more significance, as does the fact that this first occurrence establishes the relationship between God and Israel as one of concerned/impassioned parent with needy/victimized child. These factors are important because Booth argues that once a macro-metaphor such as the parent-child one is established — especially if it is done powerfully and if it is repeated — subsequent events will be seen to reinforce the metaphor.[44]

It is not surprising, then, to find God figured as a parent elsewhere in the Bible — often times quite explicitly (e.g., Deut. 1:31; 8:5; 32:6; Jer. 3:4; Ps. 68:6 [ET 5]),[45] at other times by means of the identification of Israel (or a representative thereof) as the child(ren) of the LORD (e.g., Deut. 14:1; 2 Sam. 7:14; Isa. 1:2, 4; 30:1, 9; 63:8; Jer. 3:14, 22; 4:22; 31:20; Hos. 2:1 [ET 1:10]; 1 Chron. 17:13; 22:9-10; 28:6), or, occasionally, both (see Deut. 32:5-6, 18; Isa. 43:6-7; 45:10-11; 63:16; 64:7 [ET 8]; Jer. 3:19; 31:9; Ezek. 16; Hos. 11; Mal. 2:10-11; 3:17; Pss. 2:7; 89:27-28 [ET 26-27]; Sir. 23:1, 4). Each of these texts can and should be read for how they reinforce the parent-child metaphor begun in Exodus 4

---

tempts at genocide in Exodus 1:15-22. Note also Deuteronomy 32:43: "Praise, O heavens, his people, worship him, all you gods! For he will avenge the blood of his children" (NRSV).

43. Perhaps the lack of an explicit term for a parent (whether father or mother) in Exodus 4:21-23 is a hint that in this particular instance of the metaphor the parental passion is restricted to the deity, not to be replicated (nor replicable) by humans. In this interpretation, the metaphor allows us to sympathize with YHWH's parental passion but not act/requite in the same way. For more on parental passion, mobilized in the defense of the child, see Brueggemann's essay in this volume.

44. See the next paragraph and cf. the use of *bkwr* in Exodus 22:5; 12:12, 29; 13:15; cf. 13:2, 13; 22:28; 34:20. The only other instance of *bkwr* in God's mouth with reference to Israel is Jeremiah 31:9. Cf. Psalm 89:28 [ET 27] for YHWH making the king "(as) the firstborn" (*bkwr*).

45. Mythological passages such as Psalm 82:6-7 and the like (cf. Gen. 6:2, 4; Job 1:6; 2:1; 38:7; Ps. 29:1), while not completely unrelated, lie at some remove from the concerns of the present essay.

— a task that lies outside the scope of the present essay.[46] Even so, it can be stated that *nurture and care* are aspects of some of these metaphors (see, e.g., Deut. 1:31; Jer. 31:9; Hos. 11:1, 3-4, 8-9; Mal. 3:17; Pss. 68:6-7 [ET 5-6]; 103:13; Wis. 14:3; cf. Deut. 32:10-11); *covenant and discipline* belong to others (see, e.g., Deut. 8:5; 14:1; Prov. 3:11-12; Mal. 1:6); *adoption* seems implied in still others (see, e.g., Ps. 27:10; cf. 2 Sam. 7:14; 1 Chron. 17:13; 22:9-10; 28:6; Ps. 2:7); and so on and so forth. Most of these passages figure God as a father and Israel as God's son (usually), God's daughter (cf. Lam. 2:13; Deut. 32:19; Isa. 43:6; 2 Cor. 6:18), or a (female) foundling saved by the LORD (Ezek. 16). All of them reinforce the parent-child metaphor even as they simultaneously modify it, adding various nuances to its first occurrence in Exodus 4. One way to put this is to say that these additional metaphors reveal YHWH to be not just any parent, but a certain kind of parent — a father who carries and protects, for instance (Deut. 1:31), and a mother who will not forget her child (Isa. 49:15; see further below).[47]

Another observation regarding the parent-child metaphor established in Exodus 4:22 (if not earlier) in light of Booth's work is that, as a macro-metaphor, the parent-child metaphor creates a powerful world that captures all other narratives. It co-opts (lesser) metaphors in subsequent contexts, creating a lens through which they can and will be seen as part and parcel of the macro-metaphor. In this way, the events following Exodus 4 — *all* the events, not just those that explicitly utilize the metaphor — can be "read with" the parent-child image. Assuming and granting that this is true, we can focus on two specific ways the metaphor functions when the rest of Scripture is seen through its lens: Israel's perceptions and representations of (1) God as its parent; and (2) itself as God's child. Co-inhering with both of these, but perhaps forming a third distinct category, is another function: viewing other people as God's children (see further below).[48]

---

46. Tasker, *Ancient Near Eastern Literature*, offers brief analyses of most of the father-passages. For still other passages, see further below.

47. See Terence E. Fretheim, *The Suffering of God: An Old Testament Perspective*, Overtures to Biblical Theology (Philadelphia: Fortress, 1984), p. 12.

48. As Terence E. Fretheim has reminded me (oral communication), this latter category may indicate that family is fundamentally a *creational* category (especially as opposed to a *covenantal* one). One thinks of how the book of Genesis is structured as a genealogy: "these are the generations [*tôlĕdôt*] . . ." (see Gen. 2:4; 5:1; 6:9; 10:1, 32; 11:10, 27; 25:12, 13, 19; 36:1, 9; 37:2). If so, this would indicate that Israel's self-understanding is based on the more basic creational understanding of God's relation to the entire world. See Fretheim's extensive treatment of this motif in his *God and World in the Old Testament*.

God-Perceptions

There is a tendency, perhaps even pressure, to read the parent-child meta-phor's impact on God-perceptions positively. So, for example, Tasker argues that the basic tenor of the portrait of God as a father in Scripture is God's passion for God's children,[49] such that God's parenting is best described in terms of רחם/*rḥm* ("mercy, pity") and אהבה/*ahbh* ("love").[50] He concludes his study with a list of attributes describing God's fatherhood: creative, per-sonal and loving, universal, covenantal, powerful, salvific, nurturing, vindi-cating, just and merciful, educational, proactive, relational, humanitarian.[51]

All of these divine qualities are laudable. But, as Exodus 4 demonstrates, the texts themselves reveal other qualities as well, showing that disturbing aspects can be inextricably joined to the most beautiful of things. These other, more negative qualities must not be neglected. They, too, are real and have potentially real impact on real children. And, as Exodus 4 also demonstrates, it is often the distinctly familial aspect of the metaphor that allows one to understand and empathize with, if not appropriate, the negative instances of the metaphor.[52]

1. Whether "positive" or "negative,"[53] it is clear that the parent-child meta-

---

49. Tasker, *Ancient Near Eastern Literature*, pp. 197, 207, argues that this is in contrast to other ancient Near Eastern deities. So, similarly, John W. Miller, "God as Father in the Bible and the Father Image in Several Contemporary Ancient Near Eastern Myths: A Comparison," *Studies in Religion* 14 (1985): 347-54.

50. Tasker, *Ancient Near Eastern Literature*, p. 198. Note that Phyllis Trible has argued that רחם/*rḥm* has female connotations (*God and the Rhetoric of Sexuality*, Overtures to Biblical The-ology [Philadelphia: Fortress, 1978], esp. pp. 31-59).

51. Tasker, *Ancient Near Eastern Literature*, pp. 204-6. See also Miller, "God as Father," esp. p. 353; Miller, *Calling God "Father": Essays on the Bible, Fatherhood and Culture*, 2nd ed. (New York: Paulist, 1999), p. 44; Melnyk, "When Israel Was a Child," pp. 245-59; Willem A. VanGemeren, "'*Abbā*' in the Old Testament?" *Journal of the Evangelical Theological Society* 31 (1988): 393.

52. Some readers will no doubt take issue with the suggestion that we could or should "ap-propriate" negative aspects of the parent-child metaphor. Space precludes a refutation of that objection; I can only defer and refer to Booth's work, which masterfully shows that *all* meta-phors must be evaluated and that we do, in fact, perform such evaluation all the time — indeed, every time we encounter a metaphor — and that we do so on the basis of preexisting metaphors that we already know and have already evaluated. "Appropriation," that is, is not an option and need not and must not be understood simplistically in positive or utilitarian fashion. The term Booth coins for the kind of engagement he describes is "coduction." See *The Company We Keep*, esp. pp. 70-77, 371-81.

53. These terms are heuristic; I do not wish to imply a simple dichotomy. Several of the metaphorical constructions and contexts are exceedingly complicated and do not permit easy reification.

phor impacts Israel's depictions of God. Given the urgency of the negative instances of the metaphor, these merit special attention. As a first example, one might lift up the issue of *parental impatience with children.* Simplistically (too simplistically), one might contrast a human parent's impatience with their child with God's supposedly infinite patience so as to produce a particular ethic (a work ethic, no doubt!): namely, parents who *try* to be more patient with their children. The problem with this scenario is that parent YHWH is sometimes portrayed as impatient with child Israel. Does this obviate the ideal of a truly patient parent (whether divine, ancient, or modern)? Does it, rather, recommend impatience with children? Perhaps someone would want to argue that; it makes far more sense, however, to reverse the metaphor, so to speak, and examine God's impatience through the parent-child lens. Seen in this way, God's impatience becomes quite understandable, maybe even forgivable. Who, after all, has not been similarly exasperated with their children at one point or another? Moreover, there are times when impatience with one's child(ren) is not only natural but expected, even justified. A look at the murmuring accounts in the Pentateuch casts light on this.

In the murmuring stories, Israel complains about various matters, including a lack of basic necessities during their sojourn in the wilderness: water, bread, meat. Jay A. Wilcoxen has noted a marked difference between these kinds of stories prior to Sinai (e.g., Exod. 15:22-27; 16:1-36; 17:1-7) and those after Sinai (e.g., Num. 11:1-35).[54] Prior to Sinai, there are no serious punishments associated with the Israelites' complaints regarding food and water. After Sinai, there are major punishments, including death. Sinai, in short, makes a difference: it formalizes the God-Israel relationship and, therefore, Israel's responsibilities (see, e.g., Exod. 19:1-8). When viewed through the lens of the parent-child metaphor, this narrative development can be seen on analogy with human development:

> The divine promise to the patriarchs is the "conception" of "Israel," the exodus is the "birth" (the "delivery") of "Israel," Sinai is the "bar mitzvah" of "Israel" (the point at which moral responsibility formally begins), the two parts of the wilderness period are preadolescent childhood and the period from adolescence to adulthood. . . . Prior to Sinai their responsibility in these respects had not been formalized. "Israel" was still a child to be scolded not yet a "son of the commandment."[55]

54. Jay A. Wilcoxen, "Some Anthropocentric Aspects of Israel's Sacred History," *Journal of Religion* 48 (1968): 333-50.
55. Wilcoxen, "Some Anthropocentric Aspects," pp. 347-48, 349.

Israel "grows up" at Sinai, or is supposed to at any rate. By means of the parent-child metaphor God's parental impatience is made understandable, and, in some cases — such as in the murmuring stories or the golden calf debacle (see Exod. 32:1–34:28) — it is portrayed as justifiable.

Related to the issue of impatience is that of *parental fatigue*. Perhaps the universal experience of being a tired parent affords insight into some of the habits and attitudes of "God the father." The parent-child lens suggests that parental fatigue might explain "lapses" in God's (stereo)typical qualities such as patience, tolerance, love, and the like. "If God is a parent," the metaphorical logic runs, "and parents sometimes get tired and impatient with their children, then maybe that is why God is impatient with me/us now." This logic is obviously well down the road to theodicy — making sense of or at least considering God's mysterious and problematic ways. The logic is also putting the metaphor's power to good use on the child-referent of the metaphor — that is, Israel's self-perception — a topic that will be engaged momentarily.

Third, the parent-child metaphor proves helpful in understanding *divine regret*. Parents sometimes (in truth, oftentimes) have regret regarding their parenting. Parents sometimes (oftentimes) regret things they did or did not do, or wish they had done things differently, because they realize too late that their children were incapable of certain attitudes or behaviors or were unable to understand certain concepts. Hosea 11 is a good example of this process at work in the parent-child metaphor (see also Jer. 42:10). Here YHWH is figured as a parent, loving Israel as a "young boy" *(nʿr)* and calling "my son" *(bny)* from Egypt (Hos. 11:1). But Israel rebelled, sacrificing to the Baals and offering incense to idols (v. 2). YHWH then recounts a history of parental goodness: teaching Israel to walk, carrying Israel, feeding them (vv. 3-4). This mismatch between parental beneficence and childish rebellion is more than the divine parent can stomach: Israel will return to Egypt, be ruled by Assyria; the sword rages and devours (vv. 5-6). But it is precisely at this juncture, at the very moment when the people call out to the Most High to no avail, that avail occurs.

> How could I hand you over, O Ephraim?
> How could I give you up, O Israel?
> How could I make you like Admah?
> How could I make you like Zeboiim?
> My heart is changed within me;
> all my compassion grows tender.
> I will not act upon my fierce anger;
> I will not turn to destroy Ephraim;
> for I am God, not a human,

the Holy One in your midst,
and I will not come in rage.

(vv. 8-9)

YHWH, like other parents, realizes — partially in retrospect, but also (and largely) in a self-conflicted sort of way — that he was too hard on child Israel. Divine compassion wins out: YHWH's children will return from Egypt and Assyria, YHWH returns them to their homes (vv. 10-11).

Does the parent-child metaphor "sanctify" passages like this one, which can recount divine judgment in violent detail? Or does the metaphor simply suggest the image of an abusive (divine) parent? Many have worried about the latter option, and with good cause.[56] But the ethical criticism of macrometaphors cuts both ways: the divine parent can be seen in some passages as a violent one, but the violent passages can also be reframed, chastened, modified in light of other instances and aspects of the parent-child metaphor, including (and especially) those of love and nurturance. That modification may not solve all of the problems at work in passages that involve divine violence, but it does create a heuristic matrix through which they can be seen and understood in more sympathetic fashion. Perhaps God is, at times at least, an impatient and exhausted parent. Perhaps, at times at least, God is even provoked by a child's rebellion, such that divine judgment is warranted. And perhaps, at times at least, if and when God *over*-punishes, even God regrets.[57] But the Hosea 11 passage also indicates that dissemblance is part of the parent-child metaphor. God is God, after all, not a human (v. 9b), and that predication both justifies and motivates God's decision not to punish (v. 9a, c). Perhaps it is significant to note that the term for human here is specifically *ʾîš*, which generically means "man," but which can also be used for fathers (e.g., Deut. 1:31; Eccles. 6:3). YHWH is like a father, yes, but also unlike a father: in this case, YHWH's patience and decision to forgo punishment distinguish him from human counterparts even as they set an example of forgiveness for human parents to emulate (see Part IV below).

2. Other positive aspects of the portrayal of God as a parent in the Old Testament can also be seen by means of the metaphor's power to co-opt other narratives. Positive aspects of *parental passion* have already been noted above for Exodus 4 and Hosea 11. Another example: the constant reminders of God's gift of land or other gracious acts to Israel in Deuteronomy (cf. also Jer. 3:19)

---

56. See, e.g., Terence E. Fretheim, "'I Was Only a Little Angry': Divine Violence in the Prophets," *Interpretation* 58 (2004): 365-75.

57. See further Fretheim, "'I Was Only a Little Angry,'" on the regret having to do, at least in part, with the fact that the human agents chosen and used by the LORD overdo it and go too far.

could be seen as *assurances of parental goodness.*[58] The protection and care begun in Exodus 4 are reinforced here through seemingly endless repetition, with the result that God appears — again, at times at least — as the ideal parent, one who is not above *parental indulgence,* providing the child with all of the best gifts.[59] *Parental forbearance* is another positive aspect and serves to balance instances of *parental impatience.* Indeed, both were at work in the play of the poetry in Hosea 11. Still further on this point, when some of the Pentateuchal legislation pertaining to children is seen through the metaphorical lens, God is depicted as *ultra*-patient.

According to Deuteronomy 21:18-21, the incorrigible son *(bn)* — one who is stubborn *(srr)* and rebellious *(mrh),* who will not listen *('yn + šmʿ)* to the voice of his father and mother and who will not heed *(lʾ + šmʿ)* their discipline — deserves death after a public trial with the elders at the city gate (cf. also Exod. 21:17; Lev. 20:9; Prov. 20:20). The verbs used to describe this rebellious child are often used of Israel. In fact, "most of the vocabulary that describes the rebellious son in the Hebrew Bible is used to portray Israel's rebellion against Yahweh."[60] Through the metaphorical lens — especially with a little help from the prophets — one can see child Israel often and repeatedly cursing its parent, YHWH (see, e.g., Isa. 1:2-3). But, while YHWH repeatedly engages in legal proceedings with the rebellious child (especially with a little help from the prophets), the prescribed punishments are repeatedly deferred. God's threatened punishments look increasingly like empty parental threats: they are not lies per se, but the loving parent never wishes to act on them. And, even when the death penalty is finally executed in 596/586 — if the destruction of Jerusalem and the Judean deportations into Babylonian exile can be described in such a way[61] — even this is not the final word. There is, for both parent and child, *life after death.* Moreover, the life that

---

58. See, e.g., Deuteronomy 1:8, 11, 20-21, 25, 35-36; 2:7, 12, 29, 36; 3:18; 4:1, 21, 38, 40; 5:16, 31; 6:10, 18, 23; 7:8, 12-13; 8:1, 10; 9:6, 23; 10:11; 11:9, 17, 21, 31; 12:1, 7, 9, 15; 14:24, 29; 15:4, 6-7, 10, 14, 18; 16:10, 15, 20; 17:14; 18:9; 19:1-2, 10, 14, 28; 21:1, 23; 23:21 [ET 20]; 24:4; 25:15, 19; 26:1-3, 9, 15; 27:2-3; 28:8, 11-12, 52; 30:16, 20; 31:7, 20-21, 23; 32:49, 52; 34:4.

59. Positive aspects such as these argue against McCarthy, "Notes on the Love of God," pp. 145-46, who finds no trace of tenderness or love in the parent-child metaphor, evidently because the love that is discussed is one that can be commanded. For a thorough refutation of such a position, see Jacqueline E. Lapsley, "Feeling Our Way: Love for God in Deuteronomy," *Catholic Biblical Quarterly* 65 (2003): 350-69. Note also Leo G. Perdue, "The Israelite and Early Jewish Family: Summary and Conclusions," in Perdue et al., *Families in Ancient Israel,* p. 171.

60. Melnyk, "When Israel Was a Child," p. 256. Cf., e.g., Nehemiah 9:29; Psalm 78:8; Isaiah 1:23; 30:1; 65:2; Numbers 27:14; Deuteronomy 1:26.

61. See Donald E. Gowan, *Theology of the Prophetic Books: The Death and Resurrection of Israel* (Louisville: Westminster John Knox, 1998).

happens then is, according to Jeremiah and Ezekiel, completely at God's gracious initiative. The child is resurrected, as it were, purely because of the parent's surpassing love and grace; the child does nothing to provoke or promote this restoration.[62] Whatever the case, long before the climactic drama of exile and return, parent YHWH is repeatedly shown to be "slow to anger" (see, e.g., Exod. 34:6; Num. 14:18; Jon. 4:2; Nah. 1:3; Sir. 5:4), forgiving, and non-punitive.

3. Two items bear emphasizing with regard to the impact of the parent-child metaphor on Israel's depiction of YHWH. First, the themes identified above and those like them need not and should not be seen as originating solely from within the parent-child metaphor. Each may well have its own distinct lineage. Still, the fact that each can be profitably understood by means of the parent-child metaphor underscores the metaphor's power. Simply put, it has the two characteristics (or tests) that Booth deems necessary for macro-metaphors: comprehensiveness and correspondence.[63]

Second, the fact that Israel knows the ups and downs of its parent's "moods" or "tempers" — that it can read the deity's various affect states and is able to recognize, characterize, and record them — is worth worrying about in light of Alice Miller's notion of the "gifted child." Is Israel such a gifted child, which in Miller's estimation is not a positive characteristic in the least since it is the product of inappropriate parenting?[64] Or, on the contrary, at its best moments, does the parent-child metaphor show God to be the paradigmatic "good enough" parent if not, in fact, more than that?[65] Perhaps child Israel — better, Israel as fully grown adult child — is affectively gifted because it had a parent that appropriately attended to it via mirroring, paren-

---

62. See Thomas M. Raitt, *A Theology of Exile: Judgment/Deliverance in Jeremiah and Ezekiel* (Philadelphia: Fortress, 1977). One might contrast Luke 15:11-32 where the prodigal must first return.

63. *Comprehensiveness:* "It 'covers' the essential territory with astonishing breadth: it provides a ground for our responsibilities; it accounts for our human origins and nature; it provides particular standards for choosing between plausible moral requirements; and it provides a motive for obeying the moral law that it reveals." *Correspondence:* it corresponds "to our commonsense experience of our own ambiguous natures and that of our fellows. . . . It does not deny but rather explains our capacity for nobility — and yet both acknowledges and provides remedies for our inherent love of vice. . . . It is open to new historical experience; in the domain of history, it is pluralistic. . . . [It] is implicitly *shareable* by all humankind" (Booth, *The Company We Keep*, pp. 359-61).

64. See Alice Miller, *Prisoners of Childhood,* trans. Ruth Ward (New York: Basic, 1981).

65. For the notion of the "good enough" parent, see D. W. Winnicott, *The Maturational Processes and the Facilitating Environment: Studies in the Theory of Emotional Development* (Madison: International Universities, 1965), pp. 140-52.

tal matching, empathetic attunement, and the like.[66] When the parent-child metaphor is drawn widely, given its fullest, most comprehensive scope, it certainly looks that way. The Psalms, for example, especially the laments, become a means by which God mirrors Israel's pain, granting it legitimacy and reality.[67] The canon of Scripture itself becomes a family scrapbook or picture album of sorts, preserving not only moments of the family's history for posterity's sake but also occasions for *parental pride*.

4. One final text must be mentioned: it is the notoriously difficult Ezekiel 16, which depicts Jerusalem as an abandoned baby girl, a foundling, evidently left to die of exposure (vv. 1-5). YHWH saves Jerusalem (vv. 6-7), then marries her (vv. 8-14), but after she "plays the whore" (vv. 15-34) YHWH promises punishment that is rife with themes of sexual violence (vv. 35-43).[68] Like Hosea 11, when Ezekiel 16 is viewed through the parent-child lens it seems to be at great pains to describe the heights and depths, the passion and compassion of God's parental relationship with Israel. In family contexts, of course, passion and compassion always run perilously close to "out of control." Unlike Hosea 11, however, where God's compassion wins out, Ezekiel 16 is (in)famously more complicated than that. The discussion of this terrifying text in the secondary literature is massive and cannot be rehearsed here. It is enough to sug-

---

66. See Miller, *Prisoners of Childhood*, p. 10; Miller, *For Your Own Good: Hidden Cruelty in Child-Rearing and the Roots of Violence*, trans. Hildegarde Hannum and Hunter Hannum (German orig., 1980; New York: Farrar, Straus, Giroux, 1990), p. 284: "People whose integrity has not been damaged in childhood, who were protected, respected, and treated with honesty by their parents, will be — both in their youth and in adulthood — intelligent, responsive, empathetic, and highly sensitive. They will take pleasure in life and will not feel any need to kill or even hurt others or themselves. They will use their power to defend themselves, not to attack others. They will not be able to do otherwise than respect and protect those weaker than themselves, including their children, because this is what they have learned from their own experience, and because it is this knowledge (and not the experience of cruelty) that has been stored up inside them from the beginning." One might compare, in this vein, the repeated emphases in the Torah on taking care of the stranger, orphan, widow, and similar personages. In these ways, child Israel seems to have learned from its Exodus parent. See further Part IV below.

67. See Brad D. Strawn and Brent A. Strawn, "From Petition to Praise: An Intrapsychic Phenomenon?" (paper presented at the annual meeting of the Society of Biblical Literature, Denver, Colorado, 2001); Walter Brueggemann, "The Costly Loss of Lament," *Journal for the Study of the Old Testament* 36 (1986): 57-71; Erich Fromm, *You Shall Be as Gods: A Radical Interpretation of the Old Testament and Its Tradition* (1966; New York: Henry Holt, 1991), pp. 201-23. Cf. also Tasker, *Ancient Near Eastern Literature*, p. 119, for the Psalms' depiction of God's fatherhood as the care of orphans, widows, the estranged, and released prisoners (and see previous note).

68. For a discussion of the problematics at work in the latter section and related passages, see Renita J. Weems, *Battered Love: Marriage, Sex, and Violence in the Hebrew Prophets*, Overtures to Biblical Theology (Minneapolis: Fortress, 1995) and the literature cited there.

gest that the use of the parent-child metaphor in this passage might offer another way into and through (but not around) its many difficulties.

Without wanting to oversimplify the situation, it seems that a major shift occurs at verse 15. Verses 1-14 set a more "positive" beginning to the chapter, recounting YHWH's saving of the exposed baby girl (Jerusalem), raising her, and then marrying her,[69] though it must be admitted that even this first unit is not without problems and that this "positive" beginning is quickly overturned. After the turn in verse 15, which begins to recount Jerusalem's rebellion, it is noteworthy that God's wrath in the latter part of the chapter is connected in no small degree to children and childhood: Jerusalem is criticized for having forgotten the days of "your youth" (*ymy n'wryk*; vv. 22, 43), apparently a reference to YHWH's earlier act of saving her. Even more significantly, Jerusalem is condemned for what she has done to *her own* sons and daughters, including sacrificing them (v. 20), slaughtering and offering them up (v. 21), even loathing them (v. 45). God cares about these little ones: they are the children borne by Jerusalem following her marriage to YHWH (v. 20). God explicitly calls them "*my* children" (*bny;* v. 21). The end of the chapter, which speaks of restored fortunes and consolation (vv. 53-54), also does so in terms of children — specifically daughters (vv. 53, 55; cf. 57) — and, again, mentions the days of Jerusalem's youth (*bymy n'wryk;* v. 60, cf. vv. 22, 43).

Ezekiel 16 is difficult and disturbing, but, among other things, the lens of the parent-child metaphor reveals within this chapter what might be called *God's preferential option for the child,* especially *the weakest, most vulnerable child.* God's care for the exposed baby girl Jerusalem is not unlike God's care for firstborn son Israel in Exodus 4; only the child's sex has changed. In both texts, it is the weakest, abused, left-for-dead child that is cared about and attended to. And yet, not unlike the murmuring episodes, when the child grows up, different expectations are in place. After Sinai, son Israel ought to murmur less. When grown, daughter Jerusalem ought not to forget the days of her youth, when YHWH rescued and cared for her. If (when) she does forget her parent's example of protection and care, goes after other "parents" (see Jer. 2:27), and the result is the victimization of her own (and God's own!) children, the divine parent will see to them.[70] God's parental passion is mobilized

---

69. It is twice emphasized that YHWH is not Jerusalem's biological parent: "your father was an Amorite and your mother a Hittite" (v. 3; cf. v. 45).

70. The leitmotif of "blood" (*dm*) in Ezekiel 16 is a critical point here; compare verse 22 with verses 36, 38: Jerusalem forgets how she was bloody, left for dead (v. 22), and then perpetrates violence on her children, who are bloody as a result (v. 36). So YHWH will now visit bloody fury against Jerusalem (v. 38). It is almost as if the sight of blood should automatically remind Jerusalem of her plight when the LORD rescued her. How awful, then, that the sight of blood on Je-

especially on behalf of the youngest, the weakest, the most helpless, the most victimized child. God's older children, if (when) they are grown and forget the days of their youth — how they were rescued and nurtured — and if (when) they abuse their own (and God's own) children, will find themselves on the other side of God's mercy.[71]

It is at this juncture that one might (re)consider the divine curses that threaten children (e.g., Deut. 28:54-57). Via the metaphoric lens these might be seen as *hyper*-curses: a way to shock the Israelites into an awareness of the severity of their wrongdoing and the profundity of their imminent punishment insofar as God's preferred concern — the littlest children — are here targeted. These hyper-curses show them that they *must* change their ways — if for no other reason than for the sake of their children! It is worth recalling that these types of curses are typically set in covenant contexts, where the parent-child metaphor is often at work.

Israel-Perceptions

The fact that it is the child, Israel, who presents and preserves these God-depictions says much about Israel itself. This is, after all, how Israel perceived and represented its LORD. That being granted, the parent-child metaphor also has direct bearing on Israel's self-understanding and self-representation. The world-creating lens of the parent-child metaphor means that all of Israel's life with God can be seen through it from both sides of the relationship. Here, too, a full presentation lies outside the scope of this essay; space permits mention of only two significant dyads.

1. *Special (firstborn) child* and *one of many children*. Israel is YHWH's *first-born* — it is special, favored, the recipient of unusual care and attention.[72] But

---

rusalem's own children — at her own hand — does nothing of the sort. Note also the tragic cycle of abuse recounted in verse 45.

71. Perhaps the spy debacle and the shift from old to new generation belong in this discussion (see Num. 13:1–14:45). Though no mistreatment of the children is mentioned, the faithless generation does use them in their argument: the children, they lament, will become booty (Num. 14:3). YHWH's response is to see that the children do nothing of the sort: "But your toddlers, whom you said would become war-booty, I will bring them in, and they will know the land that you have despised" (v. 31).

72. In ancient Israel primogeniture included preferential status that was manifested in a double portion of property, a special blessing from the father, and fatherly succession as the next head of household (Philip J. King and Lawrence E. Stager, *Life in Biblical Israel*, Library of Ancient Israel [Louisville: Westminster John Knox, 2001], pp. 47-48; de Vaux, *Ancient Israel*, pp. 41-42).

the very language of "firstborn child" suggests that there are *other children* who also belong to the LORD. God has "other stories," other children who are "not of this fold" (cf. John 10:16).[73] Child Israel lives in this tension: special and privileged as eldest child, but always in the presence of other children, younger ones, who threaten and compete for parental favor in various ways.[74]

2. *In need (immature)* and *growing up (maturing)*. Israel's self-presentation as a child and the self-understanding that comes by means of this metaphor constitutes a profound confession of immaturity, need for further growth, and dependent status. To return to the examples already mentioned: (a) the murmuring narratives witness an Israel that realizes (after the fact) that things were different prior to Sinai. It could get away with more back then. Following Sinai, its murmurings are not acceptable. A new stage has been reached. It is time to grow up, take more responsibility, especially given the repeated parental provision of food and drink, deliverance and care. Similarly, (b) in prophetic passages of judgment, Israel presents itself as the rebellious child, in need of parental correction, even discipline.[75] In still other places — (c) the Psalms come to mind — child Israel clings to its parent, refusing to be separated, refusing to be silenced, insisting on saying the parent's name, over and over again if necessary, until it is heard, until its questions are answered.[76]

---

73. See Carol Meyers, *Exodus*, New Cambridge Bible Commentary (New York: Cambridge University Press, 2005), p. 62. For some intriguing texts, see Deuteronomy 2:1-25; 4:19; 32:8; Amos 9:7; Isaiah 19:19-25; and the discussion in Patrick D. Miller, "God's Other Stories: On the Margins of Deuteronomic Theology," in Miller, *Israelite Religion and Biblical Theology: Collected Essays*, Journal for the Study of the Old Testament — Supplement Series 267 (Sheffield: Sheffield Academic Press, 2000), pp. 593-602.

74. See the problems between the firstborn and the younger son throughout Genesis (e.g., 4:1-16 [Cain and Abel]; 16:1-15 and 21:1-21 [Ishmael and Isaac]; 25:19-34 and 27:1-40 [Jacob and Esau]) and beyond. For discussion, see further Frederick E. Greenspahn, *When Brothers Dwell Together: The Preeminence of Younger Siblings in the Hebrew Bible* (New York: Oxford University Press, 1994); Fewell, *The Children of Israel*, pp. 43-53; Levenson, *The Death and Resurrection of the Beloved Son*.

75. On discipline, see the essay by William P. Brown in the present volume. Note also Tasker, *Ancient Near Eastern Literature*, p. 135, who points out that the parallelism at work in Proverbs 3:12 connects correction with favor. "[T]he importance of the association is that it qualifies the concept of correction-discipline and removes it from the realm of abusive father-child relationships by linking it to an everlasting covenant based on concepts of . . . mercy and truth . . . love and delight." Whether it is the poetics of Proverbs 3:12 alone that does this or the power of the macro-metaphorical lens and its relation to other, more positive sentiments, is, however, open for discussion.

76. See Ludwig Köhler, *Hebrew Man*, trans. P. R. Ackroyd (German orig., 1953; New York: Abingdon, 1956), pp. 68-69 on children's insistent and insatiable question-asking. See also the essay by Patrick D. Miller in the present volume.

Surely, if God is a parent who carries children through the wilderness (Deut. 1:31), who lifts them to God's cheek (Hos. 11:4) — surely that kind of parent will listen to this child's voice!

Even as it acknowledges immaturity by means of the parent-child metaphor, Israel also portrays itself as in process and maturing. Human maturation does not happen overnight, not even over many years. So the metaphor confesses, on the one hand, and indicts on the other. It indicts because it chastens the overbearing parent.[77] Children cannot understand everything — Israel admits that. Shouldn't God admit it too? Children are not capable of everything — Israel admits that. Shouldn't God admit it too? God gets tired, impatient, frustrated — Israel understands that (see above). But doesn't that mean that God should pause before punishing? After all, God is dealing with a *child*, one that is maturing, to be sure, but one that is still in need, still dependent — in a word, still a child — and God cares for children, especially small, weak, and vulnerable children. At this point, God's quality of being "slow to anger" (Exod. 34:6; Num. 14:18; Jon. 4:2; Nah. 1:3; Sir. 5:4) takes on increased significance.

In these examples (and others like them), the parent-child metaphor is shown to work its power on both the human community and the divine partner. One further example of this, developed more extensively below, can be briefly mentioned here: maturing Israel is given increased responsibilities, as is the case with any developing child. A process of independence might be traced; at the very least, God's use of human agency in Israel (and beyond) indicates that God and Israel are *inter*dependent — like any and every other family unit.

(M)other Metaphors

The parent-child macro-metaphor is obviously quite productive. It has had an especially lively reception in its gendered form as that of father-son. Most of the passages recounted above are crafted in this way. But several are not. In fact, the metaphor is not always explicitly marked for gender. This indicates that the male/father version of the metaphor is, in truth, *yet another macro-metaphor* that has been layered onto the macro-metaphor of

---

77. One might compare the UN Convention on the Rights of the Child article 31:1, which provides for the right of the child "to rest and leisure, to engage in play and recreational activities appropriate to the age of the child" — that is, to truly be a child and not a "miniature adult." Note Tasker, *Ancient Near Eastern Literature,* p. 203, who speaks of the child's right to veto.

parent-child. The divine parent in Exodus 4 is not explicitly gendered by means of a "father" term. The same is true for Hosea 11. Indeed, there are other metaphors — *mother* metaphors — that should be considered when we take up the parent-child metaphor. When this is done, it becomes apparent that the parent-child metaphor can just as easily be read through the lens of mother-child as that of father-child. This is, of course, most especially true for those passages that explicitly or implicitly invoke God as a mother. Famous here are the passages from Second Isaiah (Isa. 42:14; 45:10-11; 49:15; 66:13), but there are a number of other instances as well (Pss. 22:10-11 [ET 9-10]; 131:1-3; note also Luke 13:34//Matt. 23:37; cf. 2 Esdr. 1:30).[78] In fact, a closer look at the "father" texts demonstrates that several of them employ language that is an amalgam of mother and father imagery (e.g., Deut. 32:18; Jer. 31:20; Ps. 103:13; cf. also 1QH 17.35-36)[79] — underscoring by means of the mixed-metaphorical construction that God is neither mother nor father, male nor female, or at least neither of these exclusively. These are, and remain, *metaphors.*

Be that as it may, if the lens employed for the parent-child macro-metaphor is that of mother and child, many God-depictions are equally understandable if not more so. God's provision of food to Israel in the wilderness, for example, makes perfect sense within the world of mothers and their young.[80] In the wilderness, then, perhaps the parent who carries the child is a mother (cf. Isa. 46:3-4; 63:8-9).[81] Viewing some of these God-depictions through the lens of motherhood rather than fatherhood may "fix" them in some ways and "break" them in others: positive aspects are shown to be equally applicable to mothers; they are not the sole possession of fathers. But the same holds true for negative aspects: mothers are as capable of these as are fathers. But not to worry; even if mothers forget their children, YHWH will

78. Korpel, *A Rift in the Clouds*, pp. 241-42, believes that Moses' statement in Numbers 11:12 figures YHWH as a mother. For the possibility that Psalm 131 was written by a mother, see Patrick D. Miller, *They Cried to the LORD: The Form and Theology of Biblical Prayer* (Minneapolis: Fortress, 1995), pp. 239-43; see also Melody D. Knowles, "A Woman at Prayer: A Critical Note on Psalm 131:2b," *Journal of Biblical Literature* 125 (2006): 385-89.

79. In some of these texts, the maternal aspects are evoked by use of רחם/*rhm*. See note 50 above.

80. See L. Juliana Claassens, *The God Who Provides: Biblical Images of Divine Nourishment* (Nashville: Abingdon, 2004).

81. See the essay by Jacqueline E. Lapsley in the present volume, and also Frederick J. Gaiser, "'I Will Carry and Will Save': The Carrying God of Isaiah 40–66," in *"And God Saw That It Was Good": Essays on Creation and God in Honor of Terence E. Fretheim,* ed. Frederick J. Gaiser and Mark A. Throntveit, Word and World Supplement 5 (St. Paul: Luther Seminary, 2006), pp. 94-102. Gaiser's article demonstrates that the carrying motif is broader than just that of parent.

not forget Israel (Isa. 49:15).[82] That is, as was the case with fathers, YHWH is both like and unlike human mothers.

The existence of mother metaphors expressing the parent-child metaphor demonstrates that the metaphor is capable of more than one reception. The divine parent is not exclusively or irreducibly male; nor is the child invariably a son. The father-son version is just that: one version that must come in — like any metaphor — for modification and critique given the existence of female-gendered versions. Mother metaphors offer irrefutable proof that father metaphors are metaphorical — no matter how powerful — and that no metaphor is beyond reproach. Still further on this point, it should be recalled that both human and divine partners — not to mention their relationship — are described metaphorically in Scripture in ways that go beyond and that are other than the familial.[83] YHWH can be an animal: a bird or a bear, a lion or a maggot (see Exod. 19:4; Deut. 32:11; Hos. 5:12, 14; 13:8). And Israel can be a cow, a sick body, an abandoned booth, or a vineyard as easily as it can be a child (see Amos 4:1; Isa. 1:6, 8; 5:7).

What all that means is that no one cosmic myth, no one macro-metaphor will do — not even one as pervasive as that of parent-child, whether mother or father, son or daughter. While cosmic myth metaphors are all-consuming and world-constituting, it is for this very reason that they must be critiqued by means of other metaphors. "Metaphoric criticism of metaphors for ultimate commitments is one of the most important kinds of talk we can ever attempt," Booth writes, because "no single myth can give any culture all that is needed both to ensure its survival and to enable its individual inhabitants to build rewarding life stories for themselves"[84] — not even, it should be underscored, a myth that is deeply ingrained and profoundly loved.[85]

Yet even when we grant the veracity of these claims — that other metaphors are important, and that the parent-child metaphor is not above cri-

---

82. As with the father lens, the net can be widely spread with the mother macro-metaphor. For example, it seems to have been the mother's prerogative to name the children (see Joseph Blenkinsopp, "The Family in First Temple Israel," in Perdue et al., *Families in Ancient Israel*, p. 68; de Vaux, *Ancient Israel*, p. 43). What does that mean for those instances in which YHWH (re)names key individuals like Abraham and Sarah (Gen. 17:5, 15), Jacob (to "Israel"; Gen. 32:28), the people of Israel (from "not-my-people" to "children-of-the-living-God"; Hos. 2:1 [ET 1:10]), the city of Jerusalem (to "YHWH is there"; Ezek. 48:35)?

83. Perdue, "The Household," for instance, believes the sphere of kingship is the main alternative to that of the household. But according to Schloen *(The House of the Father)* and others, kingship and family structures are profoundly interrelated in the ancient Near East.

84. Booth, *The Company We Keep*, pp. 335, 350. See also p. 345.

85. It is especially the metaphors we like, repeat, and dwell on that are most tenacious and most potentially destructive (see Booth, *The Company We Keep*, p. 295).

tique — it is nevertheless clear that this particular metaphor remains a macro-metaphor *in* Scripture and *in* human society, *because* of Scripture and *because* of human society. And, because of that, this particular metaphor remains both powerful and potentially dangerous.[86] We would be remiss, then, especially if we care about our children, not to inquire after the ethics of this particular metaphor.

Part IV: The Ethics of the Divine Parent–Human Child Metaphor

If energy expended in engagement equals ethical power (see Part II), then much of ethical significance has already been said in the preceding discussion. There are nevertheless two areas deserving special attention in the ethics of the parent-child metaphor: (1) how it may have functioned in ancient Israelite families and (2) how it might function in contemporary families. In both cases the question is: Did/does the metaphor help people parent better?[87] And if so, how?

---

86. But also potentially (even especially) useful (see further Part IV below). In passing, it might be noted that the usefulness and ubiquity of the parent-child metaphor may commend its necessity at some level. It *can* be used negatively, but also positively; that it *must* be used at all is suggested by the fact that metaphors must not be too idiosyncratic or they will not communicate effectively (see Mary Kinzie, *A Poet's Guide to Poetry* [Chicago: University of Chicago Press, 1999], p. 164).

87. One should be careful not to romanticize the lives of ancient children or the parent-child relationship in antiquity. Images of family closeness — by our standards — are rare (for an exception, see depictions of the royal family in Egyptian art of the Amarna Age). It is widely acknowledged that children occupied the bottom rung of ancient societies and were largely powerless vis-à-vis the near absolute authority of their parents and other adults (see Joseph A. Grassi, "Child, Children," in *The Anchor Bible Dictionary*, 6 vols., ed. David Noel Freedman et al. (New York: Doubleday, 1992), 1:905; Blenkinsopp, "The Family in First Temple Israel," pp. 66-68; Köhler, *Hebrew Man*, pp. 59-62). Artistic depictions often portray children as "miniature adults," and we know of cruel, physical means of punishment and education in antiquity (see Prov. 13:24; 22:15; 23:13; Sir. 30:1, 12; and the essay by William P. Brown in the present volume). With these caveats duly entered, it should nevertheless be stressed that other images of children are known in Scripture (see especially Isa. 11:8-9; Zech. 8:5). Children were valued, pregnancy was a time for rejoicing, and birth was an occasion to celebrate (see Perdue, "The Israelite and Early Jewish Family," p. 171; de Vaux, *Ancient Israel*, p. 470; King and Stager, *Life in Biblical Israel*, p. 41; Grassi, "Child, Children," p. 904; and the essay by Terence E. Fretheim in the present volume).

The Metaphorical Ethics Back Then

The evidence pertaining to the impact of the metaphor on Israelite parents is mostly circumstantial, barring the discovery of a text that clearly depicts a reflex of God's benevolent parenting activities in a human familial context.[88] That being granted, the metaphor can be read "historically," investigated with reference to socio-political (i.e., familial) realities.[89] What social order permitted, authorized, and made sense of the parent-child metaphor? How does the metaphor reflect sociological realities "on the ground"? One can then investigate the instances of the metaphor for potential reflexes in "real life." One possible correlation: when YHWH is depicted as a man *('îš)* carrying his son (Deut. 1:31; cf. Hos. 11:4), it may be an indication that Israelite fathers (and mothers) — some of them at any rate — did the same. The parent-child metaphor thus casts light on theology and theological anthropology (perceptions of God and Israel) but also on real family dynamics.[90] There is a synergy of sorts in the metaphor between theology and anthropology, psychology and sociology.

88. The closest non-biblical analogue of which I am aware is the presentation of *Tkmn-w-šnm's* treatment of his father El (see Manfred Dietrich, Oswald Loretz, and Joachín Sanmartín, *The Cuneiform Alphabetic Texts from Ugarit, Ras Ibn Hani, and Other Places* [hereafter *KTU*], 2nd enl. ed. [Münster: Ugarit-Verlag, 1995], 1.114:18-22) in light of the description of the "ideal" son in the Aqhat text from Ugarit (*KTU* 1.17 i 23-33, 42-48; ii 1-9, 14-23). The parallel is inexact insofar as the parent and child here are both divine, though the list of filial duties in Aqhat applies to human children. The list may be translated as follows: "Bless him, Bull, El my father,/Prosper him, Creator of Creatures./Let him have a son in his house,/Offspring within his palace,/To set up his Ancestor's stela,/The sign of his Sib in the sanctuary;/To rescue his smoke from the Underworld,/To protect his steps from the Dust;/To stop his abusers' spite,/To drive his troublers away;/To grasp his arm when he's drunk,/To support him when sated with wine;/To eat his portion in Baal's house,/His share in the house of El;/To daub his roof when there's [mu]d,/To wash his stuff when there's dirt" (Simon B. Parker, "Aqhat," in *Ugaritic Narrative Poetry*, ed. Simon B. Parker, SBL Writings of the Ancient World 9 [Atlanta: Scholars Press, 1997], pp. 52-53). For discussion, see Schloen, *The House of the Father*, pp. 343-45, 352; A. van Selms, *Marriage and Family Life in Ugaritic Literature* (London: Luzac, 1954), pp. 100-103; and David P. Wright, *Ritual in Narrative: The Dynamics of Feasting, Mourning, and Retaliation Rites in the Ugaritic Tale of Aqhat* (Winona Lake: Eisenbrauns, 2001), pp. 48-69, who thinks the list is synecdochic.

89. Cf. Booth, *The Company We Keep*, p. 335: "Whenever we look closely at any powerful cluster of metaphors, we can infer from it the maker's world"; and Schloen, *The House of the Father*, p. 350: "the programs of action evident in Ugaritic literary texts are best explained in terms of a patrimonial conception of the social order. . . . These programs of action are thus subplots within a larger plot formed by the typical lifecourse of the ideal (male) protagonist."

90. This kind of analysis is facilitated by metaphorical constructions in which the source domain is real, knowable, and derived from common, lived experience (as, e.g., in Deut. 1:31). In other constructions, with different source domains, analysis is more difficult. But note Schloen, *The House of the Father*, p. 356, who finds the relationship of the Ugaritic gods El and Baal to

If so, the parent-child metaphor can be seen as both descriptive of and (potentially) prescriptive for actual parent-child relationships in ancient Israel. The latter item makes it imperative that we investigate "negative" aspects of the metaphor because the stakes are so high. Given negative instances, their prescriptive potential, and possible deleterious outcome scenarios, we need to work hard to uncover and critique the metaphor even as we work equally hard to reclaim its best possible outcomes. Again, some steps toward critique and reclamation are evident in the preceding discussion. But, given the extent and power of the parent-child metaphor, there is more work to be done and much grist for the ethical mill. As but one example, we might consider the role of instruction.[91] Could the role of Israelite parents in the (religious) instruction of their children, especially as that is emphasized in Deuteronomy, be a reflection on and the result of the divine instruction found throughout Scripture itself (even and especially in Deuteronomy)? If so, then, as parent YHWH teaches child Israel, so Israelite parents instruct their children.[92] Moreover, the fact that the divine instruction in Deuteronomy so often concerns life and well-being, not to mention care for others, including persons who lie outside of the immediate kinship structure (e.g., debt slaves, widows, fatherless children, etc.), is no small ethical point.[93]

As another example, consider Proverbs 19:18 (NRSV):

Discipline your children [*bnk*] while there is hope;
do not set your heart on their destruction.

In the human family, this instruction sounds like encouragement for parents to imitate YHWH as the long-suffering parent painted in several passages by means of the parent-child metaphor (see above). Or, via the mother-child version of the metaphoric lens, one might note that in Isaiah 66 the consolation mother Jerusalem offers corresponds in no small way to the consolation mother YHWH extends:

---

nevertheless capture "fundamental experiences of fatherhood and sonship and their dynamic interrelation that constituted the social world of those who sacrificed to these gods, heard and recited the myth, and wrote it down."

91. On education/instruction, see King and Stager, *Life in Biblical Israel*, pp. 45-47; de Vaux, *Ancient Israel*, pp. 48-50; Perdue, "The Israelite and Early Jewish Family," p. 190; Köhler, *Hebrew Man*, pp. 68-69; and Patrick D. Miller's essay in the present volume. It is apparent that both mothers and fathers were active in education (Prov. 1:8; 6:20; de Vaux, *Ancient Israel*, p. 49).

92. See William P. Brown's essay in the present volume and his comparison of the father's teaching in Proverbs 6:21-22 with the Shema in Deuteronomy 6:6-9.

93. Perdue, "The Israelite and Early Jewish Family," pp. 171-72; see also the essays by Jacqueline E. Lapsley and by Walter Brueggemann in the present volume.

[Mother Jerusalem]

that you may nurse and be satisfied
    from her [Jerusalem's] consoling [√*nḥm*] breast;
that you may drink deeply with delight
    from her glorious bosom
For thus says the LORD:

. . .

[Mother YHWH]

As a mother comforts [√*nḥm*] her child,
so I will comfort [√*nḥm*] you;
you shall be comforted [√*nḥm*] in Jerusalem.

(Isa. 11:11-13, NRSV)

The Metaphorical Ethics Now

At many points the preceding discussion has drifted into, or revealed potential for, today's parents and children. Ultimately, for our children's sake, it is
the contemporary significance of the parent-child metaphor that is most important. Can it, does it, help us parent better? Many parents would have to admit that they have said things to their children like "I should only have to tell
you *once.*" But in the play of the parent-child metaphor, that dictum is simply
not true. If God tells God's children the same thing more than once — at
times over and over again, even if to no avail — why do we imagine that our
parenting will be "better" than that?

Many writers have argued that the image of God as a parent does (and
should) impact human parenting.[94] The point is especially pressing in the
light of studies that have demonstrated the effect — both direct and indirect
— that parents have on children's images of God.[95] These two — the divine
and human parent, as well as the metaphorical and real human child — are
conjoined, for better for worse.

But which is it, better or worse? There are people who have had poor par-

94. E.g., Miller, "God as Father," p. 353; Miller, *Calling God "Father,"* esp. pp. 55-70; Tasker,
Ancient Near Eastern Literature, pp. 5, 158, 195-97; Perdue, "The Household," p. 252; Fretheim,
The Suffering of God, p. 10. See also Walter Brueggemann's essay in the present volume. For the
gods as paradigms for human parenting in Greco-Roman sources, see Margaret Y. MacDonald's
essay in the present volume.

95. Dickie et al., "Parent-Child Relationships and Children's Images of God," esp. pp. 25, 31,
42.

ents and, as a result, have profound difficulty with God(-images). Given the awesome power and virtually unlimited extension of the parent-child macro-metaphor, what then? Here again the importance of ethical engagement, "metaphoric criticism," is underscored and leads to several responses. First, the perduring power of the parent-child metaphor demonstrates that it works because it has been lived.[96] Second, it has been lived in positive, not just negative ways — that is, it has been lived *well* — and this is true quite apart from the human source domain of the metaphor. Despite poor parenting, that is, some have found in God the "perfect substitute attachment figure" for an imperfect caregiver.[97] Booth points out that "surviving metaphors survive because . . . they continue to uncover truth about us."[98] There is something true about the parent-child metaphor, in part because it reflects the social reality of the family — a reality that remains crucial for the well-being, health, and future of children — even though that social reality has often fallen short.[99] So, while the parent-child metaphor is fraught with peril and checkered with actual disasters — as all metaphors are — it is not uniformly or unequivocally so. We must resist "the temptation to make global claims when what we need are discriminations. . . . Come, let us abandon these general moves and start talking, first about *this* one, and then about *that* one."[100] And let us do so armed with the full range of metaphors from the entirety of Scripture and how these not only strengthen and reinforce but also modify and critique the parent-child metaphor. The result may be an interpretation of the text as the best text possible and an understanding of God as the best possible parent[101] — one that inspires us to behave similarly toward our children.

96. Cf. Booth, *The Company We Keep*, pp. 350-52, 368.

97. Dickie et al., "Parent-Child Relationships and Children's Images of God," esp. pp. 25-26, 31, 42.

98. Booth, *The Company We Keep*, p. 368.

99. Bellamy, ed., *The State of the World's Children 2005*, p. 15: "Families form the first line of defence for children: the further away children are from their families, the more vulnerable they are to risks." Cf. the Convention on the Rights of the Child, preamble and article 7: the right to know and be raised by one's parents. For a recent statement on the importance of good fathering in particular, see Linda J. Waite and William J. Doherty, "Marriage and Responsible Fatherhood: The Social Science Case and Thoughts about a Theological Case," in *Family Transformed: Religion, Values, and Society in American Life*, ed. Steven M. Tipton and John Witte Jr. (Washington, DC: Georgetown University Press, 2005), pp. 143-67.

100. Booth, *The Company We Keep*, pp. 312-14; his italics.

101. For an argument for interpreting the biblical text as "the best text it can be," see Dale Patrick, *The Rhetoric of Revelation in the Hebrew Bible*, Overtures to Biblical Theology (Minneapolis: Fortress, 1999), p. 193, and the literature cited there. For the "good enough" parent, see note 65 above.

I conclude this section on ethics — ancient and modern — by considering an interesting facet of the parent-child metaphor that has not garnered much discussion, but which, in the end, may contain its greatest ethical power. That facet is related to this simple fact: parents age, and children grow up and, in time, become parents to their own children. And on it goes. What this means is that when the parent-child metaphor is utilized, unless it is completely frozen,[102] it carries with it implications of family dynamics that are both synchronic and diachronic. The former means that different members of the family play different roles and interact in various ways; the latter means that these family roles change and develop, again in various ways and through time, as the members mature and age (cf. 1 Sam. 2:26; Luke 2:52; Hos. 11:1; 1 Cor. 13:11).[103] In ancient Israel, as children grew up, they helped with the family's work, apprenticed themselves to their parents' tasks, and continued those tasks after the parents' death.[104] On the human level, that is, children replace their parents in no small way — as in the epigraph at the beginning of this essay from Sirach 30:4-5 (cf. also Ps. 127:3-5). That text, manifestly about *human* fathers and sons, takes on a different hue when viewed through the lens of the divine parent–human child metaphor. The child, "one like" the parent, is apprenticed to the parent's work and learns from the parent's instruction — all of that begins to place Israel's son- and daughtership in a distinctly different light. It begins to look like it has as much to do with mission and God's purposes as it does with Israel's election or status. There are, of course, connections to both status and election in the parent-child metaphor.[105] In Egypt, it was the pharaohs who called themselves the gods' sons; at Ugarit, use of the epithet "son of El (god)" for humans was apparently reserved for kings.[106] In this light, child Israel begins to look not just like an heir, but like an heir *to the throne*. But even in the royal house there are pro-

---

102. Cf. Schloen, *The House of the Father*, p. 356, on the frozen nature of the Ugaritic pantheon "around which the narrative must flow." In my judgment, the pluralistic nature of the metaphorical world of Scripture works against any similar freezing.

103. The maturational dynamic implicit in the parent-child metaphor speaks against both Freud's and Daly's concern about the metaphor confining humans to infantile states (see note 10 above).

104. For data on work in ancient Israel, see Carol Meyers, "The Family in Early Israel," in Perdue et al., *Families in Ancient Israel*, pp. 27-30; King and Stager, *Life in Biblical Israel*, p. 46; Perdue, "The Israelite and Early Jewish Family," pp. 189-90; Pamela J. Scalise, "'I Have Produced a Man with the LORD': God as Provider of Offspring in Old Testament Theology," *Review and Expositor* 91 (1994): 579-81.

105. See Tasker, *Ancient Near Eastern Literature*, p. 175; Melnyk, "When Israel Was a Child," p. 259.

106. Tasker, *Ancient Near Eastern Literature*, p. 49; Korpel, *A Rift in the Clouds*, p. 253.

found connections to mission. It was, after all, the duty of kings in the ancient Near East to care for orphans and to judge the case of widows.[107] Is it unexpected, then, to find such a concern often on the lips of YHWH's intermediaries, the prophets? The divine parent, who is also the just ruler, requires correlate behavior from the royal offspring. It is thus not surprising to find another child of God, later, saying that he "must be about his Father's business" (Luke 2:49; cf. Matt. 5:44-45).

God's (grown) child must model parental care for other children not only because the child is *God's* child, about God's business, but also because the child knows that *all* children are God's children.[108] Recall, after all, that the child prays "*our* Father," not "*my* Father"; and remember that this child is the *firstborn*, not the *only child.* Among other things, these observations suggest that care for children must extend beyond one's own biological children. And so, in this regard, even those without biological children can (and must) still be loving "parents" toward children.[109] The concern for the orphan in Scripture, commanded by the divine (adoptive) parent and modeled by the children, makes the very same point.[110] For the grown child of the LORD, parental care must be imitated whether through parenting proper, adoption, surrogate parenthood, or just plain old mentorship. Whatever the case, it clearly takes a metaphor to raise a child.

The family dynamic in diachronic mode means that child Israel develops, but so does Israel's divine parent, as does the relationship between these two. Possible connections at this point between the parent-child metaphor and

107. See Korpel, *A Rift in the Clouds,* p. 238; further, Moshe Weinfeld, *Social Justice in Ancient Israel and in the Ancient Near East* (Minneapolis: Fortress, 1995). These social-justice aspects of the parent-child metaphor obviate Daly's critique of the metaphor as devoid of such (*Beyond God the Father,* p. 24).

108. See note 73 above and the discussion there; also Tasker, *Ancient Near Eastern Literature,* pp. 198, 207; Melnyk, "When Israel Was a Child," p. 246. For the capacity of beautiful things — like an adorable child — to exert pressure on observers to care for them and to extend such care to other items of the same category (i.e., in this case, other children) and beyond, see Elaine Scarry, *On Beauty and Being Just* (Princeton: Princeton University Press, 1999).

109. Cf. P. A. H. de Boer, *Fatherhood and Motherhood in Israelite and Judean Piety* (Leiden: Brill, 1974), on various authority figures as "mothers" and "fathers" in ancient Israel. Note also the presentation of apostolic figures as parents, with their churches as their children. See Beverly R. Gaventa, "Our Mother St. Paul: Toward the Recovery of a Neglected Theme," in *A Feminist Companion to Paul,* ed. Amy-Jill Levine with Marianne Blickenstaff (Cleveland: Pilgrim Press, 2004), pp. 85-97; and her essay in the present volume. Note also de Vaux, *Ancient Israel,* p. 49, on calling priests "father" — a practice as early as Judges 17:10; 18:19.

110. See Exodus 22:21-25; Deuteronomy 14:28-29; 16:9-11, 13-14; 24:17, 19-21; 26:12; 27:19; Proverbs 23:10; etc. Perdue, "The Israelite and Early Jewish Family," p. 193, believes orphans were "children . . . from broken families that no longer provided nurture and protection" for them.

other realities are several. Steven A. Rogers, for example, has attempted to map human development onto the portrayal of God's relationship with the main figures in Genesis.[111] His schema appears too rigid and imposed, but his ability to trace stages of maturation in the parent-child relationship — including separation, individuation, and reintegration — between God and the ancestors is evocative. With each maturational stage, God seems to recede, giving more control to the human "children." That is, the parent-child metaphor, with its associated dynamism, may help to explain the slow disappearance and silence of God that has sometimes been noted in Scripture.[112] In Rogers's words, with reference to the ancestors:

> Like the parent of an adult, God's silence may be taken as respect for Joseph's psychic integration and spiritual health. This does not mean that God is inactive, but rather that God's activity is subtle and designed to operate behind human events to support and sustain Joseph's psychic integration, instead of directing and guiding it, as occurs with Abraham and even Jacob. . . . What this requires for God and any parent relating with an adult child is a comfort with paradox and metaphors.[113]

This includes, it would seem, comfort with metaphors of the family and of the maturing relationship between a parent and child with its various paradoxes (and sub-metaphors). These paradoxes encompass, on the one hand, the child who grows into an adult and continues the parent's legacy, all the while remaining the parent's child; and, on the other hand, the "good enough" parent who remains benevolent and of use to the child, largely by not-retaliation, despite the child's attempt to control the parent (cf. Prov. 19:18).[114]

Among other things, then, *growth, mission,* and *purpose* are at work in the dynamics of the parent-child metaphor. Carrying on the parental legacy is part of what is expected of children, including the children of Israel. A well-known rabbinic story gets at these issues in a delightful way:

111. Steven A. Rogers, "The Parent-Child Relationship as an Archetype for the Relationship Between God and Humanity in Genesis," *Pastoral Psychology* 50 (2002): 377-85; this is not completely unrelated to Freud's work in *Moses and Monotheism.* See also Wilcoxen, "Some Anthropocentric Aspects," esp. p. 350.

112. See especially Jack Miles, *God: A Biography* (New York: Knopf, 1995); Richard Elliott Friedman, *The Disappearance of God: A Divine Mystery* (Boston: Little, Brown, and Company, 1995).

113. Rogers, "The Parent-Child Relationship," p. 383.

114. These latter notions are taken from D. W. Winnicott, "The Use of an Object and Relating through Identifications," in Winnicott, *Playing and Reality* (1971; London: Routledge, 2005), pp. 115-27.

Again [Rabbi Eliezar] said to them: "If the *halachah* agrees with me, let it be proved from Heaven!" Whereupon a Heavenly Voice cried out: "Why do you dispute with R. Eliezer, seeing that in all matters the *halachah* agrees with him!" But R. Joshua arose and exclaimed: "*It is not in heaven* (Deut 30:12)." What did he mean by this? — Said R. Jeremiah: "That the Torah had already been given at Mount Sinai; we pay no attention to a Heavenly Voice, because Thou has long since written in the Torah at Mount Sinai, *After the majority must one incline* (Exod 23:2)." R. Nathan met Elijah and asked him: "What did the Holy One, Blessed be He, do in that hour? — He laughed [with joy], he replied, saying, 'My sons have defeated Me, My sons have defeated Me.'" (*b. B. Metzi'a* 59b)

In addition to maturation and growth, there is conflict of a kind in this account, though in this case the halakic contest is in service to the purposes of Torah, and God is said to be delighted that the children have become even more adept (!) in Torah than God. Whatever the case, at all times we should remember that children come to grips with their parents in different (and sometimes difficult) ways as they mature and age. The lament process, especially as encapsulated in the Psalms, both facilitates and attests to such maturation on the part of the pray-er. On the other side of lament, everything looks different (see, e.g., Psalm 30) — including God, the self, and the enemy. That different perspective may be quite sobering, even if it is, despite that fact, liberating in its own way. Sobriety and a lack of easy or happy endings is the way things are, sometimes, with lament. And that is the way they are, sometimes, with the complexities of family life. We should not be surprised, then, to see reflexes of that same dynamic worked out in the God-Israel metaphor, whether that is in the lament psalms or, more broadly, elsewhere in Scripture (e.g., Job or Ecclesiastes) where disappointment with the divine "father" reaches its apex (better: nadir).

But even then, the metaphor continues to operate. It is, after all, a *comprehensive* macro-metaphor. Even in the midst of parental disappointment comes the old commandment — heard afresh, perhaps, in a new metaphoric register: "Honor your father and mother, *as the* LORD *your God commanded you,* so that your days may be long *and that it may go well with you* in the land that the LORD your God is giving you" (Exod. 20:12; Deut. 5:16; cf. Mal. 1:6).[115]

---

115. Words in italics are found only in the Deuteronomic version. Scholars have long noted the connection between honoring (√*kbd*) one's parents and the honor due to the LORD (note *kĕbôd* YHWH, "the glory of the LORD"). Both of the Deuteronomic additions tie the command closely to other passages where obedience is mandated by God and directed toward God. King and Stager (*Life in Biblical Israel,* p. 42) believe that the law concerning rebellious children

One of the things children were to do in ancient Israel was honor their parents. One of the things children still do now, sometimes, is forgive them. There is more than just *growth and conflict* in the parent-child dynamic, then. There is also the possibility for *resolution and reconciliation.* Perhaps it is no coincidence, then, that, in the end, YHWH commends Job four times as "my servant" (Job 42:7-8) and that Ecclesiastes concludes with an epilogue urging proper worship of God and obedience to the commandments (Eccles. 12:13).

Conclusion

The present study has suggested that there is (and should be) something similar and familiar, perhaps even more than that, between the God-human relationship and that of the human parent and child. As demonstrated above, the metaphor of God-as-our-parent/us-as-God's-children casts light on depictions of God in Scripture, depictions of Israel in Scripture, and depictions of children in Scripture. Even more importantly and profoundly, it suggests that human parents must strain to the highest and best levels of that metaphorical construction so that their parenting, care, and nurture of their children is indeed worthy of the divine image. If so, this would be no small contribution of Scripture's parent-child metaphor to and for all children everywhere, including the children in our own midst, who are so often neglected, victimized, and abused.

(Deut. 21:18-21) "underscores the importance of showing gratitude to parents for the care that they have shown their children." The same could also hold true for the Fifth Commandment. Of course, if a parent did not show care to his or her children, keeping the commandment becomes far more complicated. See Walter J. Harrelson, *The Ten Commandments and Human Rights* (Macon: Mercer University Press, 1997), pp. 92-105.

PART II

TEXTS FROM THE NEW TESTAMENT

7   Children in the Gospel of Mark, with Special Attention to Jesus' Blessing of the Children (Mark 10:13-16) and the Purpose of Mark

Judith M. Gundry

This essay will explore the theme of children in Mark by looking at texts in the Gospel where small or young children appear, either as characters in the narrative or as subjects of Jesus' teaching.[1] My exploration will be guided by two questions. First, how does Mark's material on Jesus and children relate to the purpose of his Gospel? Second, what light does Mark shed on views of and practices toward children in early Christianity?

I will argue that Mark depicts Jesus as overcoming the religious and cultural obstacles to embracing children's full and equal participation in the eschatological reign of God, and so motivates the audience of the Gospel likewise to overcome the religious and cultural obstacles to faith in the crucified Jesus and their own participation in the eschatological reign of God.

Introductory Questions

Why and for Whom Did Mark Write His Gospel?

Mark's Gospel is a narrative of Jesus' actions and (to a lesser extent) teaching during his public ministry, ending in his death and the announcement of his resurrection. Scholars today recognize in this narrative a theological slant and

---

1. I use the traditional designation "Mark" for the author of the second Gospel, whose authorship is disputed.

This essay is dedicated to my sons, Nathanael and Aaron.

purpose.[2] Among the suggested purposes are two that are diametrically opposed to each other: (1) Mark writes to correct an understanding of Christian
discipleship solely in terms of power and authority (a "theology of glory" emphasizing the successes of Jesus) by emphasizing discipleship that includes self-
denial and cross-bearing (a "theology of suffering" emphasizing the suffering
of Jesus); (2) Mark writes to overcome the extreme offensiveness of Jesus' suffering and death on a cross by presenting him as powerful, authoritative, wise,
prescient, compassionate, innocent, divinely favored (etc.) and in this way to
encourage acceptance of the early Christian proclamation of the crucified Jesus
as God's Son (Mark 15:39, etc.) and Servant who gave his life "as a ransom for
many" (Mark 10:45). Here I will assume the second view,[3] without denying that
Mark may also have had other purposes in mind.

Mark probably wrote his Gospel for a Roman audience with a strong Gentile component. Scholars differ on whether his audience was already Christian and on the Gospel's precise dating, though a dating sometime in the second half of the first century CE is generally accepted.[4] For such an audience
the early Christian gospel was a tough sell. In the words of Martin Hengel:

> To believe that the one pre-existent[5] Son of the one true God, the mediator
> at creation and the redeemer of the world, had appeared in very recent
> times in out-of-the-way Galilee as a member of the obscure people of the
> Jews, and even worse, had died the death of a common criminal on the
> cross, could only be regarded as a sign of madness.[6]

2. It is beyond the bounds of this essay to address the historical reliability of Mark (for
which see the abundant secondary literature). The following comments should not be construed as making historical claims but as making claims regarding Mark's interpretation of early
Christian tradition about Jesus.

3. For a full-scale argument, see Robert H. Gundry, *Mark: A Commentary on His Apology for
the Cross* (Grand Rapids: Eerdmans, 1993), esp. pp. 1-15, 1022-26. He summarizes: "This gospel is
for people who are afraid to believe in a world that despises weakness and esteems power. The
Jesus of Mark is overpowering. Let the weak find in him their champion, the strong their conqueror" (p. 1026); also Craig A. Evans, *Mark 8:27–16:20*, Word Biblical Commentary 34B (Nashville: T. Nelson, 2001).

4. Some scholars date Mark between 45 and 60 CE, while others prefer a later dating during
the Jewish war ending in the destruction of Jerusalem in 70 CE, or after its destruction.

5. Pre-existence is not a feature of Markan Christology; nevertheless, Hengel's basic point
still stands.

6. Martin Hengel, *The Cross of the Son of God* (London: SCM, 1986), p. 98; cf. pp. 93-102 for
a discussion of common views on crucifixion in the Greco-Roman world. The "word of the
cross" that Christians preached was thus considered "folly" (so, Paul in 1 Cor. 1:18, 23), "mad-
ness" (so, Justin Martyr, *Apology* 1.13.4).

Crucifixion was the worst form of capital punishment imposed by the Romans, reserved for criminals and slaves because of its shamefulness and physical brutality.[7] For this reason, according to the Roman senator and orator Cicero, "the very word 'cross' should be far removed not only from the person of a Roman citizen but also from his thoughts, his eyes, and his ears. For it is not only the actual occurrence of these things or the endurance of them, but also the liability to them, the expectation, even the mere mention of them, that is unworthy of a Roman citizen and a free man" (Cicero, *In Defense of Rabirius* 16).[8]

Though some forms of death in the Greco-Roman world could even be noble, heroic, and glorious,[9] Jesus' death was not so. It was, rather, shameful and repulsive. And early Christians who did obeisance to the one who was crucified thus humiliated themselves in the eyes of others. Such self-humiliation is depicted in a graffito discovered on the Palatine Hill in Rome: a sketch of a worshiper raising his hand toward a figure on a cross with the body of a man and the head of an ass, underneath which is the inscription, "Alexamenos adores god."[10] This graffito is probably the earliest visual representation of Jesus dying on a cross, and it pokes fun at early Christian worship of the crucified Jesus.

Mark thus faced the problem of how to persuade people with such views (or fellow Christians subject to such ridicule)[11] to believe in Jesus and live as his disciples. Mark's Gospel, argues Robert H. Gundry,[12] meets such embarrassment over and criticisms of the crucified Jesus head-on by highlighting Jesus' successes displayed in his public ministry and even his suffering and death itself.[13] Mark's Jesus is magnetic; he draws crowds wherever he goes. He as-

7. Cf. Philippians 2:8; Hebrews 12:2.

8. Cf. also Tacitus *Annals* 15.44.3. Hengel (*The Cross of the Son of God*, p. 97) comments: "The heart of the Christian message, which Paul described as the 'word of the cross' . . . ran counter not only to Roman political thinking, but to the whole ethos of religion in ancient times and in particular to the ideas of God held by educated people."

9. For literary evidence, see Hengel, *The Cross of the Son of God*, pp. 189-220; for visual artistic evidence, see David L. Balch, "Paul's Portrait of Christ Crucified (Gal. 3:1) in Light of Paintings and Sculptures of Suffering and Death in Pompeiian and Roman Houses," in *Early Christian Families in Context: An Interdisciplinary Dialogue*, ed. David L. Balch and Carolyn Osiek (Grand Rapids: Eerdmans, 2003), pp. 84-108.

10. See the reproduction in Balch, "Paul's Portrait of Christ Crucified," p. 104; the original is housed in the Palatine Museum, Rome.

11. On disciples' suffering through persecution in Mark, see Adela Yarbro Collins, *The Beginning of the Gospel: Probings of Mark in Context* (Minneapolis: Fortress, 1992), pp. 66-68.

12. Gundry, *Mark: A Commentary on His Apology for the Cross*.

13. Adela Yarbro Collins ("From Noble Death to Crucified Messiah," *New Testament Studies*

tounds people with his miraculous healings, exorcisms, and authoritative words. He knows the thoughts in others' hearts and minds as well as his own God-given destiny, and he marches resolutely toward Jerusalem to fulfill it. He is the faithful Son who submits to the cross rather than being overtaken by it.

I will argue in the last section of this chapter that Mark's material on children fits into this strategy of overcoming the obstacle of Jesus' crucifixion by presenting him in an attractive and compelling way. But first an overview of Mark's material on children.

What Children Did Mark Include in His Gospel?

Mark does not begin his Gospel with a genealogy of Jesus and a birth narrative (unlike Matthew or Luke). Nor does he give any information on Jesus' childhood (unlike Luke). Mark is not interested in Jesus the infant or the small child but only in Jesus the adult "Son of God."[14] Mark starts with John the Baptist's preparing the way for Jesus' ministry, Jesus' baptism by John, Jesus' temptation in the wilderness, and then proceeds with the narration of Jesus' public ministry, culminating in death and the announcement of his resurrection.

It is in Mark's narrative of Jesus' public ministry that we discover the evangelist's interest in small or young children. Jesus performs miracles for children: he raises Jairus's twelve-year-old daughter from the dead (Mark 5:22-24, 35-43); he exorcizes an evil spirit from the Syrophoenician woman's young daughter (Mark 7:25-30); he casts out a demon causing deafness and muteness from a man's young son (presumably an epileptic, Mark 9:17-29). Jesus hugs a little child to demonstrate for his disciples how to be great in God's kingdom, and he equates their receiving a little child into their care in his name with receiving Jesus himself (Mark 9:33-37). People bring little children to Jesus, and he teaches that they are intended recipients of God's kingdom and examples of entering it, which he demonstrates by hugging them, laying his hands on them, and blessing them (Mark 10:13-16).

The young daughter of Herodias, in striking contrast to the other children in Mark, dances before Herod Antipas at his birthday party and asks him as a

---

40 [1994]: 481-503) argues persuasively that Mark does not try to win over his audience by portraying Jesus' death in the Greek tradition of the noble death. She argues instead that Mark uses a typically Jewish model, focusing on Jesus' death "for our sins" and "according to the Scriptures," which has its own persuasive power.

14. "Son of God" in Mark 1:1 is omitted in some manuscripts, and scholars are divided as to whether it is original here. But the phrase is used elsewhere for Jesus in the Gospel (see Mark 1:11, etc.).

reward for the head of John the Baptist at her mother's instigation; Herod complies (Mark 6:14-29).

The texts noted above share a common vocabulary for small or young children.[15] *Paidion* (the diminutive form of *pais*) occurs at Mark 9:36-37 for a "very young child, infant,"[16] whom Jesus takes, puts in the midst of his disciples, and takes up in his arms. The plural *paidia*, "little children," occurs at 10:13-15 for the children brought to Jesus for blessing and taken up into his arms.[17] The daughter of Jairus is also called *paidion* (5:39-41), as well as *thygatēr*, "daughter" (5:35), and the diminutives *thygatrion*, "little daughter" (5:23), and *korasion*, "little girl" (5:41, 42). Since she is said to be already twelve years old (5:42), the diminutives should be taken to indicate endearment rather than a small child.[18] *Thygatēr*, "daughter" (7:26), and *thygatrion*, "little daughter" (7:25), are also used for the Syrophoenician woman's child.[19] It is uncertain whether this diminutive indicates a small child or endearment. The daughter of Herodias, who dances before Herod, is called *thygatēr*, "daughter" (6:22), and *korasion* (the diminutive of *korē*), "little girl" (6:22, 28). This di-

15. Some Greek words for "child" do not necessarily denote the small or young child — e.g., *teknon* is used for "child" with respect to descent, not age. For a thorough discussion of terms for child/children in the New Testament, see Peter Müller, *In der Mitte der Gemeinde: Kinder im Neuen Testament* (Neukirchen-Vluyn: Neukirchener Verlag, 1992), pp. 165-200.

16. W. Bauer, W. F. Arndt, F. W. Gingrich, and F. W. Danker, *A Greek-English Lexicon of the New Testament and Other Early Christian Literature,* 2nd ed. (Chicago: University of Chicago Press, 2000) (hereafter BAGD), s.v. παιδίον, 2.a, cites Mark 9:36-37; 10:13-14 et al. for the meaning "very young child, infant," which falls under the larger umbrella of *paidion* for a child who is below the age of puberty (for which *pais* can also be used; see BADG, s.v. παῖς, 1); see also Albrecht Oepke (παῖς, παιδίον, παιδάριον, τέκνον, τεκνίον, βρέφος, *Theological Dictionary of the New Testament* [hereafter *TDNT*], ed. Gerhard Kittel and Gerhard Friedrich, trans. Geoffrey W. Bromiley [Grand Rapids: Eerdmans, 1964-76], 5:637) lists evidence supporting the upper age limit for *paidion* as six.

17. William L. Lane (*The Gospel According to Mark,* New International Commentary on the New Testament [Grand Rapids: Eerdmans, 1974], p. 359) thinks that Jesus' action of hugging, or taking up in the arms, suggests that the little children were *very* young. Luke has "infants" (*brephē,* Luke 18:15).

18. With Gundry, *Mark,* p. 275. BADG, s.v. θυγάτριον, notes the use of the diminutive for a daughter of marriageable age.

19. The girl is also referred to metaphorically as one of the "little dogs" (Mark 7:27, *kynarioi,* probably a faded diminutive, or one that has lost its original sense) who eat the crumbs of the children's bread that fall from the table. Jews referred to ritually impure Gentiles as "dogs" because of wild dogs' association with ritual impurity and in connection with the necessity of separation from non-Jews. Joel Marcus (*Mark 1–8,* Anchor Bible Commentary [New York: Doubleday, 2000], p. 464), notes, however, that "dog" sometimes has more positive associations in Old Testament/Jewish tradition and here may denote the righteous Gentile who participates in the end-time blessings promised to Israel.

minutive has been taken to indicate a child of about twelve, who is old enough to dance at a dinner party, but still a child, perhaps of marriageable age.[20] The "son" with a spirit causing deafness and muteness "since child-hood" (*paidiothen,* 9:21) is called *paidion,* "little child" (9:24). Here the diminutive is coupled with a reference to the father — "the father of the little child" (*ho patēr tou paidiou*) — and thus indicates biological relationship, not age. The fact that he is brought by his father to Jesus while not undergoing a seizure may suggest he is unable to come independently and so is still a young child (9:17; cf. the bringing of *little* children to Jesus for blessing, 10:13).[21]

In summary, Mark includes a substantial amount of material on children in his Gospel, and he ties this material together by the use of common terminology. His lack of attention to the children's precise ages, except in one case, suggests a thematic relation among these texts.[22] Taken together, they show small or young children as occupying a significant space in Jesus' public ministry and as forming a motif in Mark's Gospel. Thus, in the following comments, I will treat these texts as mutually interpretive.

What, more specifically, does Mark say about children, and why does he say it? What perspective does he bring to bear on this material, and to what end? How might Mark's Gospel affect the way his readers thought about or related to children? I will now turn to these questions.

Children in the Gospel of Mark

And they were bringing little children to him, that he might touch them; and the disciples rebuked them.[23] But when Jesus saw it he was indignant, and said to them, "Let the little children come to me, do not hinder them;

20. Roger Aus, *Water into Wine and the Beheading of John the Baptist,* Brown Judaic Studies 150 (Atlanta: Scholars, 1988), p. 49. Ross S. Kraemer ("Implicating Herodias and Her Daughter in the Death of John the Baptizer: A (Christian) Theological Strategy?" *Journal of Biblical Literature* 125 (2006): 321-49 (p. 335 with n. 34) discusses various possibilities for her age, but favors "a relatively young child."

21. The term *neaniskos* at Mark 14:51 can refer to a "young man" as old as forty (see *Exegetical Dictionary of the New Testament* [hereafter *EDNT*], ed. H. Balz and G. Schneider [Grand Rapids: Eerdmans, 1990-93], vol. 2, s.v. νεανίσκος), so I have excluded this text from the present discussion.

22. The terminology used does not reflect an understanding of precise stages in a child's development, as noted by James Francis, "Children and Childhood in the New Testament," in *The Family in Theological Perspective,* ed. Stephen C. Barton (Edinburgh: T&T Clark, 1996), p. 67.

23. "Them" (*autous*) can refer either to the children or to those bringing them. The Greek construction is unclear.

for to such as these belongs the kingdom of God. Truly, I say to you, whoever does not receive the kingdom of God like a child shall not enter it." And he took them in his arms and blessed them, laying his hands upon them. (Mark 10:13-16)

Mark 10:13-16 (par. Matt. 19:13-15; Luke 18:15-17) will be the focus of my discussion. This text is particularly significant in that it combines Jesus' *teaching about* little children and the kingdom of God and Jesus' *ministry to* children and shows the relationship between them. This teaching and ministry are occasioned by the disciples' rebuke of those bringing little children to Jesus on the way to Jerusalem, and they are set in contrast to the disciples' views and actions. Mark uses this contrast to develop both his portrait of Jesus and the motif of children in his Gospel. While closely examining Mark 10:13-16, I will weave into the discussion other Markan texts on children at appropriate points.[24]

Although a considerable amount of scholarly attention has already been devoted to Mark 10:13-16,[25] some questions remain insufficiently answered. For example, how do the intentions of the people bringing children to Jesus — "that he might touch them" — relate to Jesus' actions — hugging, laying on hands, and blessing them — and how do these actions relate to his teaching that the kingdom of God belongs to children and that one must receive it as a child does? How do the disciples' rebuke and Jesus' indignant response shed light on his actions and teaching? Further, how does Jesus' healing and exorcistic activity for individual children in Mark 5:22-24, 35-43; 7:25-30; 9:17-29 relate to his actions and teaching during the encounter with a group of children in Mark 10:13-16? After addressing these questions I will return to the matter of how these texts may contribute to the overall purpose of the Gospel.

---

24. Cf. also my discussion of Mark 9:33-37 in "The Least and the Greatest: Children in the New Testament," in *The Child in Christian Thought*, ed. Marcia J. Bunge (Grand Rapids: Eerdmans, 2001), pp. 29-60 (esp. pp. 43-46), and "'To Such as These Belongs the Reign of God': Jesus and Children," *Interpretation* 56 (2000): 469-80 (esp. pp. 475-78).

25. Matthew Black, "The Markan Parable of the Child in the Midst," *Expository Times* 59 (1947-48): 14-16; F. A. Schilling, "What Means the Saying about Receiving the Kingdom of God as a Little Child?" *Expository Times* 77 (1965-66): 56-58; W. Stegemann, "Lasset die Kinder zu mir kommen: Sozialgeschichtliche Aspekte des Kinderevangeliums," in *Traditionen der Befreiung*, vol. 1, ed. Willi Schottroff and Wolfgang Stegemann (Gelnhausen/Berlin: Stein, 1980), pp. 114-44; Ernest Best, *Following Jesus* (Sheffield: JSOT Press, 1981), pp. 106-9; Andreas Lindemann, "Die Kinder und die Gottesherrschaft," *Wort und Dienst* NF 17 (1983): 77-88; J. Duncan M. Derrett, "Why Jesus Blessed the Children (Mk 10:13-16 par.)," *Novum Testamentum* 25 (1983): 1-18; Ernest Best, "Mk 10.13-16: The Child as Model Recipient," in *Disciples and Discipleship: Studies in the Gospel According to St. Mark* (Edinburgh: T&T Clark, 1986), pp. 80-97; further literature cited in the notes below.

Children as Heirs of the Kingdom of God

Mark 10:13-16 starts out as apparently another miracle story. People bring little children to Jesus "that he might touch them." Jesus' touching people, or their touching him, has led to healing for the sick earlier in Mark (3:10; 5:27-34, 41-42; 6:56; 7:32-35; 8:22-25).[26] One of these was a child: Jesus took Jairus's dead daughter by the hand and raised her from the dead (Mark 5:22-24, 35-43). Moreover, Jesus has already performed exorcisms for children: the Syrophoenician woman's daughter (Mark 7:25-30) and the boy with a deaf/mute spirit (Mark 9:17-29). The people's motive in 10:13, "that he might touch them," and the previous miracles for children lead the reader of Mark to expect more miracles here.

But Mark mentions no miracles. Instead, Jesus hugs the little children,[27] lays his hands on them, and blesses them. Despite the shift from the previous healings and exorcisms for children to the present hugging, hand-laying, and blessing, James Francis describes our text as the "culmination" of Jesus' ministry to children.[28] Francis does not elaborate, but what this culmination entails, and how Mark 10:13-16 can have this function, requires explanation.

In Mark, Jesus' miracles for children and others, consisting in healing the sick and exorcising evil spirits, are signs of the presence of God's reign in and through him. He opens his public ministry with the announcement that "the kingdom of God is at hand" (Mark 1:15) and then inaugurates that kingdom through mighty deeds in which divine blessings associated with the end-time come to pass.

"The kingdom of God" (*hē basileia tou Theou*) refers either to God's ruling activity (thus the alternate translation, "the rule of God") or the sphere of God's rule. It "is at hand," that is, near or present (Mark 1:14-15). Mark's Jesus draws on Jewish eschatological expectation of a future kingdom of God as the unambiguous manifestation of God's already present rule over Israel and the whole world, which is obscured in times of suffering. The kingdom's coming will bring blessing and deliverance from oppression for the subjects of God's

---

26. On hand-laying to mediate healing power, see Rudolf Pesch, *Das Markusevangelium I. Teil,* Herders theologischer Kommentar zum Neuen Testament (Freiburg/Basel/Wien: Herder, 1976), p. 300.

27. In Luke, Jesus does not touch the children at all. In Matthew, the children are brought "that he might lay his hands on them and pray," and he does lay hands on them. Mark alone mentions Jesus' hugging the children, not only here, but also at 9:36. If Matthew and Luke have dropped the hugging, did it connote something incompatible with their portraits of Jesus, and if so what? See further below on the significance of hugging in Mark.

28. Francis, "Children and Childhood," p. 73.

kingdom. In Mark, Jesus is the one who inaugurates the kingdom through his preaching, teaching, exorcisms, miracles, death, and resurrection. The kingdom of God is already present in his person, yet it is still to come in full power (Mark 9:1; 14:25; 15:43). Thus, the miracles for children imply that children are those for whom the kingdom of God has drawn near; they are among the intended beneficiaries.

Jesus' teaching in Mark 10:14, "to such as these [little children] belongs the kingdom of God," makes this implication explicit. The Greek construction, *tōn toioutōn estin hē basileia tou Theou* (literally, "belonging to such as these is the kingdom of God") uses a genitive of possession *(tōn toioutōn)*[29] to describe the relation between the kingdom of God and little children such as those brought to Jesus: the kingdom is theirs. Thus it is appropriate that they now receive it.[30]

Why does the kingdom of God belong to little children? Apparently just because they need it. Need is the reason for Jesus' welcoming at his table tax collectors and sinners (who were shunned by the strictly law-observant as well as ordinary respectable people). Jesus responds to his critics: "Those who are well have no *need* of a physician, but those who are sick; I have come to call not the righteous but sinners" (Mark 2:16-17).[31] It is those who recognize their need by coming to Jesus who benefit from his ministry, as also implied in his healing and exorcizing evil spirits for those who seek him out.

The Matthean and Lukan Beatitudes are often cited as parallels to Jesus' saying in Mark about children and the kingdom of God. Mark's "to such as these [little children] belongs the kingdom of God" is almost identical to Luke's and Matthew's "to you/them belongs the kingdom of heaven" *(hymetera/autōn estin hē basileia tōn ouranōn)*, which gives the ground for Jesus' pronouncement, "blessed [or 'happy, fortunate'] are . . ." (Luke 6:20; Matt. 5:3, 10). In Luke this beatitude is spoken to "the poor," and in Matthew, to "the poor in spirit" and "those who are persecuted for righteousness' sake." Only objective need and dependence on God by "the poor" is in view in Luke,[32] whereas in Matthew a subjective or active aspect of dependence is

---

29. "Belonging to such as these [i.e., little children]" *(tōn . . . toioutōn)* refers to children not at hand who are like the children at hand, rather than referring to adults who are like children (with Gundry, *Mark,* p. 547); cf. the similar construction, "one of such little children," in 9:37.

30. In Mark the kingdom of God can be "received" in the present as well as "entered" in the future (cf. Mark 10:15), in keeping with the present and future aspects of the kingdom of God noted above (cf. Joachim Gnilka, *Das Evangelium nach Markus Bd. 2,* Evangelisch-katholischer Kommentar [Zurich/Einsiedeln/Köln: Benziger; Neukirchen-Vluyn: Neukirchener, 1979], p. 81).

31. Cf. Luke 7:36-50; 15:1-32.

32. Cf. the following beatitudes in Luke: "Blessed are you who are hungry now, for you will be

added: "poor *in spirit*" and "persecuted *for righteousness' sake.*" Thus in Matthew "*reward* in heaven" is promised (Matt. 5:12). Luke is the better parallel to Mark 10:14,[33] for like Luke's "poor," Mark's "little children" are simply objectively dependent on God, as suggested by the fact that they do not even come to Jesus on their own but are brought by others (Mark 10:13). The kingdom of God belongs to them without respect to their subjective attitude or activity.[34]

The Markan miracle stories featuring children also illustrate their sheer dependence as recipients of the kingdom of God. Again, the children are brought to Jesus, rather than coming on their own.[35] More strikingly, the miracles themselves take place apart from, and in one case over against, what the children do or think. Jairus's daughter has already died when Jesus arrives at the house, and he raises her from the dead, obviously apart from any accompanying attitude or action on her part (Mark 5:41). The Syrophoenician woman's daughter is not even present when Jesus performs the exorcism; rather, her mother goes home and finds the girl lying on the bed, the demon gone (Mark 7:30). The boy with a deaf/mute spirit not only cannot hear or speak but is thrown into a violent convulsion by the spirit when it sees Jesus, who performs the exorcism in the face of such demonically inspired resistance (Mark 9:17-29). Thus, despite children's inaction, absence, and even resistance, Mark's Jesus brings the blessings of the kingdom to children *solely* on the basis of their need. Even in the aftermath of these miracles, Mark notes no attitudinal response by the children, only that they have been restored to health: the girl who was raised from the dead stood up and began to walk around (Mark 5:42); the formerly demon-possessed girl was lying on the bed (Mark 7:30); the formerly demon-possessed boy was able to stand (Mark 9:27). Therefore, it is completely unjustified to claim, as, for example, Francis does, that the subjective manner in which children receive the kingdom of God — that is (ostensibly) with the gladness and wholehearted acceptance with which a child receives a gift[36] — is why it belongs to them. Not any par-

---

filled. Blessed are you who weep now, for you will laugh. Blessed are you when people hate you . . . on account of the Son of Man . . . for surely your reward is great in heaven" (Luke 6:21-23).

33. Cf. Gnilka, *Markus 2*, p. 81.

34. Cf. Gnilka, *Markus 2*, p. 81.

35. S. M. Anderson ("An Exegetical Study of Mark 9:14-29," B.D. Honours diss., University of Glasgow, 1994; cited in Marcus, *Mark 1–8*, p. 365) comments that the children cannot even request healing for themselves because of the condition in which they find themselves. Cf. the bringing of adults by others for healing in Mark (e.g., 2:1-12).

36. So Francis, "Children and Childhood," p. 76: "It becomes a sign of true faith to be able to welcome (to receive) the Kingdom with spontaneous joy."

ticular quality of the child,[37] but "the child's littleness, immaturity and need of assistance, though commonly disparaged, keep the way open for the fatherly love of God."[38]

To be sure, Mark stresses the *parents'* subjective faith accompanying Jesus' miracles for children. Even though the children are inactive or resistant, the parents come to Jesus, request his help for their children, and exercise faith in his power to perform the miracle (see further below). Yet the parents themselves are not models of receiving the kingdom of God, according to Jesus. Rather, the children, who do nothing, not even believe, and on the contrary resist, *are* models. So we ought to take the parents' faith and actions simply as showing what objective dependence on God looks like in adults, that is, how an adult disciple becomes childlike in order to enter the kingdom of God (see further below).

The flipside of children's need or dependence on God's giving the kingdom is God's prior initiative to give it. For Mark this divine initiative is seen in Jesus' ministry, for he is — as the voice from heaven declares at his baptism — "my beloved Son" and enjoys divine approval, "with you I am well pleased" (Mark 1:10-11). Thus interpreters are correct to portray Jesus' teaching that the kingdom of God belongs to children as attesting the grace of God and the gift-character of the kingdom. For example, C. E. B. Cranfield comments: "the reason [why the kingdom belongs to little children] is . . . to be found in their objective humbleness, the fact that they are weak and helpless and unimportant, and in the fact that God has chosen 'the weak things of the world' (1 Cor. 1.26ff.)."[39] Or — in less Pauline language — Robert Gundry takes the Gospel writer to mean that when God brings the kingdom, children simply submit to it, as only they can, being weak and helpless.[40] It should be added that, in this case, submission would not be experienced as oppression but as liberation.

Little children were the weakest and most vulnerable link in the social chain and therefore in many and profound ways dependent on God's rule be-

---

37. Suggestions include modesty, innocence, trustfulness, simplicity, freshness (cf. Dan O. Via, *The Ethics of Mark's Gospel — in the Middle of Time* [Philadelphia: Fortress, 1985], pp. 129-31).

38. Oepke, παῖς, *TDNT* 5:649.

39. C. E. B. Cranfield, *The Gospel According to Saint Mark,* Cambridge Greek Testament Commentary (Cambridge: Cambridge University Press, 1963), p. 32. Cf. Rudolf Pesch, *Das Markusevangelium 2. Teil,* Herders theologischer Kommentar zum Neuen Testament (Freiburg/Basel/Wien: Herder, 1980), p. 132: "The promise of God's kingdom to the children should be understood as the revelation of the grace of God" (translation mine).

40. Gundry, *Mark,* p. 550.

ing implemented in their lives. If Jesus' ministry has demonstrated so far that the kingdom of God is for those who are needy *because* they are needy and dependent on God, then clearly it belongs to little children. Therefore Jesus objects when the disciples rebuke those bringing little children to him and insists that they come and be blessed by him. They are heirs of the kingdom of God, and not just heirs but examples: "*whoever* does not receive the kingdom of God as a little child [receives it] will never enter it" (Mark 10:15). The disciples themselves will have to become like little children, not just give them access to Jesus, in order to enter the kingdom (see further below).

Is child baptism in view in Mark 10:13-16, as some have argued?[41] The statement, "do not prevent them [i.e., the little children] from coming to me" (Mark 10:14), has been taken to allude to a dispute over child baptism at the time Mark wrote his Gospel. For the verb "prevent" *(kōluein)* is associated with baptism in the early church, and candidates for baptism underwent testing before being admitted (cf. Acts 8:36; 10:47, 11:17; cf. Matt. 3:14). But, with Joachim Gnilka, the evidence for such a debate is too slim, even though we can take Jesus to insinuate the acceptance of children for baptism.[42]

The disciples' rebuke thus provides the occasion for Jesus to make explicit what has until now been implicit, namely, that the kingdom of God belongs to little children — for God chooses to give the kingdom to the needy and dependent — and they now participate in its blessings. This forthright explication, overturning the assumptions of the twelve disciples, brings Jesus' ministry to children to a culmination.

Children as Jesus' Own

Not only Jesus' teaching but also his actions demonstrating his teaching — he hugs, lays hands on, and blesses the children — form part of this climax, as I will try to show in the following comments. While he previously touched to heal, now he touches to *bless*. In Old Testament–Jewish tradition children were the objects of blessing on various occasions. The Jewish Talmud attests the practice of bringing children to the elders (i.e., scribes) for blessing after

---

41. Yes, according to Oscar Cullmann, *Die Tauflehre des Neuen Testaments: Erwachsenen- und Kindertaufe*, Abhandlungen zur Theologie des Alten und Neuen Testaments 12 (Zürich, 1958); Joachim Jeremias, *Infant Baptism in the First Four Centuries* (Philadelphia: Westminster, 1960). No, according to Kurt Aland, *Did the Early Church Baptize Infants?* trans. John F. Janzen (Philadelphia: Westminster, 1963), among others. For a more recent discussion, see Müller, *In der Mitte der Gemeinde*, pp. 336, 348ff., 355ff.

42. Gnilka, *Markus 2*, p. 81; cf. Cranfield, *Mark*, p. 323.

the Day of Atonement (*Soferim* 18.5), and some scholars have suggested that Jesus' action here should be seen against that background.[43] But the late dating of rabbinic texts makes this move problematic, as does the lack of connection with the Day of Atonement in Mark.[44]

Jewish parents also blessed their children on certain occasions. J. Duncan M. Derrett argues that one such blessing is alluded to in Mark 10:13-16: Jacob's blessing of Ephraim and Manasseh in Genesis 48.[45] When Jacob was near his death and it was time to pass on the blessing in the form of promises made to Abraham, to Isaac, and then to himself, he blessed Joseph through his two sons, Ephraim and Manasseh:[46] "Therefore your two sons, who were born to you in the land of Egypt before I came to you in Egypt, are now mine; Ephraim and Manasseh shall be mine, just as Reuben and Simeon are. . . . Bring them to me, please, that I may bless them. . . . So Joseph brought them near him and he kissed them and embraced *(perielaben)* them. . . . Israel stretched out his right hand and laid it on the head of Ephraim, who was the younger, and his left hand on the head of Manasseh. . . . He blessed Joseph . . ." (Gen. 48:1-22). Here the children who receive a parental blessing are *adopted* in order to be blessed. As Derrett comments, the gesture of embrace signifies "in the most emphatic manner possible" that the boys are Jacob's adopted sons.[47] Jesus, continues Derrett, "blesses children analogously with Jacob's blessing of Ephraim and Manasseh in somewhat parallel circumstances" and "confirms the prophecy [i.e., Jacob's blessing], but as activated (by himself) *now.*"[48]

Without exploring any further points of contact between the two texts proposed by Derrett,[49] what support is there for the view that Jesus' blessing of the children can be interpreted as a parental blessing like Jacob's? In parallel texts where the rare verb Mark uses for "take in the arms, hug" *(enankalizomai)*[50] appears with little children or babies as the object, the gesture of

43. Jeremias, *Infant Baptism*, p. 49; Hans-Ruedi Weber, *Jesus and the Children: Biblical Resources for Study and Preaching* (Geneva: World Council of Churches, 1979), p. 15.

44. Gundry, *Mark*, p. 551, among others.

45. Derrett, "Why Jesus Blessed the Children," p. 3, notes that the allusion was seen by seventeenth- and eighteenth-century commentators, but lost from view until he revived the suggestion.

46. Why Jacob does not bless his son Joseph directly, but only through his two children, is not clear.

47. Derrett, "Why Jesus Blessed the Children," p. 10.

48. Derrett, "Why Jesus Blessed the Children," pp. 3, 5.

49. Derrett relies on later midrash on Genesis 48 for some of his more speculative suggestions.

50. BADG, s.v. ἐναγκαλίζομαι.

hugging implies assuming a parental role in order to rescue them from death. In Diodorus Siculus 3.581-83, Cybele is called *"mother (mētēr)* of the mountain" because the babies set out to die on the mountain "were generally taken up into her arms *(enankalizomenōn)"* and "were saved *(sōzomenōn)* from death by her spells." Their rescue mirrors her own providential salvation from death as a newborn after being exposed on the very same mountain. In Plutarch, *Moralia* 492D, Roman women "take in their arms *(enankalizontai)* and honor their sisters' children" at a festival in honor of Leucothea, who took her deceased sister's child under her care. The women's hug thus symbolizes their readiness to assume a parental role for a niece or nephew in order to save a motherless child from perishing, as did Leucothea. In Mark 9:36-37 Jesus hugs *(enankalisamenos)* a little child and says to his disciples, "whoever receives *(dexētai)* one such little child in my name receives *(dechetai)* me." In similar formulations "receive" has the sense of "provide hospitality" (cf. Mark 6:11).[51] Since a little child rather than an adult is the object of the verb here, more than simple hospitality to a guest is implied; something analogous to assuming a parental role may be intended. Not only love and acceptance (in contrast to denigration) of little children[52] but attending to their needs in a more comprehensive sense is suggested by the parallelism of the verbs "hug" and "receive." W. Stegemann has suggested an allusion to the practice of taking in orphans, which is plausible, if we take the post–New Testament rabbinic texts supporting it (e.g., Megillah 13a) to be possibly attesting earlier traditions.[53]

Jesus' hug, therefore, can be seen as an adoptive embrace, an assumption of a parental role. His subsequent blessing indicates that he has adopted the children in order to pass on an inheritance[54] to them before he dies,[55] and in this way "save" them.[56] Jesus' imminent death is not only the occasion of his blessing the children but also the ratification of a new covenant that will issue in their eschatological salvation: at the Last Supper, Jesus "said to them, 'This is my blood of the covenant, which is poured out for many'" (Mark 14:24). Jesus' death procures eschatological salvation (cf. Mark 10:45), which is already

51. BADG, s.v. δέχομαι 5, cites Mark 9:37, etc., for the meaning "receive as a guest, welcome." On hospitality to Jesus' representatives, see Müller, *In der Mitte der Gemeinde,* pp. 216-18.

52. Gnilka, *Markus* 2, p. 57; Pesch, *Markusevangelium* 2, p. 106.

53. Stegemann, "Lasset die Kinder zu mir kommen," pp. 72-73.

54. Derrett ("Why Jesus Blessed the Children," p. 10) describes Jesus' gestures as "an acknowledgement in acted metaphor . . . that they [the children] are his relations and co-heirs." As David Bartlett argues in his essay on adoption in the present volume, adoption was practiced in Greco-Roman antiquity primarily to gain a suitable heir.

55. Cf. the nearby passion predictions in Mark 9:31 and 10:32-34.

56. Pesch (*Markusevangelium* 2, p. 132) describes Jesus' gestures as salvifically effective.

anticipated in his bringing near the kingdom of God by his powerful deeds. In this light Jesus' hug can be seen as a *saving* gesture (as in the texts previously cited)[57] with *eschatological* overtones. Similarly, eschatological salvation is associated with a divine "embrace" in Manuscript D of the long recension of the *Testament of Abraham* 14, line 28:[58] God said to Abraham, "I have embraced *(enēnkalisamēn)* them [the souls of dead sinners] and led them to life through my highest goodness." By a hug and a blessing, therefore, Jesus claims the little children brought to him as his own children and mediates an inheritance of salvation to them.

It is not sufficient, therefore, to take Jesus' hug as a remarkable display of love and affection, which "can only be properly appreciated within the context of calloused attitudes toward children that still prevailed within Hellenistic society in the first century."[59] This, of course, is also true,[60] and the contrast is striking against the background of the oft-quoted letter from Alexandria around 100 CE reflecting the pagan practice of exposure of newborns. In this letter an absent husband writes to his wife upon the birth of their child: "If it was a male child, let it live; if it was a female, cast it out" (Pa-

---

57. Gnilka (*Markus 2*, p. 57) notes that an embrace can be seen as a saving gesture ("Heilsgestus").

58. *The Testament of Abraham: The Greek Recensions*, trans. Michael E. Stone, Texts and Translations 2, Pseudepigrapha Series 2 (Missoula, MO: Society of Biblical Literature, 1972), p. 36. This probably Jewish writing is of uncertain date, but the extant manuscripts with medieval features may be based on an original text from the first or second century CE (see the discussion in Dale C. Allison Jr., *The Testament of Abraham*, Commentaries on Early Jewish Literature [Berlin/New York: Walter de Gruyter, 2003], pp. 34-40). Similarly, as J. Fitzmyer (*Luke*, p. 1089) notes, in the parable of the prodigal son (Luke 15:11-32) the father's hug and kiss of the returning prodigal is not just a greeting or welcome, but an act of life-generating forgiveness. When the father saw the prodigal returning from afar, he ran to him, hugged him (*epepesen epi ton trachēlon autou*, literally, "fell on his neck"), and kissed him. The prodigal's loss of sonship ("I am no longer worthy to be called your son; treat me like one of your hired hands") is reversed by the father, who gives him the best robe, a ring for his finger, and sandals for his feet and slaughters the fatted calf for a celebration in his honor. For he who was "lost" is now "found," he who was "dead" is "alive again." The point of the parable is that God is such a father, who — out of "ready, unconditioned, and unstinted love and mercy" — makes children out of those who are not, and joyfully receives them into God's family where they enjoy abundant blessing (cf. Joseph A. Fitzmyer, *The Gospel According to Luke*, Anchor Bible Commentary, vols. 28-28A [Garden City, NY: Doubleday, 1981-85], p. 1085).

59. So, Lane, *Mark*, p. 361; similarly, Gnilka, *Markus 2*, p. 57; Pesch, *Markusevangelium 2*, p. 106.

60. Jesus' treatment of little children can be seen as a particular instance of his care for the marginalized — for example, "tax collectors and sinners" (Mark 2:15-16). On God's fierce love of the most vulnerable members of society — typically, widows and orphans — see Walter Brueggemann's essay in the present volume.

pyrus Oxyrhynchus 4.744).[61] Here we see that gender played a significant role in the way little children were treated. While it is also the case that parental affection is well attested in both Jewish and Greco-Roman first-century contexts,[62] it is right to say that we cannot simply assume children received loving treatment at the hands of adults.[63]

Jesus' ministry to children in Mark thus culminates not only in his declaring them explicitly to be heirs to and beneficiaries of God's reign that has dawned through Jesus, but also in his assuming a parental role and blessing them with eschatological salvation as well as saving them from sickness and death in this life.

Children in Jesus' Family and the Parent/Child Relationship

The interpretation proposed above, that the little children brought to Jesus become his own children and heirs by his adoptive embrace and blessing, is consistent with Jesus' teaching in Mark 3:33-35 on his followers as his family members: "He said, 'Who are my mother and my brothers?' And looking at those who sat around him, he said, 'Here are my mother and my brothers! Whoever does the will of God is my brother and sister and mother.'"

This teaching is occasioned by his own mother's and siblings' opposition to his mission (Mark 3:21, 31). They want to restrain him in response to the rumor that "he has gone out of his mind." They arrive at the house where he is surrounded by followers and send to him and call him. Instead of answering their call, he says that he already *is* with his family, the ones he is "looking at," who "were sitting around him." They are further identified as those who "do the will of God." The phrase is not defined, presumably because the point is simply to identify *Jesus' followers* as the ones who do God's will, rather than those who oppose him (perhaps in this way intending to do God's will).[64] Je-

---

61. Cited in J. L. White, *Light from Ancient Letters* (Philadelphia: Fortress, 1986), pp. 111-12.

62. E.g., 4 Maccabees 15:4 (where maternal affection is a passion to be conquered by religious reasoning). See Thomas Wiedemann, *Adults and Children in the Roman Empire* (New Haven/London: Yale University Press, 1989), pp. 25-32, 84-112; John Nolland, *Luke 1–9:20*, Word Biblical Commentary 35a (Dallas: Word, 1989), p. 785.

63. In fact, a hug given to a child can be motivated by sexual attraction; see Xenophon, *Anabasis* 7.4.10: "embracing the child . . ." *(peribalon ton paida)*. Jesus' embrace of little children is clearly differentiated from the sexually motivated hugging in Xenophon, since Jesus' hug is accompanied by a blessing with ritual hand-laying, and the narrator makes no mention of sexual motives.

64. Marcus (*Mark 1–8*, p. 286) suggests that listening to Jesus' teaching is what those sitting around Jesus are doing, which makes them his family as doers of God's will.

sus' natural family, "standing outside" and sending to him and calling him (3:31), rather than sitting around him and being the object of his gaze, is portrayed as not doing God's will, not being part of his "family."

Mark does not explicitly mention children as part of this "family," though the setting in a house (*oikos,* 3:20) probably presupposes the presence of children. If children were part of the crowd assembled around Jesus that he calls his family, how ironic is the disciples' later attempt in Mark 10:13 to hinder children from coming to Jesus. It is those who do not come, but remain "outside," who do not belong to Jesus' family.

The point here is not that Jesus replaces the family of origin — he explicitly does not (see further below) — but that he "extends kinship relations to the whole community [of disciples]," as Richard Horsley argues.[65] Horsley notes the importance of "kinship" in connection with social and economic protection for individuals and families in traditional agrarian societies, and he cites the faltering of the patrilineal family through economic hardship in first-century Palestine as the social context of Jesus' teaching. Other social contexts that deserve mention are the persecution of Jesus' followers by their own family members and the sacrifices of an itinerant lifestyle required of Jesus' followers. By extending kinship relations to the community of disciples, Jesus thereby extends the *benefits* (and obligations) of such relations to his "family."

These benefits are multiplied "one hundred-fold" to Jesus' new family members: "No one who has left home or brothers or sisters or mother or father or children or fields for me and the gospel will fail to receive a hundredfold times as much in this present age: homes, brothers, sisters, mothers, children and fields — along with persecutions" (Mark 10:28-30).[66] Stephen Barton sees in this text the culmination of Jesus' teaching in the whole of Mark 10 (addressing marriage, children, and property), implying the creation of an alternative social world in which a new "household" made up of Jesus' disciples compensates (and more) for the earthly household, without replac-

65. Richard A. Horsley, *Hearing the Whole Story: The Politics of Plot in Mark's Gospel* (Louisville: Westminster John Knox, 2001), pp. 196-97.

66. Renunciation of family and possessions in the service of a (temporary?) itinerant missionary lifestyle is in view here (cf. Pesch, *Markusevangelium 2,* pp. 144-45). Against overinterpreting the demand for renunciation, see R. T. France, *The Gospel of Mark: A Commentary on the Greek Text,* New International Greek New Testament (Grand Rapids: Eerdmans; Carlisle: Paternoster, 2002), pp. 407-8. Jesus' teaching leaves out receiving a hundred-fold times as many *fathers* (cf. also Mark 3:35), presumably because it would conflict with the uniqueness of God as father for disciples (cf. Matt. 23:9). It goes without saying that a multitude of mothers or siblings is only a boon for children if it entails multiplying Jesus' own beneficial treatment of children.

ing it (cf. Acts' depiction of the early church as having all things in common in 2:44; 4:32, 34-37).[67] (Of course, the present social benefits of membership in Jesus' family do not occlude future, eschatological benefits. Jesus also promises "in the age to come eternal life," Mark 10:30b.)

For Jesus' followers to receive many more benefits in his family than those they have lost in their earthly families, they must individually take up his call to serve their fellow family members. Jesus singles out service to little children as the supreme form of exercising this call, equivalent to serving Jesus himself: "'Whoever wants to be first must be last of all and servant of all.' Then he took a little child and put it in their midst. Taking the child in his arms, he said to them: 'Whoever welcomes one such little child in my name welcomes me'" (Mark 9:34-37). By taking up the highest calling to serve little children in particular, Jesus' adult disciples will bring about a new household where the most disadvantaged receive the greatest love and care, and the benefits of the earthly family are multiplied one hundred-fold, or beyond imagination, to little children.

Jesus' extension of kinship relations to his "family" of disciples does not necessarily imply the replacement of the family of origin, as I noted above. Rather, Mark presents Jesus as both revitalizing the earthly family and incorporating it into his own "family." Jesus' ministry of healing and exorcism for children is carried out both at the request of parents (Mark 5:23; 7:26; 9:17, 22)[68] and for the benefit of parents, who counted on their children for future economic and other benefits. Mark indicates the parents' investment in the children's healing at 9:22, where the father of the deaf/mute boy presents himself as a "possible co-beneficiary of Jesus' help":[69] "But if you can do anything, take pity on *us* and help *us*." It was thus not only affection but practical necessity that motivated parents to bring their children to Jesus.

In this connection, it is helpful to recall Peter Lampe's caution against imposing an Enlightenment grid of individualism on the New Testament texts. He observes that in Roman antiquity the individual was integrated into a social body, primarily the *oikos,* or household, characterized by vertical, pyramidal relationships of dependence. Worth or value flowed from the top of the pyramid — the *paterfamilias* (household father) and, not seldom, the *materfamilias* (household mother) — to the members below, and they in turn were

---

67. Stephen C. Barton, *Discipleship and Family Ties in Mark and Matthew* (Cambridge: Cambridge University Press, 1994), pp. 103-7. Both Barton and Horsley (*Hearing the Whole Story,* pp. 196-97) avoid caricaturing Jesus' teaching as anti-familial.

68. It can be assumed that those bringing little children to Jesus in Mark 10:13 were parents or older siblings.

69. Gundry, *Mark,* p. 490.

to act in a way that reflected that worth.[70] Children were to contribute to the parents' welfare, just as parents enabled their children's contribution by training and disciplining them. Children's incapacitation or death could spell disaster for parents.[71]

Not surprisingly, then, Mark makes explicit that Jesus' miracles have restored children to a normal, functional state in which they could fulfill their roles in the *oikos*. After Jesus raised Jairus's daughter, "immediately the girl stood up and began to walk around" (Mark 5:42). Jesus' instruction to "give her something to eat" (Mark 5:43) also shows interest in her ability to function normally. The Syrophoenician woman's daughter was found "lying on the bed, and the demon gone," implying that she could now rest unimpeded by demonic disturbance (Mark 7:30). In the case of the deaf/mute, who had been rolling around on the ground and foaming at the mouth and finally was convulsed so violently that he appeared like a corpse, Jesus "lifted him to his feet, and he stood up" (Mark 9:27).

The parents to whom these children are returned in good health are characterized as persons with steadfast, proven faith. Not only do they bring their children to Jesus and request his help, but they also persevere in faith, despite great obstacles. Jairus's daughter dies before Jesus arrives, and Jesus urges him, "Don't be afraid. Just believe!" And he does, despite the unbelief of the mourners and onlookers (Mark 5:36). The Syrophoenician woman counters Jesus' initial rejection with a clever reply, which Jesus acknowledges: "for such a reply you may go; the demon has left your daughter" (Mark 7:29). The father of the deaf/mute wavers when the disciples fail to cast out the demon. But when Jesus affirms that *all* things are possible to the one who believes, the father replies: "I believe. Help my unbelief!" (Mark 9:23-24). All three parents exhibit something more than ordinary parental concern and intervention for their children's welfare. They emerge from these crises over their children as not merely loving parents but believers in the power of God through Jesus, despite obstacles. A radical faith is required of them: faith in Jesus' power to raise the dead, to perform an exorcism at a distance, to cast out a demon causing a long and nearly fatal childhood illness. It is a faith so radical that it must be granted by Jesus — "help my unbelief!" — as if faith itself requires exorcism of the "demon" of unbelief. Such characterizations of the parents by

---

70. Peter Lampe, "Menschliche Würde in Frühchristlicher Perspektive," in *Menschenbild und Menschenwürde*, ed. Eilert Herms (Gütersloh: Chr. Kaiser Gütersloher, 2001), pp. 288-304 (esp. pp. 289-91).

71. Cf. the story of Jesus' raising a widow's only son from the dead in Luke 7:11-15, which ends with the words: "The dead man sat up and began to talk, and Jesus gave him back *to his mother*," implying her salvation as well.

Mark suggest that he intends to portray Jesus not simply as revitalizing the family but as incorporating both parents and children into his own "family," extending the benefits of God's reign not just to children but to all those who are childlike in their need and dependence on God.

Children among Jews and Gentiles
in the Ancient Mediterranean World

The occasion of the culmination of Jesus' ministry to children in Mark, as already noted, is the disciples' rebuke of those bringing little children to Jesus so that he might touch them. Before we examine the reasons for the disciples' rebuke, it is important to pause here and ask how children were seen in Mark's world.

First-century Judaism was characterized by the assigning of a higher value to children than in the Greco-Roman world generally.[72] From the perspective of the Hebrew Scriptures and Jewish tradition, all of life is the Creator's work and therefore to be valued and preserved. Children were considered a prime blessing and gift from God (cf. Gen. 1:28; Pss. 127:3-5; 128:3-6). On that basis abortion, exposure, and infanticide were condemned (e.g., Josephus, Antiquities 4.287; cf. Acts 7:19). Children had a place in the religious life of Israel: they observed its religious rites and were taught its founding traditions and way of life (cf. Gen. 17:10-14; Exod. 12:26-27; Deut. 4:9-10). Strong emphasis was placed on their training and discipline for the benefit of the family and nation (cf. Prov. 1–9; 10:1; 13:24; 19:18). Honoring parents was paramount (cf. Exod. 20:12).

This great appreciation for children and attention to their needs and development, however, did not preclude denigrating them as lacking in understanding and self-willed (cf. Isa. 3:4, 12; Eccles. 10:16; Wisd. of Sol. 12:24; 15:14), naturally naughty and needing strong discipline (cf. 2 Kings 2:23-24; Sir. 30:1-13). Children were not seen as innocent but, like the rest of humanity, caught in the web of sin and guilt (cf. Ps. 51:5; Job 25:4; 2 Bar. 54:15), and not spared divine judgment (cf. Isa. 13:16; Jer. 6:11; 44:7; Ps. 137:9).[73]

Among first-century Greeks and Romans there was considerable pessimism about the child on account of his or her physical smallness, underdevelopment, and resulting vulnerability, as well as ignorance, capriciousness, and

---

72. John D. Crossan (*The Historical Jesus: The Life of a Mediterranean Jewish Peasant* [San Francisco: Harper, 1993], p. 269; cf. pp. 265-302) is thus misleading when he states that Jesus taught a "kingdom of children" in the sense of a "kingdom of nobodies," for "to be a child was to be a nobody."

73. Oepke, παῖς, *TDNT*, 5:646-49.

irrationality, qualities that were to be set aside through rigorous education and harsh discipline. The Roman philosopher Cicero wrote concerning childhood, "the thing itself cannot be praised, only its potential," and categorically denied the desirability of reverting in any sense to the state of childhood (Cicero, *De Republica* 137.3, ed. Ziegler, frag. incert. 5; cf. *On Old Age* 83). There was optimism only about the possibility of making something out of the "raw material" (cf. Plutarch, *De Liberis Educandis* 2.1-14; Seneca, *De Constantia Sapientis* 12.3).[74] A formal rediscovery of the child is evident in Hellenistic poetry, painting, and sculpture, but here interest in children and their antics was for adults' pleasure. Also noteworthy is the fact that children were seen as sexually uncomplicated or not deceptive and thus better suited to particular cultic roles than adults.[75]

Philo of Alexandria, a deeply Hellenized Jewish philosopher of religion (ca. 15 BCE–50 CE), reflects the oscillation between positive and negative perspectives on children in both Old Testament–Jewish tradition and the Greco-Roman world. He describes the "soul of an infant" as "without part in either good or evil" up to the age of seven (Philo, *Allegorical Interpretation* 2.53; cf. 2 Macc 8:4). By contrast, he also says that the little child soon veers toward the bad (Philo, *Heir* 295) and is especially vulnerable to sensual and even sexual desire (Philo, *Creation* 161).[76]

Early Christianity exhibits both modes of speaking about children as well. The apostle Paul plays on the notion of children's innocence — "be infants *(nēpiazete)* in evil"[77] — simultaneously with that of their immaturity — "do not be children *(paidia)* in your thinking . . . but in thinking be adults *(teleioi)*" (1 Cor. 14:20; cf. 13:11). First Peter speaks in a positive sense of the newborn's dependence on milk as a metaphor for Christians' need for spiritual nourishment (1 Pet. 2:1-3), while Hebrews uses the same metaphor negatively (Heb. 5:13-14).[78]

---

74. Oepke, παῖς, *TDNT*, 5:642-43; cf. Lindemann, "Die Kinder und die Gottesherrschaft."

75. See Oepke, παῖς, *TDNT*, 5:640-45.

76. Cf. also Philo, *Flaccus* 68. On the corrupted innocence of children in rabbinic literature, see Oepke, παῖς, *TDNT*, 5:647.

77. That is, inexperienced in doing evil, with Christian Wolff, *Der erste Brief des Paulus an die Korinther: Zweiter Teil: Auslegung der Kapitel 8–16*, Theologisches Handkommentar zum Neuen Testament 7/2 (Berlin: Evangelische Verlagsanstalt, 1982), p. 135.

78. Harold W. Attridge, *The Epistle to the Hebrews*, Hermeneia (Philadelphia: Fortress, 1989), pp. 159-62, notes that Hellenistic philosophical and educational imagery focusing on training for ethical discernment forms the background for Hebrews 5:13-14.

Children and Hierarchy in the Kingdom of God

Mark does not explain the reason for the disciples' rebuke. Many have pointed to children's social and religious inferiority as the reason,[79] but based on how children were viewed and valued in the ancient Mediterranean world, it seems that we should not assume that Mark is portraying the disciples simply as uncaring toward or dismissive of children, which is too flat a view of children for Mark's social context.

Further, the suggestion that the disciples rebuked the people bringing children because children were socially inferior does not explain why Jesus' disciples attempted to bar little children from coming to him *after previously* participating when Jesus responded to requests for help for children, and even assisting in the case of the deaf-mute. Indeed, the disciples have not

---

79. So, e.g., Pesch, *Markusevangelium 2*, p. 37; France, *Mark*, p. 395. For other explanations of the disciples' rebuke, see the discussion in Francis, "Children and Childhood," p. 74.

A great deal of research during the last few decades has been devoted to the family and household in antiquity, including children as a subset of the ancient family. For Greece and Rome, see Beryl Rawson, ed., *The Family in Ancient Rome: New Perspectives* (Ithaca, NY: Cornell University Press, 1986); Suzanne Dixon, *The Roman Mother* (Norman, OK: Oklahoma University Press, 1988); Thomas Wiedemann, *Adults and Children in the Roman Empire* (New Haven/London: Yale University Press, 1989); Beryl Rawson, *Marriage, Divorce, and Children in Ancient Rome* (Oxford: Clarendon, 1991); Mark Golden, *Children and Childhood in Classical Athens* (Baltimore: Johns Hopkins University Press, 1990); Keith R. Bradley, *Discovering the Roman Family: Studies in Roman Social History* (Oxford: Oxford University Press, 1991); Suzann Dixon, *The Roman Family* (Baltimore: Johns Hopkins University Press, 1992); Nancy Demand, *Birth, Death, and Motherhood in Classical Greece* (Baltimore: Johns Hopkins University Press, 1994); Suzanne Dixon, ed., *Childhood, Class, and Kin in the Roman World* (London/New York: Routledge, 2001). For early Christianity, see Peter Müller, *In der Mitte der Gemeinde: Kinder im Neuen Testament* (Neukirchen-Vluyn: Neukirchener Verlag, 1992); William A. Strange, *Children in the Early Church: Children in the Ancient World, the New Testament and the Early Church* (Carlisle, Cumbria: Paternoster, 1996); Stephen C. Barton, ed., *The Family in Theological Perspective* (Edinburgh: T&T Clark, 1996); Bettina Eltrop, *Denn solchen gehört das Himmelreich: Kinder im Matthausevangelium: Eine feministisch-sozialgeschichtliche Untersuchung* (Stuttgart: Ulrich E. Grauer, 1996); Halvor Moxnes, ed., *Constructing Early Christian Families: Family as Social Reality and Metaphor* (London: Routledge, 1997); Carolyn Osiek and David L. Balch, *Families in the New Testament World: Households and House Churches* (Louisville: Westminster John Knox, 1997); Stephen C. Barton, *Life Together: Family, Sexuality and Community in the New Testament and Today* (Edinburgh/New York: T&T Clark, 2001); Peter Balla, *The Child-Parent Relationship in the New Testament and Its Environment*, Wissenschaftliche Untersuchungen zum Neuen Testament 155 (Tübingen: Mohr Siebeck, 2003); O. M. Bakke, *When Children Became People: The Birth of Childhood in Early Christianity*, trans. Brian McNeil (Minneapolis: Fortress, 2005); Carolyn Osiek and Margaret Y. MacDonald, *A Woman's Place: House Churches in Earliest Christianity* (Minneapolis: Fortress, 2006).

barred *anyone* from getting to Jesus until now, even though Mark repeatedly reports crowds of people pursuing and gathering around Jesus and pressing on him, trying to touch him for healing of their diseases. On one occasion Jesus even has to ask his disciples to ready a boat for him to get into, lest the crowds crush him (Mark 3:9-10). I propose to explain the disciples' rebuke in terms of the development of Mark's narrative, against the background of Jewish expectations regarding the future eschatological reign of God, Jewish debates about rank in the coming kingdom, and widespread views on seniority in antiquity.

By Mark 10:11 Jesus has concluded his Galilean ministry[80] and turns toward Jerusalem: "He left that place [Capernaum] and went to the region of Judea and beyond the Jordan." And at Mark 10:32a we read: "They were on the road, going up to Jerusalem, and Jesus was walking ahead of them." Mark portrays the disciples as deeply affected by this move: "they were amazed, and those who followed were afraid [in the sense of having a profound measure of respect]"[81] (Mark 10:32b). Though Mark does not account for this reaction, it makes sense within the broader context. Soon afterward, on the way, James and John come to Jesus with the request, "Grant us to sit, one at your right hand and one at your left, *in your glory*" (Mark 10:37). The request betrays the assumption that the eschatological crisis has begun, and Jesus is going to Jerusalem to reestablish the Davidic kingdom (corresponding to Jewish expectation), or will do so soon at his future coming as Son of Man in glory (Mark 8:38; cf. 13:26).[82] James and John are characterized as expecting a key role in Jesus' kingdom, along the lines of Jesus' promise in Matthew 19:28 (par. Luke 22:30) that the twelve disciples "will sit on thrones judging the twelve tribes of Israel." Their aspirations mirror prevalent discussions about rank in the coming reign of God attested in Jewish sources contemporaneous with the New Testament (e.g., the Essene writings found at Qumran, cf. 1QSa 1, 1; 1QSa 2, 11-22; 4QS 2, 20-23) and later (in rabbinic literature; see Str-B IV 1131f.). The Gospel of Matthew especially reflects such discussions (Matt. 5:19; 11:11; 18:1-4; 20:21), and the disciples' infighting in Mark 9:33-34; 10:35-41 may be illuminated by them.

Mark lets the expectations regarding what Jesus is about to do in Jerusalem spread to others, the closer he gets to his destination. As he is leaving Jericho, the blind beggar Bartimaeus shouts out, "Son of David, Jesus, have

---

80. For Jesus' Galilean ministry, see Mark 1:24–7:23; 7:31–9:50, punctuated by a brief stint in Syrophoenicia in Mark 7:24-30.

81. The Greek verb *phobeō* can have this sense (cf. Mark 16:8; BAGD, s.v. φοβέω, 2) and is likely to have it here in parallelism with *thambeō*, "be astounded, amazed."

82. Gundry, *Mark*, p. 583. Cf. Pesch, *Markusevangelium 2*, p. 104.

mercy on me!" (Mark 10:47). The title "Son of David" either compares Jesus to Solomon, the prototypical son of David, a king with wisdom, authority, and miraculous power (cf. Testament of Solomon 20:1; Josephus, *Antiquities* 9.64), from whom one can expect mercy (cf. Matt. 15:22); or it casts Jesus in the role of the expected messianic conqueror from David's line who will liberate and save Israel (cf. Psalms of Solomon 17:23 [21]).[83] If the latter, the Bartimaeus scene portrays Jesus as having awakened Jewish hopes for a political Messiah.[84]

The pericope on Jesus' entry into Jerusalem definitely portrays him in this way (Mark 11:1-11). He enters the city on a colt, as expected of the long-awaited king (Zech. 9:9; Gen. 49:11). The crowds acclaim him with the words of Psalm 118:25-26, which are given a messianic interpretation in early Christianity (Mark 12:10b):[85] "Hosanna! Blessed is the one who comes in the name of the LORD!" (Mark 11:9b). The immediately following acclamation clearly expresses nationalistic messianic hopes: "Blessed is *the coming kingdom of our ancestor David!*" (Mark 11:10a). The first acclamation should thus be taken to identify Jesus as the one who comes in the LORD's name *as the expected Davidic Messiah to reestablish David's kingdom* and usher in a new era of salvation for all of Israel.[86] The crowds' royal treatment of Jesus also casts him in the role of a conquering king: they spread their cloaks on the colt so he will not have to ride bareback and place their cloaks and leafy branches on the road.

The amazement and awe of Jesus' disciples and followers at his turning toward Jerusalem is thus *unlikely* to betray lack of comprehension, and *likely* to express expectation of a climactic conclusion to the journey, though of course they misconstrue that conclusion (cf. the disciples' failure to understand Jesus' passion predictions, Mark 8:31-33; 9:31-32; 10:32b-45).[87]

---

83. This use of the title "son of David" rests on the Old Testament belief that the Messiah would be a descendant of David (e.g., Isa. 11:1-5; Jer. 23:5-6; Ezek. 34:23-24).

84. Pesch (*Markusevangelium 2*, p. 172) thinks it less likely that the crowds attempt to silence Bartimaeus so as not to hinder Jesus on his way to Jerusalem than that they do so in order to suppress the messianic identity of Jesus, lest his opponents do away with him prematurely (cf. Mark 8:30). But this suggestion lacks supporting evidence.

85. So also in later rabbinic and targumic literature, e.g., MidrPs 118,22-24; see Str-B 1.849-50.

86. With Pesch, *Markusevangelium 2*, pp. 184-85; Gnilka, *Markus 2*, p. 110.

87. Other explanations for the disciples' amazement and the followers' fear are: urgency and/or incomprehensibility of Jesus' march to Jerusalem (France, *Mark*, p. 412; Simon Légasse, *L'Évangile de Marc II*, Libraire Lecoffre 5 [Paris: Les Éditions du Cerf, 1997], p. 628; Pesch, *Markusevangelium 2*, p. 148; Gundry, *Mark*, pp. 570-71), the realization that Jesus was going into immediate peril (Cranfield, *Mark*, p. 335), Jesus' awe-inspiring power in general (Lane, *Mark*,

The exciting prospect of Jesus' imminent establishment of his kingdom in Jerusalem and the disciples' assumption that they in particular would benefit by sharing in his reign made eminently undesirable any delays caused by people's clamoring for Jesus' attention or bringing others to Jesus — especially when these people were little children, who seemed relatively insignificant in the grand scheme of things.[88] This, I suggest, is the explanation for the otherwise odd shift in Mark's narrative already noted, namely, the disciples' rebuke of people bringing children to Jesus at Mark 10:13, in contrast to their former behavior. It also explains a similar shift in the crowds' behavior. When Bartimaeus shouts to get Jesus' attention, "many sternly ordered him to be quiet" (Mark 10:48). This is the first time the crowds have ever tried to block someone in need from getting Jesus' help.[89]

Therefore, in my view, Mark presents the disciples' rebuke of those bringing little children to Jesus — ironically, at the very culmination of his ministry to children in Mark — as based on a now heightened expectation of the completion of Jesus' mission, however badly misunderstood by them, and preoccupation with their own rank as Jesus' closest associates. Traditional assumptions regarding the relative value of age over youth factor in as a more general backdrop to this scenario.

Mark's Jesus will have none of the disciples' assumptions. "When Jesus saw this [their rebuke] he was indignant, and said to them, 'Let the little children come to me! Do not stop them!'" (Mark 10:14). Jesus' indignation is rare in Mark, appearing elsewhere only at 3:5 (but in some manuscripts also at 1:41),[90] and thus indicates *serious* disapproval.[91] At 3:5 Jesus reacts "with anger" at his

---

p. 374), a mere framework for Jesus' prediction lending it revelatory quality (Gnilka, *Markus 2*, p. 96).

88. Cf. John M. G. Barclay, "There Is Neither Old Nor Young? Early Christianity and Ancient Ideologies of Age," *New Testament Studies* 53 (2007): 225-41, for a discussion of perceptions of the relative value of age versus youth in the ancient Mediterranean world. Barclay points to early Christian texts broadly within the Pauline tradition that agree with the prevailing ideology in the Greco-Roman world, ascribing greater value and power to the "old" than the "young" — with some exceptions (1 Tim. 4:12; Ignatius, *Magnesians* 3.1).

89. Pesch (*Markusevangelium 2*, p. 172) thinks a better explanation for the crowds' attempt to silence Bartimaeus is the desire to suppress the notion that he is a political Messiah. But suppression of Jesus' Messiahship is not something that the crowds do in Mark, and the suggestion seems inherently unlikely.

90. The variant reading "being angry" *(orgistheis)*, referring to Jesus' reaction to a leper's condition before touching and cleansing him (Mark 1:41-42), is less likely to be original since the manuscripts supporting it are not as impressive as are those which read, "being filled with compassion" *(splanchnistheis)*.

91. Horsley (*Hearing the Whole Story*, p. 189) notes a parallel between Jesus' indignation at

opponents for resisting his Sabbath-day healing of the man with a withered hand. In 10:14 he is indignant for a similar reason, resistance to his blessing little children. But now his anger is aimed at his own disciples, for they are opposing rather than aiding his mission to inaugurate the kingdom of God.[92] The double command in 10:14 — staccato-like in the lack of intervening conjunction (asyndeton) — forms a sharp and weighty rebuke. Also emphatic are the double references in 10:16 to Jesus' touching the children — "taking them in his arms . . . laying his hands on them" — and the reference to blessing them — "he blessed them" — with an intensified form of the verb, *kateulogei*.[93]

All of the above place strong emphasis on Jesus' repudiation and defeat of the attempt to hijack his true mission: to bestow the blessings of God's kingdom on children and the childlike. (Similarly, Bartimaeus is not silenced by the crowds, and Jesus hears, calls, and heals him, Mark 10:49-52.) Jesus succeeds in putting the young before the old, the disabled before the able, and the poor before the rich. Like Jacob, he overturns seniority by first blessing the younger, over the objections of their elders (cf. Joseph's objections to Jacob's first blessing the younger Ephraim, Gen. 48:17-19).[94] Jesus replaces a conventional hierarchy with one based on need: in his kingdom the most dependent have the highest priority. His blessing of the children against the wishes of the disciples shows the countercultural power of his teaching that the kingdom of God belongs to little children.[95]

Childlikeness and the Kingdom of God

Jesus' teaching in Mark 10:15 ends on a rather ominous note: "Truly I tell you, whoever does not receive the kingdom of God as a little child will never enter it." Here Jesus threatens the disciples with exclusion from the coming kingdom, because their putting a roadblock in the way of his blessing the children,

---

the disciples' rebuke of the ones bringing children to Jesus and the curse that the disciples are to speak against those who do not receive them when sent out on a mission. Matthew and Luke soften Jesus' reaction by omitting his indignation.

92. Similarly, Jesus disapproves of the disciples' attempt to stop a non-follower from exorcising in Jesus' name at Mark 9:38-40, and he rebukes Peter for resisting his teaching on the suffering, death, and resurrection of the Son of Man (Mark 8:31-33).

93. The prefix *kat-* lends an intensified sense to the basic meaning, "bless" (see BAGD, s.v. κατευλογέω). Gundry (*Mark*, p. 545) sees the complex form of the verb to stress "Jesus' authority to elevate even children to the heirship of God's kingdom."

94. Derrett, "Why Jesus Blessed the Children," pp. 6-7, notes the parallel.

95. Cf. Weber, *Jesus and the Children*, pp. 15-16.

heirs to the kingdom, signals that the disciples themselves do not know how to receive it as a little child does.[96] This ignorance[97] is also seen in their false expectations of what is about to happen to Jesus and themselves in Jerusalem. So Jesus goes from "let the little children come" to *become* "like a little child." But what does it mean to be childlike in receiving the kingdom?

The answer is unclear, for no definition of childlikeness is given. Jesus has not even defined in the previous verse how children themselves receive the kingdom of God, but merely asserts that it belongs to them, on the ground, I argued earlier, of children's need and dependence on God and, correspondingly, God's own gracious initiative in Jesus to fill their need.

What, then, does it mean to receive the kingdom of God "as a little child" receives it?[98] Willi Egger has argued persuasively that the *form* of Mark 10:15 itself suggests the answer: Jesus adapts a common formula found in Jewish apocalyptic literature (and, later, the Talmud), stating the condition for "entering the kingdom of God" (or the like).[99] The condition for entry varies from saying to saying — and is in fact disputed in rabbinic literature. In many of these formulaic sayings, the fulfillment of the law (whether ethical or cultic regulations) is the condition for participating in the future life. By contrast, Jesus makes receiving the kingdom "as a little child" the condition for entry. This sounds like a provocation,[100] since little children were precisely non-doers of the law, indeed, too young even to be obliged to do it (cf. Jub. 23:26).[101]

---

96. What is being compared with a little child by the Greek phrase *hōs paidion*, "as a little child"? The Greek construction is ambiguous. Either "the kingdom of God" itself is like a little child, and to be received as such, or people's receiving the kingdom of God is to be like a little child's receiving it. The first option can be rejected since the kingdom of God in Mark has connotations of power and is unlikely to be compared with something so weak as a little child. See further Gundry, *Mark,* pp. 550-51.

97. The disciples' lack of comprehension of Jesus' deeds and teaching is a theme in Mark (cf., e.g., 4:13; 6:52; 7:18; 8:17, etc.).

98. The *Gospel of Thomas* 22 has a similar saying of Jesus in which becoming "as children" ("infants being suckled") to enter the kingdom is interpreted in terms of being sexually innocent, or asexual. The saying is most likely a later adaptation of the canonical Gospel saying. Cf. Howard C. Kee, "'Becoming a Child' in the Gospel of Thomas," *Journal of Biblical Literature* 82 (1963): 307-14.

99. Willi Egger, παιδίον, in *EDNT,* 3:4; cf. Müller, *In der Mitte der Gemeinde,* p. 69. For a fuller discussion of the Jewish apocalyptic formula, see Hans Windisch, "Die Sprüche vom Eingehen in das Reich Gottes," *ZNW* 27 (1928): 163-92.

100. Cf. Gnilka, *Markus 2,* p. 81. Pesch (*Markusevangelium 2,* p. 133) also comments: "The call to become like children is the most concise formulation of the demand to renounce prestige, power, wealth and security" (citing K. Berger).

101. Similarly, women and persons with a bodily defect had a lesser obligation toward the law (see Müller, *In der Mitte der Gemeinde,* p. 68). Only the adult male Jew was fully obliged to

It is irrelevant whether we take Jesus to be negating the entrance requirement of the works of the law in the traditional sense — works that form a basis for future justification before God (whether understood in a legalistic way,
that works earn merit before God, as in 4 Ezra 9:7 and 2 *Baruch* 51:7,[102] or in a
synergistic way, that works contribute to justification as a response to divine
grace, as in *Mishna Sanhedrin* 10:1-4)[103] — or in the more recently popular
sense of works that function to mark out God's chosen people from others.[104]
In either case the point is that dependence on *God* for entering God's reign —
whether on account of the lack of a particular religious identity and/or the
life to back it up (as *self*-dependence) — is what Jesus *requires*.[105] It is *neces-*

---

do the law and potentially law-observant (Oepke, παῖς, *TDNT*, 5:647). The circumcision of
eight-day-old boys required by the Jewish law was a sign of their covenant membership and
foreshadowed their future obligations to keep the law when no longer under age.

102. These texts are not representative of Palestinian Judaism as a whole, which was not
monolithically legalistic, but illustrate one of several kinds of soteriology within it, as recent
scholarship has demonstrated; see the following note.

103. This synergistic soteriology is what E. P. Sanders (*Paul and Palestinian Judaism: A Comparison of Patterns of Religion* [Minneapolis: Fortress, 1977]) describes as "covenantal nomism"
and sees to be characteristic of Palestinian Judaism in general (with only a few exceptions).
Sanders's critics have argued that Judaism did not draw the distinction between grace/faith and
works, which is the presupposition of "covenantal nomism," so the designation is anachronistic
(e.g., Stephen Westerholm, *Perspectives Old and New on Paul: The "Lutheran" Paul and His
Critics* [Grand Rapids: Eerdmans, 2004], pp. 341-51).

104. So, e.g., the works of James D. G. Dunn, N. Thomas Wright, and others representing
the "New Perspective on Paul."

105. Matthew defines becoming like a little child in order to enter the kingdom of heaven as
"taking a humble place" and so, paradoxically, being the "greatest": "Truly I tell you, unless you
change and become like children, you will never enter the kingdom of heaven. Whoever becomes humble like this child is the greatest in the kingdom of heaven" (Matt. 18:3-4). W. D.
Davies and Dale C. Allison, *A Critical and Exegetical Commentary on the Gospel According to
Saint Matthew*, International Critical Commentary [London/New York: T&T Clark, 2004], vol.
2, p. 759) comment on the unusualness for first-century Jewish ears of Matthew's elevation of
childlikeness, given that Jewish piety was focused on learning and practicing the law, and in this
context the unlearned and unpracticed child could scarcely be an example of religious greatness. While this observation rings true, on the other hand, Matthew's definition of childlikeness
in terms of humble *service* — "whoever receives one such child in my name receives me" (Matt.
18:5) — avoids Mark's passive definition (note Mark's relegation of the saying on disciples receiving a little child to a different pericope, Mark 9:33-37). Matthew adds emphasis to his active
definition by warning against causing "one of these little ones who believe in me" to sin (Matt.
18:6-9) and despising "one of these little ones . . . [lest] one of these little ones should be lost"
(Matt. 18:10-14), where "little ones" presumably include the little children mentioned in Matthew 18:2-5 (cf. Robert H. Gundry, *Matthew: A Commentary on His Literary and Theological Art*
[Grand Rapids: Eerdmans, 1982], p. 361). In conclusion, Matthew's motif of childlikeness seems
less unusual for a first-century Jewish context than Mark's.

sary to occupy a state of religious need before God, like a little child without the law to stand on.

Jesus' insistence on childlikeness in this sense for entering the kingdom of God is, however, not only a "paradoxical provocation" for a first-century CE Jewish audience, as Egger has argued.[106] It is also, significantly, an echo of Old Testament traditions in which Israel is depicted as the smallest, as an infant or a child, at the point when God elected and redeemed the nation. Israel was the *littlest* of all peoples, so God's election and redemption can only spring from God's love (Deut. 7:7-8). Israel was "a child" when God loved him and called him out of Egypt, and like an infant whom God took up in his arms, bent down to feed, and taught to walk (Hos. 11:1-4). Most dramatically of all, the prophet Ezekiel depicts Jerusalem (representing Israel) as an exposed newborn Canaanite girl who is rescued, raised, and then married by God solely on the basis of divine merciful compassion and life-giving power:

> Thus says the LORD God to Jerusalem: Your origin and your birth were in the land of the Canaanites; your father was an Amorite, and your mother a Hittite. As for your birth, on the day you were born your navel cord was not cut, nor were you washed with water to cleanse you, nor rubbed with salt, nor wrapped in cloths. No eye pitied you, to do any of these things for you out of compassion for you; but you were thrown out in the open field, for you were abhorred on the day you were born. I passed by you, and saw you flailing about in your blood. As you lay in your blood, I said to you, "Live! And grow up like a plant of the field." You grew up and became tall and arrived at full womanhood. . . . I pledged myself to you and entered into a covenant with you, says the LORD God, and you became mine. Then I bathed you with water and washed off the blood from you, and anointed you with oil. I clothed you. . . . I adorned you. . . . you had choice flour and honey and oil for food. . . . Your fame spread among the nations on account of your beauty, for it was perfect because of my splendor that I had bestowed on you, says the LORD God. (Ezek. 16:3-14)[107]

In this text, the child who is the least of the least — an untended, undesired, exposed newborn girl, abhorrent to everyone except God — stands for the nation God chooses to enter into a covenant with and to bless.[108] The meta-

---

106. So Egger, παιδίον, in *EDNT*, 3.4.

107. Francis ("Children and Childhood," p. 75) notes, but does not discuss, these texts.

108. See the discussion by Moshe Greenberg, *Ezekiel 1–20*, Anchor Bible Commentary (Garden City, NY: Doubleday, 1983), pp. 273-306.

phor removes all doubt about whether God's actions toward Israel are based on anything other than divine love and mercy.

Though Israel subsequently forgot "the days of your youth, when you were naked and bare, flailing about in your blood" (Ezek. 16:15, 22, 43) and "trusted in your beauty and played the whore," God says, "I will remember my covenant with you in the days of your youth, and I will establish with you an everlasting covenant . . . when I forgive you all that you have done" (Ezek. 16:60, 63). Here the future salvation God will bring about requires the "adult Israel" to remain in the position of radical dependence on divine mercy that characterized the days of her youth. Thus, as Moshe Greenberg comments, "in the future as in the past, God's tie with Israel will be self-motivated, an expression of his concern and nature, rather than of any quality or merit of Israel."[109]

Jesus' teaching his disciples that they must receive the kingdom of God "as a little child" in order to enter it (while unparalleled in a strict sense) is strikingly reminiscent of the prophetic critique of Israel as having forgotten her former state of radical dependence on God as an exposed newborn girl and needing to occupy that same state in the new covenant that God will establish with her. It is perhaps legitimate to conclude that Jesus brings this Old Testament prophetic tradition to a climax by asserting that *only* those who stand in the least palatable, most shameful and unenviable position of dependence on God, namely, that of a little child, will enter the kingdom of God — and therefore *anyone* can enter. Though unappealing (in a first-century CE Mediterranean context), the requirement of childlikeness is thus ultimately liberating (and the alternative of failing to enter the kingdom is far worse!). James Francis captures the spirit (if not the language) of Jesus' teaching on receiving God's reign when he says that "the emphasis of the story [in Mark 10:13-16] . . . falls . . . upon an understanding of God's free grace. . . . all who are equally without merit or desert, receive the Kingdom of God and are ranked equal with Jesus himself."[110]

Jesus as the Eschatological Deliverer of Children

There is one child in Mark's Gospel whom I have not yet discussed: Herodias's daughter, who dances before Herod Antipas and receives as her re-

---

109. Greenberg, *Ezekiel 1–20*, pp. 291-92.
110. Francis, "Children and Childhood," p. 74. Francis is wrong, however, to see the flipside of God's free grace as children's "entitlement to be recognized." For "entitlement" robs grace of its free character.

ward the head of John the Baptist on a platter. This child seems to have nothing in common with the other children mentioned in Mark, who are objects of Jesus' miraculous power and blessing. What does this story contribute to the picture of children in Mark, and why is it included?

Herodias's daughter appears in Mark 6:17-29 in a flashback to the ministry of John the Baptist, Jesus' forerunner (Mark 1:2-8).[111] Jesus' powerful ministry awakens in Herod the suspicion that "John, whom I beheaded, has been raised" (Mark 6:14-16), and the parallel between the two figures prompts the flashback. Herod had imprisoned John "on account of Herodias, his brother Philip's wife, because Herod had married her." Herodias bore a grudge against John and wanted to kill him, but Herod was afraid of doing so, "knowing that he was a righteous man, and he protected him." Herodias's opportunity to do away with John came, however, when her young daughter danced so pleasingly before Herod that he solemnly swore to grant any wish of hers, up to half his kingdom. The young girl sought her mother's counsel, and Herodias told her to ask for the head of John the Baptist (surely an ironic reference to the obligation of children to honor their parents!). And she got it, on a platter. Herod was unwilling to dishonor himself in front of his guests by refusing her.

This flashback occurs between the stories of the two girls in Mark 5:21-24, 35-43 (Jairus's daughter) and Mark 7:24-30 (the Syrophoenician woman's daughter),[112] each with a parent who seeks out Jesus to help his or her child. This contrast between the children, together with their parents, does not seem accidental. But surely Mark is not simply interested in contrasting good and bad children (and parents) here. Rather, I suggest he is contrasting the ministries of John the Baptist, on the one hand, and Jesus, on the other, with respect to the vulnerability of children (and their parents) to evil. In *Jesus'* ministry children are given life and liberated from evil through a parent's request and its fulfillment. In *John the Baptist's* ministry a child is complicit in the taking away of life through a parent's request and its fulfillment. Thus, Jesus has the power to effect life and liberation for the benefit of children; but John does not: a mere child gets the better of him. Herod is thus wrong about Jesus: he is much more than John *redivivus.*

Jesus injects a new, life-generating power into first-century CE Jewish life, while John the Baptist merely prepares the way. Herod's family represents the

---

111. John's appearance and proclamation is seen as a fulfillment of Isaiah's prophecy of a messenger who will prepare the way of the LORD (Mark 1:2-4).

112. Marcus (*Mark 1–8,* p. 403) sees the flashback about the evil mother and daughter to be bracketed by Mark 5:24-34 and Mark 7:24-30 with their "two daringly positive female figures," the woman with the hemorrhage and the Syrophoenician woman. Marcus, however, overlooks the contrast between the negative and positive child-figures.

depravity of the current situation and demonstrates that children, too, are caught in the web of evil that causes so much suffering and death. John begins to address the problem by preaching a baptism of repentance for the forgiveness of sins. Yet more is needed. As John tellingly predicts, "The one who is more powerful than I is coming after me . . . he will baptize you with the Holy Spirit" (Mark 1:7-8). John's prediction has come to fulfillment in Jesus' ministry, as the flashback to John the Baptist's ministry makes obvious. Jesus is indeed the stronger one, as his encounters with children show, in contrast to John's encounter. Jesus' baptism by John explains this greater strength: the Spirit descends like a dove on Jesus and a voice from heaven identifies him as the Beloved, the Son of God (Mark 1:9-11).

Children's receiving the kingdom of God, and anyone's receiving the kingdom of God as a little child, are thus possible because of the power and authority of Jesus as God's unique Son and the bearer of the Holy Spirit. Through Jesus, in Mark's Gospel, the power of evil over this world has been broken, even for the most vulnerable, on whom evil had its strongest grip — namely, little children. Here Mark shows an indebtedness to Jewish apocalypticism, which emphasized the hope of redemptive divine intervention in a humanly hopeless situation of oppression under evil power.[113] Yet, differently from Jewish apocalypticism, in Mark divine intervention comes not to the oppressed who are characterized by the righteousness of the law but, *apart from the works of the law,* to little children and the likes of them. Such divine intervention for the sake of the *religiously* dependent is not new, of course, as I have already illustrated from Ezekiel's description of God's intervention for the exposed Canaanite newborn girl Jerusalem. What is new in Mark is the eschatological horizon of God's intervention in Jesus: he brings *the kingdom of God now* to children and the childlike, through the power of God's Spirit that has come upon him.

Children and the Purpose of Mark's Gospel

I have noted along the way in this discussion the kinds of implications Mark's Gospel has for early Christian views of and practices toward children. Now it is time to return to the question of the relation between the Markan material on children and the purpose of Mark.

113. See, further, Adela Yarbro Collins, "Is Mark's Gospel a Life of Jesus? The Question of Genre," in *The Beginning of the Gospel: Probings of Mark in Context* (Minneapolis: Augsburg Fortress, 1992), pp. 1-38.

Mark's depiction of Jesus as working miracles for children, embracing them and making them members of his family and heirs of the kingdom of God, teaching that they are exemplary recipients of God's reign, and requiring adults to receive the kingdom of God as do little children would not necessarily have made sense or been appealing to Mark's Gentile Roman audience and may even have offended them. It would have contradicted many conventional attitudes toward little children that they can be thought to have held. On the other hand, Mark weaves into his material on children an impressive and appealing Jesus, in such a way as to counteract whatever negative reactions his narrative elicited. Mark plays up attractive aspects of Jesus in his interactions with children, in the following ways:

- The Jesus who takes a demeaning servant role in attending to little children rather than engaging in much more glorious exploits as a conquering king is at the same time impressively powerful: he raises a child from the dead, exorcizes an evil spirit from a child at a distance and without a word, and casts out an evil spirit that had caused a long and nearly fatal childhood illness.
- The Jesus who hugs little children who are not his progeny and in this way symbolizes his rescuing them by giving his own life for them (cf. Mark 10:45)[114] is surprisingly reminiscent of illustrious women who rescued children in the Hellenistic world, and even of the God who rescued infant Israel.
- The Jesus who is on a death march to Jerusalem to die an ignominious death by crucifixion without ever having produced an heir[115] in whom he would vicariously live on is the same Jesus who has many children and heirs by adoption, and who passes on to them not just the promise or prefiguration of the kingdom of God but its presence as an eschatological reality.
- The Jesus who disregards seniority and teaches instead that the kingdom of God belongs to ignorant, immature, morally deficient, and socially inferior little children is at the same time the one who brings the kingdom of God near with power and mediates its blessings.
- The Jesus who unpopularly teaches adults to put themselves in the category of the youngest, from which they have escaped only with great effort and through suffering harsh discipline, at the same time shows his author-

114. We can compare Romans 5:6-8, where Paul sets Christ's death for the "weak, the ungodly, sinners" in the context of the unusualness of dying even for a righteous or good person (i.e., one with high standing).

115. Despite *The Da Vinci Code*!

ity to discipline adults who are not childlike in their attempts to receive the kingdom of God by stopping them in their tracks, rebuking them forcefully, and warning them of exclusion from the coming kingdom.

Despite the unpalatability of Jesus' actions toward and teachings about little children, therefore, Mark's Jesus can be not only swallowed but relished. Mark's readers can see him as "the stronger one," the one upon whom the Holy Spirit has come, the one who can "baptize with the Holy Spirit," God's beloved Son[116] — as Mark attractively describes him at the beginning of his Gospel.

Conclusion

In conclusion, the Markan material on children is very well suited to Mark's purpose of overcoming cultural and religious obstacles to faith/faithfulness in response to the gospel message, not only those occasioned by the offensive manner of Jesus' death, but also those brought about by his "in your face" way of treating and talking about little children. Further, Mark's Gospel illustrates how, in the light of the dawning of God's kingdom in Jesus, children's traditional social and religious inferiority can no longer justify their marginalization, but instead requires their emulation and devoted service by adult members of Jesus' "family" of disciples.

116. On the connotations of "Son of God" for Gentile Christians in Rome and elsewhere, see Adela Yarbro Collins, "Mark and His Readers: The Son of God among Greeks and Romans," *Harvard Theological Review* 93 (2000): 85-100; and for the connotations for Jewish readers, see Adela Yarbro Collins, "Mark and His Readers: The Son of God among Jews," *Harvard Theological Review* 92 (1999): 393-408.

8 "What Then Will This Child Become?":
Perspectives on Children in the Gospel of Luke

John T. Carroll

Children play a surprisingly prominent and important role in the Gospel of Luke. The narrative opens by announcing and celebrating the significance of the births of two infants, John (the prophet and baptizer) and Jesus, and pauses to open a window onto Jesus' youthful interactions with his parents (Luke 1:5–2:40; 2:41-52). On more than one occasion during his ministry Jesus heals children (8:41-42, 49-56; 9:37-43; cf. 7:11-17). Twice, when encountering young children, he provocatively points his disciples to these children as exemplars of God's work in the world and affirms that hospitality toward children reflects one's disposition toward God (9:46-48; 18:15-17). In a farewell meal with his intimate followers, he offers the young as models of authentic leadership in the community that would orient its life by his aims and commitments (22:25-27). Commenting on the less than enthusiastic welcome he and his disciples have sometimes met during their itinerant ministry, Jesus draws a lesson from the games children play in the town marketplace (7:31-35).[1]

The late-first-century social world of Luke's first audience, like that of Je-

---

1. Much of this material Luke shares with the other New Testament Gospels, particularly Matthew and Mark — including the use of a wide range of Greek words for the child and children: *brephos*, infant; *nēpios*, infant; *paidion*, young child; *pais*, child (or servant); *teknon*, child; *huios*, son; and *thygatēr*, daughter. Only Luke adds the comparative adjective *neōteros* in the sense of "younger" in 15:12, 13; 22:26; moreover, Luke diverges from both Matthew and Mark by substituting *brephē*, "infants," for *paidia*, "young children," in the pivotal scene of 18:15-17 (cf. Matt. 19:13-15; Mark 10:13-16). Although Luke is much indebted to source traditions, a distinctive Lukan profile results from this Gospel's expansive treatment of the birth and childhood narrative (1:5–2:52), its Last Supper portrait of the young as models of leadership, and its strong emphasis on status inversion — a narrative theme to which the image of the child makes a significant contribution.

sus several decades earlier, was a world of and for the adult, and especially, at least in the public realm, the male adult. Luke knows this reality well, as the male disciples' disinclination to embrace young children (Luke 18:15) or to believe the eyewitness report of women on Easter morning (24:9-11) vividly displays. Yet as this narrative begins, the pace of the action slows dramatically so as to highlight the conversation between two pregnant women, who discuss their circumstance and the fortunes and promise borne by the children to whom they will soon give birth (1:39-56). Heavenly choirs burst into song in praise of a helpless newborn laid by his mother in an animal's feeding trough (2:8-14), and rather than rush to the account of Jesus' activity as a mature adult, Luke lingers over the closing years of his childhood, pondering his identity and vocation as son not only of Mary and Joseph but also of God (2:39-52).

A narrative that opens in such a way, though perhaps reminiscent for Jewish readers of the early chapters of the Exodus narrative (Exod. 2:1-10), would be disorienting for its earliest readers, likely located in one or another major city of the Greco-Roman world late in the first century CE.[2] The cultural disorientation attending the story's beginning would prepare Luke's audience for the surprising and radical role reversals that lie ahead. For the divine deliverance to which Luke points, long awaited by Israel and now accomplished through the ministry of the Messiah, does not replicate or endorse the prevailing social, economic, and political patterns. God's work of salvation instead turns the world upside-down and inside-out, an unfolding story of reversal that continues in the book of Acts (Luke's sequel narrative), extending to the ends of the earth and drawing Gentiles, too, into the people of God. Among the most intriguing — and subversive — reversals that Luke's audience encounters, among the challenges to social convention, is that concerning children. In the realm of God, as envisioned and enacted by Jesus in his public ministry, children are honored guests, welcome even, if necessary, over the objection of the disciples. Indeed, the child becomes a paradigm for membership in the realm, or the household, of God. (Both realm and house-

2. If the shape and direction of Luke's two-volume narrative (Luke and Acts) is a reliable indicator, the first Lukan audience probably was composed mostly of Gentiles who had joined the early Christian movement, but probably including not only non-Jews already drawn to the Jewish scriptures and traditions but also some Jews. It is perhaps revealing that the book of Acts closes with Paul, under house arrest, being accorded a mixed reception by the Jewish community at Rome and then offering this climactic statement: "Let it be known to you then that this salvation of God has been sent to the Gentiles; they will listen" (Acts 28:28; with earlier anticipations in Luke 2:30-32; Acts 13:44-48; 18:5-6; 19:8-10; this translation and all subsequent translations come from the NRSV).

hold are important Lukan metaphors for the humanly constructed world as reconstructed by the activity of God.)[3] At the same time, Jesus' call to discipleship apparently disrupts and divides families, summoning children to a new household and to a new filial relationship, one that transcends the claims of the human parents and household.

Children and Families in Luke's Narrative: Multiple Perspectives

Jesus seems in Luke to speak in more than one voice regarding children and their families. On the one hand, he affirms the Decalogue commandment that children honor their parents (Luke 18:20; cf. Exod. 20:12; Deut. 5:16). And according to the narrator, Jesus himself exemplifies filial obedience and loyalty as a youth (Luke 2:51). Such an affirmation of family cohesion and of children's obedience to their parents would trouble none of Luke's first readers, whatever their cultural roots and social location; this was the culturally expected pattern in the Greco-Roman world of the late first century CE.[4]

Another perspective, however, is more insistent and less expected. Jesus challenges potential disciples to leave their households, and their parents, to join his movement. Those who would follow Jesus must "hate" father and mother (Luke 14:26), as they separate themselves from *everything* — family relationships, possessions, security, even life itself — in answering the call to discipleship, for the sake of God's reign (cf. 18:29). Jesus promises disciples who have left all to join his company an abundant return on what they have given up; the implication is that in the new (fictive) family gathered around Jesus they will experience God's abundant blessing (18:30). A new household has replaced the old one. This dimension of Jesus' message and practice of the reign of God is subversive, disrupting the most basic social institution of his culture,[5] the very institution that played a crucial role in the shaping of iden-

---

3. E.g., household: Luke 12:35-48; 14:16-24; 15:8-10, 11-32; realm [or reign] of God: 13:18-21; 17:20-21. Meal imagery often links these two metaphorical fields, as in 13:20-21, 23-29; 14:15-24; 22:15-20.

4. For a sample of statements, drawn from various authors and eras, that assume or urge the child's duty to honor, respect, and obey parents, see Plato, *Laws* 4.717B-718A; 11.932A; Iamblichus, *On the Pythagorean Way of Life* 8.38, 40; Aristotle, *Nicomachean Ethics* 9.2.7-8; Epictetus, *Discourses* 2.10.7; Valerius Maximus, *Memorable Doings and Sayings* 5.4.7; and, from the New Testament, Ephesians 6:1-3; Colossians 3:20. On the latter texts and their cultural environment, see further Margaret Y. MacDonald's essay in this volume.

5. Jesus was not the only teacher to subordinate family roles and relationships to a higher

tity, the transmission of religious tradition, and the fostering of religious commitment.[6] As for Jesus himself, Luke shows that he already realizes, at the age of twelve, whose son he really is and which filial loyalty must take precedence (2:48-49): he is the Son of God and must be about God's work. Later, when confronted by his mother and brothers, he will assert that it is those who align themselves with God's purpose who constitute his true family, not his own mother and siblings (8:19-21; cf. 11:27-28), although in Luke's narrative his mother and brothers do eventually become part of that new family, that new household of God (Acts 1:14).

Viewed from the side of parents, the narrative also offers both positive and negative images. Parents express care for their children's well-being, approaching Jesus on behalf of their sick children. The prominent community leader Jairus, for example, "fell at Jesus' feet and begged him to come to his house, for he had an only daughter, about twelve years old, who was dying" (Luke 8:41-42). With the words "Child, get up!" Jesus restores health, and life, to the young girl, and he then directs her parents to "give her something to eat" (vv. 54-55), an intriguing practical instruction that presses the parents beyond their astonishment at an extraordinary event to resume their parental responsibility for nurture and care for their daughter.

Later, a father appeals to Jesus to help his spirit-tormented son, after the disciples' attempts at a remedy have failed (Luke 9:37-43). Once again, it is an only child for whom Jesus' intervention as healer is requested: "'Teacher, I beg you to look at my son; he is my only child. Suddenly a spirit seizes him, and all at once he shrieks.' . . . Jesus rebuked the unclean spirit, healed the boy, and gave him back to his father" (vv. 38-39, 42). Perhaps parental concern for the restoration of health to young children is the motive also in 18:15-17: "People were bringing even infants to [Jesus] that he might touch them" (v. 15). Typically, in Lukan healing stories, the children Jesus aids are their parents'

loyalty. See, e.g., Epictetus, *Discourses* 3.3.5-6; Philo, *On the Special Laws* 1.316-18; Musonius Rufus, *Discourse* 14; for further discussion, see Stephen C. Barton, "The Relativisation of Family Ties in the Jewish and Graeco-Roman Traditions," in *Constructing Early Christian Families: Family as Social Reality and Metaphor*, ed. Halvor Moxnes (London: Routledge, 1997), pp. 81-100; Peter Balla, *The Child-Parent Relationship in the New Testament and Its Environment*, Wissenschaftliche Untersuchungen zum Neuen Testament 2.155 (Tübingen: Mohr [Siebeck], 2003).

6. See John G. M. Barclay, "The Family as the Bearer of Religion in Judaism and Early Christianity," in Moxnes, ed., *Constructing Early Christian Families*, pp. 66-80; cf. Halvor Moxnes, "What Is Family? Problems in Constructing Early Christian Families," also in *Constructing Early Christian Families*, pp. 13-41, esp. p. 37. Luke portrays the families of John the baptizer and Jesus as faithful custodians of Jewish tradition and practices (e.g., Luke 1:5-9, 59; 2:21-24, 39, 41).

only children (this is also the case for the only son of the widow at Nain in 7:11-17, although the age of the dead son is unknown). With this distinctive storyteller's touch, Luke raises the stakes for the healing encounter between children (with their parents) and Jesus, which lends added poignancy to the cures, to the liberation, that he effects.

The narrative also pictures parents' concern for their children's care in less extreme circumstances. For example, in a lesser-to-greater argument that highlights God's gracious provision for people, Jesus presupposes that human fathers, too, seek to provide what children need for safety and well-being (Luke 11:9-13). Indeed, if the father in the parable of the two sons is viewed as a positive character,[7] perhaps an image of the extravagantly compassionate, merciful God (15:11-32), then even wayward, disappointing, and rebellious children do not forfeit the loving care of their fathers (parents).

Nevertheless, Jesus also pictures intense conflict between parents and children. This is the other side of Jesus' call to children to leave their households in order to embrace the life of the disciple, for the sake of participation in the realm of God. Parents (siblings, too) may betray Jesus' followers in the time of crisis that is coming (Luke 21:16). Jesus even describes his own mission as purposefully precipitating division within households, setting father against son and son against father, mother against daughter and daughter against mother (12:51-53). The order here may be significant, intimating that it is father and mother, not son and daughter, who initiate conflict — although one would expect that a son's or daughter's decision to forsake the household to follow Jesus would not have found a friendly parental reception. Likewise, John the baptizer, according to the prophetic announcement by the angel Gabriel, is to assume the Elijah-like eschatological role of restoring families, turning the hearts of fathers to their children (1:17). The task is necessary, it appears, because of fault that lies in the fathers, not the children, inasmuch as the synonymous parallelism of verse 17 aligns fathers with "the disobedient" in the next line of Gabriel's message (aligning children, moreover, with "the frame of mind [*phronēsei*] of the righteous"!). If there is intergenerational conflict within the household, in the social world pictured in Luke's narrative, blame may well rest with the parents.

The depiction of children within Jesus' own social context, and in the reimagined world of God's realm, is part of a larger story of the fulfillment of

---

7. Though certainly one whose behavior defies custom and convention for the *paterfamilias:* he too easily cedes power and control, and too readily extends mercy, to his disrespectful sons. See further Bernard Brandon Scott, *Hear Then the Parable: A Commentary on the Parables of Jesus* (Minneapolis: Fortress, 1989), pp. 111, 117, 122.

God's purposes that takes the form of radical reversal. Jesus' message and practices overturn conventional arrangements of power, status, and privilege. Mary's Song highlights precisely this dimension of God's saving intervention in Israel's history (Luke 1:51-53), indicating that the social reversals — the inversion of power, status, and honor — that Jesus announces and enacts in his ministry (e.g., 4:16-21; 6:20-26; 7:18-23; 16:19-31) are part of a longer story of God with God's people. Children receive honor in God's household in ways that they do not and cannot in the social world both Jesus and, later, Luke and his audience inhabit. The upside-down world of God's reign as Jesus sees and practices it shows that, when it comes to children, God's ways are not our ways. Yet since God is the model whose gracious, compassionate mercy we are called to emulate (6:36; cf. 15:11-32), God's ways are to become ours in the world. So hospitality extended to the vulnerable one, the one of low status, becomes welcome extended to God. And the sovereign rule of God assumes the strangest of forms, power and greatness in the guise of low status, humility, and weakness.

Children and Their Parents

The beginning of Luke's narrative locates the families of John and Jesus within faithful, Torah-observant Israel. In such a community, children honor their fathers and mothers, even as all honor and seek to be faithful to God (cf. Luke 10:27; 18:20). Nevertheless, the pious Israel that Luke pictures is also expectant, awaiting the fulfillment of God's ancient promises to the people. Mary gives voice to this hope (1:46-55), but so do Zechariah (1:68-79), Simeon (2:30-32), and Anna along with a host of others (2:36-38). As the story unfolds, readers discover that eschatological fulfillment of ancient promise, at least as Jesus proclaims and embodies it, does not bless ancient social patterns but instead brings disruption. The reversals of power and position for which Mary praises God (1:51-53) necessarily mean trouble for existing households and their structures of power. The family, that is, will not only be affirmed by the ministry of the Messiah but also fundamentally challenged.

Parental Honor and Children's Nurture
(Luke 2:51-52; 11:11-13; 18:20)

Children owe their parents honor, respect, and obedience, an obligation that is grounded in the Decalogue itself:

Honor your father and your mother, so that your days may be long in the land that the LORD your God is giving you. (Exod. 20:12, with recapitulation in Deut. 5:16)

Moreover, the Torah prescribes the harshest of penalties for a rebellious son's disobedience to his father or mother:

Whoever strikes father or mother shall be put to death. . . . Whoever curses father or mother shall be put to death. (Exod. 21:15, 17)

If someone has a stubborn and rebellious son who will not obey his father and mother, who does not heed them when they discipline him, then his father and his mother shall take hold of him and bring him out to the elders of his town at the gate of that place. They shall say to the elders of his town, "This son of ours is stubborn and rebellious. He will not obey us. He is a glutton and a drunkard." Then all the men of the town shall stone him to death. So shall you purge the evil from your midst; and all Israel will hear, and be afraid. (Deut. 21:18-21)

As the latter passage indicates, more is involved in children's (here, sons') respect for and obedience to their parents than household order and parental honor, although these matter a great deal.[8] The entire community has a stake in households wherein parents receive the respect and honor their children owe them. The duty of loyalty and obedience to parents is a social — and clearly, a religious — obligation of the utmost importance. The cohesion, stability, and economic viability of the community depend on such an ordered family structure.[9]

Fittingly, therefore, Luke portrays the child Jesus as an obedient son of pious Jewish parents. On the threshold of adulthood, even when he has become aware that his identity as Son of God relativizes the claim of his earthly parents upon him (Luke 2:48-49), the narrator links his growth "in wisdom and in years, and in divine and human favor" to his ongoing submission to his parents' authority (2:51-52). In the household of Joseph and Mary, he receives nurture, protection — and awareness of his place within

---

8. As Patrick D. Miller points out in his essay in this volume, the Decalogue command that children honor parents has primarily adult children in view.

9. On Philo's reaffirmation of the reciprocal biblical injunctions relating to parents (e.g., protection, nurture, instruction, and discipline) and their children (e.g., obedience, fear, and respect), see Adele Reinhartz, "Parents and Children: A Philonic Perspective," in *The Jewish Family in Antiquity*, ed. Shaye J. D. Cohen, Brown Judaic Studies 289 (Atlanta: Scholars Press, 1993), pp. 61-88.

the people of God. Though the details are hidden from us, the narrative intimates that Jesus' emerging sense of vocation springs from his religious formation within a household where fidelity to God's ways matters, a family in which Jesus' own mother ponders everything, even what lies beyond her comprehension.

Moreover, in Jesus' world, as Luke pictures it, parents provide for and protect their children. This norm of family and village life supplies Jesus with a concrete example on which to build a lesser-to-greater argument that appeals for a life of trust in God:

> [Jesus said to his disciples], "Is there anyone among you who, if your child asks for a fish, will give a snake instead of a fish? Or if the child asks for an egg, will give a scorpion? If you, then, who are evil, know how to give good gifts to your children, how much more will the heavenly Father give the Holy Spirit to those who ask him?" (Luke 11:11-13)

Human fathers, evil though they may be, routinely provide good gifts (e.g., a fish or an egg), not harmful substitutes (a snake or a scorpion), to their children.[10] Jesus gives voice here to a commonsense assumption regarding the characteristic motivation and intention of parents toward their children. He does so in service of an appeal for trust in the provision that comes from a gracious and trustworthy heavenly parent. How much more reliable is God's provision — of the Holy Spirit, God's own empowering presence — for those who ask (v. 13b)![11]

In conversation with a would-be disciple who enjoys a position of considerable status and great wealth, Jesus later acknowledges the biblical injunction to honor parents, among other sacred obligations drawn from the Decalogue (Luke 18:20). However, before the episode has ended, this duty has taken a back seat to far more radical claims upon one's commitment and allegiance. Asked to abandon every security and comfort, to forsake wealth for the benefit of the poor and to leave all behind to follow Jesus, this rich man can only walk away discouraged — a baffling and troubling outcome in the estimation of the audience that overhears the exchange (18:22-27). Jesus' vision of God's household poses a direct challenge to human households and therefore to conventional arrangements that require loyalty and submission

---

10. Tragically, of course, human fathers (and mothers as well) do often harm their own children. For a brief reflection on this interpretive challenge posed by Luke's text, see the concluding section of this essay.

11. The phrasing ("give the Holy Spirit") comes from Lukan redaction; in Matthew 7:11 God gives "good things" to those who ask.

to parents. In the world reconfigured by God's rule, loyalty to God overrides loyalty to one's human parents — or, for that matter, any other allegiance.

God's Reign and a Clash of Family Loyalties
(Luke 2:48-50; 8:19-21; 14:26; 18:28-30; 21:16-17)

Jesus assembles a company of disciples, each of whom has answered the call to leave home and find a place in a new, fictive kinship group, one that has no *paterfamilias* other than God. Luke emphasizes that disciples "leave everything" to attach themselves to Jesus' band (Luke 5:11, 27-28; cf. 18:28-30). If the disciples come to realize that God's claim may collide with allegiance to parents and household, this is a discovery that Jesus made before them, as displayed in the Lukan account of Jesus' visit to the Jerusalem temple at the age of twelve (2:41-50). The revelatory climax of the scene comes with a stunning exchange between the youth and his mother. (Joseph is physically present yet remains intriguingly silent, as he is, indeed, throughout the narrative.)

> When [Jesus'] parents saw him, they were astonished, and his mother said to him, "Child, why have you treated us like this? Look, your father and I have been searching for you in great anxiety." He said to them, "Why were you searching for me? Did you not know that I must be in my Father's house?"[12] But they did not understand what he said to them. (2:48-50)

As Jesus navigates the transition to adulthood, his family's customary Passover pilgrimage to Jerusalem furnishes the occasion for his first words in the narrative. A less than submissive reply to his mother exhibits his awareness that he is *God's* Son — and that this filial role transcends his family ties to Joseph and Mary. *This* is the family to which he belongs, the one that defines his identity and vocation and claims his allegiance.[13]

Some two decades later, Jesus invites others to join the same family, a kin-

---

12. Or "my Father's domain"; literally, "I must be among [in] the things of my Father." On the translation of this ambiguous expression, see Raymond E. Brown, *The Birth of the Messiah* (Garden City, NY: Doubleday, 1979), pp. 475-77, 490-91; Joseph A. Fitzmyer, *The Gospel according to Luke: Introduction, Translation and Notes*, 2 vols., Anchor Bible 28-28A (New York: Doubleday, 1981-85), vol. 1, pp. 443-44; Joel B. Green, *The Gospel of Luke*, New International Commentary on the New Testament (Grand Rapids: Eerdmans, 1997), pp. 156-57; Mark Coleridge, *The Birth of the Lukan Narrative: Narrative as Christology in Luke 1–2*, Journal for the Study of the New Testament — Supplement Series 88 (Sheffield: JSOT Press, 1993), pp. 202-3.

13. This is the striking, and focal, claim of this passage, even if Jesus does return home with his parents afterward as their obedient son (Luke 2:51, discussed above).

ship group defined only by a commitment to align one's life with the purposes of God, to hear the word and do the work of God. When his mother and brothers attempt unsuccessfully to see him, he responds by radically redefining his family affiliation. The words must have sounded to Luke's audience like a shocking rebuff:

> Then [Jesus'] mother and his brothers came to him, but they could not reach him because of the crowd. And he was told, "Your mother and your brothers are standing outside, wanting to see you." But he said to them, "My mother and my brothers are those who hear the word of God and do it." (Luke 8:19-21; cf. 11:27-28)

A summons to hear and do the word of God sounds innocent enough. Who could object to such an approach? Yet this is a subversive and disruptive message when it draws sons and daughters out of their households and locates their primary identity and allegiance elsewhere, in the domain of God. The call to discipleship posed a radical challenge to parental authority and household stability, and the families of those who tied their fortunes to Jesus' band were well aware of the threat — recognition, with accompanying resistance, that is mirrored in a series of Jesus' sayings:

> [Jesus said to the crowds], "Whoever comes to me and does not hate father and mother, wife and children, brothers and sisters, yes, and even life itself, cannot be my disciple." (14:26)

> Then Peter said, "Look, we have left our homes and followed you." And he said to them, "Truly I tell you, there is no one who has left house or wife or brothers or parents or children for the sake of the kingdom of God, who will not get back very much more in this age, and in the age to come eternal life." (18:28-30)

> [In the coming time of intense crisis and persecution of which Jesus is speaking,] "You will be betrayed even by parents and brothers, by relatives and friends; and they will put some of you to death. You will be hated by all because of my name." (21:16-17; cf. 12:51-53)

The call to be Jesus' disciple, to align oneself with the rule of God, requires radical reordering of life. This amounts to a countercultural disruption of family and household. The language is extreme and forces awareness of what is at stake in one's response to Jesus' call to discipleship. To "hate" one's father and mother (and the rest) does not mean to actively (and

ragefully) wish ill for them, as a twenty-first-century reader might assume
— after all, Jesus also commended love of enemies! — but, instead, to have a
deeper commitment and devotion to something else. It is a matter of one's
"primary allegiance," which, for the disciple, cannot be to family but must be
to God's work.[14] The call to hate even oneself means to turn away from the
relationships, activities, and commitments that previously defined identity.
Heeding a summons to separate oneself from house and family, the potential
disciple is not permitted to return home to say farewell, or even to honor the
obligation to bury a parent who has died (9:59-62). Like Jesus at age twelve,
the one who follows Jesus is child of God in a filial relationship that transcends the claim of allegiance to earthly parents. These are not words designed to comfort parents, but they can be liberating and empowering for
their children, especially in a social world in which one's place as dutiful son
or daughter within the household was the primary determinant of identity,
role, and vocation. Of course, if a vigorous and healthy tension between the
command to honor parents and the call to commit oneself to the reign of
God is to be maintained and not simply dissolved in favor of the latter, one
should not forget Jesus' affirmation of the Torah's command to honor parents. Especially in cultures today in which the family is a fragile and imper-
iled institution, how might the continuing call to love and honor parents
constitute a needed corrective to too facile abandonment of family systems
to pursue the latest fad, no matter how alluring?

Children and Status in the Realm of God

Attention to the role and expectations assumed by children in relation to
their parents (and families) in Luke's narrative has yielded significant, if not
entirely consistent, discoveries. Families, including the relationships that bind
parents and children, are important; nevertheless, the call to service in the
realm of God surpasses even those sacred ties. That is already a provocative
approach, but the Lukan perspective on children features even more dramatic
and radical role reversals. Children, like the poor and others on the social
margins, participate in God's grand reversal of present circumstance: the inversion of power, privilege, and status that marks the realm of God.

14. Green, *Gospel of Luke,* p. 565.

The Child as Paradigm of Greatness and Authority
(Luke 2:7; 9:46-48; 18:15-17; 22:25-27)

Within Luke's narrative, the world of human relationships as reconstituted by God's commitments and aims is a strange place. In the realm of God to which Jesus points, the first are last and the last first (Luke 13:30); good fortune belongs to the poor, not the wealthy (6:20, 24; 16:19-31); true honor and pride of position belong to those who lack status, not those who possess it or strive mightily to acquire it (e.g., 14:7-11; 18:14). And in such a world, the young child becomes the paradigm of greatness. Even Jesus' closest disciples, who have seen deeds and heard words that witness to this upside-down reign of God, need repeated instruction on this point, which is decidedly countercultural. The child as model of life in God's realm? Surely not!

It does not require exceptional historical imagination to (re)write the cultural scripts relating to honor and status-seeking in Luke's world.[15] The disciples in this Gospel read from a script that leaves little doubt. The narrator makes equally clear that the attempts of Jesus' followers to acquire status and honor run counter to his own commitments and to the purposes of God. Luke's audience, reoriented from the start to the strange, status-inverting ways of God (e.g., Luke 1:51-53; 4:16-30; 6:20-26), may find the disciples' incomprehension remarkable. However, it is the countercultural practices of Jesus that are remarkable.

Children play a key role in two of the scenes that develop this conflict between Jesus and his disciples on the nature and source of honor or status. In the first passage, the disciples have failed to grasp Jesus' second explicit announcement of the coming death of "the Son of Man" (Luke 9:44-45). The ensuing exchange illustrates how far the disciples are from understanding their Lord's mission:

> An argument arose among [the disciples] as to which of them was the greatest. But Jesus, aware of their inner thoughts,[16] took a little child and put it by his side, and said to them, "Whoever welcomes this child in my name

---

15. See Joel B. Green, *The Theology of the Gospel of Luke,* New Testament Theology (Cambridge: Cambridge University Press, 1995), pp. 76-94; Bruce J. Malina and Jerome H. Neyrey, "Honor and Shame in Luke-Acts: Pivotal Values of the Mediterranean World," in *The Social World of Luke-Acts: Models for Interpretation,* ed. Jerome H. Neyrey (Peabody, MA: Hendrickson, 1991), pp. 25-65. The literature on honor and shame in the social world of early Jews and Christians is now voluminous.

16. Literally, "knowing the reasoning [*dialogismon,* the same word translated "argument" in v. 46] of their hearts." Luke highlights Jesus' prophetic discernment.

welcomes me, and whoever welcomes me welcomes the one who sent me; for the least among all of you is the greatest." (9:46-48)

The disciples compete with one another for the highest place of honor and influence in the company that has gathered around Jesus. He responds with an object lesson that turns their status-seeking on its head. Calling to his side a young child *(paidion)*, he commends hospitality to "this child" as the way to welcome Jesus and therefore the way to welcome God. By positioning the child at his side,[17] Jesus identifies himself with the child, who is to be treated as Jesus' own representative ("in my name").

While the disciples strive to acquire honor, to *take* (i.e., to attain status as the greatest), Jesus redirects the action, speaking of *receiving* another, of extending hospitality. If one desires to honor Jesus, and God, one will do so precisely by extending gracious hospitality — to the young child. By honoring a child, Jesus' own envoy, one honors Jesus, and in honoring Jesus one honors God.[18] But Jesus presses even further. In the realm of God, honor, status, and power are not what they seem. It is the one low in status, the child, who embodies the greatness that Jesus prizes. The one marginal in position and power is the very one whom God honors — one more reprise of the principal theme of Mary's Song.

Young children reappear later in the narrative and again figure in conflict between the perspectives of Jesus and his followers. The disciples may have forgotten the lesson learned in Luke 9:46-48, but Luke's audience will remember.

People were bringing even infants to him that he might touch them; and when the disciples saw it, they sternly ordered them not to do it.[19] But Jesus called for them [i.e., the infants] and said [to the disciples], "Let the little children come to me, and do not stop them; for it is to such as these that the kingdom of God belongs.[20] Truly I tell you, whoever does not receive the kingdom of God as a little child will never enter it." (18:15-17)

Once again, Luke's narrative sharply contrasts the disciples and children, whom Jesus honors at his followers' expense. An unidentified "they" (presumably parents) are bringing babies to Jesus. Their age underscores their vulnerability and dependence *(paidia,* "children," is the word at this point in

17. A distinctive feature of Luke's account; cf. "in their midst" in Matthew 18:2; Mark 9:36.

18. Green, *Gospel of Luke,* p. 392.

19. I would translate the phrase "began to rebuke them"; the imperfect-tense verb is *epetimōn*. With the same verb, the narrator later relates the attempt to silence a blind beggar who seeks Jesus' attention (Luke 18:39).

20. Or "God's realm is composed of ones like these."

Matt. 19:13; Mark 10:13). The motive of the approach to Jesus is likely to seek his "touch" for healing sick children, although this is not stated. Far from offering gracious welcome (cf. Luke 9:48), however, the disciples set up a roadblock, speaking words of sharp rebuke *(epetimōn)*. Jesus sides with the young against his disciples; even infants have right of access to him, because, after all, they already have a place within God's realm. Jesus rebukes the rebukers: if you want to know what God's reign is like, how God's household is constituted, then you need look no further than these children! Indeed, any who wish to have a place in God's realm should look to these vulnerable, low-status children as the model to be emulated. One enters God's realm by embracing it without pretension to status or power.[21]

The line with which Jesus closed the preceding unit — the parable of the Pharisee and the tax agent (Luke 18:9-14), which was told, the narrator reports, to those who esteemed themselves righteous and scorned others (v. 9) — alerts Luke's audience to listen for this theme in verses 15-17: "For all who exalt themselves will be humbled, but all who humble themselves will be exalted" (v. 14). The narrative throws the spotlight on the radical reversals of role and position that attend Jesus' call into the dominion of God.

Without a break in the narrative, a rich ruler now appears (Luke 18:18). He is an *archōn,* a ruler, only in Luke, which underscores both his status and his immense wealth. Thus Luke draws a stark contrast between Jesus' welcome of infants, who model the realm of God, and a ruler who cannot enter God's realm (taking "inherit eternal life" as a synonymous expression), despite his fidelity to Torah — and his status, power, and wealth (vv. 22-23).

In Jesus' acts of healing and hospitality, as in his message, God is effecting radical role reversal, as Mary's Song eloquently announced near the start of the narrative (Luke 1:51-53), and as Jesus programmatically declared in his controversial inaugural address to his hometown synagogue (4:16-30). This world of stunning reversals is well captured in 10:21, where Jesus thanks God for disclosing strange wisdom (i.e., concerning the Spirit active in Jesus' ministry) not to those who are already wise but to infants *(nēpioi)* instead.

Jesus' closest followers have not yet grasped the point by the end of the

---

21. To paraphrase the saying as I construe it: "welcome the realm of God as [*hōs*] a child *does.*" It is possible, however, that Jesus is offering participation in the realm of God to those who welcome (receive) a child, who "welcome the realm of God as he [or she] welcomes a child." The language of hospitality (welcome or receive) does link Luke 18:15-17 and 9:46-48, where it associates welcome extended to the child with that offered to Jesus (and God). In 18:15-17, though, one welcomes the realm of God, not a human being. Hospitable welcome is not the focus in this passage; rather, the central concern is the inversion of status and power in the world ruled by God.

story, so Jesus drives it home one last time in the last meal he shares with his friends. Responding to yet another argument about greatness (Luke 22:24), he attempts again to rewrite the disciples' honor code, admonishing his status-hungry disciples to aim young:

> The kings of the Gentiles lord it over them, and those in authority over them are called benefactors. But not so with you; rather the greatest among you must become like the youngest, and the leader like one who serves. For who is greater, the one who is at the table or the one who serves? Is it not the one at the table? But I am among you as one who serves. (vv. 25-27)

Finally, Jesus himself is the paradigm of greatness in the upside-down world where God is in charge. And he began his own life as a vulnerable newborn, clothed and nourished by his mother — Messiah and Savior, to be sure, but his low status symbolized by his first bed (a feeding trough for animals), the first to acclaim him shepherds living beyond the margins of the city (Luke 2:7, 8-20). Lord of the *oikoumenē* (the world of human culture and habitation), ultimately demoting Caesar (cf. 2:1), yet only by way of a manger — a powerful symbol of the reversals that lie ahead.[22]

Child's Play and a Community's Hospitality (Luke 7:31-35)

Jesus points to children as model participants in the realm of God, but he does not specify what qualities of children he has in mind. Taking a cue from larger narrative patterns in this Gospel, I have located as a central interest the lack of status and power and the vulnerability of children in Jesus' (and Luke's) social world. Children, like others on the margins of the community's life, will receive — do even now receive — honor with God, honor that human society denies them. They illustrate and themselves embody the status transformation that comes with God's reign.

In one passage, however, Luke does draw attention to a particular, and typical, activity of children: play. The routine activity of children playing games in the town market supplies Jesus with a metaphor through which to deliver a stinging indictment of his contemporaries for their failure to embrace his ministry, as well as that of the prophet John before him:

---

22. For discussion of a similar emphasis in Paul's letters on inversion of ordinary cultural values with regard to status and power, see the essay by Beverly Roberts Gaventa in this volume (particularly the section on "The Cross and Human Values").

"To what then will I compare the people of this generation, and what are they like? They are like children sitting in the marketplace and calling to one another,

'We played the flute for you, and you did not dance;
we wailed, and you did not weep.'

For John the Baptist has come eating no bread and drinking no wine, and you say, 'He has a demon'; the Son of Man has come eating and drinking, and you say, 'Look, a glutton and a drunkard, a friend of tax collectors and sinners!' Nevertheless, wisdom is vindicated by all her children." (7:31-35)

The prophet Zechariah painted a picture of children at play in the streets of Jerusalem as a sign of the restoration of the people that God would surely accomplish. In the future time when God will return to Zion, and Jerusalem will be restored as a faithful city, the streets will be populated with old men and women who sit securely, "and the streets of the city shall be full of boys and girls playing in its streets" (Zech. 8:5). In Jesus' redrawing of the image, though, children's play in the streets (or marketplace) of the town takes on a *critical* function. The failure of children to agree on the game they will play — will it be mournful dirge or festive dance? — or perhaps the refusal of some children to play any game at all exposes the refusal of Jesus' contemporaries to respond to the austere prophetic ministry of John the baptizer and then to join the joyful company that gathers around Jesus. That is to say, a breakdown in children's play in the public space of the town offers eloquent commentary on a whole town's (indeed, in an obviously exaggerated complaint, a whole generation's) failure to show hospitality to God's messengers.

The interplay of imagery relating to children and hospitality is thus complex and ironic in Luke's narrative. Welcome of young children becomes emblematic of welcome of God through acceptance of the mission of God's Messiah. Yet lack of hospitality toward the Messiah and his envoys (even more sharply depicted in Luke 9:52-56; cf. 9:5; 10:10-12) finds vivid illustration in children's frustrated attempts to play a game. Children at play in the streets of Jerusalem would be a happy symbol of the restoration of a nation; unfortunately, however, the Messiah sent by God to effect that restoration is encountering both acceptance and resistance, as Simeon's oracle anticipated (2:34). Nevertheless, in God's world, Wisdom finds vindication — God's wisdom is incarnate — in human society among all God's children (7:35): Jesus, John, and all those who embrace their ministries; perhaps even those who, for the time being, have turned away; but certainly no one if not young children, who are beloved of God and who are entitled to inhabit public spaces where they may play freely and safely.

Concluding Reflection

Surveying the surprisingly extensive materials concerning the child and children in Luke's Gospel, we have discovered vivid images of intra-familial conflict alongside affirmations of the formative power and religious significance of children's participation, with their parents, in families. For all the challenge Jesus' vision and communal embodiment of the reign of God pose to the household, he also assumes — at least in Luke 11:11-13 — as the normal pattern that parents express love for their children by providing them with what they need.[23] It would be foolish and potentially even harmful, however, for readers to make such an assumption today. Parents do often harm, do often seek what hurts rather than nourishes and nurtures their children.[24] The "evil" in human parents, which Jesus does recognize (e.g., 11:13), sometimes — whether intentionally or unwittingly — delivers snake or scorpion, not nourishing egg or fish, to a dependent child. Readers of Luke's narrative today, aware of the destructive reality of child abuse, may find in this Gospel both challenge and inspiration to develop creative communal structures that support and nurture children, assisting and reinforcing the efforts of parents but also, when necessary, intervening to stand with the child. Luke's text prompts a haunting question, as one considers the development of a child's capacity for trust, and thus for authentic faith. If human parents give their children what they need and so model, though in a flawed and imperfect way, God's benevolent, gracious care, how will capacity to trust in God emerge when parents (or other significant adults) are fundamentally untrustworthy? In such cases, the theological priority of participation in the realm of God — hence in the *fictive* family that gathers around Jesus — may prove to be as much resource and aid as it is problem for the community of God's people.

"What then will this child become?" (Luke 1:66). Friends and neighbors of

23. Paul shares this assumption about the parental role (see 2 Cor. 12:14), as Beverly Roberts Gaventa observes in her essay in this volume.

24. In this connection, I continue to find instructive and challenging, though certainly not convincing on all points, the work of Alice Miller. See, e.g., *For Your Own Good: Hidden Cruelty in Child-Rearing and the Roots of Violence,* trans. Hildegarde Hannum and Hunter Hannum (New York: Farrar, Straus, and Giroux, 1983); and *Thou Shalt Not Be Aware: Society's Betrayal of the Child,* trans. Hildegarde Hannum and Hunter Hannum (New York: Farrar, Straus, and Giroux, 1984).

the newborn John, son of Elizabeth and Zechariah, originally posed this question as they pondered his significance. However, it signals the importance of other children in the Lukan narrative, including "this child" whom Jesus, wishing to counter the misguided passion for greatness and status voiced by his disciples, called to his side (9:46-48), and those young children whom Jesus summoned after his own disciples had chastised them (18:15-17). What will these children be? In Jesus' bold vision and radical practice of the realm of God, children receive special hospitality and honor; indeed, wiser, stronger adults who yearn to have a place in God's household would do well to accept the low status and honor that belongs to children within this world. In the upside-down, inside-out world of reversal that is God's dominion, children — like others among the socially marginalized — will be specially honored guests. The community that bears Jesus' message into the future and seeks to embody his values and commitments in its practices would do well to welcome and honor them, too. And not only that. They will take a cue, for their own relationships to one another, to the world, and to the Holy, from the child among them.

9   Children in the Gospel of John

Marianne Meye Thompson

Children are essentially missing from the pages of the Gospel of John. It lacks the stories and metaphors, so dear from the other Gospels, that have undergirded Christian understanding of children for years. Unlike the Synoptic Gospels, the Gospel of John does not recount any story in which Jesus encounters a child: no pastoral paintings of Jesus taking children onto his lap and blessing them could be painted based on John (compare Mark 10:13-16; par. Matt. 19:13-15; Luke 18:15-17). Nowhere in John does Jesus hold up a child as a model of the humble status requisite for greatness in the kingdom (Mark 9:35; Matt. 18:2) or compare the way one welcomes a child to the way one welcomes him (Mark 9:37; Matt. 18:5; Luke 9:48). There are no stories from the infancy or youth of Jesus (Matt. 2:13-21; Luke 2:21-38, 41-52). No healings are recounted that obviously entail the healing of young children (compare, e.g., Mark 5:21-43; Matt. 9:18-26; Luke 8:40-56). Few persons or characters in the Gospel of John, except the royal official (John 4:48-52), even seem to have children; again, compare Jesus' many allusions to families in parables and sayings in the Synoptic Gospels (e.g., Mark 12:19; Luke 15:11-32; Matt. 21:28-32). John also lacks the explicit warnings about intra-family conflicts, such as those regarding children and parents "rising against" each other (Mark 13:12; Matt. 10:21; Luke 21:16). Finally, in John, no children cry out, "Hosanna to the Son of David!" (Matt. 21:15) at the triumphal entry. Children are simply silent.

However, the metaphor "children of God" does occur in John. While the metaphor might at first seem to offer direct access to an exploration of children and childhood in the Gospel, it actually suggests that we must come at the topic indirectly. "Children of God" does not denote children as those who are young, but refers to any and all persons as children of God. Indeed, the metaphor drives us to consider the broader theological framework of the

Gospel in which the image is lodged. In order, then, to reflect on how John might shape our thinking about children, in spite of the absence of children in its pages, and how thinking about children in John might shape our reading of the Gospel, I propose to investigate the central theme of the Gospel, namely, the theme of life, and, more specifically, the Johannine claim that God gives life to the world through his Son and by his Spirit, through which human beings are reborn as children of God. John has too often been read as a "spiritual Gospel," where "spiritual" is defined as that inner, individual, or personal religious aspect of human life that stands over against life in its material, social, and economic aspects. But this Gospel, whose central theme is life, demands that we see the needs of human beings as physical, social, economic, *and* spiritual. None of these may be left out of account in how we think about human beings and, consequently, how we think about children.

Within this framework we may then probe more carefully the metaphor "children of God" to suggest what it meant and how it might serve to focus our understanding of children. Over the years such terminology has been read as referring to the "spiritual" status of those who are "children of God," in part because it clearly does not denote any sort of physical descent from God. But increased attention in recent years to the social setting of the Gospel of John indicates that these terms of kinship served to provide the nascent messianic community with an identity when the natural human ties of kinship and family had been painfully and unfortunately severed through disagreements about the messianic identity of Jesus. Those who were "children of God" lived out that identity in this world, with particular social consequences. While John celebrates the formation of the new "family of God," centered in Jesus, the Son, it is clear that the loss of the natural or physical family that sometimes attended it is viewed as a great rift in the fabric of the way things should be.

Finally we will turn our thoughts to the one who was not merely another child of God, but the Son of God, and who sends out his followers even as he was sent, in order to ask how the shape of his life might in turn shape the lives of his disciples. Obviously John posits a significant difference between those who are born as children of God and the one who simply is the Son of God. And while more than one narrative does present Jesus as a model to be emulated, it is also clear that Jesus' life cannot be reduced to a model to be emulated. Still, those who follow Jesus carry out the work that he himself embodied, namely, to bring life and light into the world of death and darkness. Taken together, these pieces can provide a theological framework for how one thinks about ministry to and with the children of this world, who, as those who are created by God, are also called to find their identity as children of

God. Moreover, focusing on children brings into sharper view John's emphasis on life, for the process of birth and the nurturing of children provide vivid
images of human relationship to God, the Creator of all.

God's Life for the World

We will begin with an exploration of the fundamental theme in the Gospel of
John of God's life-giving purposes for the world. The narrative of the Gospel
of John is the account of the one in whom there was, is, and will be life for the
world, namely, the Word of God (1:4; 11:25; 14:6). The Gospel of John reflects
the life-giving character of the Word in its very structure: it begins with creation ("In the beginning . . . all things were created"; 1:1, 3) and anticipates the
return of Christ (21:23). In the theme of *life,* we find John's vision of what human existence is and ought to be in relationship to God who is the creator
and source of all life. This is, then, the starting point for thinking about the
lives and value of children as well.

"All Things Were Made through Him"

That God created the world through Christ is repeated in various parts of the
New Testament; these passages also tend to emphasize that *all* things were
created through Christ. In John 1:3 we read, "all things were made through
him" *(panta di auto egeneto),* and the note is insistently echoed elsewhere.
Thus Paul writes in 1 Corinthians that there is one God "from whom are *all
things* and for whom we exist, and one Lord, Jesus Christ, through whom are
all things and through whom we exist" (1 Cor. 8:6; compare Col. 1:16-17; Heb.
1:2). Such an emphasis draws upon the Old Testament portrayal of God, and
particularly Isaiah 40–55, as the sole creator of all, who consequently exercises
unique sovereignty over all things as well. God is not only the creator, but the
sole creator of the world (Isa. 44:24) and of all that is (Isa. 40:28, 45:7; 48:12-13;
cf. 42:5; 44:24; 45:11-12). Such sentiments are echoed in later Jewish literature:
the God "who lives for ever created *all things*" (Sir. 18:1 LXX); is the "creator of
all things" (2 Macc. 1:24-25); the "cause of *all things*" (Philo, *Dreams* 1.67); "the
beginning and middle and end of *all things,*" and the one who "breathes life
into *all creatures*" (Josephus, *Against Apion* 2.190; *Antiquities* 12.2.2).

Such formulations provided fruitful material for the church's struggles
with Gnosticism. In Gnosticism, a radically dualistic philosophical and religious movement, judged a heresy by the early church, salvation was a release

of the spirit from the material body. Inasmuch as matter was deemed evil, it followed that the Most High God could not have created the material world; such a role was assigned to an inferior deity. Hence, the God who created the world, according to Genesis, could not be the God and Father of the Lord Jesus Christ. The early church insisted in various ways on holding things together that the Gnostics held apart. Whereas the Gnostics dissolved the unity of God, distinguishing between a God who was creator and another who was redeemer, the New Testament and the church bore witness that the God of Israel, who created the world, is indeed the God and Father of our Lord Jesus Christ, through whom God redeems the world. The insistence on the unity of God, and on the unity of the work of Father and Son, served as a bulwark against the denigration of the material realm and against a conception of salvation as focused solely on the escape of the soul or spirit of a person from his or her body.

An insistence on the unity of God also means that the God who creates is the God who saves. Indeed, even as the prologue of John insists that "the world was made through him" (1:11), so too later in the Gospel Jesus is said to take away the "sin of the world" (1:29) and to be the "Savior of the world" (4:42). John's language may be taken to point to the universal focus of God's saving work through Christ, but it also binds together the creation and salvation of the world, so that salvation cannot be construed as a rescue of the spirit from the physical realm. Indeed, the one God who created the world also loves it and desires to save it. The life *of* this world is as much the gift of God as the life that comes *after* this world.

The Incarnation of the Word: The Unity of Spirit and Flesh

Perhaps no statement in John affirms the goodness of the material world so clearly as does the statement of the Incarnation: "The Word became flesh" (John 1:14). As Augustine notes in his *Confessions,* although he had read Greek philosophy and found numerous similarities to the doctrine of the *Logos* (Word) in it, there was one significant difference: "I did not read in them that 'the Word was made flesh and came to dwell among us'" (7.9). Augustine's comment reflects the ancient dualism of Greek thought, which understood deity as absolute, unchangeable, and transcendent, and therefore also uncontaminated by the material world, which bore none of those traits. The Logos was the "link" between the transcendent and the material but did not actually participate in the material realm. But in Christian thought, the Logos becomes flesh and enters into the material realm, without thereby ceasing to be

God. John puts it boldly: the Word became flesh and dwelled among us. As Augustine also comments, "He was counted as one of our number and he paid his dues to Caesar" (*Confessions* 5.3). In other words, he took on not only the flesh of the human condition, but the particular human flesh of a Jewish subject of the Roman empire in the first century. He became a human being.

The dualism of Greek thought, which made the genuine incarnation or "enfleshment" of the divine an impossible thought, lay behind certain ancient religious movements, particularly but not only Gnosticism. If Augustine wrote that he had not read in the Greek philosophers that "the Word had become flesh," Irenaeus commented that no heretic held the view that the Word was made flesh (*Against Heresies* 3.11.3). John's statement, "the Word became flesh," has been taken as an attack on Docetism, the belief that Jesus lacked a body of real flesh and blood and only seemed to be human (Docetism, from the Greek, *dokein,* "to seem"). Whether or not it was written to combat Docetism, the Gospel's statement that the "Word became flesh" certainly would have been impossible for a Gnostic or a Docetist.

These points are important because of the tendency to read John in solely "spiritual" terms. By that I mean the tendency to characterize what Jesus does for human beings solely in "spiritual" terms, so that the miracle of the feeding of the five thousand is really about the fact that Jesus offers "spiritual food"; the raising of Lazarus is really about the eternal (= spiritual) life that Jesus offers; and the kingdom of Jesus pertains solely to the spiritual realm ("My kingdom is not of this world"; John 18:36). But John does not characterize "life" or "eternal life" with the adjectives "physical" and "spiritual." Indeed, John uses two terms for life: he uses *zōē* (life) eighteen times and *zōē aiōnios* (eternal life) eighteen times; and he uses the verb "to live" *(zaō)* seventeen times. "Life" and "eternal life" appear to be used interchangeably (cf. 3:16; 5:24; 5:3-40; 6:47-48; 10:10, 28; 20:31) John does not characterize "real" life as "spiritual" or "eternal" over against what we might call "created life." In fact, the opposite for John of eternal life is not earthly life but death; similarly, the opposite of earthly life is also death. There is no terminological distinction in John between "spiritual death" and "physical death," and eternal life refers not to a spiritual condition but to the life one has with God after the resurrection to life. Life, in all its forms, comes from the hand of God.

Thus, for example, in John 6 Jesus feeds the five thousand with five loaves and two fishes. While modern readers of Scripture typically refer to this and other deeds as miracles, John's regular term for such deeds is "signs." As "signs," these amazing deeds point to who Jesus is and what he offers, as well as to the God of life who offers gifts of life and health through Jesus. This particular "sign" indicates that Jesus is the bread of life, who feeds those who are hungry and gives drink to those who are thirsty (John 6:35). A typical way of reading this story is to interpret "eating" and "drinking" as "spiritual" practices; that is, they have to do with coming to faith. Indeed, the story is also often read to disparage the desire to seek for physical food: the crowds seek Jesus because "they ate their fill of the loaves" (6:26). But the point of John 6 is not that Jesus provides spiritual sustenance for walking on the path of discipleship — although he does indeed provide that — but that he is the source of *all* life. Since the one who feeds the five thousand is also the one through whom the world was created (1:3), what the crowds are being asked to see is not that Jesus provides spiritual rather than physical nourishment, or that spiritual food is better than physical food, but rather that the one who has fed their bodies can do so because he is the one through whom all life was created and, hence, will also raise them to life at the last day. Put differently, the one who feeds their bodies also feeds their spirits; the bread of life nourishes both body and spirit. This one is the agent of God's life: unless this were so, he could not have fed them; unless this were so, he could not raise them to life at the last day (6:54, 58).

Thus Rudolf Schnackenburg rightly insisted on the "solidly material aspect" of the signs of Jesus.[1] In narrating the accounts of Jesus' signs, John often takes pains to paint the situation of those in need in great detail so as to emphasize their helplessness. Thus in John 5:1-9 the paralyzed man, apparently helpless, has been lying among a crowd of needy people for thirty-eight years (vv. 6-7). He cannot help himself, and no one helps him (v. 7). To the eyes of all others and likely to himself, his plight appears hopeless; that is, it appears hopeless to all but Jesus. In John 6, there is a large crowd (v. 5) with needs to be met and inadequate resources to meet them (vv. 7, 9). Again, no one else imagines that anything can be done; but Jesus does, and he undertakes to do it. These situations are real, the needs are severe, and Jesus meets those needs. Jesus has and provides the resources needed to heal the man, and he uses what little is available among the five thousand to feed the crowds. He does not tell the man at the pool that his real need is "spiritual healing," nor does he tell the crowds that their real needs are "spiritual." Neither does he simply reduce the man to his physical needs, nor the crowds to their hunger. The man needs healing, and the crowd needs food; and because Jesus is the agent of the creator God, the God of life, he can provide these gifts to the creation.

But Jesus also warns the man about the consequences of sin, and he admonishes the crowd that eating one's fill is not all there is to life. In both cases,

---

1. Rudolf Schnackenburg, *The Gospel According to St. John,* vol. 1 (New York: Herder and Herder, 1968), pp. 515-28.

Jesus interprets what he has done as an act of obedience to God. It is God's desire to feed, to heal, to forgive sin, and to bring people to faith. By interpreting such texts within the context of the prologue's emphasis on the creation of *all things* through the Word of God, and of the Incarnation as the en-*flesh*-ment or embodiment of that Word, these texts can be seen to offer quite a decidedly anti-dualistic view of the work of God in Christ. The spiritual and bodily aspects of the human being are united because they were united in Christ. It is in this framework that we should understand who and what God's purposes for the world are, and what the needs of human beings, including children, are.

Children in the Ancient World

John's emphasis on life may also be set in the context of the ancient world's familiarity with mortality, particularly with the mortality of infants and children. While the evidence regarding treatment of and regard for children in the ancient world is rather mixed, children were regularly "at risk" in ancient societies because of their physical fragility, and certain children were especially at risk of abandonment and abuse. Here we find a stark contrast with both the Jewish and Christian world in terms of their understanding of the divine mandate to care for those most vulnerable, including children and the unborn. Indeed, because God is the Creator of all, and because God cares for the poor, the orphaned, and the widowed, those who claim to worship and honor God are called to manifest similar care and compassion for those most vulnerable to the abuses of society and even to the vicissitudes of ordinary life.

At Risk: Child Mortality, Abortion, and Infanticide

In his study *Adults and Children in the Roman Empire,* classicist Thomas Wiedemann discusses the situation of children in the ancient Roman empire. As Wiedemann notes, child mortality was a simple fact of life. While numbers and statistics are notoriously difficult to compile for this period — and especially so when they involve children, and the children of the poor or slaves — it is difficult to doubt that the rate of mortality in childhood was quite high. Wiedemann conjectures that in the ancient world, where life expectancy was probably between 20 and 25 years, it was likely that a child had a fifty-fifty chance of surviving to age 10, and a less than one-in-two chance of living into adulthood.[2] In other words, in the ancient world, all children were children at risk, at least at risk of not surviving into adulthood. It should be noted that Wiedemann's statistics are drawn, to a large extent, on data gleaned (so far as they can be) from contemporary under- or pre-industrialized societies.[3] The realities inhabited by many of the world's citizens are closer to those faced in antiquity than to those dealt with by the developed world.

In view of the high mortality rates in the ancient world, it is not surprising that children were characterized as weak, vulnerable, and fragile. Thomas Wiedemann points out that in many ways children were particularly associated with the world of the gods: they were in special need of divine protection because of their vulnerability and weakness. Interestingly, however, Wiedemann interprets these data as pointing, not to the importance, but rather to the marginality of children. He writes, "Classical society saw children as especially associated with the divine world because they were *unimportant,* not because they were the same as adults."[4] Although Wiedemann does not say it in this way, it seems that children were in special need of the protection of the gods *from* other human beings who were likely to prey upon the weaknesses of children and exploit their fragility. Classical society seemed at times to view the weakness of children, and especially of deformed or female children, as grounds for their destruction rather than for their need of protection. There is no congruence between the actions of the gods and human responsibility.

There is of course truth in the evaluation of children as weak, vulnerable, and fragile because of their physical and mental immaturity. But the characterization of children — along with women, the aged, and slaves — in these terms served simply to further relegate them to inferior or secondary status and to the margins of community life. Rather than seeing the fragility of children as reason for their special need for protection and care, the negative characterization of children in these terms served as a foil for true "manhood" — and, hence, true humanity. Children did not measure up to the standards of the adult male; hence, they did not need to be afforded the same protections or privileges of adult males. In the pagan world, therefore, children were at risk not merely because of their lesser physical and mental capacities, but because as children they were at greater risk for exploitation and abuse.

2. Thomas Wiedemann, *Adults and Children in the Roman Empire* (New Haven and London: Yale University Press, 1989), pp. 11-17.

3. Wiedemann, *Adults and Children,* pp. 13-16.

4. Wiedemann, *Adults and Children,* p. 185; emphasis added.

To be sure, children were thought to deserve some protection; for example, because they were noncombatants in war, they were to be protected and not to be killed. However, there are also tales of the massacre and enslavement of children, as well as reports of infanticide and exposure of unwanted babies, particularly girls or babies that were deformed in any way. A frequently cited letter from Hilarion to his pregnant wife, Alis, demonstrates the contrast between his anticipation of the birth of a son and that of a daughter: "Know that I am still in Alexandria. . . . I ask and beg you to take good care of our baby son, and as soon as I receive payment I shall send it up to you. If you are delivered of a child [before I come home], if it is a boy keep it, if a girl, discard it."[5] The Roman statesman and philosopher, Seneca, writes, "We destroy our monstrous children and also drown our children if they are weak or unnaturally formed," adding that it is not "anger, but reason that separates the harmful from the sound" (*On Anger* 1.15.2-3). While in the ancient world all children were, in some respects, children at risk, that risk was greatly increased among those children who were additionally vulnerable, such as those born with birth defects, or those less valued in society, such as girls.[6]

How widespread the practice of infanticide was in the pagan world is not known. Some modern authors have interpreted the data to indicate that the practices of infanticide and exposure of unwanted newborns were horrifically common, but the lack of documentation renders all such conclusions tentative.[7] But what is clear is that both Jews and Christians repeatedly condemned both abortion and infanticide, because these acts were violations of God's commands and destroyed that which God had created. There is to be a definite congruence between God's own regard for children and human responsibilities toward them, a subject to which we now turn.

---

5. Papyrus Oxyrhynchus 744; it can be dated to the 17th of June, 1 BCE.

6. Indeed, the general consensus seems to be that in both theory and practice infant girls were more liable to infanticide by various means.

7. See, for example, Rodney Stark, *The Rise of Christianity: How the Obscure, Marginal Jesus Movement Became the Dominant Religious Force in the Western World in a Few Centuries* (San Francisco: HarperCollins, 1997), pp. 97-99, 118, 124-25: "Not only was the exposure of infants a very common practice, it was justified by law and advocated by philosophers" (p. 118); Wiedemann, *Adults and Children*, p. 36. But see Sarah B. Pomeroy, *Goddesses, Whores, Wives, and Slaves: Women in Classical Antiquity* (New York: Schocken Books, 1975), p. 165, who comments, "Christian authors such as Justin Martyr doubtless exaggerate the extent to which contemporary pagans engaged in infanticide, but, on the other hand, it is clear that this method of family planning was practiced without much fanfare in antiquity."

Jewish and Christian Protection of Children

In considering responsibilities to children today, it is important to note that both Jewish and Christian tradition ground the treatment of children ultimately in God's commands and in God's creation of all that is. In other words, it is not merely because children are vulnerable or fragile, or because they are the responsibility of those who brought them into the world, but because they are created by God that they have status, dignity, and inestimable value. The "lens" through which ancient Jews and Christians viewed children was essentially the dictum of Genesis 1, picked up in the New Testament, that God is the giver of all life and that the law of God protects those to whom God has given life. Thus, for example, Josephus noted that both abortion and infanticide were prohibited in the law (*Against Apion* 2.202); in couching his argument in the philosophic garb of the ancient world, Philo added that these practices violated the laws of nature (*Special Laws* 3.110-19). In the Jewish *Sentences of Pseudo-Phocylides* (50 BCE–100 CE) we read, "Do not let a woman destroy the unborn babe in her belly, nor after its birth throw it before the dogs and the vultures as a prey" (lines 184-185).

Christianity inherited its prohibition against both abortion and infanticide from its Jewish heritage. The *Didache* (or "The Teaching of the Twelve Apostles"; early second century?) states: "Thou shalt not murder a child by abortion" (2:2) and also notes that "The Way of Death is filled with people who are . . . murderers of children and abortionists of God's creatures" (5:1-2). The Epistle of Barnabas (ca. 125 CE?) also repeats the prohibition against both (19.5). Justin Martyr explained the prohibition against exposure of infants as follows:

> We have been taught that to expose newly-born children is the part of wicked men; and this we have been taught lest we should do any one an injury, and lest we should sin against God, first, because we see that almost all so exposed (not only the girls, but also the males) are brought up to prostitution. . . . And again [we fear to expose children], lest some of them be not picked up, but die, and we become murderers. (*First Apology* 27, 29; ca. 150 CE)

A second-century Christian apologist, Athenagoras, wrote to the Roman emperor Marcus Aurelius, pleading against the practices of abortion and infanticide because the fetus in the womb is "a created being, and therefore an object of God's care. . . . [We do not] expose an infant, because those who expose them are chargeable with child-murder" (*Plea for Christians* 35). Christian emperors outlawed the practice of exposure in the year 374 CE.

Both Jews and Christians interpreted the prohibitions against infanticide or exposure of infants in *theological* terms, appealing either to the law of God or to the status of the infant as created by God to argue that the one who exposed a child was guilty of murder and would have to answer to God. There is no explicit appeal to the inherent value of the child apart from that child's relationship to and creation by God. But this very relationship grants the child inestimable value and dignity. Created by God, and protected by the law of God, the child derives her identity and status from the God who created her, and this affords the child unique protection.

The data from antiquity cannot be construed to mean that pagan parents routinely disposed of their children or that there was no genuine affection for them; there are, indeed, accounts of or letters from fathers grieving the loss of children — including girls — who had died. Moreover, the ideal emperor as *pater patriae* (often translated "father of the fatherland") was painted as one who had a special concern for the weak, which included children, women, and old men. But the data does testify that, on the whole, children, and especially those particularly vulnerable, were viewed as less than fully human and, therefore, sometimes treated virtually as trash to be disposed of if inconvenient in any way. It is not hard to argue that without a doctrine of the creation of the world by one supreme God, there is no ultimate ground for arguing for the protection of the weak and vulnerable. But the view that God has created all that is and that God cares for his creation provides an immediate platform for valuing even the "least" of the world.

The Gospel of John describes human beings in their relationship to God as "children of God" in part because this metaphor for human beings develops the idea of God as the life-giving Father. Human beings receive their life and their identity from God. Thus the metaphor also serves as a lens through which we may get a picture of human life in relationship to God; that is, human beings draw their life, identity, and value from relationship to the God who created them and who gives them new birth through the Spirit.

Children of God and the Family of God

The Gospel speaks of the disciples of Jesus as "children of God" (John 1:12; 11:52); Jesus addresses his disciples as "little children" (13:33) and "children" (21:5). John does not claim, as did the Jewish writer Aristobulus (second century BCE), "We are all [God's] children" (fragment 4.6). Rather, it is clear that, in John, the designation "children of God" refers not to all humankind, but rather to those who, by God's Spirit, have become part of a new family of God

(1:12-13). The designation "children of God" does signal that identity comes from belonging — here, belonging to the God who made them — and this theme is worth probing further for the way in which the metaphor "children of God" illumines human identity with relationship to God the Creator.

Born Anew: New Life from God

The phrase "children of God" *(tekna tou Theou)* in John points to the fact that human identity is ultimately grounded in relationship to God, who created "all things" through Christ. The descriptive epithet "children of God" appears first in 1:12, where those who become God's children are contrasted with those who are born "of ordinary descent" (quite literally, "of bloods"; *ex haimaton*) and of "fleshly desire" *(ek thelēmatos sarkos)*.[8] It is not physical birth or lineage that qualifies one to be a "child of God"; rather, the children of God are those who believe in the name of the Son of God *(huios tou Theou)*. Later, in one of the best-known dialogues in the Gospel, Jesus informs Nicodemus that he needs to be "born from above" (3:3). Here Jesus speaks of a second birth that is not physical. Such birth has nothing to do with entering into a mother's womb again (3:4); rather, it is a birth effected by the Spirit of God (3:5). This description alludes to God's creation of human- kind as recounted in Genesis, where we read that God "formed man from the dust of the ground, and breathed into his nostrils the breath of life; and the man became a living being" (Gen. 2:7, NRSV). Both the Hebrew and Greek words for "breath" can also be translated "spirit." Hence, when Jesus tells Nicodemus that he must be born by "the Spirit" (John 3:5), there are echoes of the scene in Genesis 2: just as God "breathed" the breath (or Spirit) of life into the first human being, so God gives new birth through the Spirit of life. In John's perspective, all are created by God; not all are recipients of the Spirit of new birth.

Although one might call this new birth a "spiritual birth," two points are important here. First, God gives new life to those whom he had first created. God does not will death for his creation but, having given it life, now wills new life for it. Second, it is important to note that this so-called "spiritual" birth has concrete consequences and manifestations, as we shall see. Those who were "born anew" were born into a new community; but they might also have discovered that belonging to this new fellowship entailed leaving a com-

---

8. See also David L. Bartlett's discussion of the Johannine texts in "Adoption in the Bible," in this volume.

munity that included one's natural family for another community, namely, a community of those who likewise professed faith in Jesus and so had been born anew as God's children. At least in some instances, becoming a child of God means that natural family ties are severed and natural family relationships are lost.

The idea that one's religious allegiances determined and even overrode all other allegiances can be found in various Jewish authors, such as Philo of Alexandria (20 BCE–50 CE), who wrote:

> But as for these kinships, as we call them, which have come down from our ancestors and are based on blood-relationship, or those derived from marriage or other similar causes, let them all be cast aside if they do not seek earnestly the same goal, namely the honor of God, which is the indissoluble bond of affection which makes us one.[9]

In Philo, as in early Christian thinking, common religious allegiance bound its adherents not only to one and the same God but also to each other. So also the community at Qumran, with its ideals for adherence to the sect, suggests a similar subordination of family and household ties for the sake of religious commitment, including commitment to a particular community. Among pagans, one may cite the Cynics, who held that the ideal philosopher was free from all worldly distractions brought about by the duties of family and home, so that he could be free to be "wholly devoted to the service of God" and to the universal family.[10] In other words, religious — or philosophical — commitments entailed the subordination of family ties, but brought with them identification with and belonging to a new community.

Gathered by God: The New Family of Jesus

The phrase "children of God" also indicates what we may call the horizontal dimension of identity: those who belong to God belong to each other. Because John has frequently been interpreted in highly individualistic terms, it is important to note the thread of communal identity that runs throughout

---

9. Philo, *Special Laws* 1.316-17. For a fuller discussion of similar passages in ancient literature and comparison to the Gospels, see Stephen C. Barton, *Discipleship and Family Ties in Mark and Matthew,* Society for New Testament Studies Monograph Series 80 (Cambridge: Cambridge University Press, 1994); and, in this volume, John T. Carroll's discussion of the phenomenon in the Gospel of Luke and ancient literature (esp. note 2).

10. Epictetus, *Discourses* 3.22.69-72.

the Gospel. Several passages and images may be noted in this regard: Jesus is portrayed as a shepherd who gathers his flock together (John 10:16); his death serves to "gather together the children of God who are scattered abroad" (11:52), even as promised in the prophets.[11] As we have seen, the idea that religious affiliation creates a new set of kin and allegiances was not novel in the ancient world. It matters all the more, therefore, how one names the particular family or community to which one belongs. What values, relationships, and commitments are part of this particular community? From whom does this community draw its identity? Whose character determines the shape of these relationships?

In the Gospel of John, the "Father" in this community is the life-giving God who loves the world (John 3:16). The family must, therefore, follow his example in actions that bring life, and in the manifestation of love; indeed, "love one another" summarizes all the commandments in the Gospel of John (13:34-35; 15:13). So Jesus calls those who do his commands not "servants" but "friends" (15:14-15). This granting of the status of "friend" rather than "servant" or "slave" to those who belong to his family demonstrates that the designation of "children of God" likewise refers not to a secondary or inferior status, but to an honorific identity as those who are brothers and sisters to the one who is the Son of God. They have become members of the family of Jesus that has been gathered together by God.

One narrative in John calls special attention to the shape of the family that is both lost and established when the social networks that ordinarily bind parents to children are disrupted. This narrative is the story of the man born blind in John 9. It is easy to characterize this man as displaying a heroic profession of faith: he stands alone against the taunts and under the questioning of "the Pharisees" in this chapter, until ultimately they reject him. In spite of their rejection, he nevertheless professes his trust in Jesus with the simple words, "LORD, I believe." His parents appear in the cast, but not in the role of "supporting actor and actress." Quite the contrary — they distance themselves from the man and refuse to speak on his behalf, and the man must fend for himself. But in spite of the exemplary courage and faith of this man, there is clearly a critical undercurrent in the story as well. Not only do this man's parents lack courage, but they abandon him. He has become, in essence, an orphan. Furthermore, the family has been torn asunder by that which should have united them: the healing of their son by the one who embodies God's life

---

11. For the hope of the regathering of God's people or of the twelve tribes, see Isaiah 11:12; 43:5-6; 54:7-8; 56:8; Jeremiah 23:1-5; Ezekiel 34:5-11; 37:20-28; see also Sirach 35:11; 48:10; Baruch 4:37; 5:5; 2 Maccabees 1:27; 2:17-18; Jubilees 1:15; Psalms of Solomon 11:2; 17:28-31.

and light for the world. Now the man needs a family and a place to belong. Jesus takes the initiative to find the man when his own people have "cast him out" (9:35). Jesus' act of seeking and finding the man show him to be the good shepherd who keeps the flock from being scattered; a shepherd who protects his own, and does not abandon his own to the wolves; one who will not leave his followers as orphans (14:18). Later, in John 21, Jesus entrusts Peter with the care of his sheep. Following Jesus' own example, the church serves to pastor the sheep, the diverse "children of God," who are under its care, and who are often abandoned by the very parents and communities who should be responsible for them.

This new family is sealed in Jesus' words from the cross, where he entrusts his mother to the care of the Beloved Disciple, and vice versa (19:26-27). Earlier in the Gospel, Jesus had distanced himself from both his mother and his brothers. In John 2, in the account of the changing of the water into wine, Jesus' mother reports to him that the host of the wedding has run out of wine. Presumably she expects Jesus to help in some way, although the text does not specify what he is to do or why he is to do it. Some have speculated that this is a family wedding and that therefore Jesus might be particularly obligated to help. In any case, when Jesus' mother informs him of the problem, he appears to rebuff her, replying, "Woman, what does this have to do with me?" (2:4). But Jesus then provides an abundance of wine for the wedding. Similarly, when Jesus' brothers urge him to go up to the festival in Jerusalem to make himself known, Jesus says he will not go, but subsequently does go (7:1-10). Odd as they may seem, these accounts share a common pattern: a family member makes a request of Jesus; he refuses it; but then he essentially does what was originally asked — apparently not because his family has made the request, but because he has acted in accord with the will of his Father. Jesus severs natural family ties for the sake of obedience to his Father.

Then, as he is dying, Jesus entrusts his mother to the disciple whom he loves and entrusts that disciple to his mother (19:26-27). The scene can be read on two levels. On the one hand, it can be read literally, as Jesus' provision for his mother by establishing a new relationship between her and his own disciple. On the other hand, the scene has been taken figuratively or symbolically as establishing the new "spiritual" family of God, that is, the church. These options should not be taken as mutually exclusive. Jesus does create new realities, new relationships, new communities. But for John, the ideal would be the overlap of the natural family and the family of the children of God.

Children of God and the Human Family

The Johannine term "children of God" refers specifically to those who profess their allegiance to Jesus as the Messiah and Son of God. "Children of God" does not designate the entire human race, but, like the phrase "children of Israel" from which it is drawn, designates those human beings who have become, through God's initiative and grace, part of the family of God.[12] Therefore, it would not be consonant with Johannine — or, for that matter, New Testament — usage to designate all children as "children of God," and so to ground discussions of advocacy for children and contemporary debates about children's rights in the assertion that "all children are children of God."

But John does bear witness that all children — indeed, all human beings — are created by God, given the breath of life by God (Gen. 2:7; cf. John 1:3). Even as the entire world is created by God through God's life-giving breath, so that same world is loved by God (3:16-17), and the death of Jesus on the cross is intended to "draw all people" to him (12:32) and to give them the breath of life that grants new birth (3:3-5). In other words, the Gospel of John bears witness that all human beings, created by God, are intended also to belong to the "children of God," to find their identity in the family given new birth and gathered by God around Jesus. God's created work is intended to be completed in the work of the new creation; life is intended to be consummated in eternal life. In this way, then, the "children of God" become both a sign and a foretaste of what God desires for the entire human family; namely, a family with a unifying center in Jesus, which embodies the life-giving love of God to each other.[13] Indeed, that is the point for John: the human family has a center for its unity, in which all persons, including those most at risk, find that they belong, and that center is in the family that God gathers around Jesus.

As drawn from the Gospel of John, the value and dignity of children and of human life depend on two factors: first, that all persons have received life, and second, that all may receive new life from God's life-giving breath or Spirit. Precisely because John's view of creation is so all-encompassing — all things are created by God; all spiritual and material things belong to God — it can also serve to provide the basis for thinking about the needs and rights of children, their identity and status, and their place in this world. In other words, the raw material best suited to advocating for humane treatment of

---

12. On this point, see the summary comments of David Bartlett, "Adoption in the Bible," in this volume.

13. On this point, see Lesslie Newbigin, *The Light Has Come: An Exposition of the Fourth Gospel* (Grand Rapids: Eerdmans, 1982), p. 43.

children today is likely to be found in John's Gospel in the sweeping assertions that all life, in all its forms, comes from and belongs to God and that faithfulness to God leads to working for the wholeness of the world created by the one God. To do so means to engage in the mission of God, who faithfully brings life to his creation. The image of Jesus' followers as "the children of God" strengthens rather than undercuts those claims, for the fact that they are called together into a family demonstrates the loving and saving compassion of God for all his creation, that God has not abandoned the world that he created, but that he continually works for its life, wholeness, and unity. As Jesus tells his followers, he will not leave them as orphans (John 14:18).

The Life of the Son of God: Light in Darkness

As noted earlier, the Incarnation of the Word of God is central to the Johannine vision of the identity of Jesus, as well as to the coherence of the material and spiritual aspects of reality and of humanity. Human beings are flesh and spirit, and they have needs of both flesh and spirit. In John, the narrative of Jesus' life unfolds what it means for God to enter into human existence so as to provide both a revelation of the character of God and a model for human life. According to John 1:18, Jesus has made the Father known. In John 1:51, Jesus promises Nathanael and others that if they follow him they will see the "heavens opened." These claims are particularly striking, since the Gospel does not subsequently narrate heavenly visions or dramatic epiphanies. It narrates the life of one human being, Jesus of Nazareth, whose earthly life was lived in a relatively small and undistinguished part of the world's geography and encompassed a relatively short span of years. In Jesus we see both the historical situatedness, the particularity, of the Incarnation and the ordinariness of the manifestation of God's glory. This is how the glory of God is revealed, how the heavens are opened: these revelations occur in the day-to-day life of Jesus, a life that includes, but is not limited to, dramatic signs. These points are perhaps worth exploring further as we ponder the plight of children in today's world and how the church might extend its unique resources to them.

Jesus' Life and Mission

First, a comment on the historical situatedness and ordinariness of Jesus' life. It perhaps cannot be repeated too often that Jesus was a faithful Jew and that he understood his mission as a mission to his people Israel. Jesus entered the public scene in connection with the baptismal ministry of a Jewish prophet named John, called Galilean fishermen to be his disciples, discussed and disputed with Pharisees, taught in synagogues and in the temple, frequently journeyed to Jerusalem, and died by crucifixion at the hands of Roman imperial power. Much more could be said, but the manifestation of God's glory and the shape of Jesus' mission are concretely determined by these historical, social, and religious contexts. Jesus' historical mission does not take place in every physical part of the globe, or touch every single human person, or effect all peace and justice. But in his word and deed, the glory of God was nevertheless revealed as he brought life to the dead, sight to the blind, and a home to the outcast.

Jesus' life was in many ways very ordinary: he attended a wedding (John 2:1-11), got tired and thirsty after a long walk (4:6-7), had brothers who didn't believe in him (7:1-5), needed financial support from others (cf. 12:6 and Luke 8:1-3), wept at the death of a friend (John 11:35), and had close friends for whom he cared (13:23). To be sure, there were unusual events, such as his death by crucifixion and the signs that he worked, but it is striking that at times people do not even know that these wondrous deeds had occurred. At the wedding feast in Cana, few seem to know what has happened to suddenly provide wine for the wedding. The man healed at the pool of Bethzatha does not even know the name of the man who did it. Jesus simply does what he does because it is the life-giving work of God who loves the world. Thus when Jesus sends out his disciples with the words, "As the Father has sent me, so send I you," what is implicit is the understanding that human beings find themselves in specific, concrete situations in which they manifest the life-giving work of God, and that often the manifestation of such life comes in very ordinary packaging. To do the life-giving work of God means to meet the material and spiritual needs of human beings and to understand that human identity must be construed both in its theological aspects — in relationship to God — and in its communal aspects — in relationship to other human beings.

While John does speak of the manifestation of glory in the signs of Jesus, he also paradoxically speaks of the revelation of God's love through the cross. There Jesus himself takes on the position of one of the most vulnerable, and least powerful, participants in society; he takes on the role of a slave in washing the feet of his disciples, an act that foreshadows his death by crucifixion, that is, the death often meted out to slaves. Here the one with "all power" dies at the hands of Roman power; this is foreshadowed in his humble act of washing the disciples' feet at his last meal with them. On the one hand, it is clear that Jesus' act is intended to accomplish something for his disciples that they cannot accomplish for themselves. On the other hand, however, this act is also presented as a model for the disciples to emulate. To be sent as Jesus is sent means to take the risk of love for the other, for the vulnerable, weak, and fragile in the world. While it is easy to think of Jesus as the "powerful" ministering to the "weak," we can also think of Jesus as the vulnerable ministering to others who are also vulnerable. Jesus is sent "from above" and has often been said to enter the world in John as a "stranger from heaven," but his incarnation is real and his life is lived not among the elite or powerful of his people or the world. Precisely because there are ungodly uses of power, often exercised against the vulnerable children of the world, those who name the name of Jesus must follow his example, exercising power in willed self-giving of love for the other. As noted, Jesus here sets an example for his disciples to emulate.

Children as Participants in Jesus' Mission

When we think of children in relationship to Jesus' act on the night of his betrayal, we should think of them not so much in terms of those being ministered *to,* but as those who are called to emulate the ministry of Jesus as well. Children need to be meaningful participants in the mission of Jesus in the world. Children can neither be ignored nor idealized, nor made to serve adult programs, projects, and desires, nor can they be left out of the call to discipleship or the mission of the church. They, too, are called to love as Jesus commanded, and so to imitate the one in and through whom they are created. We will do the children of the world a disservice, again relegating them to inferior or secondary status, if we assume that they do not need or crave an understanding of their identity, value, and belonging that is drawn from relationship to the God who made them. The status and dignity of being a "child of God" refers to adults and children who together are members of the family gathered by Jesus. Augustine's oft-quoted dictum, "Our hearts were made for thee, O God, and we are restless until we rest in thee," does not apply merely to adult males, but to all, including all those whom society is prone to relegate to the margins.

John's theology of incarnation and mission indicates that the children of God of all ages participate in God's mission in the world. The presentation of the life of the Word of God as enfleshed, so that his glory was seen in ordinary life, serves to suggest how the lives of the children of God of all ages are similarly embodiments of the glory of that Word, lived out in ordinary life. Here is where the divine mission touches the human world: through and in the lives of those who manifest the life-giving love of God. Jesus acts with life-giving love even when he does not speak of his own identity and even when it is not recognized. That is not the whole story, but it is an important part of the story of what happens when the Word of God becomes incarnate and the light shines in the darkness.

And it is clear that, for John, the power of darkness is at work in the world. The Word was made flesh so that his glory could be seen; this one was "the light of the world" (John 8:12; 9:5). Although the children of God are not light to the world as Jesus was and is, nevertheless the ordinary lives of the children of God reflect the light of God in the world as they reflect the work of the God of life. Even as we commented on the ordinariness of Jesus' life, and how through it the light of God shone in the darkness, so we might see that it is in the ordinariness of human life that God's light continues to shine in the dark-ness. To be sure, the work of vanquishing the darkness is properly the work of God, and no doubt much evil has been done through the abuse of power by those who have usurped this divine office for themselves. Ultimately, it is God's work to dispel the darkness. But if, first and foremost, the revelatory light of the glory of God shines in the life-giving and loving deeds of Jesus, it shines secondarily also through those who bear testimony to that light, who are sent as the Son of God is sent. God's light "still shines in the darkness" through them as they embody the life and love of Jesus.

Concluding Reflection

Jesus' earthly life ended with the establishing of a new family, a family that be-comes the point of identity for all who are children of God, a family that is to be the point of identity for all who are created by God — namely, all human-kind. This is a family that includes the children of all ages, and so it is through and in this family that the light of God shines in darkness. To this family is given the prime command to "love one another" even as Jesus has loved them: they manifest to each other the love of God for the world, as demon-strated in Jesus. The description of those who follow Jesus as the children of God, as a new family with God as the life-giving Father, serves as a reminder that everyone in this family answers both to each other and to God. This dual responsibility can be ignored only to the detriment of the lives of all — and especially to the detriment of children, those still most vulnerable to neglect and abuse.

10   "Tell Me a Story":
     Perspectives on Children
     from the Acts of the Apostles

Joel B. Green

Those who follow the narrative from the Gospel of Luke into the Acts of the Apostles may rightly feel astonished at the apparent move from the children-rich environment of the Gospel to a narrative virtually devoid of the presence of children. Luke's Gospel begins with the births of two children, John and Jesus, in celebrated accounts of the miraculous and of promise (Luke 1:5–2:52). Among the New Testament Gospels, Luke alone includes in his narrative an episode from Jesus' childhood, demonstrating the boy's growth in wisdom, years, and favor (2:40-52). Jesus blesses children, heals them, presents them as exemplars of kingdom service, and urges hospitality toward them (e.g., 8:40-56; 18:15-17; 22:24-27).[1] Acts presents itself as the follow-on to the Gospel of Luke (see Acts 1:1), as volume two, so to speak.[2] Turning the page from Luke 24 to Acts 1, then, we might justifiably wonder, Where have all the children gone?

This is not to say that children, defined loosely as persons who have yet to achieve adulthood, are entirely absent from Acts. In a book in which children appear so infrequently, the attention Luke gives to children in Israel's past is remarkable. Relevant material is found in Stephen's speech before the Jerusalem Council, in which Stephen rehearses the history of Israel. Early on, he refers to God's provision of a son, Isaac, to Abraham, immediately after having declared Abraham childless (Acts 7:5-8). Stephen's words may remind us of that earlier account in Luke's Gospel, of Elizabeth and Zechariah, also child-

---

1. See John T. Carroll's essay in this volume; see also Joel B. Green, *The Theology of the Gospel of Luke*, New Testament Theology (Cambridge: Cambridge University Press, 1995), pp. 89-90, 117-18.

2. I assume the narrative unity of Luke-Acts. The authorship of this two-volume work is debated; I will refer to the narrator as "Luke" without bias as to the identity of the actual author.

less, whom God blessed with a son, John the Baptist (Luke 1:5-7, 13). After this, Stephen mentions a policy of the Egyptian Pharaoh mandating that the newly born babies of "our ancestors" be abandoned at birth. But Moses was rescued from this early practice of exposing infants when he was adopted into the home of Pharaoh's daughter and trained in the wisdom of the Egyptians (Acts 7:19-22). Stephen also reports Moses' fathering of two sons (7:29). Given the highly selective nature of Stephen's historical summary, it is difficult to imagine that such references would be "irrelevant" to the narrative, as one commentator has it.[3] Instead, in these references we can follow an emphasis on God's provision of children, against odds of all kinds, in order to ensure that God's purpose and promises come to fruition — and thus the serendipitous role of children in the realization and progression of God's work. This latter emphasis is picked up elsewhere in Acts. In 12:12-16, the "slave-girl" (παιδίσκη, paidiskē) Rhoda expends great effort to extend hospitality to the apostle Peter, miraculously rescued from prison. Even though the believers had gathered at the house where she served for the expressed purpose of praying for his release, in order to welcome Peter Rhoda persisted beyond the ridicule of those who disbelieved her report of the apostle's presence at the gate. In 23:16-22, the son of Paul's sister courageously intervenes with the Roman tribune in order to foil a plot against Paul's life, a plot that, if successful, would have frustrated Paul's call to proclaim the good news in Rome. Three other texts pay tribute to the importance of parent-child relations by drawing attention to them, even if they do not develop those relationships further (Mary, mother of John Mark — 12:12; the parents of Timothy — 16:1; and the four daughters of Philip — 21:9).

With this, however, we have gone about as far as we can go in our examination of Luke's direct treatment of children and youth in the Acts of the Apostles. One or two additional references appear, and, even though they add little, these will be mentioned in the discussion that follows. Since Acts is the second longest document in the New Testament (second only to Luke's first volume, the Gospel of Luke), and since it is the New Testament's only narrative account of the character and mission of the fledgling church, we might be disappointed by how little it has to offer on the subject of children and child-

---

3. With reference to Acts 7:29, so C. K. Barrett (*A Critical and Exegetical Commentary on the Acts of the Apostles*, 2 vols., International Critical Commentary [Edinburgh: T&T Clark, 1994/ 1998], pp. 359-60), following Kirsopp Lake and Henry J. Cadbury, *The Acts of the Apostles*, vol. 4: *English Translation and Commentary*, ed. F. J. Foakes Jackson and Kirsopp Lake, Beginnings of Christianity 1 (London: Macmillan, 1933; reprint ed., Grand Rapids: Baker, 1979), p. 76. Barrett also speculates that Moses' two sons would have tied him to Midian, had it not been for the divine call.

hood. As I will attempt to show, however, this does not render pointless an exploration of the book of Acts, though it does require that we adjust our lens somewhat so as to entertain the relevance of evidence of a more subtle nature. Sharply put, the narrative of Acts provides us with almost nothing by way of raw material for assembling how we might think about children or act toward them. However, Acts does promote the formation of communities and persons-in-community whose discipleship of Jesus, whose allegiance to God, and whose empowerment by the Holy Spirit lead to dispositions and practices of faith and hospitality among children, together with other inhabitants of the margins of our world.

What of "Household Baptism"?

Depending on their ecclesial tradition, some may query my observation regarding the absence of children in the Acts of the Apostles by drawing attention to Luke's reports of household baptisms. Surely, some will say, these would have included the baptism of children. Household baptisms form a subset of the household conversion accounts in the Lukan narrative,[4] and there are three: the baptism of Cornelius and his household (see esp. Acts 10:2, 24, 27, 33, 44-48), the baptism of Lydia and her household (see esp. Acts 16:14-15), and the baptism of the Philippian jailor and his household (see esp. Acts 16:31-34).[5] This is a potentially potent area of study since, as Thomas Wiedemann observes, to baptize small children might well have signaled within Christian communities that the lives of the young were just as significant as those of adults.[6] Within the horizons of the Roman world — in which children were not only the weakest, most vulnerable of the populace but also possessed little implicit value as human beings[7] — this would have marked a

4. These have been profitably examined in David Lertis Matson, *Household Conversion Narratives in Acts: Pattern and Interpretation*, Journal for the Study of the New Testament — Supplement Series 123 (Sheffield: Sheffield Academic Press, 1996).

5. See also, perhaps, Acts 18:8b. I have discussed "household baptisms" more fully in Joel B. Green, "'She and Her Household Were Baptized' (Acts 16:15): Household Baptism in the Acts of the Apostles," in *Dimensions of Baptism: Biblical and Theological Studies*, ed. Stanley E. Porter and Anthony R. Cross, Journal for the Study of the New Testament — Supplement Series 234 (Sheffield: Sheffield Academic Press, 2002), pp. 72-90.

6. Thomas Wiedemann, *Adults and Children in the Roman Empire* (New Haven: Yale University Press, 1989), pp. 6-7.

7. For more nuance on the representation of children in the Roman Mediterranean, see, e.g., Beryl Rawson, ed., *The Family in Ancient Rome: New Perspectives* (Ithaca, NY: Cornell University Press, 1986); Rawson, ed., *Marriage, Divorce, and Children in Ancient Rome* (Oxford: Ox-

stunning innovation. A conclusion in favor of the participation of children in those household baptisms would be supported by the casual reference in Acts 21:5 to the "women and children (τέκνον, *teknon*)," numbered along with the disciples at Tyre, who knelt and prayed with Paul and his companions before sending them on their way to Jerusalem. This novelty would also be fully coherent with the larger Lukan narrative in which conventional concerns with status are often subverted.[8] Nevertheless, the difficulties with this line of argument were well documented a half-century ago in the dispute over whether we might find in Acts a biblical-theological foundation for infant baptism, between Kurt Aland and Joachim Jeremias, summarized in George R. Beasley-Murray's discussion of the question, "Infant Baptism a New Testament Institution?"[9] The Aland-Jeremias debate itself is enough to demonstrate the ambiguity of the evidence in Acts. Indeed, we might be pardoned for concluding that, if Luke were interested in scoring theological points with regard to the baptism of young children, he might have done so in a more decisive and transparent way.

Thinking with Acts about Children

What would happen were we to shift our attention from what Acts might tell us about children in the first century to how Acts might shape the church's theology and practices regarding children? Among possible avenues for exploration, I will highlight three: the importance of narrative in identity development and moral formation, Luke's theology of the Holy Spirit, and Luke's interest in those persons who occupy society's margins.

---

ford University Press, 1991); and Rawson, *Child and Childhood in Roman Italy* (Oxford: Oxford University Press, 2003).

8. With regard to the status of children in particular, cf., e.g., Luke 9:46-48; 18:15-17. See further the article by John Carroll in this volume. Luke would thus be a prominent witness of the transformation of the church's social world with respect to the status and treatment of children; see James Francis, "Children and Childhood in the New Testament," in *The Family in Theological Perspective*, ed. Stephen C. Barton (Edinburgh: T&T Clark, 1996), pp. 65-85 (esp. pp. 80-84).

9. G. R. Beasley-Murray, *Baptism in the New Testament* (Grand Rapids: Eerdmans, 1962), pp. 306-52. Kurt Aland, *Did the Early Church Baptize Infants?* (London: SCM, 1963); Aland, *Die Stellung der Kinder in den frühen christlichen Gemeinden — und ihre Taufe*, Theologische Existenz heute 138 (Munich: Kaiser, 1967); Joachim Jeremias, *Infant Baptism in the First Four Centuries* (London: SPCK, 1960); Jeremias, *The Origins of Infant Baptism: A Further Study in Reply to Kurt Aland*, Studies in Historical Theology 1 (London: SCM, 1963).

The Importance of Narrative

To a degree that we are only beginning to realize, our formation as persons and communities, the shaping of our identity and practices, is "storied." The question, then, is, What sort of persons and what sort of communities might be formed in relation to the story Luke narrates? After some initial comments about the importance of narrative, I want to sketch what it might mean to begin to write oneself into the narrative of Acts — that is, to allow it to shape our lives decisively.

Whose Story?

"Tell me a story" is a request we might associate with children, but narrativity is pivotal for all human development. "*Story* is a basic principle of mind. Most of our experience, our knowledge, and our thinking is organized as stories," writes cognitive scientist Mark Turner, who adds that "narrative imagining is our fundamental form of predicting" and our "fundamental cognitive instrument for explanation."[10] If it is true that narrative is the means by which we make sense of the world and our experiences in the world, then what happens among subcultures, like that of the childhood and youth population in the United States, generally vacated of narratives or whose narratives accord privilege to violence and/or to short-term resolution of dilemmas? I am thinking, for example, of the stories that shape the lives of children in those parts of our world torn by inter-tribal warfare, but also of those who are invited to stamp vicariously through war zones in increasingly realistic video games or weaned on a diet of fast-paced television. The stories we tell about ourselves, through which we construct our sense of self, are woven out of the threads and into the cloth of the stories present to us in our social world and communal traditions. The story we accept sets the terms of what we take to be true, normal, and good. It shapes our patterns of thinking, feeling, and acting and serves as a conceptual scheme that is at once *conceptual* (a way of seeing things), *conative* (a set of beliefs and values to which a group and its members are deeply attached), and *action-guiding* (we seek to live according

10. Mark Turner, *The Literary Mind: The Origins of Thought and Language* (New York: Oxford University Press, 1996), pp. v, 20. On the role of narrative forming and recounting beliefs, see, e.g., William Hirstein, *Brain Fiction: Self-Deception and the Riddle of Confabulation* (Cambridge, MA: The MIT Press, 2005) (who demonstrates the incredible lengths to which humans will go to make sense of reality in narrative terms); and Gary D. Fireman et al., eds., *Narrative and Consciousness: Literature, Psychology, and the Brain* (Oxford: Oxford University Press, 2003) (a multidisciplinary exploration of the role of narrative in personal formation).

to its terms).[11] And this presses hard on the question, What narratives are being nurtured in our communities, our churches, and our families?

Reflecting on the contemporary theological problematic in the United States, James McClendon referred to a "contest of stories." From an early age, he observes, we learn a consensus story that forms us as Americans, a narrative with such stable elements as these: brave pilgrims set out in search of freedom from tyranny; they find the promised land where they must conquer the indigenous population as well as battle for independence; they engage in civil war in order to liberate all persons; they move westward across the continent, to realize their dreams, depending only on themselves; and, blessed by God, they are able to fight for the liberty of those outside their borders as well. Without wanting to belittle the American Story, which has underwritten hope for millions of families, McClendon nevertheless observes that one of the most visible constants of that story is the violence repeatedly regarded as necessary in the face of threats to freedom. Contrast this, he says, with a story that pivots upon a savior who comes on a donkey, who is acclaimed as the prince of peace, and in whose death peace is won. The pressing question for McClendon is this: "Which story, the cultural or the biblical one, really engages me?"[12]

The plot lines of the master drama McClendon has outlined have been deeply etched into the psyche of generations of Americans. Its influence waned in the last thirty-five years of the twentieth century, so much so that we may wonder whether the children reared in the United States during this period share this common story. Since September 11, 2001, however, that drama, or something like it, has resurfaced with a vengeance, again ensuring the apparent relationship between violence and freedom — a relationship that manifests itself in all sorts of cultural products: for example, video games, music, and movies. The challenge of "narrative" remains whether we are thinking of this historic American master drama, a guiding narrative like those embodied in such stories as "The Little Engine That Could" or "Humpty Dumpty," or the rootlessness and despair accompanying an apparent lack of stories by which to make sense of life (which is itself a kind of guiding story).

11. I have borrowed this way of conceiving "conceptual scheme" from Owen Flanagan, *The Problem of the Soul: Two Visions of Mind and How to Reconcile Them* (New York: Basic, 2002), pp. 27-55.

12. James Wm. McClendon Jr., *Systematic Theology*, vol. 3: *Witness* (Nashville: Abingdon, 2000), pp. 358-62 (at 362); I have adapted the version of the American Story that McClendon recounts.

Perspectives on Narrative from the Neurosciences

A few comments at the interface of theology and neuroscience will underscore what is at stake in this question.

Human beings are always in the process of formation. "People don't come preassembled, but are glued together by life,"[13] writes neuroscientist Joseph LeDoux, who describes how, at a basic level, formative influences are encoded in the synapses of the central nervous system, those points of communication among the cells of the brains, or neurons. Though the organization of the brain is hardwired genetically, genes shape only the broad outline of our mental and behavioral functions, with the rest sculpted through our experiences. From birth, we are in the process of becoming, and this "becoming" is encoded in our brains by means of synaptic activity. Simply put, in our early years, far more synapses are generated than are needed, so that the formation of the brain proceeds under the principle, "Use it or lose it." Those neural connections that are used are maintained and remodeled, while those that fall into disuse are eliminated. Particularly formative in this regard are the first years of life and those of late adolescence, though fresh connections are generated in response to our experiences even into adulthood, until the very moment of death. Hence, both nature and nurture end up having the same effect: shaping our neuronal interactions in ways that form and reform the developing self.

Embodied human life performs, then, like a cultural, neuro-hermeneutical system, locating (and thus making sense of) current realities in relation to our grasp of the past and expectations of the future.[14] To speak thus of past, present, and future is of course already to frame meaning in narrative terms. Scientist-theologian Anne Foeret refers to humans as "*Homo Narrans Narrandus* — the storytelling person whose story has to be told," who tells stories to make sense of the world and to form personal identity and community.[15] From neurobiology and its interactions with cultural anthropology and philosophy, then, we have a heightened interest in and recognition of *narrativity* as a meaning-making enterprise. This is not first and foremost a statement about exegetical method, though the narrative form of Acts invites narrative-

13. Joseph LeDoux, *Synaptic Self: How Our Brains Become Who We Are* (New York: Viking Penguin, 2002), p. 3.

14. Cf. Stephen P. Reyna, *Connections: Brain, Mind, and Culture in a Social Anthropology* (London: Routledge, 2002); Daniel J. Siegel, *The Developing Mind: How Relationships and the Brain Interact to Shape Who We Are* (New York: Guilford, 1999).

15. Reported in S. Jennifer Leat, "Artificial Intelligence Researcher Seeks Silicon Soul," *Research News and Opportunities in Science and Theology* 3 (4 December 2002): 7, 26 (at 7).

critical interests, but rather about narrativity as an essential aspect of our grasp of the nature of the world and of human identity and comportment in it. Foreshadowing emphases that would surface in the ensuing two decades, Hayden White observed, "To raise the question of narrative is to invite reflection on the very nature of culture and, possibly, even on the nature of humanity itself."[16] Accordingly, it is crucial to inquire, What stories are shaping the worlds we indwell? What stories are we embodying?

As a narrative representation of historical events, as historiography, the Acts of the Apostles is implicated in such aims as identity formation and legitimation.[17] What sorts of identity, formation, and performance are the consequence of inhabiting this narrative?

Acts: A Narrative of Conversion

Manifestly, the narrative of Acts prioritizes conversion as the (re)orientation of one's allegiances toward the God of Israel known to us in the life, death, and resurrection of Jesus of Nazareth. This orientation gives rise to and is confirmed in community-nested practices that are appropriate to those allegiances and that open the way to ongoing (trans)formation as one comes more fully to embrace this new life-world and make it one's home. Life is apprehended within this structure of meaning, within the grand story of YHWH's purpose and Israel's history — as this is interpreted in relation to the advent of Jesus.

Acts underscores especially the communal dimension of conversion. Conversion is in the context of a multiethnic people of God, whose very make-up represents and broadcasts God's purpose, and whose characteristic practices enflesh God's *praxis* even as they serve to conform God's people ever more fully to the contours of God's character and will. Thus, Acts locates the meaning of life not simply in the sum of one's life experiences, but rather within the community of God's people and within the grand mural of God's purposes. We are called to participate in something bigger than ourselves and to participate in the writing of God's narrative within which our choices make a

16. Hayden White, *The Content of the Form: Narrative Discourse and Historical Representation* (Baltimore: Johns Hopkins University Press, 1987), p. 1.

17. On the aims of historiography, see David Lowenthal, *The Past Is a Foreign Country* (Cambridge: Cambridge University Press, 1985); Albert Cook, *History/Writing: The Theory and Practice of History in Antiquity and in Modern Times* (Cambridge: Cambridge University Press, 1988); more particularly regarding Acts, see Clare K. Rothschild, *Luke-Acts and the Rhetoric of History: An Investigation of Early Christian Historiography*, Wissenschaftliche Untersuchungen zum Neuen Testament 2:175 (Tübingen: Mohr Siebeck, 2004).

difference. Acts highlights an orientation-to-the-other, whether the other be the needy within one's own community or those who dwell in lands far away, promoting the disposition of hospitality as an essential response to God and the world.

This is a narrative in which God has not yet been figured out, but is capable of surprising innovation, even to the point of overturning centuries of tradition in keeping with the revelation of his character and aims in Israel's Scriptures. As a result, this is a narrative in which God's people repeatedly find themselves simply trying to catch up with God, to get in sync with God's initiatives. The inclusion of the Ethiopian within the people of God constituted a theological and missional departure of such magnitude that Luke must pepper his narrative with multiple proofs that this was God's doing (e.g., Acts 8:26, 29, 39). Sharing the table with Gentiles countermanded Jewish norms so unexpectedly that Luke recounts the story of Cornelius and his household with multiple visions — and even then Luke must tell the story twice (Acts 10:1–11:18). This is not because God was doing a "new thing," since these missional expansions were fully congruent with Israel's recognition of YHWH as the creator and Lord of the cosmos (and not only of one nation) and the foundation narrative that declared Abraham the progenitor of "many nations" (and not only one). Rather, these innovations drew attention both to overlooked aspects of Israel's Scriptures and to alternative interpretations of those Scriptures. For Luke, the ways of God are very old, even if Luke's narrative takes surprisingly fresh turns as it documents how the ancient plan of God is coming to fruition.

This is a narrative in which prayer is pivotal as a critically reflexive practice for God's people. Through prayer, the faithful community discerns God's agenda, with the result that, over and over, it finds itself becoming more and more oriented toward outsiders. Prayer becomes an avenue by which God forms God's people as a community for mission. As Luke repeatedly observes, it is in the context of prayer that God sketches the horizons of a mission that extends to the end of the earth (e.g., Acts 9:10-12; 10:3-4, 9-16, 30-31; 11:5; 22:17-21).

This is a narrative in which engagement with Scripture functions similarly to stretch the self-understanding of the community and its mission, especially where scriptural interpretation is shaped by the presence of outsiders within the community. The same can be said of the church's understanding of the significance of Jesus — who, of course, was not yet written into "Scripture," but whose life and mission nonetheless function as a norm or pattern for the life of the community. That is, the presence of outsiders helps the church to understand better the ramifications of the advent, death, and resurrection of their savior and to order their lives as believers accordingly. Thus, Peter's interaction with Cornelius is revelatory for Peter, leading him to exclaim, finally, that Jesus is "Lord of all" (Acts 10:36). Similarly, the problem of the status of Gentiles in the people of God presses the Christian leadership to reexamine the Scriptures and to discover in their own holy writings that "we should not trouble those Gentiles who are turning to God" (15:19).[18]

For those of us engaged with Luke's narrative, conversion is the consequence of embracing this story as our own and seeing the plot line of our lives as continuous with and an ongoing extension of the narrative that, for Luke, begins with the promise to Abraham, celebrates New Exodus in the advent of Christ, continues on in the expansion of the mission to all people, and leans forward into the eschaton.

The Democratization of the Spirit

Irrespective of how one resolves the debate on "household baptism," there is no escaping the inclusion of children in the "all flesh" of Acts 2:17. Likewise, the promise of the salvation that comes via the gift of the Spirit includes not only "you" (presumably, the adults present at Pentecost as well Luke's readers) but also "your children" (Acts 2:39).[19] The latter text manifestly refers to "children" in the sense of "posterity" or "tribe" (τέκνον, teknon, cf. Matt. 2:18; 27:25; Acts 13:33), but we have no reason to exclude young people from this promise. "Your sons and your daughters shall prophesy, and your young men shall see visions" (Acts 2:17), and, indeed, the "four unmarried daughters" of Philip are endowed with the gift of prophecy (Acts 21:9). In Acts 21:9 the NRSV translates παρθένος (parthenos) as "unmarried," but the connection with another parthenos, Mary, also a virgin and identified in part thus for her

18. The contemporary fecundity of this hermeneutic is illustrated with regard to the status and role of women in the people of God in John Christopher Thomas, "Reading the Bible from within Our Traditions: A Pentecostal Hermeneutic as Test Case," in Between Two Horizons: Spanning New Testament Studies and Systematic Theology, ed. Joel B. Green and Max Turner (Grand Rapids: Eerdmans, 2000), pp. 108-22.

19. Luke's summary of the community of Jesus' followers united in prayer (Acts 1:14) names the apostles "with the women, including Mary the mother of Jesus, and his brothers." One textual witness (D) adds καὶ τέκνοις (kai teknois, "and children") after "the women," but this reading has little to commend it. γυνή (gynē) could refer to the women gathered (as in the NRSV) or could qualify those women further as "wives," an ambiguity that would have been resolved by the addition of "and children," ensuring that women were not represented as having an independent status in the community (see Walter Thiele, "Eine Bemerkung zu Act 1:14," Zeitschrift für die neutestamentliche Wissenschaft 53 [1962]: 110-11).

youth (Luke 1:27),[20] should not be overlooked and may suggest the relative youth of Philip's daughters.

Such texts as these begin to incarnate within the life of the community the emphasis on children as participants in God's dominion (e.g., Luke 18:16). However, we need to recognize that, in these texts, the terms "child" and "daughter/son" allow no facile or even obligatory distinctions with regard to age,[21] nor to "children" in the genetic sense required in images of the nuclear family; instead, they refer to a network of relations defined in familial and household terms.

Care for the Least and Left-out

If we think of "child" less in familial terms and more with reference to a network of relations including those who would have occupied the margins of

20. *Parthenos* refers to a female of marriageable age, with an emphasis on her having not yet engaged in sexual intercourse. In the world of Luke, this would suggest a young girl, perhaps 12-13 years old, not yet or only recently having achieved puberty. In Roman law, the minimum age of marriage for girls was 12 (for boys, 14), with betrothal no earlier than age 10 (Beryl Rawson, "The Roman Family," in *The Family in Ancient Rome: New Perspectives*, ed. Beryl Rawson [Ithaca, NY: Cornell University Press, 1986], pp. 1-57 [at 21]). Jewish practices were comparable, with marriage ideally having taken place by the time a young girl reached 12+ years of age (see Léonie J. Archer, *Her Price Is Beyond Rubies: The Jewish Woman in Graeco-Roman Palestine*, Journal for the Study of the Old Testament — Supplement Series 60 [Sheffield: Sheffield Academic Press, 1990], pp. 151-71). This benefited the two males involved — the father, who could thus better ensure his daughter's purity (i.e., virginity; cf. Sir. 7:24; 42:9-11) and receive the economic benefit of the "bride price"; and the husband, for whom she was available for the whole of her child-bearing years. Evidence that this ideal was actually practiced is too scarce to support generalizations, but it is clear that, though women who were older, in the late teens or 20s, continued to marry, others were in fact given in marriage at the onset of puberty (see Tal Ilan, *Jewish Women in Greco-Roman Palestine* [Peabody, MA: Hendrickson, 1996], pp. 65-69).

21. For example, νεανίσκος, *neaniskos*, usually translated "young man," appears in Acts 2:17. The same term identifies those who bury Ananias and Sapphira in 5:10, but in 5:6 they are νεώτεροι (*neoteroi*, the comparative form of νέος, *neos*, "young"); then, in 5:9, they are "men" (ἀνήρ, *anēr*). Moreover, in 7:58 Saul is identified as a νεανίος, *neanios*, also customarily translated as "young man." This record of usage leads me to conclude that Luke does not deploy these terms in a semi-technical way to refer to persons of a certain age group. Peter Balla thus overstates the case when he writes that Luke's linguistic choices imply the presence of "young people" at Pentecost and "corroborate the view that children were present in the congregations in the early Christian church" (*The Child-Parent Relationship in the New Testament and Its Environment*, Wissenschaftliche Untersuchungen zum Neuen Testament 2.155 [Tübingen: Mohr Siebeck, 2003], pp. 204, 206).

those communities we might consider, then additional evidence becomes more interesting.

Care for the Needy

Reflecting on the early church's attitude and practices regarding possessions, Luke observes that "there was not a needy person among them" (Acts 4:34). For Luke, this is important, first, because of the apparent interpretive relationship between the apostolic testimony to the resurrection of the Lord Jesus and care for the needy in the community. Note that reference to proclamation of the resurrection is situated between dual references to economic koinonia (Acts 4:32-34a). The correlation of the message of the resurrection and this sharing or partnership is supported by the several occasions in the Lukan narrative in which resurrection and nourishment are woven together (e.g., Luke 8:49-56; 15:11-32; 24:13-35; Acts 10:41). Jesus' resurrection is intertwined with the pervasive Lukan interest in hospitality: nourishment for the hungry, inclusion of the needy and outcast, redemptive fellowship, and the general subversion of conventional concerns with honor and status. The community of goods is a tangible expression and substantiation of the resurrection of Jesus from the dead.

Selling what one has is customary within the community Luke depicts, but such giving is voluntary and is oriented toward addressing the plight of the needy. The profundity of this practice is urged by its relation to Deuteronomy 15, from which Luke draws his observation: "there was no needy among them." In this way, he borrows the qualification of God's people delivered from Egypt in the Exodus in order to portray followers of Jesus as God's people restored in New Exodus. Also of importance are Greco-Roman patterns of friendship. It was proverbial that "friends hold all things in common";[22] accordingly, the scene Luke paints is that of discipleship as friendship with the needy — giving freely, without expectation of return (see Luke 6:27-35).

Counterexamples drive home the importance of this message for Luke. When Ananias and Sapphira conspire to withhold from the community of believers, even while masquerading as persons committed to sharing all things, they fall under judgment (Acts 5:1-11). When, under the apostles' leadership, a class of widows is ignored during the daily distribution of food, leadership of the mission-church passes from them to others (6:1-7). On a

---

22. For the relation of economic factors to models of friendship, see, e.g., Peter Garnsey and Richard Saller, *The Roman Empire: Economy, Society and Culture* (Berkeley: University of California Press, 1987), pp. 148-59.

grander scale, when the believers in Judea suffer because of famine, the disciples in Antioch provide economic support (11:27-30). In his departing address to the Ephesian elders, Paul includes within his proclamation of "the whole purpose of God" his assurance that he had "coveted no one's silver or gold or clothing," but had worked with his own hands to support himself and his companions. "In all this," he states, "I have given you an example that by such work we must support the weak, remembering the words of the Lord Jesus, for he himself said, 'It is more blessed to give than to receive'" (20:33-35).

The significance of such dispositions and practices with respect to our thinking about children is transparent when we consider the violence done to children in antiquity and today, the commodification of children and youth, and, today, the unrelenting presence of children as representatives of the poor of the world's population. In Acts, the commodification of the young is illustrated by "a slave-girl who had a spirit of divination and brought her owners a great deal of money by fortune-telling" (16:16). Predictably, when Paul liberates her from the spirit, her "owners" drag Paul and his companion, Silas, before the magistrate; after all, "their hope of making money was gone" (16:19). In one of the few references to children in the book of Acts, the exposure of little children under Egypt's king in the time of Moses is condemned as an act of treachery (7:19). What reminders do we need of the sorry treatment of children today, whether as child-soldiers in Somalia, as models for Internet pornography, as voiceless persons in the world's systems of social care, as conduits for the realization of adult dreams, or as persons sold into slavery or into modern-day harems? What reminders do we need of the endangerment of children today, whether through the widespread use of abortion as a means of state-sanctioned birth control or gender selection, or in the stunning reality that the United States has one of the highest infant mortality rates among nations of the "developed world." Salvation in Lukan theology, grounded in Jesus' resurrection and modeled after it, may well find concrete expression in the raising up of the quintessentially needy among us: children.

Strange Households

If the occurrence of the terminology of "children" is minimal in the book of Acts, the same cannot be said of the language of "household." To take one particularly noteworthy example, in the section of Luke's narrative that runs from Acts 9:32 to 11:18, we find an impressive array and number of references to houses, households, and household hospitality:[23] the saints "make their

---

23. This is noted in Beverly Roberts Gaventa, *From Darkness to Light: Aspects of Conversion*

homes" in Lydda (9:32); Aeneas was homebound (9:33); Tabitha is laid in an upstairs room (9:37); Peter lodges with and enjoys the hospitality of Simon (9:43; 10:5-6, 17-18, 32); Peter prays from the rooftop of this house and extends the hospitality of the house to Cornelius's ambassadors (10:23); Cornelius "feared God with all his household" (10:2), an extended family that includes household slaves (10:7); Cornelius prays in his house (10:3, 30); Cornelius gathers together into his house both "relatives and close friends" (10:24), welcomes Peter and his entourage into his home (10:23, 25, 27; 11:12), and asserts that God is present in his house (10:33); Cornelius and his household invite Peter to stay with them for several days (10:48); upon returning to Jerusalem, Peter is upbraided for entering Cornelius's home and sharing his hospitality (11:3); Peter explains how he and his companions entered Cornelius's household (11:12); and, finally, Peter reports that an angel had preceded him into the house (11:13) and had instructed Cornelius to send for Peter, who would bring a message that would be effective for "your salvation" as well as that of "your household" (11:14).

Why is this important? The punch-line for this lengthy account of Peter's mission comes in Acts 10:33, where all of this talk about houses, homes, and homebodies finds its focal point in Cornelius's astounding claim that, *in his home*, all have gathered *in the presence of God*. This is astonishing, first, because God's presence is associated with God's "house," the temple in Jerusalem, and not with the house of a Caesarean centurion; and second, because the Cornelius who claims for his residence the presence of God is a Gentile, albeit a God-fearing one. The household thus becomes the site of struggle over competing perspectives on God's interface with the world. As God's house, the temple structured the socio-religious world of the Jewish people, the lines of its architecture radiating outward to establish boundaries segregating priest from non-priest, Jew from Gentile, male from female, clean from unclean. Luke's account of Peter's entry into the home of an unclean dead woman (Acts 9:36-42), his temporary residence in the home of an unclean tanner (9:43), and his entry into the home of a Gentile (see especially 10:28: "You yourselves know that it is unlawful for a Jew to associate with or to visit a Gentile") overturns this ideology. Locating this scene in this house — a Gentile household where God is present — Luke reports that God has established a new center of worship and mission, the home. The gift of the Spirit that falls upon Cornelius and his household is an irrefutable sign of God's acceptance of these persons, and their baptism establishes the household as the new center for God's people.

---

in the New Testament, Overtures to Biblical Theology (Philadelphia: Fortress, 1986), p. 113; Matson, *Household Conversion Narratives,* pp. 102-24.

In a second set of scenes, Acts 16:11-40, the home has a similarly pivotal role. With no synagogue to attend, Paul and those traveling with him enter the home of Lydia, where she and her household become believers and are baptized. Using her home as a base of mission, Paul and Silas soon find that their missionary activity has landed them in jail. After they are liberated from their shackles by an earthquake, we next find them in the home of the jailor, where they receive hospitality in the form of health care and food. Finally, they return to Lydia's home, which again becomes a mission center.

Why is this important? It is because of the significance of the house(hold) for the Roman Empire. The household was regarded, as Cicero put it, as "the seed-bed of the state."[24] The orderliness of household relations was both a model for and the basis of order within the empire, with persons "assigned a precise place in a vast system of orders, classes, tribes, and centuries."[25] Rome regarded itself as a household with the emperor as *paterfamilias.* In other words, the center of the Roman world was, first, the home, from whence the world took shape; by extension, Rome performed this function, ordering life and setting boundaries: everyone with a place, everyone in their place.

Yet, the households that receive attention in Acts 16 are not at all "orderly." As a dealer in purple dye, Lydia may have had wealth, but in a society where the currency of status was not money but honor, she would still be marked as a woman (and thus of lower status by accident of gender), as a single woman (who thus would not have enjoyed whatever benefit might have accrued to her on account of her husband), and, perhaps as a divorcée.[26] Adding to

---

24. Cicero, *On Duties* 1.53-55; cited in *The Roman Household: A Sourcebook,* ed. Jane F. Gardner and Thomas Wiedemann (London: Routledge, 1991), p. 2.

25. Claude Nicolet, "The Citizen: The Political Man," in *The Romans,* ed. Andrea Giardina (Chicago: University of Chicago Press, 1993), pp. 16-54 (at 26).

26. The suggestion that Lydia was a divorcée is based on general regulations for household economics in the Roman empire and on census returns. Regarding the former, husband and wife were not a single economic unit, and whatever she brought into the marriage, including the dowry itself, was hers to reclaim should the marriage dissolve. Divorces brought with them no expectation of alimony, and this underscores the woman's relative independence vis-à-vis material holdings. Property owned by the male head of the household (*paterfamilias*) was almost always bequeathed to the children, not to his surviving wife. Children, if they were considered legitimate, typically but not always went to the father. For relevant background, see Suzanne Dixon, "Family Finances: Terentia and Tullia," in *The Family in Ancient Rome: New Perspectives,* ed. Beryl Rawson (Ithaca, NY: Cornell University Press, 1986), pp. 93-120; J. A. Crook, "Women in Roman Succession," in Rawson, ed., *The Family in Ancient Rome,* pp. 58-82; Rawson, "Roman Family," pp. 19, 32-37. For census returns, see D. C. Barker, "Census Returns and Household Structures," *New Documents Illustrating Christianity,* vol. 4, ed. G. H. R. Horsley (Grand Rapids: Eerdmans, 1997), no. 21, pp. 87-93; his reading of the data supports the likelihood that Lydia, as a head of household, would have been a divorcée rather than a widow; his

Lydia's ambiguous status, she is described as a God-fearer — that is, a sympathizer who was nonetheless marginal to the Jewish community. Notwithstanding all of this, she is the first and model convert on European soil. For his part, the jailor is numbered both among the enemy and among those who inhabit the bottom rung of an oppressive system. Having heard the good news, though, this jailor (who because of his own oppressed status must fear for his life even though he has made a livelihood as the instrument of oppression for others), and with him his whole household, are transformed. In short, in a narrative sequence where issues of civic pride, honor and shame, and Roman custom and order are so much emphasized, it is surely extraordinary that Lydia, the jailor, and their households, who in no way exemplify these Roman values, serve as exemplars.

Through reflecting on households, our discussion thus has wandered far from any explicit focus on children and childhood. Let me try to bring us back by outlining two important ramifications of these observations. First, in a world obsessed with order (and which confused order with peace), the household portraits Luke has painted are decidedly out of order. Because of the pivotal role of the household in propagating the values of the empire, Luke's critical engagement with the norms of the household is tantamount to introducing a virus into the system, the effect of which could only be the unraveling of norms as the Christian movement spread. Indeed, writing of the "important mediatory role" of the home, François Bovon observes, "The disciples or apostles have it as their mission to reach the city; but if the city is to believe, the home must be converted."[27] But if this is so, then, likewise, the unenviable place of children in household and community must undergo metamorphosis. Those transformative values that take root in the household will propagate transformation beyond its boundaries. More simply, to change the household is to change the world.

Second, Luke's presentation of these households urges certain roles for the household in relation to the faith.[28] As a center of hospitality (note: not of

---

discussion is summarized in Bradley Blue, "Acts and the House Church," in *The Book of Acts in Its Graeco-Roman Setting*, ed. David W. J. Gill and Conrad Gempf, Acts in Its First-Century Setting 2 (Grand Rapids: Eerdmans, 1994), pp. 119-222 (esp. 184-85).

27. François Bovon, "The Importance of Mediations in Luke's Theological Plan," in *New Testament Traditions and Apocryphal Narratives*, Princeton Theological Monograph Series 36 (Allison Park, PA: Pickwick, 1995), pp. 51-66 (at 55).

28. For historical perspective, see Roger W. Gehring, *House Church and Mission: The Importance of Household Structures in Early Christianity* (Peabody, MA: Hendrickson, 2004); for contemporary perspective, see Christine D. Pohl, *Making Room: Recovering Hospitality as a Christian Tradition* (Grand Rapids: Eerdmans, 1999).

entertainment), the household is the locus of care for the distressed, of sharing the faith with others, of community formation through the sharing of meals, of teaching and worship, and of mission-sending. Whatever else we make of the model Luke has provided, it is worth reflecting on the wisdom of our having relegated these practices of hospitality to the "hospitality industry" or to church buildings. The result is generations of children who are provided with less and less contact with faithful agents of Christian mission, fewer and fewer models of relationship-building, and so for whom faith becomes so personalized that it need not even find expression within one's own household.

On Doing a Theology of Children with Acts

On the one hand, Acts has little to offer by way of a biblical perspective on children and childhood. Children appear infrequently in the narrative and never find themselves as the center of attention. No one repeats Jesus' practice of welcoming children, nor do we find explicit instruction about the roles of children in or beyond the household. If theology is known by its propositions, then, because it has no propositions regarding children to offer, we would be well advised to bypass Acts in developing a theology of children and childhood. If, on the other hand, theology is critical and constructive reflection on the practices of the church in the world,[29] then such a negative judgment could not be justified. If theology is a craft oriented toward developing particular intuitions, forming particular dispositions, cultivating particular practices, sculpting a particular kind of people, then Acts has much to offer after all.

Even if Acts does affirm the importance of children in the actualization of God's redemptive plan, this is not its particular focus or contribution. Instead, hardly by mentioning children at all, Acts nonetheless promotes the formation of communities and persons-in-community whose discipleship of Jesus, whose allegiance to God, and whose empowerment by the Holy Spirit is oriented toward the extension of faith and hospitality to persons who occupy the margins of the world. For Acts, the "end of the earth" includes an Ethiopian and a Gentile centurion, to give only two of many examples. Undoubtedly, in our world ethnic and racial and vocational categories also determine inside and outside status, but in today's marketplace it is difficult to argue

29. See Charles M. Wood, *The Formation of Christian Understanding: An Essay in Theological Hermeneutics* (Philadelphia: Westminster, 1981).

against the conclusion that the most at-risk sectors of society are occupied by children (though the aged poor or ill must also be considered). The prophylactic and antidote that Luke offers are perhaps all the more potent for their not being directed specifically at child-oriented practices. Instead, he both calls for and helps to mediate a conversion of one's dispositions — one's deepest commitments, allegiances, attitudes, and patterns of thinking, feeling, and believing — that cannot help but revolutionize one's practices with children.

11 Finding a Place for Children in the Letters of Paul

Beverly Roberts Gaventa

The letters of Paul have figured prominently in a number of recent ecclesiastical discussions, most notably those having to do with human sexuality, the roles of women in the church, the relationship between Christians and Jews, and the doctrine of justification by faith. Yet few readers of the Bible would turn to Paul's letters in eager expectation of help when thinking about questions concerning children and their welfare. And those readers who do turn to Paul's letters for help will find little support in the scholarly literature. Recent decades have witnessed a proliferation of books on children, families, and households in Greece and Rome,[1] but very little work has been done on the place(s) of children in the epistles of Paul.[2] The reason for this paucity of

---

1. Beryl Rawson, ed., *The Family in Ancient Rome: New Perspectives* (Ithaca, NY: Cornell University Press, 1986); Thomas Wiedemann, *Adults and Children in the Roman Empire* (New Haven: Yale University Press, 1989); Suzanne Dixon, *The Roman Mother* (Norman, OK: Oklahoma University Press, 1988); Mark Golden, *Children and Childhood in Classical Athens* (Baltimore: Johns Hopkins University Press, 1990); Keith R. Bradley, *Discovering the Roman Family: Studies in Roman Social History* (Oxford: Oxford University Press, 1991); Beryl Rawson, *Marriage, Divorce, and Children in Ancient Rome* (Oxford: Clarendon, 1991); Suzanne Dixon, *The Roman Family* (Baltimore: Johns Hopkins University Press, 1992); Nancy Demand, *Birth, Death, and Motherhood in Classical Greece* (Baltimore: Johns Hopkins University Press, 1994). On families in early Christianity, see Halvor Moxnes, ed., *Constructing Early Christian Families: Family as Social Reality and Metaphor* (London: Routledge, 1997); Carolyn Osiek and David L. Balch, *Families in the New Testament World: Households and House Churches* (Louisville: Westminster John Knox, 1997); Peter Balla, *The Child-Parent Relationship in the New Testament and Its Environment*, Wissenschaftliche Untersuchungen zum Neuen Testament 155 (Tübingen: Mohr Siebeck, 2003); Carolyn Osiek and Margaret Y. MacDonald, *A Woman's Place: House Churches in Earliest Christianity* (Minneapolis: Fortress, 2006).

2. Dorothy W. Martyn, "The Child and Adam: A Parable of the Two Ages," in *Apocalyptic and the New Testament: Essays in Honor of J. Louis Martyn*, ed. Joel Marcus and Marion L.

233

scholarly literature is easy to identify, since Paul has little to say on the topic. There may be more here than is currently acknowledged, however. This chapter will begin by surveying the references, both explicit and implicit, to the actual children who comprise part of the Pauline congregations. It then will examine the ways in which Paul refers to children metaphorically. Finally, in addition to these descriptive tasks, the chapter will take up the more constructive task of considering ways in which Pauline theology may have contributions to make to contemporary reflection about children, quite apart from his explicit and implicit references to children. It is Paul's theology, with its claims about God's grace-filled intervention in human life, that calls for a radical reconsideration of who children are, how they are to be assessed, and what roles they play in human community.

Children in the Churches of Paul

The references to actual flesh-and-blood children who inhabit the Pauline communities are rare indeed. There is no clear reference to children themselves as believers although there are passages that suggest the presence of children in the communities. At the conclusion of Paul's letter to the Romans, he greets a number of people by name (16:3-16). Within this list of greetings, he refers to the households of certain believers:

> Greet also the church in their [i.e., Prisca and Aquila's] house. (16:5)

> Greet those who belong to the family of Aristobulus. (16:10b)

> Greet those in the Lord who belong to the family of Narcissus. (16:11b)[3]

Although no child is named or addressed here individually, the presence of children may be inferred from the fact that households in the Roman world

---

Soards, Journal for the Study of the New Testament — Supplement Series 24 (Sheffield: Sheffield Academic Press, 1989), pp. 317-33; O. Larry Yarbrough, "Parents and Children in the Letters of Paul," in The Social World of the First Christians: Essays in Honor of Wayne A. Meeks, ed. L. Michael White and O. Larry Yarbrough (Minneapolis: Fortress, 1995), pp. 126-41; Balla, The Child-Parent Relationship, pp. 157-64, 182-95, 198-201; Reidar Aasgaard, "Paul as a Child: Children and Childhood in the Letters of Paul," Journal of Biblical Literature 126 (2007): 129-59.

3. In Romans 16:10b and 11b, the word "family" does not actually appear in the Greek, but the expression "those who are from among the people of Aristobulus" or "Narcissus" clearly refers to the households of those individuals, hence the translation of the NRSV. On the phrase and its connotation, see Wayne A. Meeks, The First Urban Christians: The Social World of the Apostle Paul (New Haven: Yale University Press, 1983), pp. 75-76.

consisted of extended families, including slaves and their own families.[4] In the same way that the presence of women in these communities is now understood to extend well beyond the explicit naming of female believers, the presence of children may also be assumed.

In a few places Paul makes reference, at least indirectly, to adult offspring. Romans 16:13 greets both Rufus and his mother. Paul castigates the Corinthians for their tolerance of a man who is living with his father's wife (presumably meaning his stepmother; 1 Cor. 5:1-5). In Galatians 1:16, Paul refers to himself as having been set apart for the apostleship from before his birth, from the womb of his mother.[5]

A few other biological offspring are mentioned in the letters, although these references are not to physical offspring among Paul's congregations. Romans 4 never actually discusses the child Isaac, but it does recount Sarah's barrenness and the promise to Abraham that he would be the father of many. Galatians 4:22 mentions the two sons of Abraham. Romans 9 refers to the children born to Sarah (vv. 6-9) and Rebecca (vv. 10-13; and see also Gal. 4:28). Second Corinthians 3:7 and 13 speak of the children (lit., "sons"; "people" in NRSV) of Israel. Galatians 4:4 describes Jesus as "born of a woman," just as Romans 1:3 refers to Jesus' descent from the line of David (see also Rom. 9:5).

One further text touches on the relationship between children and parents. At the end of Romans 1, Paul includes a list of accusations against human beings, ranging from murder to gossip. Within that list, there is a reference to those who are "rebellious toward parents" (v. 30). Lists of vices of this sort are conventional, appearing elsewhere in the New Testament and its literary environment,[6] so that the charge of being "rebellious" toward parents merely reflects the widespread assumption that children should treat their parents with respect (see also 2 Tim. 3:2-5).

In 1 Corinthians 7 Paul does explicitly mention the children of believers. In the context of instructing Christians at Corinth about questions of sexual relations and marriage, Paul takes up the emerging problem of marriage between believers and unbelievers: What should converts do if they find themselves married to unbelievers, especially in view of Jesus' instructions against divorce (1 Cor. 7:10-11; see Mark 10:2-13; Luke 16:18; and cf. Matt. 5:31-32; 19:3-

---

4. Meeks, *The First Urban Christians*, pp. 29-31.

5. English translations generally obscure this wording, but Galatians 1:16 literally reads, "the one who called me from the womb of my mother."

6. E.g., Galatians 5:19-23; Colossians 3:5, 8; 1 Timothy 1:9-10; 2 Timothy 3:2-4; 1 Peter 4:3. For a brief introduction to the virtue and vice lists, see John T. Fitzgerald, "Virtue/Vice Lists," *Anchor Bible Dictionary*, ed. David Noel Freedman, 6 vols. (New York: Doubleday, 1992), 6:857.

9)? Paul advises these believers that, if their spouses agree to continue in the marriage, they should not seek a divorce:

> For the unbelieving husband is made holy through his wife, and the unbelieving wife is made holy through her husband. Otherwise, your children would be unclean, but as it is, they are holy. (1 Cor. 7:14 NRSV)

What exactly Paul means by this assertion is unclear. Judith Gundry-Volf concludes that Paul understands these children as being "consecrated to God through their familial or genealogical relationship to believers"; they do not yet participate in salvation, but Paul anticipates that their relationship with their parents will eventually lead them to faith.[7] Yet, as Gundry-Volf also notes, elsewhere in Paul the vocabulary of holiness has to do with God's own action of rendering human beings holy (e.g., 1 Cor. 1:2; 6:11; 1 Thess. 5:23), and it seems unlikely that God's action is altogether absent here, especially in light of the discussion of divine calling in 1 Corinthians 7:17-24. Probably the holiness ascribed to these children reflects their location in the body of Christ through God's calling of their household; that is, their holiness is a statement about God's action, not about their own faith or achievement. Whatever the precise connotation of Paul's remarks, as O. Larry Yarbrough points out, the context even here is not a consideration of children per se and their thriving; instead, Paul is addressing some questions about marriage and touches on the situation of children only very briefly.[8]

Even by casting the net this widely, it is impossible to make Paul's letters into a consideration of children or childhood. The reasons for this silence are not hard to find and do not suggest indifference to children, much less hostility. To begin with, as is often noted, Paul's eschatological expectations were such that he did not imagine himself to be constructing a church that would endure and thrive in the generations that followed his own (e.g., 1 Thess. 4:17; 1 Cor. 15:51; Rom. 13:11). He did not treat questions about the rearing of children any more than he treated questions about identifying church leadership for coming generations. In addition, as 1 Corinthians 7:14 suggests, Paul probably assumed that the actions of parents automatically involved their children, so that his comments on Christian proclamation, worship, and fellowship may be taken as having implications for the lives of children, whether or not they are specifically mentioned (see below).

---

7. Judith Gundry-Volf, "The Least and the Greatest: Children in the New Testament," in *The Child in Christian Thought*, ed. Marcia J. Bunge (Grand Rapids: Eerdmans, 2001), pp. 29-60 (quotation on p. 51).

8. Yarbrough, "Parents and Children in the Letters of Paul," pp. 128-30.

Children in the Rhetoric of Paul

In addition to these references to biological children, Paul's letters also make use of metaphorical language concerning children and childhood. In a few places, Paul draws on the language of childhood to denote childlikeness, which may be understood either negatively or positively. More strikingly, Paul characterizes the relationship between himself and his congregations as that between parent and child. In addition, of course, Paul speaks of Jesus Christ as God's Son[9] and employs adoption language to refer to believers as God's children, fellow-heirs with Jesus Christ.

The following offers a sketch of Paul's metaphorical language about children, which Reidar Aasgaard explores more fully in the chapter that follows. And the chapter by David Bartlett in Part III of this volume examines the important motif of adoption in Pauline letters as well as other biblical texts.

Children and Childlikeness

First Corinthians 13 offers what is probably the most familiar instance in which Paul writes of children:

> When I was a child, I spoke like a child, I thought like a child, I reasoned like a child; when I became an adult, I put an end to childish ways. (1 Cor. 13:11)

The analogy is simple and straightforward. In the lines that follow, Paul contrasts what is seen in a mirror with what is seen in a face-to-face encounter, and what is seen at present with its eschatological fulfillment. To speak, think, and reason as a child does not, in this context, reflect negatively on children so much as it acknowledges that adults have greater capacities.

A few other passages similarly play upon the immaturity or innocence of children. In 1 Corinthians 3:1, Paul compares the Corinthians themselves with children who must still consume only milk, because they are not ready for solid food.[10] In 1 Corinthians 14:20, he encourages the audience to resist being "childlike" in their thinking, encouraging them to be "childlike" with respect to evil. And in Romans 2:20, Paul chastises those who imagine themselves (in

---

9. E.g., Romans 1:3-4; 5:10; 8:32; 1 Corinthians 1:9; 2 Corinthians 1:19; Galatians 1:16; 4:4; 1 Thessalonians 1:10. Jesus is identified as God's Son in many strands of the New Testament (e.g., see Matt. 14:33; 16:16; Mark 3:11; Luke 1:35; John 1:34; 20:31; Acts 9:20; Heb. 4:14; 1 John 3:8; Rev. 2:18).

10. See below for more on this verse.

this case wrongly) to be "a guide to the blind, a light to those who are in darkness, a corrector of the foolish, a teacher of children." In some other context, to be sure, "a teacher of children" could be a neutral or even positive reference to children; here, however, the context may suggest otherwise, especially when the reference to children follows a reference to those who are "foolish."[11]

Paul as Parent

In addition to these metaphorical expressions that have to do with being young or immature in perception or behavior, at several points in his letters Paul analogizes his relationship to believers in his congregations with that between a parent and children.[12] A few times the analogy applies to a single individual, as when he writes of Timothy as his beloved son (Phil. 2:22; see also 1 Cor. 4:17) and when he writes of Onesimus as having become his child during his imprisonment (Philem. 10). More often, the analogy pertains to Paul's relationship to a congregation rather than to an individual. When he recalls for the Thessalonians their initial time together, Paul declares that "we dealt with each one of you like a father with his children" (1 Thess. 2:11). While admonishing the Corinthians, he reminds them somewhat sharply that he is the one who "begot" them and that they have only one father in the faith (1 Cor. 4:14-21).

Much less attention has been paid to the fact that, in addition to referring to himself as the father of believers, Paul also refers to himself as their mother. In Galatians 4:19, he employs the language of birthing to express his concern:

My little children, for whom I am again in the pain of childbirth until Christ is formed in you.

In 1 Thessalonians 2:7, the language becomes even more intimate with the declaration that Paul and his co-workers were "like a nurse tenderly caring for her own children." And in 1 Corinthians 3:2, he complains that he had to continue to breastfeed the Corinthians, who were not ready yet for solid food.[13]

---

11. In her essay in this volume, Judith M. Gundry contrasts Paul's use of childlikeness as something negative with the Gospels' metaphorical use childlikeness for total dependence on God.

12. See the extensive study of this feature of Paul's letters by Christine Gerber, *Paulus und seine 'Kinder': Studien zur Beziehungsmetaphorik des paulinischen Briefe*, Beihefte zur Zeitschrift für die neutestamentliche Wissenschaft 136 (Berlin: Walter de Gruyter, 2005).

13. On these passages, see Beverly Roberts Gaventa, "The Maternity of Paul: An Exegetical Study of Galatians 4:19," in *The Conversation Continues: Studies in Paul and John in Honor of*

Two other passages touch on this parent-child relationship. In 2 Corinthians 6:11-12, Paul concludes a lengthy passage sketching the nature of his own ministry, a ministry that has been challenged among the Corinthians, with a declaration of his own sense of the emotional connection between them:

> We have spoken frankly to you Corinthians; our heart is wide open to you. There is no restriction in our affections, but only in yours. In return — I speak as to children — open wide your hearts also.

Later in 2 Corinthians, Paul again draws on the parent-child analogy to explain his sense of obligation to the community in Corinth:

> And I will not be a burden, because I do not want what is yours but you; for children ought not to lay up for their parents, but parents for their children. I will most gladly spend and be spent for you. (2 Cor. 12:14b-15a)[14]

Victor Paul Furnish rightly characterizes these scattered references as terms of "endearment."[15] They scarcely amount to a Pauline doctrine about children, their education and nurture, or even their place in the community of faith. They do, however, reveal his awareness of the deep and mutual obligations between parents and children. Paul chooses these metaphors (consciously or unconsciously), he understands himself as both father and mother to these believers, and that in itself makes a claim about the importance of children to parents and vice versa. If Paul never gives actual advice to parents about the raising of their children,[16] he does nevertheless assume and draw upon the parent-child relationship in ways that reflect positively upon the valuation of children for their parents and the larger community.

J. *Louis Martyn,* ed. Robert T. Fortna and Beverly R. Gaventa (Nashville: Abingdon, 1990), pp. 189-201; "Apostles as Babes and Nurses in 1 Thessalonians 2:7," in *Faith and History: Essays in Honor of Paul W. Meyer,* ed. John T. Carroll, Charles H. Cosgrove, and E. Elizabeth Johnson (Atlanta: Scholars Press, 1990), pp. 193-207; "Mother's Milk and Ministry in 1 Corinthians 3," in *Theology and Ethics in Paul and His Interpreters: Essays in Honor of Victor Paul Furnish,* ed. Eugene H. Lovering Jr. and Jerry L. Sumney (Nashville: Abingdon, 1996), pp. 101-13; "Our Mother St. Paul: Toward the Recovery of a Neglected Theme," in *A Feminist Companion to Paul,* ed. Amy-Jill Levine with Marianne Blickenstaff (Cleveland: Pilgrim Press, 2004), pp. 85-97; and *Our Mother Saint Paul* (Louisville: Westminster John Knox, 2007). See also Susan Eastman, *Recovering Paul's Mother Tongue* (Grand Rapids: Eerdmans, 2007).

14. On parallels to this statement in Paul's literary environment, see Yarbrough, "Parents and Children in the Letters of Paul," pp. 134-38.

15. Victor Paul Furnish, *II Corinthians,* Anchor Bible 32a (New York: Doubleday, 1984), p. 361.

16. As Yarbrough rightly notes ("Parents and Children in the Letters of Paul," p. 138).

Children are seldom seen and never heard in these letters, but the letters nevertheless reflect a robust sense of their importance.

A Place for Children in the Theology of Paul?

These bits and pieces drawn from varying contexts in the Pauline letters barely touch upon the questions contemporary readers might like to have Paul discuss, questions about the value to be assigned to children and their contributions, the place children occupy within believing communities and society as a whole, and the responsibility of communities for the formation and welfare of all children. The letters simply will not yield direct answers to those questions. To take up those questions, it is essential to move beyond individual passages that refer directly and indirectly to children and to consider Paul's theology and the implications of that theology for an understanding of children and our obligations to them. Here the attempt is to think *with Paul's letters* about children and their flourishing. Several significant Pauline motifs that may be suggestive include: (1) the corruption and restoration of human speech in relation to God and the family, (2) Paul's understanding of the gospel as ushering in a radically altered epistemology and hence a radically altered assessment of children, and (3) the body of Christ motif as that motif relates to the fragility and significance of all human beings, particularly children.

The Corruption and Redemption of Human Speech

The first several chapters of Paul's letter to the Romans offer a penetrating analysis of human sinfulness, characterizing the human being as living in captivity to powers of sin and death.[17] Although Paul says nothing here about children's sinfulness per se, the universal grasp of sin that emerges from these

---

17. On this feature of Romans, see Beverly Roberts Gaventa, "The Cosmic Power of Sin in Paul's Letter to the Romans: Toward a Widescreen Edition," *Interpretation* 53 (2004): 229-40. Paul's understanding of the universal extent of sin's grasp has been neglected in recent scholarly discussion, but it is theologically significant, especially for an understanding of children. Marcia Bunge reminds me that the notion that "all are sinful" has, for example, helped some Christian theologians to recognize children's growing moral responsibility and to see all children as equals, therefore paving the way for a more humane treatment of all children and including all children in educational and health care reforms. See "Introduction" in Bunge, ed., *The Child in Christian Thought,* pp. 13-16.

chapters would seem to include children as well.[18] This larger analysis of the work of sin culminates in a lengthy compilation of scriptural quotations (Rom. 3:10b-18) that forms an emphatic conclusion to the point Paul has been developing since 1:18 about the power of sin in human life. The collection of scriptural quotations has long interested scholars, but scholarly interest has focused more on the origin and function of the collection than on its content. As a result, a feature of this passage that remains neglected is its emphasis on human speech.

The collection opens and closes with general assertions about the faithlessness of human beings:

> There is no one who is righteous, not even one:
> there is no one who has understanding,
> there is no one who seeks God.

(Rom. 3:10b-11)

> There is no fear of God before their eyes.

(v. 19)

At the center of the collection, however, stand three striking quotations having to do with human speech (Rom. 3:13-14):

> Their throats are opened graves;
> they use their tongues to deceive.

(Ps. 5:10 LXX)

> The venom of vipers is under their lips

(Ps. 139:4 LXX)

> Their mouths are full of cursing and bitterness.

(Ps. 10:7)

In these terse lines drawn from the psalms, Paul depicts the thoroughgoing corruption of human speech, graphically imaged in terms of throat, tongue, lips, and mouth.[19]

This focus on human speech takes on more importance when we recall

18. For an insightful discussion of children and the power of sin in Paul's thought, see Dorothy W. Martyn, "The Child and Adam: A Parable of the Two Ages."

19. For a more extended discussion of this text, see Beverly Roberts Gaventa, "From Toxic Speech to the Redemption of Doxology in Paul's Letter to the Romans," forthcoming in *The Word Leaps the Gap: Essays on Scripture and Theology in Honor of Richard B. Hays*, ed. J. Ross Wagner, A. Katherine Grieb, and C. Kavin Rowe (Grand Rapids: Eerdmans, 2008).

that the indictment that begins in Romans 1:18 also strongly features the corruption of human speech. The practices that Paul so relentlessly adduces in the vice list of 1:29-30 include corrupt acts of speech (at least those he identifies as deceit, gossip, slander). More to the point, the indictment itself actually begins with human repression of the truth (1:18), with the refusal to give thanks to God (1:21), and with exchanging truth about God for a lie (1:25). In Paul's analysis, at the very root of the human entrapment in the power of sin lies corrupt speech to and about God. Paul pulls this entire section together with the conclusion that the law itself "speaks" in order that "every mouth may be silenced" (literally, "every tongue might be stopped"). The juxtaposition of the vileness of human speech and the declaration that the law stops human speech seems too neatly parallel to be accidental.

In later parts of the letter, where Paul considers humanity as it has been released from the power of sin and placed under the power of the gospel as God's own children (see especially Romans 6 and 8), there are at least hints that human speech is made healthy. Several of the spiritual gifts that are bestowed on the community are gifts that involve speech (at least those of prophecy, teaching, and exhortation; see 12:6-8). More important, in chapter 15, at what many regard as the climax of the letter's argument, Paul celebrates the glorification and praise of God by Jew and Gentile together ("with one voice," 15:6):

> Rejoice, O Gentiles, with his people.
> Praise the Lord, all you Gentiles,
>   and let all the peoples praise him.
>
> (Rom. 15:10-11)

The restoration of human speech, indeed the speech of all creation, comes into view also in the Philippians hymn, which anticipates the eschatological praise of God by every tongue in creation:

> So that at the name of Jesus
>   every knee should bend,
>   in heaven and on earth and under the earth,
> and every tongue should confess
>   that Jesus Christ is Lord,
>   to the glory of God the Father.
>
> (Phil. 2:10-11)

While this motif of the corruption and restoration of human speech concerns all of humankind, it is suggestive to ask what this preoccupation with speech might have to contribute to reflection on the lives of children. In the most obvious instance, the connection lies in the ever-present challenge that speech poses to the nurture of children: How does adult speech call children forth in ways that are healthy or crippling? How does speech shape their self-understandings? With what tone are they addressed? What information is revealed to and concealed from children? Do children hear speech from "mouths full of cursing and bitterness," speech that merely belittles and malforms? Despite the childhood boast that "sticks and stones may break my bones, but words can never hurt me," words can and do actually break the spirit.[20]

This point, taken in isolation, seems no different from what might be found in the works of child psychologists, such as Dr. Spock and T. Berry Brazelton. It is crucial here not to lapse into a kind of utilitarianism with a theological veneer, and a thin veneer at that, in which Scripture is employed merely to underscore the conventional wisdom. Something far more challenging comes to expression in Paul's letters than in contemporary parenting manuals. Paul locates the "mouths full of cursing and bitterness" within the more fundamental problem of human rebellion against God, the failure to acknowledge God as God (Rom. 1:18-32; 3:10b-11, 18). Malformed human speech is not simply a bad habit or a bad practice; it stands as a symptom of humanity's unwillingness to understand itself as created rather than as Creator. At the very least, Paul's letters raise the question of what it means for children to hear, first and foremost, words that acknowledge God as Creator and Lord and honor Jesus Christ as God's own Son, what it means for children to hear words of acknowledgment and honor, words of praise and gratitude.[21] As Charles Marsh has astutely observed, gratitude "lifts us out of our natural instinct to find fault and to belittle others."[22] Genuine acknowledgment and gratitude to God will come to expression in a myriad of ways that allow human beings of all ages to flourish.

---

20. It may be objected, and with some justification, that this is a problem largely born out of luxury, one that scarcely touches children in poverty, children whose daily lives are consumed with the search for food and shelter and clothing. Yet surely the hopes of such children are also reinforced or crushed by the language used around and for them, and perhaps especially by the language they never hear.

21. Christian educator Carol Wehrheim encourages new parents to pray aloud while holding their infants or while standing beside their cribs: "Let the sound of your voice giving thanks to God and asking for God's love and care be among the earliest words that your child remembers" (*The Baptism of Your Child: A Book for Presbyterian Families* [Louisville: Geneva Press, 2006], p. 31).

22. Charles Marsh, *The Beloved Community: How Faith Shapes Social Justice, from the Civil Rights Movement to Today* (New York: Basic Books, 2005), p. 214.

The Cross and Human Values

In popular understandings of Paul's letters, human response to God's actions in the gospel is largely cast in terms of faith (in the sense of assenting to the gospel's content or to its propositions). Texts such as Romans 1:16 and 3:22, particularly read through a Protestant emphasis on justification by faith, underwrite emphasis on human believing and, consequently, on human acting. Pauline studies in the last several decades have relentlessly criticized such presentations, but often both the adherents and the critics of this traditional view overlook yet another feature of Paul's letters, and that is Paul's understanding of the epistemological divide brought about by the gospel. The gospel is not so much a set of propositions to which people give assent as it is an *event*, an action of God that calls into being a new way of thinking and perceiving.

Two passages from the Corinthian correspondence offer the most direct access to this epistemological divide. In 1 Corinthians 1:18, Paul writes that

The word of the cross is foolishness to those who are perishing,
but to us who are being saved it is the power of God.

The inverted parallelism underscores the point: two groups of people (those who are perishing and those who are being saved) simultaneously look at the same event (the cross) and see two different things, either foolishness or power.[23] The second passage, 2 Corinthians 5:16-17, can be read as giving an account of this divide. Translated somewhat loosely:

So from now on we understand no one in a merely human way. Even if we earlier understood Christ in a merely human way, now we no longer do so. So that if someone is in Christ, there is nothing less than new creation. The old has passed away. Behold, the new has come.

In a classic article on this passage, J. Louis Martyn argued that it understands the Christ event, especially the cross itself (see vv. 14-15, and recall 1 Cor. 1:18, as well as 1 Cor. 2:2 and Gal. 3:1), as revealing that God's perceptions, God's knowledge, God's values are radically at odds with those of human beings.[24]

---

23. That Paul contrasts "foolishness" with "power" instead of the more predictable "wisdom" has much to do with the setting at Corinth, where some people apparently thought they were in possession of wisdom. Notice that, having defined the terms to his liking, Paul does return in verse 24 to affirm that the gospel is God's wisdom as well as God's power.

24. J. Louis Martyn, "Epistemology at the Turn of the Ages," in *Theological Issues in the Letters of Paul* (Nashville: Abingdon, 1997), pp. 89-110. For a compelling explication of what this

Those who have been overtaken by the gospel actually perceive things differently, beginning with perceptions of the death of Jesus Christ on the cross and extending to include perceptions about all human beings.

Paul does not unpack this difference in perception directly, but certain features of it may be glimpsed in his letters. To begin with, the cross demolishes any claims to privilege and any manner of perception that relies on birth or social status. First Corinthians 1:26-31 sharply reminds the Corinthians of the fact that they were not called on the basis of their status or birth, precisely so that they might not be able to boast about such matters. The cross also demolishes assessment of human beings based on their achievements, including achievements in the arena of religious life. Paul's clearest statements of this point come when he speaks of his own calling in Galatians 1:11-17 and in Philippians 3:2-11. In both instances, there is a radical disjuncture between his earlier zealous pursuit of religious achievement and the gospel that overturns that same zeal. He concludes that he has endured the loss of "all things" and regards them as mere "rubbish" (Phil. 3:8). In addition, the cross undermines conventional notions of strength and weakness, since the cross itself displays Jesus Christ as the pinnacle of weakness and simultaneously the place of human redemption. In 2 Corinthians 10–13 Paul glories in his own weakness, castigating those who demand from their leaders powerful speech and charismatic gifts.[25]

Paul does not specifically mention children in connection with this epistemological shift, but it is not difficult to extend his argument to include them. If the Corinthians are called to account for boasting about their birth and social standing, then surely Paul would castigate those cultures (especially North American culture) in which childhood evaporates due to the pervasive commodification that not only robs children of their childhoods but actually places them in harm's way. Many of the world's children are at risk because they are early on commodified in terms of what they can produce, so that children in developing countries are assessed only in terms of what work they can do and for how long. Children in affluent countries are also at risk from a commodification that is far less easy to unmask. By assessing these children in terms of their achievements — intellectual, athletic, artistic — society also commodifies them, rendering their childhood merely an extended training ground for the marketplace.

---

epistemological crisis looks like, see also Martyn's "From Paul to Flannery O'Connor with the Power of Grace," also in *Theological Issues in the Letters of Paul*, pp. 251-66.

25. In his essay in this volume, John T. Carroll considers a similar reversal of human values in the Gospel of Luke.

What might it mean to perceive the world's children — all of them — not in this merely human way, but from the vantage point of their value to God? To put the question pointedly, if the cross itself is God's power, what does that imply about the way in which we think about the earth's children? It would seem obvious that the care and nurture of children — without regard to their productivity, success, birth, or income — would be a first priority.

The Body of Christ: To Whom Do We Belong?

Twice in his undisputed letters, Paul draws on language about the "body of Christ" to instruct his addressees about the life of the believing community. In 1 Corinthians 12, he analogizes believers with a single human body in order to respond to problems that have to do with worship and the use of spiritual gifts in worship. All those who are baptized, according to Paul, are baptized into a single body (1 Cor. 12:12-13). This baptism means that, while there are "weaker" parts of the body and "stronger" parts of the body, there should be no conflict among these various parts since the various members "have the same care for one another. If one member suffers, all suffer together with it; if one member is honored, all rejoice together with it" (vv. 25b-26). On this basis, Paul goes on in 1 Corinthians 14 to offer specific instruction about how worship should be conducted in a way that respects the differing gifts granted to individuals without lionizing one gift over against another. In Romans 12, he again draws on this analogy, although less extensively, to address the use of spiritual gifts in leadership of the community. That this is not a passing whim becomes clear in Galatians 3 with its language about being baptized into Christ. Although the discussion of disputes in Romans 14:1–15:6 does not draw on the image of the body of Christ, that passage operates with a similar notion of the location of believers in a single household, which it is their obligation to support and upbuild.

The Pauline conviction that believers belong together to the single body of Christ proves enormously provocative for reflection about children. To begin with, the singularity of this body means that what happens to a part of it affects the whole. It is not possible, in Paul's analysis, for affluent North Americans to imagine that what happens to impoverished children in China or to children with HIV in Africa or to immigrant children in southern California is a matter of indifference to the whole of this body. These and other "at risk" children render the whole of the body of Christ "at risk." Their fragility exposes that of the entire body. By the same token, whatever strength there is in the body of Christ is strength that affords protection for the world's children.[26]

As Paul employs this motif of the body of Christ as a way of arguing for the importance of all the spiritual gifts within a Christian community, it is important also to reflect on the roles children occupy in the body of Christ or in the household of God. What gifts do children bring to that body, gifts that often go unnoticed? Perhaps the most obvious gift is the gift of love, since it is in receiving and being received by children that many parents (and not only parents) find their capacity for love enlarged past all imagining. Children also contribute to the human capacity for doxology and wonder, since their own delight in discovery proves contagious for those who watch and listen. While these may be the contributions of the "weaker" members of the body, they are by no means negligible.

Conclusion

Virtually at every point in this essay, as we attempt to discern what Paul might have to say about children or related to children, his convictions about God come into play. That is most readily seen in the constructive part of the essay, since it asks specifically about the implications of Paul's theology, his talk about God. It is also the case, however, in the descriptive part of the essay, where the children who are mentioned (whether actual or metaphorical children) are the objects of God's creation or redemption or preservation. While this preoccupation with God is to be expected in early Christian letters, it stands in sharp contrast with the way in which many of Paul's contemporaries thought about children and their families. It also stands in contrast with the way in which many people currently think about children and their families.

---

26. In Paul's letters, to be sure, those who are part of the body of Christ are those who have been baptized into the body (1 Cor. 12:13), so that a very literal construal of this phrase would hold that this point applies only to Christians. Yet there is much in Paul's letters that underscores the universal extent of God's intervention in human life, as in Romans 5:12-21 and 11:32. See also Victor Paul Furnish, "Inside Looking Out: Some Pauline Views of the Unbelieving Public," in *Pauline Conversations in Context: Essays in Honor of Calvin J. Roetzel,* ed. Janice Capel Anderson, Philip Sellew, and Claudia Setzer, Journal for the Study of the New Testament — Supplement Series 221 (Sheffield: Sheffield Academic Press, 2002), pp. 104-24, and "Uncommon Love and the Common Good: Christians as Citizens in the Letters of Paul," in *In Search of the Common Good,* ed. Dennis P. McCann and Patrick D. Miller (New York: T&T Clark, 2005), pp. 58-87.

For many of Paul's contemporaries, the household existed for the sake of the *polis,* the city or state. The Stoics, for example, speak of families as miniature cities and of children as being raised for the sake of the *polis.*[27] Such a notion seems bizarre to contemporary readers. But in North America, for example, our thinking about the household may be no less instrumental or utilitarian. The family, in our case a nuclear family consisting of parents and children in a single generation, belongs to itself. At least we imagine that our families are independent and even self-sufficient. In practice, however, it may be that our families actually belong to the marketplace, since it is the business of buying and selling that overshadows much of what our families do.

By sharp contrast with both these views, Paul locates the family in the household of God. The family does not belong to itself, and children do not belong to their parents. They belong, all of them, to God's household. We may then take some comfort from Paul's reminder to the Romans that the Lord of this household is able to sustain all who are within it (Rom. 14:4).

---

27. The second-century Stoic Arius Didymus writes that the household is "the source for a city.... For the household is like any small city, if, at least as is intended, the marriage flourishes, and the children mature and are paired with one another; another household is founded, and thus a third and a fourth, and out of these a village and a city" (quoted in David L. Balch, "Household Codes," in *Greco-Roman Literature and the New Testament,* ed. David E. Aune, Society of Biblical Literature Sources for Biblical Study 21 [Atlanta: Scholars Press, 1988], p. 41). Consistent with this viewpoint, Hierocles, also a second-century Stoic, comments that "our country especially urges us to do so [marry and have children]. For I dare say that we raise children not so much for ourselves as for our country by planning for the constitution of the state that follows us and supplying the community with our successors" (quoted in Abraham J. Malherbe, *Moral Exhortation: A Greco-Roman Sourcebook* [Philadelphia: Westminster Press, 1986], p. 104).

12   Like a Child: Paul's Rhetorical
Uses of Childhood

Reidar Aasgaard

The apostle Paul very rarely mentions real, living children, as is clearly shown in this volume's article by Beverly R. Gaventa. Still, children turn up on virtually every leaf of his letters, especially in the shape of metaphors drawn from the world of childhood and parent/child relations.[1] For example, Paul often speaks of his readers as children and of himself as a parent to them. Sometimes this is expressed in ways that imply parental care and concern. At other times he can speak in seemingly negative terms about being like a child. Surprisingly, he also on some occasions characterizes himself as a fetus, a premature baby, and a child.

Paul's use of kinship and childhood language is complex, and scholars have recently devoted more attention to it, especially to his use of sibling and parent/child terminology.[2] In this kind of language, which is usually em-

1. The terms "metaphor" and "metaphorical" are in the following used in a general and rather non-technical sense, on a level with "figurative," "transferred," and "imagery." On the use of kinship metaphors in Paul, see my book *"My Beloved Brothers and Sisters!": Christian Siblingship in Paul* (London/New York: T&T Clark Int./Continuum, 2004), pp. 23-31, 118-36; I apply the metaphor theory of George Lakoff and Mark Johnson to the material. Trevor J. Burke, *Family Matters: A Socio-historical Study of Kinship Metaphors in 1 Thessalonians* (London/New York: T&T Clark Int./Continuum, 2003), pp. 18-28, builds on my book.

2. See, for example, Daniel von Allmen, *La famille de Dieu* (Göttingen: Vandenhoeck & Ruprecht, 1981); Norman R. Petersen, *Rediscovering Paul: Philemon and the Sociology of Paul's Narrative World* (Philadelphia: Fortress, 1985); John L. White, "God's Paternity as Root Metaphor in Paul's Conception of Community," *Forum* 8 (1992): 271-95; Hellerman, *The Ancient*

This chapter is an abridged and slightly revised version of my article "Paul as a Child: Children and Childhood in the Letters of the Apostle," *Journal of Biblical Literature* 126 (2007): 129-59. I refer to this article for a more detailed presentation and discussion of the issue.

ployed metaphorically of Christians, many see a reflection of ideas associated with being family in antiquity: Christians are to relate to one another in ways similar to those of the family, with its structures and mentalities. Several scholars have also focused on how Paul uses kinship language as a rhetorical means to regulate his relations to fellow Christians, and in particular to further his own authority, with some even maintaining that Paul with this language aims at exercising a strong control over his communities.[3]

Although the literature about Paul's use of kinship language has been steadily growing, scholars have generally focused on one specific aspect of this, namely his "parent" language, particularly about God or Paul as "father," and about Paul as "mother." Far less effort has been put into the study of the *place of children* in Paul's thinking.[4] Furthermore, this literature has not fully addressed many of the apparent contradictions in Paul's use of childhood imagery. For example, although Paul speaks in seemingly authoritarian and patriarchal terms about himself as a father to his childish congregations, he can

---

Church as Family (Minneapolis: Fortress, 2001); S. Scott Bartchy, "Who Should Be Called Father? Paul of Tarsus between the Jesus Tradition and Patria Potestas," *Biblical Theology Bulletin* 33 (2003): 135-47. See many of the entries in the select bibliography in the present volume, including Beverly Roberts Gaventa, *Our Mother Saint Paul* (Louisville: Westminster John Knox, 2007); Susan Eastman, *Recovering Paul's Mother Tongue* (Grand Rapids: Eerdmans, 2007); and Christine Gerber, *Paulus und seine 'Kinder': Studien zur Beziehungsmetaphorik der paulinischen Briefe* (Berlin: Walter de Gruyter, 2005).

3. This has particularly been emphasized by scholars studying Paul from the perspectives of power and of gender. For instance, Elisabeth A. Castelli, *Imitating Paul: A Discourse of Power* (Louisville: Westminster John Knox, 1991), esp. pp. 98-111, 115-17, has brought attention to Paul's idea of imitation in 1 Corinthians and of the Corinthians imitating Paul as children do a father (4:16-21). She argues that this forms part of a discourse of power that aims at leaving his authority uncontested and at securing sameness instead of difference. Her view is also supported by Vernon K. Robbins, *The Tapestry of Early Christian Discourse: Rhetoric, Society and Ideology* (London: Routledge, 1996), pp. 195-99, and Sandra Hack Polaski, *Paul and the Discourse of Power* (Sheffield: Sheffield Academic Press, 1999), pp. 12-13, 14-15. Similarly, Lone Fatum, "Brotherhood in Christ: A Gender Hermeneutical Reading of 1 Thessalonians," in *Constructing Early Christian Families*, ed. Halvor Moxnes (London: Routledge, 1997), pp. 183-97, maintains that Paul employs parent/child metaphors in 1 Thessalonians to strengthen his authority and further male prominence, to the effect that women only become associate members of the Thessalonian "brotherhood" through their men.

4. A few of the scholars have — to an extent — employed this perspective. With regard to the New Testament in general, see Peter Müller, *In der Mitte der Gemeinde: Kinder im Neuen Testament* (Neukirchen-Vluyn: Neukirchener, 1992), and William A. Strange, *Children in the Early Church: Children in the Ancient World, the New Testament, and the Early Church* (Carlisle: Paternoster, 1996). On the obedience of children, see Peter Balla, *The Child-Parent Relationship in the New Testament and Its Environment* (Tübingen: Mohr Siebeck, 2003). On 1 Thessalonians, see Burke, *Family Matters.* On Paul, see Aasgaard, *"My Beloved Brothers and Sisters!"*

also speak of himself as their mother. In fact, he can even present himself from the reverse perspective: as himself being a child to them.

The aim of this chapter is to explore more fully the language of children and childhood in the seven undisputed Pauline letters: Romans, 1 and 2 Corinthians, Galatians, Philippians, 1 Thessalonians, and Philemon. By exploring this issue in his letters, the chapter helps address the following central questions: What is the nature and scope of Paul's childhood language? What does it reveal about his attitudes to actual children and his views of child/parent relationships? In what ways do Paul's attitudes conform to or deviate from Greco-Roman ideas and ideals of childhood and family life?[5] Does he in any manner have a profile of his own? And — importantly — in what ways do children and childhood play a role in the rhetoric of his letters?

The chapter addresses these and related questions by exploring Paul's childhood language in the interface between his socio-cultural setting and his rhetorical and theological strategies. The purpose is of course not to give an exhaustive presentation of the lives of children and of ideas about childhood in antiquity. Rather, the chapter highlights aspects of Greco-Roman attitudes to children that are relevant to Paul's letters by focusing on four primary categories regarding children: *kinship, social position, formation,* and *belonging.*

As will be argued below, by exploring Paul's childhood language through these four categories, we come away with a fuller understanding of his attitudes toward children and also of the seemingly contradictory elements in his view. And by observing closely how he makes use of childhood language in his rhetoric in ways that are sometimes startling and daring, we may even add a new dimension to our overall understanding of Paul.[6]

Analysis of Paul's Childhood Language

Paul's childhood language can be categorized in various ways.[7] One is to distinguish between *concrete* and *metaphorical* usage, that is, when Paul speaks

5. For a survey of research on childhood in antiquity and early Christianity, see Reidar Aasgaard, "Children in Antiquity and Early Christianity: Research History and Central Issues," *Familia* (Salamanca, Spain) 33 (2006): 23-46. Although there were clearly cultural and regional differences in antiquity, one can nonetheless speak of certain general attitudes.

6. This does not mean, of course, that we have access to what Paul "really" thought about these matters. What will be dealt with are the ideas displayed by Paul as an "implied author"; these ideas may very much concur with that of the "real" Paul, but this is of course impossible to confirm.

7. For a survey of Paul's children/childhood language, see Aasgaard, "Paul as a Child," *Journal of Biblical Literature* 126 (2007): esp. Table 1-2; also Müller, *In der Mitte der Gemeinde,* pp. 165-200, esp. 174-75, 188, 191, 196-200.

about actual children and when he employs the term metaphorically. His attitudes toward children are likely to be reflected in both types of language and in parallel ways. For instance, his notions about being a child of God would probably be quite similar to those about being a child of a human being.[8] Sometimes the distinction is hard to uphold: Is Paul's idea that Christians are adopted as sons of God (Rom. 8:15, 23) only "metaphorical" or does it have some kind of more real sense?[9]

A second way of categorizing Paul's childhood language is to distinguish between *relational* usage and *life-stage* usage.[10] In the former, emphasis is on familial relationships — for example, parent/child relations (e.g., God as father). Within such usage, age is often of minor relevance (e.g., Christians as children of God). Many instances in Paul are of such a relational kind. In life-stage usage, however, the language refers to children proper. Such usage also occurs a number of times in Paul — for example, of an underage child as heir (νήπιος, Gal. 4:1). This example also shows that it is not always possible to distinguish clearly between the two: relational and life-stage usage may intersect.

Although these two approaches are helpful, I shall in the following primarily employ a third approach: organizing Paul's childhood language according to *semantic fields*. Peter Müller has usefully outlined the word field "child" within the New Testament as a whole by dividing the field into four main areas: *kinship, social position, formation,* and *belonging.*[11] This form of categoriziation is valuable not least because these four main areas, each with its own sub-areas, are very much in keeping with the main dimensions of children's life in antiquity. In addition, it allows for a more dynamic and multifaceted analysis of the material, since it enables us to view Paul's statements

---

8. See Aasgaard, *"My Beloved Brothers and Sisters!"* pp. 24-29, 306-12, and Burke, *Family Matters,* pp. 27-28, 250-56, for discussions of this.

9. James M. Scott, *Adoption as Sons of God: An Exegetical Investigation into the Background of YIOTHESIA in the Pauline Corpus,* Wissenschaftliche Untersuchungen zum Neuen Testament 2:48 (Tübingen: Mohr Siebeck, 1992), esp. pp. 267-70; and the chapter by David Bartlett in this volume.

10. This distinction is particularly focused by Müller, *In der Mitte der Gemeinde,* and Balla, *The Child-Parent Relationship.* Andreas Michel, *Gott und Gewalt gegen Kinder im Alten Testament,* Forschungen zum Alten Testament 37 (Tübingen: Mohr Siebeck, 2003), has developed this theoretically and as concerns children in the Hebrew Bible. Even though he deals exclusively with children in a concrete sense, his distinctions are nevertheless fully applicable to the New Testament material. Stephen Bertman, ed., *The Conflict of Generations in Ancient Greece and Rome* (Amsterdam: Grüner, 1976), deals extensively with parent/youth relations.

11. *Verwandschaft, Gesellschaftliche Stellung, Erziehung,* and *Zugehörigkeit,* respectively. See the map in Müller, *In der Mitte der Gemeinde,* p. 197; for a detailed survey, see pp. 165-200, esp. pp. 197-200, in Müller's book.

from various angles — for example, from the perspectives both of social position and of formation.

Kinship

A majority of Paul's childhood language belongs to the *kinship* field, and these instances are often stereotypical in character.[12] They deal with only a few, interconnected issues, have traditionally been termed metaphorical (e.g., God as father/Christians as children), and are usually of a relational type (parent/child relations without reference to age).

Both in frequency and in character, this parent/child language reflects central concerns in antiquity: producing children was a means of securing succession and of transferring property (material inheritance and cultural heritage).[13] The former was also very much seen as a measure taken by parents in order to secure their own safety in old age.[14]

Succession

In Paul, succession is by far the most common category. It can be divided into four subgroups, of which the first three give little information beyond stating a relationship: (1) Jesus as Son of God (e.g., Rom. 1:3-4); (2) believers as children of God (e.g., Rom. 8:14-21); and (3) believers as descendants of Israel (e.g., 2 Cor. 3:7, 13), of Abraham (e.g., Rom. 9:7-9), and of Sarah and of Hagar (Gal. 4:21-31). Within this system of succession Jesus occupies an in-between position: he is God's "Son, born of a woman" (Gal. 4:4) and also descended from David (Rom. 1:3-4). In addition, he is viewed as "the firstborn among many siblings" (Rom. 8:29).[15]

The last subdivision, (4) Christians as children of Paul, sheds more light on the Pauline texts. In Philippians 2:22, he presents himself as the father of Timothy, his (adult) "son," who obeys and supports his father, in accordance with common expectations.[16] In Philemon 10, the runaway slave Onesimus is called

12. In addition, the high frequency of sibling language serves to make this group numerically even more dominating; see Aasgaard, *"My Beloved Brothers and Sisters!"* pp. 3-4, 130-36.

13. Aasgaard, *"My Beloved Brothers and Sisters!"* pp. 45-46.

14. Tim G. Parkin, *Old Age in the Roman World: A Cultural and Social History* (Baltimore/London: Johns Hopkins University Press, 2003), pp. 203-36, esp. pp. 205-15.

15. See Aasgaard, *"My Beloved Brothers and Sisters!"* pp. 137-50, for a discussion of this passage.

16. Balla, *The Child-Parent Relationship,* p. 196 n. 60; Carolyn Osiek, *Philippians, Philemon,* Abingdon New Testament Commentaries (Nashville: Abingdon, 2000), pp. 76-77.

Paul's child, whom he has borne, or "fathered," "begotten" (ἐγέννησα).[17] If the term is here a general reference to parent/child relations, Onesimus is depicted as an adult child, and the usage is relational.[18] However, if ἐγέννησα refers to giving birth, the slave is in the position of a small child, a "new-born." The latter understanding appears the more likely, and this finds support in Galatians 4:19, in which Paul speaks of the Galatians as children whom he — like a woman — must once more give birth to: "My little children, for whom I am again in the pain of childbirth." Paul's use here of himself as a birth-giving mother is striking.[19] In both texts, he appears to focus on the burdensome aspect of childbirth: in Philemon, he is giving birth "in chains" (cf. also v. 13);[20] in Galatians, he is "in . . . pain."[21] The final example to be mentioned is 1 Corinthians 4:14-16. In this passage, Paul calls the Corinthians his children, whom he has "fathered" in Christ — here, ἐγέννησα is explicitly male-oriented (cf. v. 15b) — and over whom he has a right that goes far beyond that of "guardians." I shall return to this passage later.

Property Transfer

The texts on transfer of property are the second largest use of childhood terms in the kinship group.[22] Usually, Paul deals with property transfer in a

17. See Markus Barth and Helmut Blanke, *The Letter to Philemon: A New Translation with Notes and Commentary,* Eerdmans Critical Commentary (Grand Rapids: Eerdmans, 2000), pp. 324-29, 329-35 (excursus), 336-38, for a discussion of the meaning of this term.

18. Ronald F. Hock, "A Support for His Old Age: Paul's Plea on Behalf of Onesimus," in *The Social World of the First Christians: Essays in Honor of Wayne A. Meeks,* ed. L. Michael White and O. Larry Yarbrough (Minneapolis: Fortress, 1995), pp. 78-80. Hock holds that Paul is here playing on ideas of children's responsibilities for taking care of parents in their old age.

19. See Beverly Roberts Gaventa, "The Maternity of Paul: An Exegetical Study of Galatians 4:19," in *The Conversation Continues: Studies in Paul and John in Honor of J. Louis Martyn,* ed. Robert T. Fortna and Beverly Roberts Gaventa (Nashville: Abingdon, 1990), pp. 191-94, 198-99. See also Gaventa, "Our Mother St. Paul: Toward the Recovery of a Neglected Theme," *Princeton Seminary Bulletin* 17 (1996): 37-39, reprinted in *A Feminist Companion to Paul,* ed. Amy-Jill Levine and Marianne Blickenstaff (Cleveland: Pilgrim, 2004), pp. 85-97; and Gaventa, *Our Mother Saint Paul* (Louisville: Westminster John Knox, 2007).

20. It is likely that Paul is not only using a technical term for being in prison but also underscores the burdensome nature of this birth; cf. Barth and Blanke, *Letter to Philemon,* p. 336.

21. On the use of ὠδίνω in connection with birth, see Gaventa, "The Maternity of Paul," pp. 192-94. A metaphor of birthing is also employed in Romans 8:22-23 (συνωδίνει, of creation "groaning in labor pains"); see Luzia Sutter Rehman, "To Turn the Groaning into Labor: Romans 8.22-23," in Levine and Blickenstaff, eds., *A Feminist Companion to Paul,* pp. 74-84. Rehman emphasizes that Paul's use of the metaphor does not imply passive suffering, but action: giving birth as active work.

22. Surprisingly, Müller has not included inheritance within the semantic field of kinship,

metaphorical sense, that is, with reference to his Jewish and Christian heritage: of being heirs of Abraham (Gal. 3:29) and God (Rom. 8:17), and of inheriting the kingdom of God (1 Cor. 6:9-10). However, he can also on occasion address issues of material inheritance: 1 Corinthians 6:1-11 may be about Christians taking one another to court over inheritance matters.[23]

Generally, Paul's use of this language shows that he shares current notions about inheritance and transfers and exploits them in the religious — that is, Christian — domain. Galatians 4:1-7 is characteristic. In this passage Paul speaks of the position of a child in the household and also introduces the concept of adoption. This is one of very few examples within the category of kinship in which Paul has a child proper in view: such a νήπιος equals slaves in rights and "remain[s] under guardians and trustees until the date set by the father" (v. 2). Here, Paul employs near-technical terms related to inheritance laws and making of wills;[24] and the picture he presents of childhood is a period of dependency and inferiority. However, he also considers Christians to be beyond this: in Christ they are no longer in a slavish position (v. 3) but have become adult children (v. 6). As heirs of God they will "receive adoption" (v. 5), and they have already — as a deposit — been gifted with the Spirit (v. 6). The idea of adoption recurs in more detail in Romans 8:15, 23 and 9:4.[25]

Importantly, Paul not only focuses on the position of children as heirs but also consciously turns the tables. In 2 Corinthians 12:14-15, a passage that Gaventa also addresses, Paul underscores his obligation as a spiritual father to the Corinthians. He is to give and not to take from them: "for children ought not to lay up for their parents, but parents for their children." Thus Paul views the relationship from the perspective of the "weaker" party: it is the older generation who must act for the benefit of their descendants, whereas they are relieved from such a burden. Although Paul is probably echoing a traditional saying in antiquity, it is nonetheless striking that he emphasizes such a

---

even though it is one of the most important elements; see Aasgaard, *"My Beloved Brothers and Sisters!"* pp. 66-70, 77-81, 89-92, also 144-45, 224-26.

23. Aasgaard, *"My Beloved Brothers and Sisters!"* pp. 222-26, 235-36.

24. Frank J. Matera, *Galatians*, Sacra Pagina 9 (Collegeville: Liturgical, 1992), pp. 148-49, with references; also Hans Dieter Betz, *Galatians: A Commentary on Paul's Letter to the Churches in Galatia* (Philadelphia: Fortress, 1979), pp. 203-4; Derek R. Moore-Crispin, "Galatians 4:1-9: The Use and Abuse of Parallels," *Evangelical Quarterly* 60 (1989): 203-23.

25. For a detailed discussion of the meaning of υἱοθεσία in these texts, see Scott, *Adoption as Sons of God*, esp. chs. 3 and 5; for adoption, foster children, and displaced children in general, see Beryl Rawson, *Children and Childhood in Roman Italy* (Oxford: Oxford University Press, 2003), pp. 250-63, with references. Cf. also Müller, *In der Mitte der Gemeinde*, p. 300.

thought so strongly.[26] He even develops this idea of parental renunciation by stating in verse 15 that he himself "will most gladly spend and be spent for you."

Children within Marriage

As discussed by Gaventa, Paul deals only once with an issue in which children are directly involved, namely, in 1 Corinthians 7:14. Here, Paul addresses an instance of (potential or experienced) family conflict. In verses 12-16, he discusses whether a believer should remain in marriage with a non-believer. In his opinion, the Christian should stay married, since an unbelieving spouse in this way is "made holy" and — as an additional result — the children are not "unclean."[27] Although the precise meaning of the statement is uncertain, Paul here has an eye to children's welfare: the marriage secures their religious standing as "holy." At the same time, however, children are obviously not his primary concern. This is clear from verse 15, in which he permits divorce if this is the wish of the non-believer,[28] and from verse 16, where he appeals to the believing spouse's concern for the partner. In neither case are the children mentioned: focus is on the interests and responsibilities of adult Christians.[29] Paul may have had an idea that children in cases of divorce would stay holy if they remained with the Christian parent.[30] But in light of verse 14b it seems more likely that he views the holiness of children as depending on two elements: that the parents are married and that at least one of them is a believer. It is also worth noting that he does not spell out the implications for the children of a divorce; clearly, such a perspective is not the first to come to his mind.

26. See O. Larry Yarbrough, "Parents and Children in the Letters of Paul," in White and Yarbrough, eds., *The Social World of the First Christians,* pp. 131, 134-36, with references.

27. Paul's formulations may here indicate that he thinks of children who are not baptized; cf. Müller, *In der Mitte der Gemeinde,* p. 358.

28. On Paul's restrictive view of divorce, see O. Larry Yarbrough, *Not Like the Gentiles: Marriage Rules in the Letters of Paul,* Society of Biblical Literature Dissertation Series 80 (Atlanta: Scholars, 1985), pp. 112-14; also Yarbrough, "Parents and Children in the Letters of Paul," pp. 139-40.

29. Yarbrough, "Parents and Children in the Letters of Paul," pp. 129-30; also J. Dorcas Gordon, *Sister or Wife? 1 Corinthians 7 and Cultural Anthropology,* Journal for the Study of the New Testament — Supplement Series 149 (Sheffield: Sheffield Academic Press, 1997), pp. 123-24, with references.

30. And thus also remain part of the local Christian community ("the holy"); cf. Müller, *In der Mitte der Gemeinde,* pp. 360-61; L. William Countryman, *Dirt, Greed, and Sex: Sexual Ethics in the New Testament and Their Implications for Today* (Philadelphia: Fortress, 1988), pp. 209-10. Normally, the father and his family of origin would have the right to children in case of divorce.

Social Position

The second main group of texts deals with the position of children within society and family life. Usually, these texts refer to children proper. The texts are few, but of much interest, since they have more to say on the issue of children than did the kinship material, and present a more complex picture of Paul's attitudes and strategies.

The Fetus and the Premature Child

Paul refers twice to a fetus — in both cases himself. In the first, Galatians 1:15, he speaks of himself as already chosen by God in his mother's womb. The statement echoes Psalm 139:13, of the psalmist being "knit . . . together in . . . mother's womb," and also alludes to Isaiah 49:1, 5-6, thus implying that Paul's calling is parallel to that of Isaiah. By this, Paul skillfully employs Scripture to support his claim to apostleship. Implicitly, he also gives expression to certain ideas about a fetus: it is formed, "knit," by God; it is human (at least potentially); and its "person" is already present in core. With this, Paul very much mirrors Jewish notions about the fetus. Though differences should not be overstated, the Jewish idea about human beings being created in the likeness of God (Gen. 1:26) appears to have contributed to a higher status for the fetus than was customary in antiquity, including more restrictive attitudes toward abortion.[31] Although it is clearly beyond his scope, Paul indirectly reflects such a valuation of the fetus here.

The other mention is the striking statement in 1 Corinthians 15:8. Here, Paul tells about his own calling: "Last of all, as to one untimely born (ἐκτρώματι), he appeared also to me."[32] The way he characterizes himself here is both unusual and unexpected. The phenomenon of premature birth was very common in antiquity.[33] Due to the general living conditions, a great number of infants died, and the status of newborns was very low.[34] A prema-

---

31. For abortion practice and views in antiquity, see Andreas Lindemann, "'Do Not Let a Woman Destroy the Unborn Babe in Her Belly': Abortion in Ancient Judaism and Christianity," *Studia Theologica* 49 (1995): 253-71; O. M. Bakke, *When Children Became People: The Birth of Childhood in Early Christianity* (Minneapolis: Fortress, 2005), pp. 110-39, 149-51.

32. The word ἔκτρωμα can also be translated "miscarriage" or "aborted child."

33. Rawson, *Children and Childhood in Roman Italy,* pp. 103, 116-17.

34. This is reflected *inter alia* in the (occasional) practice that fathers at birth should lift up the child from the ground as a sign of his acceptance of it and of its right to enter into the society of human beings; see, e.g., Eva Marie Lassen, "The Roman Family: Ideal and Metaphor," in Moxnes, ed., *Constructing Early Christian Families,* pp. 104-5, esp. note 5, with references;

ture child would be even more vulnerable and socially marginal, given its small chances of survival.

The word ἔκτρωμα, which occurs only here in the New Testament, is extremely rare in non-biblical classical sources.[35] It is used only three times in the Septuagint, all regarding a state of great unhappiness: Numbers 12:12; Ecclesiastes 6:3; Job 3:16. Paul's usage probably echoes texts such as these, although he does not, like them, use the term in the sense of stillborn; rather, he uses the term in the sense of prematurely born, or possibly born with some kind of physical defect.[36] In any case, the harshness of his expression is obvious, and the question becomes pressing: Why is Paul describing himself in this way?

One answer to this is to say that he is here simply making use of a very striking metaphor to refer to his apostolic call at Damascus (1 Cor. 9:1). A more contextually related — and more likely — explanation, however, is that he is here responding to opposition in Corinth. As part of their criticism, the opponents have branded him as an ἔκτρωμα, that is, as lacking a calling that could legitimate his apostleship. Instead of protesting, Paul adopts their description, but uses it positively, in favor of himself and his message, possibly modeled on the practice of self-derogation known from the prophets (e.g., Isa. 6:5).[37] According to such an interpretation, Paul employs a consciously

---

Mireille Corbier, "Child Exposure and Abandonment," in *Childhood, Class and Kin in the Roman World,* ed. Suzanne Dixon (London/New York: Routledge, 2001), pp. 58-60. For the living conditions of children in antiquity, see, e.g., Aasgaard, *"My Beloved Brothers and Sisters!"* pp. 37-39, with references.

35. According to the *Thesaurus Linguae Graecae,* the term occurs before Paul (in securely datable sources) only once in Aristotle (384-322 BCE), in *De Generatione Animalium* 4.5.18 (Loeb Classical Library edition), in the sense of "abortion," and twice in Philo (20 BCE–40 CE), *Legum Allegoriae* 1.76 (Loeb Classical Library edition), in the sense of "miscarriage" or "stillborn." The passage in Philo, which is an interpretation of Numbers 12:12, has some features in common with Paul. See also "ἔκτρωμα," in W. Bauer, W. F. Arndt, F. W. Gingrich, and F. W. Danker, *Greek-English Lexicon of the New Testament* (hereafter BADG), 3rd ed. (Chicago: University of Chicago Press, 2000), p. 311, with references. For discussions of various interpretations of Paul's use of the word, see George W. E. Nickelsburg, "An ἔκτρωμα Though Appointed from the Womb: Paul's Apostolic Self-Description in 1 Corinthians 15 and Galatians 1," in *Christians among Jews and Gentiles,* ed. George W. E. Nickelsburg and George W. MacRae (Philadelphia: Fortress, 1986), pp. 198-205; Markus Schaefer, "Paulus, 'Fehlgeburt' oder 'unvernünftiges Kind'?" *Zeitschrift für die neutestamentliche Wissenschaft* 85 (1994): 209-17 (who sees in 1 Cor. 15:8 a reference to Hos. 13:13).

36. If the latter is the case, Paul may be referring to his "thorn . . . in the flesh (σκόλοψ τῇ σαρκί)," 2 Corinthians 12:7, or he may have been indicating that he was small in stature (*paullus* — "small").

37. See Nickelsburg, "An ἔκτρωμα Though Appointed from the Womb," pp. 198-99; Raymond F. Collins, *First Corinthians,* Sacra Pagina 7 (Collegeville: Liturgical Press, 1999), p. 537.

drafted strategy by which he defends his position as an apostle.[38] Whatever the explanation, it must nonetheless be said that his use of ἔκτρωμα here is daring — indeed, so daring that the question must be raised whether the idea of such a strategy is tenable. This is a matter to which we shall return in the final discussion. In any case, the expression serves to emphasize the contrast between what he himself is and what he has attained, that is, between his own humble position and the magnitude of his message and of God's grace (cf. v. 10).[39] Thus, he is not to be judged on what he or others say about him, but on what he has achieved, particularly by making the Corinthians into believers (v. 11).[40]

The Orphaned Child

In 1 Thessalonians 2:17 Paul mentions his brief but sorrowful separation from the Thessalonians, and he describes this as being "orphaned," ἀπορφανισθέντες, the only occurrence of this word in the New Testament. The term has been read in two different ways. Traditionally, it has been understood in a general sense, as Paul being "bereft of" or "taken/torn away from" the Thessalonians.[41] Interpreted thus, Paul depicts himself as being separated from them, or even — in the position of a father — as being made childless.[42] If, however, the term is instead read in accordance with its basic and more pregnant meaning, Paul appears in the position of a child who has been orphaned. The former interpretation seems usually to take its point of departure from a general idea of his superiority as apostle, or in the description in 2:11 of him as father; and the notion of Paul as orphan is seen as incompatible with this. However, the latter understanding is for several reasons the more likely:[43] the word is in other Greek

38. For such an interpretation, see Collins, *First Corinthians*, pp. 532-33.

39. Nickelsburg, "An ἔκτρωμα Though Appointed from the Womb," pp. 204-5; Schaefer, "Paulus, 'Fehlgeburt' oder 'unvernünftiges Kind,'" pp. 216-17.

40. This "turning of the tables" usage does not necessarily imply that Paul here intends to upgrade the status of an ἔκτρωμα; rather, he bases his argument on its low position. In effect, however, the use of this metaphor may serve to enhance the status of such a child.

41. See the brief presentation in Earl J. Richard, *First and Second Thessalonians*, Sacra Pagina 11 (Collegeville: Liturgical, 1995), pp. 128-29, and the discussion in Burke, *Family Matters*, pp. 157-60. For the former understanding, see the translations in NASB, AMP, NAB; for the latter, see the translations in KJV, NIV.

42. This is the interpretation of, e.g., Traugott Holtz, *Der erste Brief an die Thessalonicher*, Evangelisch-katholischer Kommentar zum Neuen Testament 13 (Zürich: Benziger/Neukirchener, 1986), p. 115; Richard, *First and Second Thessalonians*, pp. 128-29.

43. This is also the interpretation of a growing number of scholars. See also Abraham J. Malherbe, *The Letters to the Thessalonians: A New Translation with Introduction and Commen-*

sources always used as meaning "orphaned."[44] It also seems strange that Paul should employ such a special term unless he is using it in its more pregnant sense. In addition, Paul need not be consistent in his use of metaphors: he can often — sometimes all of a sudden — change perspective.[45] An example of this in fact occurs in the abrupt shift from child (or nurse) in 2:7 to father in 2:11.

Consequently, Paul here characterizes himself from the perspective of a child, and a child in a very vulnerable position, a parentless child. His way of expressing himself in 1 Thessalonians 2:17 — and in much of the passage — appears strongly emotionally colored,[46] and the metaphor must have been intended, and perceived, as striking.[47] Thus, Paul does not here present himself as a father longing for his children, but as an orphan yearning — hopelessly — for its parents. What is conveyed through the metaphor in terms of power is not parental care or authority, but the helplessness and marginalization of an orphaned child.[48]

The Immaturity of Children

In antiquity, children were viewed as immature: they were undeveloped of character, bodily weak, emotionally unstable, and intellectually deficient, and were thus unable to reach the standard of the ideal human being, which was the (male) adult. Although people had an understanding of childhood as a life stage with its own characteristics and value, children were often seen as unfinished, as humans-to-be.[49]

Paul very much conforms to this pattern. Interestingly, the imagery of the

---

tary, Anchor Bible 32B (New York: Doubleday, 2000), pp. 187-88; Burke, *Family Matters,* pp. 158-60, with references; Aasgaard, *"My Beloved Brothers and Sisters!"* pp. 288-89.

44. On the basis of an analysis of the occurrences of the term in Greek literature, this has been argued convincingly by John B. Faulkenberry Miller, "Infants and Orphans in 1 Thess. 2.7," unpublished paper delivered 20 November 1999 at the Annual Meeting of the Society of Biblical Literature, Boston, Massachusetts.

45. Cf. Aasgaard, *"My Beloved Brothers and Sisters!"* pp. 287-89, also 29-31.

46. Also emphasized by Burke, *Family Matters,* p. 159, and others.

47. This is the opinion of Beverly Roberts Gaventa, *First and Second Thessalonians,* Interpretation (Louisville: John Knox, 1998), p. 41; Burke, *Family Matters,* pp. 159-60.

48. Paul may, however, also have had Old Testament and Old Testament Apocrypha notions in mind, with their emphasis on God's special concern for widows and orphans (Exod. 22:22; Deut. 10:18, etc.; also John 14:18; James 1:27). If so, Paul is also an orphan under the protection of God.

49. See, e.g., Thomas Wiedemann, *Adults and Children in the Roman Empire* (New Haven: Yale University Press, 1989), pp. 17-25; Mark Golden, *Children and Childhood in Classical Athens* (Baltimore: Johns Hopkins University Press, 1990), pp. 1-12.

immature child surfaces particularly in his advice to the Christians in Corinth. In 1 Corinthians 2:6–3:4 he addresses their misperception of wisdom and their internal strife. He characterizes this as a lack of maturity: they risk being "un-spiritual" or "natural" (v. 14) and even being "as people of the flesh" (3:1). And they fall short of the ideal, which is to be "spiritual" (v. 15) or "perfect" (v. 6) and to have the mind of Christ (v. 16b), that is, the spiritual faculties and attitudes characteristic of him. In sum, they are like children. Even more, he has to communicate with them as if they were babies (3:1), and he must again feed them with milk, not solid food (v. 2). Here, infancy is employed to indicate religious inadequacy: the Corinthians have fallen down to a stage below what is required. And Paul puts himself in a position of power: he is the one able to nurture them. It is nonetheless conspicuous that he also here (cf. above on Gal. 4:19) views himself in a female role, as a breastfeeding mother or a nursemaid; such a metaphor does not primarily signal authority and correction, but rather care and provision.[50]

In 1 Corinthians 14:20, Paul strikes a similar note: when criticizing the misuse of spiritual gifts, he admonishes the Corinthians not to "be children in . . . thinking (φρεσὶν)" and rather "in thinking be adults (τέλειοι)." Again, they are likened to children, and even infants, and the ideal set up is to become adults, that is, mature (cf. also "perfect" in 2:6, τέλειοι). Φρήν occurs in the New Testament only here and connotes mature reflection as opposed to childish emotionality.[51]

The idea of the child as unfinished is developed in greatest detail in 1 Corinthians 13, the "love hymn." Here, in 13:11, Paul follows up the "I"-perspective introduced in 12:31b–13:3. It is a matter of debate whether or not the first-person singular refers to Paul or to human beings more generally. In 12:31b, however, he is clearly referring to himself, and it seems reasonable that this is also the case in the following verses, but as an archetypical model for human — and Christian — development. If so, Paul is here explicitly speaking of his own childhood experience. By referring to his own maturing, he shows the Corinthians a "way" (cf. 12:31b) from childishness to adult maturity. Once again, the latter is described as a state of completeness (τὸ τέλειον), whereas the former is depicted as partial (v. 10).

In the course of the chapter, Paul develops the idea of love in a way that goes beyond human limits and turns it into a divine and eschatological en-

50. Müller, *In der Mitte der Gemeinde*, pp. 298-99; Gaventa, "Our Mother St. Paul," pp. 32-33; Collins, *First Corinthians*, pp. 140-41, 143; Balla, *The Child-Parent Relationship*, pp. 183-84, 191-92. See also p. 267 below.

51. Collins, *First Corinthians*, p. 507; also Müller, *In der Mitte der Gemeinde*, pp. 297-98. Cf. also Romans 2:20.

tity. It is to describe the contrast between what is and what will be that he employs the metaphors of childhood and adulthood.[52] In 1 Corinthians 13:11, childhood and adulthood are contrasted in a number of areas: as concerns speech, thinking, and reasoning: "When I was a child, I spoke . . . thought . . . reasoned like a child." Here, the child is seen as having rational faculties similar to an adult's. At the same time, however, its ability to utilize them falls short of what is required, and Paul underscores the deplorable state of the child — and of the immature human being — by his triple repetition of "like a child." The transition from the one state to the other he describes as to "nullify" or "do away with" (καταργηθήσεται) what is childish.[53] Although Paul is primarily concerned with contrasting the present human state with what is to come, and thus may overstate his case as concerns the relation between child and adult, the contrast between the two nonetheless appears very marked.

In 1 Corinthians 13:12, Paul develops his idea of the preparatory and imperfect character of childhood, now with a particular view to knowledge, the special interest of the Corinthians: being a child implies seeing "in a mirror, dimly," having only fragmentary knowledge, as opposed to the adult state of seeing "face to face," of having a full understanding. Although the characterization does not necessarily imply that Paul downgrades childhood in terms of value,[54] it nonetheless emerges as something negative within the context of the letter — although Paul is also aware of children's potentials.

The opposite of a childish state is maturity, or, more precisely, the mature man (1 Cor. 13:11). It is likely that Paul here has himself as a male adult in view, although he may also indirectly refer to human beings in general, both male and female, but from the perspective of maturity as a male characteristic.[55]

As for his presentation of himself, provided that "I" is self-referential, Paul's point in verses 11-12 is to communicate that his childish state is passé and that he now possesses the qualities of an adult. He has moved beyond the

---

52. This seems to have a parallel in Philo, *De Fuga et Inventione* 172-73, who in a context of formation and learning holds that only God is able to provide supreme perfection; cf. also pp. 269-70 below.

53. Καταργέω occurs frequently elsewhere in 1 Corinthians and in other of his letters. The term is often, and here too, used emphatically, marking a drastic difference between what was and what is.

54. This is the view of, e.g., Collins, *First Corinthians,* p. 486.

55. See, e.g., Collins, *First Corinthians,* p. 486; Colleen M. Conway, "'Behold the Man!' Masculine Christology and the Fourth Gospel," in *New Testament Masculinities,* ed. Stephen D. Moore and Janice Capel Anderson, Semeia Studies 45 (Atlanta: Society of Biblical Literature, 2003), pp. 164-67.

childish ways of the Corinthians and can speak to them with the authority of a mature man.

The Child as Beloved

In antiquity, children were also looked upon as objects of care and affection, but often in a sentimentalizing way.[56] Such a focus can also be observed in Paul, although the number of texts is limited.

In 1 Corinthians 4:14-16, Paul's attitude toward the Corinthians is as a father's should be: they are "beloved" (v. 14).[57] Similarly, in verse 17, Timothy is described as his "beloved and faithful child." Thus, Paul presents himself as a loving father of both the addressees and Timothy, his co-worker. It may be that Paul here has the relationship of a father and grown-up children in mind. However, although Timothy is presented as a loyal son performing an adult commission as messenger, it seems likely that Paul primarily views the Corinthians in terms of underage children (cf. below).

An interesting instance in which Paul depicts himself as a child is the greeting in Romans 16:13 to Rufus's mother, who has been "a mother to me also." It is clear that she somehow has given him the sense of being taken care of. Although Paul does not develop the issue of age, the setting implies that he is here thinking in terms of a mother and an adult son.[58]

A conspicuous case of parental concern toward underage children occurs in the much debated 1 Thessalonians 2:7. Here Paul likens the relations between the Thessalonians and himself to "a nurse tenderly caring for her own children." The parent/child relation is described with a metaphor signaling a strong bond of affection: τροφός may refer to a breastfeeding mother, but it is more likely employed with its specific meaning, namely, nurse.[59] Thus, Paul here visualizes the care shown by a nurse toward her own children, a care going beyond the professional care she is to show toward the children of oth-

---

56. See, e.g., Emiel Eyben, "Fathers and Sons," in *Marriage, Divorce, and Children in Ancient Rome*, ed. Beryl Rawson (Oxford: Clarendon, 1991), pp. 116-21; Dixon, *The Roman Family*, pp. 98-108.

57. For a brief discussion of this passage, see also p. 254 above; cf. also Yarbrough, "Parents and Children in the Letters of Paul," pp. 131-32.

58. For a brief discussion of this passage, see Balla, *The Child-Parent Relationship*, pp. 182-83.

59. For the former view, see, e.g., Burke, *Family Matters*, pp. 151-52; for the latter, see, e.g., Malherbe, *The Letters to the Thessalonians*, p. 146, with whom I agree. Cf. also the discussion in Abraham J. Malherbe, *Paul and the Popular Philosophers* (Minneapolis: Fortress, 1989), pp. 35-48.

ers.[60] In verse 8 Paul again underscores this loving relationship: he deeply cares for them, and they have "become dear" to him.

The main reason for the scholarly discussion of verse 7, however, is the textual problem in verse 7b. Should the original text be read: "But we were *gentle* among you," ἐγενήθημεν ἤπιοι, or: "But we were *babies* among you," ἐγενήθημεν νήπιοι?[61] The answer given to this question is of little consequence for the understanding of the metaphor itself, though the "gentle" alternative serves to enhance the tenderness of it. What is significantly altered, however, is the role allocation within the relationship: Does Paul see himself as a nurse and the Thessalonians as his small children? Or does he put himself as a baby in their motherly arms? If the former is the case, the metaphor is — for antiquity — a conspicuous one: Paul, a man, depicts himself in the position of a woman.[62] If the latter is the case, however, the metaphor is even more striking: Paul presents himself as a helpless baby, dependent on the (likely) goodwill of a mother! Although both interpretations are possible, I am strongly inclined to opt for the latter, since text-critically both external and internal attestation weigh in favor of νήπιοι being original. Thus, Paul here depicts himself as a baby in his relations to the Thessalonians.[63]

Such a conclusion has, rhetorically speaking, considerable consequences

---

60. The verb θάλπῃ, which connotes warmth, cherishing, and comfort, also emphasizes this. See Malherbe, *The Letters to the Thessalonians*, p. 146; "θάλπω," *BADG*, 3rd ed., p. 442; Burke, *Family Matters*, p. 152; cf. also Ephesians 5:29.

61. For the former view, see NA[25] and the translations in NRSV, NIV, NASB, AMP, NAB, KJV; for the latter, see NA[27] and the alternative translations in the notes of NRSV and NASB.

62. See the discussion in Burke, *Family Matters*, pp. 154-57 (with references), with whom I agree; also Balla, *The Child-Parent Relationship*, pp. 191-92.

63. External attestation is clearly in favor of νήπιοι with broad support by texts such as P[65] ℵ* B C* D* F I. The many corrections of νήπιοι to ἤπιοι also point in the direction of "gentle" as a later polishing of a more original textual stratum. Internal evidence is more divided. On the one hand, ἤπιος occurs elsewhere in the New Testament only in 2 Timothy 2:24 and may thus be regarded original from a *lectio difficilior* point of view. However, νήπιος can also be *lectio difficilior*, since it makes Paul's use of metaphor more clumsy and maybe even embarrassing. In addition, νήπιος is a favorite word generally in Paul and also fits in very well with the metaphor field here (familial care). Thus, internal evidence also weighs in favor of νήπιοι being original. I here support the argument and conclusions of Timothy B. Sailors, "Wedding Textual and Rhetorical Criticism to Understand the Text of 1 Thessalonians 2.7," *Journal for the Study of the New Testament* 80 (2000): 81-92; Jeffrey D. Weima, "'But We Became Infants Among You': The Case for NHΠIOI in 1 Thess 2.7," *New Testament Studies* 46 (2001): 547-64; see also Burke, *Family Matters*, pp. 154-57; Bruce M. Metzger, *A Textual Commentary on the Greek New Testament*, 2nd ed. (Stuttgart: Deutsche Bibelgesellschaft, 1994), pp. 561-62. Sailors, "Wedding Textual and Rhetorical Criticism," pp. 92-97, and Burke, *Family Matters*, pp. 155-56, also argue well for different punctuation (with full stop after "among you," and with vv. 7c-8 as one sentence).

for Paul's construction of his own role and of his relationship to the Thessalonians: according to this interpretation, Paul is in 1 Thessalonians 2:7 putting himself at their mercy.[64] Although he is here appealing to the emotions of his addressees, he is clearly not ironic or manipulative; given the positive relations between him and them, he has nothing to gain from being so. Rather, Paul appears to be sincere and straightforward. He does not appeal to paternal authority or to maternal care: instead, he strips himself of power and renounces a position in a hierarchy above them (cf. also v. 7a). The strategy seems drastic indeed, and it will be made the object of closer scrutiny later in this essay.

The Child as Obedient

In antiquity obedience was regarded as a central virtue at all stages of life, but particularly with regard to children's relations to parents. Such an obligation was especially due to the father, as household leader, *paterfamilias*. The appropriate virtue was that of piety *(pietas)*, which in Greco-Roman tradition implied a considerable degree of subservience. However, there were also important limits to the obligation, though more so in a Greek than in a Roman setting.[65]

For Paul, too, obedience is a self-evident and basic value. In this, he clearly reflects current attitudes, although he does not deal at length with the issue. He can see disobedience toward parents as a hallmark of ungodliness (Rom. 1:30).[66] He emphasizes his "child" Timothy's faithfulness and expects the Corinthians to comply with Timothy's teaching of Paul's "ways in Christ" (1 Cor. 4:17). Similarly, his frequent use of moral exhortation in the letters presupposes obedience as a commonly approved virtue.[67] Finally, he also expects children to accept as a matter of course the conditions set by a father as concerns inheritance (Gal. 4:2).

The Innocent Child

In antiquity, children were not only valued negatively as compared to adults. Childhood also had qualities lacking in other stages of life: children were in-

---

64. The first-person plural form of the verb may imply that Paul is here also including his co-workers; nonetheless, the focus is primarily on the role of Paul himself.

65. Eyben, "Fathers and Sons," pp. 142-43; Richard P. Saller, *Patriarchy, Property and Death* (Cambridge: Cambridge University Press, 1994), pp. 102-32, esp. 130-32; Balla, *The Child-Parent Relationship*, esp. pp. 76-79, 109-11; Aasgaard, *"My Beloved Brothers and Sisters!"* pp. 49-51.

66. Yarbrough, "Parents and Children in the Letters of Paul," pp. 130-31.

67. Balla, *The Child-Parent Relationship*, pp. 76-79, 109-11, 229-32.

nocent and pure and not yet tainted by human affairs. As marginal beings they were perceived to have special contact with the "other world," and they could on occasion mediate divine messages, for example as oracles.[68]

A reflection of this kind of thinking may surface in Philippians 2:14-15. Here, Paul describes how he expects the children of God to behave: they are to "do all things without murmuring and arguing" and thus be "blameless and innocent" and "without blemish in the midst of a crooked and perverse generation."[69] The following phrase, "in which you shine like stars in the world," may support the idea of children as mediators of the divine world: as "children of God" they portend the heavenly time to come.[70] Although Paul probably here primarily refers to adults, his characterizations have much in common with ancient idealizations of children: they are clean and without guilt and are still uncorrupted by this — swiftly deteriorating — world.

Formation

Since children were imperfect and immature, they were in need of formation. Such formation had to be rendered in a way adapted to their skills, and children were expected to go through a process that eventually would turn them into adults.[71] Paul very often refers to elements contributing to this process through verbs and nouns containing the Greek root παιδ-.

Formation as a Process

Formation was from early childhood seen as a continually ongoing process. Antiquity's view on character development was more static than is common today: people were thought to show their personality — for good or for bad — from early on, and continuity in character was more emphasized than change.[72] Nevertheless, much emphasis was put on cultivation of one's per-

---

68. Wiedemann, *Adults and Children in the Roman Empire,* pp. 176-86; also Golden, *Children and Childhood in Classical Athens,* pp. 46, 49-50.

69. In this passage, Paul obviously makes a play on the murmuring of the Israelites in the desert; cf. Exodus 16:1-12 (LXX); see, e.g., Osiek, *Philippians, Philemon,* pp. 70-71.

70. On the eschatological element, see, e.g., Osiek, *Philippians, Philemon,* pp. 71-72.

71. Wiedemann, *Adults and Children in the Roman Empire,* pp. 143-75; Tor Vegge, *Schule und Bildung des Paulus* (Berlin: De Gruyter, 2006), pp. 233-50.

72. See, e.g., Bruce J. Malina and Jerome H. Neyrey, *Portraits of Paul: An Archaeology of Ancient Personality* (Louisville: Westminster John Knox, 1996), esp. pp. 1-18.

sonality, on training (παιδεία) and the need for progress.[73] To this end, several pedagogical manuals were produced.[74] To reach full maturity, people — even grown-ups — had to be led; they were in need of "soul-guidance" (psychagogy).[75]

Elements of such thinking are also reflected in Paul. He has to speak to the recalcitrant Corinthians as to infants (1 Cor. 3:1) and as to children (2 Cor. 6:13). They have again to be nourished with milk (breastfed) before they can go on with solid food (1 Cor. 3:2; cf. above).[76] Such metaphors are also known from philosophical texts on formation, and the occurrences in Paul are likely to be parallel to or even to reflect such usage.[77] He approves the ideal of progress (Phil. 1:25; also Gal. 1:14). The Corinthians have to mature from being children "in thinking" to being adults (1 Cor. 14:20; cf. above). Such a process of maturing involves not only children or relapsing Christians (cf. also 1 Cor. 4:14-21), but Christians in general: they have to receive teaching (Rom. 16:17; Phil. 4:9); they all need to be disciplined (1 Cor. 11:32);[78] and they even need to be trained through chastising hardships (2 Cor. 6:9).

The Agents and Tools of Formation

The professional formation of children was usually the task of teachers. Sometimes, a pedagogue (παιδαγωγός, often a slave) was responsible for following children to school or for giving them their basic education himself.[79] On a more advanced level, soul-guidance was the task of the educated man, in particular the philosopher.[80] Usually, however, education was the responsibil-

---

73. Rawson, *Children and Childhood in Roman Italy,* pp. 136-38; Vegge, *Schule und Bildung des Paulus,* pp. 312-29.

74. See, e.g., Vegge, *Schule und Bildung des Paulus,* pp. 190-228; Abraham J. Malherbe, *Moral Exhortation: A Greco-Roman Sourcebook,* Library of Early Christianity (Philadelphia: Westminster, 1986), pp. 85-109.

75. Clarence E. Glad, *Paul and Philodemus: Adaptability in Epicurean and Early Christian Psychagogy,* Novum Testamentum Supplements 81 (Leiden: Brill, 1995), pp. 17-23, 53-69.

76. Yarbrough, "Parents and Children in the Letters of Paul," pp. 132-33; cf. also the comments above on 1 Corinthians 13:11-12.

77. For references, see, e.g., Collins, *First Corinthians,* p. 143; Vegge, *Schule und Bildung des Paulus,* pp. 326-29.

78. The text can be translated both "when we are judged by the Lord, we are disciplined" and "when we are judged, we are being disciplined by the Lord" (cf. NRSV). The notion of need for discipline is the same in both cases, however.

79. Bradley, *Discovering the Roman Family,* pp. 37-43, 49-55; Vegge, *Schule und Bildung des Paulus,* pp. 22-29.

80. Malherbe, *Moral Exhortation,* pp. 30-47.

ity of parents, particularly as far as character formation was concerned. Fathers and mothers were viewed as role models for boys and girls respectively, but with a special focus on the role of the father.[81]

Similar features recur in Paul: the Corinthians need to have pedagogues in Christ (1 Cor. 4:15). In the history of God's people, the law served for a long period as such a guardian (Gal. 4:24-25). And just like children, non-Jews are lacking in knowledge and truth and need the teaching of the law-abiding Jew to grasp the fullness of the law (Rom. 2:20). Clearly, Paul is here also dependent upon common philosophical-religious language.[82]

Guidance of children could in antiquity be carried out in a hortatory way.[83] This is reflected in Paul: like a father he would be "urging," "encouraging," and "pleading with" the Thessalonians "to lead a life worthy of God" (1 Thess. 2:11-12). And as the father of the Corinthians, he does not want to shame them but to admonish them — νουθετῶν in 1 Corinthians 4:14 implies firm admonition (see also Rom. 15:14; 1 Thess. 5:12, 14). In return, he expects the Corinthians to do the duty of children, which is to cherish him as their main authority figure (1 Cor. 4:15), as their only father in Christ, and as a model person: "Be imitators of me" (4:16).[84]

According to the ancients, even stricter measures were often needed in the formation of children: they had to be controlled.[85] Paul mentions such discipline on a number of occasions, a little more frequently than he does milder forms of guidance.[86] In Galatians 3:23-26 he speaks of believers as formerly under a guardian, namely, the law. Here, believers are viewed as

81. See, e.g., Eyben, "Fathers and Sons," pp. 112-43; Rawson, *Children and Childhood in Roman Italy,* pp. 157-68, 187-88, 197-98; O. Larry Yarbrough, "Parents and Children in the Jewish Family of Antiquity," in *The Jewish Family in Antiquity,* ed. Shaye J. D. Cohen (Atlanta: Scholars, 1993), pp. 41-49; John M. G. Barclay, "The Family as the Bearer of Religion in Judaism and Early Christianity," in Moxnes, ed., *Constructing Early Christian Families,* pp. 66-72; Balla, *The Child-Parent Relationship,* pp. 62-73, 86-104, with references.

82. See, e.g., Malherbe, *Moral Exhortation,* pp. 57, 80, 136; Vegge, *Schule und Bildung des Paulus,* pp. 326-29.

83. Malherbe, *Moral Exhortation,* pp. 23-29; Balla, *The Child-Parent Relationship,* pp. 102-3.

84. Elizabeth A. Castelli, *Imitating Paul: A Discourse of Power* (Louisville: Westminster John Knox, 1991), pp. 97-103; Collins, *First Corinthians,* pp. 193-94; Balla, *The Child-Parent Relationship,* p. 184.

85. Saller, *Patriarchy, Property and Death,* pp. 133-53; also Richard P. Saller, "Corporal Punishment, Authority, and Obedience in the Roman Household," in Rawson, ed., *Marriage, Divorce, and Children in Ancient Rome,* pp. 144-65.

86. His language of discipline is sometimes employed in adult contexts, in which notions of childhood do not seem to be prominent (e.g., 1 Cor. 11:32). In 2 Corinthians 6:9, he describes the hardships of the servants of God: they are not being killed but experience punishment (παιδευόμενοι).

minor children. With the breaking in of the new age and with faith in Christ, they are still children, that is, sons of God (v. 26). However, they are no longer underage but have the rights of adult children: they are heirs (cf. 4:1-7), no longer dependent on the protection of a pedagogue (3:25, NRSV "disciplinarian").

Discipline in antiquity was often performed by physical means, which were regarded as a natural and necessary part of children's formation.[87] Paul appears to have shared such attitudes. However, he mentions physical punishment of children explicitly on only one occasion, namely in 1 Corinthians 4:21. Here, at the end of his fatherly admonition of the Corinthian Christians, he asks warningly: Should he come with love and gentleness, or "with a stick" (ἐν ῥάβδῳ)? ῥάβδος was the traditional instrument for the punishing of small children at home and in school, and it was a main metaphor for *paideia* in the sense of discipline.[88] By speaking of the stick, Paul discloses that he views the Corinthians not as children in a relational sense, but as children who are minors, either as his own underage children or possibly — if "father" is to be understood as meaning "teacher" — as his primary school pupils.[89] And it is clear that, although he prefers to abstain from using the stick, he is prepared to employ it if necessary.

The Goal of Formation

As noted above, in antiquity a child was viewed as unfinished and on its way toward full humanity; this was the state of the mature male, a person able to speak, feel, reason, and act in a way not partial, but perfect (τέλειος, cf. 1 Cor. 13:10-12; 14:20).[90] To reach such maturity, the person under formation should strive to conform to current ideals, particularly the models presented by religion or philosophy, for example the ideal of "the wise man."[91] Here, Paul on

---

87. Eyben, "Fathers and Sons," pp. 121-24; Saller, "Corporal Punishment," pp. 144-65; Saller, *Patriarchy, Property and Death,* pp. 133-53, esp. 151-53; also Rawson, *Children and Childhood in Roman Italy,* pp. 175-77.

88. Collins, *First Corinthians,* p. 202; "ῥάβδος," in *BADG,* 3rd ed., p. 902; cf., e.g., Proverbs 22:15 (LXX). See also the interpretation of Bartchy, "Who Should Be Called Father?" pp. 142-43.

89. For references, see Wolfgang Schrage, *Der erste Brief an die Korinther,* Evangelischer-katholische Kommetar VII/1 (Zürich: Benziger/Neukirchener, 1991), pp. 353-57.

90. The idea of a mirror (1 Cor. 13:12) in the context of formation is also used in Philo, *De Fuga et Inventione* 213; cf. Vegge, *Schule und Bildung des Paulus,* pp. 243-44, 305-12.

91. Vegge, *Schule und Bildung des Paulus,* pp. 233-301. For a presentation of Stoic views on this, see Troels Engberg-Pedersen, *Paul and the Stoics* (Edinburgh: T&T Clark, 2000), pp. 45-79, and for Epicurean views, see Glad, *Paul and Philodemus,* pp. 60-88. Cf. also Malherbe, *Paul and the Popular Philosophers.*

several occasions refers to himself as a model for imitation (1 Cor. 4:16; 11:1; Gal. 4:12; Phil. 3:17; 1 Thess. 1:6-7; 2:14; also 1 Cor. 13:11-12).[92]

However, the single most important model of human maturity for Paul is Christ: the aim of Christian formation is becoming like him. Paul does not see this only as an outward matter but also as an inner change, in which the character of the Christian is radically transformed, in body and mind, into the likeness of Christ. This will reach its ultimate goal only in the world to come (cf. Rom. 8:29; also 1 Cor. 13:11-12; Phil. 3:21).[93] But Paul also views this as a process at work in the present. In Galatians 4:19, he says that he — like a mother (cf. above) — must again deliver (πάλιν ὠδίνω) the Galatians, his "little children," if they are to receive formation. However, they are not only to be formed "in Christ." Paul goes a considerable step further: Christ is to be formed in them (μορφωθῇ Χριστὸς ἐν ὑμῖν).[94] Thus, the aim is not only imitation, but integration: believers are to be shaped into the maturity of Christ.

Paul hints at what this formation implies in Philippians 3:10-11: it is "becoming like" (συμμορφιζόμενος) Christ in his sufferings and death. Thus, Paul depicts Christian maturing very much in accordance with his understanding of Christ as crucified and resurrected (cf. also Rom. 6:1-11). Although Paul shares a general idea about the aim of human formation with his contemporaries, this idea has also taken on a distinctive Christian shape: the mature man is Christ, the one who gave his life in the service of all human beings — an ideal that would deviate considerably from other ideals of human perfection in antiquity.[95]

Belonging

Peter Müller's fourth semantic domain was that of *belonging*, which comprises elements such as religious affiliation, loyalty, and identification. Many of the childhood metaphors in Paul can be sorted into this group, such as

---

92. These passages are discussed by Castelli, *Imitating Paul*, pp. 89-117.

93. Brendan Byrne, *Romans*, Sacra Pagina 6 (Collegeville: Liturgical, 1996), pp. 268-69, 272-73; Andrzej Gieniusz, *Romans 8:18-30, "Suffering Does Not Thwart the Future Glory,"* University of South Florida International Studies in Formative Christianity and Judaism 9 (Atlanta: Scholars, 1999), pp. 266-76; also Aasgaard, *"My Beloved Brothers and Sisters!"* pp. 139-41, with references.

94. See the discussion of this passage in Gaventa, *The Maternity of Paul*, pp. 194-97. However, "in" (ἐν) may here be interpreted as "among" and may refer to the relations among the Galatians; cf. Matera, *Galatians*, pp. 162, 166.

95. See the brief discussion in Osiek, *Philippians, Philemon*, pp. 93-95.

Christians as "children of God" and Christians as "descendants of Abraham"; these have already been dealt with as part of the kinship category and are nearly exclusively of a relational kind.

Within the fourth category, however, Müller also includes belonging to a *community,* that is, the place of children within the local churches. Surprisingly, Paul deals with children in such a setting in only one instance. The single passage is, again (cf. above), 1 Corinthians 7:14, on children in mixed marriages. Clearly, Paul is attentive to children and to their place within the church, signaled by their holiness (ἄγια). But he does not here, or elsewhere, develop what kind of status they would have. Considering Paul's frequent use of childhood language and his strong interest in practical community life — and also the focus on children in the later household codes — this is striking.

Consequently, issues on the place of children within the communities are almost untouched by Paul. Why this is so we can only guess. It may be that such an issue was beyond his horizon as a male and a person of relatively high standing — although this is hard to believe considering his frequent use of childhood language. It may also be that it was beyond the general horizon of his churches, in view of the manifold other challenges they had to cope with. Or it could be that no sufficiently serious problem concerning children had turned up, at least in the eyes of Paul — with the possible exception of 1 Corinthians 7:14. Whatever the reasons for this lack, it indicates a limited attention on the part of Paul as far as children and community life is concerned.

Children and Childhood in Paul: Attitudes and Strategies

It is now time to synthesize and to reflect upon Paul's ideas about children and childhood and how he employs them rhetorically and theologically. The first to be noted is the *omnipresence of childhood language:* its use is conspicuous, in both frequency and variety. Thus, the topic of childhood appears to play a noticeable role in the apostle's thinking. For a male, middle-class person in antiquity this is not exceptional, but nonetheless it is far from usual: in comparison to others writing about children, Paul as a single and childless man appears to have had an above average attention to the issue.[96]

At the same time there appears to be an *incongruity* in his use of this language. Considering its frequency, it is striking that he speaks so little of real

---

96. Cf., e.g., family men such as Cicero (106-43 BCE), *Epistulae ad Atticum, Epistulae ad Familiares,* and *De Oratore;* Plutarch (ca. 46-121 CE), *De Liberis Educandis* and *De Fraterno Amore;* and Pliny the Younger (61–ca. 112 CE), *Epistulae.*

children, concerning their place both in the family and in church. It is worth noting that he never addresses children directly so as to single them out as a group or to assign to them specific roles. There is also little in the letters to suggest that he has an interest in changing their living conditions or to influence people's notions and evaluation of them. This forms a contrast to the focus on children in the Gospels' depictions of Jesus (e.g., Mark 9:33-37 par.) and in the deutero-Paulines and Pastoral Epistles (e.g., Eph. 6:1-4; 1 Tim. 3:4-5). Whereas children are made an explicit topic there, they are — at the most — an *ad hoc* issue in Paul. Instead, childhood language is used for other means, namely, toward adults and for dealing with general matters such as human development, Christian maturing, and interpersonal relations.

Furthermore, it is clear that Paul in many respects *conforms to contemporary ideas* about children. Indeed, some of his notions may stem from his own childhood experiences (e.g., 1 Cor. 13:11) or his observation of children. More certain, however, is his dependence on common mentality and on philosophical and literary *topoi* concerning children. These, his cultural frame of reference and his own rhetorical education, are likely to be the most important sources for his childhood language.

Paul's presentation of the matter shows that he sees children from the perspective of ancient patriarchy. He shares antiquity's view on children's place within kinship structures (succession and inheritance), on their social position (qualities and shortcomings), and on their formation (means and ends). This is not surprising, but it is still important to note, since it shows his dependence on current structures and mentalities. In fact, if Paul's childhood language is to be rhetorically effective at all, it is vital that it take its point of departure from common and mutually accepted ideas about children, both when he employs these ideas in conventional ways and when he uses them in ways less conventional.

Paul's conformity to such patterns can be observed in his *theological use* of childhood language; this is particularly visible in his parent/child metaphors. For example, he uses it to place Christians within the history of the people of God: they are children of God, their Father (e.g., Rom. 8:14-17), and offspring of Abraham, their forefather (e.g., Gal. 3:29). Also, Christ is the Son of God and the descendant of David (Rom. 1:3-4). Consequently, both Christians and Christ are heirs to the kingdom of God (Rom. 8:17, etc.). Paul clearly shows an ability to exploit current notions theologically. For example, in Galatians 3:23–4:7 he develops ideas of inheritance and depicts Christians as children who are yet minors, growing up to become of age, ready to receive their heavenly patrimony. Here, the metaphors contribute in a fundamental way to shaping Christian self-understanding, and they operate in competition with traditional Jewish thinking (cf. Gal. 4:21-31). Due to their frequency, these parent/child metaphors are important for the establishing of Christian identity in Paul.

Equally important is Paul's use of childhood metaphors as means *to regulate the relations between himself and his co-Christians*. Rhetorically, he adapts the childhood and family/kinship language to the situation of each letter and to his relations to his addressees. Such language is, for instance, far less common in Romans, which reflects a more distant relationship between him and the addressees, than in his close and very positive interaction with the recipients of 1 Thessalonians.[97]

This kind of usage, however, is characterized by a notable tension. On the one hand, Paul conforms to patriarchal patterns. He often uses the metaphors to depict Christians in a position inferior to himself: he is their father, they his children. And as children they are to obey and imitate him (1 Cor. 2:6–3:4) and to reach the same maturity as him (1 Cor. 13:11-12). Sometimes he rebukes them: the Corinthians turn out to be immature babies, needing to be breast-fed (1 Cor. 3:1-3). Quite often, then, Paul signals the authority of a *paterfamilias*, even threatening the Corinthians with physical punishment if they disobey (1 Cor. 4:21).

On the other hand, the nuanced way in which he portrays himself as father is also worth noting. What emerges is not a picture of a harsh, authoritarian father, but of a father concerned with his children and attentive to their abilities and needs: he communicates with them according to their level (2 Cor. 6:13), acts lovingly (1 Cor. 4:14-17), strives to increase their inheritance (2 Cor. 12:14), and exhorts them in a benevolent way, as a firm, yet loving father (e.g., 1 Thess. 2:11-12). Such attitudes do not necessarily imply that Paul differs from current ideals of father/child relations. Rather, his attitudes are likely to be in keeping with them: the father role of antiquity was more flexible than has often been allowed for, and Paul seems to utilize the whole spectrum given for this role in how he relates to his "children."[98] In fact, his focus appears to be more frequently on an understanding and supportive type of father than on an authoritarian one.

Another central part of the picture is displayed in Paul's *mother/child metaphors;* this is clearly more uncommon than his use of the father/child metaphors. In them, he puts himself in a female role, as a birth-giving mother (Gal. 4:19), a breastfeeding mother (1 Cor. 3:1), and — possibly, though less likely —

---

97. See the analysis in Aasgaard, *"My Beloved Brothers and Sisters!"* pp. 261-84 (esp. 283-84), 285-95 (esp. 292-95).

98. Cf., e.g., the variation described by Eyben, "Fathers and Sons," pp. 112-43; Saller, *Patriarchy, Property and Death,* pp. 102-33, esp. 131-33; also Balla, *The Child-Parent Relationship,* chs. 1-3.

a nurse (1 Thess. 2:7). In fact, Paul uses metaphors of himself as a mother as often as, or even more frequently than, a father.[99] Although maternal metaphors may belong among stock rhetorical or philosophical *topoi,* they nonetheless here give evidence for Paul's ability to identify with such a role and to view parent/child relations from the angle of a female parent.[100] This impression is strengthened by the fact that such metaphors occur in several of his letters. Together, they make this a truly conspicuous feature in Paul.[101]

Of special interest here, however, is Paul's use of metaphors related to *childhood as a phase of life.* Once again, tensions become visible. On the one hand, he seems — in keeping with views at that time — to idealize children as innocent and untouched by the world (Phil. 2:15). He also ascribes to them serious shortcomings: they do not have the necessary mental and physical capacities for adult maturity. On the other hand, he values their intellectual capacity positively, maybe even more so than many contemporaries (1 Cor. 13:11). And, more importantly, although he shares the idea about the goal of children's formation — the mature male adult — his view of the *contents* of this is significantly different from prevailing views: it is not shaped by current philosophical-religious ideals, but by the model of Christ giving himself for others (Rom. 8:29; Gal. 4:10; Phil. 3:10).

Deserving particular attention here are the texts in which Paul depicts *himself as a child.* One of them is primarily relational, namely, his mention of Rufus's mother as his own mother too (Rom. 16:13). In the other instances, however, he speaks of himself as an underage child, and in quite drastic ways: as a fetus (Gal. 1:15), as prematurely born (1 Cor. 15:8), as a child depending on its nurse-mother (1 Thess. 2:7), and as an orphan (1 Thess. 2:17). Clearly, these Paul-as-child metaphors are so striking that they, like the parent/child metaphors, need to be accounted for.

This can be done in several ways. One approach is to view the metaphors primarily in light of the rhetorical situation of each letter: for example, in 1 Corinthians Paul is turning criticism to his own benefit, and in 1 Thessa-

---

99. Gaventa, "Our Mother St. Paul," pp. 30-37. Some of the father/child language mentioned in the preceding paragraph can also be classified as maternal; cf. 2 Corinthians 6:13; 12:14; Philemon 10; cf. Balla, *The Child-Parent Relationship,* pp. 194-95.

100. See, e.g., Gaventa, "The Maternity of Paul," pp. 191-94, with references; Malherbe, *Paul and the Popular Philosophers,* pp. 35-48.

101. Cf. also Gaventa, "Our Mother St. Paul," p. 35; Gaventa, *First and Second Thessalonians,* pp. 31-34. It is worth noting that Paul uses maternal metaphors when he refers to his ongoing "nurturing" of his communities, but paternal metaphors when characterizing the initial (momentary) stages of Christian preaching and conversion; see Gaventa, *First and Second Thessalonians,* pp. 34, 36, 41-42.

lonians his writing reflects the amiable relations between him and his addressees, as well as his uncontested authority there.[102] This is saying far too little about the metaphors, however: although this can make them more understandable, it falls short of accounting sufficiently for their usage. They should not only be viewed as employed *ad hoc*, but as playing a more central part in Paul's letters. This is clear from his frequent, thoroughgoing, varied, and often conspicuous use of them.

Thus, another way of accounting for the metaphors of Paul-as-child and those of parent/child is by seeing them as part of a strategy by which Paul wants to further his authority and control over his communities; this is — as noted at the beginning of this essay — what some scholars do.[103] Within such a view, even Paul's "gentle" metaphors become means for strengthening his power and can be disclosed as both authoritarian and male biased. For example, the parent/child metaphors aim at displaying his graciousness; the metaphor of the untimely born is a deft rhetorical counter-strike in defense of his apostleship; and the modesty in his self-presentation as a baby and an orphan is pretense or pandering to the Thessalonians to gain their good will. Even Paul's theological motivations can be made to fall victim to such readings: his meekness toward God, the gospel, his apostolic calling, or his fellow Christians may all be unmasked as his seeking to secure his authority by a claim to live up to his message.

Such an approach is rather problematic, however, not least because it will often take its point of departure in models that make it downplay texts and interpretations that do not fit in.[104] Within such a view, in 1 Thessalonians — usually without the exegetical problems being taken into consideration — Paul is likely to be depicted as a nurse and an orphaned father, not as a child.[105] This view is also sometimes reinforced by a simplistic perception of the socio-historical context, especially through a one-sided, and obsolete, idea of an all-authoritarian father, with Paul seen as reflecting only the life-and-death power of the Roman *paterfamilias*.[106]

---

102. As for 1 Thessalonians, I basically agree with Burke, *Family Matters*, p. 157. For a broader discussion of Paul's rhetorical strategies in his use of kinship metaphors, see Aasgaard, *"My Beloved Brothers and Sisters!"* pp. 285-95.

103. As indicated by Gaventa, "Our Mother St. Paul," p. 44.

104. For a similar criticism particularly of Castelli, see Bartchy, "Who Should Be Called Father," p. 143.

105. See, e.g., Lone Fatum, "Brotherhood in Christ," in Moxnes, ed., *Constructing Early Christian Families*, p. 186; Fatum, "Tro, håb og gode gerninger," in *Den nye Paulus og hans betydning*, ed. Troels Engberg-Pedersen (København: Gyldendal, 2003), p. 132.

106. See, e.g., Castelli, *Imitating Paul*, p. 111; partly also Fatum, "Tro, håb og gode gerninger,"

In my opinion, we are correct in seeing the Paul-as-child and the parent/ child language as part of a general strategy in Paul. But instead of employing generalizing, and sometimes circular-reasoning, approaches to the matter, we should pay more heed to the material itself, namely, to Paul's *socio-cultural context,* which is more nuanced than has been allowed for; to his *texts,* which have turned out to be more versatile than assumed; and to the *interplay* between context and texts, which betrays a Paul with considerable freedom of movement within the given paths — and maybe even outside of them. Neither Paul nor his contemporaries should be underestimated in these matters.[107]

Read in such a way, several of Paul's childhood metaphors emerge as fundamentally daring. By associating himself with beings at the rim of the human world — one untimely born, a baby, an orphan — Paul presses his matter far indeed. Thus, what can be seen as rhetorical cleverness may just as likely be interpreted as the opposite, namely, as Paul here employing metaphors that in fact are not meant to enhance his authority *but to make him vulnerable and left to the mercy of his addressees.* Indeed, this (apparent folly) seems to be the case.[108] To liken oneself to such kinds of children would be to risk forfeiting the respect one could have secured by other, more favorable self-descriptions. Paul could easily have applied a number of such metaphors to attain his aims. But he does not.[109] The way he uses father/child and mother/child metaphors also supports this impression. Thus, the picture given is of a Paul able to deal with such matters from an unusual, sometimes extraordinary angle, even when it does not serve, or is not intended to serve, his interests. Consequently, Paul in these instances expresses himself in a way paradoxical not only on a rhetorical level but also on a social and ideological level.[110]

---

pp. 131-36. I fully subscribe to the questioning of this position by Gaventa, "Our Mother St. Paul," pp. 43-44. For nuanced views, see Eyben, "Fathers and Sons," pp. 142-43; Saller, *Patriarchy, Property and Death,* pp. 102-32, esp. 130-32; Balla, *The Child-Parent Relationship,* esp. pp. 76-79, 109-11; Aasgaard, *"My Beloved Brothers and Sisters!"* pp. 49-51.

107. I here agree with the point of view indicated by Gaventa, "The Maternity of Paul," p. 199.

108. This is an idea also hinted at by Jennifer Larson, "Paul's Masculinity," *Journal of Biblical Literature* 123 (2004): 96.

109. And they are not the only expressions of such an attitude in Paul; for a discussion of some aspects of this, see Timothy B. Savage, *Power through Weakness: Paul's Understanding of the Christian Ministry in 2 Corinthians,* Society for New Testament Studies Monograph Series 86 (Cambridge: Cambridge University Press, 1996), esp. pp. 187-90.

110. A similar kind of thinking is also seen elsewhere in 1 Corinthians, particularly in Paul's description of his apostolic ministry: "we have become the rubbish of the world, the dregs of all things" (4:13).

The portrait of Paul to emerge from this is more complex, but also far more interesting, than usually supposed. Obviously, it shows an apostle very much on a level with current attitudes on parenting, children, and childhood; this is the main part of the picture. But an essential part is also that of a Paul who — to a surprising degree — can view these matters from an alternative perspective, a perspective from below. True, the "deviating" metaphors must be balanced against his many statements claiming authority and power for himself. Nevertheless, the sensitivity and openness — and maybe even the countercultural nature — of his use of these metaphors should be taken far more seriously than has been customary.[111]

Conclusion

Paul was a child of his time, clearly reflecting current notions on children and childhood. But he was also an adult in his time, able to have his own say vis-à-vis traditional attitudes, capable of putting himself in the place of others, in this case particularly of children, and even willing to renounce his power in accordance with his understanding of Christ as a model for Christian service.

---

111. Indeed, the burden of proof for accounting differently for them lies with those who see Paul as mainly an "authority figure."

13 A Place of Belonging: Perspectives on Children from Colossians and Ephesians

Margaret Y. MacDonald

Colossians and Ephesians form part of the collection of New Testament works often known as the disputed letters of Paul (including also 2 Thessalonians, 1 Timothy, 2 Timothy, and Titus). In other words, biblical scholars dispute whether Paul was the author of these documents because of apparent differences in thought, language, and style compared to the other letters. Some scholars claim that Colossians and Ephesians were written by close associates or disciples of the apostle during his imprisonment or in the decades that followed his death in order to allow his legacy to speak to a new generation. Although they are by no means identical, there are close resemblances between Colossians and Ephesians — with Ephesians frequently viewed as in some way dependent upon Colossians — and they are often treated together.[1]

For the purposes of this essay, the complicated arguments concerning the authorship and distinctive features of Colossians and Ephesians in comparison to the undisputed letters of Paul are generally of secondary significance. Nevertheless, in one important respect these arguments do have a direct bearing on our discussion. Instruction directed at children and concerning the parent-child relationship appears in a type of ethical teaching that emerges for the first time in the disputed letters of Paul: the household code. At its most basic, the code comprises a series of commands aimed at different

---

1. Note that I have argued elsewhere in favor of the deutero-Pauline authorship of Colossians and Ephesians (see Margaret Y. MacDonald, *Colossians and Ephesians*, Sacra Pagina, ed. D. J. Harrington, S.J. [Collegeville: Liturgical Press, 2000]). By those who view the works as pseudonymous, Colossians is frequently dated between 60 and 80 CE and Ephesians between 80 and 90 CE.

I am grateful to my research assistant Gillian Pink for her helpful suggestions and attention to detail.

relationship pairs (typically husband-wife, master-slave, and parent-child) with the intent of ensuring correct behavior and attitudes in all roles. As will be discussed in detail below, the development of this type of teaching corresponded to a growing need to explain the identity of early church groups in the midst of rising tensions between these groups and the outside society. As the second century CE approached, Pauline communities sought to define behaviors and patterns of relations in house churches that were rooted in ancient conventions and expectations concerning the family.

There are, admittedly, some references to childbirth, infancy, and childhood in the undisputed letters of Paul, but these are largely metaphorical and indirect (e.g., 1 Thess. 2:7; 1 Cor. 3:1-2; 4:14-17; Gal. 3:19–4:7; 4:19-20; Rom. 8:22-25). Paul does once refer to children in a way that informs us that they were valued members of the community: in his argumentation in 1 Corinthians 7:10-16, children are presented as "holy" evidence for the desirability of preserving marriages between believers and nonbelievers.[2] With the epistles to the Colossians and the Ephesians, however, references to childhood move from the metaphorical and the indirect (cf. Col. 1:15; 3:6; Eph. 1:5; 2:3; 4:14; 5:1, 8) to the concrete and direct. That the household codes address children as one of the groupings requiring exhortation for life in the Lord indicates their presence within the assembly before which the epistle is to be read (Col. 3:18–4:1; Eph. 5:21–6:9).

The references are short — two reciprocal verses in Colossians 3:20-21, which are expanded somewhat in Ephesians 6:1-4. But their significance far outweighs their length. First, Colossians and Ephesians arguably offer the earliest explicit and indisputable evidence of the valuing of the parent-child relationship in early Christian communities.[3] It is in fact interesting to reflect upon why so little has been made of this by commentators, compared to the frequent recognition of Ephesians 5:22-33 as the first significant endorsement of marriage in early Christian literature. Second, Colossians and Ephesians

2. Peter Balla has drawn attention to two other texts that deal with real child-parent relations, but indirectly (Rom. 1:30 — rebellion against parents, and 1 Cor. 5:1 — a man living with his father's wife). See Balla, *The Child-Parent Relationship in the New Testament and Its Environment,* Wissenschaftliche Untersuchungen zum Neuen Testament 155 (Tübingen: Mohr Siebeck, 2003), pp. 160-65. For other indirect references, see also Beverly Gaventa's essay in this volume, "Finding a Place for Children in the Letters of Paul."

3. These documents overlap in dating with the Gospels (see note 1). As a whole, the Gospels offer more ambiguous evidence with respect to the parent-child relationship. It is nevertheless important to note the presence of the command to honor one's parents (Mark 7:10 and 10:19; Matt. 15:4-9 and 19:19; Luke 18:20), which is also cited in Ephesians 6:2-3. The healing stories in the Gospels offer an indication of a strong bond between child and (usually one) parent, and there are narratives that reveal the assumption that children should obey parents. See the discussion in Balla, *The Child-Parent Relationship,* pp. 114-26.

infuse the parent-child relationship with the values that have shaped it throughout Christian history, notably obedience, discipline, restraint, and encouragement. Finally, though it has rarely been recognized as such, Ephesians 6:4 is the earliest expression in the New Testament of the education of children as a community priority.

Understanding the significance of what is being said about children in Colossians and Ephesians, however, requires a twofold interpretative process. First, we must pay attention to literary issues: the genre, the implications of heavy reliance on traditional material and themes, and the nature of the relationship between Colossians and Ephesians themselves, including the distinct perspective of each epistle.[4] Second, certain issues concerning the historical context are especially important: the relationship between the authority of fathers and the influence of mothers over their children, the overlap between children and slaves as subordinates both in reality and in ideological discourse, the parameters of domestic space, and the role of the house church as the educator of children. Moreover, in dealing with context, it is particularly valuable to take into account recent advances in the study of children and childhood, especially by historians of the Roman family but, increasingly, also by scholars of early Christianity. Often, these studies point the way to a variety of ancient sources — pagan, Jewish, and Christian — that can shed light on the teaching in Colossians and Ephesians concerned with the child-parent relationship. In this essay, comparison of Colossians and Ephesians to the Pastoral Epistles (1 Timothy, 2 Timothy, Titus) proves to be especially enlightening.

Children in Household Code Discourse

Introduced for the first time in Colossians, and offering the most succinct example of the genre, household code teaching became a typical form of early Christian discourse (Col. 3:18–4:1; cf. Eph. 5:21–6:9; 1 Pet. 2:18–3:7; 1 Tim. 2:8-15; 3:4-5; 6:1-2; Tit. 2:1-10; 3:1; Ignatius, *Letter to Polycarp* 4.1–5.1; Polycarp, *Letter to the Philippians* 4.2–6.1).[5] No precise parallel to these codes has been

---

4. For a more thorough comparison than is possible here, see Balla, *The Child-Parent Relationship*, pp. 165-78.

5. Some scholars have argued that only Colossians and Ephesians should be thought to contain true examples of the household code genre, with the other texts containing only certain elements. See Balla, *The Child-Parent Relationship*, p. 168. While it is true that Colossians and Ephesians contain the strictest examples of this genre (including all three pairs of relationships), this should not be overemphasized. First Peter, the Pastorals, and the Apostolic Fathers also clearly reflect the same type of household code traditions, even if they are interpreted more freely.

found in other traditions, addressing subordinate groups directly rather than via the *paterfamilias* (the senior male head of the household). Nonetheless, it is generally accepted among scholars today that the household code has its origins in Hellenistic discussions of "household management" among philosophers and moralists from Aristotle (see *Politics* 1.1253b-1260b26) onward, including Stoics, Neo-Pythagoreans, and Jews.[6] As is especially clear in the case of the household codes of the Pastoral Epistles and the Apostolic Fathers, Aristotle's wider interests in the ruling of the state, of which the household is a microcosm, parallel the broader preoccupations of the early church authors in the organization of the house church.

Children in Classical and Hellenistic Texts

In Aristotle's *Politics*, as in the early church household codes, children play a comparatively minor role: they, along with women and slaves, are an example of the classes who "by nature" are intended to be ruled (1260a8-14). The child (ὁ παῖς) — at least the male child — is arguably the "greatest" among the inferiors, for he possesses the deliberative part of the soul in an undeveloped form, while the female has it "but without full authority," and the slave lacks it altogether. The same emphasis on the potential of the male child is found in the statement that the education of both women and children "to be good" is desirable for the goodness of the state; while women make up half of the free population, "the children (τῶν παίδων) grow up to be the partners in the government of the state" (1260b15-26). This emphasis on the potential of the child, however, does not overshadow the practical requirements of managing behavior, requirements that put children in a significantly different position vis-à-vis their fathers from that of wives vis-à-vis their husbands. In governing the household, the head of the house was to administer his rule using a republican model with respect to his wife, but a monarchical model in the case of his children. As a ruler by virtue "both of affection and of seniority," the rule of the father is nothing less than that of a king (1259b10-18). Yet elsewhere, Aristotle makes it clear that kingly authority does not mean tyrannical rule over one's children (*The Nicomachean Ethics* 8.1160b23-1161a10); paternal rule among Persians is said to be tyrannical, for they use their sons as slaves.[7]

---

6. The groundbreaking work is David L. Balch, *Let Wives Be Submissive: The Domestic Code in 1 Peter*, Society of Biblical Literature Monograph Series 26 (Chico, CA: Scholars Press, 1981).

7. Quotations from Aristotle's *Politics* are from the Loeb Classical Library edition. The quotation from *The Nicomachean Ethics* is cited in Balch, *Let Wives Be Submissive*, p. 35.

Since David L. Balch's groundbreaking study on the domestic code in 1 Peter, scholars have identified parallels, increasingly close both in form and in content, between the New Testament household codes and other household management texts, thus cautioning against viewing the codes as containing unique ethical norms.[8] As these ancient ideas evolved in a wide range of philosophical and political circles, certain themes repeated themselves, themes that also surface clearly in the household codes of Colossians and Ephesians. For example, in Neopythagorean traditions, which many scholars now date to the first centuries BCE and CE, we find a repeated emphasis on the obedience of children.[9] Here, it is important to note that reference to the obedience (ὑπακούω) of children is found in both Colossians 3:20 and Ephesians 6:1. Ephesians 6:2 also speaks of children "honoring" their parents, an obvious allusion to the commandment from the Decalogue (LXX Exod. 20:12; Deut. 5:16).[10] Although it is impossible to determine the precise age of the children in view by the author of Ephesians, the reference to honoring par-

8. While it is true that certain features of the household code schema seem to have developed in the early church groups (such as the repeated emphasis on "the Lord" or "in the Lord" in clauses offering justification for the ethical exhortations), the parallels between household management texts from the ancient world and the New Testament household codes are increasingly being viewed as a matter of form and not only of theme. For discussion of especially close parallels, see David Balch, "Neopythagorean Moralists and the New Testament Household Codes," *Aufstieg und Niedergang der römischen Welt* 2, no. 26.1 (1992): 389-404, concerning texts from Hellenistic street philosophy, which offer particularly good parallels especially to the genre of the Colossian code. These parallels also extend to inscriptional evidence. Angela Standhartinger has noted the similarities in form between the Colossian household code and the Philadelphian inscription found on a stele referring to ethical requirements of a household cultic association. See Angela Standhartinger, "The Origin and Intention of the Household Code in the Letter to the Colossians," *Journal for the Study of the New Testament* 79 (2000): 117-30, and further discussion below. See also the useful chart setting forth parallels to many elements in the Colossian and Ephesian household codes in Balla, *The Child-Parent Relationship*, p. 173 (Balla cites Georg Strecker's 1989 study). For arguments in favor of distinct early Christian features of the household code, see especially David C. Verner, *The Household of God: The Social World of the Pastoral Epistles*, Society of Biblical Literature Dissertation Series 71 (Chico, CA: Scholars Press, 1983).

9. See, for example, Perictyone, *On the Harmony of a Woman* 145.8-18, 23-26; Iamblichus, *Life of Pythagoras* 22.13, 18-19; 23.8-9, cited in Balch, "Neopythagorean Moralists," p. 402. See also Balch, *Let Wives Be Submissive*, p. 57.

10. This commandment is called "the first commandment with a promise" in Ephesians 6:2. The nature of the promise is explained in verse 3 with further adapted material from Exodus 20:12. Commentators have frequently been puzzled by the reference to the first commandment, since an earlier commandment (forbidding the making of graven images) speaks of a jealous God who punishes disobedience but promises rich rewards to the obedient (cf. Exod. 20:4-6). For full discussion, see MacDonald, *Colossians and Ephesians*, p. 333.

ents certainly is meant to include a respectful attitude toward the parents of grown children, precluding any maltreatment and extending to their physical care in old age (cf. Exod. 21:15, 17; Prov. 19:26; 20:20; 28:24; Mark 7:9-13; Matt. 15:4-6).[11] Closely related to the notion of obedience — for rebelliousness and stubbornness constitute dishonor (Deut. 21:18-21) — honoring parents was a basic orientation or value of the ancient Mediterranean person.[12] The concept of honoring (τιμάω) parents is also found in Neopythagorean traditions, albeit somewhat less frequently than in the biblical tradition.[13] David L. Balch succinctly summarizes the implications of these parallels as follows: "For Neopythagorean moralists, children were both to obey and honor their parents. The command in Exod. 20:12 would not have sounded strange to them, and the language of Col. 3:20 would have been even more familiar."[14]

Philo and Josephus: Jewish Models

Some of the discussions of household management that come from the period of Colossians and Ephesians present rather extreme views on the obedience of children, emphasizing children's status as subject to the authority of their parents.[15] Philo, for example, in his comments on the fifth commandment (also cited in Ephesians), groups children with slaves in relation to the authority of parents: "For parents belong to the superior class of the abovementioned pairs, that which comprises seniors, rulers, benefactors and masters, while children occupy the lower position with juniors, subjects, receivers

11. See Andrew T. Lincoln, *Ephesians,* Word Biblical Commentary 42 (Dallas: Word, 1990), p. 405; E. Best, *A Critical and Exegetical Commentary on Ephesians,* International Critical Commentary (Edinburgh: T&T Clark, 1998), p. 554; and Patrick D. Miller's essay in this volume, "That the Children May Know." On the concept of honoring parents in Jewish literature, see Balla, *The Child-Parent Relationship,* pp. 86-91.

12. Joseph Plevnik, "Honor/Shame," in *Biblical Social Values and Their Meaning: A Handbook,* ed. J. J. Pilch and B. J. Malina (Peabody, MA: Hendrickson, 1993), p. 97.

13. See, for example, Pempelus, *On Parents* 141.14-19; 142.4-6, 11-13; Bryson, *On Household Management* 4.142; Zaleucus, *Preface* 227.23-25; Charondas, *Preface* 61.1-3. Cited in Balch, "Neopythagorean Moralists," pp. 402-3. See also discussion of honor and reverence as a duty of children to their parents in Greek and Latin sources of this era in Balla, *The Child-Parent Relationship,* pp. 62-64.

14. Balch, "Neopythagorean Moralists," p. 403.

15. It is interesting here to consider texts from Proverbs that emphasize the radical consequences of disobedience for children. See especially Proverbs 30:17 and 20:20 as discussed by William P. Brown, "To Discipline without Destruction: The Multifaceted Profile of the Child in Proverbs," in this volume.

of benefits and slaves" (Philo, *Decalogue* 166; cf. *Hypothetica* 7.3, 5; cf. Josephus, *Against Apion* 2.206).[16] It is worth noting in passing that while the author of Colossians tempers the authority of fathers/masters to a certain degree (see below), the opening of the exhortations to both children and slaves uses virtually identical language: they are to obey fathers/masters "in everything." In a second, very similar text, Philo justifies the hierarchical relationship between parents and their children by means of a highly suggestive analogy: "For parents are midway between the natures of God and man, and partake of both. . . . Parents, in my opinion, are to their children what God is to the world" (Philo, *Special Laws* 2.225-27; cf. 2.231; 4.184; cf. Josephus, *Against Apion* 2.206).

Two features of Philo's thought deserve special attention here. First, it is clear that, writing in the Roman era, he interprets the Decalogue in light of Platonic and Aristotelian political ethics.[17] But, as noted above, Aristotle resisted the equation of slave and son when it came to the authority of the *paterfamilias*. According to Balch, the Roman concept of the authority of fathers and heads of households — *patria potestas* — often increased the emphasis on the obedience of children in household management ethics in comparison to earlier Greek models.[18] Indeed, we have a clear example of this in the encomium of Rome given by Dionysius of Halicarnassus (30-7 BCE), which includes the three pairs of relationships in the same order as Colossians and, like Colossians, speaks of children honoring and obeying parents in all things (*Roman Antiquities* 2.26.1-4). Dionysius stresses the severe punishment of children who disobey and notes that Roman law actually gives greater power to the father over his son than to the master over his slaves (2.27.1).[19] Second, Philo's analogy recalls ancient notions of the gods as models for parents/fathers. Hierocles in "How to Conduct Oneself towards Parents," for example, describes parents as images of the gods (see Stobaeus, *Anthology* 4.25.53; cf. Iamblichus, *Life of Pythagoras* 22.18-19).[20] A less obvious partial parallel of such ideas is also found in Josephus's thought when he proclaims: "Honor to the parents the Law ranks second only to honor to God" (Josephus, *Against Apion* 2.206).

16. Quotations from Philo and Josephus are from the Loeb Classical Library edition. In his essay in this volume, Brown also notes the interchangeable social positions of children and slaves in Jewish traditions when he comments on Proverbs 17:2 and 29:21.

17. Balch, *Let Wives Be Submissive*, pp. 53-54.

18. Balch, *Let Wives Be Submissive*, p. 54.

19. On the physical discipline of children, see also Proverbs, especially Proverbs 13:24; 22:15; 23:13-14, as discussed by Brown in this volume.

20. On this issue and for further reference, see Peter Müller, *In der Mitte der Gemeinde* (Neukirchen Vluyn: Neukirchener, 1992), p. 320.

Although it is not explicit in the case of children, a similar analogical principle is at work in Ephesians, where the authority of Christ as head of the church mirrors the authority of husbands over wives: wives are to be subject to their husbands as to the Lord. But here, as elsewhere in the household codes, it is important to note that human authority in familial relations is qualified and only secondary to the authority of the Lord (with respect to the authority of parents, Ephesians seems closer to Josephus than to Philo). In addition, the codes ultimately place the household within the broad arena of God's realm rather than specifically within the city or state (cf. Eph. 2:19). The call for mutual submission in Ephesians 5:21 qualifies all calls for submission as rooted in reverence for Christ. The motivation or justification clauses, often using the expression "in the Lord" (found also in the teaching for children in Col. 3:20 and Eph. 6:1), play a fundamental role in weaving this message into the household codes.[21] Thus, Judith M. Gundry-Volf notes: "the household codes do not draw a parallel between parents and God/gods in order to motivate appropriate behavior as do some ancients. Parents stand alongside children under the Lord."[22] For Gundry-Volf, the household codes reveal the potential for critical tension between the authority of children and the authority of parents and, "in particular cases, release children from the obligation toward parents (as in Jesus' teaching), although the codes do not explicitly envision such a conflict."[23] While not made explicit, as will be discussed further below, it is likely that the codes spoke to an audience that included the children of nonbelievers,[24] and therefore the potential for such conflict was in fact quite high.

The Apologetic Function of Household Codes

Because of the tendency to engage in mutual instruction "in the Lord," it is easy to fall into the mistaken assumption that the household codes of Colossians and Ephesians were primarily intended to ensure internal cohesion and were solely focused on inter-believing relationships. It is important to bear in mind, however, that scholars have sought to understand the codes

21. The expression "in the Lord" (Eph. 6:1) is missing from some ancient manuscripts. The longer reading, however, is probably to be preferred. See Lincoln, *Ephesians*, p. 395.

22. Judith M. Gundry-Volf, "The Least and the Greatest: Children in the New Testament," in *The Child in Christian Thought*, ed. Marcia J. Bunge (Grand Rapids: Eerdmans, 2001), p. 56.

23. Gundry-Volf, "The Least and the Greatest," p. 56.

24. *Pace* Lincoln, *Ephesians*, p. 403, and Best, *A Critical and Exegetical Commentary on Ephesians*, p. 524.

within the context of household management material, which frequently displays apologetic intent. There is, admittedly, significant disagreement concerning the extent to which apologetic interest is displayed by particular documents. First Peter, with its explicit reference to relations with nonbelievers within the code (1 Pet. 3:1-6), lies at one end of the spectrum and Ephesians, with its highly idealized "Christian" view of marriage and lack of explicit reference to concrete relations with non-believers, at the other.[25] But at some level, all New Testament household codes carry apologetic connotations, for they constituted essential projections of identity in a society where family structure and relations were fundamental to establishing honor in one's own eyes and in the eyes of others.[26]

Hierarchy, Harmony, and Education in the Household

Little attention has so far been paid to how references to children may have played a role in such apologetic interests. Here, it is especially useful to examine how children figure in Josephus's treatment of the theme "concerning household management" in the midst of his apologetic discourse. In *Against Apion*, he responds to anti-Jewish propaganda by and for the Flavian dynasty after the destruction of the Temple in 70 CE, and the context of the work is

25. Balch *(Let Wives Be Submissive)* argues in favor of an apologetic purpose for the household code in 1 Peter, and many have taken up his views and applied them to other household codes. J. D. G. Dunn has argued for a double apologetic slant in the household code of Colossians, aimed not only at pagan outsiders but also at Jews. See *The Epistles to the Colossians and to Philemon: A Commentary on the Greek Text,* New International Greek Testament Commentary (Grand Rapids: Eerdmans, 1996), p. 250. For reservations with respect to the apologetic function of the Ephesian household code, see especially Sarah J. Tanzer, "Ephesians," in *Searching the Scriptures 2: A Feminist Commentary,* ed. Elisabeth Schüssler Fiorenza (New York: Crossroad, 1993), p. 330.

26. Here it is important to keep in mind that even explicitly apologetic texts have dual inward/outward functions. L. Michael White, for example, has argued that apologetic literature offers insiders a means of looking toward their margins with the larger society. See "Visualizing the 'Real' World of Acts 16: Toward Construction of a Social Index," in *The Social World of the First Christians: Essays in Honor of Wayne A. Meeks,* ed. L. M. White and O. L. Yarbrough (Philadelphia: Fortress Press, 1995), pp. 159-69. On apology and Ephesians 5:21–6:9, see detailed discussion in Carolyn Osiek and Margaret Y. MacDonald (with Janet Tulloch), *A Woman's Place: House Churches in Earliest Christianity* (Minneapolis: Fortress Press, 2006), pp. 234-35. On how the pivotal values of honor and shame in ancient Mediterranean culture may have influenced early church teaching concerning children, see O. M. Bakke, *When Children Became People: The Birth of Childhood in Early Christianity* (Minneapolis: Augsburg Fortress, 2005), pp. 154-58.

therefore roughly contemporary with Colossians and Ephesians.[27] In an effort to convince his audience that Judaism is compatible with the values of the literate classes of Rome, Josephus gives a prominent place to the treatment of children by Jews.

Josephus draws extensively on values and ideas associated with the ideal Roman *paterfamilias* and family in his apologetic discourse. Perhaps most striking of all is the description of the Jews living under the Law as under a father and master (ὑπὸ παρτὶ τούτῳ καὶ δεσπότῃ) (cf. Gal. 3:24); the heart of the Jewish way of life is thus explained with direct reference to the authority structures of the household (*Against Apion* 2.174). As the head of the family enjoys the honor of a harmonious and ordered household, Jews are united in belief under the Law; consequently, even women and dependents (τῶν οἰκετῶν, children and probably also slaves) will state that piety (εὐσέβειαν, a concept closely associated with Roman devotion to matters of family and state) is their primary motivation (2.181).[28]

In Josephus's thought, the Law is something that is observed and absorbed from infancy (*Against Apion* 2.173, 178). In maintaining the most extreme rights of the head of the household over the life of his children, Josephus notes that the Law sanctions the stoning of sons who rebel against their fathers' will (2.206; Deut. 21:18-21; Lev. 20:9; cf. Philo, *Special Laws* 2.232). The honor that is owed to parents extends even to the fact that the mere intent of wronging them or of impiety is enough to lead to death (*Against Apion* 2.217; Deut. 21:18-21; Lev. 24:13). Josephus also makes it abundantly clear, however, that Jews treasure their children, eschewing practices associated with other nations: they raise all of their children, and women are not to cause abortions, lest they be charged with infanticide (*Against Apion* 2.202-3; cf. Philo, *Special Laws* 3.108-19). Rather than providing a pretext for such raucous celebration as might follow the birth of a Roman child, the birth of a Jewish child is an occasion for sobriety, followed by dedicated efforts to educate, including the teaching of reading and training in the laws and the traditions of the forefathers (*Against Apion* 2.204; cf. Philo, *Hypothetica* 7.14). At one point, Josephus even identifies the education of children as the highest

27. See Martin Goodman, "Josephus' Treatise *Against Apion*," in *Apologetics in the Roman Empire: Pagans, Jews, and Christians,* ed. Mark Edwards, Martin Goodman, and Simon Price, in association with Christopher Rowland (Oxford: Oxford University Press, 1999), pp. 50-51. *Against Apion* was composed sometime after the *Antiquities* in 90 CE. On the dating of Colossians and Ephesians, see note 1 above.

28. The Romans prized the virtue of *pietas,* which they associated with loyalty to gods, state, parents, and family. It was a virtue frequently linked to the obedience of children. See Beryl Rawson, *Children and Childhood in Roman Italy* (Oxford: Oxford University Press, 2003), p. 223.

priority of Jews: "Above all we pride ourselves on the education of our children, and regard as the most essential task in the life the observance of our laws and pious practices, based thereupon, which we have inherited" (*Against Apion* 1.60).

Comparison of Colossians 3:20-21 and Ephesians 6:1-4 to Josephus's apologetic discourse can help us to interpret household code teaching with respect to the parent-child relationship. There are some obvious parallels. Although severe consequences for disobedience are not spelled out as in the case of Josephus's discourse, the emphasis on obedience, especially on obedience "in everything" in Colossians 3:20, highlights the seriousness of the demand. The interplay with the extreme authority of fathers according to Roman law that one also senses in Josephus's thought is suggested by the move to address fathers directly in the deutero-Pauline works, although in these texts there is an explicit attempt to moderate expressions of authority (Col. 3:21; Eph. 6:4). Moreover, the references to education and to the Law being learned from infancy, so emphatically stressed by Josephus, can help us to appreciate the significance of bringing up children "in the discipline and instruction of the Lord" (Eph. 6:4), to be discussed further below. The concept of religious instruction being absorbed by young children (but here under the influence of mothers and grandmothers) is also suggested by 2 Timothy's reference to faith being passed down to Timothy from his grandmother Lois, via his mother Eunice (2 Tim. 1:5; cf. 1 Pet. 2:2-3). On the other hand, the Greek term παιδεία (discipline) employed in Ephesians 6:4 can refer not only to the upbringing of a child but also to the training or orientation of an adult — suggesting the life-course process that is also inherent in the teaching of the Law.[29] Second Timothy 3:16 refers, in fact, to "training in righteousness" as one of the purposes of Scripture. That the whole life course is in view is suggested by a call for Timothy to continue in what he has already learned, including the sacred writings that he has known from childhood (βρέφος, literally "infancy"). Although it is unlikely to be referring mainly to adult children, Ephesians 6:4 has connotations of lifelong learning and echoes of a fatherly authority that extends even over adult children.[30]

---

29. On the close association between discipline and instruction in Hebrew and on the importance of this association for understanding Proverbs, see the essay by Brown in this volume.

30. Note that M. Gärtner (*Die Familienerziehung in der alten Kirche* [Cologne: Bohlau, 1985], pp. 36-37) has argued that Colossians 3:20-21 refers to adult children. This, however, is clearly a minority opinion, though it has been stressed that the children mainly in view must have been old enough to understand the content of the exhortations. For a good summary of the discussion in the secondary literature about the age of the children, see Bakke, *When Children Became People*, p. 320 n. 5. On the process of lifelong learning (but specifically with re-

Valuing Children

With references to abortion, infanticide, and exposure, Josephus seeks to illustrate that Jews choose the moral high ground in comparison to their Roman contemporaries. Such references are notably absent from New Testament works, including Colossians and Ephesians, but do appear in works from the early second century (*Didache* 2.2; *Epistle of Barnabas* 19.5; cf. *Sibylline Oracles* 2.279-82). Interestingly, the close association of such ideals with traditional household ethics is suggested by the *Epistle of Barnabas,* which links teaching against abortion and infanticide with calls for firm physical punishment of sons and daughters ("Thou shalt not withhold thy hand") and for teaching children to fear God from their youth onwards (19.5). By the time the Christian apologists of the middle and latter decades of the second century were writing, early Christian attitudes to abortion, infanticide, and exposure had become the kind of explicit boundary markers we find in Josephus's work. It would be naïve to think that such practices disappeared completely in early church groups,[31] but when taken together with texts that point to the care of orphans as an early church priority (James 1:27; *Epistle of Barnabas* 20.2; Hermas, *Mandates* 8.10; Hermas, *Similitudes* 9.26.1-2) there is good reason to suspect that the rearing of infants was a concern that early Christians shared with Jews and other groups in the Roman world.

That the care of orphans was an important aspect of early Christian identity is suggested by the fact that, at the beginning of the second century CE, Ignatius of Antioch cites the neglect of orphans and widows among the vices of his "heretical" adversaries (Ignatius, *Letter to the Smyrnaeans* 6.2). Even more telling in the evidence from this period is the instruction found in the Shepherd of Hermas that Grapte, a literate female early church leader, should teach the widows and orphans (Hermas, *Visions* 2.4.3). We do not know precisely what kind of care was involved here, but it clearly included a teaching element. Moreover, given the house-church base of early Christianity, we should think of these widows and orphans as living and learning together.

In this ancient Mediterranean context, a fatherless child would be considered orphaned. Therefore, widows who joined church groups might often have been accompanied by their own "orphaned" children, despite the custom of appointing male guardians whose influence seems to have depended on a variety of factors, such as the social status of the family involved and the mother's

---

spect to female members of the community), see Osiek and MacDonald, *A Woman's Place,* pp. 90-92. See also note 11 above.

31. See full discussion in Osiek and MacDonald, *A Woman's Place,* pp. 51-53.

capacity for autonomy. The dedication to caring for widows (Acts 6:1; 1 Tim. 5:16) that emerges in early Christian literature implicitly carries concern for destitute children. However, we should probably think of the obligation to widows and orphans as extending beyond these mother-child groupings to encompass children — both slave and free — with no living parents. These children could find themselves associated, sometimes simply by chance, with believers and/or believing households. Unfortunately, the evidence does not offer details about how these children were cared for or whether they were officially adopted in some fashion.[32] Certainly, the metaphorical language in Pauline literature, including the concept of inheritance applied to slaves (who by law could not inherit) in the Colossian household code (Col. 3:24), suggests that Pauline Christians were very comfortable in defining the household of God in a manner that transcended legal familial boundaries (Eph. 2:19).[33]

That an ethos encouraging the protection of children could easily take root in household associations like the house churches of Pauline Christianity is suggested by an inscription found on an ancient monument. This marble stele, offering instruction to an unknown Philadelphian household and/or religious association, probably dates from the late second or early first century BCE. Although she does not draw detailed attention to the material concerning children, Angela Standhartinger notes significant parallels between the Colossian household code and this inscription, which seeks to regulate the interactions between the familial groupings also found in Colossians 3:18–4:1. Standhartinger argues that, like the household code material, this inscription served an apologetic function for the cultic association, assuring onlookers that the familial relations between group members were respectable and of a hierarchical nature, despite societal suspicions to the contrary.[34] For our purposes, it is especially important to note that this group sought to project an image of itself in

---

32. It is interesting here to note the reference, coming from a significantly later period than Pauline Christianity — the third century CE — to the infant of the martyred Felicitas being adopted by a Christian woman of the community in *The Martyrdom of Perpetua and Felicitas* (15). See full discussion in Osiek and MacDonald, *A Woman's Place*, p. 47.

33. For metaphorical treatment of adoption in Paul's letters, see especially Galatians 3:19–4:7. On the question of inheritance, see the further discussion of the situation of slave children below.

34. See Standhartinger, "The Origin and Intention of the Household Code," pp. 117-30. It is important to note that the inscription does not deal directly with the relationship between parents and their children. As explained below, however, it does deal with the treatment of children. For the inscription, see *Sylloge inscriptionum graecarum* 3.985, 3rd ed., ed. W. Dittenberger, 4 vols. (Leipzig, 1915-24). For Greek text and English translation (cited in this essay) and detailed discussion of the diverse and complex issues raised by the text, see S. C. Barton and G. H. R. Horsley, "A Hellenistic Cult Group and the New Testament Churches," *Jahrbuch für Antike und Christentum* 24 (1981): 7-41.

which abortion, infanticide, and exposure were ruled out. Even marriages between slaves (having no legitimate status in law) were shielded from the sexual designs of the "Lord" of the house, and virgins and boys (probably slaves) were protected from corruption.[35] None of this is made explicit in Colossians or Ephesians, but both documents place emphasis on sexual ethics. Moreover, the highly sexual nature of the marriage imagery running through Ephesians 5:22-33 suggests that the family ideals of the household codes were deeply intertwined with sexual ideals — ideals that in this context could easily spill over into norms relating to abortion, exposure, and abandonment. As we explore the probable nature of the audience of the Colossian and Ephesian household codes, we will see that the significance of the direct address to children may extend far beyond the simple fact that children are being taken for granted as members of the community. It may offer an indirect indication that the rearing of infants was an early church priority because the community was swelling its ranks with rescued, previously abandoned children and the offspring of slaves who may or may not have been part of the community. The image portrayed is one of obedient children who dutifully honor their parents, but the reality may often have been quite different indeed.

Boundaries Transgressed: The Case against the Christians

Although scholars have paid little attention to the matter, second-century pagan critics accused the early Christians of encouraging the recruitment of unruly, rebellious, and inadequately supervised children. The most detailed record of such impressions is found in Celsus's account, which refers to children in house and workshop settings being encouraged "to leave father and their schoolmasters, and go along with the women and little children who are their playfellows to the wooldresser's shop, or to the cobbler's or the washerwoman's shop, that they may learn perfection" (Origen, *Against Celsus* 3.55).[36] But Lucian of Samosata's association of orphans with "old hags called widows"

35. The inscription instructs men not to have sexual relations with married women, whether slave or free, and to avoid defiling or corrupting boys or virgins (μὴ φθερῖν μηδὲ παῖδα μηδὲ παρθένον), calling to mind the accessibility of household slave children for sexual use by masters and by those to whom he wished to offer his slaves (25-27). Concern for the protection of children, including slave children, is also revealed in the inclusive prohibition against making use of "a love potion, abortifacient, contraceptive, or any other fatal thing to children [a probable reference to exposure and/or infanticide]" (20-21).

36. Origen, *Contra Celsum*, trans. Henry Chadwick (Cambridge: Cambridge University Press, 1953).

who together keep vigil for an imprisoned Christian is equally damning (*The Passing of Peregrinus* 12-13). With a more specific focus on sexual corruption, the anti-Christian polemic of Marcus Cornelius Fronto singles out the presence of children at the immoral banquets of Christians and the use of children in the most abominable of rites (Minucius Felix, *Octavius* 8-9). These attacks are highly stereotypical and clearly designed to put down Christians, but they are also in keeping with some of the real practices of early Christians that can be established on the basis of other sources: house church meetings that sometimes violated the prerogatives of a pagan *paterfamilias,* providing sustenance to orphans and widows, and inclusive banqueting practices.

The transgression of inter- and intra-familial boundaries in the process of its self-definition was one of the central reasons why second-century critics found early Christianity offensive, and such transgressions most certainly did occur. Although the process is barely hinted at in the early Christian texts (cf. 2 Tim. 1:5), it is not difficult to find Gospel texts to support the recruitment and teaching of children (both slave and free) belonging to non-Christian homes with a concomitant lack of deference to the received tradition emanating from one's elders: "At that time Jesus said, 'I thank you, Father, Lord of heaven and earth, because you have hidden these things from the wise and the intelligent and have revealed them to infants" (Matt. 11:25, NRSV).[37] The involvement of children in church groups may well have been an important factor in the evolution of Christian apologetic discourse, of which the household codes offer an early example. While this example comes from the first decades of the third century, it is interesting to note that in response to the anti-Christian polemic of Marcus Cornelius Fronto cited above, Minucius Felix does not hesitate to feature the treatment of children in the ideological battle between paganism and Christianity. In addition to defending Christians against charges of grotesque rites involving the drinking of infants' blood, he launches his own attack, highlighting the brutal practices of pagans, including exposure and infanticide (*Octavius* 30.1-2).

Ideal Families and the Authority of Fathers

In addition to exploring the possible apologetic functions of the New Testament household codes, recent scholarship has stressed their idealized nature. The overall impression one gains is that of a harmonious believing family unit

---

37. See James Francis, "Children and Childhood in the New Testament," in *The Family in Theological Perspective,* ed. S. Barton (Edinburgh: T&T Clark, 1996), pp. 76-77.

(especially in the case of Ephesians, where marriage serves as a metaphor for the relationship between Christ and the church). The codes address the community in a manner that seems to assume that all listeners will find their place in the categories, even though they may be living lives that depart from the ideal in significant ways — the instructions subsume groups without breaking down categories or considering overlapping categories. In the case of children, several scenarios come to mind: What of the child whose father was a nonbeliever? Should he or she obey him in all things? What of the slave whose father was a believer living in another house in the neighborhood, but whose master was a nonbeliever? How would such a child "hear" the household code instructions? It is evident, especially in the case of Colossians, that the codes do not state that members belonging to the various pairs of relationships are all Christians.[38] Other Pauline texts remind us of the complex nature of the audience, which included subordinate members of the household of a pagan *paterfamilias* (e.g., 1 Cor. 7; 1 Tim. 6:1-2). As will be explored further below, we should think of the audiences addressed in Colossians and Ephesians as diverse groups of people, often living in complex family circumstances. We will see that children were most likely at the center of this diversity and complexity.

Christian Parenting Practices: How Different Were They?

Recognizing the idealized nature of the household codes involves adopting a critical stance in relation to the structures of power and authority reflected in the codes. There is a certain tension inherent in the household codes themselves, between the obvious emphasis on the authority of the *paterfamilias* (in keeping with the image of the honorable male who must maintain dominion over his house) and the attempt to temper the potential severity of that authority in his dealings with wife, children, and slaves.[39] With respect to the

38. Specifically referring to Ephesians, but equally applicable to other texts that contain household codes, Turid Karlsen Seim has argued that the code may well have spoken (even primarily) to women and slaves who were subject to non-believing heads of households ("A Superior Minority: The Problem of Men's Headship in Ephesians 5," in *Mighty Minorities? Minorities in Early Christianity — Positions and Strategies*, ed. D. Hellholm, H. Moxnes, and T. K. Seim [Oslo/Copenhagen/Stockholm/Boston: Scandinavian University Press, 1995], pp. 167-81). With respect to Colossians, Jean-Noël Aletti has argued that the author of Colossians does not make the Christian allegiance of both partners explicit. See *Saint Paul: Épître aux Colossiens* (Paris: J. Galbalda, 1993), p. 250.

39. On ideologies of masculinity in the Roman world, see Craig A. Williams, *Roman Homosexuality: Ideologies of Masculinity in Classical Antiquity* (Oxford/New York: Oxford University Press, 1999), pp. 141-42.

parenting of children, at least, while Christian motivations may have led to the encouragement of more moderate approaches, there is no evidence of novelty. In fact, in setting forth the responsibilities of parents toward their children, Colossians only calls on fathers not to provoke their children, lest they lose heart (Col. 3:21). This succinct recommendation may reflect some sensitivity to the fact that children who became members of Pauline churches were potentially subject to ridicule and maltreatment because of their new allegiances,[40] or could be accused of rebelliousness if not closely monitored (cf. Tit. 1:6). But this text, along with the virtually identical passage in Ephesians 6:4, is also clearly in keeping with the warnings against excessive severity toward children found in other ancient texts (e.g., Pseudo-Plutarch, *Moralia* 8F [*De Liberis Educandis*]; Pseudo-Phocylides 207).[41]

Nor can new patterns of behavior be read into the recommendations directed at the children. Ephesians 6:1 commands obedience to parents "in the Lord," while Colossians 3:20 refers to obedience "in all things." The justification for the call for obedience in Ephesians 6:1 includes "for this is right or just (δίκαιον)" instead of the command to do what is "pleasing in the Lord" (Col. 3:20). The instruction to children in Ephesians appears to be more distinctly "Christianized" than the one found in Colossians: Ephesians 6:1 echoes the reference to righteousness (δικαιοσύνη), which appears as one of the elements that set believers apart from nonbelievers (Eph. 4:24; 5:9). Moreover, the exhortation to children in Ephesians 6:2-3 amplifies citations from Scripture. But, despite clear efforts to "Christianize" household management materials, none of the recommendations concerning the parent-child relationship in Colossians and Ephesians can be said to encourage behavior that could be deemed distinctly Christian in concrete terms, with the possible exception of the Christian content in the teaching that fathers are to impart to their children, according to Ephesians 6:4 (to be discussed further below). Even the reference to "what is right" fits with the repeated treatment of household management material in discourses on justice.[42] The most that can be said is that, in general, the vision of the child-parent relationship re-

---

40. See Dunn, *The Epistles to the Colossians and to Philemon*, p. 252.

41. Some ancient authors argue that under certain circumstances children might actually disobey their fathers, especially in the interests of philosophy. Musonius Rufus's writings on this subject are often cited. See the discussion in Balla, *The Child-Parent Relationship*, pp. 74-75. See also p. 175, where he notes that Epictetus, like the author of Colossians, recommends that children obey their parents in everything, while at the same time cautioning that the philosopher's commitment to "good" should represent the top priority. On limitations of the power of the *paterfamilias*, see p. 46.

42. For examples, see Balch, "Neopythagorean Moralists," pp. 403-4.

flected in Colossians and Ephesians resembles more moderate approaches, especially when it comes to articulating the authority of the head of the household. In keeping with some apologetic texts, Colossians and Ephesians stress the obedient, orderly, and respectful conduct of children, though Colossians stops short of advocating the need for discipline, and neither text mentions the harsh consequences for disobedience that we see in other pagan, Jewish, and (later) Christian documents.

Father . . . and Mother: The Real Balance of Power

Complementing the insights of New Testament scholars on the idealized nature of the household codes, recent work on the Roman family reminds us that traditional statements concerning the father's authority should not be taken at face value. In particular, the emphasis on the authority of the *paterfamilias* that runs through the household code, spanning his role as father, master, and teacher, needs to be considered in relation to the real influence of mothers. Research on the Roman family has revealed that even very restrictive legal pronouncements upholding the formal authority of the fathers in the house need to be understood in conjunction with a multitude of conventions lacking formal authority but nevertheless constituting a coordinating sphere of maternal influence. It is therefore important to remember that those who heard the household codes of Colossians and Ephesians probably assumed that mothers were being granted informal authority in managing household affairs. Certainly, the idealized image of marriage as unity in Ephesians 5:22-33 has much in common with contemporary descriptions of marriage, which preserved the essential hierarchy of relations in the household but emphasized mutual responsibility, companionship, and coordinating duties (see Plutarch, *Conjugalia Praecepta* 142F-43A).[43] In the Roman era, wives were praised for exhibiting such good management virtues as the able hosting of guests and frugality (see Pliny, *Epistulae* 4.19). But it is especially interesting for our purposes to note that as Roman women gained increasing autonomy, not only in Rome itself but also in the Eastern provinces, they pushed the limits of the legal rights of the *paterfamilias* and other male guardians by playing a central role in mapping out futures for their children, including education and marriage. Mothers increasingly participated in finding good matches for their children and, often in widowhood, for all practical purposes managed the affairs of their children quite autonomously, at least until they remarried.[44]

43. See full discussion in Osiek and MacDonald, *A Woman's Place,* pp. 131-32.
44. See Susanne Dixon, *The Roman Mother* (London/Sydney: Croom Helm, 1988). On the

One fascinating example illustrating the powerful voice of a mother who speaks up on behalf of a young adult daughter (or by our standards probably an adolescent) is recounted in the writings of Aulus Gellius (Latin author and grammarian who wrote the twenty-book compendium entitled *Attic Nights*). The mother in question had assisted her daughter through the very difficult delivery of her first-born child; she became an advocate for her well-being by insisting that her daughter was too exhausted to breastfeed. In response, a group of the father's philosophical friends, in keeping with more conservative mores, protested against reliance on wet-nurses (*Attic Nights* 12.1.1-5; cf. Tacitus, *Dialogus de oratoribus* 28.4-5). In this case, the circumstances involve a distinguished senatorial family, but, according to Susanne Dixon, for lower-class women, in particular within slave and freed-slave families, the role of mother advocate and protector of her children may well have been tantamount to that of "an anchor in a very uncertain world."[45]

The shift from a command for obedience to parents (Col. 3:20 and Eph. 6:1-3), where both mothers and fathers are included, to the direct address of fathers (Col. 3:21 and Eph. 6:4), as the ones whose formal authority must at once be recognized and tempered, is in keeping with this picture. Once again, comparison to the household code material in the Pastoral Epistles is suggestive. There is the clear reinforcement of the image of a masculine authority rooted in conventional notions of masculine honor, which involves the formal authority of the father over his children. For example, the criteria for the selection of elders in Titus 1:6 include their having believing children who are accused neither of debauchery nor of unruliness.[46] Similar criteria are listed in 1 Timothy 3:4-5 for the selection of bishops, but this time the political consequences of the violation of these norms and the concern with image become explicit: "For if someone does not know how to manage his own household, how can he take care of God's church?" (NRSV). The links between such a statement and conventional household values are immediately clear,

---

increasing autonomy of Roman women and how that may have influenced the life of the early church communities, see Bruce W. Winter, *Roman Wives, Roman Widows: The Appearance of New Women and the Pauline Communities* (Grand Rapids: Eerdmans, 2003). Here we might consider also the set of papyrus documents associated with a Jewish woman named Babatha from the second century CE, which point to efforts to curtail the influence of male guardians over the life of her son after the death of his father. For detailed discussion of these documents, see Ross Shepard Kraemer, "Jewish Women and Women's Judaism(s) at the Beginning of Christianity," in *Women and Christian Origins*, ed. R. S. Kraemer and M. R. D'Angelo (New York: Oxford University Press, 1999), pp. 53-62.

45. Dixon, *The Roman Mother*, p. 233.

46. On the role of fathers in relation to their children in the Pastoral Epistles, see Bakke, *When Children Became People*, p. 154.

given the resemblance between this statement and Plutarch's observation: "a man therefore ought to have his household well harmonized who is going to harmonize state, forum, and friends" (Plutarch, *Conjugalia Praecepta* 144C).[47] In both Plutarch's discourse and the Pastoral Epistles, household norms are explicitly intertwined with formal recognition of male leadership in the body politic for either the state (Plutarch) or the church (the Pastorals). This explicit recognition is notably absent from Colossians and Ephesians, suggesting perhaps that in the context in which these documents were produced the reinforcement of male authority had more do with image than with actual church leadership structures. Indeed, Nympha's leadership of the house church (Col. 4:15) points to the fact that, in the later decades of the first century, there were currents in the Pauline churches that ran counter to the most conservative manifestations of household ethics that were coming to be articulated in the household codes.

Despite the explicit link between male church leadership and household norms in the Pastoral Epistles, the documents contain much material that confirms the insights emerging from Roman family studies about the real, but informal, authority of mothers and grandmothers in the household. The Pastorals restrict women's formal leadership opportunities; but, at the same time, instructions such as we find in 1 Timothy 5:14, that young widows should marry, bear children, and manage their households, would have created opportunities for women to exercise influence in a house-based movement. In those limited avenues explicitly recognized for women to exercise leadership, children also play a role. Although drawing on past experience, the list of criteria for the enrollment of widows (1 Tim. 5:9-10), including such home-based activities as hospitality, caring for children, and relieving the afflicted, should probably be understood as implying that these women were to continue providing acts of service after enrollment; the list opens up many possibilities for general service to children in church groups, both in sickness and in health.

Most intriguing of all, given the prohibition against women engaging in public/official teaching in 1 Timothy 2:12, is the exhortation in Titus 2:3-5 that they be good teachers (καλοδιδάσκαλοι). Here, teaching refers to older women instructing younger women (by our standards, often adolescent girls) to love their husbands and children and to be good managers of their households. Although different roles for men and women are being articulated, the choice of terminology — the use of the recognized word for teacher (διδάσκαλος) — implies that women's coordinating role is highly valued by the author. Despite its probably conventional manifestations, the significance of this recognition of women's authority should not be underestimated. In addition, this text offers a window into intergenerational exchanges among women, from young girls to wise grandmothers.[48] As we have seen above, in outlining the role played by Timothy's mother and grandmother in the development of his faith, the author of 2 Timothy likewise points to the importance of maternal influences in the teaching of boys (2 Tim. 1:5).

The Pastoral Epistles offer important evidence for the informal authority of mothers (and grandmothers) that was often associated by convention with traditional hierarchical visions of households in the Roman world. Given what we know about family life in this context and the community house church setting, there is little reason to doubt that the informal authority of mothers was also a prominent feature in the communities of Colossians and Ephesians. Despite the greater focus on the authority of fathers in these texts, we should keep in mind that the relationship with the mother was a key part of parent-child interactions; mothers almost certainly made an important contribution to the creation and maintenance of the infrastructure of communities.

Children in the Neighborhood:
Survival, Childcare, and Education

Fluid Boundaries and Shared Space

In addition to alerting us to the influence of mothers, recent scholarship on the Roman family can help us to explore the tension between the ideological discourse of the household codes and the real lives of children by enhancing our understanding of the physical space of childhood. In her groundbreaking study of childhood and children in the Roman world, Beryl Rawson has argued that Celsus's description of early Christianity contains highly believable physical images reflecting the intermingling of freeborn children, slave children, and adult slaves.[49] Despite the distance in ideological discourse between

---

48. See Osiek and MacDonald, *A Woman's Place*, p. 91. Note also that Neopythagorean traditions associated with Perictyone, who is presented as the author of the treatise *On the Harmony of a Woman*, envision a process of teaching whereby mothers teach their daughters virtues including prudence (σωφροσύνη). This term is associated with women in 1 Timothy 2:9 and Titus 2:4-5. See Balla, *The Child-Parent Relationship*, pp. 49-50.

49. Rawson, *Children and Childhood in Roman Italy*, p. 216.

the legitimate children of the freeborn and slaves, childhood for freeborn persons in the Roman world would often have involved *de facto* membership in the slave *familia:* free and enslaved babies were frequently nursed by the same slave women, and free and slave children would grow up playing together. This vision of "shared space" adds one more complicating element to our understanding of the audience receiving the household code instruction. Many of the children addressed in the household codes were probably slave children (some with no knowledge of and/or contact with biological parents), and many of the adult slaves who were instructed no doubt had children.

In keeping with the comments above concerning the presence of Christians belonging to non-believing households in the audience of Colossians and Ephesians, it is important not to take the categories of relationships as rigid descriptions of groups. Many members would have belonged to more than one category, and some key facets of their identity simply are not recognized within the pairs of relationships. For many children, for example, a mother's or father's authority may have been balanced by, or even replaced with, the influence of grandparents, stepmothers or stepfathers, nurses, nannies, and slave-attendants of various kinds. When it came to the children of nonbelievers, women like Nympha (Col. 4:15), who were probably widows themselves, may have stepped in as pseudo-mothers, offering a combination of spiritual formation and childcare. Indeed, such seems to be the role of Grapte in the Shepherd of Hermas (*Visions* 2.4.3) and possibly also of the enrolled widows of 1 Timothy 5:9.

Rawson has identified "the neighborhood" as an important source of protection and identity, especially for poorer families living in urban tenement houses.[50] Given the fact that the street may have been the only playground for many children, there must have been many cases when a child disappeared and the child's absence went unnoticed, or it was assumed that a friend was providing for the child. As noted above, children must sometimes have been adopted by default, sometimes being saved from particularly harsh circumstances, as seems to be presupposed in the comments of the second-century apologist Aristides, who refers to Christians rescuing orphans from those who treat them harshly (*Apology* 15). But the intermingling of free and slave children, often under the care of slave caregivers, must have created many opportunities for contact with early church groups, even among freeborn children who were part of a large household with a considerable retinue of slaves and clients. A highly moving epitaph from Rome for a six-year-old boy, Marcianus, testifies to the importance of the neighborhood as a social context

---

50. Rawson, *Children and Childhood in Roman Italy,* p. 211.

for freeborn children as well: a huge crowd is said to have attended the little boy's funeral, and the whole street wept.[51]

The House Church: A Locus of Education

The merging of household and house-church space in the New Testament era created unique opportunities for the evangelization of children. Children must often simply not have distinguished between being at home, at the house of playmates, or in the church community. For example, the house church could easily have been a place where their conductors to school (the slave *paidagogoi*) regularly took them as part of their daily routine — to and from school, to visit friends, or sometimes even to a house where a teacher had been hired to instruct the children of the household and some additional children.

In the Roman world, the education of very young children — roughly until age five to seven — was a home-based affair. The question of whether beyond this point it was better to educate children at home or to send them out to school was debated by intellectuals. Despite the advantages of what we would call today "socialization" (see Quintilian, *Institutes of Oratory* 1.2), some members of the elite classes certainly preferred private tutors. Education in the home probably especially benefited slaves and girls, who might otherwise not have had access to higher forms of education. Elevated conversations during dinners where slave children might act as servers, entertainers, or readers (see Nepos, *Atticus* 14) provided opportunities for learning, and sometimes these were enhanced by the presence of visiting intellectuals.[52] It is in the context of a long association of education with the household — beginning, in the mind of some thinkers, with the careful selection of wet-nurses for their speech and moral example (Quintilian, *Institutes of Oratory* 1.1.4-5) — that we should read the call for fathers to raise their children "in the discipline and instruction of the Lord" in Ephesians 6:4. This text probably points to a "specifically Christian body of instruction" that was to be imparted to children in a home setting.[53]

Ephesians 6:4 marks the beginning of considerable interest in the Chris-

---

51. *Corpus inscriptionum latinarum* 6.7578. For translation and discussion of the inscription, see Beryl Rawson, "Education: The Romans and Us," *Antichthon* 33 (1999): 81-98.

52. Rawson, *Children and Childhood in Roman Italy*, pp. 154-56; on the education of slave children, see also pp. 187-91.

53. See John M. G. Barclay, "The Family as the Bearer of Religion," in *Constructing Early Christian Families*, ed. H. Moxnes (London/New York: Routledge, 1997), p. 77.

tian socialization of children during the period of the Apostolic Fathers (cf. *1 Clement* 21.6, 8; *Didache* 4.9; Polycarp, *Letter to the Philippians* 4.2). As we noted above concerning the authority of the *paterfamilias,* it is important to recognize that the formal authority of fathers with respect to education needs to be considered in relation to more informal expectations about the role of mothers. There are ample indications of the important educational influence of mothers, and not only in the case of little children (Quintilian, *Institutes of Oratory* 1.1.6-7).[54] Interestingly, the Christian socialization of the child is explicitly presented as the duty of wives in Polycarp's *Letter to the Philippians* (4.2).

Christianity's Impact on the Situation of Slave Children

The household continued to be a key center for the education of Christian children for centuries beyond the period of the house churches. Some Christian children attended pagan schools, with their Christian education fostered at home and in church.[55] It is difficult to know whether this contributed to a specifically Christian way of raising children beyond the Christian content of instruction. For our period, there are many intriguing questions to consider, especially concerning the treatment of slave children: Did perceptions concerning the holiness of children (1 Cor. 7:14) affect the treatment of slave children, including the use of corporeal punishment (more severe punishments such as whipping were generally viewed as appropriate for slaves but not for free children)[56] and the sexual use of their bodies? Were some of the children directly addressed in Colossians and Ephesians previously abandoned infants now adopted by early Christian families? Were they generally adopted as slaves? The rescuing of exposed infants was commonplace in the Roman world, but most often these children were raised as slaves.[57] Were limits placed on the education of slave children in early church communities? Were these communities perhaps less inclined to separate slave families?

---

54. See discussion in Rawson, *Children and Childhood in Roman Italy,* p. 155.

55. For a good summary of the issues and a discussion of relevant primary and secondary sources, see Mary Ann Beavis, "'Pluck the Rose but Shun the Thorns': The Ancient School and Christian Origins," *Studies in Religion* 29 (2000): 411-23.

56. See R. P. Saller, "Corporeal Punishment, Authority, and Obedience in the Roman Household," in *Marriage, Divorce, and Children in Ancient Rome,* ed. B. Rawson (Oxford: Oxford University Press, 1991), pp. 144-65.

57. Jennifer A. Glancy, *Slavery in Early Christianity* (Oxford: Oxford University Press, 2002), pp. 7-8; Rawson, *Children and Childhood in Roman Italy,* p. 118. See also notes 32 and 33 above.

We have seen that the mingling of slave and free children was a central feature of childhood and upbringing in the Roman household. Inscriptional evidence suggests that sometimes slave children were raised with the aspiration that they would share in the promise of the free children of the family, and the affection between children brought up together must sometimes have lingered into adulthood and cut across social boundaries.[58] But it was far more common for traditional cultural norms to dominate so that adulthood brought a wide social chasm between slave and free. Even Seneca, who is well known among ancient authors for his comparatively liberal and humanitarian attitude toward slavery, makes his disdain clear for a former slave playmate, now feeble, who hopes to be recognized by him (Seneca, *Epistles to Lucilius* 12.3).

While our conclusions must be tentative, there are some indications that the communities underlying Colossians and Ephesians were pushing the limits of cultural acceptability in their treatment of children and slaves (including slave children). James Francis has raised an intriguing question regarding a possible link between the teaching of Jesus on children and the structure of the household codes. Noting that the instructions to subordinates typically precede the instructions to superiors in the household codes of Colossians and Ephesians (thereby reversing the Aristotelian model of consideration of household relations), he wonders whether "we might just detect the influence of a wider perspective based upon that logion of Jesus which echoes the metaphorical significance of childhood, 'let the greatest among you become as the youngest' (Luke 22:26)."[59] Francis's suggestion receives support from the text of the Colossian household code itself, which implies a bestowing of honor upon slave members, who would have included slave children. Colossians 3:24 indicates that slaves will receive inheritance (κληρομία; cf. 1:12; Rom. 8:14-17), thus reversing cultural expectations concerning the legal rights of inheritance as belonging only to the freeborn.[60] Moreover, slave and free are listed among the groups united in Christ (Col. 3:11), and the humiliation of the

---

58. See the Roman inscription *Corpus inscriptionum latinarum* 6.22972 dedicated by Publicia Glypte to two little boys, her own son Nico and her house-born slave Eutyches. The fact that both boys are dressed in the garb of well-educated citizens and hold scrolls, with a scroll box between them, indicates Glypte's intention to grant the slave boy his freedom and raise him as a foster brother to her own son. See Rawson, *Children and Childhood in Roman Italy,* pp. 259-61.

59. Francis, "Children and Childhood in the New Testament," p. 82.

60. See Margaret Y. MacDonald, "Slavery, Sexuality and House Churches: A Reassessment of Col 3.18–4.1 in Light of New Research on the Roman Family," *New Testament Studies* 53 (2007): 94-113.

slave trade (Col. 2:14-15), involving triumphal processions of slaves as bounty of war, acts as a powerful image for explaining what God has accomplished through Christ in relation to the "rulers and authorities" who are now the true captives. This must have made a powerful impression on the Colossian audience. We gain some sense of this from the remnants of Rome's monuments, which, especially in the second century, used captive children to great visual effect "as symbols of Rome's power and her enemies' humiliation."[61]

Conclusion

An examination of the teaching on parents and children found in the Colossian and Ephesian household codes in relation to the treatment of household management in other ancient texts has revealed the thoroughly conventional character of the New Testament teaching. In fact, of all the categories of relationships treated in these codes, the parent-child relationship is arguably the most conventional, offering little by way of direct evidence of transformation in the Lord (in contrast, for example, to the teaching on slavery in Colossians or the teaching on marriage in Ephesians). We must assume that the parents who received this instruction valued the education of their children and used methods of discipline (including physical methods) like their Jewish and Gentile contemporaries. At the same time, however, it is worthy of note that the deutero-Pauline authors avoided articulating the call for obedience in the strongest possible terms, resisting setting forth harsh consequences for the disobedience of children. In general, the exhortations of Colossians 3:20-21 and Ephesians 6:1-4 are in keeping with the moderate approaches of certain ancient authors, especially regarding the authority of the male head of the household.

When we keep in mind that the codes are idealizations of family life that must be understood in the context of a far more complex social reality, however, this straightforward picture of mutual but hierarchical relations becomes increasingly complicated. Historians of the Roman family have highlighted the fact that traditional statements of the authority of the *paterfamilias,* such as we find in the household codes, operated in a world that included the informal authority of mothers over their children. Moreover, children were generally cared for by a much wider group than simply their parents and grandparents, extending to nurses, nannies, and tutors, many of whom were slaves. Within early church communities of this period, a child's circle of influence

---

61. Rawson, *Children and Childhood in Roman Italy,* pp. 53-54.

could embrace caregivers who were either believers or nonbelievers, and, in the case of the believing child of a nonbelieving *paterfamilias,* the lines of authority were by no means clear. Although not emphasized by scholars who have tended to view the codes as inter-believing directives, the comments of second-century pagan critics on early Christianity invite us to wonder whether the recruitment and education of children and the rescuing of abandoned and orphaned children may have been related to the apologetic function of the codes.

The overlap between the categories of slave, parent, and child is also a key feature of this complex picture. The language of liberation in Colossians is highly metaphorical and must be treated cautiously, but it invites us to think of slaves and slave children as honored members of the community even though the hierarchical structures of the household are not eradicated. Although it might strike modern interpreters as paternalistic and of little real social consequence, the impact of welcoming slaves into a mixed group united by a common moral standard should not be underestimated. It is certainly not beyond the realm of possibility that the audience of Colossians included slaves and slave families who had been kidnapped or captured in war as well as slaves born into households or adopted as foundlings.[62] In an urban neighborhood, the house church may have offered a place of belonging and safety for children with very uncertain futures. By means of their direct address to children, the household codes of Colossians and Ephesians ensure that all children are acknowledged, have a place, and are welcomed. It is in this capacity that the teaching on the child-parent relationship finds lasting significance.

---

62. Glancy notes that, after the Jewish War, the slave markets of the empire were flooded with captives. Many have dated Colossians to approximately this time period, about the year 70. Glancy notes that Rome's great wars of expansion had slowed down by the first century, "but occasional wars throughout the provinces and at the edges of the Empire meant a continuing, if episodic, supply of captives as slaves" (p. 77). She speculates that at least a small number of these slaves would have been members of the emerging Christian group (p. 78).

PART III

THEMATIC ESSAYS

14   Children and the Image of God

W. Sibley Towner

Child advocates and religious leaders around the world who represent a wide range of faith-based organizations and agencies are actively involved in efforts to address the needs of children today. They work with others in their own religious traditions as well as with a range of secular and not-for-profit organizations to offer assistance to children at risk. They are also interested in the spiritual development of children and how to nurture the spiritual lives and religious identities of children in complex and pluralistic social contexts.

Those whose religious convictions are informed by the Bible often refer to biblical passages that speak of caring for the poor and orphans and loving and serving the neighbor. Another central way they speak about the dignity and value of all children is with the help of the biblical notion that human beings are created in the image of God.

The primary biblical references for the claim that human beings are made in the image of God are found in chapters 1, 5, and 9 of Genesis:

> Then God said, "Let us make humankind in our image, according to our likeness, and let them have dominion over the fish of the sea, and over the birds of the air, and over the cattle, and over all the wild animals of the earth, and over every creeping thing that creeps upon the earth." So God created humankind in his image, in the image of God he created them; male and female he created them. God blessed them, and God said to them, "Be fruitful and multiply, and fill the earth and subdue it; and have dominion

---

A somewhat different version of this essay called "Clones of God: *Genesis* 1:26-28 and the Image of God in the Hebrew Bible" appeared in *Interpretation* 59 (2005): 341-56.

over the fish of the sea and over the birds of the air and over every living thing that moves upon the earth." (Gen. 1:26-28)

When God created humankind, he made them in the likeness of God. Male and female he created them and named them "Humankind" when they were created. (Gen. 5:1b-2)

Whoever sheds the blood of a human, by a human shall that person's blood be shed; for in his own image God made humankind. (Gen. 9:6)[1]

Other biblical texts that are dependent on these primary texts include Wisdom of Solomon 2:23; Sirach 17:3; 1 Corinthians 11:7; 2 Corinthians 3:18; 4:4; Colossians 1:15; 3:10; and James 3:9. Two of these references focus on Jesus as the image of God (2 Cor. 4:4; Col. 1:15). Psalm 8 is often thought to stand in this tradition, speaking of human beings as made "a little lower than God, and crowned . . . with glory and honor" (Ps. 8:5).

Although references to the image of God are prevalent in discussions about the needs of children today, the precise meaning of the biblical term is often unclear. Furthermore, although biblical scholars have explored and examined the term in depth and offered rich interpretations of it, they have rarely directly discussed the term in relationship to children. Theologians and ethicists who build on the work of biblical scholars and the notion of the image of God to articulate contemporary perspectives on human rights or human dignity have also generally neglected to include children.

Thus, the primary aim of this chapter is to offer an introduction to a biblical understanding of the image of God and its application to children, treating them with respect and seeing them as human beings. The first two parts of the chapter outline a range of interpretations of the image of God and some of the difficult exegetical issues that any interpretation of the biblical passages must address. The chapter then considers some of the central elements of the meaning of the image of God and affirms that, from a biblical perspective, children, too, are made in the image of God, thereby underscoring the full humanity and dignity of all children. By outlining a biblically informed view of the image of God, this chapter provides biblical resources for contemporary conversations and consultations on the needs, rights, and responsibilities of children. By examining the notion of the image of God with

---

1. This text links an apparently early law against murder with one of the three *imago dei* passages attributed to the late Priestly source (P). The fact suggests that the "image" concept may have had a history prior to its elevation to fundamental status by P. See J. Maxwell Miller, "In the 'Image' and 'Likeness' of God," *Journal of Biblical Literature* 91 (1972): 289-304.

the "lens" of "the child," this essay also highlights often neglected aspects of biblical understandings of the image of God, revealing its radical breadth. It also helps emphasize the importance of interpreting biblical notions of likeness and image, not only in terms of God-human, adult-adult, or male-female relationships — which is often the case today — but also in terms of the complex and dynamic relationships that are highlighted throughout the Bible between God and children, adults and children, children and children, and parents and children.

Introduction to Some of the Proposals on the Table

The meaning of the image of God has been variously interpreted, and a comprehensive survey of the many proposals regarding the exact meaning of the image of God in human beings is beyond the scope of this essay. However, following the lead of Claus Westermann,[2] I note that a number of larger categories of interpretation of this dramatic concept emerge. Some of these categories overlap. Readers can refer to primary texts and other secondary sources that outline these and other proposals in depth.[3]

Among these proposals are those that interpret the image of God as:

1. consisting primarily in spiritual endowments such as memory, self-awareness, rationality, intelligence, spirituality, even an immortal soul (e.g., Philo, Gregory of Nyssa, Augustine, Thomas Aquinas, Friedrich Schleiermacher);
2. manifested in our ability to make moral decisions, which presupposes free will and a knowledge of good and evil (e.g., G. W. Bromiley, Michael Morrison);
3. also seen in the sometimes denigrated or "base" human emotions, especially love, qualities not shared with animals (Augustine, a view rejected by Gregory of Nyssa[4]);
4. expressed in the unique human capacity for self-transcendence, from which, in turn, beauty and the recognition of beauty emerge (Farley);

---

2. C. Westermann, *Genesis 1–11*, trans. John J. Scullion, S.J. (Minneapolis: Augsburg, 1984), pp. 147-55.

3. A greatly expanded survey of modern proposals is offered in Gunnlaugur A. Jónsson, *The Image of God: Genesis 1:26-28 in a Century of Old Testament Research*, trans. Lorraine Svendsen (Lund: Almqvist & Wiksell International, 1988).

4. J. Pelikan, *Christianity and Classical Culture* (New Haven: Yale University Press, 1993), p. 129.

5. seen in the external appearance of human beings (e.g., Gunkel, Humbert, von Rad, Zimmerli);

6. displayed when the human being serves as God's deputy on earth, an idea often expressed in royal ideology (e.g., Hehn, von Rad, Wildberger, W. H. Schmidt);

7. seen fully in the person of Jesus Christ and interpreted in relationship to other biblical passages, such as Colossians 1:15; cf. 2 Corinthians 4:4;

8. seen primarily as the human being's relationship to God as God's counterpart or partner, the "thou" who is addressed by the divine "I" (e.g., Buber, Brunner, Westermann);

9. signifying "existence in confrontation," and more particularly the "juxtaposition and conjunction" of male and female (e.g., Karl Barth).[5]

This is not an exhaustive list by any means, and the vast range of proposals on the table can be and have been categorized in a number of different ways. For example, Douglas John Hall divides various ways of approaching the meaning of the phrase "image of God" into two broad categories: "substantialist" and "relational" understandings.[6] He claims that substantialists perceive the image of God as embodied in us in some physical, emotional, or spiritual attribute, some substance or endowment, such as physical appearance, rationality, immortality, or freedom. A relational approach, on the other hand, "conceives of the imago as an inclination or proclivity occurring within the relationship."[7] Hall himself supports this relational understanding because, as he notes, all the basic notions of biblical belief (shalom, justice, righteousness, love) are relational ones. And given Hall's broad categories, we could divide the list above into two parts: 1-7 as substantialist and 8-9 as relational, and we could add a number of proposals to each category.

Other contemporary biblical scholars caution that the "image of God" cannot be pinned down to one meaning, whether substantialist or relational.

---

5. See Karl Barth, *Church Dogmatics* III/1, trans. J. W. Edwards, O. Bussey, and H. Knight (Edinburgh: T&T Clark, 1958), p. 195. In his discussion of Genesis 1:26-27 (pp. 191-206), Barth focuses on verse 27 and its parallel in Genesis 5:1-2, asking, "Could anything be more obvious than to conclude from this clear indication that the image and likeness of the being created by God signifies existence in confrontation, i.e., in this confrontation, in the juxtaposition and conjunction of man and man [sic] which is that of male and female?" (p. 195). Barth claims that his ideas are built on those of Dietrich Bonhoeffer. See also Dietrich Bonhoeffer, *Creation and Fall*, trans. John C. Fletcher (London: SCM, 1959), pp. 33-38.

6. Douglas John Hall, *Imaging God: Dominion as Stewardship* (Grand Rapids: Eerdmans, 1986).

7. Hall, *Imaging God*, p. 98.

James Barr, for example, claims that the biblical writers deliberately used the vague and multivalent terms "image" and "likeness" because they meant only to call attention to the God/human likeness not shared by animals, but they had no "definite idea about the content or location of the image of God."[8] In a recent essay, Andreas Schuele describes the *imago dei* as "a *thick* but nevertheless *vague* symbol."[9]

An Inventory of Seven Exegetical Issues
Raised by the Foundational Texts

Interpreting the precise meaning of the image of God is also made more difficult because of a number of complex and highly debated exegetical issues raised by the texts. This section of the chapter gives some examples of these issues and how they are generally addressed by biblical scholars today. For example:

1. *Location of the texts within Genesis 1–11.* The foundational biblical texts on the image of God are found within Genesis 1–11 (Gen. 1:26-28; 5:1b-2; 9:6). Biblical scholars acknowledge two major sections of the book of Genesis: chapters 1–11 (the creation and primeval story) and chapters 12–50 (the ancestral narrative). Furthermore, they often recognize two accounts of creation (Gen. 1:1–2:4a and 2:4b-25) in view of the literary break at Genesis 2:4b when the account is retold in a different style and with a different order of events. Many scholars claim that these two accounts emerged out of different traditions that were passed down orally and then eventually merged into one text in Genesis 1–2: Genesis 1:1–2:4a is often called the Priestly account and 2:4b–2:25 the Yahwistic account.

In the Priestly account, the creation of humankind takes place in the overall order of creation on God's sixth and final working day, after the creation of all other land animals; and it appears that for the Priestly narrators, humankind is God's crowning work. Although other living creatures in this account are, like human beings, blessed and told to "be fruitful and multiply" (Gen. 1:22), no other creature is made in God's image or told to "subdue" the earth and "have dominion over the fish of the sea and over the birds of the air and over every living thing that moves upon the earth" (1:28). Such language is

---

8. James Barr, "The Image of God in the Book of Genesis — A Study of Terminology," *Bulletin of the John Rylands Library* 51 (1968-69): 11-26, esp. p. 13.

9. Andreas Schuele, "Made in the Image of God: The Concepts of Divine Images in Genesis 1–3," *Zeitschrift für die altestamentliche Wissenschaft* 117 (2005): 1-20, esp. p. 7.

unparalleled in the Yahwistic account, but the special role of the human being is evident in texts that lift up the distinctive role of tilling (caring for) the ground (2:5, 15) and naming the animals (2:19-20).

2. *Plural subject*. At the moment prior to the creation of humankind, God says, "Let us make humankind in our image, according to our likeness" (Gen. 1:26a; see also 3:22; 11:7). What does the "us" and the "our" mean in this context? Pre-critical Christian interpreters typically heard a reference to the Holy Trinity in these words. Others have argued that God simply uses a "plural of majesty" here. On the whole, critical scholarship has settled on the notion of the divine council as the best explanation for this unexpected use of the plural by the Creator.[10] The text is speaking to the retinue of divine beings that cluster around God, the heavenly king.[11]

The implication of the latter solution to the plural reference for understanding the meaning of *imago dei* in the Priestly creation account is this: whatever it is in human beings that mirrors God mirrors the divine realm as a whole. Gerhard von Rad put it elegantly: "The extraordinary plural ('Let us') is to prevent one from referring God's image too directly to God the Lord. God includes himself among the heavenly beings of his court and thereby conceals himself in the majority."[12] More recently, Dean McBride has said, "Adamic beings are animate icons; they are empowered by the 'image' and its correlative blessing to be a terrestrial counterpart to God's heavenly entourage."[13]

3. *Adam as a collective or generic concept*. A third issue raised by the Priestly language of Genesis 1:26-28 is the meaning of the Hebrew noun *'adam*, now translated by the NRSV as "humankind."[14] This collective sense inheres in the noun, as the use of the plural imperative in 1:26b ("let them") shows. The noun *'adamah*, "earth," looks like a feminine form of a masculine *'adam*, and indeed, the similarity of these words to one another has led some

10. The evidence is assembled by P. D. Miller, *Genesis 1–11: Studies in Structure and Theme*, Journal for the Study of the Old Testament — Supplement Series 8 (Sheffield: University of Sheffield Press, 1978), pp. 9-18.

11. Even though it may be a pale remnant of earlier polytheism, the heavenly court is by no means suppressed in the Hebrew Bible. See, for example, 1 Kings 22:19-23; Job 1:6–2:6; Psalms 82; 89:6-7; Isaiah 6:1-8; Jeremiah 23:18.

12. G. von Rad, *Genesis*, trans. John H. Marks, Old Testament Library (Philadelphia: Westminster, 1961), p. 57.

13. Dean McBride, "Divine Protocol: Genesis 1:1–2:3 as Prologue to the Pentateuch," in *God Who Creates: Essays in Honor of W. Sibley Towner*, ed. William P. Brown and S. Dean McBride (Grand Rapids: Eerdmans, 2000), p. 16.

14. This is not another instance of NRSV periphrasis intended to eliminate a gender-specific English noun (KJV, RSV: "man").

scholars to translate *'adam* as "earth-creature."[15] Although the term *'adam* itself is sometimes used in the Bible as a proper name of the first man, especially in genealogies (e.g., Gen. 4:25; 5:1-5; 1 Chron. 1:1), the word *'ish* is usually employed when the reference is to a single male individual (see Gen. 2:23, where *'ish* and its feminine form *'ishshah* are explicitly linked together). Although with the definite article *ha'adam* can refer to a single male individual (e.g., 3:8), the definite form can also be construed as collective (even in our key texts, 1:27 and 9:6). The collective sense in Genesis 1:26-28 is conveyed, as noted above, by the plural verb "and let them have dominion," and also by the added remark of verse 27c, namely, "male and female he created them."

4. *Significance of male and female.* Unlike the Yahwist in Genesis 2:18-23, for the Priestly writer both genders exist in this *'adam* from the outset. The collective noun *'adam* denotes the first exemplar of all of us, that is, "humankind." Image of God as male and female reveals the fundamentally relational character of image. Relationality is thus understood to be intrinsic to both God and those made in the divine image.

5. *Semantics of "image" (ṣelem) and "likeness" (demut).* What do the terms "image" and "likeness" precisely mean in the various texts in which they are used, and how are the terms related? The Hebrew word for "image," *ṣelem*, occurs seventeen times in the Old Testament. The usual etymology of the word relates it, among other cognates, to an Arabic verb for "cut off," and, though no verbal stem for the term occurs in biblical Hebrew, the notion of "carving" is maintained in texts in which the term denotes free-standing idols (e.g., 2 Kings 11:18 = 2 Chron. 23:17; perhaps Amos 5:26). The usage broadens to include molten or cast idols in Numbers 33:52 and Ezekiel 7:20 and 16:17, as well as the curative golden replicas of the pesky mice and tumors that the Philistines sent back to Israel along with the purloined ark (1 Sam. 6:5, 11). An "image" can be either three-dimensional or a painted one (Ezek. 23:14). It is instructive that in modern Hebrew, the related noun *ṣillum* is a photograph.

Twice *ṣelem* is used in a sense exactly opposite these examples of very physical representation. In Psalm 39:6, the poet says of the human plight, "Surely everyone goes about like a shadow *(ṣelem)*. Surely for nothing (*hebel* [the opening word of Ecclesiastes]) they are in turmoil." In a similar vein, another psalmist acknowledges to God the fate of the wicked: "They are like a dream when one awakes; on awaking you despise their phantoms *(ṣelem)*" (73:20). So an "image" can be a mere semblance of a person.

All but one of the remaining occurrences of the term in the Hebrew Bible

15. E.g., Phyllis Trible, *God and the Rhetoric of Sexuality* (Philadelphia: Fortress, 1978), pp. 77-87.

are in our key examples, where God and human beings share the "image." Should the evidence from the other uses of *ṣelem* in the Hebrew Bible tilt our understanding toward physical resemblance? Are we dealing with a major anthropomorphism here, where people are like living, walking statues of God sent to speak and act for the king in all corners of the royal dominion? Further support for this view can be gained from the only other use of the term, in Genesis 5:3, where physical family resemblance is clearly in view: "When Adam had lived one hundred thirty years, he became the father of a son in his likeness *(demut)*, according to his image *(ṣelem)*, and named him Seth." Or should we infer from the two uses in the Psalter that the *imago dei* is not a physical thing at all, but some other kind of semblance? Or as great writers and theologians are wont to do, has the Priestly writer simply dared to recast a familiar term into a very new shape? Or is it possible at all to discern exactly what this writer had in mind when he used the term *ṣelem*?

The semantic issues of Genesis 1:26 also include the word that is set there in parallel to "image," namely, "likeness" *(demut)*. This term occurs some twenty-one times in the Hebrew Bible as a noun, and it has another five adverbial uses. It is derived from a fairly common Hebrew verbal root, also well attested in other Semitic languages, meaning "resemble, liken." It is a somewhat more abstract term than *ṣelem* and can refer to similarities other than visual ones (e.g., Isa. 13:4a).[16] Nearly half of the nominal occurrences are found in Ezekiel's inaugural vision, wherein the prophet avoids saying that he saw God and the heavenly court by using such circumlocutions as "the appearance of the likeness *(demut)* of the glory of the Lord" (Ezek. 1:28). In Daniel 10:16, the prophet reports that "one in human form *(demut)* touched my lips," by which he means an angel (apparently Gabriel). These usages seem to imply a reflection or projection of a reality, more than the reality itself. But the resemblance can be very revealing of the prototype, as, once again, Genesis 5:3 demonstrates when it says that Seth was in the "likeness *(demut)*, according to [the] image *(ṣelem)*" of his father, Adam.

In only two of our three key examples, Genesis 1:26 and 5:1, are "image" and "likeness" set in parallel to each other. Remembering that these texts tie together theology and anthropology, the divine and the human realms, we may be drawn from the physicality implied in "graven image" in the direction of resemblance, as in a face in a mirror or a photograph. For those who have eyes to see, something about human beings, including their children, is reminiscent of God and the heavenly beings! The psalmist saw it and exclaimed, "You have made them a little lower than God [or: the divine beings]" (Ps.

---

16. J. M. Miller, "In the 'Image' and 'Likeness' of God," p. 293.

8:5).[17] The audacity of the claim is underscored by Isaiah of the Exile, who sweeps away all human attempts to compare the incomparable Creator God to any images of our own making: "To whom then will you liken God, or what likeness *(demut)* compare with him?" (Isa. 40:18).[18] On the contrary, reply the Priestly writers, decades later, in Genesis 1:26-28. According to them, there is one likeness after all, and it still inheres in the little child, the President of the United States, Great-aunt Millie, you and me, and billions of other exemplars, living and dead, of the creature called *'adam*.

6. *Connection with "dominion" in Genesis 1:26b.* Syntax, too, raises an issue in our key verses. Following God's injunction to the divine council to create *'adam* in the divine image, God uses a forceful third-person imperative (jussive) to define the role of the newly created *'adam:* "and let them have dominion" over the newly created fauna of the earth. The etymology of the Hebrew word *radah*, "to have dominion," has been much discussed, its parallel with *kabash*, "to subdue" the earth, in 1:28 canvassed, and the sense both words have in other texts of trampling, enslavement, and harsh rule by the powerful over the weak (e.g., *radah* in Ezek. 34:4; see also *kabash* in Jer. 34:11, 16; Zech. 9:15) explored. Clearly it means that God is conferring a kingly status upon *'adam* and invites humankind to rule over the rest of the living creatures as God's viceroy. "God is a power-sharing, not a power-hoarding God."[19] But in what manner is *'adam* going to rule over all the living things that God made and pronounced "good" (Gen. 1:25b)? When the other creatures look upon *'adam* as a royal or even god-like figure, what will they see? A tyrant, an exterminator, a satanic figure? Or will they experience the ruling hand of *'adam* as something as tender and gentle as that of their Creator?

This is where syntax comes into play. For a number of years now, critical scholarship has been in general agreement that the "dominion" that God assigns to the first tiny human community over all the creatures of land, sea, and air flows from the "image" of God that God places within *'adam* alone of all the creatures. This flow is best seen if the conjunction *waw* that introduces the clause "and let them have dominion" is construed not as the coordinating conjunction "and" but as a subordinating conjunction, "so that." The Hebrew vocalization would support this proposal. The result would be a purpose

---

17. Note, however, that Psalm 8, reflective as it is of Genesis 1:26-30, never uses terms like "image" or "likeness," but leans more toward "honor" and "glory." See Barr, "The Image of God in the Book of Genesis," p. 12.

18. For a contrary view, see Frederick Gaiser, "To Whom Will You Compare Me?" *Word and World* 19 (1999): 141-52.

19. Terence E. Fretheim, "Creator, Creature, and Co-Creation in Genesis 1–2," *Word and World*, Supplement Series 1 (1992): 11-20, esp. p. 15.

clause that could be translated: "Let us make 'adam in our image, according to our likeness, so that they may have dominion. . . ." Although the NRSV reading implies it, too, this reading would make very clear the source of the "dominion" or hegemony with which God commissions humankind. They are to exercise their kingly rule within the ecosphere in God's manner, the way God would do it. That means treating the creation with tenderness and appreciation for its intrinsic goodness and beauty. (Incidentally, such a meaning coheres nicely with the natural curiosity about and admiration of other creatures that are exhibited by children.)[20]

Although biblical commentators and theologians disagree about the precise relationship between human beings and other living creatures that is suggested in these and other biblical passages, and although they define this relationship in various ways (such as the "primacy" of human beings, their "hierarchy" over other creatures, their "stewardship" over them, or the "equality in value" of all living creatures), they generally agree that the texts clearly reject human exploitation of or tyrannical rule over other living creatures and affirm human solidarity with and nurturing care of them.

7. *Sexuality.* A final issue raised by the key texts themselves is the relationship of human sexuality to the image of God in us. Does the Priestly notice that God created 'adam in the binary form of male and female (Gen. 1:27; 5:3) imply that God has a sexual nature and that sexuality itself discloses the divine image? The text is not explicit about this. On the one hand, sexuality here can be seen as conferred on humankind as a separate blessing (1:28 and 9:7), as a kind of separate implementing action necessary to answer the imperative to "have dominion."[21] There have to be children, generation after generation! Genesis 5:1-3 underscores this understanding; there, the binary nature of the 'adam created in the "likeness" of God is reiterated, but the transmission of the "image" of Adam to Seth occurs as a separate event of sexual generation. On the other hand, it may be said that the gendered nature of humankind is revealing of the nature and activity of God (e.g., both paternal and maternal imagery is used to speak of God, especially in Isaiah 40–66). In either case, "image" is manifested in the very plurality and consequent fellowship of male and female.

20. For a discussion that questions the use of kingly language for speaking of the image of God, see T. Fretheim, *God and World in the Old Testament: A Relational Theology of Creation* (Nashville: Abingdon, 2005), pp. 46-56.

21. See Phyllis A. Bird, "'Male and Female He Created Them': Gen. 1:27b in the Context of the Priestly Account of Creation," *Harvard Theological Review* 74 (1981): 129-59. Bird warns against splitting off the command or blessing of biological reproduction in Genesis 1:28 from the other aspects of image in verses 26-27. The image of God is manifested in men and women enlarging their sphere of "dominion" as they multiply over the face of the earth.

The Meaning of *Imago Dei*

Now that we have laid these proposals and issues on the table and have recognized the complexity of the biblical texts on the image of God and the long and varied history of the interpretation of these passages, what can we say about the meaning of the image of God and how it might apply to children and childhood?

Much in line with Hall's proposal and other contemporary biblical scholars, I believe that the image of God must be interpreted primarily in relational terms.[22] In general, Genesis 1:26-28 and its echoes in 5:1-2 and 9:6 point human relationships in three directions.[23]

First, of course, human beings are related to their creator, God, who placed the divine image in them. From a biblical perspective, this relationship is expressed in worship and in obedience to the covenant will of God for human beings.

Second, human beings relate to each other, beginning with the simple fellowship of male and female. They express this relationship in love and loyalty, and often do so sexually, with the result that the bonds of love and loyalty are extended to children, too.[24] Other primary forms of human relationship expressed in Genesis and throughout the Bible involve children and adults in extended familial relationships of parents, grandparents, aunts, uncles, children, and grandchildren. The signal importance of parent-child relationships begins as early as the tragic story of Cain and Abel in Genesis 3, reaches a peak of intensity in the father-son story of the near-sacrifice of Isaac in Genesis 22:1-19, and inheres in the tender care for children by the extended family in such texts as Genesis 31:55 (Laban's farewell) and Genesis 49 (Jacob's final blessing of his sons) and in lovely wisdom sayings like this one: "Grandchildren are the crown of the aged" (Prov. 17:6).[25]

Third, human beings find themselves in relationship with the animals, the plants, and the rest of the created order. The text calls this relationship "do-

---

22. See also the discussions regarding the centrality of relational understandings in J. Richard Middleton, *The Liberating Image: The* Imago Dei *in Genesis 1* (Grand Rapids: Brazos, 2005); and Fretheim, *God and World in the Old Testament*, pp. 13-22, 46-56.

23. I owe insight on this triangle of relationships to Alan G. Padgett, "The Image of God in Scripture" (videotaped lecture on Gen. 1:26 and 1 Cor. 11:7-16 given at Azusa Pacific University, 1993).

24. See Benedict M. Guevin, *Christian Anthropology and Sexual Ethics* (Lanham, MD: University Press of America, 2002).

25. Indeed, much of the Hebrew wisdom tradition is couched as instruction of children within the family.

minion," and, as we have seen, dominion should be understood as a just and nurturing rule done on God's behalf.[26] Genesis 1–11 emphasizes the goodness of creation, and other biblical passages give tender and wonderful glimpses of God's own care for the world, from which human beings can extrapolate their own best behaviors toward our fellow creatures (see, for example, Prov. 30:24-28; Job 38–41; Ps. 104). These and other biblical passages help to clarify the nature of the relationship of human beings with other creatures. The task of human beings is to enact God's image and to announce to the natural orders of the world, to the water and the air and the wild things, "We bring a new respect to our relationship with you. We seek with you a genuine encounter." We owe the creatures an outpouring of charity, providential in the sense that it knows no bounds and is unwilling to stop until it includes all of creation. We seek the long-term discipline of stewardship, which learns how to do things right so that our skills really enhance life around us.

Though the literal terminology of the Priestly account in Genesis ("image" and "likeness" of God) is used nowhere else in the Hebrew Bible, the view that all human beings are made in the image of God and are defined by these three primary relationships permeates the entire Old Testament. The praise of God in the Psalms, the codification and acceptance of the covenant in the Pentateuch, and the expressions of human love and love for the created order in the wisdom writings and elsewhere all invite the reader of Scripture to consider how the inspired writers of the Hebrew canon reflected back to God the divine image in their narratives, laws, and poems.

Biblical scholar J. Richard Middleton helpfully points out the radical and "democratizing" nature of this notion of the image of God in the ancient world. In his book *The Liberating Image: The* Imago Dei *in Genesis 1,* he discusses notions of sacral kingship in other ancient Near Eastern cultures. In such cultures, only kings and related elites were living images of the high god. Israel "democratized" and generalized the *imago dei* concept to the point that all human beings bore it and bore the consequent responsibility of exercising rule over the earth as kings would do. As Middleton puts it, "All persons have equal access to God simply by being human. . . . Humans are the only *legitimate* or *authorized* earthly representations of God."[27]

Middleton concludes with a final chapter called "Imaging God's Primal Generosity." He argues that rejections of social stratification, self-aggrandizement

26. William P. Brown discusses the "biblical work ethic," its relationship to *imago dei,* and its implications for understanding Qoheleth's unique discovery of joy in the midst of toil in his essay, "'Whatever Your Hand Finds to Do': Qoheleth's Work Ethic," *Interpretation* 55 (2001): 271-84.

27. Middleton, *The Liberating Image,* p. 207.

through the abuse of power, even violence itself (which is given ontological status in other cultures by the cosmogonic myth of the gods making war on the enemy, chaos, in the very process of creation) all flow from this belief in a universal *imago dei*. Understanding the *imago dei* this way leads to "an ethic characterized fundamentally by power with rather than power over."[28]

Middleton's points are especially important as we turn directly to children. Before we do, however, I would like to add two qualifications that we must also keep in mind regarding the image of God. These I have discussed in more detail and along with other qualifications elsewhere.[29] First, *although human beings are made in God's image, they remain distinct from God.* Although human beings are made in God's image, the distinction between God and humankind should not be minimized or erased. Human beings are blessed with a capacity to relate to God, neighbor, and world; indeed, we are invited into fellowship with God and commissioned by God to do godly work in the world. That work flows from the *imago dei* in us. God's image enables the relationship, as Genesis understands it. However, it is in the nature of relationship that it be reciprocal, that there be two or more freestanding parties, able and willing to enter into the relationship or free to say no to it, as well. That truth may be only implicit in Genesis 1:26-28, but the free give-and-take between God and humankind throughout the narrative, historical, and prophetic books of the Bible demonstrates that the relationship is between two separate and free parties. We are neither gods, nor participants in the heavenly council, nor embodiments of the great Absolute. We are God's friends and partners, creatures made by God out of earth and spirit (Gen. 2:7), and given awesome responsibility in relationship to other living creatures.

Second, *although the image of God in human beings can be obscured or distorted, it cannot be smashed or erased.* Since early times, many Christian theologians have taken the "fall" recounted in Genesis 3 to be the story of the smashing of the mirror, the irreparable loss of the "image of God" within us. The notion that the image of God can be erased or defaced is expressed in a number of Protestant statements of faith. The Scots Confession of 1560, for example, makes this loss explicit when it says that through "original sin, the image of God was utterly defaced in man, and he and his children became by nature hostile to God, slaves of Satan, and servants to sin."[30]

---

28. Middleton, *The Liberating Image*, p. 297.

29. See Towner, "Clones of God: *Genesis* 1:26-28 and the Image of God in the Hebrew Bible," *Interpretation* 59 (2005): 341-56.

30. "The Scots Confession," ch. 3. Actually, this view differs very little from that expressed in

The problem with these antithetical juxtapositions of Genesis 3 with Genesis 1 is that nothing in either Genesis text suggests that a basic change in human nature, a new anthropology, as it were, could or did occur in the Garden. Assuming that Genesis 3 is from the hand of the Yahwist and is therefore much earlier than the Priestly first chapter of Genesis, the position is even more dramatic. Even after centuries of additional theological reflection, the inspired Priestly writers of Genesis 1:26-28 could celebrate more clearly than ever the inalienability of the divine gift of image to humankind. Indeed, they reiterate the language of "image of God" in post-"fall" narratives (i.e., Gen. 5:1b-2; 9:6). Sin and rage, human frailty and perverseness can obscure or distort the capacity — indeed, the inborn need — for relationships with God, people, and the world around us. That cannot be doubted. But human nature, shaped in the divine image, remains constant. That is the biblical witness. If "image" is an innate propensity toward relationship, that capacity would, in the Priestly view, presumably always be present from childhood to maturity as a fundamental element of biblical anthropology.

In an elegantly written essay on "The Self in the Psalms and the Image of God," James L. Mays notes that Genesis 3 posits a second "likeness" between God and humankind, one that we might describe as the shadow side of the *imago dei* of Genesis 1:26-28. After Adam and Eve have completed their primal rebellion in the garden, Yahweh says, "Behold, the human being has become like one of us, knowing good and evil" (Gen. 3:22). Expulsion from paradise follows. "[This] self-centered enterprise to take possession of life is a radical disconnection with the original likeness."[31] From it flow the alienations between peoples, siblings, and parents and children that form the warp and woof of the Genesis narratives. Mays applies these two "likenesses" manifest in human beings to explain the "deafening" dissonance between Psalm 8, which he takes to be a poetic version of Genesis 1:26-28 and which ranks humanity "a little lower than God" (Ps. 8:5), and the anguished prayers of individual lament that surround it in the Psalter. In my opinion, these two "likenesses," one God-given and the other self-imposed, sum up two sides of the human experience. The former assures us of our intrinsic worth; the latter acknowledges that we do not grow from childish innocence to autonomous adulthood without sinning.

And grow we will. The *imago dei* is displayed in individuals and commu-

---

the 1546 "Decree Concerning Original Sin" of the Roman Catholic counter-reformation Council of Trent.

31. In *God and Human Dignity*, ed. R. Kendall Soulen and Linda Woodhead (Grand Rapids: Eerdmans, 2006), pp. 27-43, at 38.

nities differently as maturation, experience, or character-building take place. The sages of Israel understood this, too, when they summoned their pupils to the discipline of their elders and obedience to God's Torah: "Fools despise wisdom and instruction" (Prov. 1:7b). Accepting correction and teaching does not mean settling for static personhood. On the contrary, because God is a living God, and "we are made in God's image, we are not 'making ourselves up' as we go along."[32] It would be better to say that we continually draw upon that proclivity which, according to Genesis, inalienably exists in human nature, and that we enact it — less than perfectly to be sure, except by the man from Nazareth — in varying degrees of fullness.

Children as Human Beings Who Are Created in the Image of God

Middleton and other biblical commentators do not directly discuss the subject of children and the image of God, and nowhere does the Hebrew Bible say explicitly that children are made in the image of God. In fact, the word "image" alone is applied to a child only once, namely in Genesis 5:3, where it is noted that Seth was in the image and likeness of his father, Adam.

Nevertheless, taking into account some of the central elements of a biblical understanding of the image of God, and taking seriously Middleton's point about the radical universality of this term, we must affirm that the image of God also applies to children. Full humanity presupposes the inherent divine image, and no child or any other human being is excluded.[33]

This application of the image of God to refer to children is affirmed by other biblical texts. For example, from the very beginning of the Hebrew Bible, children are regarded as a blessing. The sexual relationship that leads to the birth of children enjoys a special divine blessing in the first *imago dei* passage: "Be fruitful and multiply" (Gen. 1:28). The history of Israel is inaugurated when childless Abram is promised descendants as numerous as the stars (Gen. 15:1-21). The psalmist revels in the multiplication of progeny:

32. Ellen Davis, *Getting Involved with God: Rediscovering the Old Testament* (Boston: Cowley, 2001), p. 100.

33. This essay does not address the issue of the *imago dei* in fetuses and the related issue of abortion, because the biblical writers do not speak of these matters. For discussions of abortion in antiquity, see, *inter alia*, Andreas Lindemann, "'Do Not Let a Woman Destroy the Unborn Babe in Her Belly': Abortion in Ancient Judaism and Christianity," *Studia theologica* 49 (1995): 253-71; and O. M. Bakke, *When Children Became People: The Birth of Childhood in Early Christianity* (Minneapolis: Fortress, 2005).

Like arrows in the hand of a warrior
are the sons of one's youth.
Happy is the man who has his quiver full of them.

(Ps. 127:4-5)

Other biblical texts point out the intimate relationship of God and human beings from the beginnings of their lives. For example, in the view of the psalmists there is never a time in the conception and birth of children when the hand of God is not present.

For it was you who formed my inward parts;
you knit me together in my mother's womb.
I praise you, for I am fearfully and wonderfully made. . . .
Your eyes beheld my unformed substance.
In your book were written all the days that were formed for me,
when none of them as yet existed.

(Ps. 139:13-14, 16)

Conception and birth inaugurate destiny for a child who bears the image of God within. That destiny is drawn out in the Fifth Commandment, "Honor your father and your mother, so that your days may be long in the land that the Lord your God is giving you" (Exod. 20:12). Long, full tenure in the land is, generally speaking, secured by honorable behavior and by a way of life that is passed from elders to their offspring. Parents recite the narrative of God's providential care for the covenant people (e.g., Exod. 12:26-27; 13:8-16; Deut. 4:9-12). As learning occurs, children gradually take upon themselves the joys and the burdens of the *imago dei.* That image, however, is there from the beginning.

The social, ethical, and religious implications for the treatment of children that follow from an understanding that children, too, are made in the image of God are tremendous. For example, the inherent image of a generous, loving God lays the groundwork for the schooling of children in nonviolence, in caring relationships with other creatures, and in acceptance from God of a share in the creative process.[34] Such perspectives take Middleton's

---

34. Another article that draws out the implications of Genesis 1:26-28 for children is by Douglas McConnell, "God Creates Every Unique Person as a Child with Dignity," in *Understanding God's Heart for Children: Toward a Biblical Framework,* ed. Douglas McConnell, Jennifer Orona, and Paul Stockely (Colorado Springs: Authentic Pub., 2007), pp. 13-22. The "interdependency" that characterizes all human relationships applies to the created order as well: "The health and well-being of humans is inextricably linked to the health and well-being of the earth" (p. 21). Children, living in a community that nurtures the idea of stewardship, can readily understand and accept that.

claims seriously and agree that a proper understanding of the image of God leads to "an ethic characterized fundamentally by power with rather than power over."[35]

Conclusion

Genesis 1:26-28 and related biblical texts affirm that human beings — regardless of gender, race, social status, or nation — bear within them the image of God from infancy through old age. Further, they affirm that from a right relationship with God flows nurturing "dominion" in the world. Human beings are neither mini-gods nor "miserable offenders," wholly incapable of good. From childhood onward, they are God's creatures and chosen partners in the work of the creation. They are given ever greater opportunity to be bearers of the divine image, that is, to follow the path of wisdom and to live in obedience to Torah in their relationships to God, one another, and the rest of the world.

---

35. Middleton, *The Liberating Image,* p. 297.

15 Child Characters in Biblical Narratives: The Young David (1 Samuel 16–17) and the Little Israelite Servant Girl (2 Kings 5:1-19)

Esther M. Menn

Children and adolescents figure prominently as characters in a surprising number of biblical narratives. Some of these young characters have names, are well known, and play central roles. David defeats Goliath. Joseph has a splendid embroidered coat. Rebekah dares to leave her family. Samuel is called to be a prophet. Other young characters are named but play seemingly minor roles in the story. Moses' sister Miriam finds the nursemaid for her brother. Jacob's youngest son Benjamin never says a word. Still others are not named at all and are dwarfed by adults who are named, and yet these young people also play a role in the story. A servant girl seeks healing for Naaman, the commander of the Syrian army. The Shunammite's son returns to life through the prayerful healing of Elisha. Jephthah's daughter consents to be sacrificed to fulfill her father's vow. A boy shares his meal when Jesus speaks to a hungry crowd.

Although the Bible includes many examples of child characters of various ages, from the very young to teenagers, they are rarely the focus of biblical interpretation. Minor characters are sometimes overlooked. Major characters might be treated, but their particular roles in events or stories are rarely examined in depth. The tales of the young David, for example, are well known but often regarded as a prelude to the "real" story of his actions as an adult king. As a result, some of the child characters in the Bible are ignored in biblical scholarship and highlighted primarily in children's Bibles. Perhaps because they are small, child characters are easy to dismiss or to stereotype as simple, innocent, and insignificant.

This chapter closely examines two of the many child characters found in the Bible: the young David (1 Samuel 16–17) and the little servant girl of the wife of Naaman, the commander of the Syrian army (2 Kings 5:1-19). The stories of the young David are well known, and he is a central character in these particular chapters of Samuel. David is also remembered as the greatest of all Israelite kings in the Bible, and he is a prominent figure in many other biblical passages and in Israelite history. Unlike David, the servant girl is a minor character. She is not featured prominently in the narrative. So small is her role in the story that she is given no name, and she never reappears as an adult later in the narrative of Israel's history.

Although the stories and characters are very different, a close examination of these texts finds that both characters play important and even similar roles in the narratives. Both stories depict young people finding solutions to problems, intervening when adults are threatened and ineffectual, offering theological insights into God's ways, and acting within the context of international conflict and tensions between cultures and national identities. The essay also illustrates that these and other complex and surprising roles can be found in other biblical stories about children and adolescents as well.

By examining just two of the many possible examples of child characters in biblical narratives, the essay illustrates how focusing closely on the roles of children, broadly defined as those not yet attaining full adult status, helps to uncover often neglected aspects of particular texts. The lens of the child enables readers to see familiar stories and characters in fresh ways and to recognize the amazing range and depth of young characters and their essential contributions. Their agency, insight, and presence determine the course and outcome of many stories, whether they dominate the front stage of the narrative or appear briefly and remain for the most part behind the scenes. Their speech often articulates the central themes of the narrative and provides a theological witness otherwise absent in the story. Children emerge as leaders, protagonists, and witnesses in the Bible perhaps not in spite of their youth but because of it. Close attention to child characters in the Bible also serves to challenge some of our own contemporary conceptions about the vulnerabilities and strengths of children and about what it means to be a child.

The Young David

Although the activities of David as king are highly significant in Israelite history, some of the most memorable events in his life's story occur before he has come to power, when he is still a youth. On one level, David's childhood narratives serve as an introduction to the adult king's life and work. They are much more than that, however, since these narratives portray a young person's ability to affect everything from the dynamics of his family to the outcome of international power relations. They show that the qualities, actions, and words of a child make a big difference in the course of human events. In the narratives about his early life, David exhibits the personality, intelligence, and initiative that he later shows as king of Israel.

Passages about David's childhood and youth are found in 1 Samuel 16–17. There are three introductions to David's life in these chapters, two of which clearly present David as a youth. These include the story of David's anointing by Samuel (1 Sam. 16:1-13) and his victory over the Philistine champion Goliath (1 Sam. 17:1-58). These narratives highlighting David's early identity as a king and as a warrior, respectively, are secondary to the main body of narratives that follows in 1 and 2 Samuel. Sandwiched between these stories is a third introduction (1 Sam. 16:14-23), which relates how David came to the royal court as a skilled musician to soothe Saul in his manic moods. This narrative portrays a somewhat older hero, who is already an accomplished young man, "skillful in playing [the lyre], a man of valor, a warrior, prudent in speech, and a man of good presence; and the LORD is with him" (1 Sam. 16:18).[1]

Since this essay focuses on child characters in biblical narratives, it will concentrate on the two introductory stories about David as a youth (1 Sam. 16:1-13 and 17:1-58). These narratives deserve to be taken seriously, even though they are clearly later traditions that have been edited together with little attempt at harmonization.[2] The introduction of David as a young musician (1 Sam. 16:14-23), by contrast, fits with the theme of the conflict between David and Saul for the kingship that is featured in the remainder of 1 Samuel and therefore appears to be from an early stratum of David narratives. The motif of David as musician appears elsewhere in the Bible (Amos 6:5), and David's connection with the Psalms has long been celebrated.[3]

---

1. Biblical quotes are taken from the NRSV, although at times the author offers alternative translations of specific words to highlight particular points.

2. The secondary character of David's secret anointing at Bethlehem (1 Sam. 16:1-13) is suggested by the fact that this scene is never mentioned again in the David narratives, in which this king is publicly anointed at Hebron by the tribe of Judah in 2 Sam. 2:1-4 and by the northern tribes of Israel in 2 Sam. 5:1-3. Saul continues to be called "the LORD's anointed" in the stories of his conflict with David in the remainder of 2 Samuel (for example, in 1 Sam. 24:6). The introduction to Jesse and his eight sons in 1 Sam. 17:12-16 is redundant, following the earlier story of David's anointing in 1 Sam. 16:1-13, indicating that the story of David and Goliath stood independently at some point. See Ralph W. Klein, *1 Samuel*, Word Biblical Commentary, 10 (Waco, TX: Word Books, 1985), pp. 157-62, 168-89; and Kyle P. McCarter, *II Samuel*, Anchor Bible (Garden City, NY: Doubleday, 1984), pp. 273-78, 279-309.

3. See Allen Cooper, "The Life and Times of King David according to the Book of Psalms," in *The Poet and the Historian: Essays in Literary and Historical Biblical Criticism*, ed. R. E. Friedman (Chico, CA: Scholars Press, 1983), pp. 117-31; James L. Mays, "The David of the Psalms," *In-

Israel's folk memory apparently could not rest content with a single introduction emphasizing David's ability as musician, important as that quality was for the traditional author of the Psalms. Nor was the lack of a childhood for the archetypal king tolerable. Portraits of David's youthful rise to royalty and fame in battle emerged, much in the same way that the early church produced secondary vignettes from the boyhood of Jesus.[4] Childhood seems to be an indispensable stage of life for pivotal characters in religious history.[5]

As an aside, it is curious to note the lack of a birth narrative associated with David, even though in the Bible the lives of many great male protagonists are introduced by such stories. One thinks of the birth narratives of Ishmael, Isaac, Jacob, Samson, Samuel, and Solomon in the Hebrew Scriptures, and of John the Baptist and Jesus in the New Testament. At one time Israel's first king, Saul, may have had a birth narrative. In the pro-David material preserved in the Bible, however, it has been incorporated into the birth narrative of the prophet Samuel, who anointed both Saul and David. Evidence for this conclusion may be seen in the repeated play on the name "Saul" *(šā'ûl)* from the Hebrew word "to ask" or "to lend" in Hannah's explanation that she has "asked him" *(šě'iltîw)* from the LORD (1 Sam. 1:20; cf. 1:17) and "lent him" (Hebrew, *hiš'iltihû)* to the LORD, so that he is "lent" (Hebrew, *šā'ûl)* to the LORD (1:28).

There is a birth narrative involving foreign ethnic identity, bold female initiative, and incest that serves as the story of Davidic origins in the Bible. This story, set at a safe remove from David himself in the ancestral period, depicts the interactions of the royal ancestress Tamar and her father-in-law Judah, leading to the birth of twins (Genesis 38). In this narrative, David's ancestor Perez bursts forth as the surprising firstborn son, symbolizing David's unexpected eruption on the scene of Israelite history.[6]

---

terpretation 40 (1986): 143-55; and Esther M. Menn, "Sweet Singer of Israel: David and the Psalms in Early Judaism," in *Psalms in Community: Jewish and Christian Textual, Liturgical, and Artistic Traditions,* ed. Harold W. Attridge and Margot E. Fassler (Atlanta: Society of Biblical Literature, 2003), pp. 61-74.

4. For examples, see Luke 2:40-52, which depicts Jesus wisely conversing with the teachers in the temple, and the *Infancy Gospel of Thomas,* which portrays the miracles that he worked as a child.

5. See, for example, stories depicting scenes from the childhoods of Jacob and Esau, Joseph and his brothers, Moses, and Samuel. An exception to this general rule is the figure of Abraham, who first appears as an adult in Genesis 12.

6. Esther Marie Menn, *Judah and Tamar (Genesis 38) in Ancient Jewish Exegesis: Studies in Literary Form and Hermeneutics* (Leiden: Brill, 1997), pp. 82-105.

Anointed by Samuel

The first introduction to David involves the prophet Samuel's anointing of a new king of Israel (1 Sam. 16:1-13). Immediately before this episode, God has rejected Saul as king of Israel because he disobeyed the divine commandment to put all of the Amalekites and their animals to the sword in accordance with the practice of the ban, or holy war. Saul spared King Agag, as well as some of the best animals for sacrifice. The prophet Samuel announces to Saul that because he did not obey, "The LORD has torn the kingdom of Israel from you this very day, and has given it to a neighbor of yours, who is better than you" (15:28). The neighbor who is better than Saul turns out also to be much younger. He is the young David.

The story of David's replacement of Saul begins with God's commission of Samuel to go to Bethlehem to anoint one of Jesse's sons as king over Israel. After seven of Jesse's sons are rejected in turn, their youngest brother, David, is brought in from tending his father's flocks. At God's prompting, Samuel anoints David king, and immediately the spirit of God comes upon him as a sign that he has been empowered as God's royal servant.

From Absent to Chosen

David's role in the scene of his anointing is especially remarkable in that he remains absent for most of the narrative. He appears in person only after being called in the concluding verses (1 Sam. 16:11-13). Jesse's missing son is first mentioned in his father's explanation of his absence, immediately before he is summoned: "There remains yet the youngest, but he is keeping the sheep" (v. 11). As the smallest of eight brothers in this version of the story (vv. 10-11; cf. 17:12; but one of seven brothers in 1 Chron. 2:13-15), David is of little account. He is not included among Jesse's sons as Samuel calls the family together, sanctifies them, and partakes with them of the festival sacrifice as the context for the anointing ritual (1 Sam. 16:5). David is still absent when Jesse makes each of his older sons pass by Samuel, only to have them disqualified from the throne one by one (vv. 6-10).

On one level, the young David exemplifies the exclusion of children from important events in the life of the family, community, and nation. So completely ordinary is the smallest child's absence that it is not initially noted by the narrator nor by any other character. Jesse has a respectable family representation at the sacrifice without his youngest son, and his oldest son, Eliab, seems worthy of the throne in the prophet Samuel's estimation: "Surely the LORD's anointed is now before the LORD" (1 Sam. 16:6).

On another level, however, the story also emphasizes that God marks the absence of the youngest son and sees beyond outward appearance and stature. According to the text, God looks at the heart and certainly not at the tall stature of the eldest son:

> But the LORD said to Samuel, "Do not look on his appearance or on the height of his stature, because I have rejected him [David's brother Eliab]; for the LORD does not see as mortals see; they look on the outward appearance, but the LORD looks on the heart." (1 Sam. 16:7)

In the end, all of David's older brothers are passed over, and the "handsome" latecomer with "ruddy" cheeks and "beautiful eyes" is chosen to be anointed within this family circle (v. 12).

A Little Child Shall Lead Them

Samuel is instructed by God to rise in the presence of this boy who arrives from the pasture (1 Sam. 16:12). Similarly, in the previous verse, when Samuel learns that there still remains the youngest son, he informs those assembled for the sacrifice that they will not sit down to eat until he comes (v. 11). Refraining from sitting and rising to one's feet are both unusual actions to take on behalf of a child. With his erect posture, the venerated judge and prophet honors the divine choice of Jesse's youngest son as the anointed one, as the messiah designated to lead Israel. David does not have any of the expected qualifications or political experience that would mark him as a choice for kingship by human standards. It is his heart and the LORD's anointing that make this youth a king.

Upon being anointed by Samuel, David becomes the sudden recipient of the LORD's spirit: "Then Samuel took the horn of oil, and anointed him in the presence of his brothers; and the spirit of the LORD came mightily upon David from that day forward" (1 Sam. 16:13). The child does not need to be instructed into a mature faith nor mentored until he qualifies to lead. From the moment of his anointing David becomes the inspired servant of God. Young David's gift of the spirit contrasts with the situation of the old King Saul, from whom the spirit of God departs, to be replaced by an "evil spirit" that afflicts him (v. 14).[7]

In this account of David and in other biblical stories, we see a child desig-

---

7. The theme of God's spirit coming upon David and departing from Saul provides a link between this first introduction to David in the story of his anointing and the second introduction that follows (1 Sam. 16:14-23). Reading the material synchronically, the newly anointed and spirit-filled David is able to calm the old king, who is deprived of God's spirit and plagued by an evil spirit that has replaced it.

nated for leadership early in life. Here, the young David emerges as the unexpected leader of a whole people. Other famous kings in Israel were also slated for leadership early in life. For example, Solomon, who is best known for his wisdom, was given the throne name "Jedidiah" ("Beloved of Yah") shortly after his birth, since "the LORD loved him" (2 Sam. 12:24-25). King Josiah, who went on to lead a major religious reform, was only eight years old when he began to rule in Jerusalem (2 Kings 22:1-2). The boy Joash or Jehoash alone preserved the Davidic lineage when all the other heirs to the throne were killed by Queen Athaliah, the daughter of Ahab from the northern Omride Dynasty (2 Kings 11:1–12:21). Supported by the high priest Johoiada, Joash assumed the throne when he was only seven years old and enjoyed a long reign that included a religious reform.

Ascendancy of the Youngest Son

Another pattern seen in the story of David's anointing by Samuel and in other biblical stories, as well as in folk narratives of many cultures, is the unexpected ascendancy of the youngest son. It is Isaac rather than his older half-brother Ishmael who remains the focus of the Abrahamic covenant (Gen. 17:18), just as in the next generation it is Jacob rather than his older twin brother Esau (Gen. 25:19-34; 27:1-40). Jacob's son of his old age, Joseph, sees his childhood dreams fulfilled when his older brothers bow down to him in Egypt (Gen. 42:6-9; cf. 37:5-10). Moses is Aaron's younger brother (Exod. 6:20-25), and yet it is he and not his priestly brother who leads the Israelites out of slavery in the exodus narrative. The deference of John the Baptist to his younger relative Jesus, from the womb (Luke 1:39-45) to the baptismal scene at the Jordan (Matt. 3:1-17; Mark 1:1-11; Luke 3:15-22; John 1:19-36), is an adaptation of this same pattern. In view of this biblical convention, it is only fitting that David, the youngest of all of Jesse's sons, should be anointed king by Samuel (1 Sam. 16:11-13). Also in keeping with this pattern, the young David emerges as the amazing victor over the Philistine giant Goliath (17:33, 50), while his elder brothers and the rest of Saul's army cower in fear.

David as Young Warrior

The story of David and Goliath remains the most popular story of David's youth. It is also the one in which David appears centrally as the main character, hero, and witness to the God of Israel. This narrative apparently involves a late transfer of a valiant deed from one of David's mighty men to David himself. In 2 Samuel 21:19 there is this brief notice: "There was another battle with the Philistines at Gob; and Elhanan son of Jaare-oregim, the Bethlehemite, killed Goliath the Gittite, the shaft of whose spear was like a weaver's beam." The expanded treatment of this same heroic episode in 1 Samuel 17 presents another Bethlehemite as its victor. In this unforgettable tale, young David, fresh from the sheepfold and confident of God's help, defeats the giant Philistine warrior Goliath using only his sling and stones.

The celebrated story of David's victory in an unequal one-on-one contest was retold in different forms, two of which have been intertwined in the biblical text itself,[8] and it was highlighted in literature from the Second Temple period (e.g., Sir. 47:4-5; 1 Macc. 4:30; Septuagint Ps. 151:6-7). No doubt much of the popularity of this narrative stems from David's exemplification of Israel's identity as a small nation surviving under seemingly impossible odds. For present purposes, the story may also be read with an eye toward David's role as a child, albeit the extraordinary and peerless child of legend.[9]

Overlooked Dimensions

The story is so familiar that it hardly needs summarizing. Usually, however, the narrative is stripped of its historical context, its territorial dimensions, and its gory details in order to render it suitable for the Sunday school curriculum. The opening situation involves a standoff between the armies of the Israelites and the Philistines, who are camped on opposite hills with the valley of Elah sloping westward toward the Mediterranean as the battleground between them (1 Sam. 17:1-3, 19). As was frequently the case during the early Israelite monarchy, Israel was at war with the Philistines over border issues. The Philistine troops had advanced eastward to occupy Socoh, a small town to the

---

8. The story in 1 Samuel 17 represents at least two stages in the growth of the story of David and Goliath, edited together as a single narrative. The older version consists of 1 Sam. 17:1-11, 32-54, and the newer version, which is entirely missing in the oldest Greek manuscripts, consists of 1 Sam. 17:12-31, 55-58, and some verses in 1 Samuel 18. For the present essay, the narrative will be considered as a whole, despite the gaping seams that are apparent, for example in the secondary introduction of David and his family in 1 Sam. 17:12-16, and in the concluding dialogue in 1 Sam. 17:55-58 that ignores the previous conversation between David and Saul in 1 Sam. 17:31-37. For an analysis of the textual issues of this narrative in 1 Samuel 17, see Klein, *1 Samuel*, pp. 168-89; and McCarter, *II Samuel*, pp. 284-309.

9. While most of the numerous recent books on David from the 1990s and the 2000s treat the story of his combat with Goliath, the focus seldom remains long on David's character and role as a youth. For an example of a very interesting discussion that illustrates this point, see Baruch Halpern, *David's Secret Demons: Messiah, Murderer, Traitor, King* (Grand Rapids: Eerdmans, 2001), pp. 4-11.

west of Bethlehem toward the Philistine coast that was claimed by Judah (1 Sam. 17:1; Josh. 15:35), but actually lay on a contested border (2 Chron. 11:7; 28:18). The story ends with the victorious Israelite army pushing the Philistines back to Gath and Ekron, two of the five famous Philistine cities located near the Mediterranean.[10]

In this story of violent international relations, the name of the site of the Philistine encampment, Ephes-dammim (literally "End of Blood" in Hebrew), has a peculiar resonance.[11] Goliath's challenge to the Israelites to select a champion to fight with him, with the provision that the defeated man's army would become the servants of the winning man's side (1 Sam. 17:8-10), was intended to prevent bloodshed.[12] But beginning with David's slaying and cutting off of Goliath's head with the giant's own sword (vv. 50-51, 54, 57), much blood is spilled, as wounded Philistines fall along the route of their hasty retreat all the way back to the coastal plain (v. 52). Perhaps had Goliath defeated David the battleground would have been just as red. But judging from Goliath's taunt that he intends to "give [David's] flesh to the birds of the air and to the wild animals of the field" (v. 44), the Philistine champion has a limited goal of defeating his opponent in single combat. In his response, David similarly envisions dispatching his opponent, by striking him down and cutting off his head (v. 46), but he has much more in mind. Using the same imagery of carrion that Goliath employs, David expands the scope of the conflict and envisions a slaughter of the entire Philistine army:

> "I will give the dead bodies of the Philistine army this very day to the birds of the air and to the wild animals of the earth, so that all the earth may know that there is a God in Israel, and that all this assembly may know that the LORD does not save by sword and spear; for the battle is the LORD's and he will give you [*'etkem*, plural] into our hand." (vv. 46-47)

These are examples of the story's international and bellicose details, rarely emphasized when it is summarized. The basic contours of the story being well known, it is possible to skip further summary and move directly to more focused observations about the young David's character and roles in the story.

---

10. For the geographical setting of this story, see John A. Beck, "David and Goliath: A Story of Place: The Narrative-Geographical Shaping of 1 Samuel 17," *Westminster Theological Journal* 68 (2006): 321-30.

11. An alternative name, Pas-dammim (1 Chron. 11:13), meaning "Stripe of Blood," would seem to be a more appropriate name for a contested border region and certainly reflects the ending of the story in 1 Samuel 17 with the rout and slaughter of the Philistines.

12. The common use of captives of war as servants also forms a backdrop for the story of the little servant girl from Israel in 2 Kings 5:1-19.

In the Middle

The reader finally meets David after a lengthy description of the military stalemate between the Philistine and Israelite troops and of the challenge presented by the Philistine champion Goliath (1 Sam. 17:1-11). When David is introduced at last, there is no mention of his previously being anointed king (16:1-13). Nor is there any acknowledgement of his position as a musician in Saul's court (16:14-23); in fact, Saul does not even recognize David after he fells Goliath (17:55-58). In what is clearly an independent tradition, David is introduced *de novo* as Jesse's youngest son and errand boy. David's routine is to go back and forth between Saul's camp to the west of Bethlehem, where on behalf of his father he checks on his three eldest brothers in the Israelite army, and Bethlehem, where he feeds his father's sheep (17:12-16). While he is entrusted with a remarkable level of responsibility and fulfills it in an exemplary fashion,[13] David plays roles typically assigned to children. His chores include caring for the family's animals and delivering messages and other items on behalf of adults.

The main action of the story begins when David's father Jesse sends him on one of his errands. David is instructed to bring food supplies to his brothers and to inquire about their health (ironically, to inquire about their "peace," Hebrew *šālôm*, in a time of war; 1 Sam. 17:17). He is also charged with bringing back some token from them. Additionally, David is given presents to deliver to his brothers' commanding officer (vv. 15, 17-18, 20; cf. 16:20, where he brings gifts from his father to Saul). In these assignments, David acts as a go-between, as a representative on behalf of older people in interpersonal transactions.

Once David arrives at the Israelite camp in compliance with his father's command (1 Sam. 17:20), he is in constant interaction with various adults. He finds his brothers in the battle ranks and greets them, acting as his father's intermediary (vv. 22-23). From this point on, however, David's conversations begin to move him beyond the orbit of his own family, toward a more substantive intermediary role, as the unlikely representative of the Israelite army and even of Israel's God in hand-to-hand combat with the Philistine champion Goliath. When David hears the Philistine's defiant challenge (v. 23) and learns from the frightened soldiers how the king would reward the man who dared to strike him down (v. 25), he begins to seek confirmation about this situation from others among the troops (vv. 26-27). David does not halt his

---

13. Of interest in this respect are the text's descriptions of how David himself delegated certain responsibilities, when he was not able to attend to them himself, leaving the sheep with a keeper (1 Sam. 17:20) and entrusting his deliveries to the keeper of the baggage (1 Sam. 17:22).

investigation into this larger intermediary role, even when his eldest brother, Eliab, chides his presumption and tries to put him in his place by taunting him about his lowly position within the family hierarchy (vv. 28-29).[14] He continues to seek corroboration about the terms of engagement (v. 30).

In response to Eliab's criticism, David protests that he hasn't done anything meriting rebuke, since he was just talking: "Is it not [just] a word?" (dābār, 1 Sam. 17:29). But David's conversations with the troops signal his interest in fighting the Philistine warrior, so that eventually King Saul hears of David's "words" (now plural, dĕbārîm, v. 31) and summons him to his presence. After David describes his qualifications for battle, gained through defending the flock, and testifies to his confidence that the LORD would deliver him from the Philistine as he had previously delivered him in his encounters with wild beasts (vv. 32-37), the Israelite king sends him forth as the champion who will represent the Israelites with God's help: "Go, and may the LORD be with you" (v. 37).

If David's initial role as errand boy places him in an intermediary position between family members and other adults that is more or less typical for some children (cf. Joseph in Gen. 37:12-14), the intermediary role that King Saul sanctions for him, as a representative of the Israelite army and even of the "LORD of hosts, the God of the army of Israel," in whose name David confronts Goliath (1 Sam. 17:45), is absolutely extraordinary. Goliath, the Philistine champion, is twice called in Hebrew a "man between" ('îš habbēnayim, vv. 4, 23) the two armies. David, too, plays this intermediary role on behalf of the Israelites and their God, although he is no adult man at all, but just an adolescent.

Boy in a Man's World

David's youth and inexperience in war are, of course, what makes his victory so amazing and memorable. The world of war is a world of men, as the narrative stresses when it repeatedly refers to the ranks of Israel as "every man of Israel" ('îš, 1 Sam. 17:19, 24; cf. vv. 2, 25, 26), no matter how terrified and ineffectual they may be to face the Philistine threat. Goliath, besides being a champion, a "man between" the armies ('îš habbēnayim, vv. 4, 23), is also described as a "man of war" ('îš milḥāmâ, v. 33), a "warrior" (gibbôr, v. 51), and most simply as a "man" ('îš, vv. 10, 24, 25). Goliath calls for another "man" ('îš, vv. 8, 10) to fight as a worthy opponent, not the laughable youth that finally

---

14. Eliab's anger may stem from the fact that even though he was the eldest son he was rejected as God's anointed in favor of his youngest brother, David (1 Sam. 16:6-7).

dares to approach him (v. 42). Saul and the Israelite soldiers also expect a "man" (*'îš*, vv. 25, 27; cf. v. 26, where David echoes their assumption) to volunteer for combat, a mature adult who can accept the king's largess and his daughter's hand in marriage, as well as freedom for his whole household (v. 25).

David is decidedly not a man. He is instead the "son of a man" (*ben-'îš*, 1 Sam. 17:12, 55, 58), Jesse the Bethlehemite, who is described as old in contrast to his youthful offspring (v. 12). David has "big" brothers (*haggĕdōlîm*, vv. 13, 14; cf. v. 28), the three oldest of whom serve in Saul's army (vv. 13, 14, 17-19).[15] The narrator stresses that David is the "smallest" in the family (*haqqāṭān*, v. 14).

Throughout the story, the narrator calls David simply by his name, but in Goliath's eyes he is a mere "youth" (*na'ar*, 1 Sam. 17:42), which is also what King Saul repeatedly calls him (vv. 33, 55, 58; cf. v. 56, where Saul calls him an "adolescent" or "stripling" in the NRSV, *'ālem*). It is Saul who draws the contrast between David and Goliath into sharpest relief, when he cautions David against volunteering: "You are not able to go against this Philistine to fight with him; for you are just a boy (*na'ar*), and he has been a man of war (*'îš milḥāmâ*) from his youth (*minnĕ'urâw*)" (v. 33). Saul's incredulous inquiry at the end of the narrative about the identity of the unknown victor also emphasizes David's immaturity. The king's question to Abner concerns whose son the victor is (v. 55), since he is apparently not yet a man in his own right, and David responds by identifying himself not by his own name but simply as the "son of your servant Jesse the Bethlehemite" (v. 17:58).[16]

Other elements in the story dramatize David's immaturity. One is the contrast in size between the giant Goliath, who is 6 cubits and a span (over nine feet tall, 1 Sam. 17:4), and David, who cannot even walk in Saul's adult-sized heavy armor nor lift his sword (v. 38). Lack of experience also marks David's young age. David himself admits that he is not practiced with military equipment (vv. 38, 39, 40), and Saul notes this same lack of training when he observes that, in contrast to David, Goliath has been a man of war from his youth (v. 33). David instead trusts the simpler weaponry that he has used in his youthful occupation as a shepherd. The detail of David's gathering five smooth stones for his sling from the dry river bed (v. 40) is indicative of his improvisational tactics.

Goliath's scornful perception of David highlights David's juvenile status.

15. When they are named, the three oldest are called the "eldest," the "second," and the "third" (1 Sam. 17:13), which stresses their status in the family. Eliab is also called David's "big" brother in 1 Sam. 17:28.

16. As the story continues, Saul takes David away from his own father and family into the royal household following his victory over Goliath (1 Sam. 18:2).

David appears to the Philistine as "a youth, ruddy and handsome in appearance" (1 Sam. 17:42).[17] With his staff in his hand (v. 40), David is just a little
boy waving sticks at a dog, in Goliath's deprecating analogy (vv. 42-43). This
comparison is ambiguous, however. While boys sometimes do get bitten by
the dogs that they tease, there is a chance that a boy with a stick may hurt a
dog badly. Even more telling is that Goliath's implicit identification of himself
as a mere dog suggests that he is less of a threat than the lions and the bears
that David has killed in the past (vv. 36-37).

Being a youth does have its advantages, even in the military arena. David's
unorthodox choice of the slingshot that he had mastered in his early years
eliminates Goliath's advantage of size, strength, and experience with conventional weaponry. The stone hits a place on Goliath's head left vulnerable by
his bronze helmet even before David had come into range of the giant's
sword, spear, and javelin (1 Sam. 17:48-49).[18] "The LORD does not save by
sword and spear" is David's assertion (v. 47; cf. v. 45). A second advantage that
David has is that he is swift of foot, due at least in part to his youth. There is
much running in this narrative, including the terrified fleeing first of the Israelite ranks (vv. 2, 24) and finally of the Philistine soldiers, closely pursued by
the Israelites (vv. 51-52). David's speed is not part of any fearful collective
movement, however, but rather defines his character. Even before David encounters Goliath, he is expected to quickly comply with his father's command
(v. 17), and he runs to the battle line to find his brothers (v. 22). Because David
is not weighted down with heavy armor and weapons as Goliath is, he remains mobile in their encounter. In contrast to the Israelite troops who flee
from Goliath, David runs quickly toward the approaching Philistine and
takes his shot (v. 48), and then he runs to the fallen body to kill him and cut
off his head with his own sword (v. 51).

Looking at this narrative closely, it becomes apparent that David's youth
assumes multiple valences. At first, David's age is simply a fact, due to his position in the family birth order. Then it becomes a sure disqualification as a
serious contender, as in the scornful reaction of his eldest brother, Eliab. It appears to be a serious disadvantage from Saul's perspective, and it is a cause for
ridicule from the giant Goliath. On the battlefield, however, David's youth becomes an unexpected advantage. With his victory, it becomes a source of
amazement, expressed through the reaction of none other than the great King
Saul himself.

17. This description of David resembles the one found in 1 Sam. 16:12.

18. The bronze helmet is the first item mentioned in the lengthy description of Goliath's
military equipment (1 Sam. 17:5), foreshadowing the place of his vulnerability.

As a youth in this legendary tale, David plays the champion's role that all of the adults are too fearful to perform. Usually the champion representing an army would be the most mature, experienced, and virile of men. In this story, David rises to the occasion and takes on this function, not on adult terms, but as an adolescent whose confidence rests in God.

Out of the Mouth of Babes

It is young David, and none of the more mature and experienced characters, who articulates the theological dimensions of the challenge presented by Goliath. The Philistine's loud threat, "Today I defy the ranks of Israel!" (1 Sam. 17:10), leaves King Saul and his men terrified and speechless (v. 11). David later hears Goliath utter similar words, which cause the Israelites to flee (vv. 23-24). The soldiers accept Goliath's perspective when they talk among themselves: "Surely he has come up to defy Israel" (v. 25). Saul's only response is to appeal to his troops' self-interest and ambition, by offering an attractive reward to whoever might slay the defiant giant (v. 25). Before David intervenes, Goliath's challenge remains entirely a matter of superior physical force, with no recognition of God's presence on the battlefield or with the troops.

When David begins to speak to the soldiers, he first affirms the common view that the Israelite army has been insulted, when he inquires about the reward set for the man who "takes away the reproach from Israel" (1 Sam. 17:26). David does not stop with this perspective, however. He adds a question that begins to shift the definition of what is at stake: "For who is this uncircumcised Philistine that he should defy the armies of the living God?" (v. 26; cf. vv. 36, 45). According to David, the outsider Goliath has no right to challenge Israel's ranks, because they are supported by the God of life, who is present even in war, where death constantly threatens. Goliath's insults are an attack against the reputation of Israel's God.

When David is summoned before King Saul, he takes the initiative in their conversation and volunteers to do what no adult man has dared: "Let no one's heart faint because of him; your servant will go and fight with this Philistine" (1 Sam. 17:32). David's encouraging words refer to the "human heart" (*lēb 'ādām*), using the generic Hebrew term for "human being" (*'ādām*) rather than the masculine term for "man" (*'îš*), which describes the adult members of the Israelite army and their Philistine challenger. David thus moves the ideal of the narrative away from heroic bravado to human trust in God, exemplified by this youth himself.[19]

---

19. Note that earlier David's eldest brother, Eliab, had chided David for the evil of his heart

In response to Saul's fixation on David's youth and inexperience in what appears to be an unequal contest, David protests that he has extensive experience in fighting ferocious predators that threatened the flock (1 Sam. 17:34-35). He then goes on to repeat his earlier assertion to the soldiers that Goliath defies not only the Israelite army but Israel's God as well: "Your servant has killed both lions and bears; and this uncircumcised Philistine shall be like one of them, since he has defied the armies of the living God" (v. 36; cf. v. 26). David's basis of confidence in the present crisis is his prior experience with God: "The LORD, who saved me from the paw of the lion and from the paw of the bear, will save me from the hand of this Philistine" (v. 37).

At the end of David's inspiring theological oration, Saul sends him into combat with a blessing: "Go, and may the LORD be with you" (1 Sam. 17:38). Saul is the only other character besides David who verbally recognizes Israel's God, and he does so only in a formulaic response to David's lengthy, personal testimony.

Goliath, for his part, calls upon his gods to curse David (1 Sam. 17:43). David responds to his barrage of mockery and threats (vv. 42-44) by reiterating directly to the Philistine what he has said before, that in defying the Israelite army Goliath is actually opposing Israel's God: "You come to me with sword and spear and javelin; but I come to you in the name of the LORD of hosts, the God of the armies of Israel, whom you have defied" (v. 45). David understands the fight not just as between two human combatants.

According to this narrative, David's divinely bestowed victory serves a larger purpose: "so that all the earth may know that there is a God in Israel, and that all this assembly may know that the LORD does not save by sword and spear; for the battle is the LORD's and he will give you into our hand" (1 Sam. 17:46-47). This same rejection of conventional military power symbolized by the sword and spear appears earlier when David declines to borrow Saul's weaponry (vv. 38-40).[20]

David's defeat of Goliath and the subsequent rout of the Philistines confirm the theological position that David articulates. But the narrative retains some contradictions. Whereas David repeatedly refutes reliance on military might in favor of trust in God, it is through military means that the Israelites defeat the Philistines. David ultimately uses a sword to kill and behead Goliath, albeit the giant's own sword, and he treats the severed head as a gory tro-

---

(1 Sam. 17:28), because he was inquiring about the terms offered by Saul for the man who defeated Goliath.

20. This same perspective is also suggested in the concluding summary of the combat scene, which stresses that "there was no sword in David's hand" (1 Sam. 17:50).

phy of war (1 Sam. 17:51, 54, 57). God is entirely absent in the violent scenes at the conclusion of the narrative.[21] The earlier accusation brought against David by his eldest brother, Eliab, concerning his presumption and bad intentions (v. 28) never entirely subsides. Eliab is responding to the bald self-interest of the very first words that David speaks in the entire Bible: "What shall be done for the man who kills this Philistine?" (v. 26). In light of this calculating question, it is notable that David's opportunistic rise to power in Saul's palace begins immediately after he defeats the Philistine (18:2). The youthful figure of David in this story therefore embodies a complex range of positions, including a pious rejection of military power since "the battle is the LORD's" (17:47), the celebration of cunning, underhanded violence to preserve a people under threat from territorial invaders, and the temptation to justify lethal conflict in the name of God for opportunistic and self-serving purposes.

Vocation of a Shepherd Boy

David's work as a shepherd provides a common backdrop for both of the narratives that we have explored. While David's tending of the flock is never front and center in these narratives concerning his anointing and his defeat of Goliath, this pastoral occupation defines his character. The very first glimpse of the future king in the Bible points to this childhood employment, when in response to Samuel's question about David's whereabouts his father Jesse notes that "he is keeping the sheep" (1 Sam. 16:11). In the next chapter, when his brother Eliab questions David about his interest in the challenge posed by the Philistine warrior Goliath, he taunts him for shirking his usual occupation in favor of the excitement of the battlefield: "Why have you come down? With whom have you left those few sheep in the wilderness? I know your presumption and the evil of your heart; for you have come down just to see the battle" (17:28).

While tending sheep appears to be a minor task relegated to the youngest son, David's humble chores foreshadow his future. Shepherding is a metaphor for royalty in the Bible (2 Sam. 5:2; 7:7-8), as well as elsewhere in the ancient Near East. Hammurabi, the great Babylonian king, presents himself as the shepherd of the dark-haired people in the introduction to his famous law code. In the Bible, Moses is a shepherd of his father-in-law's flocks until he is

---

21. Nor does Saul offer any theological perspective in the last verses of the chapter, but rather inquires about the identity of the victorious youth (1 Sam. 17:55-58).

commissioned at the burning bush as God's prophet and the leader of the Israelites (Exod. 3:1-2).[22] God's kingship is also portrayed through shepherding
imagery (Gen. 48:15; Ps. 23:1; 80:1). David's childhood pursuits on the margins
of his family therefore point to his future role as king.

The pasture is also a training ground for combat. Through his shepherding, David gains experience in fighting predators and learns a lesson in faith,
to trust in God to give him the victory. David recalls his work as formative
when he justifies his confidence to Saul:

> David said to Saul, "Your servant used to keep sheep for his father; and
> whenever a lion or a bear came, and took a lamb from the flock, I went after
> it and struck it down, rescuing the lamb from its mouth; and if it turned
> against me, I would catch it by the jaw, strike it down, and kill it. Your ser-
> vant has killed both lions and bears; and this uncircumcised Philistine shall
> be like one of them, since he has defied the armies of the living God." David
> said, "The LORD, who saved me from the paw of the lion and from the paw
> of the bear, will save me from the hand of this Philistine." (1 Sam. 17:34-37)

Shepherding Beyond the Bible

Depictions of David as a youthful shepherd have been popular both in later
literary representations and in the history of art.[23] Very often in these later
portraits, David is presented playing his harp and composing music while
tending the sheep. While David as a youthful musician is not part of his depiction in the stories of his anointing and of his fight with Goliath, there is a
tendency to read backwards from the remaining introductory scene where
David is identified as a young man "skillful in playing the lyre" (1 Sam. 16:16).
It was logical to conclude that the origins of his genius in music-making must
be traced back to his time as a shepherd.

For example, an extra Davidic composition known as Psalm 151, found in
the early Greek translation of the Bible known as the Septuagint, as well as in
a Hebrew version discovered at Qumran (known as 11QPs[a]), portrays David
as praising God with his music when he was a shepherd boy:

> I was small among my brothers, and the youngest in my father's house; I
> tended my father's sheep. My hands made a harp; my fingers fashioned a
> lyre. And who will tell my Lord? The Lord himself; it is he who hears. It was

---

22. King Mesha of Moab is stated to be a sheep breeder in 2 Kings 3:4.

23. Artistic renditions of David as a youth often portray him in shepherd clothing, holding
his staff and pouch (1 Sam. 17:40).

he who sent his messenger and took me from my father's sheep, and anointed me with his anointing oil. (Ps. 151:1-4)[24]

Viewed in light of this image of David as a musical shepherd, Psalm 23 emerges as his autobiographical statement of trust in God from the days of his youth. David's early occupation as a shepherd shapes his destiny in ruling over Israel, in fighting enemies, and in praising God. Much of David's adult identity stems from his early experience with the flock.

In later Jewish tradition, fascination with the young David's work tending sheep during the formative period of his life continues. The classic rabbinic commentary on the Psalms known as the *Midrash on the Psalms (Midrash Tehillim)* develops the preparatory aspect of David's work as a shepherd, when it portrays him vowing to build a temple for God during his pastoral exploits with a mythological animal known as the reem.[25] Thinking that this enormous creature was a mountain, David climbed on its back while following the flock. Once the animal arose from its sleep, however, David found himself stranded high off the ground on the horns of the reem. At that point, the future king vowed that he would build a temple as tall as the length of the reem's horn, if God would help him get down safely. This fanciful midrash projects David's interest in the construction of the Jerusalem temple back to his youthful days as a shepherd and thereby demonstrates the ongoing project of connecting David's childhood with his adult commitments and projects.

Shepherding as Identity Forming

A general observation that might be drawn from the example of David as a shepherd boy both in and outside of the Bible is that the tasks and occupations of childhood, however humble and ordinary they may seem, may already manifest the core of a person's character and vocation. Certainly youthful pursuits prepare a person for future tasks, much as David's youth as a shepherd prepared him to be king, warrior, musician, and even temple patron. But childhood involves much more than preparation for adult occupa-

---

24. This version is taken from the Septuagint. The Hebrew version from Qumran develops David's musical skill to an even greater extent: "The mountains do not witness to him, nor do the hills proclaim; the trees have cherished my words and the flocks my works. For who can proclaim and who can bespeak and who can recount the deeds of the Lord? Everything has God seen, everything has he heard and he has heeded."

25. *Midrash Tehillim* 22.28. See Esther M. Menn, "Praying King and Sanctuary of Prayer, Part I: David and the Temple's Origins in Rabbinic Psalms Commentary *(Midrash Tehillim),*" *Journal of Jewish Studies* (2001): 1-26.

tions. The activities and accomplishments of a young person can be taken as an achievement and an end in themselves. Childhood may be viewed as a time of essential formation and embodiment of personality, commitments, and vocation. In this perspective, the adult simply lives out the identity created as a child.

The Little Israelite Servant Girl

The second example of a child character in a biblical narrative also appears during a time of war. She is the little Israelite girl who serves the wife of Naaman, the commander of the army of Aram (Syria) featured in the narrative of healing and conversion in 2 Kings 5:1-19.[26] The nation of Aram was Israel's greatest enemy during the reign of the Omride kings in the ninth century BCE. According to the biblical story, none other than Israel's God gave victory over the Israelites to the Arameans through the leadership of Naaman (2 Kings 5:1). Yet despite Naaman's greatness as a military strategist and mighty warrior,[27] he suffers from leprosy.[28] The little Israelite girl is able to identify to her mistress a source of healing for Naaman's dread skin disease: "If only my lord were with the prophet who is in Samaria! He would cure him of his leprosy" (v. 3).

Naaman reports the little girl's words to the king of Aram, and this king in turn sends Naaman to the Israelite king in Samaria with rich payments and a document demanding healing for the commander. When the king of Israel despairs because of his inability to comply with such an impossible request, which he takes as a provocation to further battle, the prophet Elisha comes forward to remedy the situation.[29] Naaman feels insulted by Elisha's simple cure of dipping seven times in the Jordan River, but his healing is immediate once he complies. Naaman then acknowledges Israel's God as the only God "in all the earth" (2 Kings 5:15) and makes arrangements to bring back a cartload of earth from Israel upon which to offer his burnt offerings to the LORD, even from his home in Aram (v. 17).

---

26. See Cogan Mordechai and Hayim Tadmor, *II Kings,* Anchor Bible (Garden City, NY: Doubleday, 1988), pp. 61-67; and Jean Kyoung Kim, "Reading and Retelling Naaman's Story (2 Kings 5)," *Journal for the Study of the Old Testament* 30 (2005): 49-61.

27. Like the warrior (*gibbôr,* 1 Sam. 17:51) Goliath, Naaman is a mighty warrior (*gibbôr ḥayil,* 2 Kings 5:1).

28. Naaman's name means "pleasant," which accords with his success in life but contrasts with his leprous condition.

29. Elisha's name means "My God Saves," which resonates with the "salvation" that the Lord gave to Aram through Naaman (2 Kings 5:1).

Valuing Things Big and Small

The nameless little Israelite girl appears in only three verses (2 Kings 5:2-4) of the story of Naaman's healing and conversion to the worship of the LORD, the God of Israel (2 Kings 5:1-19). In her minor role, she has only one brief appearance and one spoken line. Her small role matches her insignificance as a spoil of war and a house servant for the wife of the commander who defeated her people. Her marginality as a child captive in enemy territory represents the weakness of the northern kingdom of Israel, which was unable to protect her and no doubt many others like her in time of war. Yet, in her vulnerability as a captive in a foreign land the little girl's words challenge the pretensions of the mighty and offer hope for healing and life.

This narrative presents a sustained and ironic contrast between what appears "big" and important and what appears "small" and insignificant that ultimately inverts their usual valuation. Naaman, the commander of the army of the king of Aram, is introduced up front as a "big man" (*'îš gādôl,* 2 Kings 5:1), whereas the child captive from Israel with no name is described as a "little girl" (*na'ărāh qĕṭannāh,* 2 Kings 5:2) in the following verse.[30] This initial contrast between size and gender accentuates the small female child's placement within overwhelming world events dominated by men, involving armies and kings, commanders and prophets. In the big world into which the conflict between Israel and Syria has forced her as an enslaved captive of war, the child is introduced simply as "little," as if that is the one thing that matters, her smallness in the midst of everything mighty, powerful, and gross.

As the story progresses, we find other remarkable uses of the adjectives "big" and "little." When Naaman becomes miffed at the simple instructions that Elisha gives through a messenger, his servants note that if the prophet had given him a "big" task to do (Hebrew, *dābār gādôl,* 2 Kings 5:13), he would have simply done it. A "big" demand from the prophet would have been in keeping with Naaman's important status as a "big" man (2 Kings 5:1). His servants' observation overcomes Naaman's resistance to washing in the waters of the Jordan, a river that seems less desirable than the Abana and the Parpar rivers flowing through Damascus (2 Kings 5:12). After he dips in the Jordan, Naaman's flesh is restored, like the flesh of a "little boy" (*na'ăr qāṭōn,* 2 Kings 5:14). Naaman becomes like the "little girl" at the beginning of the story in his pure flesh, and also ultimately in his recognition of the God of

---

30. For the Hebrew term *na'arah,* see Carolyn S. Leeb, *Away from the Father's House: The Social Location of* na'ăr *and* na'ărāh *in Ancient Israel,* Journal for the Study of the Old Testament — Supplement Series, 301 (Sheffield: Academic Press, 2000).

Israel who works for healing through the prophet in Samaria (2 Kings 5:15-18).

The Power of a Wish

What is "little" in this narrative is certainly not to be dismissed. As the narrative spotlight turns to the little Israelite servant girl for the briefest moment, the display of everything grand and significant in the world of war suddenly comes to a halt. Although she is small and lacks any official power, the girl's few words are the first spoken in the narrative. All subsequent action of the more important characters hinge on them:

> She said to her mistress, "If only my lord were with *(lipnê)* the prophet who is in Samaria! He would cure him of his leprosy." (2 Kings 5:3)

What kind of words does the little girl offer to Naaman's wife? Her single line contains no lament or complaint, no cursing or whining, which we might expect from a diminutive captive of war forced to serve the enemy. Her words are also not a command, nor a report, nor any other kind of speech that would have its place in times of war and in the high circles that manage war. Instead, the little girl's words express a wish contrary to fact: "if only" (*'ahălê*, 2 Kings 5:3). The girl has a heart full of compassion and wishes only for the enemy commander's healing, despite his role in defeating her people and taking her into captivity. She also wants to make known the power for life that is among her own people, through the prophet in Samaria. In a time of killing and destruction, she focuses her attention on healing and restoration, even for the military leader on the other side.

The little girl no doubt wishes that many things were different. She would certainly like to be at home, to be with her parents and neighbors and country people. But the only words that we have in this story express her wish that Naaman could be with *(lipnê)* the prophet in Samaria. Simple presence is what she wishes for Naaman, just as proximity and immediacy are what children want most from their parents and others whom they love and trust to make things right. Her words express confidence that this kind of closeness to the prophet would lead to Naaman's healing.

The words that the little girl speaks seem to offer a childlike, indiscriminate hope that things might be better for everyone, everywhere. Her wish envisions a world without sharply drawn national borders and without clear-cut divisions between enemies and friends. Her words lack rancor or resentment for what has happened to disrupt her life; they are full instead of abundant forgiveness and trust that there is a force for life and healing more powerful than any army. If only the power of healing and life possessed by the prophet in Samaria were the power that was recognized and respected in international relations.

From Wish to International Crisis

The information about the healing power of the prophet at Samaria presented in the little girl's wish causes something of an international crisis when it falls into the hands of the military leader Naaman and the king of Aram. These important adults take a child's wish and attempt to turn it into an economic and political transaction, as if incredibly large amounts of silver, gold, and expensive garments could buy the healing that the little girl's words locate in enemy territory. The adults also bully a child's wish into a command, and not only a verbal command, but a formal, written command, carried in a letter by none other than the leprous leader of the Aramean army himself.

Although the Aramean king demands that the king of Israel perform a healing for his leprous commander, the power of healing is not the power of kings. Their area of expertise is war, killing, and death. To his credit, the king of Israel realizes that the power to restore the health of a leper belongs to God alone. He tears his clothes as a sign of mourning and extreme distress and asks: "Am I God, to give death or life, that this man sends word to me to cure a man of his leprosy?" (2 Kings 5:7).

But even though the king of Israel recognizes God as the source of all healing and acknowledges that he is not God, still he is unable to see the real human need that the enemy commander embodies in his leprous flesh. He panics because he cannot see behind this clumsy international pressure the sincere desire for health, but can only conclude that it must be a pretext for more conflict: "Just look and see how he is trying to pick a quarrel with me" (2 Kings 5:7). The crisis in the palace in Samaria indicates a fear that the enemy's search for wholeness is yet another cause for violence and killing, a prelude to further defeat. The little girl's wish for the enemy's health becomes in the king's palace an impossible order and an international crisis.

By contrast, the little girl was able to see the humanity of the Aramean general, his basic frailty and mortality, even though he was so great and important a man. She also pointed to the power of God's prophet in Samaria.

The prophet Elisha himself also desires to let Naaman know that there is a prophet in Israel through his healing, as he tells the Israelite king: "Let [Naaman] come to me, that he may know that there is a prophet in Israel" (2 Kings 5:8). Elisha's words confirm that the little girl has spoken the truth when she located the power of healing in the prophet in Samaria.

The role of the prophet in healing is entirely overlooked in the international crisis caused by the search for Naaman's cure. The Aramean king demands that the Israelite king heal his leprous commander, and the Israelite king knows that he does not have that power. But neither of them, nor Naaman himself, acting as a messenger to convey the order for his own healing, remembers the little girl's wish that Naaman could be with the prophet in Samaria (2 Kings 5:3), nor do they comprehend that it is God's prophet who has the power of healing (v. 8).

Conjuring the Prophet

It is not within the power of kings to command the prophets, who have their independent source of authority through their direct relationship to God, as spokesperson, intercessor, and conduit of divine power, including the power to heal. The prophet Elisha is not summoned by the king in Samaria, but rather he sends his own message to the king (2 Kings 5:8). Elisha apparently becomes involved in the situation because the Israelite king acknowledges his own weakness and impotence by rending his garments. Elisha acts to bring the focus back on the role of the prophet, which is what the little girl had stressed in her wish for her master.

Elisha summons Naaman to his home, but then he does not go out to meet the military leader personally when he arrives with his horses and chariots, in a display of military might and political importance (2 Kings 5:8-10). Naaman does not get the big fanfare that he no doubt expected. Nor does he receive the healing ritual or the "big" therapeutic protocol that he anticipated (v. 11). The prescription is simply to dip seven times in the Jordan (v. 10). This modest regimen is in keeping with the theme of the power of small things, exemplified also in the power of the "little" girl to recognize the healing gift of the prophet in Samaria.

Naaman is angry that he is not treated as the "big," important man that he is, that the prophet does not officially welcome and acknowledge him as powerful and worthy of a private audience. He is also angry about the commonness of the means of healing that the prophet identifies, since the Jordan is insignificant in comparison with the larger rivers of Damascus, the Abana and the Pharpar (2 Kings 5:12). Naaman's servants observe that if he had been given a difficult task, some "big thing" (*dābār gādôl*, 2 Kings 5:13) to do, he would have done it immediately. The commander is used to mounting major operations, to moving large companies, to bearing up under strain and duress. He does not seem to be able to accept a small assignment for the sake of health and life.

Once Naaman does acquiesce to being treated as a person of no special consequence, as a child might be treated summarily, once he acknowledges the modest river of the Jordan as a potential means of healing and dips in the river seven times, he is healed immediately, and his skin becomes like that of a little boy (*na'ar qāṭōn*, 2 Kings 5:14). This comparison of course emphasizes the complete healing of his skin, since there is no finer and more beautiful skin than the skin of a child, without blemish, even in tone and in texture, with quick healing properties. In this context, where the "little girl" wished her master good health, it also seems significant that when he taps into the power for healing that she articulated, he himself becomes childlike. He becomes a "little boy," the counterpart of the "little girl," at least skin deep.

Dirt and Worship

The mighty Naaman becomes a worshiper of Israel's God through his experience of the power of small things. He attended to what his wife's little servant girl said, he was healed through contact with the humble river of the Jordan, and his skin was transformed from leprous to pure, like that of a little boy. Naaman's reaction to the effectiveness of what appears insignificant is to return with the rest of his company to stand "before" the man of God who restored his flesh (*lĕpānâw*, 2 Kings 5:15). This action fulfills the little girl's wish that her master were with or "before" this prophet in Samaria (*lipnê*, v. 3). Elisha the healer in turn stands "before" the LORD (*lĕpānâw*, v. 16), whom Naaman now also recognizes as the only God.[31]

Naaman urges Elisha to accept a reward (2 Kings 5:15-16), but the prophet refuses because the economy of healing is distinct from the plunder of kings and armies.[32] Since Naaman cannot give anything, he requests instead to take something. He plans to take back a load of soil from Israel, in keeping with

31. To stand "before" *(lipnê)* indicates acceptance of the authority of a superior. Note that at the beginning of the story Naaman was an important man "before" *(lipnê)* his master, the king of Aram (2 Kings 5:1), and the little girl captured from Israel was serving "before" *(lipnê)* Naaman's wife (2 Kings 5:2).

32. The continuation of the story in 2 Kings 5:20-27 depicts the negative consequences of entangling the prophet's vocation with monetary transactions. Elisha's servant Gehazi secretively claims a payment from Naaman, but as a result he becomes afflicted with Naaman's leprosy.

the understanding that each land had its own deity who was worshiped in that particular territory.[33] Naaman's cartload of earth seems like a small gesture, but it is symbolic of his total allegiance to the God of his wife's little servant girl. At the end of the narrative, the big Syrian commander and the little girl from Israel worship the same God.

The little slave girl living on foreign soil testifies to the power of healing that Israel's God offers through the "man of God" (2 Kings 5:15) living in Samaria. Her witness in a foreign land started a whole string of events that led finally to the enemy captain's healing and to his acknowledgment of his enemies' deity. The little girl had wished something good for the foreign enemy of her people, and now this enemy has become a fellow worshiper of the LORD, the God of Israel, and no other gods (v. 17). Instead of the usual spoils of war, including captive children for servants, Naaman takes home dirt. He carries back a bit of earth from Israel upon which he plans to sacrifice to the LORD, the God of Israel (v. 17), whom he acknowledges as God over all the earth, even if upon occasion he must accompany the king of Aram in his official worship of the Aramean god Rimmon (v. 18).

Like the little girl, Naaman becomes a servant on foreign soil. As he makes plans to bring back his cartload of earth, this army commander repeatedly calls himself the servant ('ebed, 2 Kings 5:15, 17, 18) of Elisha, the prophet of Israel's God who was able to heal him of his leprosy. The little servant girl had insight into the true power of health and life. She had made possible the crossing of national boundaries in search of these good gifts, even during a time of war, when power generally means the ability to kill and defeat and establish new borders to be defended. She testified to God's power over all life through her wish that initiated Naaman's quest for health and eventually led to the even bigger step of his acknowledging Israel's God as the only God in all the earth.

That a little Israelite servant girl should have such insight points to the perceptiveness of children about matters of faith. Much later in the rabbinic period, a midrash from the classic commentary on Exodus known as the *Mekhilta of Rabbi Ishmael* portrays the perceptiveness of another servant girl. In remarking on a verse from the Song of the Sea in Exodus 15, "This is my God, and I will glorify him" (Exod. 15:2), Rabbi Eliezer claims that "a maidservant saw at the sea what Isaiah and Ezekiel and all the prophets never saw."[34] The passage continues with an explanation that, unlike the entire generation

33. In light of the narrator's acknowledgment that Israel's God was acting beyond the borders of Israel in giving victory to Aram through Naaman (2 Kings 5:1), this act of transporting dirt in order to be able to worship the Lord outside of the land seems superfluous.

34. *Mekilta de-Rabbi Ishmael*, trans. Jacob Z. Lauterbach, vol. 2 (Philadelphia: The Jewish Publication Society of America, 1976), p. 24.

of the exodus from Egypt who perceived God directly at the sea, the Israelite prophets perceived God only in similitudes (Hos. 12:10) and visions (Ezek. 1:1). While the larger dynamics of this midrash would require more exploration than this essay allows, it is worth noting that later tradition acknowledges the theological astuteness of another nameless servant girl.

Common Threads

Although the stories of David and the little Israelite servant girl are very different, they share several common threads. These are especially worth noting since other stories that feature child characters pick up some of the same themes and develop them in distinctive ways.

Perhaps most obvious is that David and the little Israelite servant girl intervene and find solutions to problems that confound adults and that threaten lives. David defeats the Philistine giant who terrified the Israelite troops, when no one else in Saul's army dared to fight Goliath. The little servant girl alone offers insight into a source of healing for the powerful commander of the Syrian army.

There are other examples of young people in the Bible who solve difficult problems that pose a threat to life when adults for some reason are unable to intervene. For example, Miriam, the older sister of Moses, takes personal initiative in negotiating with the daughter of Pharaoh an arrangement that spares her brother from Pharaoh's decree that all male Hebrew infants must be thrown into the Nile (Exod. 2:5-10). In this instance, Miriam's solution of identifying Moses' own mother as his nurse until he is old enough to be taken as an adopted son into the palace is especially elegant. Not only is Moses spared from drowning, but Moses' mother gets paid for caring for her own son, and the family relationship is preserved, at least for the short term.[35]

Another common thread is that both children express theological insights and witness to their faith. The words of David and the little servant girl introduce God into the narrative and change the course of events. In both cases, a

---

35. Other suggestive instances in which young people, perhaps teenagers or young adults, intervene to preserve life include the work of Jonathan and Michal, the children of Saul, who work together to spare David from their father's anger and violence (1 Sam. 19–20), and a "young Hebrew" named Joseph (Gen. 41:12) who interprets the dreams of Pharaoh and organizes Egypt to save lives in a time of famine (Gen. 41:14-57). A less well known instance involves Jehosheba, princess daughter of King Jorah (and Ahaziah's sister), who hid Joash son of Ahaziah and his nurse for six years, sparing him from slaughter (2 Kings 11:1-3). This boy became king of Judah when he was seven, as the only remaining heir to the throne of David.

child's words are central to the story and express a particular understanding of the community's relationship with God.

The role of children's speech and theological insight could be fruitfully explored in other biblical stories. For example, Samuel was just a boy when he was called as a prophet (1 Sam. 3:1-18), and "as Samuel grew up, the LORD was with him and let none of his words fall to the ground" (1 Sam. 3:19). Daniel and his three companions are portrayed as youths when they were brought to Nebuchadnezzar's court in Babylon (Dan. 1:4-7), and yet they were full of wisdom and insight, and they had the courage to speak up about their religious convictions and distinctive practices, in some cases bringing the foreign king to acknowledgment of the true God.[36]

Remarkably, the stories of David and the Israelite girl also portray children acting on the borders between cultures and national identities, negotiating divides that sometimes baffle and hobble older people. Children are depicted not as isolated and protected individuals, but rather as actors embedded within complex familial and international structures and relationships. The story of David and Goliath, for example, is not only about "trust in God as a singular and isolated act of piety" but also about "a faithful act with profound political consequences that changed the course of the nation and in doing so brought hope."[37] The Israelite girl acts with compassion and kindness not simply to a stranger and foreigner but to her people's enemy.

There are other examples in the Bible of children as agents of change in complex political or international settings and in relationship to strangers, foreigners, and enemies. A number of the examples that have already been mentioned in this section exemplify this dynamic: Miriam negotiates with Pharaoh's daughter and her Egyptian maids (Exodus 2); Joseph interacts with Pharaoh and his household (Genesis 41); Daniel and his companions are taken as youths to live in the Babylonian court, where they use all of their skills as counselors on behalf of the foreign power, while still maintaining their religious identity (Daniel 1); Rebekah offers water to a stranger and his camels when they appear at the local well (Genesis 24).[38]

---

36. See also Jeremiah, who was a youth when he was commissioned in his prophetic role, and yet God instructed him to speak wherever he would be sent (Jer. 1:6-7).

37. Stephen Tollestrup, "Children Are a Promise of Hope," in *Understanding God's Heart for Children*, ed. Douglas McConnell, Jennifer Orona, and Paul Stockley (Colorado Springs: World Vision, 2008), p. 192. Tollestrup adds in a footnote on the same page: "The transformational and social content of the David and Goliath episode is almost entirely missing in any Sunday school or children's training material. Faithfulness and obedience are stressed above the possibility of social impact. Children need to know that they can impact and change their world."

38. In some cases, such as the teenager Dinah who visited the daughters of the land (Genesis

Although the child characters in both stories are agents of change amid international conflict, both stories also illustrate children's vulnerability and marginalization. Despite their intelligence and skill in negotiating their circumstances, both David and the Israelite girl are separated from their families or communities due to war. David must leave his father and travel to get word of his brothers because of the war with the Philistines. The Israelite girl is more tragically and permanently absent from her family, as a captive of war now serving the wife of the enemy commander. Both stories point to the vulnerability of children of all ages, who are caught in the violence and upset of communal or national conflicts.

Other children in biblical narratives also exemplify the vulnerability of children to become marginal or separated from their families and communities. Rebekah's favorite son, Jacob, had to flee from his older twin brother Esau's anger to live with his Uncle Laban, never to see his mother again. Joseph was sold into slavery by his older brothers and taken down to Egypt, to the enduring grief of his father Jacob. The biblical narratives about Jacob and about Joseph present their separation from their families as an unwelcome hardship; however, God brought success and blessing to both of these youthful characters, even in their isolation and vulnerability.

Conclusion

Each of these additional examples and others not mentioned would warrant further study in order to develop a comprehensive treatment of child characters in biblical narratives. The expansive list of examples that comes quickly to mind in thinking through the common aspects between the stories of David and the little Israelite girl shows that children in the Bible play important and sometimes unexpected roles. Their noteworthy qualities can include intelligence, altruism, and ethical impulses. While children are vulnerable and dependent, they also show themselves willing to take risks and to become involved in situations that adults sometimes find overwhelming or even defeating.

Biblical narratives of children show God at work in families, communities, and nations not only through the mighty and the powerful by human standards, but also through the weak and insignificant. It is "not by might, nor by power, but by my spirit, says the Lord of hosts" (Zech. 4:6). God's

---

34), children who cross borders become vulnerable to harm, rape, and violence between different tribes and groups of people.

spirit is surprisingly present and active through what might appear to be weakness, vulnerability, and trust that children in particular represent so well.

David and the little servant girl, as well as all the other child characters who act and speak in the Bible, challenge our concept of what it means to be a young person. These small characters are by no means the least. They witness to the integrity and full humanity of children and adolescents, both in the Bible and outside of its pages to our own day.

16 "He Placed a Little Child in the Midst": Jesus, the Kingdom, and Children

Keith J. White

The interaction between Jesus and his disciples described in Matthew 18:1-14 includes some of the most significant child-related actions and teachings of Jesus. In this passage, Jesus is asked by his disciples: "Who is the greatest in the kingdom of Heaven?" Jesus responds in this way:

> He called a child, whom he put among them, and said, "Truly I tell you, unless you change and become like children, you will never enter the kingdom of heaven. Whoever becomes humble like this child is the greatest in the kingdom of heaven. Whoever welcomes one such child in my name welcomes me." (Matt. 18:2-5)

Jesus then warns his disciples sternly about the dangers of causing little ones who believe in him to sin or of despising them. The episode concludes with the story of a shepherd losing one of a hundred sheep and searching for it until he finds it: "So it is not the will of your Father in heaven that one of these little ones should be lost" (Matt. 18:14).

In this pericope and its variations in the other Synoptic Gospels (Mark 9:33-37; 10:13-16; and Luke 9:46-48; 18:15-17),[1] Jesus freely and deliberately chooses a little child as a way of challenging and illuminating the disciples' theological "discussion" or "argument" about the kingdom.[2] Throughout the Synoptics, there are many who come to Jesus, including those who are un-

---

1. Although they are treated as distinct and separate incidents in the three Gospels, there is some overlap in the teaching of Jesus between the event where he places a child in the midst (Matt. 18:1-14; Mark 8:33-37; Luke 9:46-48), and the time when people bring children to Jesus (Matt. 19:13-15; Mark 10:13-16; Luke 18:15-17).

2. "Argument" rather than "discussion" is the word used in Luke 9:46.

clean, poor, beggars, Gentiles, women, and sinners. However, at no point does Jesus choose one of these as a sign of the kingdom of heaven by placing them in the midst of the disciples.[3]

Jesus' startling action of putting a *child* in the midst of his disciples raises certain issues of interpretation. One such question is what becoming like little children means in relation to the kingdom of heaven. Some have claimed that becoming like a child has to do with a subjective state of mind or personal qualities such as trust, dependency, honesty, simplicity, or transparency, which are supposedly inherent or intrinsic to children.[4] Others believe that it is the objective reality, the real life and humble (marginal, if not invisible) status of children that holds the key to this passage.[5]

A second critical question is whether the "child placed by Jesus" in Matthew 18 is part of a running theme of the Gospel or is placed distinctively and exceptionally at this point in the narrative. The question is of theological significance in the light of what theologians have written about the relationship between the child Jesus in Matthew 1–2 and the child placed in the midst by Jesus in chapter 18. Writers like Hans Urs von Balthasar and Robin Maas have stressed the links,[6] but to do so they have used the other Gospels, including John.

The placing of a child in the midst of a theological discussion also prompts questions about one of the central and continuous themes in Matthew's Gospel: the kingdom of heaven. Although the nature of the kingdom of heaven — as taught, signed, and demonstrated by Jesus — is also central to the two other Synoptic Gospels,[7] it is only in Matthew that the message first

3. This comparison is not developed in this paper. One distinctive of children is their universality. Not every person is poor, a woman, or black, but every person either was or is a child. The idea of "child" is associated with growth and development, and therefore with hope. Jürgen Moltmann develops child as a metaphor of hope in "Child and Childhood as Metaphors of Hope," *Theology Today* 56, no. 4 (January 2000): 592-601.

4. Roy Zuck, *Precious in His Sight* (Grand Rapids: Baker Books, 1996), p. 206, lists a sample of what commentators have read into the phrase "become like little children." They include being receptive, amenable, simple, teachable, modest, unspoiled, trusting, in need of instruction, and sinless.

5. Hans-Ruedi Weber, *Jesus and the Children* (Geneva: WCC, 1979), pp. 31-32.

6. See Hans Urs von Balthasar, *Unless You Become Like This Child* (San Francisco: Ignatius Press, 1991), p. 11, who speaks of the "very being of Christ, whose identity is inseparable from his being a child in the bosom of the Father"; and Robin Maas, "Christ as the Logos of Childhood," *Theology Today* 56, no. 4 (January 2000): 456-68.

7. In stressing the centrality of the kingdom of heaven in Matthew's Gospel, it is important to acknowledge that this contrasts with the view of those who see it as about "church." Although the Gospel is about the nature of a new community, the people of God, it is not, in the view of this writer, a book about "church." It is the one Gospel to include the word *ekklēsia,* and there is

announced by John the Baptist is reiterated word for word by Jesus: "Repent, for the kingdom of heaven is at hand."[8] One common interpretation of the Gospel as a whole focuses on Matthew's Jewish audience and the ways in which Matthew connects the kingdom of heaven with God's (or YHWH's) developing kingdom on earth, commonly interpreted as the church. If so, then what particular light does Jesus' unusual action of placing a child in the midst of his discussion about the kingdom shed on the precise meaning of *basileia tōn ouranōn* (the kingdom of heaven) and the Gospel as a whole?

The primary aim of this chapter is to explore these and other questions and to reexamine the Gospel of Matthew as a whole from a specific perspective: with the child placed by Jesus in mind.[9] This approach of "foregrounding the child" allows the action and teaching of Jesus in Matthew 18 both to inform the view of children and childhood in Matthew and to illustrate core themes of the narrative. The chapter therefore serves as a corrective to commentaries that regard children in Matthew as only background material[10] or metaphors in the teaching of Jesus.[11] Although it focuses primarily on Matthew, the chapter also prompts reflection on complex relationships expressed in all three Synoptic Gospels between children and the kingdom of heaven.

---

teaching for the community of faith all through, but it is not about the "institutional paraphernalia which the word 'church' tends to suggest to us" (R. T. France, *The Gospel According to Matthew*, Tyndale New Testament Commentary [Grand Rapids: Eerdmans, 1985], p. 55). An alternative view can be found in K. Stendahl, "Matthew," in *Peake's Commentary on the Bible*, ed. M. Black and H. Rowley (London: Nelson, 1975), p. 769, who calls it "a handbook for teaching and administration within the church" and compares it to the "Manual of Discipline" from Qumran. Stendahl (p. 770) agrees that Matthew is concerned with who will inherit the kingdom of heaven but concludes that this means the church. In my view the teaching and actions of Jesus in relation to children and the kingdom of heaven may well have been marginalized because "church" has been uppermost in the minds of many commentators and theologians.

8. Matthew's Gospel is unique in this respect: it is the only one in which the teaching of John and Jesus are shown to be identical in their core and focus.

9. I am grateful to my friend and colleague Professor Haddon Willmer for his wise counsel and comments on this chapter flowing from our work together on Matthew 18, and to Daniel Jarratt and Marcia Bunge for their editorial skills and assistance.

10. I am using the term "background" here not in the usual sense of the historical, social, and cultural context of the Gospel but rather in the sense of the narrative as a whole of which children are a part. The use of the terms "foreground" and "background" in this paper derives from the hermeneutic principle of Marshall McLuhan (written with Bruce Powers) in *The Global Village: Transformations in World Life and Media in the Twenty-first Century* (Oxford: Oxford University Press, 1988).

11. This action and teaching of Jesus with a child in the midst has become a starting point for what has become known as "child theology." This recent approach to doing theology is not restricted to a concern for children or childhood but has set out in the hope of exploring the full range of biblical, historical, and systematic theology using the child placed by Jesus as a lens.

The chapter takes a narrative approach to the text, focusing on three main sections of the Gospel: birth narratives (Matt. 1–2); an extended section describing the kingdom of heaven (3:1–21:16); and the suffering, death, and resurrection of Jesus (21:17–28:20). There are different ways of analyzing Matthew, a common one being to suggest that it is woven around five great discourses.[12] By way of contrast this chapter is organized around the narrative, summarizing the content of each of these three divisions of the material and highlighting critical insights regarding children and their relationship to Christ and the kingdom.[13]

By taking a more narrative approach to the text and by foregrounding the child, the chapter finds the following:

1. Children in the Gospel are depicted as integral to the narrative and clues to its meaning.
2. The placing of a child in the midst of Jesus' disciples is a unique sign or acted parable and represents a surprising new way of understanding the way of the cross and the kingdom of heaven.[14]
3. A triad comprising Jesus, the kingdom of heaven, and the little child placed in the midst form an important motif in Matthew's Gospel. Each part of the triad illuminates the other two; to attack or marginalize one is to despise the other two; in welcoming or receiving one, the other two are also accepted.

The conclusion is that children, whatever their age, are not only active participants in the unfolding story but are also essential for a true reading of the Gospel, understanding the identity and person of Jesus Christ, modeling the way of the cross, and representing the radical nature of ecclesial community.

This reflection on the Gospel of Matthew and some of its central themes brings together my study and experience in a number of varied contexts. For

---

12. An example of this is usefully set out in France, *Matthew*, pp. 59-61.

13. This is not intended to imply that the Gospel as we have it was written as a continuous sequential narrative. For example, the birth and passion narratives may have been formed separately from the stories and teaching of Jesus' ministry. Neither is it an attempt to detract from the fact that its primary purpose is to tell the good news of Jesus through using elements, and partly in the genre, of narrative.

14. In arriving at this view I am indebted to the insights and writings of Haddon Willmer. Davies and Allison use the term "enacted parable" of this incident in their commentary: W. D. Davies and D. C. Allison, *A Critical and Exegetical Commentary on the Gospel according to Matthew, Volume 2, Chapters 8–18* (Edinburgh: T&T Clark, 1991), p. 756.

the past twenty years I have worked on a new edition of the Bible.[15] While working on this project, and like my mentor Pandita Ramabai (1858-1922) in India, I was living alongside and caring for children in a residential community. In my case this was in my family home, Mill Grove, which has opened its doors to children in need since 1899. In establishing the Child Theology Movement (CTM) I have been privileged to participate in theological consultations on every continent comprising both practitioners who are working directly alongside children and theologians who are seeking to establish how children and childhood relate to the study and activity of theology as they understand it. My background extends beyond biblical studies and child theology and includes literature and the sociology of religion and childhood.

All of these contexts have combined to shape my particular approach (literary, theological, and sociological) to the narrative of Matthew's Gospel, using the action and teaching of Jesus in chapter 18 as a primary clue to understanding the text.

The Birth Narratives (Matthew 1–2)

Matthew's Gospel is introduced by way of genealogy and then describes the birth of Jesus, the coming of the Magi, the flight to Egypt, and the return to Nazareth. Joseph in the birth narrative is called "son of David." This title is also applied to Jesus when the children in the temple sing "Hosanna to the Son of David" (21:12-16).

Herod tells the Magi from the East to make a careful search for "the child."[16] Matthew records that "they saw the child with his mother Mary, and they bowed down and worshiped him."

This reception of the Christ child is set against child suffering that echoes the slaughter of the boy-children in Egypt in the days of Moses. Jeremiah's prophecy (Jer. 31:15) is fulfilled: "A voice is heard in Ramah, weeping and great mourning, Rachel weeping for her children and refusing to be comforted because they are no more." The child Jesus is taken to Egypt by his parents to avoid the slaughter.

Without reading too much into the birth narratives, it would be wanton not to notice that the focus of the narrative is on Jesus as a child. Much has been written about how the birth narratives prepare the reader/listener for

---

15. *The Bible: Narrative and Illustrated* (London: IBS-STL and WTL Publications, 2008).

16. For the record, the word "child" occurs ten times in the story of the birth of Jesus, quite apart from the references to "son."

what is to come, but the fact that a child is central to this drama is rarely noticed or commented upon.[17]

This child is conceived through the Holy Spirit and is the one of whom the prophet Isaiah prophesied: "A virgin [young woman] will be with child and will give birth to a son, and they will call him Immanuel, which means, God with us" (Isa. 7:14). Robin Maas sums it up thus: "The clear intent of the birth narratives in Matthew and Luke is to record the advent of the long-awaited Messianic child,"[18] and Jürgen Moltmann sees this Messianic child as a metaphor for hope realized in every child.[19] Both writers stress the fact that we are not encountering simply incarnation (that is, God in *human* form) but the Creator or God-self in the Christ *child*.

In taking care not to imply a thematic or theological link between the childhood of Jesus and the little child of Matthew 18 (which Jesus himself at no point makes), it is vital not to go to the other extreme and detach the umbilical cord between the birth narrative and the rest of Matthew. The child in question ("this child": Jesus Christ) is not only the fulfillment of prophecy; his birth story is also an account of God placing a child, his beloved Son, at the center of history.[20]

Any reading of the birth narratives needs to recognize the tension between those who argue that the rest of the narrative (especially the cross) is set within the context of this eternal child,[21] and those who believe that this view overemphasizes the significance of the child Christ in the narrative and in Matthew's theology. The former suggest that "this child" has center stage not just in this part of the narrative but in Matthew's understanding of the whole of God's purposes; in Jesus, God has placed a child, the eternal child, at the center of all things. The latter hold that the birth stories are there to embed Jesus in the whole biblical narrative of God and to insist that Christ has really come in the flesh, that he has real humanity. But it is not the baby as baby who is savior, whereas in chapter 18 it is precisely this child, to whom no

17. A reading of the major commentaries on the text of Matthew's Gospel confirms this tendency to marginalize "the child." It is as if there is no room for the child in the inn of theology (to borrow an image from Luke's birth narrative).

18. Maas, "Christ as the Logos of Childhood," p. 460.

19. Moltmann, "Child and Childhood as Metaphors of Hope," p. 592.

20. I explored this theme of the child Jesus placed in the center of history in an unpublished sermon given at the Malaysian Baptist Theological Seminary on 5 November 2002.

21. Balthasar, *Unless You Become Like This Child*, p. 64: "This primacy of the trinitarian Childhood over the work of redemption. . . ." This is also the implication of the work of Rahner as described by Mary Ann Hinsdale, "'Infinite Openness to the Infinite': Karl Rahner's Contribution to Modern Catholic Thought on the Child," in *The Child in Christian Thought*, ed. Marcia J. Bunge (Grand Rapids: Eerdmans, 2001), pp. 406-45.

promise about what he will become in adulthood is attached, who is theologically significant. Because Jesus never made a specific link between his birth and the child he placed in the midst, it is probably wise to avoid conflation, preferring instead an open anagogical relation between the two.[22]

The Kingdom of Heaven (Matthew 3–21)

The birth narratives conclude with the account of how Joseph took "the child and his mother to Nazareth" (Matt. 2:21-23), and this next section of the text begins with the words, "In those days." At this point Matthew describes John the Baptist and his ministry, summarizing his message thus: "Repent, for the kingdom of heaven is near" (3:2). This is the announcement of the most important news (good news, or *gospel*) of which Matthew can conceive. It is also the commencement in this reading of the Gospel of one of its overarching themes.

There will be over thirty subsequent references to this kingdom in the rest of the Gospel, and nearly all of Jesus' teaching and actions reveals something of its nature and dynamics, with the child placed by Jesus in the midst having a special if not unique role in this revelation (Matt. 18).

The Initial Section of the Narrative

As Jesus is baptized the heavens open and he is identified as God's beloved Son: the kingdom is not only near but is revealed in and through his person. The essential testing or temptation that ensues in the wilderness is between God's kingdom or commands, on the one hand, and alternative (more predictable worldly, political, religious) ways of seeking to go about his mission (to save his people from their sins), on the other. John is imprisoned, and Jesus begins his ministry in Galilee, with the words, "Repent, for the kingdom of heaven is near" (Matt. 4:17).

Jesus calls four disciples, all of whom are fishermen, and then teaches, preaches, and introduces the good news by his action of healing disease and sickness. His teaching is summarized in the Sermon on the Mount, in which the radical nature of the newly announced kingdom of heaven is described

---

22. This is the pattern used to deal with the different question of the relation between faith and politics, church and state, in Karl Barth, "Christian Community and Civil Community," in *Against the Stream* (London: SCM, 1954).

(Matt. 5:1–7:29). Arguably, the main theme of this collection of teachings is "Seek first his kingdom and his righteousness" (6:33). If the disciples are surprised later by the teaching of Jesus with a little child in their midst, part of the reason may be that they had not digested just how revolutionary this "sermon" was.

Greatness in the Kingdom

It is in the Sermon on the Mount that Jesus (not the disciples) introduces the theme of greatness in the kingdom of heaven. There is a reversal of expected roles and experiences, and at one point Jesus says: "Anyone who breaks one of the least of these commandments and teaches others to do the same will be called the least in the kingdom of heaven, but whoever practices and teaches these commands will be called great in the kingdom of heaven" (Matt. 5:19). Jesus does not specifically refer to children in this collection of teachings, but what he advocates is consonant with the meaning he gives to the child, notably his stress on not storing up treasures on earth or worrying about tomorrow (6:19-34).

The Lord's Prayer

Some time later Jesus teaches his listeners to pray, "Our Father" (Matt. 6:9). The prayer assumes that those who pray are children of a heavenly Father.[23] So by now the reader has been presented with the child both as a physical, personal reality (in the Christ child) and as a metaphor for the follower of Jesus (child of God). This interplay between the real child and the child as metaphor for Christians will continue throughout the Gospel. In the efforts of scholars to seek a proper balance between the two, it seems as if the stress on the metaphor has tended to eclipse the real child in much work of the commentators to date.[24]

---

23. Joachim Jeremias, *New Testament Theology* (New York: Scribner, 1971), pp. 155-56, argues that becoming like a child means learning to say "abba" again.

24. See Weber, *Jesus and the Children*, pp. 22-33, for a discussion of the relation of actual children and children as metaphors in the Gospels.

Healing

There follows a period (Matt. 8–9) when Jesus heals people from different backgrounds of a range of illnesses and conditions and also calms a storm. Significantly, one of those healed is a twelve-year-old girl (9:18-26). Then, having demonstrated the kingdom of heaven (God's way of doing things) in practice, he sends his twelve disciples to take part in what might be seen as an inauguration of the kingdom (ch. 10).

Jesus, John the Baptist, and Children's Games

In Matthew 11:11 Jesus uses John the Baptist's greatness to illustrate one aspect of the kingdom of heaven: a person "who is least in the kingdom of heaven is greater than" John, celebrated prophet and eventual martyr. It is Jesus who continues to focus on the question that comes to dominate much of the thinking of the disciples: Who is the greatest in the kingdom of heaven?

In contrasting John's abstemious preaching and way of life with his own, Jesus uses what some commentators take to be children's rhymes or games.[25] Before we pass on we should be aware that in making one of the most important comparisons between his ministry and that of John the Baptist, Jesus does so by use of a metaphor based on children's play: "To what shall I compare this generation? They are like children sitting in the marketplaces and calling out to others: 'We played the flute for you, and you did not dance; we sang a dirge and you did not mourn'" (Matt. 11:16-19).

Revealed to Little Children

Matthew uses the phrase "at that time" [*en ekeinō tō kairō*] (Matt. 11:25) to mark the occasion when Jesus prays to his Father: "You have hidden these things from the wise and learned, and revealed them to little children.[26] Yes, Father, for this was your good pleasure" (11:25-26). In the narrative context it is clear that "these things" are to do with reading the signs that point to the heart of the kingdom of heaven: understanding the nature of God's way.[27] In

---

25. See a detailed reference to this passage in Weber, *Jesus and the Children*, pp. 1-13.

26. We know from what Jesus teaches later on, when he was in the temple at Jerusalem (Matt. 21:12-16), that he saw great significance in the cries of babies as described in Psalm 2.

27. The equivalent passage in Luke's Gospel, 10:21-22, comes after the successful mission of

any reading of the Gospel this statement of Jesus is exceptional: the King of the kingdom is announcing how the kingdom of heaven is advancing, despite the fact that it is being resisted or rejected by whole cities. By way of contrast, it is the will of his Father that children are given the capacity to sense the reality of what is going on in the world around with specific reference to Jesus, and to make a right living response to it. And this revelation includes "knowing the Father" (11:27). Children, the King, and the kingdom are inextricably linked in the story from now on.

But is this revelation of the kingdom to all children? Or is Jesus describing the way in which he and his message are actually being received by particular children? We cannot be sure, but as a corrective to the idea that children play no part in the crowds that follow Jesus we should note that there is good reason to suppose that they eagerly followed him, listened to his stories, and rejoiced in the signs that he did. They may symbolize young followers/disciples, but they also understand as children much that the disciples and the learned miss or reject.

As the narrative continues, the conflict deepens between traditional understandings of God's will and the new revelations of Jesus. The mother and brothers of Jesus arrive (in Mark's account, Mark 3:20-21, to rescue him because they were so concerned about his well-being), and Jesus refers to the will of his Father in heaven, by implication showing that the kingdom redefines what people understand by family ties (Matt. 12:46-50). A group of simple and direct parables about the kingdom of heaven follows (Matt. 13:24-52).

When the disciples fail to understand a parable (Matt. 15:15-20), Jesus asks: "Are you still so dull?" and then praises the faith of a Gentile (Canaanite) woman, who is pleading with him to heal her daughter. In this remarkable conversation the word "children" is used to describe the descendants of Israel (Jacob). Thus the term may include many generations: a reminder that we are all children (15:21-25). The Pharisees meanwhile continue to ask for a sign, despite the fact that in Matthew's narrative they have been seeing repeated signs (16:1-12). The wise and learned simply cannot understand the kingdom of heaven.

A Turning Point

At this stage (Matt. 16:13-28) there is a major turning point in the narrative, in the ministry of Jesus, and in the disciples' understanding of the way the king-

---

the followers of Jesus and confirms this reading. Luke stresses the contrast between those who accept and those who reject the kingdom of God and its King.

dom of heaven operates. At Caesarea Philippi Peter confesses that Jesus is truly the Christ, the Son of the living God. Jesus tells Peter that this insight has been revealed by his Father in heaven (as the truths about the kingdom had been revealed to little children). So though Peter was quite unlike a child, as his behavior often showed, God had treated him as a child, in the sense that the Father chose to reveal this to him. The Father chose to regard Peter and expected him to respond as a child to the revelation made known. God's revelation found a voice in Peter, and maybe some perception behind the voice, and in giving voice in this way Peter was like the children of Matthew 11.

But "from that time on" (Matt. 16:21) Jesus begins to reveal to his followers for the first time his destiny on earth: he will suffer at the hands of the elders, chief priests, and elders of the law, and he will be killed in Jerusalem before being raised to life on the third day.[28] Peter protests. The insight he has been given is a momentary occurrence, which Peter proceeds to invalidate and wipe out. Overall the set of his mind and spirit is not receptive to the revelation when that reception requires childlikeness. Instead, because he has a bossy blind spirit that is Satan, Jesus rebukes him (16:23).

There follows the Transfiguration, when the divine identity of Jesus is confirmed in a dramatic and powerfully symbolic way. From now on Jesus moves south toward Jerusalem to "drink his cup" (see Matt. 20:22), and he reveals the nature of the kingdom of heaven in increasingly direct terms by his actions and teaching.

Children as Signs of the Kingdom

We have reached a sequence in the narrative (Matt. 17:14–21:16) when children become a key sign of the kingdom. One of the ways of understanding the significance of this point is to consider Jesus on the final stage of his journey and during the last period of his teaching. He is seeking to remind his disciples of what he has already taught and to sharpen their understanding of truths about the kingdom of heaven.[29] On coming down from the

---

28. Jesus speaks three times of his death in Matthew's Gospel (16:21; 17:22-23; 20:17-19), and each time there is a significant reaction from his followers and friends.

29. I have explored this section of Matthew's narrative in an unpublished paper called "A Walk with Jesus from Caesarea Philippi to Jerusalem," originally delivered to the Episcopal Church in Camp Allen, Texas, 2004, and in a modified form to the Anglican Children's Advisers' Conference, at High Leigh, London, in 2005. The incidents involving children are interspersed with conflicts between the kingdom of heaven and daily life and issues such as a tax, forgiveness and debt, divorce, and wealth.

mountain Jesus finds a boy suffering from seizures (17:14-23). His disciples cannot help. Jesus heals the boy, talks of faith like a mustard seed, and reiterates his destiny (this is the second of three occasions) in such a way that the disciples are filled with grief. The issue of payment of taxes is a rude reminder of the intersection between the kingdom of heaven and "the kings of the earth" (17:14-27).

Now comes the moment in the narrative when Jesus places a little child (*paidion*) in the midst of his disciples. Although there are similarities between the Synoptic Gospels at this point, Matthew has the fullest account of Jesus' teaching here.[30] As noted above, it includes the phrase "unless you change and become like little children you will never enter the kingdom of heaven" and also the challenge to "become humble like this child." This teaching seems to stand everything on its head. The disciples have the greatest claim to be insiders of this kingdom: that is why they are talking about their positions within it. They are sure they are in: the main unanswered question concerns their future status. Peter, James, and John are the front runners, having been with Jesus on the mountain. But now Jesus introduces a rank outsider (the little child) and indicates that the reality is the very opposite of what the disciples believe to be the case. The outsider is inside; and they, unless they change, are outsiders!

To them this kingdom is beginning to seem bizarre, if not crazy. It is completely upside down, inside out, and back to front. A little later (Matt. 19:27), Peter asks what is in it for those who have followed Jesus all through his ministry, but the consistent teaching of Jesus that began in earnest with the Sermon on the Mount has not changed. True happiness and blessing belong to the most surprising people. And these people are epitomized by the little child, who is negligible to the point of invisibility. The child has no merit or value compared to those who have made sacrifices for the kingdom. This is real humility (perhaps "marginalization" is a contemporary dynamic equivalent), the sort that characterizes Jesus as he hangs on the cross. The child is perhaps a sign of the ultimate marginalization and despising of Jesus.

Jesus also places the warning about the millstone immediately after his teaching about the child and the kingdom: "If any of you put a stumbling block before one of these little ones who believe in me, it would be better for you if a great millstone were fastened around your neck and you were drowned in the depth of the sea" (Matt. 18:6). Welcoming or rejecting the kingdom is synonymous with welcoming or rejecting a little child or little one

---

30. The parallel passages are helpfully compared in Zuck, *Precious in His Sight*, pp. 202-4.

who believes in Jesus.[31] You cannot follow (and that includes welcoming and accepting) Jesus without welcoming children. You cannot reject (and that includes refusing and marginalizing) children without rejecting Jesus.

The parable about a lost sheep is told by Jesus to ensure that "you do not look down on one of these little ones, for I tell you that their angels in heaven always see the face of my Father in heaven" (Matt. 18:10-14). Twice as Jesus tells the story he refers to his Father in heaven. He is identifying himself with children, literal and metaphorical. In some readings of the text, however, the link between this parable and the little child placed by Jesus in the midst is lost.[32]

Jesus then teaches about forgiveness and responds to a question about divorce (Matt. 18:15–19:12). The kingdom of heaven is set in the real (sociopolitical) world, and the contrast between their two value systems and modi operandi continues to be stressed.

Despite Jesus continually teaching about and demonstrating the kingdom of heaven, there is no shred of evidence that the disciples are any nearer to understanding what Jesus means. Little children are brought to Jesus for him to place his hands on them and pray for them ("bless them," possibly with the Aaronic blessing), but his disciples "rebuked those who brought them" (Matt. 19:13-15). Jesus tells them to let the children come to him, "for the kingdom of heaven belongs to such as them." Once again there are actual children in the presence of Jesus and the disciples as he teaches and acts.

Whatever else they may stand for metaphorically, they are real children, and their actual participation in the narrative cannot be allowed to be eclipsed by other readings of the Gospel. Real children have enormous metaphorical potential. They are provocative of ideas and visions. Grown-ups see themselves, their experience, their world, and their futures through what the child sparks off in them. Children scatter metaphors without limit as real children. They are despised and violated if in any way people take flight on the metaphor and abandon the real child.

A rich young man (Matt. 19:16-22) comes to Jesus wanting to enter the kingdom of heaven ("get eternal life"). Jesus tells him to sell everything to gain treasure in heaven and then to follow him. The man goes away saddened, and when Jesus explains how hard it is for a rich man to enter the kingdom of heaven the disciples are alarmed. Giving no indication of having heard what

---

31. It may be that in challenging his male disciples to welcome children Jesus is making a radical point in refusing to accept that the rearing of little children is solely the responsibility of women.

32. For example, Stendahl, "Matthew," p. 789, where he sees the guardian angels as relating to "rank-and-file disciples."

Jesus taught with the child in the midst, they wonder who can be saved (19:23-30). Jesus consoles them but reminds them that the kingdom of heaven is a back-to-front realm. A parable follows confirming that God's kingdom does not work on the principle of human merit, fairness, or effort (20:1-16). Jesus then tells of his coming destiny and death for the third time (20:17-19).

And once again the matter of entry and position in the kingdom of heaven arises (Matt. 20:20-27). This time it is the mother of two of the disciples who has a question. In response to it Jesus spells out to his restive followers in no uncertain terms that the kingdom of heaven is a complete contrast to the ways of earthly kingdoms. Greatness is about servanthood, and the Son of Man came not only to serve but to give his life as a ransom for many (20:26-27).

Two blind men call out to Jesus (just like uninhibited children), and then Jesus enters Jerusalem. From the point at which he reveals his destiny and how the kingdom really operates (Matt. 16:21), children have been the most consistent sign of the kingdom.

In the temple (Matt. 21:12-16) Jesus continues to demonstrate the kingdom by cleansing the temple of inappropriate activity (which has more in common with the kingdoms of the earth than the kingdom of heaven?), and he heals the blind and the lame. It seems as if an awkward, possibly fearful silence has replaced the earlier Hosannas. But no, children continue to acknowledge the Chosen One: "Hosanna to the Son of David!" Jesus is confronted by indignant leaders and points them to Psalm 8: "From the lips of children and infants you have ordained praise." This is the climax of this section of the narrative of the life of Jesus, in which children and the kingdom have been inextricably linked. And it is the final journey from Caesarea Philippi to Jerusalem, from the slopes of Mount Hermon to Mount Moriah, from the transfiguration to the cross.

Reflections on the "Child in the Midst" and Real Children or "Little Ones of Faith"

In the story of the little child placed by Jesus in the middle of his disciples, Jesus calls the child and teaches the surprising truths about the kingdom and how important children are both as signs of it and as examples of how to enter it. There is a special chemistry between children and the kingdom of heaven, and also between children and the King of that kingdom, Jesus himself.[33]

---

33. The forthcoming book *Reception Class* (London: SPCK) by myself and Haddon Willmer takes this chapter as its framework. Others, notably Judith Gundry, have underlined the impor-

One way of reading this incident is as an echo of the birth narratives. The first two chapters of Matthew's Gospel place Jesus at the center of God's saving acts, theology, history, and revelation; now Jesus places a child in the center of his followers and in the middle of a theological discussion about the kingdom of heaven.

Readings that emphasize children as representatives of little ones of faith have the virtue of recognizing that Jesus is not making the little child the focus of attention or of his teaching. He certainly does not list the virtues of the child as a model citizen of the kingdom of heaven. The child is signed by Jesus in a specific theological (and narrative) context.

However, such readings hardly do justice to the fact that a little child is actually standing beside Jesus and in the middle of, and as a contrast to, the group of disciples, and that we have no warrant to suppose that the child is not present throughout the discourse until the end of the parable of the Lost Sheep (Matt. 18:14). This is a matter of critical importance in reading this passage, and commentators generally tend to ignore or overlook the question of how long the child placed by Jesus actually stood in the midst of the disciples. If the child remained standing there throughout the discourse until the end of the parable about the lost sheep, then it makes a difference to the interpretation of the whole of Jesus' teaching.[34]

Readings that stress the child as symbolic of Christians bring to the text an assumption that Matthew in general and this passage in particular are really about the church.[35] The debate is unresolved, but suffice it to say that any attempt to conflate church and kingdom of heaven is one that is difficult to substantiate in this reading of the Gospel. Whereas Matthew has introduced

---

tance and significance of the pericope. See also Zuck, *Precious in His Sight,* pp. 201-16. We will not dwell on this chemistry here, but one fruitful line of inquiry concerns the congruity between the kingdom of heaven, which is both "now and not yet," and children, who are also fully human and yet still in the process of becoming mature adults. Both manifest the tension between the present reality on the one hand and the future development or realization on the other. See Keith J. White, "Childhood and the Kingdom," unpublished paper given at the Westminster School of Theology, 7 May 1999.

34. Zuck, *Precious in His Sight,* p. 208, makes this point in relation to Mark's Gospel where the child is sitting on the lap of Jesus.

35. D. Hagner, *Matthew 14–28,* Word Biblical Commentary (Dallas: Word, 1995), p. 520, puts it like this when writing about verse 6: "The shift in terminology [from children to little ones] is a deliberate one, intended to show that now . . . those in view are not little children but disciples, i.e. Christians in the church who are being likened to little children. Pursuing the theme of this discourse, which can be characterised as life in the Kingdom of Heaven on earth (or here we might say 'the church') Matthew turns to the importance of not causing others or oneself to stumble."

"the child" in chapters 1 and 2 and reintroduced little children in his later narrative about the kingdom of heaven, there is arguably not the same degree of reference to church, although it is present in 16:18 and 18:15-20.

The present reading of the Gospel with a child foregrounded is not seeking to exclude the metaphor of children as "little ones" and reject the idea of any connection between children and disciples, but rather to see how this relationship is developed by Jesus. In so doing we can assume that it would be most unlike Jesus to take a real child as a sign without being genuinely interested in and committed to the well-being of that particular child. Jesus does not use people as teaching illustrations: they may become that, but his primary motivation is love and compassion for the individual concerned.[36]

But there is another exegetical problem: Even if "child talk" is part of "church talk" for Matthew here, why should church be the dominant determining category? Why should Jesus not be questioning and subverting church pretensions, by making "child talk" the language in which he wants to speak, the way in which he wants to say what church is called to? Matthew is concerned about religious community but not dominated or contained by church. He knew the difference between Jesus and church, played out visibly: Jesus had resources to be both for the church and against it, both inside and outside. Matthew can be read thus as subverting or relativizing church, whether from the inside or from outside, where Jesus often finds himself with the child.

So it is possible to read the Gospel as a way of challenging the way the disciples understand not only their own company and relationships but also kingdom and church. If child simply represents church, then how could a child be placed in their midst as a critical over-against?

There seems to be little reason why the references to a little child should not be taken to refer both to a child and also symbolically to other little ones, and so by extension to "big ones as little ones."[37] After centuries of marginalization, we should be careful not to render children marginal to the point of invisibility, particularly where and when Jesus chose to place them in the midst, as signs of the kingdom of heaven and of welcoming him. We must beware lest for whatever seemingly good reason we find ways of losing the significance of what God in Christ is seeking to communicate to us, whether as individuals or as a community of faith.

Read in this way, Matthew 18 (in the context of the narrative so far) allows

---

36. W. A. Strange, *Children in the Early Church* (Carlisle: Paternoster, 1996), p. 57.

37. Zuck, *Precious in His Sight*, p. 208, lists the commentators who take this line. They include Lenski (1961), Beasley-Murray (1962), France (1985), Lightner (1977), and McNeile (1955).

the little child to be a recipient of the kingdom of heaven, a model of what it means to enter the kingdom of heaven, a sign of the humility required in the kingdom of heaven, and also one who, when welcomed, becomes the means of welcoming Jesus.[38]

The Climactic Clash of Kingdoms (Matthew 21:18–28:20)

The story enters its final dramatic phase. There is a parable about the kingdom of heaven (Matt. 22:1-14: the wedding banquet), but the specific teaching about the nature of the kingdom is basically over. It is the endgame, in terms of both the life of Jesus and the eschatological focus of his teaching.

There is no more teaching directly about children (except perhaps obliquely in the reference to a hen gathering her chicks in Matt. 23:37) and little more teaching about the kingdom of heaven. Why? Because the grain of mustard seed is falling into the ground. The time for teaching is over: the pivotal crisis on the way toward the realization of all that this kingdom is and means has arrived. The full scandal of the kingdom is there for all to see, not least the disciples. This is what taking up the cross means. It is an upside-down kingdom, back to front and inside out. If the mother of Zebedee's sons (James and John) had known that this was what the kingdom meant, she would have kept silent rather than asking for what she considered to be a great favor on behalf of her sons. Hence the reply of Jesus: "You do not know what you are asking." He ends the conversation with the words: "the Son of Man did not come to be served, but to serve, and to give his life as a ransom for many" (20:20-28).

The Gospel closes with the resurrection and what is often called the Great Commission (Matt. 28:16-20).

Reflections on the Clash of Kingdoms in the Light of the Child

Even in this section, the teaching of the kingdom and its relation to children has not been lost, and for a profound reason. From the time Jesus began to teach his disciples about the fact that the Son of Man must suffer and die, the presence of children as signs of the kingdom can be detected. And what is the

---

38. See J. Gundry-Volf, "The Least and the Greatest," in Bunge, ed., *The Child in Christian Thought*, pp. 37-48, for an exposition of these themes.

essence of the sign? It is that the kingdom of heaven has got absolutely nothing to do with status, hierarchy, or merit, and everything to do with genuine humility. The greatest is the least; the Son of Man has come to be the servant of all. Jesus is not part of the political trading game. His kingdom is not of this world, not in the sense that it is "other-worldly" or wholly mystical or of the human heart and spirit without reference to daily life and politics, but because it operates by completely different principles to the organizations, culture, religion, and politics that dominate the life of this world.

He makes himself of no reputation, and takes upon himself the form of a servant, and becomes obedient unto death, even death on a cross (cf. Phil. 2:8). This is the core of the message of the kingdom of heaven. Everything that seemed to count for something becomes nothing. There is no competition or contest. Now the kingdoms of the world pronounce their verdict on the kingdom of heaven in Jesus and carry out the sentence: the King and his kingdom are vanquished. That is the obvious worldly meaning of the cross.

If the King and kingdom of heaven are vanquished, then all the discussions or arguments between the disciples about who was the greatest in this kingdom have been rendered obsolete, irrelevant. The kingdom of heaven is no more, and therefore there is no position to be had in it. All that remain are the earthly kingdoms where competing for greatness is normal.

But the kingdom of heaven is not destroyed at the cross, though the kings of the earth rage and do their worst (Ps. 2). The Lord carries through his project, unswervingly, bloodied indeed but unbowed, and so the cross represents the unmasking and defeat of these kingdoms. The King of the kingdom, who has become the least of all, has given his life as a ransom for many.

However unlikely and surprising it may seem, the little child is the chosen sign of Jesus to point to this central truth.

The Great Commission

In the light of this exploration of the text, there is a telling and possibly underestimated element: "teaching them to obey everything I have commanded you" (Matt. 28:20). For the avoidance of doubt, part of this teaching (commandment) of Jesus has been to welcome children in his name, to become humble like this child, because in doing so the King of the kingdom himself is welcomed. Is it possible to omit children from the scope and coverage of this commission, given what we have traced in the narrative?

Sadly, the answer is yes. It seems as if the church, Christian commentators, and theological studies over the centuries have often been as dull (or resistant) as the disciples when it has come to the significance of children and the kingdom of heaven.[39] It is to be hoped that one effect of the increasing study of children and childhood in a theological and biblical context, and the study of the Scriptures with children foregrounded, will be the realization that the Great Commission includes implicitly the command to change to become like, to welcome, and not to despise children. For this is what the teaching and actions of Jesus include explicitly. As the Magi received the infant Jesus (by worshiping him), and as Jesus received children, the community of followers of Jesus is called to receive them, too, as signs of the kingdom of heaven and representatives of its Servant King.

Summary

This particular reading of Matthew has revealed much about the view of children in this Gospel.

(1) *Children as part of the kingdom.* Children of different ages are depicted as receiving, whether consciously or instinctively, the kingdom of heaven in ways that others in the story, including the disciples, the leaders of the Jewish people, and the Galilean towns, do not. Matthew portrays the kingdom as potentially accessible to all through the ministry of Jesus, but children and those with childlike humility and lack of concern for status or reputation (notably the Canaanite woman and the two blind men) were those who received it. Various interpretations have been proffered, notably that entry is not according to a person's fulfillment of the Law, because Jewish children were not required to fulfill the Law. But the narrative simply records that, while children were able to receive the kingdom, many adults were not.

(2) *The humility of Jesus and children.* In the narrative the vulnerability of Jesus as a baby is stressed, and throughout his ministry he accepts a lowly status and deliberately acts with humility.[40] Children likewise are singled out by Jesus in the narrative for their humility. Receiving children as a mark of true greatness is exactly what Jesus did. Serving his disciples was a form of serving children. Children were the least, the lowest, and the last in terms of social status. The kingdom of heaven was a reversal of earthly rankings: it was an upside-down, inside-out, and back-to-front kingdom.[41] Children, when

39. John Carroll, "Children in the Bible," *Interpretation* 55, no. 2 (April 2001): 132, links the reluctance of the disciples to welcome children with that of followers of Jesus since.

40. This is the primary theme of David Jensen, *Graced Vulnerability: A Theology of Childhood* (Cleveland: The Pilgrim Press, 2005).

41. Donald Kraybill, *The Upside-Down Kingdom* (Scottdale: Herald Press, 1978), p. 33;

372   KEITH J. WHITE

made the prime objects of love and service, confirmed that kingdom values or ways of doing things were operating.

(3) *The identity of Jesus and children.* Set in a context in which the teaching of Jesus about his suffering and death is rejected by his disciples, welcoming or rejecting children has great poignancy. Jesus identifies with the marginalization and rejection of children from the mainstream discourses. Knowing the true identity of Jesus is the crucial element of the whole story. When a person welcomes a child, with no thought of reward or gain, then that person has welcomed the real Jesus, King of the kingdom of heaven.

(4) *Welcoming children.* This welcome and acceptance is the beginning of a community (body) of believers. Although children are not specifically referred to in his book, the insightful statement of B. Callen about life together with Jesus applies perfectly here: "True Christian community is faithful life together on the margin with the Master."[42] If community (shared living) is essential to the process of following Jesus, then welcoming children is at its heart.[43] Peter's confession is a watershed, but it is in the temple (perhaps the symbolic *center* of the kingdom of heaven) that *liminal* children, and only children, recognize and acknowledge the Son of David. Matthew presents the signs of the kingdom actually performed in the temple as incontrovertible evidence of the Messiahship of Jesus, but it is mostly hidden from the wise and learned.

(5) *Matthew as a whole.* This study has also made discoveries about central themes of the Gospel as a whole. Children, Jesus, and the kingdom of heaven in Matthew's Gospel inform one another and are congruent to such an extent that they might be said to be inseparable. This is consistent with the teaching of the parable about the sheep and the goats in Matthew 25:31-46. To see, to welcome, and to receive one is to receive the others. And to reject one is to risk rejecting the others. They are part of the same discourse. Each is God's gift. Each is God's revelation. Once identified and welcomed, everything becomes crystal clear; but from those who are already convinced of the wisdom of their learned way of life and belief systems, the simplicity and transparency of the truth is hidden. It is all or nothing: either children, kingdom of heaven, and Jesus, the serving king; or blindness, deafness, and sadness.

G. Ladd, *The Presence of the Future* (Grand Rapids: Eerdmans, 1974); C. N. Kraus, *The Community of the Spirit* (Grand Rapids: Eerdmans, 1974); J. Bright, *The Kingdom of God* (Nashville: Abingdon, 1953).

42. B. Callen, *Radical Christianity: The Believers' Church Tradition in Christianity's History and Future* (Nappanee: Evangel Publishing House, 1999), p. 23.

43. Kraybill, *The Upside-Down Kingdom,* pp. 303-8, stresses the importance of community in the kingdom of heaven.

It follows that to abuse and to mar children, "the least of these little ones who believe in me" (Matt. 18:6), is to strike at the heart of the kingdom of heaven and at the heart of Jesus. It is blasphemy, taking God's chosen language in vain. It is to take up sides against God and his will. The words of Jesus in Matthew make it clear that such action is evidence of Satan's work through human activity. It is not a peripheral matter affecting those who do not count, but rather a fundamental attack on God.

Conclusion

Though unremarked by Matthew, children are in a real sense God's language in and through which he reveals his true nature and therefore the nature of his kingdom. It is not just that children are signs whose message has to be read and interpreted (though they are also that); rather, as children *qua* children they are God's language.[44] They are God's language not because, like prophets, they have been entrusted with a particular message (like little Samuel, for example) but by virtue of being children, playing games, speaking out when others fall silent, responding to the invitation of Jesus. The medium is the message. According to Matthew, God has chosen to reveal himself and to speak in many ways. God is not bound to one language or medium. But it could be argued that it is children who are the language or medium through which the kingdom of heaven is most easily and naturally conveyed.

As we have noted, the important truth in Matthew 18 is not that the little child possesses or demonstrates a number of desirable qualities (virtues), but that the child is there, called by Jesus to stand in the midst. The child standing beside Jesus, among the disciples, is the language and the revelation. Insofar as we are in touch with children, we are open to God's chosen language. But this openness is not to be confused with adult labels of childhood. The child must be known for his or her own sake, as an agent, not an object or instrument. It is exactly the same with Jesus. We know him only insofar as we are able to know him as he is, not as we would like him to be.

---

44. I have resisted using the word "sacrament" here, not because it is inappropriate or inaccurate, but because it is not a term used by Matthew and requires more detailed consideration than this brief paper allows. Maas, "Christ as the Logos of Childhood," p. 458, does so: "The human child, vulnerable, utterly dependent and trusting, now becomes the real presence of Christ — a living sacrament of the kingdom of heaven." See also Pamela Couture, *Seeing Children, Seeing God: A Practical Theology of Children and Poverty* (Nashville: Abingdon, 2000), p. 13, where she sees caring for vulnerable children as a way in which God "makes himself known to us."

If the Gospel of Matthew is interpreted as being largely about adult understandings of church, then major themes, insights, and challenges of the Gospel will continue to be marginalized. On the other hand, anyone who wrestles with Matthew as a depiction of the kingdom of heaven in action will find it demands radical new priorities and attitudes in every area of life. No one should underestimate the degree of change required when seeking first this kingdom and becoming like little children. This is not facilitated by way of infantile regression, but in following Jesus and the way of the cross: that is, in being humble, lowly, and liminal.

This new way of living is not always about literal death and renunciation. It is about the willingness to see everything and everyone in a fresh light, to be willing to turn and to change, and to welcome the questions of stubborn or inquiring children as potential signs of God's way of doing things. A good place to start is to consider what real greatness is with a little child standing beside Jesus in the shadow and light of the cross.

17 Adoption in the Bible

David L. Bartlett

The Bible is a rich resource for reflection on adoption. In different ways both Moses and Jesus are portrayed as adopted children. In some psalms when the king is enthroned in glory the texts suggest that God is the adoptive parent of the human sovereign. Paul uses the idea of adoption as a description of the way in which believers are brought into fellowship with Christ. He is particularly concerned to show how adoption can bring Gentiles into God's family, where they can join with Jews.

Adoption is also a widespread and widely honored practice in contemporary society. Private, religious, and state institutions are devoted to placing adopted children with suitable adoptive parents. In some communities there is controversy over whether single parents or gay and lesbian couples should be allowed to adopt children, but there is no controversy over the claim that adoption itself is both a personal privilege and a social good.

It is striking that in most cases the biblical texts about adoption do not apply directly to the most widespread adoption practices today. While it is clear that the Old Testament presupposes that people will take almost parental responsibility for offspring not their own, it is not clear that ancient Israel had formal adoption practices. Many of the examples of adoption in both Old and New Testaments involve or suggest the adoption of adults, and the practice in the Greco-Roman society of New Testament days often involved the adoption of adults as well. This essay will therefore look at an ancient practice that sometimes applied directly to children but by no means always did so.

Special thanks to my colleagues William Brown, Charles Cousar, and Elizabeth Johnson for their help in preparing this essay.

Nonetheless, with the study of these sources in mind, it will be possible to say something both about adoption as an image of the life of faith and about the biblical understandings of adoption as clues for how faith communities deal with children today, especially in the practice of child adoption.

The center of our inquiry is Paul's remarkable claim to the Galatian Christians:

> But when the fullness of time had come, God sent his Son, born of a woman, born under the law, in order to redeem those who were under the law, so that we might receive adoption (*huiothesia*) as children. And because you are children, God has sent the Spirit of his Son into our hearts crying, "Abba! Father!" So you are no longer a slave but a child, and if a child then also an heir through God. (Gal. 4:4-7)

In order to deepen our reading of this passage, we will explore other passages on adoption, first in the Hebrew Bible, then in the Greco-Roman world of the first century, then in other New Testament passages, and finally in Paul. From Paul we will move to the issues of children and adoption today.

Some of the current issues this essay will address are these. How does the metaphor of adoption help us to understand the role of faithful persons and of communities of faith today? How do adoption narratives in the Bible help contemporary people to understand our responsibility toward children? How do these narratives help us understand a whole range of social and theological issues through the lens of the child? How might we rethink personal and social practices in using the adoption material in Scripture as a central part of our reflection and action?

Adoption in the Hebrew Bible

God Adopts Israel

Janet L. R. Melnyk has suggested that in the Old Testament there are a number of references to God as the one who adopts Israel.[1] One central text is Hosea 11:1-5:

---

1. Janet L. R. Melnyk, "When Israel Was a Child: Ancient Near Eastern Adoption Formulas and the Relationship between God and Israel," in *History and Interpretation: Essays in Honor of John H. Hayes*, ed. M. Patrick Graham, William P. Brown, and Jeffrey K. Kuan, Journal for the Study of the Old Testament Supplement Series 173 (Sheffield: Sheffield Academic Press, 1993), pp. 245-59.

When Israel was a child I loved him,
And out of Egypt I called my son.
The more I called them
The more they went from me;
They kept sacrificing to the Baals,
And offering incense to idols.
Yet it was I who taught Ephraim to walk,
I took them up in my arms
But they did not know that I healed them.
I led them with cords of human kindness,
With bands of love.
I was to them like those who lift infants to their cheeks.
I bent down to them and fed them.
They shall return to the land of Egypt,
And Assyria shall be their king,
Because they have refused to turn to me.

Looking at parallels from other ancient Near Eastern literature, Melnyk sees in this passage three typical marks of the adoption narrative. First, the parent claims the child in adoption (YHWH loves but does not beget Israel and calls — adopts — him out of Egypt). Second, the parent promises that the child will have an inheritance (here perhaps implicit in YHWH's teaching Israel to walk). Finally, the parent vows to discipline the child when necessary (thus the sending back to Egypt).

Hosea 1:10 is a kind of dis-adoption followed by adoption again. Other possible adoption texts include Deuteronomy 7:6-7 and 14:1, and Jeremiah 3:19, where the relationship between sonship and inheritance is more clear:

I thought
How I would set you among my children
And give you a pleasant land,
The most beautiful heritage of all the nations.
And I thought you would call me,
My Father,
And would not turn from following me.[2]

Jeremiah 3:20-21 goes on to describe the adopted Israel's apostasy and the punishment and weeping that follow.

---

2. See Melnyk, "When Israel Was a Child," pp. 248-51, for reference to this and other passages.

In closing her essay, Melnyk speculates on the possible reason for the stress on God's relationship to Israel as that of an adoptive parent to a child:

> The biblical writers were interested in portraying Israel as chosen and adopted by God. One wonders why the parent-child relationship was often portrayed as one of adoption rather than as one of biological birth. Perhaps because the metaphor of YHWH as parent is almost exclusively a male image, there must be a mother if YHWH is to father a nation. Although the land is sometimes given this role, the adoptive process conveniently circumvents the need for a birth-mother, and YHWH is shown to be capable of every other maternal nurturing. By conceiving the relationship as adoption, God's election of Israel, his beloved son, was emphasized. This, in turn, distinguished Israel as the people chosen by God over all other nations, and as the recipient of a desirable land for all generations of God's *bet-'ab* to enjoy. By identifying Israel as God's child, the biblical writers wrote Israel into a sense of legitimacy, recognition, and inalienable inheritance.[3]

God Adopts the King

In other passages in the Hebrew Bible it is not Israel but the (Davidic) king whom God adopts.

2 Samuel 7:11-15a

> [The Lord speaking to David:] When your days are fulfilled and you lie down with your ancestors, I will raise up your offspring after you who shall come forth from your body, and I will establish his kingdom. He shall build a house for my name, and I will establish the throne of his kingdom forever. I will be a father to him, and he shall be a son to me. When he commits iniquity I will punish him with a rod, such as mortals use, with blows inflicted by human beings. But I will not take my steadfast love from him.

Kyle McCarter makes clear how dependent this text is on the language and concept of adoption:

> The language used here . . . has nothing to do with physical descent or, therefore, with divine kingship. It is adoption language. . . . Its purpose is to qualify the king for the patrimony YHWH wishes to bestow on him.

3. Melnyk, "When Israel Was a Child," p. 259.

Calderone . . . and Weinfeld . . . have illuminated this concept by demonstrating that the model from which the language is drawn was the grant of land and/or "house" made by a king or lord to a loyal vassal. Such grants were made patrimonial and thus permanent by means of the legal adoption of the vassal as the son of the Lord. Here the establishment of a "house" for David is legitimated in the same way. Israel becomes, in effect, the patrimonial estate of David's family.[4]

One reason for adoption (often of adults) in the ancient world was the death of the biological father. Here God seems to promise David that when he dies God will be adoptive father to David's biological son. Further, as McCarter points out, the function of adoption is not to guarantee emotional support or spiritual security for the one who is adopted. The purpose of adoption is to provide a secure patrimony — an inheritance. Adoption becomes a covenant between the adoptive parent and the adopted child — the parent is guaranteed the right to keep property in the family; the child is guaranteed the right of inheritance.

Furthermore, the adopted heir, the king, takes on all the rights and privileges and responsibilities pertaining to being a son. When he goes astray, he will be punished. But the adoptive relationship, the covenant, is unconditional. "I will not take my steadfast love from him."[5] We note here that the steadfast love has a concrete manifestation: it is the inheritance, the patrimony, that will not be removed.

Psalm 2:7

I will tell of the decree of the Lord:
he said to me, "you are my son;
today I have begotten *(yalad)* you."

Though there is some dispute as to whether this represents some kind of standard adoption formula, there seems little doubt that as in 2 Samuel God is here taking the king into God's family. The use of "begotten" may be contrasted to the simple use of the verb "to be" in 2 Samuel 7, but the text seems to function again as a formula whereby God adopts the king at his enthrone-

---

4. P. Kyle McCarter Jr., *II Samuel: A New Translation with Introduction and Commentary*, Anchor Bible (New York: Doubleday, 1984), p. 207. Similarly see James M. Scott, *Adoption as Sons of God*, Wissenschaftliche Untersuchungen zum Neuen Testament, 2.48 (Tübingen: J. C. B. Mohr/Paul Siebeck, 1992), p. 100.

5. McCarter, *II Samuel*, p. 208.

ment. Artur Weiser thinks that the "begotten" formula may have originated in the Near Eastern myths of the divine parentage of royal figures, but the psalmist "transforms that alien idea into the idea of adoption, that is to say, into the declaration of the sonship of the king that took place on the day of his enthronement. By that act special importance is attributed not to the person of the king as such but to his function as king."[6] Note the use of "begotten" (*yalad*) and see our discussion of John 1:13 below.

Psalm 89:26-33 [in this part of the psalm YHWH is speaking of David]

He shall cry to me, "You are my Father,
My God, and the Rock of my salvation!"
I will make him the firstborn
The highest of the kings of the earth.
Forever I will keep my steadfast love for him,
And my covenant with him will stand firm.
I will establish his line forever,
And his throne as long as the heavens endure.
If his children forsake my law,
And do not walk according to my ordinances,
If they violate my statutes
And do not keep my commandments
Then I will punish their transgressions with the rod
And their iniquity with scourges;
But I will not remove from him my steadfast love
Or be false to my faithfulness.[7]

Here the claim that David is "firstborn" seems to represent both an allusion to adoption and a metaphor to compare David with all other kings, who may be "sons of God" but are not God's firstborn son.[8] Again the adoption carries with it the promise of patrimony — that the line will endure forever. Again YHWH promises that like a strong parent God will punish their transgressions but not remove steadfast love, not destroy the covenant.[9] Whether

6. Artur Weiser, *The Psalms: A Commentary*, trans. Herbert Hartwell (Philadelphia: Westminster, 1962), p. 113.

7. In the Masoretic Text the quoted passage begins with verse 27.

8. Weiser sees this as an adoption text (*The Psalms*, p. 208).

9. Scott presents evidence of early messianic interpretations of this psalm and notes that its themes are picked up in the New Testament, especially Romans 8:29b. Scott, *Adoption as Sons of God*, pp. 252-53; see also Weiser, *The Psalms*, pp. 592-93.

Psalms' references to the king as God's son draw more prominently on Near Eastern mythology of kings begotten by deities or on formulas for adoption, James Mays draws the essential theological implication of such rhetoric:

> In interpreting Psalm 2 and its companion royal psalms, we must remember that this way of believing and speaking about the king had a specific social location where it had its meaning and function. Its subject is the relation between God and king. It is really more about God than about the king. It is confessional, formulaic, poetic, and ideal. It is not the language of actual or practical politics, nor is it individual or biographical. Israel had other ways of talking and believing about kings and kingship. . . . The idiom found in the psalms was used to express faith in what the Lord, the God of Israel, was working out through the office of the Davidic kingship. The office, not the individual or the particular historical situation, was its theme.[10]

Adoption of Particular Persons

There are at least three other passages in the Hebrew Bible where we have evidence of something like adoption.[11] Moses is "adopted" in Exodus 2:10: "When the child grew up, she [Moses' mother] brought him to Pharaoh's daughter, and she took him as her son. She named him Moses, 'because,' she said, 'I drew him out of the water.'" It is possible here that the adoption and the naming are part of one act. The Hebrew reads, more woodenly: "When the child grew up, she brought him to Pharaoh's daughter and she took him as her son and she named him Moses."

In the book of Esther, the NRSV translates the verses that introduce Esther in this way:

> Mordecai had brought up Hadassah, that is Esther, his cousin, for she had neither father nor mother; the girl was fair and beautiful, and when her father and her mother died, Mordecai adopted her as his own daughter. (Esther 2:7)

10. James L. Mays, *Psalms*, Interpretation (Louisville: John Knox Press, 1994), p. 46.

11. Michael J. Broyde shows that the idea of legal "adoption" is foreign to Jewish legal precedents — and presumably also to the Hebrew Bible — because fatherhood is a biological concept rooted in the stories of creation. What is appropriate to Jewish practice is a kind of custodial care-giving that does not change the legal status of a child in relationship to a biological parent. Broyde, "Adoption, Personal Status, and Jewish Law," in *The Morality of Adoption: Social-Psychological, Theological, and Legal Perspectives*, ed. Timothy P. Jackson (Grand Rapids: Eerdmans, 2005), pp. 128-47.

When the turn came for Esther, daughter of Abihail the uncle of Mordecai, who had adopted her as his own daughter, to go in to the king, she asked for nothing except what Hegai, the king's eunuch, who had charge of the women, advised. Now Esther was admired by all who saw her. (Esther 2:15)

In both these passages, the root of the Hebrew phrase that is translated "adopted her" is *laqaḥ,* and the phrase means literally "took her for himself." It is unclear whether this represents any kind of legal adoption or (perhaps more likely) a kind of foster care provided by Esther's relative in his role as part of the extended family.[12] Certainly in the story Mordecai takes a kind of parental role in regard to his relative.

In Genesis 48:5 Jacob takes parental authority for Joseph's sons, Ephraim and Manasseh: "Therefore your two sons, who were born to you in the land of Egypt before I came to Egypt, are now mine; Ephraim and Manasseh shall be mine, just as Reuben and Simeon are." Jacob's claim on his two "sons" or "foster sons" is indicated simply by the Hebrew preposition "*l,*" "to" or "for" with a pronominal ending: "They shall be mine."

James Scott argues that the three texts taken together suggest the existence of a Hebrew adoption formula.[13] Furthermore, says Scott, "The fact that Ex. 2:10 contains an adoption formula is corroborated by the analogy of the Old Testament marriage formula . . . (1 Sam. 25:42; 2 Sam. 11:27, Ruth 4:13)."[14]

Given the fact that the people of Israel wanted to deal compassionately with orphans in their midst,[15] it is perhaps surprising that there are not more biblical references to the role of women in adopting orphans. The story of Moses is the clear exception. We can suggest two reasons for this. First, the care of orphans was probably the responsibility of the extended family. The caregivers certainly would have included (perhaps especially) women, but there is no evidence of legal or institutional formulas by which such arrangements were formalized. Second, insofar as something like official adoption was a factor in the life of Israel, what was at stake for the adoptee was financial security and inheritance. Most often, to promise such inheritance and to provide such security would have been the responsibility

---

12. "Although there is no specific word for adoption in the Old Testament, there are prominent instances of fosterage or legitimization (taking a child as son), which resemble adoption." Jeanne Stevenson-Moessner, *The Spirit of Adoption: At Home in God's Family* (Louisville: Westminster John Knox, 2003), p. 29.

13. Scott, *Adoption as Sons of God,* p. 74.

14. Scott, *Adoption as Sons of God,* p. 75. Philo also interprets the text as an adoption in *The Life of Moses* 1.19. See Scott, *Adoption as Sons of God,* p. 76.

15. See the essay by Walter Brueggemann in this volume.

of men in the community. Thus we have the stories of Jacob and Mordecai promising to support their relatives and the implicit promise of God to make the king also an heir.

Thus, whether or not there were formal adoption proceedings in the world of the Old Testament, it is clear that elders took responsibility for people who were biologically the sons and daughters of other people. In the case of Moses and Esther that responsibility clearly included care and guidance; in the case of Joseph's sons, Jacob presumably makes them not only his wards but also his heirs along with Reuben and Simeon and his other sons. This begins to move us toward the world of the New Testament where for Paul adoption is also adoption into an inheritance.

Adoption in the Greco-Roman World of the First Century

Paul Veyne describes the main features of adoption in Roman families in the early years of the Common Era:

> The frequency of adoption is yet another proof that nature played little part in the Roman conception of the family. Apparently one gave a child for adoption as one might give a daughter in marriage, particularly a "good" marriage. There were two ways to have children: to conceive them in legitimate wedlock or to adopt them. Adoption could prevent a family line from dying out. It was also the means of acquiring the quality of *paterfamilias,* which the law required of candidates for public honors and provincial governments. . . . Just as a testator, in choosing an heir, also made him a continuator of the family name, a man who adopted a youth was careful to choose a successor worthy to bear his name. . . . The most striking instance of an inheritance linked to adoption involves a certain Octavius, who became the son and heir of Caesar and eventually the Emperor Octavius Augustus.[16]

Because in Roman law and society the father of a household continued to have authority over his offspring for as long as he lived, it was often mutually beneficial for a father to adopt a son. The son could benefit from the security

---

16. Paul Veyne, *A History of Private Life,* vol. 1, *From Pagan Rome to Byzantium,* trans. Arthur Goldhammer (Cambridge, MA: The Belknap Press of Harvard University Press, 1987), p. 17. Veyne points out that the economic advantages of adoption could work both ways. A father-in-law, for instance, might adopt his wealthy son-in-law so that as *paterfamilias* he would have some control over the adopted son's fortune.

and wealth of the father and finally receive some of the patrimony; the father could provide for himself the support and alliance that he might desire.

There is a fascinating collection of judicial decisions regarding adoption in Roman society in *A Casebook on Roman Family Law.* Clearly those adopted were most often not infants. The standard procedure was that the adoptive father should be older (preferably at least eighteen years older) than the adopted son. The procedure of adoption involved a kind of legal fiction whereby the son was freed by his biological father, then reclaimed, then freed again, and on the third time finally claimed by the new parent. The whole procedure was ratified before a praetor, when in a kind of version of a property dispute the new father claimed the son as his own and the biological father simply declined to dispute the claim.

Though we do not have the exact words used in such a legal procedure, it seems clear that the "dispute" and awarding of sonship included some kind of formula of claiming on the part of the adoptive father:

> In the case of a son given in adoption, three mancipations and two intervening manumissions are made, just as occurs when the *pater* releases him from power in order to make him *sui iuris*. Then he is remancipated to his father, from whom the adopting person claims him (the son) as his own before the praetor.[17]

It was also the case that the adopted son perpetuated the name of his new family "by taking the full name of the adoptive father (except non-hereditary *agnomina* such as 'Africanus') and by retaining only the previous *gentilicum* (ending in *ius*) in a modified form."[18] It is not clear whether the naming was part of the official adoption rite, but it was certainly a consequence of the adoption.

The relationships set up by adoption ran through the male line only; so if Julius adopted Caius, Julius was his legal father, but Julius's wife, Julia, was not his legal mother. Women as well as men could be adopted, though this happened far less frequently. Women, since they had no familial *potestas* — power or authority — could not adopt children. Adoption was not nearly so much a matter of affection as it was of pragmatic distribution of wealth and power.[19]

---

17. Gaius, *Institutiones* 1.134, in Bruce W. Frier and Thomas A. J. McGinn, *A Casebook on Roman Family Law,* American Philological Association Classical Resources Series (Oxford: Oxford University Press, 2004), p. 306. See also Scott, *Adoption as Sons of God,* p. 12.

18. Scott, *Adoption as Sons of God,* pp. 12-13.

19. See Frier and McGinn, *A Casebook on Roman Family Law,* pp. 304-12.

Sometimes adoptions were arranged posthumously, through a will, since that became a way to continue the family line or to bring one's daughter's sons into their grandfather's line of successors and inheritors.[20] Adoption did not sever all ties with the biological family any more than marriage might do, but "in general adoption altered hereditary succession and the adoptee was subject to the same legal privileges and limitations of a legitimate biological son."[21]

Again we can see that practices that began with the attempt to continue a family line evolved into a strategy for a variety of political and property advantages — often on both sides. To enter into adoption was not so much to enter into a family as to enter into the financial, social, and political orbit of the adoptive father.

Adoption in the New Testament

In our review of the Old Testament material we noted that some biblical references to adoption claim that Israel is God's adopted child while others claim that the Davidic king is God's adopted child. In the New Testament some adoption texts refer to Jesus' adoption — either by God or by Joseph — while others refer to the adoption of believers.

The Adoption of Jesus

Mark 1:9-11

In those days, Jesus came from Nazareth of Galilee and was baptized by John in the Jordan. And just as he was coming up out of the water, he saw the heavens torn apart and the Spirit descending like a dove on him. And a voice came from heaven: "You are my son, the Beloved; with you I am well pleased."

God's word to Jesus at Jesus' baptism may well be an adoption formula. "You are my Son, the beloved; with you I am well pleased" (Mark 1:11). If, as I think, Mark is here drawing on Psalm 2:7, the question here is not whether Psalm 2:7 was originally an adoption text (see above). The question is how Mark uses

20. Suzanne Dixon, *The Roman Family* (Baltimore: Johns Hopkins University Press, 1992), p. 112.
21. Dixon, *The Roman Family,* p. 112. See also Scott, *Adoption as Sons of God,* pp. 7-13.

that text in his Gospel.[22] In order to answer that question, we need to see if there is material from around the turn of the eras in which phrases like "You are my son" or "You are my daughter" are actually used in adoptions. Certainly the text from Gaius's *Institutiones* that we quote above suggests just such a claim as part of the legal action of adoption. If Mark is following this pattern, then God, at the baptism, claims Jesus as God's own Son. The term "beloved" *(agapētos)* may here, as frequently in the Old Testament, suggest that Jesus is God's *only* son. (See Genesis 22:2.)

We all know that Mark is entirely devoid of a birth narrative. Though it is not a major motif, I suspect that there is at least an allusion to an adoption ceremony here. C. S. Mann is right to see Mark's baptism story as a kind of tapestry composed of various threads and motifs, but adoption seems to be one of those threads: "The complexity of the declaration in this verse — composed as it is of elements of Genesis 22, Psalm 2 and Isaiah 42 and 44 — can hardly be exaggerated, since it combines motifs from the soteriological ideas of Genesis 22, a messianic designation in Psalm 2, and the Servant of Isaiah 42."[23] If there is an allusion to adoption here, what does that mean for our understanding of the adoption of believers elsewhere in the New Testament, for our understanding of baptism, and for a biblical perspective on the adoption of children today?

Matthew 1:20-25

But just when [Joseph] had resolved to do this, an angel of the Lord appeared to him in a dream and said, "Joseph, son of David, do not be afraid to take Mary as your wife, for the child conceived in her is from the Holy Spirit. She will bear a son, and you are to name him Jesus, for he will save his people from their sins." All this took place to fulfill what had been spoken by the Lord through the prophet: "Look, the virgin shall conceive and bear a son, and they shall call him Emmanuel," which means "God is with us." When Joseph awoke from sleep, he did as the angel of the Lord commanded him; he took her as his wife, but had no marital relations with her until she had borne a son; and he named him Jesus.

One plausible reading of the material is that Joseph adopts Jesus: "The future indicative (You are to name him) serves as an imperative. . . . Joseph, the son of David, is being instructed by the angel to name Jesus and thereby ac-

---

22. Another possible allusion is to Isaiah 42:1, where the reference is to the choosing of a servant rather than the choosing (adoption) of a son.

23. C. S. Mann, *Mark,* Anchor Bible (New York: Doubleday, 1986), p. 201.

cept him as his own. Jesus will therefore himself be a Davidid. Compare Isa 43:1: 'I have called you by name, you are mine.'"[24] Just as in Exodus 2:10 Pharaoh's daughter claims the child as her own by giving him his name, Moses, here Joseph claims the child as his own family by naming him Jesus. If Matthew wants the reader to recognize the parallel between the two adoption stories, it will not be the only time where Matthew uses Moses as a type for Jesus (see Matt. 2:16; 5:1). It is this adoption that makes possible the claim that Jesus is not only Son of God but also (still) son of David, Messiah, through his adoptive father.[25] In this sense Joseph follows the pattern both of Old Testament and of first-century Greco-Roman adoption: he claims Jesus for his own and by claiming him makes him part of his patrilineal family — son of Joseph, son of David. "Matthew's change of address to Joseph . . . underscores the adoption of Jesus by Joseph as his legal, though not physical, offspring. Joseph must bring Jesus into David's line in order that Jesus may become the messianic king. Naming by Mary will not avail."[26] If the naming is a kind of adoption, we have a reversal of the pattern we will see in Galatians. In Galatians Christians are biologically Gentile or Jew but adoptively children of God. In Matthew, Jesus is begotten Son of God and adoptively son of Joseph. Therefore he can be both Messiah and Son of God — both Jesus (the one who saves) and Emmanuel (God with us). Matthew uses two names for two aspects of Jesus' mission and authority.

Romans 1:1-6

> . . . his Son, who was descended from David according to the flesh and was declared to be Son of God with power according to the spirit of holiness by resurrection from the dead, Jesus Christ our Lord . . . (Rom. 1:3-4)

Psalm 2:7 may be an example of an adoption (as the New Oxford Annotated Bible suggests) or an example of installation.[27] The Romans text seems to have the same kind of ambiguity we find in the psalm. If this is an adoption passage, it places Jesus' adoption as God's Son at the time of his resurrection

24. W. D. Davies and D. C. Allison, *The Gospel According to St. Matthew*, vol. 1 (New York and London: T&T Clark, 1988), p. 209.

25. See Raymond E. Brown, *The Birth of the Messiah: A Commentary on the Infancy Narratives in the Gospels of Matthew and Luke* (New York: Doubleday, 1993), p. 132.

26. Robert H. Gundry, *Matthew: A Commentary on His Handbook for a Mixed Church Under Persecution,* 2nd ed. (Grand Rapids: Eerdmans, 1994), p. 23.

27. *The New Oxford Annotated Bible,* ed. Bruce M. Metzger and Roland E. Murphy (New York: Oxford University Press, 1991), p. 675.

and suggests that the spirit (or the Spirit) was an essential agent in that adoption. (We note how the Spirit also validates the adoption of Christians in Galatians 4 and Romans 8:15 and perhaps Mark 1:9.) I am inclined to agree with those who think that Paul here uses and revises some kind of liturgical formula for this salutation, since so many of the themes seem quite different from Paul's usual emphases. However, the fact that Paul may have borrowed this formula doesn't change the fact that this is the formula he borrowed. Paul's Christology is always a mélange of metaphors more than a systematic exposition of consistent claims, and this metaphor of adoption at resurrection is consistent with two familiar Pauline claims: (1) that Jesus has a peculiar and redemptive relationship to God; and (2) that resurrection is a major part of what makes this so.

The Adoption of Believers

Adoption in the Fourth Gospel

While John's Gospel does not have any material directly on adoption, it does suggest at two points that believers have standing as children of God and that this standing is not validated by biology but by the spirit.

In the Prologue the evangelist writes about "children of God, who were begotten, not of blood, nor of the will of the flesh nor from the will of a male, but from God" (John 1:12c-13). While this is not strictly speaking the language of adoption, it does suggest that the Christian believer's true family is not a matter of biology but of faith. God is the true *paterfamilias.* "That this gift can be received only by those who believe is brought out again by the Evangelist. . . . These are the men who . . . by virtue of their faith are God's children, God's offspring. In order to underline the miraculous nature of man's relation to God as his child, the divine act of procreation which establishes the relation is sharply contrasted with man's origins in the human sphere."[28]

In the discussion with Nicodemus, Jesus says that the believer must be born again/born from above (one Greek word — *anōthen* — means both things). To be born from above is to be born (again) not from flesh but from Spirit. "Do not be astonished that I said to you, 'You must be born from above.' The wind (or spirit) blows where it chooses, and you hear the sound

---

28. Rudolf Bultmann, *The Gospel of John,* trans. G. R. Beasley-Murray (Philadelphia: Westminster, 1971), pp. 59-60.

of it, but you do not know where it comes from or where it goes. So it is with everyone who is born of the Spirit" (John 3:8). In Paul and perhaps in Mark 1:10-11, the Spirit is the agent of adoption. In John the Spirit is the agent of second birth. In both cases it is not genealogy but God's intentionality that establishes the true "childhood" of believers.

Adoption in Paul

James M. Scott argues persuasively that the standard meaning for the Greek term *huiothesia* in the first century was "adoption."[29] There are three passages in Paul's letters where the apostle refers explicitly to adoption.

Galatians 4:1-7

My point is this: heirs, as long as they are minors, are no better than slaves, though they are the owners of all the property; but they remain under guardians and trustees until the date set by the father. So with us; while we were minors, we were enslaved by the elementary spirits of the world. But when the fullness of time had come, God sent his Son, born of a woman, born under the law, so that we might receive adoption as children. And because you are children, God has sent the Spirit of his Son into our hearts, crying: "Abba! Father!" So you are no longer a slave but a child, and if a child then also an heir, through God.

Paul writes his letter to the Galatians because he is appalled that they are being seduced to take on at least some of the prescriptions of the Jewish law, though they themselves are Gentiles and came to Christ, not through the law, but through faith and the working of God's Spirit. In the extended simile of our passage the details are not entirely clear and may be a bit confused, as is often the case when Paul tries to write parabolically.[30] The basic idea is that the Galatians were formerly slaves to false gods (the elemental spirits) just as Jews were enslaved to the law. They were rescued from their bondage by God's sending of the Son, but that rescue was also an adoption. Through the mission of God's firstborn Son, they have been brought into God's family as adopted sons and daughters.

Other features of the passage help us further to understand what Paul

---

29. See Scott, *Adoption as Sons of God*, pp. 3-116.

30. See Scott, *Adoption as Sons of God*, pp. 184-86, on how puzzling this is. He seeks to solve the puzzle by seeing the whole section as a kind of typological analogy to Israel's time as a "minor" in Egypt.

means here by adoption. First, the proof of adoption is the gift of the Spirit. (We remember the Spirit as the instrument of Jesus' own adoption in Mark 1:9.) The presence of the Spirit is evident in the Spirit-filled cry of Christian worship: "Abba!" "Abba" is the Aramaic for "Father" — perhaps even with a connotation of particular intimacy. Because Gentile Christians who were formerly under the sway of elementary spirits, false gods, call God "Father" and do so truly, they know that their adoption is valid. A friend tells the story of adopting a daughter who was no longer an infant, and how the mother did not know if the relationship was "real" until one night the new daughter needed her and cried out: "Mommy!"

Second, the gift of adoption carries with it an inheritance. We remember that in our Greco-Roman sources one of the main purposes of adoption was to guarantee to the father that the family wealth would be preserved in the (expanded) family and to promise the adopted son that he would inherit his share of the patrimony. "So you are no longer a slave but a child, and if a child, then also an heir through God" (Gal. 4:7).[31]

Third, the verses leading up to the passage on adoption make clear that, as in other biblical and secular adoption stories we have studied, to be adopted is to take on, if not a new name, at least a striking new identity: "But now that faith has come, we are no longer subject to a disciplinarian, for in Christ Jesus you are all children of God through faith. As many of you as were baptized into Christ have clothed yourselves with Christ. There is no longer Jew or Greek, there is no longer slave or free, there is no longer male and female, for all of you are one in Christ Jesus" (Gal. 3:25-28).

However unclear the details of his simile, it seems clear that Paul wanted to find language that would make clear that Jews and Gentiles both had a place in God's community and God's purposes, without both having to be subject to the law of circumcision. The claim Paul makes in Galatians 4:1-7 is that Jesus is God's "birth" son and that all other believers, Jews and Gentiles alike, are adopted into God's family to become Jesus' sisters and brothers.[32] For Paul, in Galatians, all believers are children of Abraham through faith and children of God through adoption.[33] Abraham Malherbe puts it well:

---

31. On the central importance of inheritance as a theme in Galatians, see Yon-Gyong Kwon, *Eschatology in Galatians* (Ph.D. dissertation, King's College, The University of London, 2000).

32. I do not see the text as referring to a claim about the virginal conception of Jesus one way or the other.

33. J. Louis Martyn shows how the redemption from slavery and the adoption as sons may not work with rhetorical consistency but do show forth theological power. Martyn, *Galatians*, Anchor Bible (New York: Doubleday, 1997), pp. 390-92.

New relationships came about as a result of conversion and baptism. Paul understood the experience of the Spirit in conversion as a change from ignorance to knowledge of God. This knowledge was expressed in the new self-understanding that the believer was a child of God, but that experience was to Paul possible only in a new community. In his interpretation, the Spirit baptized Jews and Greeks, slaves and free, male and female, into one body (cf. 1 Cor. 12:13). The baptismal language in Gal. 3:26–4:6 represents the convert's initiation into the Christian community as an adoption by God through which the convert is admitted into a new family of brothers and sisters.[34]

Paul writes:

For all who are led by the Spirit of God are children of God. For you did not receive a spirit of slavery to fall back into fear, but you have received a spirit of adoption. When we cry, "Abba! Father!" it is that very Spirit bearing witness with our spirit that we are children of God, and if children, then heirs, heirs of God and joint heirs with Christ — if, in fact, we suffer with him so that we may also be glorified with him. (Rom. 8:14-17)

Again for the Pauline faithful the evidence of being God's son or daughter is the privilege of crying "Abba!" That cry is itself a gift of the Spirit. Christians do not choose to be God's children; they are chosen. Again, as in so many of our passages, the fruit of adoption is an inheritance. Christians share this inheritance with their firstborn brother, Jesus. And their inheritance, like his, is an inheritance both of suffering and of glory. Suffering and glory are what you get when you are adopted into this particular family. Leander Keck suggests how theologically appropriate this image is for Paul: "The imagery fits Paul's theology because adoption confers on the 'son' a new status to which he has no right but which he receives solely because of the father's decision — theologically, adoption is an act of grace."[35]

Paul goes on to say:

I consider that the sufferings of this present time are not worth comparing with the glory about to be revealed to us. For the creation waits with eager longing for the revealing of the children of God; for the creation was subjected to futility, not of its own will but by the will of the one who subjected

---

34. Abraham J. Malherbe, *Paul and the Thessalonians* (Philadelphia: Fortress Press, 1987), pp. 48-49.

35. Leander E. Keck, *Romans,* Abingdon New Testament Commentaries (Nashville: Abingdon Press, 2005), p. 206. See the very helpful fuller discussion on pp. 205-8.

it, in hope that the creation itself will be set free from its bondage to decay and will obtain the freedom of the glory of the children of God. We know that the whole creation has been groaning in labor pains until now; and not only the creation, but we ourselves, who have the first fruits of the Spirit, groan inwardly while we wait for adoption, the redemption of our bodies. For in hope we were saved. Now hope that is seen is not hope. For who hopes for what is seen? But if we hope for what we do not see, we wait for it with patience. (Rom. 8:18-24)

Here the metaphor shifts again. In the earlier part of Romans 8 (as in Galatians 4), adoption, sonship, seems to be a present reality that points toward a future inheritance. Now the sonship, the adoption, is itself part of the inheritance: believers wait for what they do not yet see. The dueling metaphors of Galatians 4 — redemption from slavery, adoption as sons — are now combined. What Christians hope for is that adoption which is at the same time redemption. Paul's language of adoption in Galatians 4 and Romans 8:15 is eschatological in that it participates in the present in-breaking of God's reign. In Romans 4:23 the language is eschatological in that it is part of the promise for which we hope.

The link between the present reality of sonship and the future hope of sonship and redemption is the Spirit. The Spirit helps us to cry "Abba!" now, and the Spirit provides those groaning prayers by which Christian believers await the fullness of their place in God's glorious family.[36]

Leander Keck points out that Romans 8:18-23 holds forth the promise of God's reversing the curse of Eden and delivering nature and human nature from decay. The Spirit is itself the first fruits of this eschatological promise:

Does verse 23 contradict what Paul had said only a few lines before? Not really — precisely because the Spirit of adoption/son-making . . . is itself the inauguration, not the completion, of the new status; so the sequence of benefits ends with future glorification. "Putting to death" the "deeds of the body" by the Spirit (v. 13) is a sign that the inauguration has occurred, but the complete "redemption of the body" is yet to come. In short, the tension between verses 15-16 and verse 23 is nothing other than the tension between "the already" and the "not yet."[37]

If, as many believe, Romans is written in part to remind the Roman Christians that God's people consist both of Jews and Gentiles, one of the epistle's major themes is that all believers are God's children through adoption. Nei-

36. See Scott, *Adoption as Sons of God,* pp. 259-60.
37. Keck, *Romans,* p. 213.

ther Jew nor Gentile has the advantage of birth when it comes to this family.[38] Romans also makes clear that the present adoption is the first stage in a glory yet to be revealed — that inheritance wherein humankind and finally all creation will rejoice in God's gracious redemption.

> Blessed be the God and Father of our Lord Jesus Christ, who has blessed us in Christ with every spiritual blessing in the heavenly places, just as he chose us in Christ before the foundation of the world to be holy and blameless before him in love. He destined us for adoption *(huiothesia)* as his children through Jesus Christ, according to the good pleasure of his will, to the praise of his glorious grace that he freely bestowed on us in the Beloved. In him we have redemption through his blood, the forgiveness of our trespasses, according to the richness of his grace that he lavished on us. With all wisdom and insight he has made known to us the mystery of his will, according to the good pleasure that he set forth in Christ, as a plan for the fullness of time, to gather up all things in him, things in heaven and on earth. In Christ we have also obtained an inheritance, having been destined according to the purpose of him who accomplishes all things according to his counsel and will, so that we, who were the first to set our hope on Christ, might live for the praise of his glory. In him you also, when you had heard the word of truth, the gospel of your salvation, and had believed in him, were marked with the seal of the promised Holy Spirit; this is the pledge of our inheritance toward redemption as God's own people, to the praise of his glory. (Eph. 1:3-14; see also 3:14-15)

Whether Ephesians was written by Paul or by one of his disciples, the theme of adoption we found in Galatians and Romans is continued and expanded here. Markus Barth nicely catches the significance of the meaning of adoption in this passage:

> Among the NT writers Paul alone speaks explicitly of adoption. Others speak of the father-child relationship between God and man, but they prefer biological imagery and mention a specific role which the word of God, the Spirit, the resurrection of Christ, or the reception of Christ in faith has in the act of birth or rebirth. Paul's utterances on adoption emphasize the causative and cognitive power of the Spirit and at the same time the juridical-economical implication of adoption: those adopted receive an in-

---

38. On the theme of unity between Jews and Gentiles in Romans, see David L. Bartlett, *Romans,* Westminster Bible Commentary (Louisville: Westminster John Knox, 1995), esp. pp. 1-7.

heritance. His specific concern is always the inclusion of the Gentiles among the children adopted by God.[39]

We note here motifs that have already been important. Adoption is the free gift of God, and it brings together disparate people — in Ephesians, especially Gentiles and Jews. Adoption includes inheritance, and therefore there is a strong eschatological component to the notion of being adopted. Adoption is sealed and certified by the Spirit. Whereas in Galatians believers become heirs along with Christ, in Ephesians they become heirs through the agency of Christ (Eph. 1:5). The whole section, Ephesians 1:5-13, strongly suggests baptismal formulas and themes.[40] The reference to Christ as "the beloved," while it uses a participle rather than an adjective to refer to Jesus, does perhaps recall his baptism in Mark's Gospel, where Jesus is named as beloved, touched by the Spirit, and perhaps (!) adopted as God's own Son.[41]

The significance of a biblical image cannot be measured by the number of times biblical writers use that image. Its significance rests more in two capacities: (1) the capacity to illumine a wide range of biblical literature, and (2) the capacity to provide insights for the lives of interested people in every age.

Because the image of adoption can be used fruitfully to refer to Israel, to Israel's King, to Christ, and to Christ's people, it touches on a remarkable range of biblical themes and claims. Because we can use the image to help us reflect on issues related to adoption and especially to the adoption of children in our own society, it has the power that comes with applicability — it counts.

Implications

Adoption as Metaphor

Despite the diversity of the material we have studied, it is possible to make some general claims about how the language of adoption is used in the Bible. Not surprisingly, the biblical language and images also reflect something of the cultural worlds in which the biblical writers lived. The narratives, metaphors, and images of adoption help us to view, and to view anew, major biblical concerns through the perspective of children, their hopes, their needs, and their appropriate claims.

---

39. Markus Barth, *Ephesians 1–3*, Anchor Bible (Garden City, NY: Doubleday, 1974), p. 81.

40. See Nils A. Dahl, *Studies in Ephesians* (Tübingen: J. C. B. Mohr, 2000), pp. 413, 424.

41. For further helpful insights on Ephesians and adoption, see Stevenson-Moessner, *The Spirit of Adoption*, pp. 111-14.

Adoption is a powerful image for God's activity with humankind because it makes clear that membership in God's family is always the result of God's activity.

Adoption is a powerful image because adoption transcends the boundaries and barriers set by biological and ethnic identity. Jews and Gentiles, slaves and free — all can be adopted. And all become part of the same family.

Adoption is a powerful image because it can be used both of individuals and of peoples. Israel is adopted by God's activity, but so are King David and the kings that follow him. Jesus is adopted at his baptism or at his resurrection, but the whole Christian community is adopted into the family along with its elder brother.

Adoption language often implies that the adoptive parent names the newly adopted child. It reminds us that the identity of faithful people is in the identities God gives us rather than the identities we give ourselves.

Adoption language points both to the present reality of God's grace and to the future promise of participation in God's glory. In different ways believers from many faiths have received adoption, and we can lay hold of the inheritance that comes with that adoption. For Paul, at least, adoption is the beginning of a fuller membership in God's redeemed family — and even God's redeemed cosmos, a membership whose fullness is yet to be revealed.

Adoption language allows believers to lay hold of the two sides of God's parental role as we see it in the adoption poems in the prophets. On the one hand, they are called to live under the parental discipline of a wise God and to expect dire consequences if they fail. On the other hand, we know the God who adopts them may chastise them but will not let them go.

"Adoption" in Communities of Faith

There are a number of ways in which the image of Israel or of the church as God's adoptive family can help us ponder the place of children "in the midst" of our lives. Here are some suggestions.

1. The language of adoption makes clear that all of us have our place in God's family by sheer grace. We are part of this community not by our choosing but by God's activity. No one is more adopted than any other. For Christians, the only "elder" member of this community is Christ. All the rest are equally children of our adoptive father, whatever our age, experience, or degree of self-satisfaction.

2. The language of adoption always points beyond the present toward hope. In the biblical world, to be adopted is to be assured of an inheritance.

While we are all properly wary of pie-in-the-sky-by-and-by theology, the apostle who most loves the language of adoption also reminds us: "If for this life only we have hoped in Christ, we are of all people most to be pitied" (1 Cor. 15:19). Adoption stakes a claim on the future for us and for our children, too. Jews and Muslims will read that future somewhat differently, but the language of adoption reminds all that it is God's future still.

3. The language of adoption helps us remember the diversity of God's family and to honor the diversity we find in the children who are part of that family. We all rejoice in those adoptive families we know where the racial mix of the family becomes a kind of parable of the marvelous complexity of the family of God.

4. The language of adoption can help Christians understand baptism, whether for infants or for adults. Adoptive language proves more helpful in discussing the rationale for infant baptism than the ambiguous texts about the baptism of "households" in Acts. Adoptive language reminds those committed to believers' baptism that they were chosen before they chose — and that that choosing does not begin when people are old enough to make a "decision" for Christ. Christ has made the first decision for believers — and for their children, too. Other faiths may also find in the image of adoption a perspective to help understand rites of passage, maturity, and belonging.

Adoption and Social Policy

The language of adoption in the Bible also raises questions about adoption in our society today.

1. What guidelines do we get for understanding the role of adoption for today? In particular, if adoption is a "norm" for some streams of Christianity, are we turning the criteria upside down when we use the biological, male-female, two-parent model as the norm for appropriate adoptions? The Bible is not the only place to understand "family" — but note that not one passage we studied in this chapter showed a husband and a wife adopting a child. And God of course is the prototypical single parent.

Timothy P. Jackson powerfully argues that suffering children have the right to be adopted, even by would-be parents who are marginalized. He spells out the social implications:

> Rather than focusing on the rights of marginalized would-be parents, we should accent the rights of suffering children to be adopted by the marginalized. . . . What is abominable — that is, what is against God's will,

or stifling of humanity, is to deny a suffering child a loving home that he or she might otherwise have. Many singles and homosexuals could provide such a home to the hundreds of "unadoptables" trapped in foster care or warehoused in large institutions. It is not being raised in a nontraditional family that causes needless human suffering, but rather being uncared for, in utero or out.[42]

2. What insights do the biblical texts on adoption provide when we consider broader issues of social policy? Some "pro-choice" groups appropriately advocate adoption as an alternative to abortion.[43] Assuming that faithful Christianity requires at least a modicum of realism, we are required to ask whether in our nation in this century there is any realistic chance that we could provide the necessary homes for new adoptions if abortion were to end tomorrow.

3. How do we deal with those tough cases where adoption fails? There are foster parents who enter a relationship hoping to adopt, and there can be guilt and disappointment on all sides when the relationship fails. God never quite gave up on Israel, but our passages from Jeremiah and Hosea show that it was tempting. And we are not God or gods; what comfort is there for less than perfect parental love, for a relationship that may have to end? There are children who are "hard to adopt" — how do the hopeful words of Galatians or of Hosea help us understand them and our responsible ministry to them? What is the relationship between the very fragile "sonship" or "daughterhood" they may now feel and that glory as God's adopted children that we are told is our inheritance — and theirs?

4. What is the role of faith communities in supporting families living out the challenges and gifts of adoption? How do we adopt the children in our own communities of faith?

There is both wisdom and hope in these words from the Christian ethicist and theologian Mark Douglas:

> Supporting families with children is no less an act of neighbor love than loving one's biological children. Adoption and foster care can be breathtaking acts of neighbor love — of learning to love others as God loved us by adopting us as children (Gal. 4:5). Indeed, from the perspective of Jesus'

---

42. Timothy J. Jackson, "Suffering the Suffering Children," in Jackson, ed., *The Morality of Adoption*, p. 203.

43. I wish we could find more honest labels for the options in this discussion. I know of no one who is anti-life or against choice. I know many people who disagree about the issues of legalized abortion.

Lordship, we might think of adoption rather than childbirth as normative for understanding our relationships with all our children: not as natural consequences of sexual activity so much as remarkable gifts that we could not bring into existence on our own.[44]

44. Mark Douglas, *Confessing Christ in the Twenty-first Century* (Lanham: Rowan & Littlefield, 2005), p. 215.

18 Vulnerable Children, Divine Passion, and Human Obligation

Walter Brueggemann

God's Passionate Commitment to Children

The following paper considers compassionate care for needy, vulnerable children. That is a central human obligation. That *human obligation* is rooted in a sense of *divine commitment* to the most vulnerable in society. That profound divine obligation is articulated in a metaphor bespeaking ferocious and tenacious concern, a ferociousness and tenacity that constitute a summons to human obligation. I will exposit this summons of obligation and commitment with reference to the Christian Old Testament. From that text and its counterpart in the Hebrew Bible have come communities of care that have led to the enactment of a compassionate, justice-seeking human ethic. This metaphor is expressed in three texts in the Old Testament:

1. In 2 Samuel 17:8, Hushai, friend of David and advisor to Absalom, reminds Absalom of the ferocious way in which his father David will fight:

> Hushai continued, "You know that your father and his men are warriors, and that they are enraged, *like a bear robbed of her cubs* in the field. Besides, your father is expert in war; he will not spend the night with the troops."

2. In Proverbs 17:12, the wisdom teacher wants to say how dangerous a fool is, more dangerous than a she-bear:

> Better to meet *a she-bear robbed of its cubs*
> than to confront a fool immersed in folly.

3. In Hosea 13:8 the prophet describes the immense anger of YHWH who will savage disobedient Israel with a profound intensity:

I will fall upon them *like a bear robbed of her cubs,*
  and will tear open the covering of their heart;
there I will devour them like a lion,
  as a wild animal would mangle them.

All three texts play with imagery drawn directly from the lived observation that a she-bear is very dangerous if one interferes with her cubs. The attachment of the she-bear to the cubs is an intense one whereby the cubs are to be valued and protected in every circumstance. That intense attachment becomes deeply instructional. In 2 Samuel it is used to speak of *ferocious warriors;* in Proverbs this attachment is cited as the most dangerous thing imaginable, such that only *a fool in folly* is more dangerous; and finally, in Hosea the image is a way to speak of *the passion of* YHWH, the God of Israel, whose offended, betrayed love makes YHWH dangerous to beloved Israel. The imagery has many interpretive uses. But here we stay with the image itself: an irreducible, deeply instinctual, intense attachment and loyalty of the she-bear to the cubs.

What better way for us to think about children: we, the *she-bears* and *he-bears,* the children, the *cubs,* and we having for them an irreducible, deeply instinctual, intense attachment and loyalty? And yet we go beyond "she-bears" because we are made in the very image of God, whose own self is as tenacious as a she-bear toward those God created and saved and loved. For the rest of what I have to say, ponder the ferocious quality of a she-bear and think simply about how we live out the deep instinctual intensity of attachment and loyalty to our young, an intensity *engraved* in nature but at the same time *imitated* from the she-bear God of covenant who defends with limitless passion that special relationship.[1] Under this image of a she-bear — engraved in nature and imitated from God's own holiness — I consider care for children, who are to be cared for in the way that a she-bear cares for her cubs; in the same way, God is evoked to care in powerful, even reckless ways for those whom God loves.

Nurturing Our Own Young

In the Old Testament, Israel is a family, a tribe, a clan, a people.[2] It sought to do something never done before, an unprecedented act that is continued in

---

1. On such intensity of attachment, see the defining study of John Bowlby, *Attachment and Loss* (New York: Basic Books, 1969, 1980).

2. There is a growing literature on a social-scientific approach to the family in ancient Israel; see the representative study of Leo G. Perdue et al., *Families in Ancient Israel,* The Family, Religion, and Culture (Louisville: Westminster John Knox Press, 1997).

derivative communities of faith. It sought to sustain a peculiar community of care and commitment without regard to race, language, or territory, a community drawn together only by the gifts of God, miracles of origin and transformation, in order to live in responsive obedience.[3] Ancient Israel is a dangerous, revolutionary effort in the Old Testament, an effort that endlessly falls back into easier seductions. But its core commitments to the human enterprise are beyond doubt.

For our purposes it is important to notice that Israel, if it was to amount to anything significant, had to be sustained over time and through the generations. A pivotal task in that sustenance, then, was to nurture, socialize, and recruit its young into its peculiar memories and hopes. Thus ancient Israel sustained its revolutionary identity by inculcating its young into its peculiarity. Every child in Israel needed to know the memories and hopes into which it was born. Concerning *our own young* in contemporary society, I shall argue that such socialization is to be done with the tenacity of a she-bear; for if our own cubs are not summoned to peculiar memories and hopes, then the community fails and our treasured cubs revert to a life that is thinner and cheaper than the one we have been given by the grace of God.

For the most part those of us living in Western society have not been as tenacious as she-bears about this nurture, carelessly expecting sustenance to come in through the woodwork, and letting our peculiar identity be dissolved into the ways of consumerism and militarism and a dozen other seductive options. Thus I propose that our fresh agenda in "children at risk" concerns first of all our own children who are deeply at risk in a pathological society if they are not nurtured into "the ways of life."[4] To this end, I remind you of three central texts that exhibit the tenacity of a she-bear in order to make sure that *our own young* fend off the risk of losing our identity in an ocean of lesser options.

---

3. There is no doubt, however, that such expansiveness and openness were greatly resisted as well. Thus there is a pervasive tension in Israel concerning the question of who is in and who is not. My reading accents the generous side of the response made in Israel.

4. I have elsewhere provided my inventory of the way in which contemporary U.S. society may be judged as pathological. This inventory includes excessive trust in technology, excessive confidence in "therapeutic" society, mad pursuit of consumer goods and the reduction of life to commodity, and the embrace of a pervasive militarism, the purpose of which is to maintain inordinate consumerism. See Walter Brueggemann, "Living with the Elusive God: Counterscript," *Christian Century*, November 29, 2005, pp. 22-28.

1. *Exodus 12–13*

It is most remarkable that in the narrative of Exodus 1–15, where Israel recites its founding miracle, the narrative itself is interrupted in chapters 12–13 to provide guidelines for the way in which this exodus wonder is to be transmitted didactically and liturgically to the young. It is perhaps telling that Jewish interpreters who must attend to community maintenance linger long over these chapters, while Christians tend to skip over them in disregard. No doubt Christians in our society have been able to skip over such intentional practices of socialization because hegemonic cultural power would keep children in our faith in any case. But now, since Christian faith is no longer hegemonic in Western culture, we may look again to these texts:

Exodus 12:26-27

[Moses said:] "And when your children ask you, 'What do you mean by this observance?' you shall say, 'It is the Passover sacrifice to the Lord, for he passed over the houses of the Israelites in Egypt, when he struck down the Egyptians but spared our houses.'" And the people bowed down and worshiped.

The Passover concerns what is material and visible in the form of blood and lamb and lentils. These odd practices are to be done "as a perpetual ordinance for you and your children" (v. 24). These practices are to evoke an interaction between parents and children in order to sustain an odd communal identity. In this undertaking, moreover, the children are always on the horizon of the community in its practice. The purpose of these actions is to induct the young into a distinctive identity. The exercise is to evoke a child's question, "Why?" The parental generation stands ready to give an answer, the response upon which they have staked their lives. The entire enterprise is to assert that the Lord treated Israel differently. The Lord did not simply spare Israel in that night of dread but set Israel on a new course. The purpose is that the children may imagine the public world as an arena in which the liberating power of yhwh is at work. The story is filled with violence and runs toward Manicheism — "us good, Egypt evil" — but these difficult questions will come later. For now the aim is to enwrap the children into an empowering narrative that can be enacted in high drama or that can be given *in nuce* in a single sentence.

After Exodus 12:26-27, the details of the liturgical celebration continue, building toward the paragraph of 12:29-32, which tells of the departure of the slave community at the behest of Pharaoh. The central preoccupation here concerns unleavened bread, the bread of rushed departure, the bread of hurried emancipation (13:3-7).

Exodus 13:8-9

[Moses said to the people,] "You shall tell your child on that day, 'It is because of what the Lord did for me when I came out of Egypt.' It shall serve for you as a sign on your hand and as a reminder on your forehead, so that the teaching of the Lord may be on your lips; for with a strong hand the Lord brought you out of Egypt."

We do this because of what YHWH did "for me." So speaks the mother, the father, the grandparents, some adult, many generations after Pharaoh. Each of them says, *"for me."* And unspoken are the words, *"for you,"* child of the narrative. This did happen! But it is not a scientifically recoverable event. It need not be. It is a narratively available event *for me,* and *to you* "child of the narrative" (child of the miracle) — "from me to you."

The child is invited to the sacramental signs of oddness: (1) a sign on your forehead, oddness unashamed; (2) a sign on your hand, highly visible; and (3) a teaching on your lips, so familiar, so precious, that it is a fallback expression of "mother-tongue" whenever you appear before the authorities and can think of nothing else to say (see Luke 21:12-15). This is what you shall say: "With a strong hand the Lord brought you out of Egypt." Look at your hand now marked, and it will remind you of the divine hand of power that opened the path for your emancipation! You shall wear these gestures and talk the talk that together attest to the way in which YHWH has walked the walk of freedom and justice and mercy, all with immense compassion matched by power unafraid.

Exodus 13:13-16

"But every firstborn donkey you shall redeem with a sheep; if you do not redeem it, you must break its neck. Every firstborn male among your children you shall redeem. When in the future your child asks you, 'What does this mean?' you shall answer, 'By strength of hand the LORD brought us out of Egypt, from the house of slavery. When Pharaoh stubbornly refused to let us go, the LORD killed all the firstborn in the land of Egypt, from human firstborn to the firstborn of animals. Therefore I sacrifice to the LORD every male that first opens the womb, but every firstborn of my sons I redeem.' It shall serve as a sign on your hand and as an emblem on your forehead that by strength of hand the Lord brought us out of Egypt."

This particular text is somewhat differently embedded. Now there is talk of offering the firstborn animals to yhwh, that is, something of value. These tent-makers are farmers who can count. They know very well that you do not easily yield a firstborn donkey to the Lord; you can, however, substitute a firstborn sheep (of lesser value) in order to redeem the life of the donkey — that is, to save the donkey for better economic reality.

And, says the text, now that I have introduced the theme of redemption of firstborn animals and have acknowledged the value of a donkey that may be saved, let me up the ante in verse 13:

Every firstborn male among your children you shall redeem.

The entire cast of this teaching is patriarchal, and valuing concerns "sons"; in contemporary interpretation we must of course extend beyond patriarchy and the valuing of sons to include daughters. But the point is clear: the child is to be "redeemed," peculiarly valued, so that the offering made to the Lord is something of lesser value as a substitute for the precious child. The entire arrangement of redemption, a saving of something of value by the offer of something of less value, attests to the children that they are valued above all else. Indeed, it will not be very long before this verse receives the familiar echo of Micah:

With what shall I come before the Lord,
    and bow myself before God on high?
Shall I come before him with burnt offerings,
    with calves a year old?
Will the Lord be pleased with thousands of rams,
    with ten thousands of rivers of oil?
Shall I give *my firstborn* for my transgression,
    the fruit of my body for the sin of my soul?
He has told you, O mortal, what is good;
    and what does the Lord require of you
but to do justice, and to love kindness,
    and to walk humbly with your God?

(Micah 6:6-8)

Yes, give something of value. The proposed list of offerings builds in value from *calves* to *a thousand rams* to *ten thousand rivers of oil* and, finally, to "*my firstborn.*" Don't give that! Let the cherished, valued firstborn — and all the treasured children — be redeemed by acts of mercy and justice and humility. Thus our third text is a stratagem to communicate to the children how deeply valued they are. So Israel tells the children, when they ask about the tradeoff rules of animal sacrifice: the Lord brought us out by a great show of power. That power, more violent than can be justified, killed the firstborn of Pharaoh in order to send a message about value, from the human firstborn to the firstborn of animals. (Note: Exod. 12:29 adds, "the firstborn of prisoners.") The deathliness of the narrative does not extend to the storytelling community. But *not us!* But *not you!* Not you, beloved firstborn son of Israel. Not you, beloved firstborn daughter in Israel. Not you, beloved children in Israel. Not you, beloved Israel of whom was said earlier in the text:

> Then you shall say to Pharaoh, "Thus says the Lord: Israel is *my firstborn son.*" I said to you, "Let my son go that he may worship me." But you refused to let him go; now I will kill your firstborn son. (Exod. 4:22-23)

The reasoning of course is somewhat complicated; nonetheless, even the smallest child will not miss the point. That is why every year in that ancient community there was sacrifice of firstborn animals, in order to remember the treasuring God has done for us and for our children.[5] Much, much later in Israel the text echoes:

> For I am the Lord your God,
> the Holy One of Israel, your Savior.
> I give Egypt as your *ransom,*
> Ethiopia and Seba in exchange for you.
> Because you are precious in my sight,
> and honored, and I love you,
> I give people in return for you,
> nations in exchange for your life.
> Do not fear, for I am with you;
> I will bring your offspring from the east,
> and from the west I will gather you;
> I will say to the north, "Give them up,"
> and to the south, "Do not withhold;
> bring my sons from far away
> and my daughters from the end of the earth."
>
> (Isa. 43:3-6)

---

5. On the sacrifice and/or redemption of children in ancient Israel, see Jon D. Levenson, *The Death and Resurrection of the Beloved Son: The Transformation of Child Sacrifice in Judaism and Christianity* (New Haven: Yale University Press, 1993).

That echo, moreover, is not finished before we get to the now-familiar ca-
dences of Mark 10:45:

> For the Son of Man came not to be served but to serve, and to give his life a
> *ransom for many.*

It all comes down to being redeemed because each one is too valuable to be
given up.

It turns out that the whole of the liturgy that is embedded in the narrative
of emancipation is aimed at the children:

- Exodus 12:26-27: how odd we are!
- Exodus 13:8: how strong is God's power on our behalf!
- Exodus 13:14-15: how treasured we are!

Generation after generation, those who have kept this liturgy with its instruction program have sustained the young in the vision of oddness because they
did not want the children to grow up in an identity given by a culture of oppression, fear, and anxiety. From its first cadence, this ancient liturgy is a
contestation for the children who are, syllable by syllable, situated in this
practice of *treasuring,* of being of quintessential value, of being wholly protected while God's requirements are paid in other ways.

2. *Deuteronomy 6*

The contestation for the children continues in the tradition of Deuteronomy.
Indeed, Michael Fishbane proposes that the fact that Deuteronomy 6 begins
with the *shema'* evidences that the younger generation was resistant and recalcitrant toward this odd identity:

> Deuteronomy 6:20-25 discloses a tension between two generations' memo-
> ries, sets of experiences, and commitments. It questions the ability of fa-
> thers to transmit their laws and faith to their sons, who see these as alien
> and do not feel the same responsibility concerning them. But, one wonders,
> is there any reason to expect these sons to be obligated through the memo-
> ries and achievements of their fathers? That the fathers would want a conti-
> nuity through their sons of their special relationship with God is under-
> standable. But what was subjective and immediate to them is seen as
> objective and mediate to their sons. These latter have not experienced the
> experiences of the fathers, nor have they subjectivized and internalized

them. One, in fact, suspects that Moses felt this intergenerational tension most poignantly. He undoubtedly felt, so shortly before his death, full dependence on generational continuity for the realization of his labors.

The teaching of the fathers in Deuteronomy 6:20-25 is an attempt to involve their sons in the covenant community of the future, and undoubtedly reflects the sociological reality of the settlement in Canaan. The attempt by fathers to transform their uninvolved sons from "distemporaries" to contemporaries, i.e., time-life sharers, is an issue of supreme and recurrent significance in the Bible.[6]

Thus the tradition proposes *saturation nurture in oddness:*[7]

> Keep these words that I am commanding you today in your heart. Recite them to your children and talk about them when you are at home and when you are away, when you lie down and when you rise. (Deut. 6:6-7)

The text says that affluence will produce amnesia; by contrast, the sons and daughters of oddness will recognize that they have been treasured. Consequently, steps must be taken against amnesia:

> When the Lord your God has brought you into the land that he swore to your ancestors, to Abraham, to Isaac, and to Jacob, to give you — a land with fine, large cities that you did not build, houses filled with all sorts of goods that you did not fill, hewn cisterns that you did not hew, vineyards and olive groves that you did not plant — and when you have eaten your fill, take care that you do not forget the Lord, who brought you out of the land of Egypt, out of the house of slavery. (Deut. 6:10-12)

It is predictable that in this saturation nurture some impatient, nearly contemptuous teenager will ask, "What is the meaning of the decrees and the statutes and the ordinances that the Lord our God has commanded you?" (Deut. 6:20).

> Then you shall say to your children, "We were Pharaoh's slaves in Egypt, but the Lord brought us out of Egypt with a mighty hand. The Lord displayed before our eyes great and awesome signs and wonders against Egypt, against Pharaoh and all his household. He brought us out from there in order to

---

6. Michael Fishbane, *Text and Texture* (New York: Schocken Books, 1979), pp. 80-81.

7. On such nurture, see chapter 4, "Beloved Children Become Belief-ful Adults," in Walter Brueggemann, *Biblical Perspectives on Evangelism: Living in a Three-Storied Universe* (Nashville: Abingdon Press, 1993), pp. 94-131.

bring us in, to give us the land that he promised on oath to our ancestors. Then the Lord commanded us to observe all these statutes, to fear the Lord our God, for our lasting good, so as to keep us alive, as is now the case. If we diligently observe this entire commandment before the Lord our God, as he has commanded us, we will be in the right." (Deut. 6:21-25)

The response of the adult community is not unlike the three responses we have noticed in Exodus 12–13; this response also tells of the exodus. But then in Deuteronomy 6:23 the response moves beyond *the exodus miracle*, as the earlier texts did not, in order to speak of *the gift of the land*. And then in verse 24 the response moves further to tell about *"statutes to observe."* This response raises the question about obligation, responsibility, and obedience. It may be, then, that Deuteronomy 6 addresses older children whereas the three Exodus texts I have cited are for younger children. Soon or late, the children of oddness must come to see that the oddness is about a demanding ethic that anticipates response to the requirements of YHWH. This community not only receives the world differently from YHWH; it also enacts the world differently in glad response to the many gifts of YHWH.

3. Joshua

The final text in this inventory is in the book of Joshua. Now we are in a very different venue. Nonetheless, the community is still engaged in *sacramental nurture*. Now the community is moving stones around in the Jordan River. The narrative knows that if you move stones long enough through a complex narrative, some child will ask: "What do these stones mean?" (Josh. 4:21). And then, once again, the adults are ready with an informed response: "Then you shall let your children know, 'Israel crossed over the Jordan here on dry ground'" (Josh. 4:22). That first response is obvious. We are moving these stones around in replication of the way the stones were first moved around when our family crossed the river into the promised land. They crossed the Jordan and received the promised land; so we cross the Jordan and receive the promise yet again. And as often as you do this, you proclaim the promise and acknowledge that we live by that promise.

But then, in verses 23-24, the interpretive comment makes a remarkable move:

For the Lord your God dried up the waters of the Jordan for you until you crossed over, *as* the Lord your God did to the Red Sea, which he dried up for us until we crossed over, so that all the peoples of the earth may know that the hand of the Lord is mighty, and so that you may fear the Lord your God forever. (Josh. 4:23-24)

Yes, the Lord stopped the waters of the Jordan so that we could receive the land of promise. These waters could not resist the intention of the land-giving God:

> Why is it, O sea, that you flee?
> O Jordan, that you turn back?
>
> (Ps. 114:5)

But then this: "*as* the Lord dried up the Red Sea." This "*as*" is Garret Green's "copula of imagination" through which in liturgy "this" signifies "that," or, as we say, this becomes that.[8] This Jordan is liturgically embraced as the Red Sea. It turns out that all these stones are in order to perform the exodus as a "moveable feast" that can be re-enacted anywhere with the right props of symbolization. Thus the liturgy pushes the wandering children back behind the Jordan to the quintessential founding miracle of oddness and of being treasured.

All of that is done, moreover, *so that . . .* and now there are two indicated consequences:

- *so that* all peoples may know yhwh is powerful; the liturgical act that engages the child is cosmic in its intention, and we may imagine that it has a trace of missional intentionality;
- *so that* you, you children, you Israel, you people of God, may hear and love and trust and obey yhwh your God forever; the nations are now on the horizon of the liturgy, but the bottom line is still Israel drawn to oddness.

*   *   *

This entire set of transactions between parents and children represented in these three central texts is designed to inculcate the children into a particular version of reality that is rooted in *miracle* and that eventuates in *covenantal obligation*. It is clear that these intergenerational families greatly value familial coherence and continuity and have taken specific steps to ensure the entry of the children into the lore, vision, and responsibility of the family through time; the intensity of the texts in the tradition of Deuteronomy indicates a sense of urgency about the process. With the fierce dedication

---

8. Garrett Green, *Imagining God: Theology and the Religious Imagination* (San Francisco: Harper & Row, 1989), pp. 73, 140.

of a she-bear, the parents intend to situate their children in this particular version of reality; the educational process is intense and insistent, because the life and identity of the children are at stake through this interaction, for life and identity of a particular kind are of course in jeopardy if children fall out of the lore of the family, whether by negligence, resistance, or seduction to other versions of reality.

Expanding Our Embrace: A Transitional Interlude

But now a transitional interlude. Family nurture and socialization concern *our* children. Nurture and socialization are a process — through education, liturgy, and many forms of saturation — concerned for and contained within family and clan. Indeed, this horizon stays inside the in-group of a particular "us." This process of socialization is inherently particular and wants at the outset to exclude all matters that concern the others who are not like us. Thus in that ancient world, society included all manner of people termed "Canaanites" who did not share in the memories of exodus and land and Sinai commandments. The purpose of the nurture of children was to distinguish between "us" within this memory and ethic and "them" outside it:

> Now therefore revere the Lord, and serve him in sincerity and in faithfulness; put away the gods that your ancestors served beyond the River and in Egypt, and serve the Lord. Now if you are unwilling to serve the Lord, choose this day whom you will serve, whether the gods your ancestors served in the region beyond the River or the gods of the Amorites in whose land you are living; but as for me and my household, we will serve the Lord. (Josh. 24:14-15)

This nurture is committed to a radical either/or that enhances *us* and *our* values to the derogation of *them* and *their* values.

There is no doubt that the Old Testament expends immense energy on the "in group," a fact attested by current scholarship on ethnology.[9] Given that fact, however, it is also clear that the Old Testament, in its final form, also knows that "the others" are on the horizon of faith and cannot be excluded from covenantal perspective. Thus the text pushes beyond the "in group" to

---

9. On the study of ethnography in the Old Testament, see E. Theodore Mullen, *Narrative History and Ethnic Boundaries: The Deuteronomistic Historian and the Creation of Israelite National Identity* (Atlanta: Scholars Press, 1993); and *Ethnic Myths and Pentateuchal Foundations: A New Approach to the Formation of the Pentateuch* (Atlanta: Scholars Press, 1997).

the others. For our concern in this volume, it is clear that the text moves beyond "our children" to "other children," that is, from *family* to a more *public perspective*. This interpretive move is grounded, for ancient Israel, in the theological affirmation that the God who delivered Israel in the Exodus — and so attends to Israel — is also the creator of heaven and earth — and so governs and cares for all peoples.

Given such a move beyond "us" to "the others," this text for contemporary readers constitutes a mandate toward other children beyond our own. In a contemporary society of narcissistic fear and acute self-preoccupation, it is important to make the connection between familial peculiarity and a more inclusive awareness that issues in larger responsibility. Care for *our children* is no alternative to caring for *other children* who also belong to our charge. The question posed by this volume is how we look and act effectively toward other children beyond our own treasured children. The answer given in these biblical texts is that action toward children other than our own must be rooted in the religious passion of a she-bear translated into funded policies of protection, care, and valuing that are as unconditional as the unconditional regard we know for our own children.

Protecting All Children, Ours and Others

We begin theologically by asking about this she-bear of a God who is ferocious in care for all children, ours and others. The Old Testament to a large extent is preoccupied with "widows, orphans, and sojourners," almost a mantra for the unprotected, to which the category of "the poor" is sometimes added.[10] This triad includes:

10. See the important studies of Harold V. Bennett, *Injustice Made Legal: Deuteronomic Law and the Plight of Widows, Strangers, and Orphans in Ancient Israel* (Grand Rapids: Eerdmans, 2002), and Enrique Nardoni, *Rise Up, O Judge: A Study of Justice in the Biblical World* (Peabody, MA: Hendrickson, 2004). It is important to note that Bennett reads the Deuteronomic provisions for widows and orphans negatively, as a strategy of the dominant class for episodic acts of generosity that in fact sustain the economic status quo. Building upon the theoretical work of Ira Goldenberg and Iris M. Young, Bennett judges that the commandments are acts of ideology and that "these regulations contributed to their oppression" (p. 124). Bennett may be correct, but in fact he offers no evidence; he simply reads the texts through this theory. A more positive reading of the provisions to which I am inclined may be suggested by the provision for the "year of release" that is much more than episodic (Deut. 15:1-18).

In any case, if one extrapolates Bennett's arguments to contemporary society, the conclusion would be that welfare provisions stigmatize the poor. That is an argument that is frequently made among neo-conservatives, though of course Bennett does not make such an interpretive move. That conclusion, which goes well beyond Bennett's argument, is one I would of course reject.

- *orphans* who have no parents as advocates;
- *widows* who have no husband as advocate;
- *immigrants* who have no legal standing.

The formula, characteristically repeated, refers to these three categories of human persons in a patriarchal society who are without a male protector (e.g., Deut. 16:11-12, 14; 24:17-22). In such a society those without male protection were exceedingly vulnerable to violence and exploitation of every kind imaginable. Our concern in this triad, of course, is *the orphan,* the one without parental advocate who is the subject of the worst kinds of exploitation.[11] While we may imagine our own contemporary society to be a more "enlightened" society, it is nonetheless the case that those without adult advocacy in our society are left, like their ancient counterparts, in the same profoundly vulnerable position.[12] Thus we may take "orphan" to be the "other" beyond our own children for whom we have profound obligation, an obligation that depends not simply on good intentions but on well-funded provisions of protection and sustenance. It is plausible to conclude that in the biblical context such "welfare" concerned not only food and physical safety, but also nurture in respect, dignity, and well-being.[13]

It is remarkable that in the biblical text this large obligation toward children other than our own is rooted in the very character of God. It is this God, of whom we have told our children in the texts I have cited above, who is a "she-bear" for orphaned children, acting as their "male" advocate in a patriarchal society when there is no other effective "male" advocate. We will look at several Old Testament texts that speak to this character of God.

1. Deuteronomy 10

In the Torah teaching, it is asserted that YHWH, the great God, has a preferential inclination toward these unprotected members of the community:

For the Lord your God is God of gods and Lord of lords, the great God, mighty and awesome, who is not partial and takes no bribe, who executes

---

11. See Bennett, *Injustice Made Legal,* pp. 48-56.

12. The term "orphan" does not refer only to children who have no parents; it refers to any child who lacks an adult safety net. Thus, for example, the "Hershey School for Orphans" in Hershey, Pennsylvania, has as its governing category "social orphans," those who may have biological parents but who have no sustaining adult relationship of care and protection. The scope of such care for children is as broad and inclusive as the community can imagine.

13. On the broad intent of the commandments in the Old Testament, see Frank Crüsemann, *The Torah: Theology and Social History of Old Testament Law* (Edinburgh: T&T Clark 1996).

justice for *the orphan* and the widow, and who loves the strangers, providing them food and clothing. (vv. 17-18)

Indeed YHWH's propensity for these unprotected persons concerns exactly justice, which, in the parlance of Deuteronomy, means enough social goods, social access, and social entitlement to share life in security and in dignity. That passion for justice, moreover, is grounded in the material specificities of "food and clothing."

2. Hosea 14

Hosea is the prophet who has pondered most deeply the capacity of YHWH for passionate love. In a remarkable one-liner in Hosea 14:3, the whole case is made:

Assyria shall not save us;
    we will not ride upon horses;
we will say no more, "Our God,"
    to the work of our hands.
In you the orphan finds mercy.

The connection of YHWH to orphans is immediate, direct, and unqualified.

3. Psalm 10

The Psalter never quits celebrating this God of public life whose primal commitments pertain to the unprotected. In Psalm 10 the poet speaks of the "atheists" who say, "There is no God" (v. 4) and who therefore fully exploit the unprotected (vv. 8-10). The psalmist, however, has no doubt that YHWH is more than an antidote to such barbarism. The psalm voices a vigorous petition that YHWH should "rise up" (v. 12). The petition reminds God of God's covenantal character, which pertains to social commitment and social obligation:

But you do see! Indeed you note trouble and grief,
    that you may take it into your hands;
the helpless commit themselves to you;
    you have been the helper of *the orphan.*

(v. 14)

YHWH must notice because the helpless have no other help and because YHWH is already known as the "helper of orphans." That is who YHWH is, and now YHWH must enact divine policy in appropriate ways. The psalm ends in a confident lyrical hope:

> O Lord, you will hear the desire of the meek;
>> you will strengthen their heart, you will incline your ear
> to do justice for *the orphan* and the oppressed,
>> so that those from earth may strike terror no more.
>
> (vv. 17-18)

When YHWH arises, YHWH does justice primarily for orphans who have no other source of justice.

4. Psalm 68

Psalm 68 is a vigorous, extended doxology that alludes to YHWH as the powerful creator who gives rain and as the God who shook Mt. Sinai. In the midst of such sweeping motifs, however, the psalm pauses to notice the core passion of this she-bear God:

> *Father of orphans* and protector of widows
>> is God in his holy habitation.
> God gives the desolate a home to live in;
>> he leads out the prisoners to prosperity,
>> but the rebellious live in a parched land.
>
> (vv. 5-6)

This is the father — the masculine protector in a patriarchal society — of orphans and of widows. The phrase "father of orphans" is odd and worth noting, because orphans are exactly those without a father. Thus the very character of God contradicts the social definition of orphan. These are not the children "without a father," for this father assures that none will be without a male protector in a patriarchal society. One may imagine orphans to be homeless, but the father gives the desolate a home, a home with many rooms! This unit of poetry concludes in verse 10:

> Your flock found a dwelling in it;
>> in your goodness, O God, you provided for the needy.
>
> (v. 10)

The needy are cared for. The vulnerable are given prosperity. The orphans are given a home. No wonder the church prays "Our Father" to the one who contradicts the identity of all those labeled as "orphans."

5. Psalm 146

In Psalm 146:9 the doxology of Israel sings of the God who executes justice:

> The Lord sets the prisoners free;
> the Lord opens the eyes of the blind.
> The Lord lifts up those who are bowed down;
> the Lord loves the righteous.
> The Lord watches over the strangers;
> *he upholds the orphan* and the widow,
> but the way of the wicked he brings to ruin.
>
> (vv. 7b-9)

This is the God with powerful active verbs: "sets," "lifts," "loves," "watches," "upholds." These verbs of divine passion, moreover, are aimed at those beyond the pale of well-being. What an unlikely collection of folk that constitute the beneficiaries of YHWH's big verbs: "prisoners," "blind," "bowed down," "stranger," "orphan," "widow." These are the ones who have no other protector and who cannot make it on their own. This doxology articulates the elemental Israelite conviction that the character of YHWH overrides pathological social conditions. The orphan ceases to be orphaned, because YHWH upholds in passion, upholds in court, upholds economically, upholds in order to permit the orphan to be *at home* safely, securely, in dignity.

*   *   *

These five texts, Deuteronomy and Hosea and three from the Psalter, attest to the very character of God. The world is governed by the one who wants none to be unprotected, who wants there to be no unprotected, at-risk child. The famous invitation of Jesus to "let the children come unto me" is not about a pious, bourgeois suburban Sunday school class (Matt. 19:13-15). Rather, it is about economic viability that sets a curb on exploitation and challenges that which cheapens human life and puts the weakest at risk. YHWH will not have it so!!

This theological characterization of God is readily transposed in Israel into ethical obligations. What YHWH wills, Israel must enact. Israel's theological imagination characteristically moves to human obligation. What YHWH intends, Israel performs. All of these texts about YHWH's protective propensity are readily transposed into Israel's mandate.[14] *Doxology* about YHWH turns to *commandment* concerning Israel. Israel acts out the orphan-vetoing character of YHWH. The connection between the two is clearest in Deuteronomy 10:17-19.

First comes the affirmation of YHWH, which I have already cited:

> For the Lord your God is God of gods and Lord of lords, the great God, mighty and awesome, who is not partial and takes no bribe, who executes justice for the *orphan* and the widow, and who loves the strangers, providing them food and clothing. (Deut. 10:17-18)

Then comes the ethical exhortation to Israel:

> You shall also love the stranger, for you were strangers in the land of Egypt. (Deut. 10:19)

Here it is the "love of the *stranger*," but the equivalent, of course, is the love of the *orphan* on behalf of the God who executes justice for the orphan. In both of the primary cases I have cited concerning family values and child nurture — Exodus 12–13 and Deuteronomy 6 — one can see these *affirmations* turned by the tradition to *mandate.*

In Exodus 12–13 we have seen three times the children's question and the adult answer about YHWH. It is not many pages away in the book of Exodus where Moses rules on behalf of orphans:

> You shall not abuse any widow or orphan. If you do abuse them, when they cry out to me, I will surely heed their cry; my wrath will burn, and I will kill you with the sword, and your wives shall become widows and your children orphans. (Exod. 22:22-24)

Those who abuse orphans (the ones who are of course vulnerable to abuse) will have their own children become orphans. The sanctions indicated are harsh indeed, indicating the seriousness of the issue. Israel is on notice that

---

14. On theological thinking in the Old Testament as a mode of praxis, see José Miranda, *Marx and the Bible: A Critique of the Philosophy of Oppression* (Maryknoll, NY: Orbis Books, 1974). Specifically see his discussion of "knowledge of God" and his reference to Jeremiah 22:15-16 on pp. 47-50. Israel *knows* by its *actions.* Thus God-talk in ancient Israel is surely God-walk.

the God in whom orphans find protection and mercy will not tolerate abusive treatment of orphans, even if they are socially exposed and vulnerable.

In Deuteronomy 6 we saw the same question of children posed for adults to answer. In this latter case the answer concerns obligation to commandments. The book of Deuteronomy unfolds the commands that the children need to know. Among them are mandates to provide abundant food for orphans and widows (Deut. 14:29; 16:11, 14; 26:12-13). In two other cases, however, commandments particularly warrant our attention. The first is in Deuteronomy 24:

> You shall not deprive a resident alien or an *orphan* of justice; you shall not take a widow's garment in pledge. Remember that you were a slave in Egypt and the Lord your God redeemed you from there; therefore I command you to do this.
>
> When you reap your harvest in your field and forget a sheaf in the field, you shall not go back to get it; it shall be left for the alien, *the orphan,* and the widow, so that the Lord your God may bless you in all your undertakings. When you beat your olive trees, do not strip what is left; it shall be for the alien, *the orphan,* and the widow.
>
> When you gather the grapes of your vineyard, do not glean what is left; it shall be for the alien, *the orphan,* and the widow. Remember that you were a slave in the land of Egypt; therefore I am commanding you to do this (Deut. 24:17-22)

Orphans, along with widows and immigrants, are an object of special concern in the Torah. While the texts articulate YHWH's concern and action, such texts surely function in terms of Israel's praxis.

Two times, moreover, appeal is made to exodus deliverance, "for you were slaves in Egypt," a status of vulnerability shared by orphans, widows, and immigrants. Most interesting, however, is the special protection offered orphans, widows, and immigrants from loan sharks who take advantage of the economically needy.

And then in verses 19-22, provision is made for positive reparation to provide economic sustenance to those who are economically disadvantaged. The mandate requires that the ones addressed — the propertied class — curb their exacting quest for profit in order to share with those without resources. Frank Crüsemann terms these sorts of provisions in the book of Deuteronomy the "first social safety net" in history.[15] The community is required — on behalf of YHWH — to do for orphans what will not be done for them in any other way.

---

15. See Crüsemann, *The Torah,* p. 224.

The other text in Deuteronomy that we may notice is Deuteronomy 27:19:

> Cursed be anyone who deprives the alien, the orphan, and the widow *of* justice. All the people shall say, "Amen!"

To "twist justice" (= deprive) means to fail to give justice to those who are powerless to acquire it for themselves; aliens, widows, and orphans are entitled to sustenance by the community and must receive their fair share of the community's resources.

The same mandate rooted in YHWH's own character also pervades Israel's prophetic texts. Among the prophets come these assertions:

> Wash yourselves; make yourselves clean;
>   remove the evil of your doings from before my eyes;
> cease to do evil, learn to do good;
> seek justice, rescue the oppressed,
> defend the *orphan,* plead for the widow.
>
> (Isa. 1:16-17)

> If you do not oppress the alien, *the orphan,* and the widow, or shed innocent blood in this place, and if you do not go after other gods to your own hurt, then I will dwell with you in this place, in the land that I gave of old to your ancestors forever and ever. (Jer. 7:6-7)

> Thus says the Lord of hosts: Render true judgments, show kindness and mercy to one another; do not oppress the widow, *the orphan,* the alien, or the poor; and do not devise evil in your hearts against one another. (Zech. 7:9-10)

And in parallel fashion the wisdom teachers know in their wise discernment that a society cannot prosper if its members are powerless or not honored. Thus:

> Do not remove an ancient landmark
>   or encroach on the fields of *orphans,*
> for their redeemer is strong;
>   he will plead their cause against you.
>
> (Prov. 23:10-11)

In his articulation of a regulative ethic in Israel, moreover, Job knows that treatment of orphans is the litmus test for fidelity,

Because I delivered the poor who cried,
 and *the orphan* who had no helper.
The blessing of the wretched came upon me,
 and I caused the widow's heart to sing for joy.

(Job 29:12-13)

If I have withheld anything that the poor desired,
 or have caused the eyes of the widow to fail,
or have eaten my morsel alone,
 and *the orphan* has not eaten from it —
for from my youth I reared *the orphan* like a father,
 and from my mother's womb I guided the widow —
. . . if I have raised my hand against *the orphan*,
 because I saw I had supporters at the gate;
then let my shoulder blade fall from my shoulder,
 and let my arm be broken from its socket.

(Job 31:16-18, 21-22)

All parts of Israel's text attest to this primal obligation that the powerful and monied are mandated to utilize their capacity and their resources to create protected space for children other than our own who are defenseless. This mandate is a part of the distinctiveness of the Torah tradition of Israel and thus part of Israel's peculiar identity.

Making the Biblical Connection

I have now traced two series of texts that concern the following:

- nurture and socialization of *our children* into faith;
- attentiveness to *other children* who are a special concern of the tradition.

The first, I have suggested, is at the center of *family nurture,* and the second reaches beyond family into *the wider community.*

The urgent issue before contemporary society concerns the connection between *our children,* to whom our devotion is limitless, and *the others,* who are at the edge of our passion. Here is the connection that occurs to me. The ultimate content of family nurture in this tradition is in order that our own children in faith have front and center in their vision the protection of orphans, a concern that is defining for faith. Family nurture in this tradition cannot be a narrow little enterprise about purity and safety; rather, it concerns inculcation into the peculiar ethical patterns of our faith. As is characteristic in Old Testament texts, these texts do not venture far into the "how" of public policy. They rather function to subvert the imagination of Israel, and so to clear space and provide materials out of which venturesome public policy may be imagined.

There is, I have attempted to show, no dimension of ethical passion more central in the tradition of the Bible than the protection of orphans. I can imagine a child asking in time to come what lentils and doorposts and stones all mean; the adult answer might properly be: "We know, directly from God, that protection of vulnerable children outside our own family is a central requirement of faith." Any other reading of the Bible runs the risk of being a misreading.

Conclusion

My conclusion is a simple one. *Nurture* for our own children and *defense* of other vulnerable children are elements of the same agenda. It will not do to invest in the former as a parochial matter to the neglect of the latter as a public matter. I finish with four texts that seem peculiarly pertinent to our concern.

1. Matthew 7:9-11

> Is there anyone among you who, if your child asks for bread, will give a stone? Or if the child asks for a fish, will give a snake? If you then, who are evil, know how to give good gifts to your children, how much more will your Father in heaven give good things to those who ask him!

This teaching of Jesus moves from our parenting to that of "your Father in heaven." I have shown how the argument moves theologically in the reverse direction. Because this heavenly parent gives good things to children, so may we — not only to our children, but to all the children of the heavenly parent, for all are in purview of this community that replicates YHWH's own passion.

2. James 1:27

> Religion that is pure and undefiled before God, the Father, is this: to care for orphans and widows in their distress, and to keep oneself unstained by the world.

James, of course, is a corrective to any casual notion of grace that imagines that we are loved without letting that love of God move through us and beyond us to needful neighbors. I suppose to be "stained by the world" would cause us to be indifferent to these very orphans and widows who are in distress. The epistle suggests that early Christians were quite concrete about the enactment of a radical social ethic.

3. Malachi 4:5-6

The Old Testament ends in an expectation of Elijah coming again:

> Lo, I will send you the prophet Elijah before the great and terrible day of the Lord comes. He will turn the hearts of parents to their children and the hearts of children to their parents, so that I will not come and strike the land with a curse.

This coming herald of the new age will turn adults toward children and children toward adults, making new solidarity and well-being possible. That anticipation is taken up in the promise of the angel to Elizabeth concerning John who is to come:

> With the spirit and power of Elijah he will go before him, to turn the hearts of parents to their children, and the disobedient to the wisdom of the righteous, to make ready a people prepared for the Lord. (Luke 1:17)

The coming of the new age is the time when the disobedient will be transformed into the wise and righteous. Disobedience is lack of care about the things of God. The righteous by contrast are wise in enacting God's embrace of unprotected children. One could imagine that the care of orphans is the ultimate test of readiness for the coming of the new kingdom. Protecting the unprotected is the work of all those who receive God's gift of newness.

4. John 14:18

In his Farewell Discourse, Jesus makes this astonishing assurance: "I will not leave you orphaned; I am coming to you" (John 14:18). The Greek is *orphanous,* quite literally, "you will not be orphaned." Indeed, the God given us in Jesus intends none to be orphaned, none to be defenseless, none to be uncared for, unprotected, unloved, unembraced. *None at all!* The reason for this passion is that the God who comes bodied in Jesus is indeed like a she-bear who will let nothing of abuse, exploitation, marginalization, or poverty come between "her" and her cubs. This God will not be robbed of her cubs, not even the ones left abandoned by the world.

*   *   *

It is our hope that we also may be given the passion of a she-bear to care for every cub, our own and all the others who will not be left orphaned by the God who gives mercy to the orphans. Beyond all the benignity of much faith, we reckon with a God capable of ferocious, tenacious caring. In the image of that God, we are summoned to the same ferociousness and tenacity. The implications for public policy concern the safety, dignity, respect, and economic wherewithal for every child, whose value is attested by the protection and care of society. Such commitment and obligation, of course, have nothing to do with the imposition of a narrow religious morality that is preoccupied with a rigid family and/or social ethic. Social policy rightly concerns economic guarantees that are to be embedded in particular communities of nurture.

Select Bibliography

Aasgaard, Reidar. *The Childhood of Jesus: Decoding the Apocryphal Infancy Gospel of Thomas*. Forthcoming.

————. "Children in Antiquity and Early Christianity: Research History and Central Issues." *Familia* (Salamanca, Spain) 33 (2006): 23-46.

————. *"My Beloved Brothers and Sisters!" Christian Siblingship in Paul*. London/New York: T&T Clark International/Continuum, 2004.

————. "Paul as a Child: Children and Childhood in the Letters of the Apostle." *Journal of Biblical Literature* 126 (2007): 129-59.

Akoto, Dorothy B. E. A. "Women and Health in Ghana and the Trokosi Practice: An Issue of Women's and Children's Rights in 2 Kings 4:1-7." In *African Women, Religion, and Health: Essays in Honor of Mercy Amba Ewudziwa Oduyoye*, edited by Isabel Apawo Phiri and Sarojini Nadar, 96-110. Maryknoll, NY: Orbis Books, 2006.

Allmen, Daniel von. *La famille de Dieu: La symbolique familiale dans le paulinisme*. Éditions Universitaires' Fribourg Suisse. Göttingen: Vandenhoeck & Ruprecht, 1981.

Bailey, James L. "Experiencing the Kingdom as a Little Child: A Rereading of Mark 10:13-16." *Word & World* 15 (Winter 1995): 58-67.

Bakke, O. M. *When Children Became People: The Birth of Childhood in Early Christianity*. Minneapolis: Fortress, 2005.

Balch, David L., and Carolyn Osiek, eds. *Early Christian Families in Context: An Interdisciplinary Dialogue*. Grand Rapids: Eerdmans, 2003.

————. *Families in the New Testament World: Households and House Churches*. Louisville: Westminster John Knox Press, 1997.

Balla, Peter. *The Child-Parent Relationship in the New Testament and Its Environment*. Wissenschaftliche Untersuchungen zum Neuen Testament 155. Tübingen: Mohr Siebeck, 2003.

Balthasar, Hans Urs von. *Unless You Become Like This Child*. San Francisco: Ignatius Press, 1991.

Barclay, John M. G. "The Family as the Bearer of Religion in Judaism and Early Christianity." In *Constructing Early Christian Families: Family as Social Reality and Metaphor,* edited by Halvor Moxnes, 66-80. London: Routledge, 1997.

———. "There Is Neither Old Nor Young? Early Christianity and Ancient Ideologies of Age." *New Testament Studies* 53 (2007): 225-41.

Bartchy, S. Scott. "Who Should Be Called Father? Paul of Tarsus between the Jesus Tradition and Patria Potestas." *Biblical Theology Bulletin* 33 (2003): 135-47.

Barton, Stephen C. *Discipleship and Family Ties in Mark and Matthew.* Cambridge: Cambridge University Press, 1994.

———. "Jesus — Friend of Little Children." In *Contours of Christian Education,* edited by Jeff Astley and David Day, 30-40. Essex: McCrimmons, 1992.

———. "The Relativisation of Family Ties in the Jewish and Graeco-Roman Traditions." In *Constructing Early Christian Families: Family as Social Reality and Metaphor,* edited by Halvor Moxnes, 81-100. London: Routledge, 1997.

Bertman, Stephen, ed. *The Conflict of Generations in Ancient Greece and Rome.* Amsterdam: Grüner, 1976.

Birge, Mary K. *The Language of Belonging: A Rhetorical Analysis of Kinship Language in First Corinthians.* Leuven: Peeters, 2002.

Block, Daniel I. "Marriage and Family in Ancient Israel." In *Marriage and Family in the Biblical World,* edited by Ken M. Campbell, 33-102. Downers Grove, IL: InterVarsity, 2003.

Borowski, Obed. *Daily Life in Biblical Times.* Society of Biblical Literature Archeological and Biblical Studies 5. Atlanta: Society of Biblical Literature, 2003.

Bosch, David. *Transforming Mission: Paradigm Shifs in Theology of Mission.* Maryknoll: Orbis Books, 1993.

Boswell, John. *The Kindness of Strangers: The Abandonment of Children in Western Europe from Late Antiquity to the Renaissance.* New York: Vintage/Random House, 1990.

Botha, Pieter J. J. *Everyday Life in the World of Jesus.* Pretoria: Biblia, 2000.

Bradley, Keith R. *Discovering the Roman Family: Studies in Roman Social History.* Oxford: Oxford University Press, 1991.

Brooke, George J., ed. *The Birth of Jesus: Biblical and Theological Reflections.* Edinburgh: T&T Clark, 2000.

Brown, William P. *Character in Crisis: A Fresh Approach to the Wisdom Literature of the Old Testament.* Grand Rapids: Eerdmans, 1996.

Brown, William P., and John T. Carroll, eds. "The Child." *Interpretation* 55, no. 2 (April 2001): 119-73.

Browning, Don, and Marcia J. Bunge. *Children and Childhood in World Religions.* New Brunswick, NJ: Rutgers University Press, 2009.

Browning, Don, Bonnie J. Miller-McLemore, Pamela D. Couture, K. Brynolf Lyon, and Robert M. Franklin. *From Culture Wars to Common Ground: Religion and the American Family Debate.* Louisville: Westminster/John Knox Press, 1997.

Brueggemann, Walter. "The Family as World-Maker." *Journal for Preachers* 8, no. 3 (Easter 1985): 8-15.

―――. *Isaiah 1–39.* Westminster Bible Companion 65, vol. 1. Louisville: Westminster John Knox, 1998.

―――. "Remembering Rachel's Children: An Urban Agenda for People Who Notice." *Word & World* 14 (Fall 1994): 377-83.

Bunge, Marcia J., ed. *The Child in Christian Thought.* Grand Rapids: Eerdmans, 2001.

Burke, Trevor J. *Family Matters: A Socio-Historical Study of Kinship Metaphors in 1 Thessalonians.* London/New York: T&T Clark Int./Continuum, 2003.

―――. "Paul's Role as 'Father' to His Corinthian 'Children' in Socio-Historical Context (1 Corinthians 4:14-21)." In *Paul and the Corinthians: Studies on a Community in Conflict. Essays in Honour of Margaret Thrall,* edited by Trevor J. Burke, 95-113. Leiden and Boston: Brill, 2003.

Carroll, John T. "Children in the Bible." *Interpretation* 55, no. 2 (April 2001): 121-34.

Claassens, L. Juliana. *The God Who Provides: Biblical Images of Divine Nourishment.* Nashville: Abingdon, 2004.

Cohen, Martin Samuel. "Ishmael at Sixteen." *Conservative Judaism* 53, no. 4 (Summer 2001): 36-43.

Cohen, Shaye J. D., ed. *The Jewish Family in Antiquity.* Atlanta: Scholars, 1993.

Cox, Cheryl Anne. *Household Interests: Property, Marriage Strategies, and Family Dynamics in Ancient Athens.* Princeton: Princeton University Press, 1998.

Crenshaw, James. *Education in Ancient Israel: Across the Deadening Silence.* Anchor Bible Reference Library. New York: Doubleday, 1998.

Crüsemann, Frank. "Gott als Anwalt der Kinder!? Zur Frage von Kinderrechten in der Bibel." *Jahrbuch für biblische Theologie* 17 (2002): 183-98.

Dasén, Veronique, ed. *Naissance et petite enfance dans l'Antiquité.* Göttingen: Academic/Vandenhoeck & Ruprecht, 2004.

Dearman, J. Andrew. "The Family in the Old Testament." *Interpretation* 52, no. 2 (April 1998): 117-29.

de Boer, P. A. H. *Fatherhood and Motherhood in Israelite and Judean Piety.* Leiden: Brill, 1974.

Delaney, Carol. *Abraham on Trial: The Social Legacy of Biblical Myth.* Princeton: Princeton University Press, 1998.

Delkurt, Holger. "Erziehung nach dem Alten Testament." *Jahrbuch für biblische Theologie* 17 (2002): 227-54.

Demand, Nancy. *Birth, Death, and Motherhood in Classical Greece.* Baltimore: Johns Hopkins University Press, 1994.

Dickie, Jane R., Amy K. Eshleman, Dawn M. Merasco, Amy Shepard, Michael Vander Wilt, and Melissa Johnson. "Parent-Child Relationships and Children's Images of God." *Journal for the Scientific Study of Religion* 36 (1997): 25-43.

Dixon, Suzanne. *The Roman Family.* Baltimore: Johns Hopkins University Press, 1992.

―――. *The Roman Mother.* Norman, OK: Oklahoma University Press, 1988.

Dixon, Suzanne, ed. *Childhood, Class and Kin in the Roman World.* London and New York: Routledge, 2001.

Doody, Margaret Anne. "Infant Piety and the Infant Samuel." In *Out of the Garden: Women Writers on the Bible,* edited by Christina Büchmann and Celina Spiegel, 103-22. New York: Fawcett Columbine, 1994.

Eastman, Susan. *Recovering Paul's Mother Tongue: Language and Theology in Galatians.* Grand Rapids: Eerdmans, 2007.

Ebner, Martin. "'Kinderevangelium' oder markinische Sozialkritik? Mk 10,13-16 im Kontext." *Jahrbuch für biblische Theologie* 17 (2002): 315-36.

Eltrop, Bettina. *Denn Solchen Gehört Das Himmelreich: Kinder im Matthäus-evangelium. Eine Feministisch-Sozialgeschichtliche Untersuchung.* Stuttgart: Verlag Ulrich E. Grauer, 1996.

———. "Kinder im Neuen Testament. Eine sozialgeschichtliche Nachfrage." *Jahrbuch für biblische Theologie* 17 (2002): 83-96.

Eyben, Emiel. *Restless Youth in Ancient Rome.* London and New York: Routledge, 1993.

Fatum, Lone. "Brotherhood in Christ: A Gender Hermeneutical Reading of 1 Thessalonians." In *Constructing Early Christian Families,* edited by Halvor Moxnes, 183-97. London: Routledge, 1997.

———. "Tro, håb og gode gerniger. Kristusfællesskabet som social konstruktion." In *Den nye Paulus og hans betydning,* edited by Troels Engberg-Pedersen, 120-55. København: Gyldendal, 2003.

Fayer, Carla. *La familia Romana: aspetti giuridici ed antiquari, parte prima.* Problemi e ricerche di storia antica 16. Roma: Bretschneider, 1994.

Fensham, F. Charles. "Father and Son as Terminology for Treaty and Covenant." In *Near Eastern Studies in Honor of William Foxwell Albright,* edited by Hans Goedicke, 121-35. Baltimore: Johns Hopkins Press, 1971.

Fewell, Danna Nolan. *The Children of Israel: Reading the Bible for the Sake of Our Children.* Nashville: Abingdon, 2003.

Finsterbusch, Karin. "Die kollektive Identität und die Kinder. Bemerkungen zu einem Programm im Buch Deuteronomium." *Jahrbuch für biblische Theologie* 17 (2002): 99-120.

Fischer, Irmtraud. "Über Lust und Last, Kinder zu haben. Soziale, genealogische und theologische Aspekte in der Literatur Alt-Israels." *Jahrbuch für biblische Theologie* 17 (2002): 55-82.

Francis, James. *Adults as Children: Images of Childhood in the Ancient World and the New Testament.* Religions and Discourse 17. Oxford et al.: Peter Lang, 2006.

———. "Children and Childhood in the New Testament." In *The Family in Theological Perspective,* edited by Stephen C. Barton, 65-85. Edinburgh: T&T Clark, 1996.

Fretheim, Terence E. *Abraham: Trials of Family and Faith.* Columbia: University of South Carolina Press, 2007.

———. "God, Abraham, and the Abuse of Isaac." *Word & World* 15 (Winter 1995): 49-57.

———. *God and the World in the Old Testament: A Relational Theology of Creation.* Nashville: Abingdon, 2005.

———. "'I Was Only a Little Angry': Divine Violence in the Prophets." *Interpretation* 58 (2004): 365-75.

———. *The Suffering of God: An Old Testament Perspective.* Overtures to Biblical Theology. Philadelphia: Fortress, 1984.

———. "Which Blessing Does Isaac Give Jacob?" In *Jews, Christians and the Theology of Hebrew Scriptures,* edited by Joel Kaminsky and Alice Bellis, 279-91. Atlanta: Society of Biblical Literature, 2000.

Gaiser, Frederick J. "'I Will Carry and I Will Save': The Carrying God of Isaiah 40–66." In *"And God Saw That It Was Good": Essays on Creation and God in Honor of Terence E. Fretheim,* edited by Frederick J. Gaiser and Mark A. Throntveit, 94-102. St. Paul: Word & World, Luther Northwestern Theological Seminary, 2006.

Gaventa, Beverly Roberts. "Apostles as Babes and Nurses in 1 Thessalonians 2:7." In *Faith and History: Essays in Honor of Paul W. Meyer,* edited by Paul W. Meyer, John T. Carroll, Charles H. Cosgrove, and E. Elizabeth Johnson, 193-207. Atlanta: Scholars Press, 1990.

———. "The Maternity of Paul: An Exegetical Study of Galatians 4:19." In *The Conversation Continues: Studies in Paul and John in Honor of J. Louis Martyn,* edited by Robert T. Fortna and Beverly R. Gaventa, 189-201. Nashville: Abingdon, 1990.

———. "Mother's Milk and Ministry in 1 Corinthians 3." In *Theology and Ethics in Paul and His Interpreters: Essays in Honor of Victor Paul Furnish,* edited by Eugene H. Lovering Jr. and Jerry L. Sumney, 101-13. Nashville: Abingdon, 1996.

———. *Our Mother Saint Paul.* Louisville: Westminster John Knox, 2007.

———. "Our Mother St. Paul: Toward the Recovery of a Neglected Theme." In *A Feminist Companion to Paul,* edited by Amy-Jill Levine with Marianne Blickenstaff, 85-97. Cleveland: Pilgrim Press, 2004.

George, Michele, ed. *The Roman Family in the Empire: Rome, Italy, and Beyond.* Oxford: Oxford University Press, 2005.

Gerber, Christine. *Paulus und seine "Kinder": Studien zur Beziehungsmetaphorik der paulinischen Briefe.* Beihefte zur Zeitschrift für die neutestamentliche Wissenschaft und die Kunde der älteren Kirche 136. Berlin: Walter de Gruyter, 2005.

Golden, Mark. *Children and Childhood in Classical Athens.* Baltimore: Johns Hopkins University Press, 1990.

Grassi, Joseph A. "Child, Children." In *The Anchor Bible Dictionary,* 6 vols., edited by David Noel Freedman et al., 1:904-7. New York: Doubleday, 1992.

Green, Joel B. "'She and Her Household Were Baptized' (Acts 16.15): Household Baptism in the Acts of the Apostles." In *Dimensions of Baptism: Biblical and Theological Studies,* edited by Stanley E. Porter, 72-90. New York: Sheffield Academic Press, 2002.

Greenspahn, Frederick E. *When Brothers Dwell Together: The Preeminence of Younger Siblings in the Hebrew Bible.* New York: Oxford University Press, 1994.

Gruber, Mayer I. *The Motherhood of God and Other Studies.* South Florida Studies in the History of Judaism 57. Atlanta: Scholars Press, 1992.

Guijarro Oporto, Santiago. *Fidelidades en Conflicto. La Ruptura Con la Familia Por Causa del Discipulado y de la Misión en la Tradición Sinóptica.* Vol. 4, *Plenitudo Temporis.* Salamanca: Publicaciones Universidad Pontificia Salamanca, 1998.

Gundry-Volf, Judith M. "Child, Children." In *New Interpreter's Dictionary of the Bible,* vol. 1, A-C, edited by Katherine Doob Sakenfeld, 588-90. Nashville: Abingdon, 2006.

————. "The Least and the Greatest: Children in the New Testament." In *The Child in Christian Thought,* edited by Marcia J. Bunge, 29-60. Grand Rapids: Eerdmans, 2001.

————. "To Such as These Belongs the Reign of God: Jesus and Children." *Theology Today* 56, no. 4 (January 2000): 469-80.

Harlow, Mary, and Ray Laurence. *Growing Up and Growing Old in Ancient Rome: A Life Course Approach.* London: Routledge, 2002.

Heard, R. Christopher. "Hearing the Children's Cries: Commentary, Deconstruction, Ethics and the Book of Habakkuk." In *Bible and Ethics of Reading,* edited by Danna Nolan Fewell and Gary A. Phillips, 75-90. Semeia Studies 77. Atlanta: Society of Biblical Literature, 1997.

Hellerman, Joseph H. *The Ancient Church as Family.* Minneapolis: Fortress, 2001.

Herzog, Kristin. *Children and Our Global Future: Theological and Social Challenges.* Cleveland: Pilgrim Press, 2005.

Heskett, Randall J. "Proverbs 23:13-14." *Interpretation* 55, no. 2 (2001): 181-84.

Horne, Cornelia B. "Children's Play as Social Ritual." In *Late Antique Christianity,* edited by Virginia Burns, 95-116. Minneapolis: Fortress, 2005.

Ihne, Hartmut. "Menschenwürde und Kinderrechte in der Einen Welt." *Jahrbuch für biblische Theologie* 17 (2002): 3-20.

Jackson, Timothy P., ed. *The Morality of Adoption: Social-Psychological, Theological, and Legal Perspectives.* Grand Rapids: Eerdmans, 2005.

Jacobsen, Thorkild. *The Treasures of Darkness: A History of Mesopotamian Religion.* New Haven: Yale University Press, 1976.

Janowski, Christine. "'Was wird aus den Kindern . . . ?' Einige Anfragen an die klassische Theologie in Zuspitzung auf die eschatalogische Perspektive." *Jahrbuch für biblische Theologie* 17 (2002): 337-68.

Jensen, David H. *Graced Vulnerability: A Theology of Childhood.* Cleveland: Pilgrim Press, 2005.

Jungbauer, Harry. *"Ehre Vater und Mutter": Der Weg des Elterngebots in der Biblischen Tradition.* Tübingen: Mohr Siebeck, 2002.

Keck, Leander E. *Romans.* Nashville: Abingdon Press, 2005.

Kertzer, David I., and Richard P. Saller. *The Family in Italy from Antiquity to the Present.* New Haven and London: Yale University Press, 1991.

King, Philip J., and Lawrence E. Stager. *Life in Biblical Israel.* Library of Ancient Israel. Louisville: Westminster John Knox, 2001.

Kleijwegt, Marc. *Ancient Youth: The Ambiguity of Youth and the Absence of Adolescence in Greco-Roman Society.* Dutch Monographs on Ancient History and Archaeology. Amsterdam: J. C. Gieben, 1991.

―――. "Kind." In *Reallexikon für Antike und Christentum,* edited by Georg Schöllgen et al., 866-931 (cols.). Stuttgart: Anton Hiersemann, 2004.

Knowles, Melody D. "A Woman at Prayer: A Critical Note on Psalm 131:2b." *Journal of Biblical Literature* 125 (2006): 385-89.

Korpel, Marjo Christina Annette. *A Rift in the Clouds: Ugaritic and Hebrew Descriptions of the Divine.* Münster: Ugarit-Verlag, 1990.

Kottsieper, Ingo. "'We Have a Little Sister': Aspects of the Brother-Sister Relationship in Ancient Israel." In *Families and Family Relations as Represented in Early Judaisms and Early Christianities: Texts and Fictions,* edited by Jan Willem van Henten and Athalya Brenner, 49-80. Studies in Theology and Religion 2. Leiden: Deo, 2000.

Kraemer, David. "Images of Childhood and Adolescence in Talmudic Literature." In *The Jewish Family: Metaphor and Memory,* edited by David Kraemer, 65-80. New York: Oxford University Press, 1989.

Kraemer, Ross. "Jewish Mothers and Daughters in the Greco-Roman World." In *The Jewish Family in Antiquity,* edited by Shaye J. D. Cohen, 89-112. Atlanta: Scholars, 1993.

Kraybill, Donald. *The Upside-Down Kingdom.* Scottdale: Herald Press, 1978.

Kügler, Joachim. "'Denen aber, die ihn aufnahmen . . .' (Joh 1,12). Die Würde der Gotteskinder in der johanneischen Theologie." *Jahrbuch für biblische Theologie* 17 (2002): 163-80.

Lacey, W. K. *The Family in Classical Greece.* London: Thames and Hudson, 1968.

Laes, Christian. *Kinderen bij de Romeinen: Zees eeuwen dagelijks leven.* Leuven: Davidsfonds, 2006.

Landy, Francis. "Do We Want Our Children to Read This Book?" In *Bible and Ethics of Reading,* edited by Danna Nolan Fewell and Gary A. Phillips, 157-76. Semeia Studies 77. Atlanta: Society of Biblical Literature, 1997.

Lapsley, Jacqueline. "Feeling Our Way: Love for God in Deuteronomy." *Catholic Biblical Quarterly* 65, no. 3 (2003): 350-69.

Levenson, Jon D. *The Death and Resurrection of the Beloved Son: The Transformation of Child Sacrifice in Judaism and Christianity.* New Haven: Yale University Press, 1993.

MacDonald, Margaret Y. *Early Christian Women and Pagan Opinion: The Power of the Hysterical Woman.* Cambridge: Cambridge University Press, 1996.

―――. "Early Christian Women Married to Unbelievers." *Studies in Religion/Sciences Religieuses* 19, no. 2 (1990): 221-34.

―――. "The Ideal of the Christian Couple: Ign Pol 5:1-2 Looking Back to Paul." *New Testament Studies* 40, no. 1 (January 1994): 105-25.

―――. "Rereading Paul: Early Interpreters of Paul on Women and Gender." *Women and Christian Origins,* edited by Ross Shepard Kraemer and Mary Rose D'Angelo, 236-53. New York: Oxford University Press, 1999.

———. "Slavery, Sexuality and House Churches: A Reassessment of Col 3:18–4:1 in Light of New Research on the Roman Family." *New Testament Studies* 53, no. 1 (2007): 94-113.

Marty, Martin E. *The Mystery of the Child.* Grand Rapids: Eerdmans, 2007.

Martyn, Dorothy W. "A Child and Adam: A Parable of the Two Ages." In *Apocalyptic and the New Testament: Essays in Honor of J. Louis Martyn,* edited by Joel Marcus, Marion L. Soards, and J. Louis Martyn, 317-33. Journal for the Study of the New Testament Supplement Series 24. Sheffield: Sheffield Academic Press, 1989.

Mays, James Luther. "The Self in the Psalms and the Image of God." In *God and Human Dignity,* edited by R. Kendall Soulen and Linda Woodhead, 27-43. Grand Rapids: Eerdmans, 2006.

McCarthy, Dennis J. "Notes on the Love of God in Deuteronomy and the Father-Son Relationship between Yahweh and Israel." *Catholic Biblical Quarterly* 27, no. 2 (1965): 144-47.

McConnell, Douglas, Jennifer Orona, and Paul Stockley, eds. *Understanding God's Heart for Children: Toward a Biblical Framework.* Colorado Springs: Authentic, 2007.

Melchert, Charles F. *Wise Teaching: Biblical Wisdom and Educational Ministry.* Harrisonburg, PA: Trinity Press International, 1998.

Melnyk, Janet L. R. "When Israel Was a Child: Ancient Near Eastern Adoption Formulas and the Relationship between God and Israel." In *History and Interpretation: Essays in Honor of John H. Hayes,* edited by M. Patrick Graham, William P. Brown, and Jeffrey K. Kuan, 245-59. Journal for the Study of the Old Testament Supplement Series 173. Sheffield: Sheffield Academic Press, 1993.

Mercer, Joyce Ann. *Welcoming Children: A Practical Theology of Childhood.* St. Louis: Chalice Press, 2005.

Meyers, Carol. *Discovering Eve: Ancient Israelite Women in Context.* New York: Oxford University Press, 1988.

———. "Everyday Life: Women in the Period of the Hebrew Bible." In *The Women's Bible Commentary,* edited by Carol A. Newsom and Sharon H. Ringe, 251-59. Louisville: Westminster John Knox, 1998.

Michel, Andreas. *Gott und Gewalt gegen Kinder im Alten Testament.* Tübingen: Mohr Siebeck, 2003.

Miller, John W. *Calling God "Father": Essays on the Bible, Fatherhood and Culture.* 2nd ed. New York: Paulist, 1999.

———. "God as Father in the Bible and the Father Image in Several Contemporary Ancient Near Eastern Myths: A Comparison." *Studies in Religion* 14, no. 3 (1985): 347-54.

Miller, Patrick D. "The Many Faces of Moses: A Deuteronomic Portrait." *Bible Review* 4, no. 5 (October 1988): 30-35.

————. "Moses My Servant: The Deuteronomic Portrait of Moses." *Interpretation* 41, no. 3 (July 1987): 245-55.

————. "Teaching the Faith." *Theology Today* 53, no. 2 (July 1996): 143-47.

Miller, Patrick D., and Ellen T. Charry, eds. Issue devoted to the theme of children. *Theology Today* 56, no. 4 (January 2000): 451-603.

Miller-McLemore, Bonnie. *Let the Children Come: Reimagining Childhood from a Christian Perspective.* San Francisco: Jossey-Bass, 2003.

Moxnes, Halvor. "What Is Family? Problems in Constructing Early Christian Families." In *Constructing Early Christian Families,* edited by Halvor Moxnes, 13-41. London: Routledge, 1997.

Moxnes, Halvor, ed. *Constructing Early Christian Families: Family as Social Reality and Metaphor.* London: Routledge, 1997.

Müller, Peter. *In der Mitte der Gemeinde: Kinder im Neuen Testament.* Neukirchen-Vluyn: Neukirchener, 1992.

————. "Die Metapher vom 'Kind Gottes' und die neutestamentliche Theologie." *'. . . was ihr auf dem Weg verhandelt habt': Beiträge zur Exegese und Theologie des Neuen Testaments,* edited by Peter Müller, Christine Gerber, and Thomas Knöppler, 192-203. Festschrift für Ferdinand Hahn zum 75. Geburtstag. Neukirchen-Vluyn: Neukirchener, 2001.

————. "Gottes Kinder. Zur Metaphorik der Gotteskindschaft im Neuen Testament." *Jahrbuch für biblische Theologie* 17 (2002): 141-62.

Nathan, Geoffrey S. *The Family in Late Antiquity: The Rise of Christianity and the Endurance of Tradition.* London/New York: Routledge, 2000.

Neils, Jenifer, and John H. Oakley. *Coming of Age in Ancient Greece: Images of Childhood from the Classical Past.* New Haven/London: Yale University Press, 2003.

Newsom, Carol A. "Woman and the Discourse of Patriarchal Wisdom: A Study of Proverbs 1–9." In *Gender and Difference in Ancient Israel,* edited by Peggy L. Day, 142-60. Minneapolis: Fortress, 1989.

Niskanen, Paul. "Yhwh as Father, Redeemer, and Potter in Isaiah 63:7–64:11." *Catholic Biblical Quarterly* 68, no. 3 (July 2006): 397-407.

Ohler, Annemarie. *The Bible Looks at Fathers.* Translated by Omar Kaste. Collegeville: Liturgical, 1999.

Osiek, Carolyn. "The Family in Early Christianity: 'Family Values' Revisited." *Catholic Biblical Quarterly* 58, no. 1 (January 1996): 1-25.

————. "Family Matters." In *Christian Origins: A People's History of Christianity,* edited by Richard A. Horsley, 201-20. Minneapolis: Fortress, 2005.

————. "The New Testament and the Family." In *The Family,* edited by Lisa Sowle Cahill and Dietmar Mieth, 1-9. Maryknoll: Orbis Books, 1995.

Osiek, Carolyn, and Margaret Y. MacDonald, with Janet H. Tulloch. *A Woman's Place: House Churches in Earliest Christianity.* Minneapolis: Fortress, 2006.

Ostmeyer, Karl-Heinrich. "Jesu Annahme der Kinder in Matthäus 19:13-15." *Novum Testamentum* 46, no. 1 (2004): 1-11.

Parker, Julie Faith. "You Are a Bible Child: Exploring the Lives of Children and

Mothers through the Elisha Cycle." In *Women in the Biblical World: A Survey of Old and New Testament Perspectives,* edited by Elizabeth A. McCabe. Lanham, MD: University Press of America, forthcoming 2009.

Parvis, Paul, and Kathleen Marshall. *Honouring Children: The Human Rights of the Child in Christian Perspective.* Edinburgh: Saint Andrews Press, 2004.

Patterson, Cynthia B. *The Family in Greek History.* Cambridge, MA/London: Harvard University Press, 1998.

Perdue, Leo G., Joseph Blenkinsopp, John J. Collins, and Carol Meyers. *Families in Ancient Israel.* Louisville: Westminster John Knox, 1997.

Phillips, Gary A. "The Killing Fields of Matthew's Gospel." In *The Labour of Reading: Desire, Alienation, and Biblical Interpretation,* edited by Fiona C. Black, Roland Boer, and Erin Runions, 249-65. Semeia Studies 36. Atlanta: Society of Biblical Literature, 1999.

Pitkin, Barbara. "Psalm 8:1-2." *Interpretation* 55, no. 2 (April 2001): 177-80.

Prest, Eddie. *God's Word on Children.* Cape Town: TFL, 1999.

Rashkow, Ilona N. *Taboo or Not Taboo: Sexuality and Family in the Hebrew Bible.* Minneapolis: Fortress, 2000.

Rawson, Beryl, ed. *Children and Childhood in Roman Italy.* Oxford: Oxford University Press, 2003.

————. *The Family in Ancient Rome: New Perspectives.* Ithaca, NY: Cornell University Press, 1986.

————. *Marriage, Divorce, and Children in Ancient Rome.* Oxford: Oxford University Press, 1991.

Rawson, Beryl, and Paul Weaver, eds. *The Roman Family in Italy: Status, Sentiment, Space.* New York: Oxford University Press, 1997.

Rehman, Luzia Sutter. "To Turn the Groaning in Labor: Romans 8.22-23." In *A Feminist Companion to Paul,* edited by Amy-Jill Levine and Marianne Blickenstaff, 74-84. Cleveland: Pilgrim, 2004.

Reinhartz, Adele. "Parents and Children: A Philonic Perspective." In *The Jewish Family in Antiquity,* edited by Shaye J. D. Cohen, 61-88. Brown Judaic Studies 289. Atlanta: Scholars Press, 1993.

Rogers, Steven A. "The Parent-Child Relationship as an Archetype for the Relationship Between God and Humanity in Genesis." *Pastoral Psychology* 50, no. 5 (May 2002): 377-85.

Sakenfeld, Katharine Doob. "In the Wilderness, Awaiting the Land: The Daughters of Zelophehad and Feminist Interpretation." *Princeton Seminary Bulletin* 9, no. 3 (1988): 179-96.

————. "Zelophehad's daughters." *Perspectives in Religious Studies* 15, no. 4 (Winter 1988): 37-47.

Saller, Richard P. *Patriarchy, Property and Death in the Roman Family.* Cambridge: Cambridge University Press, 1994.

Sandnes, Karl Olav. *A New Family: Conversion and Ecclesiology in the Early Church with Cross-Cultural Comparisons.* Bern: Peter Lang, 1994.

Sasso, Sandy Eisenberg. "When Your Children Ask: A Jewish Theology of Childhood." *Conservative Judaism* 53, no. 4 (Summer 2001): 9-18.

Scalise, Pamela J. "'I Have Produced a Man with the LORD': God as Provider of Off-spring in Old Testament Theology." *Review and Expositor* 91, no. 4 (Fall 1994): 577-89.

Schäfer, Klaus. *Gemeinde als "Bruderschaft": Ein Beitrag zum Kirchenverständnis des Paulus.* Frankfurt am Main: Peter Lang, 1989.

Schloen, J. David. *The House of the Father as Fact and Symbol: Patrimonialism in Ugarit and the Ancient Near East.* Studies in the Archaeology and History of the Levant 2. Winona Lake: Eisenbrauns, 2001.

Scott, James M. *Adoption as Sons of God: An Exegetical Investigation into the Background of huiothesia in the Pauline Corpus.* Wissenschaftliche Undersuchungen zum Neuen Testament 2.48. Tübingen: J. C. B. Mohr (Paul Siebeck), 1992.

Sharon, Diane M. "Rivalry in Genesis: A New Reading." *Conservative Judaism* 53, no. 4 (Summer 2001): 19-35.

Shier-Jones, Angela. *Children of God: Towards a Theology of Childhood.* Peterborough: Epworth, 2007.

Stager, Lawrence. "The Archaeology of the Family in Ancient Israel." *Bulletin of the American Schools of Oriental Research* 260 (1985): 1-36.

The State of the World's Children. Annual Report of the United Nations Children Fund.

Stevenson-Moessner, Jeanne. *The Spirit of Adoption: At Home in God's Family.* Louisville: Westminster John Knox, 2003.

Strange, William A. *Children in the Early Church: Children in the Ancient World, the New Testament, and the Early Church.* Carlisle: Paternoster, 1996.

Tasker, David R. *Ancient Near Eastern Literature and the Hebrew Scriptures about the Fatherhood of God.* Studies in Biblical Literature 69. New York: Peter Lang, 2004.

Thatcher, Adrian. *Theology and Families.* Oxford: Wiley-Blackwell, 2007.

Thompson, Marianne Meye. *The Promise of the Father: Jesus and God in the New Testament.* Louisville: Westminster John Knox, 2000.

Toorn, Karel van der. *Family Religion in Babylonia, Syria and Israel: Continuity and Change in the Forms of Religious Life.* Studies in the History and Culture of the Ancient Near East 7. Leiden: Brill, 1996.

Towner, W. Sibley. "Clones of God: Genesis 1:26-28 and the Image of God in the Hebrew Bible." *Interpretation* 59 (2005): 341-56.

Tropper, Amram. "Children and Childhood in Light of the Demographic of the Jewish Family in Late Antiquity." *Journal for the Study of Judaism* 37, no. 3 (2006): 299-343.

Uzzi, Jeannine Diddle. *Children in the Visual Arts of Imperial Rome.* Cambridge: Cambridge University Press, 2005.

VanGemeren, Willem A. "'Abba' in the Old Testament?" *Journal of the Evangelical Theological Society* 31, no. 4 (1988): 385-98.

van Henten, Jan Willem, and Athalya Brenner, eds. *Families and Family Relations as*

Represented in Early Judaisms and Early Christianities: Texts and Fictions. Leiden: Deo, 2000.

Waite, Linda J., and William J. Doherty. "Marriage and Responsible Fatherhood: The Social Science Case and Thoughts about a Theological Case." In *Family Transformed: Religion, Values, and Society in American Life,* edited by Steven M. Tipton and John Witte Jr., 143-67. Washington, DC: Georgetown University Press, 2005.

Weber, Hans-Ruedi. *Jesus and the Children: Biblical Resources for Study and Preaching.* Geneva: WCC, 1979.

White, Keith J. "Rediscovering Children at the Heart of Mission." In *Celebrating Children: Equipping People Working with Children and Young People Living in Difficult Circumstances Around the World,* edited by Glenn Miles and Josephine-Joy Wright, 189-200. Carlisle: Paternoster, 2004.

Wiedemann, Thomas. *Adults and Children in the Roman Empire.* New Haven: Yale University Press, 1989.

Wilcoxen, Jay A. "Some Anthropocentric Aspects of Israel's Sacred History." *Journal of Religion* 48 (1968): 333-50.

Winnicott, D. W. *The Maturational Processes and the Facilitating Environment: Studies in the Theory of Emotional Development.* Madison: International Universities, 1965.

———. *Playing and Reality.* London: Routledge, 2005.

Yarbrough, O. Larry. "Parents and Children in the Jewish Family of Antiquity." In *The Jewish Family in Antiquity,* edited by Shaye J. D. Cohen, 39-59. Atlanta: Scholars, 1993.

———. "Parents and Children in the Letters of Paul." In *The Social World of the First Christians: Essays in Honor of Wayne A. Meeks,* edited by L. Michael White and O. Larry Yarbrough, 126-41. Minneapolis: Fortress, 1995.

Yust, Karen-Marie. *Real Kids, Real Faith: Practices for Nurturing Children's Spiritual Lives.* San Francisco: Jossey-Bass, 2004.

Zuck, Roy B. *Precious in His Sight: Childhood and Children in the Bible.* Grand Rapids: Baker Books, 1996.

Contributors

Reidar Aasgaard
Project Leader
Norwegian Bible Society
Oslo, Norway

David L. Bartlett
Distinguished Professor of New Testament
Columbia Theological Seminary
Decatur, Georgia

William P. Brown
Professor of Old Testament
Columbia Theological Seminary
Decatur, Georgia

Walter Brueggemann
Professor Emeritus
Columbia Theological Seminary
Decatur, Georgia

Marcia J. Bunge
Professor of Humanities and Theology
Christ College
Valparaiso University
Valparaiso, Indiana

John T. Carroll
Harriet Robertson Fitts Memorial Professor of New Testament
Union Theological Seminary and Presbyterian School of Christian
    Education
Richmond, Virginia

Terence E. Fretheim
Elva B. Lovell Professor of Old Testament
Luther Seminary
St. Paul, Minnesota

Beverly Roberts Gaventa
Helen H. P. Manson Professor of New Testament Literature and Exegesis
Princeton Theological Seminary
Princeton, New Jersey

Joel B. Green
Professor of New Testament Interpretation
Fuller Theological Seminary
Pasadena, California

Judith M. Gundry
Research Fellow and Associate Professor (Adjunct) of New Testament
Yale University Divinity School
New Haven, Connecticut

Jacqueline E. Lapsley
Associate Professor of Old Testament
Princeton Theological Seminary
Princeton, New Jersey

Margaret Y. MacDonald
Professor, Department of Religious Studies
St. Francis Xavier University
Antigonish, Nova Scotia

Claire R. Mathews McGinnis
Associate Professor
Loyola College in Maryland
Baltimore, Maryland

Esther M. Menn
Professor of Old Testament
Director of Advanced Studies
Lutheran School of Theology at Chicago
Chicago, Illinois

Patrick D. Miller
Professor of Old Testament Theology Emeritus
Princeton Theological Seminary
Princeton, New Jersey

Brent A. Strawn
Associate Professor of Old Testament
Candler School of Theology
Emory University
Atlanta, Georgia

Marianne Meye Thompson
George Eldon Ladd Professor of New Testament
Fuller Theological Seminary
Pasadena, California

W. Sibley Towner
Professor Emeritus of Biblical Interpretation
Union Theological Seminary and Presbyterian School of Christian
    Education
Richmond, Virginia

Keith J. White
Associate Lecturer
Spurgeon's College
London, United Kingdom

Consultants

Carol Bartlett
Team Leader/Social Worker
United Methodist Children's Home
Decatur, Georgia

Don Browning
Alexander Campbell Professor of Religious Ethics
   and the Social Sciences, Emeritus
University of Chicago Divinity School
Chicago, Illinois

John Collier
Secretary to the Child Theology Movement
London, England

Susan Greener
Dean of Students
Trinity Evangelical Divinity and Graduate Schools
Deerfield, Illinois

Richard Hardel
Senior Fellow
The Youth and Family Institute
Bloomington, Minnesota

Bonnie Miller-McLemore
E. Rhodes and Leona B. Carpenter Professor of Pastoral Theology
Vanderbilt University Divinity School
Nashville, Tennessee

Michael Welker
Professor of Systematic Theology
University of Heidelberg
Heidelberg, Germany

Index of Names

440

Index of Subjects

Index of Scripture and Other Ancient Literature

DATE DUE
